THE OFFICIAL® PRICE GUIDE TO

CLASSIC VIDEO GAMES
CONSOLE, ARCADE, AND HANDHELD GAMES

David Ellis

House of Collectibles
New York

House of Collectibles and colophon are registered trademarks of Random House, Inc.

RANDOM HOUSE is a registered trademark of Random House, Inc.

This book is available for special discounts for bulk purchases for sales promotions or premiums. Special editions, including personalized covers, excerpts of existing books, and corporate imprints, can be created in large quantities for special needs. For more information, write to Special Markets/ Premium Sales, 1745 Broadway, MD 6-2, New York, NY, 10019 or e-mail *specialmarkets@randomhouse.com*

Please address inquiries about electronic licensing of reference products for use on a network, in software or on CD-ROM to the Subsidiary Rights Department, Random House Reference, fax 212-572-6003.

Visit the Random House Web site: *www.randomhouse.com*

Library of Congress Cataloging-in-Publication Data is available.

First Edition

0 9 8 7 6 5 4 3 2 1

ISBN: 0-375-72038-3

To Meghan—supporter of my hobbies and believer in my dreams.

ACKNOWLEDGMENTS

A collector's guide that covers as much information as this one is hardly the work of one person. Many people helped me greatly throughout the writing of this book, and it's only right to acknowledge each and every one of them here.

At Random House/House of Collectibles, I'd like to thank Dorothy Harris for believing in this project—without her, this book would not exist. Thanks also to Lindsey Glass and Roger Generazzo for their help and input. I'd also like to thank David Richardson at Prima Publishing for forwarding my initial proposal to House of Collectibles for consideration.

A number of fellow collectors contributed a great deal of time and effort to help me in my research and to provide me with information and photos that I otherwise would not have been able to find. First and foremost, thanks to Dan Cage—my longtime friend and one of the most avid and passionate collectors in the community—who has believed in and supported this project from the start. Dan introduced me to many of the other people who helped me out with this book.

Thanks to Cassidy and Nicole Nolen, Albert Yaruso, James Bright, Rik Morgan, Steve Orth, and William Cassidy for their patience, pictures and (most importantly) their willingness to go out of their way to help me with this book. I quite literally couldn't have done it without them. Also thanks to Bill Burton for being my unofficial photographer at classic gaming events and auctions throughout the past year.

Finally, thanks to *you,* the collector (or collector-to-be) who has purchased this book. It's because of people like you who love classic video games that this hobby continues to grow. Thanks to you, the games of the past live on and are lovingly preserved for the enjoyment of future generations.

David Ellis

CONTENTS

FOREWORD: CATCHING THE CLASSIC GAME BUG

I grew up playing video games. My generation was the first for which video games were the "in" thing. They were our answer to the Hula Hoop or Yu-Gi-Oh cards.

Everyone was playing video games in the late '70s and early '80s. At the height of this period, it was estimated that Americans spent over 75,000 man-years playing video games every year! Kids cut school to head over to the local convenience store and pump quarters into *Space Invaders*. Businessmen took extended lunch breaks and briefly escaped from the corporate world by guiding *Pac-Man* through his dot-filled maze. Arcade games appeared in every imaginable retail venue from hotel lobbies to grocery stores, and home video game consoles had found their way into millions of households.

Not everyone was a fan of video games, of course. Parents and teachers complained about the detrimental effects the games were having on children. Their complaints of video game-inspired violence and truancy caused many towns to impose strict curfews and laws governing access to arcades. Hollywood and other centers for nonvideo game entertainment bemoaned the loss of revenue they suffered as billions of consumer dollars that might normally be spent on movies and theater were instead spent on consoles and cartridges. The only solace shared by most of the antivideo game crowd was that the popularity of this new form of entertainment was, at best, a passing fad.

As the 1980s wore on, it looked as if they were right. Around 1983, the juggernaut of video game sales suddenly stopped dead. Thousands of game cartridges and consoles were sold off at bargain prices, and video game manufacturers turned their attention to the burgeoning home computer game market to bolster their sagging revenues. The arcades died a slower death, but by the late '80s most of them had disappeared. Arcade operators moved their machines by the hundreds into dusty warehouses and garbage dumps. It seemed that, after only a little over a decade, the age of video games had ended.

Of course, as we all know, the death of video games in the mid-'80s was nothing of the sort—it was merely the calm before an even bigger storm. In 1985, Nintendo introduced the Nintendo

Entertainment System (NES) in the United States to a skeptical retail community. Everyone expected the NES to be "another Atari," but they were wrong. The graphics and sound of the new game system were far superior to anything that had come before it, and the games, the quality of which were tightly controlled by Nintendo, were outstanding. The overwhelming retail success of the NES sparked the modern era of video games, and led to the multibillion-dollar video game industry that exists today.

But even now, when the Xbox, GameCube, and PlayStation 2 deliver games that are graphically and sonically superior to anything that game players ever dreamed of back in the '80s, those of us who grew up in the arcades and playing our Atari 2600s and Intellivisions at home have a soft spot in our hearts for the games of the classic era. Modern games are far flashier than the games of two decades ago, but a lot of them are all flash. Many of the "primitive" classics have gameplay that rivals the best selling games of today.

Collecting classic video games is a hobby that has grown steadily in popularity over the years. The reasons for the recent surge in interest are as varied as the collectors themselves. Some hobbyists have been accumulating collections since the '80s, and continue to collect for pure nostalgia. Others long to show their children the roots of video games—the recreational equivalent of telling the kids how we had to walk to school barefoot, uphill, through three feet of snow back in our day. Other collectors are actually young players who see the merit in the games of a simpler era.

I caught the collecting bug about five years ago when I bought one of my favorite arcade video games from the 1980s—Sega's *Star Trek: Strategic Operations Simulator*. When I plugged in that full-sized arcade video game, I realized that my high school dream of having an arcade of my own was now actually possible. I now have twelve arcade video games in my collection, and only the size of my garage limits the size of my personal arcade. Interest in the arcade side of the hobby naturally led to an interest in home video game consoles. I am currently the proud owner of ten classic consoles and around 100 game cartridges.

The growth of the classic game collecting hobby is phenomenal, and it doesn't show signs of slowing down. There are hundreds of Web sites dedicated to console, handheld, and arcade video game collecting. National and local Internet newsgroups exist everywhere. Every year there are dozens of arcade and console game collecting shows in cities all over the country. Everywhere there are people like you and me just waiting for the opportunity to meet and talk to more people like themselves, and to lure more classic game fans into this fascinating hobby.

If you're new to classic game collecting, good for you! You are about to take the first step into a fun and exciting hobby. This book is designed to help ease you in and provide the vital information you need to start and maintain your game collection. If you're a game collecting veteran, there's information in here for you as well. To date, this is the only book that provides classic game collecting info for three aspects of the hobby: console, handheld, and arcade collecting. Herein, you'll find a well-rounded view of all aspects of the hobby with extensive price guides and plenty of advice for collectors of all levels of experience.

Fair warning, though: once you've caught the classic game collecting bug, you're hooked for life. After you purchase your first classic video game, it's next to impossible to stop. Not that there's anything wrong with that.

Happy collecting!

ABOUT THIS BOOK

The *Official Price Guide to Classic Video Games* is the first price and collector's guide that covers nearly every aspect of the classic video game collecting hobby—console systems, handheld and tabletop games, and full-sized, coin-operated arcade machines. This book was written to introduce new hobbyists to the exciting world of classic video game collecting. It also serves as a reference to collectors who are already familiar with the hobby.

Games Covered in this Guide

Although the video game industry has existed for only a little over 30 years, there have already been a vast number of video games, consoles, and arcade machines released. A guide covering every video game-related item that exists up to this point in time would be a thick volume indeed!

For this reason, the *Official Price Guide to Classic Video Games* covers only items from the "classic" era: from the release of the first arcade and console video games in the early 1970s to the first big video game industry "crash" that signaled the end of the classic game era in the mid-1980s.

This time period was selected for a couple of reasons. First, this was one of the most technologically exciting time periods in the industry. Over the course of a decade and a half, the video game industry started literally from nothing and grew to become one of the most profitable fields that ever existed in the business world. During this time, the game concepts and basic technology that laid the foundation for the video game industry as it exists today were invented and refined.

The second reason, the one most pertinent to a collector's guide, is that the video games of this era are those that are most widely considered to be collectible items. With a few notable exceptions, video games produced after this time period, while very popular, are still too "new" to have much collectible value.

The console chapters of this guide cover video game consoles and handheld games produced between 1970 and 1984. The one exception to this rule is the Atari 7800, which was released in

1987. This console is included because it is the last of Atari's consoles that was compatible with game cartridges produced in the classic video game era. Consoles and handhelds produced from 1985 onward, such as the Nintendo Entertainment System (NES), Nintendo GameBoy, and the Sega Master System and their game cartridges are still easily and inexpensively available (for the most part), and aren't considered collectibles by most hobbyists.

The continuing growth of the classic game collecting community has prompted many individuals and companies to produce new game cartridges for many systems, most notably for the Atari 2600. Because these games are produced in small quantities and become instantly collectible in most cases, all new "homebrew" games released through August 2003 are included in the price lists in this guide.

The arcade game chapters cover a similar span of time, from 1970 to 1985. As is true in the console chapters, there are some exceptions to this rule. Many arcade games have had a succession of sequels that stretches beyond the classic era. Sequels to popular games, such as the *Pac-Man* series, are included for completeness regardless of the year they were produced. Other select newer games, such as *Mortal Kombat* and other popular titles released in the late '80s and early '90s are also included because these games are becoming rather popular among collectors and are starting to achieve "classic" status. New releases of classic arcade titles, such as the *Ms. Pac-Man/Galaga* combo machine released by Namco in 2000, are also included.

In both the console/handheld chapters and the arcade game chapters, this guide covers only games that were released in the United States. Including console and arcade games released worldwide would easily have doubled the size of this guide. At any rate, these are the games that are most commonly available in the video game collectible market in the United States.

How Much Is It Worth?

As this book is primarily a price guide, this question is probably in the forefront of many readers' minds when they pick it up. The price listings in this guide provide information on the monetary value assigned to classic video game hardware and software based on current trends in the hobby. There are a lot of factors that go into determining these values such as rarity, completeness, physical condition, variations in packaging and labeling, and so on. All of these factors are described in detail throughout this book.

But, to be perfectly honest, the prices listed in this guide don't really matter.

That might seem like an odd statement for the author of a price guide to make, but it's completely true. When you strip away all of the nostalgia and mystique, classic video game consoles and cartridges are nothing more than molded plastic and circuit boards populated with 20- and

30-year-old technology. Classic arcade games are pretty much the same thing, with a monitor and a particleboard cabinet thrown in for good measure.

When you look at things in that light, the answer to the question "what is it worth?" when applied to a classic game collectible is, invariably, "not much." The value of a classic video game that really matters is the value that you as a collector assign to it. You have to determine what an item is worth to you, and act accordingly when you decide to add that item to your collection.

If a rare cartridge that regularly sells for $500 holds no value for you personally, there are better ways for you to spend your $500 than to add that cartridge to your collection. If a common cartridge is a game that you remember fondly from your youth and would enjoy playing again, it is probably worth more to you than the $2 price tag that this guide assigns to it.

If you're an arcade game collector, a game that brings back memories of the local arcade that you visited on the way home from school every day is worth more to you than a rare classic that you seldom, if ever, played. *Robotron: 2084* is invariably very expensive, while a lesser-known game like *Bump 'n Jump* is usually quite inexpensive. If you loved *Bump 'n Jump* and hated *Robotron* as a kid, *Bump 'n Jump* is worth more to you than *Robotron* regardless of what the price lists say.

Keep this in mind as you build your classic video game collection. If you stick to this simple rule of valuation, you'll find that your collecting experience will be much more satisfying and fulfilling.

About the Price Guides

Obviously, one of the main features of any collector's guide is the price guide. One of the main reasons collectors delve into a book like this one is to see what their collection is worth—or to see what they can expect to pay for those few missing items they need to make their collections complete.

The price guides in this book are designed to provide that information and more. In addition to price ranges, the guides provide a number of other pertinent details on the item including, in most cases, a brief description of the item's history and/or important info you should know when you set out to collect it.

Price List Information

The following information is included in the price lists in this book:

- Game/Item Name: The name of the console, game cartridge, accessory, or arcade game.

- Manufacturer: The name of the company that created and/or distributed the item.

- Year: For arcade games, dedicated consoles, and handhelds, the year of each game's release is listed. Games with unknown release dates are indicated with a question mark (?).

- Label: For some classic cartridge systems, particularly the Atari 2600, there are two or more label variations for many cartridges that can affect the value of the game. This is omitted in price lists where label variations do not apply.

- Rarity: Every item in this guide is assigned a rarity rating between 1 and 10—the higher the number, the more rare the item.

- Prices: For console systems and handheld games, there are two price listings for each item. The first listing shows the price range for a "loose" item (no box, instructions, and so on). The second listing shows the price range for a "complete" item (in the original box, instructions, all accessories intact, and so on). For arcade games, there is a single price listing.

- Notes: This section provides background information and/or important collecting information for selected games.

How the Prices Were Determined

The prices in this book were compiled from data accumulated from November 2002 through October 2003, and represent the price trends for that time period. The sources for the price data include:

- eBay auction results

- Online dealer prices

- Dealer and trader prices at classic game conventions and events

- Live auction prices (in the case of arcade machines)

Price data from all of these sources was analyzed to create a range of prices for each item. The factors that determine the pricing for individual items are covered in the descriptions that appear before each price list in the ensuing chapters, but generally the better the condition of the item, the higher you can expect the price to be. You can also expect dealer and (in some cases) online auction prices to run closer to (or even beyond) the high end of the range, while prices from other collectors and live auction prices tend toward the middle or lower end of the range.

In some instances, prices are marked with an asterisk (*). This indicates that these items are so rare or are so seldom seen on the market that no accurate pricing information is available. The estimated prices listed for these games represent a best guess estimate based on the value of similar games. Items with a question mark (?) in the price column are items that are so rare that no price determination can be made.

In all cases, the prices in this book refer to items that are in working condition and in good physical condition (no significant rips, tears, chips, blemishes, and so on). As a general rule, the better the condition of an item, the higher its price is. New, sealed items always fetch a higher price than used items, and may sell for well above the price ranges listed here. Nonworking or damaged items always command a lower price, and can in some cases be far less expensive than the ranges listed herein.

The prices in this book are meant to serve as guidelines only. For the most part, you can expect prices for the items listed to fall within the listed range. However, as is true in any collecting hobby, prices rise and fall based on current supply and demand. There's no law that says that a going price for an item on any given day won't be well below or above the price range listed for it in this guide. By the same token, there's no guarantee that you'll get top dollar for a rare cartridge you're trying to sell just because it sold for that price in the past.

Use the price guides in this book to help you determine what you can expect to pay for a given item. If you can get it for less, good for you! If the demand for the item grows and you have to pay more...well, that's the way it goes sometimes. As a collector, you'll get used to it.

1 A Brief History of Video Games

In the Beginning...

Although most people had never seen a video game until 1971, the story of video games actually begins more than a decade earlier.

In 1958, a physicist at the Brookhaven National Laboratory in Upton, New York, came up with a way to allow visiting guests to interact with some of the lab equipment during an otherwise dull tour. Willy Higginbotham programmed a five-inch oscilloscope to display a horizontal line (the court) and a vertical line (the net), as well as a point of light (the ball). Guests could serve and return the ball and control its angle using two handheld controllers, each of which had a knob and a single button. This simple technology demonstration, which Higginbotham called *Tennis for Two*, has the distinction of being the first known video game.

Higginbotham's tennis game never left Brookhaven and, as a result, it is often overlooked in the annals of video game history. A game that was created four years later is widely considered to be the one that ultimately gave birth to the video game industry.

In 1962, Steve Russell and several other members of the Tech Model Railroad Club (TMRC) got their hands on the Massachusetts Institute of Technology's newest toy—a DEC PDP-1 mainframe computer. Using this machine and a couple of homemade controllers, they created *Spacewar*, the first computer game. This simple game of two dueling spaceships was an instant hit among the TMRC members, and word of the game spread like wildfire to students on the campus. Eventually, the game was passed on to other university campuses that were equipped with PDP-1 computers, including the University of Utah and Stanford University in California.

Up to this point, no one had considered any commercial possibilities for video games. *Tennis for Two* was a hardwired game that couldn't easily be reproduced, and *Spacewar* could only be played on a computer that cost $120,000 and took up half of a room. This was about to change thanks to a couple of visionary men: Ralph Baer and Nolan Bushnell. Each of these pioneers found a different way to bring video games to the masses.

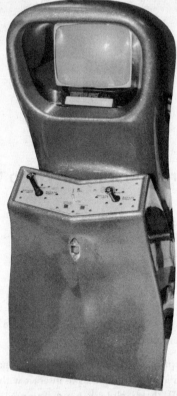

NOTE ❖❖

Throughout the text,
BOLD indicates that an
item appears in a picture.

a **The "Brown Box,"** Ralph Baer's
prototype for the world's first video
game console, the Magnavox
Odyssey.

b **A 2-player version** of Computer
Space, the first coin-operated
video game. (From the collection
of Cassidy Nolen; photo by Bill
Burton.)

c **Pong**—the game that gave birth
to the arcade video game industry.
(Photo courtesy of James Bright,
http://www.quarterarcade.com.)

The Birth of an Industry

In 1966, television engineer Ralph Baer presented a proposal and schematic for a game system that would play on an existing television set by sending signals through the TV's antenna input. The company he was working for at the time, Sanders Associates, gave him the go-ahead for the project based on the proposal and a prototype device that allowed two players to move spots around on the screen. The object of this simple chase game was for one player to maneuver his dot so that it touched the dot controlled by the other player.

Over the next couple of years, Baer and his team created several other simple games, including a target game that used a rifle to "shoot" moving targets on the screen and a number of simple paddle games. Finally, in 1967, Baer created what he called the **"Brown Box,"** a game system with a number of variations of paddle, shooting, and chase games built in.

With the technology now in place, Sanders Associates attempted to market Baer's television game. Eventually, the technology was purchased by Magnavox and, in 1972, was marketed as the Magnavox Odyssey—the first home video game system.

At about the same time that Ralph Baer began his TV game project, an engineering student at the University of Utah discovered the irresistible lure of *Spacewar*. Unlike others who had already spent countless hours playing Steve Russell's game, Nolan Bushnell saw potential that extended beyond the campus computer lab. Bushnell, who had spent his summers working in amusement park arcades and midways, realized that people would pay money to play *Spacewar* just as they paid to play pinball machines and Skeeball. After he graduated, Bushnell set out to turn a backroom campus hobby into a thriving commercial enterprise.

Commandeering his daughter's bedroom to use as his computer lab, Bushnell started building a coin-operated version of *Spacewar*. Instead of using a programmable computer, which proved to be too slow and expensive, Bushnell built a dedicated system that *only* played the game. After adding a simple black-and-white television for a monitor and a set of pushbutton controls, his prototype of *Computer Space* was complete.

A company called Nutting & Associates released **Computer Space**, the first commercial coin-operated video game, in 1971. While it was a hit on college campuses, the complicated nature of the game prevented it from catching on in bars and other locations. In other words, *Computer Space* was less than a commercial success.

The Dawn of the Video Game Age

Undeterred by the commercial disappointment of *Computer Space*, Bushnell soon embarked on his next venture. He left Nutting & Associates and, along with his friend Ted Dabney, he founded his own company—Atari. Shortly thereafter, they hired an engineer named Al Alcorn. Little did they know at the time that the first game they would produce would be the cornerstone of what would become a multibillion-dollar industry.

Pong was a simple game—just two paddles and a ball, and an instruction card that described the game's in-depth strategy: "Avoid missing ball for high score." The prototype machine was tested in Andy Capp's tavern in Sunnyvale, California, not far from Atari's offices. Within a few days, there were lines of people waiting to play the game, and the coin box was overflowing. *Pong* was a hit.

Although Bushnell had originally intended to sell the manufacturing rights for *Pong* to an existing amusement company, the success of the *Pong* prototype encouraged him to manufacture and distribute the game at Atari. So, in 1972, the first *Pong* machines started rolling off the assembly line in an old roller-skating rink in Santa Clara, California. This was the birth of one of the fastest growing companies in history, and the start of the arcade video game boom.

At about the same time, Magnavox put the final touches on Ralph Baer's TV game system and released it to the public. **The Magnavox Odyssey** sold for $100, and included 12 games and a slew of accessories, including game boards, dice, and play money that were used in conjunction with the on-screen action. Also included were plastic overlays that the player taped to the TV screen. Because the primitive Odyssey's graphics were very limited, the overlays added graphic features—maps, mazes, racetracks, and so on—to make the games more visually appealing.

Magnavox continued marketing the Odyssey through 1975 and sold a total of between 100,000 to 200,000 units. Although not a huge hit by today's standards, the Magnavox Odyssey firmly established the idea of home video games and set the stage for the home game boom that was to come.

The Golden Age Begins

Following the arcade success of *Pong*, the early- to mid-'70s saw the introduction of a huge number of *Pong*-like games both at the arcades and in homes. It seemed like everyone was trying to get a piece of Atari's success, from known electronics manufacturers like Radio Shack to toy manufacturers like Coleco. Atari themselves also reaped the benefits of *Pong*'s success by selling a **home version** in 1976. Soon, a glut of *Pong* clones inundated the home market. Atari increased their hold on the market by releasing dedicated home versions of other arcade games such as *Stunt Cycle* and *Video Pinball*.

Eventually, a couple of manufacturers came up with the idea to create versatile game consoles that could play a variety of games stored on separate cartridges rather than just a few games that were built into the unit itself. In 1976, Fairchild Camera and Instrument, RCA, and Coleco released cartridge-based game systems. The Fairchild Channel F, the RCA Studio II, and the Coleco Telstar Arcade made very little impact on the market, but they did provide a glimpse of the new direction the home video game market would soon take.

Following the new cartridge-based game console model, Atari released the **Atari Video Computer System (VCS)** in 1977. The VCS, which eventually became known as the Atari 2600, had only nine games available when it was introduced, and wasn't an immediate hit. In November 1978, Bushnell, who was now chairman of Atari after selling the company to Warner Communications, advocated selling off the VCS inventory at bargain prices and starting work on a more powerful home system. Warner executives decided to stick with the VCS. This decision turned out to be a very profitable one, due in part to the resurgence of video game popularity at arcades and a shrewd marketing decision on the part of Warner/Atari.

Before the Atari VCS gained popularity, however, the home market had become saturated with game consoles, and their popularity fell off. Mattel, one of the few companies that opted to stay out of the video game business up to this point, introduced a line of handheld light-emitting diode (LED) sports games that became an instant hit. Coleco, who by this time was losing a lot of money in the video game industry, bolstered their sales by introducing their own handheld line to compete with Mattel's games. Both companies reaped big profits from these games which, for a couple of years, dominated the home electronic game market.

Coin-operated video games had also stopped pulling in the big money. This decrease in popularity was largely due to a lack of creativity on the part of game manufacturers. While there were some innovative new games during this era, most games released prior to 1978 were variations on the *Pong* theme. It looked as if the craze started by *Pong* was going to be a passing thing. That is until a Japanese company, Taito, released a game called **Space Invaders.**

Space Invaders was so popular in Japan that it caused a nationwide coin shortage. When it was imported into the United States by Midway, the response here was nothing short of fanatical. Its popularity started the trend of putting arcade video games in every possible venue. There was hardly a hotel lobby, airport, or convenience store that didn't have one or more video games in the corner by the end of the 1970s.

The *Space Invaders* craze touched off a new wave of video game innovation. Hits by other manufacturers started appearing on the scene. Other 1978 hits included *Atari Football* and Cinematronics *Space Wars*—an updated take on Steve Russell's *Spacewar* game. Unlike Bushnell's *Computer Space*, Cinematronics' game was an instant arcade hit.

Seeing the renewed interest in arcade games, Atari made a marketing decision that changed the course of the company. They bought the home video game rights to *Space Invaders* and released it for the Atari VCS in 1980. Fans of the arcade game raced to the stores to buy the VCS just to play *Space Invaders*, and the VCS quickly became the most popular home game system available. Converting arcade titles to home titles became the cornerstone of Atari's ongoing strategy for the VCS, allowing the console to remain the most popular home video game system on the market even in the face of graphically and technologically superior competition.

The Unstoppable Industry

As the new decade approached, the video game industry was the fastest growing form of entertainment in history. Arcades were packed with patrons eagerly awaiting the release of the next new hit. And there were a *lot* of hits.

In 1979, Atari met the *Space Invaders* juggernaut head-on at the arcades with the release of *Asteroids*, which soon eclipsed Midway's hit as the most popular game around. Midway struck back with *Galaxian*, the first video game to feature full-color graphics.

On the home scene, the first true video game console war was brewing. Several companies released new systems to challenge Atari's hold on the home market. The Atari VCS's most notable opponents were Magnavox's Odyssey^2 (released in 1978) and **Mattel's Intellivision** (released in 1980).

Odyssey^2 , although heavily advertised, never gained mass appeal in the United States. Although the console's built-in keyboard gave it the potential to play more sophisticated games and to become an educational tool, the Odyssey^2 never lived up to its potential. In other countries, where the library of software titles for the system was larger and more diverse, the Odyssey^2 did fairly well.

Intellivision was clearly graphically superior to any game system on the market at the time, and its games—especially its sports titles—offered far more realistic gameplay than Atari's. The console never attained the sales numbers of VCS, however, largely due to its lack of recognizable arcade titles. Even so, the fan base for the system was sizeable.

As the '80s began, the popularity of arcade video games continued to soar. In the first year of the new decade, some of the most memorable arcade classics appeared on the scene. *Battlezone, De-*

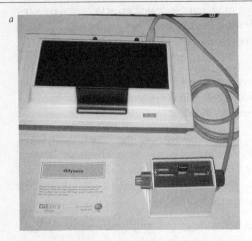

a **The Magnavox Odyssey**—*the first home video game console.*

b **Atari's original home version of** Pong, *which was also marketed by Sears under the Tele-Games label.*

c **The Atari VCS** *(later known as the 2600) went on to become one of the most popular home video game consoles in history.*

d **Space Invaders Deluxe.** Space Invaders *took the video game world by storm when it hit the arcades in 1978. Pictured is the sequel,* Space Invaders Deluxe. *(Photo courtesy of James Bright, http://www.quarterarcade.com.)*

fender, Missile Command, Star Castle, and *Berzerk* all made their debut in 1980. A number of other closet classics like *Carnival*, *Crazy Climber*, and *Red Baron* also hit the arcades that year. (Legend has it that a *Red Baron* competition between software pioneers Bill Stealey and Sid Meier led to the formation of the computer game company MicroProse.)

This was also the year that introduced the first video game to feature a main character. In 1980, an epidemic known as **Pac-Man** fever swept the video game world. Almost immediately, *Pac-Man* the game was in just about every video game location imaginable, and *Pac-Man* the character was everywhere else—lunch boxes, beach towels, coloring books, cereal, pasta, and even Saturday morning television. *Pac-Man* went on to inspire a total of nine sequels and variations.

In the home game market, 1980 was a landmark year for game developers. Tired of the lack of recognition and royalties they were receiving, a number of Atari programmers left the company and founded Activision, the first video game company that produced games for another company's console. This was an important step in the video game industry in that it provided players with a wider selection of game titles. At the same time, Activision unknowingly started a trend that would almost devastate the video game industry.

In the arcades, 1981 saw the introduction of the first *Pac-Man* sequel, *Ms. Pac-Man*, which was even more popular than the original game and went on to become the best-selling arcade video game in history. The second year of the decade also introduced such classics as *Centipede*, *Tempest*, *Galaga*, *Frogger*, *Gorf*, and *Qix*. This was also the year that introduced (arguably) the best-known video game character ever created. Although he was called "Jumpman" at the time, Nintendo's corporate symbol Mario made his first appearance in 1981 in a hit game called ***Donkey Kong.***

Following Activision's lead, new software-only game companies started popping up everywhere in 1981. Some, like Imagic, were founded by programmers who defected from other game companies. Others, like Apollo, were established by individuals who knew little about games, but saw the potential profit in the business. Even companies that had no prior connections to the entertainment industry like Ralston-Purina (the pet food manufacturers) and Quaker Oats started making games. Most of the new companies concentrated on the Atari 2600, which was still the most popular game system on the market, but some—notably Activision and Imagic—produced games for other consoles as well.

The video game juggernaut showed no signs of slowing in 1982. The arcades saw another round of classic favorites including *Joust, Robotron: 2084, BurgerTime, Dig Dug, Q*bert, Donkey Kong Junior,* and *Pole Position*. Games based on movies and television shows also started showing up in force. *Tron* and *Popeye* were among the forerunners in 1982.

In the home market the console wars raged on, with the Atari 2600 and the Intellivision firmly entrenched as the top two contenders. No other home system had posed any significant threat to the leaders until Coleco released a new console in 1982.

The **ColecoVision** was superior in every way to both the 2600 and the Intellivision. It was an instant hit, thanks in part to the fact that Coleco took a lesson from Atari and secured the rights to a major arcade hit—*Donkey Kong*—and packaged it with the system. The ColecoVision went on to sell hundreds of thousands of consoles, and 170 games were eventually produced for the system. Coleco even hedged their bets by offering an adaptor that allowed people to play Atari 2600 cartridges on the system. (Mattel eventually followed suit and offered a similar expansion for the Intellivision.)

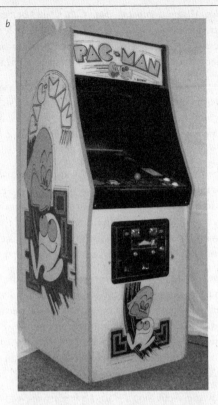

a *Mattel's **Intellivision** was the only real competition for the Atari VCS in the early '80s.*

b ***Pac-Man** made history not only by becoming one of the most popular coin-operated video games ever, but also by launching the first video game-inspired character. (Photo courtesy of James Bright, http://www.quarterarcade.com.)*

c ***Donkey Kong,** which debuted in 1981, introduced Mario—a game character that went on to become the corporate symbol of one of the most powerful companies in the industry. (From the author's collection.)*

Although ColecoVision was clearly the frontrunner of the new systems released in 1982, it wasn't alone. While still supporting the aging 2600, Atari released a new graphically superior system, the Atari 5200, to compete with the ColecoVision.

Milton Bradley, best known for its board games up to this point, entered the video game market with the revolutionary Vectrex—a system with a built-in nine-inch vector monitor (the type of monitor used in popular arcade games like *Asteroids*). Milton Bradley also entered the hand-held game market with Microvision. Although it was never a huge hit, Microvision pioneered the idea of cartridge-based handheld games.

There were now nine home video game consoles competing for consumer attention: the Atari 2600 and 5200; Intellivision; ColecoVision; **Vectrex**; Odyssey^2; Bally Astrocade (which had been introduced in 1978); the Fairchild Channel F (which was reintroduced in 1982 after having been off the market for several years); and the Emerson Arcadia 2001 (introduced in 1982). Hundreds of game cartridges lined retailers' shelves. The number of software-only game companies—most of whom were producing games primarily for the 2600 and Intellivision—grew exponentially, and were joined by major entertainment companies like 20th Century Fox and CBS who formed game divisions to cash in on their share of the profits.

In the fourth quarter of 1982, Mattel lost money for the first time since they had entered the video game business and Atari reported lower earnings than they had originally forecast. Stock in both companies dropped significantly and the resultant panic caused stock in other video game companies and retailers who carried their products to drop as well.

The Crash

As 1983 rolled around, the home game market continued to suffer. One of the major causes for the escalating problems was the competition. The wealth of new games and consoles on the market outpaced consumer demand. For the Atari 2600 alone there were, at one point, nearly 50 companies producing games. None of these companies adequately took into account the impact their competitors would have on the marketplace and predicted far higher sales figures than they could possibly meet. Retailers simply didn't have the space to carry all of the titles and began slashing prices to get rid of existing stock. Huge numbers of cartridges ended up in "dump bins" and were often sold for discount prices. The new, high-profile releases by bigger companies like Atari, Activision, and Imagic—generally priced in the $30 range—couldn't compete for the consumer dollar. Parents buying games for their children had the choice of buying a single cartridge for $30 or six cartridges for $5 each. As a result, game companies were stuck with warehouses full of unsold games. Although sales of both consoles and cartridges increased in 1983, the heavy discounts on both hardware and software in retail stores cut deeply into the manufacturers' profits.

Throughout 1983, most game consoles disappeared from the market. All of the companies that remained in the business scaled back their operations and continued dumping their excess inventory at bargain prices. Of all of the competitors, only Coleco managed to have a strong year.

Despite the shakedown that was going on in the home market, the arcade game industry wasn't showing any ill effects. Some of the most memorable classic games made their first appearance in 1983, including *Spy Hunter, Star Wars, Track and Field, Elevator Action,* and *Mario Bros.*

Of all the new arcade game releases of 1983, the one that made the most impact was probably Cinematronics' **Dragon's Lair**, an interesting combination of video game and laser disc technology.

a **ColecoVision**, released in 1982, was the first game console to significantly challenge Atari and Mattel in the classic-era home market.

b **Vectrex** offered arcade-quality graphics on its built-in vector monitor.

c **Dragon's Lair,** one of the most popular arcade games of 1983, was the first arcade game to feature laser disc technology. (Photo courtesy of James Bright, http://www.quarterarcade.com.)

The graphics were feature film-quality cel animation, unlike anything seen in an arcade up to that point. The gameplay was less than stellar—the player merely moved the joystick or pressed a button in response to the on-screen action to determine the next scene that would appear—but it was an eye-catching addition to the arcades and was one of the biggest successes of the year.

Because of *Dragon's Lair*'s success, many arcade game manufacturers saw laser disc technology as a hot new trend in arcade games. Laser disc games began arriving in droves throughout 1983 and into 1984. Many, like *Cliff Hanger* and *Space Ace*, followed the interactive cartoon model established by *Dragon's Lair*. Others like Atari's *Firefox* and Sega's *Astron Belt* used laser disc footage as a backdrop for traditional video game elements. Every theme from science fiction to sports was covered during this short period. Despite the number of titles, the novelty of the new technology wore off quickly.

As 1983 wound down, some companies remaining in the home video game market turned their attention to the growing home computer market in hopes of finding new sources of revenue. Many console manufacturers had promised upgrade devices that would turn their game machines into computers, but few had actually delivered on those promises. Coleco was an exception to this rule. They produced the **ADAM computer** in both stand-alone form and as an upgrade to the ColecoVision console. Technical difficulties led to the company delivering fewer than half of the promised 500,000 ADAM computers to the marketplace by the end of 1983, and Coleco suffered a huge stock downturn as a result. Atari, meanwhile, was holding its own in the burgeoning home computer market with its stand-alone 400 and 800 computer lines. Mattel also tried their hand at the computer business by releasing the Aquarius computer system and the ECS computer add-on for the Intellivision.

As the console game market continued its downward slide, stand-alone and handheld games enjoyed a brief surge of popularity. Coleco's line of tabletop games (styled like miniature versions of their arcade counterparts) was a huge hit, as were many of the palm-sized handheld games introduced at the time.

In 1984, the video game industry in the United States finally hit rock bottom. Although the arcade business had been unaffected by the travails of the home market, things changed for the worse as the new year rolled around. Arcades all over the country closed their doors forever, and arcade game manufacturers responded by releasing fewer and fewer games. Many of the arcade games released at this point were actually conversion kits—circuit boards, control panels, and artwork—that arcade owners used to change existing games into new ones without having to replace the entire cabinet. This cost-cutting strategy actually led manufacturers to design cabinets specifically for repeated conversion. One of the most notable (though short-lived) of these conversion games was Atari's System 1 cabinet. Atari released a total of five games compatible with this cabinet, the most popular of which was the classic *Marble Madness*.

Despite the widespread decline of the arcade industry, several notable classics were released in 1984, including *Punch-Out, Gauntlet, Karate Champ,* and the quirky game *I, Robot. Karate Champ* is arguably the most influential game of the bunch—it was the first two-player martial arts fighting game ever released. Although primitive by today's standards, it is nevertheless the predecessor of the *Street Fighter* and *Mortal Kombat* fighting game series of the late '80s and early '90s, as well as modern 3-D fighting game series like *Dead or Alive* and *Tekken*.

Perhaps the most notable event in the arcade industry in 1984 was Nolan Bushnell's return to the video game business. Part of his agreement when he left Atari in 1978 prevented Bushnell

a **The ADAM computer** *resulted in huge losses for Coleco, one of the few companies that had weathered the onset of the video game crash of the '80s.*

b **The Atari 7800,** *announced in 1984, didn't make it into the stores until 1986.*

from working in the industry for five years. In December 1983, Bushnell held a huge party to announce his triumphant return, introducing his new company, Sente. "Sente" is a term from the Japanese game Go which is the equivalent of "Checkmate." Bushnell chose the name to emphasize competition with his former company, "Atari," a Go term that means "Check." Starting in 1984, Sente introduced a number of new arcade games. The games never caught on, and the troubled company was purchased by Bally, which shut it down soon thereafter.

The home video game market continued to decline sharply. The discounts on software and hardware continued as retailers devoted more and more shelf space to home computers. The most popular video game systems, the Atari 2600 and Intellivision, were both priced below $50 at this point, and even high-end systems like the Atari 5200 and ColecoVision were priced below $100. The low prices caused an increase in console sales resulting in an increase in demand for game cartridges. Unfortunately, because profits were nonexistent, few companies were producing new high-end games for any of their consoles. Many of the smaller independent video game publishers, who had come into existence only a few years earlier, had now disappeared, and those who remained, including Activision, were shifting their development focus to home computers.

One of the first of the remaining major video game manufacturers to bow to the pressures of a sagging market was Mattel, who closed down their Mattel Electronics division in March 1984. A senior member of the Mattel Electronics team, along with several other investors, purchased the division from Mattel and promised to continue producing both software and hardware under the name Intellivision, Inc. This company, which eventually changed its name to INTV Corporation, continued producing Intellivision games and consoles until 1990.

Coleco was also feeling the pinch, and decided to shift their focus to the ADAM computer despite the fact that a large percentage of the units shipped at the end of 1983 had been returned as defective. This proved to be a disastrous move on their part, as sales for the computer were dismal at best. The failure of Coleco's electronics division almost killed the company. If it hadn't been for Coleco's toy division (which started selling the super-popular Cabbage Patch Kids dolls at about the same time), the company would have disappeared altogether. Even so, the company filed for bankruptcy. The ColecoVision hung on (barely), but was discontinued the following year along with the ADAM.

Atari, meanwhile, was in a state of transition. Outwardly, they seem to have a great deal of confidence about the future of the gaming industry. They were exploring the possibility of delivering games to their home consoles via telephone and cable television connections. They formed a partnership with LucasFilm to release two new games for the Atari 5200, *Ballblazer* and *Rescue on Fractalus*. They even announced that they were working on a brand new console, the **Atari 7800**, which would be fully compatible with existing 2600 games and feature the best graphics of any home system available.

Internally, Atari was suffering. Although they continued to support the 2600 to some extent, the 5200 was discontinued. Most of the products promised for 1984 never materialized and the 7800 didn't make it into stores until nearly two years later.

As Atari continued to decline, Warner Communications decided to sell most of their share in the company. Most of the arcade division was sold to Namco in Japan, while the remainder was held by Warner and renamed Atari Games. Warner retained about a quarter of the home division, and sold the rest to former Commodore Computer president Jack Tramiel. Tramiel slashed Atari's workforce and shifted the company's focus almost entirely to the home computer market.

After the Classic Era—The Rebirth of an Industry

As far as the United States was concerned, the video game market was dead by the middle of 1985. Two years earlier, you couldn't go anywhere without bumping into an arcade video game. Now, chances were that you had to travel quite a distance to find an arcade. With consumer interest shifting to the rapidly growing home computer market, it looked as if the home video game market was dead as well. Most retailers were of the opinion that the video game craze had been a fad after all, and took steps to eliminate their remaining video game stock and move on.

In Japan, things were different. In 1983, Nintendo had introduced a new video game system called the Nintendo Family Computer (Famicom). Millions of consoles and cartridges had been sold, and Nintendo decided to try their luck in the United States. Although they had a strong presence in the arcades, Nintendo had virtually no experience in the US home market. They first contacted Atari and tried to work out a distribution deal, but that never came to pass. So Nintendo decided to go it alone.

When the Famicom (renamed the **Nintendo Entertainment System [NES]** in the United States) was introduced at the Consumer Electronics Show in summer of 1985, it was met with great skepticism. Having been burned by the recent video game crash, retailers had no interest in selling a new video game system. The future looked bleak for the new console, but Nintendo of America's president Minoru Arakawa was encouraged to test market the NES in one American city during the Christmas season. Arakawa chose New York.

To coax stores into carrying the NES, Arakawa made the retailers an offer they couldn't refuse. The stores didn't have to pay Nintendo a penny for 90 days. In exchange, the retailers had to be willing to devote some of their floor space to Nintendo's products. Arakawa and his team even set up the displays and stocked the shelves for them. On top of this, Nintendo promised to mount a multimillion-dollar advertising campaign to promote its products. Given these generous terms, hundreds of retailers in the New York area agreed to give the NES a try.

Although the test didn't go quite as well as planned, Nintendo nevertheless sold about 50,000 NES consoles during the 1985 Christmas season, enough to warrant a second test in Los Angeles in February 1986. Despite the fact that the post-Christmas season was usually slow in the toy industry, Los Angeles sales were encouraging. By the end of 1986, the NES was available in most cities across the country, and sales had topped 1 million consoles. In 1987, an additional 3 million consoles were sold, and Nintendo was becoming a household name, a name that was synonymous with video games—as Atari had been a decade earlier.

Nintendo was well aware of the factors that contributed to the crash of the video game market in the United States. First and foremost was the glut of substandard software, mostly from third-party manufacturers. Nintendo immediately instituted a strict licensing program that limited the number of titles that third-party software companies could produce for the NES each year. They also imposed strict quality guidelines for new cartridges. Games had to pass a rigorous "fun" test at Nintendo before they got the green light for publication. Although many companies complained about these standards, Nintendo's guidelines ensured a flow of games that were consistently fun.

Consumers responded favorably to the NES, and by 1990 there were over 30 million Nintendo Entertainment Systems in U.S. homes. Popular cartridges sold as many as 2 to 3 million copies. Nintendo proved that the video game industry wasn't dead—it had just been hibernating until the next big innovation came along.

The proven success of the NES led other companies to try their hand in the market. Nintendo's primary competition was Sega, whose Master System and Genesis consoles were the first to give Nintendo a run for their money in the American marketplace. Other systems like the Neo-Geo, TurboGrafix, and the Atari 7800 made comparatively little impact on the marketplace.

Nintendo was king of the hill, and enjoyed continued success with the NES. In 1989, Nintendo introduced the Game Boy, a black-and-white handheld game system that quickly jumped to the top of the sales charts and remained there even after the release of technically superior handheld games such as the Atari Lynx and the Sega Game Gear. Game Boy remained so popular in its original form that the Game Boy Color, which Nintendo had planned to release in 1996, was pushed back to allow continued sales of existing units. Nintendo Game Boy and the compatible Game Boy Color remained the standard in handheld gaming for over a decade.

In an industry that had seen much change during the late '70s and early '80s, Nintendo managed to hold the number-one position for nearly 10 years. They endured all competition and

a **The Nintendo Entertainment System** *was first introduced in 1985; at the time, few people realized that it would signal the rebirth of the sagging video game industry.*

b **The Sony PlayStation,** *released in 1995, unseated Nintendo as the undisputed leader in the video game marketplace.*

emerged on top every time. That is until consumer electronics giant Sony decided to give the video game business a try. Ironically, Nintendo helped to engineer their fall from the top position in the industry.

While planning the release of a CD-ROM add-on for their 16-bit Super Nintendo console, Nintendo entered into an agreement with Sony to manufacture the drive that would be called the "Play Station." Sony wanted to produce their own software for the new drive, exempt from the licensing restrictions Nintendo imposed on other developers. Nintendo was adamantly opposed to this and secretly entered into an agreement with Phillips Electronics to manufacture the Super NES CD-ROM drive.

Angered by this turn of events, Sony decided to release their CD-ROM game system as a stand-alone unit. The **Sony PlayStation** debuted in 1995, and was a great success. Sony sold nearly 200,000 consoles in the last two months of the year. Their closest competitor was the Sega Saturn, which sold just over half that number. Nintendo, who had announced a new system to compete with Sega and Sony, failed to deliver their Ultra 64 (later renamed the Nintendo[64]) by the end of the year. Other competitors like the Atari Jaguar (which had been released the year before) and the 3DO (a CD-based system built by Electronic Arts founder Trip Hawkins's new company by the same name) never came close to the popularity of Sony's new system.

The Video Game Industry Today

The popularity of the PlayStation set the stage for the video game industry as it exists today. In the face of stiff competition from Sony, the Sega Saturn failed and the Nintendo[64], which continued to use the more expensive cartridge game format rather than CD-ROMs, didn't make much of a dent in the marketplace.

In 1999, Sega was the first of the major video game manufacturers to release a 128-bit video game system. More than a million Sega Dreamcast consoles were sold during the first few months in the United States, but sales dropped steadily, primarily because of Sony's announcement that the PlayStation 2 would be released the next year. Meanwhile Nintendo, while still enjoying huge sales from their handheld Game Boy and Game Boy Color lines, was falling steadily behind in the console market. Their new Dolphin system (which later became the GameCube) was announced in 1998, but didn't debut until well after the PlayStation 2.

Predictably, the PlayStation 2 was a rousing success. It was compatible with all of the original PlayStation software, giving the new system an instant library of over 1,000 games in addition to its lineup of new titles. The introduction of this console dealt the final blow to Sega, whose Dreamcast sales continued to decline. In 2001, Sega discontinued the Dreamcast and walked away from the video game console business.

In 2000, Nintendo released the follow-up to their popular Game Boy handheld, the Game Boy Advance. The following year, they released their new console, the GameCube. At about the same time, software giant Microsoft joined the console war by introducing the Xbox—a console that is basically a scaled down Pentium III computer made for playing games.

Today, the arcades that originally gave birth to the video game industry have all but disappeared. There are still a few major manufacturers that continue to produce arcade games, but arcade pioneers like Atari and Williams are gone. The arcade game market represents only a small fraction of the video game industry today, an industry that now nets in excess of $50 billion worldwide every year.

So, the console wars continue as the three major competitors—PlayStation 2, Xbox, and Game-Cube—vie for their share of the profits. With technology constantly evolving at an exponential rate, the next big revolution in video game technology is always just over the horizon. It's impossible to tell what the next big hit will be. But one thing is certain—there *will* be a next big hit. Whatever critics might want to call the video game phenomenon, it's not a fad. It's a reality.

And it's here to stay.

2 The Basics of Console and Handheld Video Game Collecting

Getting started in the hobby of collecting classic video game consoles requires little more than desire and a little bit of expendable income. You don't need to be an expert on the history of video games, nor do you need to be an accomplished game player. There are, however, a few things you should know before you dive headlong into the hobby.

Why Collect Classic Console Games?

Every person has a different reason for getting into this hobby, and each reason is just as valid as the next. After all, like any hobby, video game collecting is a means of personal expression.

Nostalgia is probably the number-one reason for collecting classic consoles. Video game nostalgia is a comparatively new phenomenon. Some toy-related and game-related collectibles like Barbie figures and Hot Wheels cars have been around for nearly half a century. Others, like tin and wooden toys, have been around even longer. Video game consoles and handheld video games, on the other hand, have only been around for a little over 30 years. The earliest of these—the ones from the 1970s and 1980s—have just started falling into what could be considered the "seriously collectible" category over the last ten years or so.

Video game nostalgia comes in many forms. Some collectors fondly remember the game console that they owned in their youth and are seeking to rebuild their old collection.

Other collectors simply enjoy the home video games of the classic era and choose to play them in addition to (or instead of) the modern alternatives available today. Despite the fact that most classic video games are now available for play on PCs (using emulator software) or on modern consoles (in nostalgic game collections), there's something about the feel and the look of the consoles, cartridges, and controllers that makes owning the games in their original form the only valid way to truly relive the classic gaming experience.

Still other collectors simply see video game consoles and cartridges as icons of an era, and want to display them as a reminder of the time when video games first became the focus of nearly everyone's attention.

The other main reason that people collect classic video games is money. Like any other collecting hobby, there are many video game items that are considered rare or are otherwise highly sought-after commodities. Some console accessories that were produced in limited numbers, like the 3-D Imager for the Vectrex, regularly sell for many times their original retail price. Certain rare game cartridges, like the coveted *MagiCard* for the Atari 2600, can fetch $1,000 or more in an online auction.

Getting into this (or any) collecting hobby strictly to make money is a risky endeavor at best. If you happened to buy a ton of consoles, accessories, and games at closeout prices when the video game market crashed in the late '80s and you still have these items stored in good condition, you stand to make a healthy profit.

If, on the other hand, you are currently acquiring classic console items simply to resell them, your chances of making a profit are becoming slimmer every day. As the video game collecting hobby grows steadily in popularity, more and more people are realizing what their old games and accessories are worth to collectors. Chances are that, unless you luck out and find a terrific deal on a highly coveted item, you'll get little more than your original price for the item if you intend to sell it immediately. The best chance you have to turn a profit on something you buy today is to hold onto the item and hope it increases in value sometime in the future. This is, of course, a crapshoot since the market values of video game collectibles fluctuate just like the prices in other collectible markets.

When it comes down to it, the reason to start collecting has to be a personal one. The first section of this book isn't meant to convince you to start a console or handheld game collection, but to provide you with the information you need to fulfill whatever collecting objectives you've already set for yourself—where to find the items you're looking for regardless of why you're looking for them, and what you can expect to pay to build the collection you're attempting to build.

The Collecting Community

One of the most rewarding experiences for many classic video game collectors is meeting other hobbyists who share their interests. People have been collecting classic game consoles since the games were first released in the 1970s and 1980s. Before the Internet, it was the tight-knit community of hardcore collectors who kept in contact with one another over the years, exchanging ideas, advice, and games, that kept classic video games alive and allowed the hobby to develop into the popular pastime that it is today. The kinship among members of the classic game collecting community is nothing short of amazing. Many prominent members of this family of collectors have contributed information and photographs to this guide.

Today, with the Internet providing easy connections between collectors across the country and all over the world, making contact with other video game collectors is easier than ever. There are local collectors' organizations all over the country that meet regularly, either physically or "virtually" through e-mail lists and Internet newsgroups. There are also national organizations dedicated entirely to supporting and furthering the classic video game collecting hobby.

a

a   **Philly Classic**, which is held each
spring in Philadelphia, and other
classic video game conventions are
excellent places to become an active part of the collecting community and meet game designers and
programmers from the golden age
of video games. (Photo by Bill Burton.)

In addition to all of the "official" clubs, mail lists, and newsgroups, there are literally thousands of fan-created web sites that show off the collections of individual collectors. Collector
sites offer a glimpse of the collections amassed by other hobbyists, and many provide valuable
collecting advice. Many collectors start their own web sites specifically to share what they've
learned about the hobby with other members of the collecting community.

Both national and local organizations regularly hold video game collecting events all over the
country. These events range from small local swap meets where collectors buy, sell, and trade
games, to huge conventions such as the **Philly Classic**, with extensive collector and dealer support and guest speakers from the classic game industry. Attending events like these is the best
way to immerse yourself in the collecting community. They allow you to meet the collectors
you've talked to online face to face. Like any hobby, collecting classic video games is one that
is most rewarding when you can share it with others who understand your passion for the
subject.

Appendix B at the back of this book provides an extensive list of Web sites and events related
to classic video game collecting.

Which Console(s) to Collect

When you decide to create a classic video game console collection, you need to set collecting goals. It is unrealistic—at least for most collectors, who operate under at least *some* financial and space limitations—to collect *every* classic console and game cartridge ever produced. As you can see from the extensive price lists later in this book, there are dozens of classic video game consoles and *thousands* of classic video game cartridges.

When you start your collection, decide what it is that you want to accomplish. Do you want to collect a sampling of video game consoles from a particular era, or do you want to purchase a single console and collect a complete set of games for that console? Do you want to limit your collection to programmable consoles (ones that use cartridges) or do you want to include dedicated consoles (ones with the games built in)? Are you interested in handheld and stand-alone games or only games that play through a television?

For most collectors, these decisions aren't very difficult. As discussed earlier, every collector has his or her own reasons for getting into the hobby in the first place, and these reasons usually define their collecting goals.

My personal console collection, for example, includes the most popular consoles of the late 1970s and early 1980s—the Atari 2600, Intellivision, ColecoVision, Magnavox Odyssey², and Vectrex—along with a small assortment of game cartridges for each. I have also collected a few of the more pivotal and interesting dedicated consoles—Atari's original *Pong* and Coleco's Telstar *Combat*, for example. I consider my collection fairly complete because I have all of my favorite consoles and games from the classic era.

A collector friend of mine, on the other hand, chose to collect only **Atari 2600 consoles and cartridges**. His collection includes nearly every 2600 cartridge ever released in the United States, and many foreign releases as well. His collection is constantly growing, as new games are still being released for the 2600 to this day.

In the end, it is up to you to decide what makes your own collection "complete." Other than space and monetary concerns, there is no reason that you ever have to stop adding to your collection. There are hard-core collectors who will always debate the completeness of your collection if given the opportunity, but the bottom line is that your collection is complete when it includes all of the items you have set out to collect.

Looking for some inspiration to get your collection started? Read on to see what's out there in the world of classic video game collectibles.

Dedicated Consoles

The earliest home video game systems had one or more games (and the game controllers) built directly into the console. These systems, known as "dedicated consoles," were popular throughout the 1970s.

Most of the earliest dedicated consoles were based on Atari's *Pong*. After this game proved to be an arcade success, countless manufacturers followed Atari into the home market with clones and variations on the *Pong* theme. Some dedicated consoles branched out into other game types, but most stuck to the *Pong* formula.

A complete collection of dedicated consoles is probably impossible to amass because so many were made, and many of them were produced in limited quantities and/or in limited distribution. A collection of this type also takes up a lot of space.

a **Atari 2600 cartridge collection.**
The size and scope of your classic
game collection is a personal decision. Only you can decide when
your collection is "complete."
(Photo courtesy of Dan Cage.)

On the other hand, collecting dedicated consoles tends to be fairly inexpensive. Many *Pong*-
type dedicated consoles are available for under $20 in working condition.

Cartridge-Based (Programmable) Consoles

In the mid- to late-1970s, game manufacturers realized that a programmable console—one
that could play many interchangeable games rather than a few built-in games—might have
greater appeal to the consumer and, at the same time, reduce manufacturing costs.

There were many cartridge-based game consoles in the classic era, but only a handful
achieved commercial success. The three most successful consoles from that time period—the
Atari 2600, Mattel Intellivision, and Coleco's ColecoVision—tend to be the most popular
among collectors today. Because of their immense popularity when they were new, there are
still a vast number of these systems (and most of their accompanying games) in existence
today. Less popular systems, like the Fairchild Channel F and the RCA Studio II are much
harder to find and are not as widely collected by casual hobbyists.

While cartridge-based systems (especially the popular ones) are the easiest to find, they are
also among the hardest to collect if your goal is to amass a collection that includes every game
and accessory ever produced for a given system.

21

For example, there have been well over 700 Atari 2600 game titles (including variations, homebrews, reproductions, and hacks) produced in the United States alone, and hundreds more were produced worldwide. There were also a huge number of accessories and add-on components for the 2600 (only some of which are covered in this guide). To build a collection that is truly complete when such a vast number of items exist is very difficult—impossible, in fact, for collectors of limited means (like most of us).

Building a modest collection of cartridge-based consoles and games can be very rewarding and challenging. It can also be fairly inexpensive if you shop around and stick to the more common items.

Handhelds and Tabletops

Starting in the mid-1970s, a number of companies began producing self-contained electronic games that were portable alternatives to game consoles played through television sets. These games generally used light-emitting diodes (LEDs), liquid crystal displays (LCDs), or vacuum fluorescent displays (VFDs) to present the game image.

Most games of this type in the classic era were handheld games—the size of an electronic calculator or smaller. Others, like the miniature arcade games produced by Coleco, were slightly larger and known as tabletop games. Like the dedicated consoles that preceded them, the portable games of this time period were generally capable of playing only a single game. There were exceptions, like Milton Bradley's Microvision and Entex's Adventure Vision, which used interchangeable cartridges. Cartridge-based handheld and portable games were rare in the classic era, and as a result can be difficult to find today.

As is true when collecting dedicated consoles, it is difficult to amass a collection of *every* handheld and tabletop classic game. However, many of these games are still readily available. Because of their small size and, in some cases, their fragility, handheld and tabletop games aren't as common as most consoles. Many of the more popular models often command higher prices than consoles, making this branch of the classic video game collecting hobby a bit pricier.

Where to Find Classic Consoles

Locating the items you want to add to your collection is part of the fun and challenge of classic video game collecting, and there are a number of places you can find new additions for your growing collection.

Online Auctions

Although you often hear collectors—buyers, at any rate—complain about online auctions because of the way that they have inflated the prices of video game collectibles, most everyone in the collecting community agrees that auction sites like eBay (http://www.ebay.com) have made it easier than ever to locate hard-to-find items. On any given day, there are hundreds of auctions for classic console, handheld, and tabletop video games and accessories. Using an easy to navigate search engine, you can zero in on the item or items you're looking for in a matter of minutes.

Online auctions can be the source of great bargains for console collectors. For example, cartridge-based classic video game systems are often sold as packages—the console, controllers, and a number of cartridges are bundled together for a single price that is often lower than the total price of the items if they were sold individually. By browsing the listings, you can often jumpstart your classic game collection by picking up such a package deal. For example, I was able to obtain an Intellivision package in an eBay auction that included two consoles (an Intellivision and an Intellivision II) and over 30 games for under $90. You can also obtain common cartridges and accessories at extremely low prices in online auctions. Some of the more common Atari 2600 and Intellivision cartridges regularly sell for under a dollar apiece (plus shipping).

On the other hand, online auctions (like their live counterparts) often generate bidding wars where prices spiral out of control. This is particularly true when a rare item comes up for bid. To make matters worse, there are some unscrupulous sellers out there who "shill" their auctions. That is, they get friends to place bids on their items to artificially inflate the price. It is difficult to spot someone who is shilling an auction, especially if you are new to the hobby. If you notice a particular seller who has multiple auctions frequented by the same bidders and whose auctions invariably close at prices that are higher than those of similar products up for auction at that time, chances are that there is some shilling involved.

You can avoid the personal financial pitfalls of bidding wars by setting an upper limit on the price you're willing to pay and sticking to it. When the price goes over your limit, stop bidding. There are few items that are so rare that you will *never* see them again, especially if you regularly attend conventions and browse online resources.

A major disadvantage associated with buying from an online auction is that there is no guarantee that the items you bid on are in working condition. By and large, most sellers are honest about the condition of their products. Many of them are collectors themselves, and they know that in such a tight-knit community their reputation will precede them if they repeatedly misrepresent the condition of their merchandise.

For the most part, you have to take it on faith that what you buy in an online auction is working. You can minimize your risk by only bidding on items that are described as tested and working. "It was working 20 years ago when I stored it in the closet" doesn't count. Avoid items described as untested unless the price is low enough so that you don't mind taking a loss if the item doesn't work. You should particularly avoid consoles that have all of their parts but are listed as untested. It takes only a couple of minutes to hook a game console up to a television and see if it's working. Usually, when a seller lists a complete console as "untested," he or she is simply trying to pawn off a nonworking console without admitting that it is broken. By putting "untested" in the item description, the seller dodges any liability when the buyer finds that the item doesn't work.

Another downside to online auctions is shipping and handling. When setting a limit on what you're willing to pay, remember to factor in the shipping charges. Some sellers charge abnormally high shipping and handling fees. A slight markup over the shipping rates is acceptable to cover packing materials and transportation costs on the seller's part, depending on the shipping method, but more than a few dollars over the actual shipping price is pushing it. Take time to study the going shipping rates for various shippers so that you know when someone is trying to take advantage of you.

Dealers and Conventions

As the classic video game collecting hobby grows, so does the number of retailers who sell classic consoles and games. Most of these retailers sell strictly through online stores, but many also frequent classic game conventions and other events.

The upside to dealers is selection and quality. Classic game dealers usually have a wider selection of rare titles than you can find by chance in online auctions or through other sources. Dealer stock is generally tested and in working order, and is usually in very good physical condition.

The downside to dealers is the price. When you buy from a dealer, expect to pay more than you would from most other sources. Dealers are middlemen—they buy at discount prices and sell their stock for a profit. There's nothing wrong with that—it's called capitalism. This is the way dealers make a living. Most dealers charge only a nominal markup on most items, with a slightly larger markup for uncommon and rare items. The guarantee of quality and functionality is usually worth the extra money.

Unfortunately, some dealers are out to take collectors for as much money as possible. These unscrupulous dealers buy up uncommon and rare titles and mark them up to incredibly high prices, usually far exceeding the accepted value of the item. This is where price guides like this book come in handy. Although you can't wave a price guide in a dealer's face and expect the dealer to sell you a cartridge at a lower price just because the book says the dealer's price is too high, you can use the price guide as a tool for determining the generally accepted value for an item. Armed with this data, you can make an informed decision as to whether or not you should make a purchase.

Collectors' Web Sites and Newsgroups

One advantage to integrating yourself into the game collecting community is that you make contact with other collectors throughout the country and all over the world. Items may be readily available in some locales that are nearly impossible to find in others. Collector web sites often include a "wanted" list of items that the site owner is looking for and a "for sale" list of items that the site owner is selling or trading. By communicating with other collectors through their personal web sites and through mail lists and newsgroups, you can often arrange purchases and trades for items you want but cannot find through other sources. Most collectors are in this hobby for the fun of it and, as such, usually treat fellow collectors fairly when making deals for trades and purchases.

When dealing with other collectors directly through their personal web sites, you should exercise courtesy. Many collectors post a list of the games in their collections on the site. Don't treat this list as a "for sale" list and bombard the site owner with requests for prices. Unless an item is specifically listed as being for sale, assume that it is *not* for sale.

Antique and Thrift Shops

Because the video game collecting hobby is still in its infancy, most antique shops—even those that sell toys and electronic items—still haven't caught on to this new collectible trend. However, as time goes on and the hobby grows in popularity, more and more classic console and handheld games are beginning to show up amongst the old furniture and crystal. This trend is both good and bad for collectors. The upside is that selling video game collectibles in these venues adds a great deal of legitimacy to the hobby. The downside is that such legitimacy means higher prices. Tagging any item with the adjective "antique" instantly increases its price by a significant percentage.

While classic video games are just starting to carve a niche for themselves in the antique world, they're often readily available in second-hand, consignment, and thrift shops. Many of these stores conceal numerous classic video game treasures if you're willing to dig for them.

Because most retailers haven't yet realized the worth of 20- and 30-year-old electronic games, you can often find some incredible bargains in these shops.

Even when a dealer does know that classic games have some value, you can often obtain good deals. For example, a store owner might price all of his Atari 2600 cartridges at $7.50 apiece because he knows that these games can be valuable. This is an outrageous price for common cartridges like *Combat* and *Pac-Man*. However, if *all* of the cartridges are priced the same, chances are that rare games like *Swordquest: Waterworld* that are worth hundreds of dollars to collectors will also be marked at $7.50 when they show up in that dealer's pile.

Yard Sales and Local Classifieds

Sometimes the old methods still work best. It's always worth browsing local flea markets, yard sales, and newspaper classifieds for classic video game consoles and cartridges. Often, you can find some excellent deals mingled with the old kitchenware and baby clothes. One person's junk is another person's treasure.

Classified ads for classic console and handheld games are few and far between these days, but they're not unheard of. Like the package deals you can get in online auctions, classified ads often advertise a game system and a ton of cartridges and accessories for a single low price. Take a few minutes to browse the classifieds. You never know what you might find.

Things to Look for When Collecting

While every console game system has its own set of guidelines for determining rarity and accepted value, there are several things that you should always look for when selecting a classic console collectible:

- Physical condition: Make sure the item is in good physical condition. Classic consoles, cartridges, and handhelds *are* 20 or more years old, so some wear is to be expected, but make sure that there are no major cracks, that electrical cords are intact, and that there is no battery corrosion (in the case of games and accessories that use batteries). On cartridges, check the condition of the label. Cartridges with ripped or missing labels should generally sell for less than identical cartridges with the labels intact.

- Functionality: If possible, test the console or game to make sure it works before you purchase it. When you don't have physical access to the item (as in an online purchase) obtain the seller's assurance and guarantee (if possible) that the game is functional.

- TV format: All of the consoles and cartridges covered in this book were released in the United States and conform to NTSC, the television format used in the United States (see Appendix A for definitions of the various television formats). In other parts of the world, television displays are subtly different. PAL, the television format used in most of Europe, is the most common TV format outside of the United States. Many of the games listed in this guide are available in both NTSC and PAL versions. Make sure that the cartridges you purchase are NTSC versions rather than PAL. PAL cartridges, while they will play on U.S. game systems, do not display correctly on most NTSC televisions.

- Completeness: The more complete a product is, the more money you can expect to pay for it. A boxed cartridge with the manual, for example, is worth more than the cartridge alone. In the case of the consoles themselves, make sure that all of the parts—especially the controllers, power supply, and TV switchbox—are included. It is important to note that some classic consoles used proprietary TV switchboxes and/or proprietary power supplies and *will not function* without them. (These systems are detailed later in this book so that you know what to look for when buying.)

- New items: Occasionally, stashes of unopened classic video game items are found in warehouses or other storage facilities and released to the public. Unopened items—especially if they are rare—usually command a higher price than opened/used items.

3 Dedicated Consoles

When you think of a home video game console today, what comes to mind is a game system that plays an almost endless variety of games that are sold individually on cartridges or discs (CDs, DVDs, or dedicated-format optical discs). This was not always the case, however. The earliest home video game consoles were dedicated—the games were built directly into the console hardware. Typically, these consoles were limited to playing a single game or a limited number of very similar games.

The first home video game console, the Magnavox Odyssey, was released in the spring of 1972. The unit's sales were bolstered somewhat by Atari's *Pong* arcade game released later that year, the reason being that the Odyssey played a game similar to *Pong*. It is a matter of debate whether Atari founder Nolan Bushnell had seen the Magnavox Odyssey demonstrated at a trade show prior to producing *Pong*. The results of a lawsuit in which Magnavox prevailed, seems to indicate that this was the case.

At any rate, the Odyssey paved the way for a seemingly endless array of dedicated home video game consoles that flooded the market in the mid-1970s. Although the Odyssey itself didn't do as well as Magnavox had hoped, many of the ensuing dedicated home video game consoles sold hundreds of thousands of units.

Most of the dedicated home consoles of this time period played only *Pong* and *Pong*-like games, and were quite similar to one another. The continuing popularity of *Pong* in the arcades fueled the market for these clone systems. Later, as the novelty of TV tennis games began to dwindle both in the arcades and at home, video game manufacturers turned to newer, fresher game ideas. Although most of the newer innovations only found their way into the arcades at first, a number of manufacturers produced dedicated home consoles that departed from the *Pong* concept.

Dedicated classic console collecting isn't quite as prevalent as that of cartridge-based console systems. Because so many manufacturers produced so many consoles that were, essentially, interchangeable with one another—that is, they all played pretty much the same game—it is very difficult to compile a definitive list of all *Pong*-clone dedicated consoles. Consequently, it is also difficult to amass a collection of all of these systems. Nevertheless, many classic video game collectors have at least a small collection of dedicated consoles, and some of the consoles—such as the Magnavox Odyssey and Atari's original *Pong*—are considered quite collectible.

This chapter hits the highlights of the dedicated console systems and provides a price guide for the systems that are most commonly found in the collectors' market today.

The Magnavox Odyssey (1972)

Note: *Magnavox used the "Odyssey" name for its entire line of home video games. This section describes the original Magnavox Odyssey. Later Odyssey models were appended with numbers (Odyssey 300, for example) to differentiate them from one another.*

Because of its historical significance as the first home video game console, the original Magnavox Odyssey is one of the most collectible dedicated video game consoles. It was introduced in 1972 and remained on the market for only about two years.

Unlike the home consoles that followed it, the Odyssey didn't use integrated circuits. Instead, it used transistors and diodes, making this console somewhat bulkier than those that followed it. Despite the fact that this technology sounds quite primitive by today's standards, the Odyssey has many advanced features that were copied (to some extent) in later consoles. For example, instead of a single game, the Odyssey plays 12 games (although most are variations on the basic ball-and-paddle theme). Unlike later dedicated multigame consoles that have switches or dials to choose between the game options, the Odyssey uses interchangeable plug-in circuit board cartridges to change games. The Odyssey circuit boards contain no game programming; they merely act as electronic switches that tell the console which game to play. Even so, the concept of interchangeable plug-in cards was the forerunner to the cartridges used in the programmable systems introduced later in the decade.

Odyssey includes two controllers, each of which has three knobs: two to move paddles (or other objects) horizontally and vertically and a third that allows players to put "spin" on the game ball.

The Odyssey is capable of producing only simple black-and-white images. The extent of the console's graphic capabilities is two paddles and a ball. There is no sound and no scoring. To make up for these shortcomings and provide game variety, Magnavox included an extensive array of accessories that were used in conjunction with the games. Each game has two-color plastic overlays (one for 19-inch TVs and one for 25-inch TVs). These overlays, which are taped to the television screen, provide the necessary playfields for the games. For example, *Haunted House* has an overlay that shows the house in which the game takes place. In addition to the overlays, many of the games require supplemental materials like dice, cards, play money, and score cards—all of which were included in the package.

Because there are so many accessories for the system, it is difficult to find an Odyssey that is 100% complete today. The following is a list of all of the **game pieces and overlays** that were included with the base system:

- Game cartridges 1-6

- *Analogic* overlays (2)

a

NOTE ✱✱

Throughout the text,
BOLD indicates that an
item appears in a picture.

b

a **The Magnavox Odyssey,** *released in 1972, is one of the most collectible classic console systems. (From the collection of Cassidy Nolen.)*

b **The Odyssey overlays and game pieces,** *which are included with the original Odyssey system, are essential for playing most of the games. Without all of these pieces, the Odyssey cannot be considered complete. (From the collection of Cassidy Nolen.)*

- *Cat and Mouse* overlays (2)

- *Football* overlays (2)

- *Haunted House* overlays (2)

- *Hockey* overlays (2)

- *Roulette* overlays (2)

- *Simon Says* overlays (2)

- *Ski* overlays (2)

- *States* overlays (2)

- *Submarine* overlays (2)

- *Tennis* overlays (2)

- A sheet of stick-on numbers

- *Football* game board/*Roulette* game board
- Odyssey stadium scoreboard with attached yardage markers
- "Pass" cards (20)
- "Run" cards (20)
- "Kick-off" cards (20)
- "Punt" cards (20)
- "Clue" cards (30)
- *Simon Says* cards (28)
- *States* cards (50)
- "Secret Message" cards (13)
- Red, white, and blue chips (16 each)
- Play money (100 each in denominations of $5, $10, $50, and $100)
- Affairs of States answer folder
- *States* study map
- Dice (2)

In addition to the game-related accessories, the following items were included in the box:

- Game controllers (2)
- Antenna/game switch
- Game cord
- Eveready red-label C batteries (6)
- Documentation (36-page user manual; "How to Get Service" card; Thank You card; Notice card; key punch inspection cards (2); and free bonus game coupon)

Note that the above lists refer to the U.S. version of the Odyssey. Accessories included with export versions of the console were somewhat different.

When you purchase an Odyssey today, make sure that the accessories are included. Although you can do without the documentation and (certainly) the 30-year-old batteries, the game accessories and the antenna/game switch are required if you intend to play the games.

A number of accessories and add-ons were released for the Odyssey during its short lifespan, including the **Shooting Gallery** (a light gun with target shooting games included), a carrying case, and an AC adaptor that eliminated the need for batteries.

There were also a number of additional games, each with their own overlay and accessories. Some, but not all, of these games include new cartridges. The games that don't include cartridges are simply new overlays and accessories that are used in conjunction with one or more of the six cartridges included with the basic Odyssey system. The games that include additional cartridges are generally considered to be more collectible. The additional game cartridges are

a

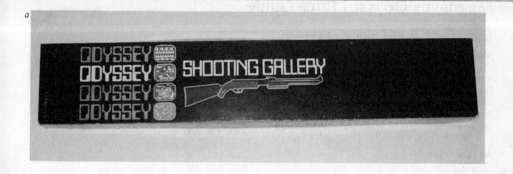

a **The Odyssey Shooting Gallery add-on,** *which included a rifle and four games, was produced in limited quantities. Only about 20,000 were sold. (From the collection of Cassidy Nolen.)*

numbered 7-10 and 12. To date, cartridge 11 is a mystery—apparently, no game using this cartridge number was ever produced.

The Odyssey games were packaged in long boxes that were big enough to accommodate the game overlays and other accessories required for the games. Like the games included with the console, it is difficult (if not impossible) to play these games without their overlays and accessories.

There were a total of eleven additional games produced (in addition to the four games included with the Shooting Gallery). A twelfth game, *Soccer,* replaced *Football* in export versions of the Odyssey, but this cartridge was never sold separately. One game, *Percepts,* was only available through mail order by sending in the free bonus game coupon included with the Odyssey system.

It should be noted that it is very uncommon to find any of the cartridges originally packaged with the Odyssey console (cartridges 1-6) for sale separately since they were never offered for individual sale. On the rare occasion that they do turn up for sale individually, you can expect to pay about $5 to $10 apiece for them.

Between 100,000 and 200,000 Magnavox Odyssey consoles were sold before the system was discontinued in 1973.

Due to the age of the console and the older technology upon which it was built, finding a working Odyssey unit is becoming increasingly difficult. Because the system uses up batteries quickly, an AC adaptor is highly recommended if you intend to play the game. The original adaptors released by Magnavox in 1972 are difficult to find, but a universal 9 Volt AC adaptor (available at any electronics store) works just as well.

An extensive archive of information on the Magnavox Odyssey, including the history, schematics, and details on both U.S. and export versions of the console is available at http://www.pong-story.com/odyssey.htm.

Magnavox Odyssey Price Guide

CONSOLES & ACCESSORIES

MAGNAVOX ODYSSEY CONSOLE
Manufacturer: Magnavox
Rarity: 6
Loose: $40–60
Complete: $100–150
Notes: Must include all game accessories, overlays, cartridges, and the proprietary antenna/game switch in order to be fully functional

AC ADAPTOR
Manufacturer: Magnavox
Rarity: 7
Loose: $9–12
Complete: $14–16
Notes: 9 Volt AC adaptor made specifically for the Magnavox Odyssey; not included with the console—only sold separately

ANTENNA/GAME SWITCH
Manufacturer: Magnavox
Rarity: 7
Loose: $10–15
Complete: N/A
Notes: The antenna/game switch used for the Odyssey had a proprietary connector rather than a standard RCA connector; difficult to find

CARRYING CASE
Manufacturer: Magnavox
Rarity: 9
Loose: N/A
Complete: $85–100*
Notes: Hard plastic carrying case for the Odyssey console; difficult to find one that is in good condition

GAMES

SHOOTING GALLERY
Manufacturer: Magnavox
Rarity: 7
Loose: $40–50*
Complete: $50–90*
Notes: Light gun rifle add-on; packaged with 2 game cartridges (#9 and #10) and 2 overlays each for *Pre-Historic Safari, Shooting Gallery, Dogfight,* and *Shootout*

BASEBALL
Manufacturer: Magnavox
Rarity: 7
Loose: $10–15*
Complete: $20–30
Notes: Includes 2 overlays, game board, score board, 26 line-up cards, 10 "Power" cards, 10 "Big Freak" cards, 12 runner tokens, and 2 dice; no cartridge (uses cartridge #3, included with the console)

BASKETBALL
Manufacturer: Magnavox
Rarity: 9
Loose: $25–35*
Complete: $40–80*
Notes: Includes 2 overlays, scoreboard, and cartridge #8

BRAIN WAVE
Manufacturer: Magnavox
Rarity: 9
Loose: $25–35*
Complete: $40–80*
Notes: Includes 2 overlays, game board, Thought Tiles (2 sets of 48), 2 dice, 2 Memory Banks, and 2 Power Markers; no cartridge (uses cartridge #5, included with the Odyssey system)

FUN ZOO
Manufacturer: Magnavox
Rarity: 7
Loose: $10–15*
Complete: $20–30
Notes: Includes 2 overlays and 28 Fun Zoo cards; no cartridge (uses cartridge #2, included with the Odyssey system)

HANDBALL
Manufacturer: Magnavox
Rarity: 7
Loose: $10–15*
Complete: $20–30
Notes: Includes 2 overlays and cartridge #8

INTERPLANETARY VOYAGE
Manufacturer: Magnavox
Rarity: 9
Loose: $25–35*
Complete: $40–80*
Notes: Includes 2 overlays, game board, 40 mission cards, 72 knowledge cards, 4 spaceship tokens, a number of message chips (exact number unknown), and cartridge #12

INVASION
Manufacturer: Magnavox
Rarity: 7
Loose: $10–15*
Complete: $20–30*
Notes: Includes 2 overlays, game board, 40 "Treasure Loot" cards, 300 army tokens, 4 ship tokens and 2 dice; no cartridge (uses cartridges #4, #5, and #6, included with the Odyssey system)

PERCEPTS
Manufacturer: Magnavox
Rarity: 9
Loose: $25–35*
Complete: $40–80*
Notes: Includes 2 overlays and Percepts cards (15 green, 15 purple); no cartridge (uses cartridge #2, included with the Odyssey system); available only through mail-order; no box

VOLLEYBALL
Manufacturer: Magnavox
Rarity: 8
Loose: $10–15
Complete: $20–30
Notes: Includes 2 overlays and cartridge #7

WIN
Manufacturer: Magnavox
Rarity: 9
Loose: $25–35*
Complete: $40–80*
Notes: Includes 2 overlays, 18 word cards, 9 image cards, 18 number cards, 4 slates, and 4 markers; no cartridge (uses cartridge #4, included with the Odyssey system)

WIPEOUT
Manufacturer: Magnavox
Rarity: 7
Loose: $10–15*
Complete: $20–30*
Notes: Includes 2 overlays, game board, 25 "Pit Stop" cards, and 4 car tokens; no cartridge (uses cartridge #5, included with the Odyssey system)

Pong and *Pong*-Clone Consoles

In the early '70s, the Magnavox Odyssey was the one and only home video game on the market. With the introduction of inexpensive microchip technology in the mid-1970s, however, many electronics companies decided the time was ripe to introduce home video games on a larger scale.

Pong was still a huge commercial success in the arcades, and Atari decided that it was time to bring their popular game home. The dedicated Atari *Pong* home console was released in 1975. Initially, the game was sold exclusively through Sears stores, but after the initial rollout Atari sold the console under its own label as well. Around 150,000 consoles sold during the 1975 Christmas season for $100 apiece.

The following year, a huge number of rival companies jumped into the home video game market, releasing a slew of *Pong* knock-offs upon the eager public. One of the companies that joined the rush was Magnavox, who reintroduced a simplified and more advanced line of Odyssey home consoles. Soon, more than 50 companies were vying for a piece of the home *Pong* market.

The retail lifespan of dedicated *Pong* and *Pong*-clone consoles was short-lived. When Fairchild Camera and Instrument released its cartridge-based Channel F video game system in 1976, it was obvious to everyone that greater game variety would mean longer shelf life for a console. Even so, variants on the *Pong* theme dominated the home video game market for the better part of two and a half years and, as a result, hundreds of different variations on the home *Pong* theme await the diligent collector today.

A number of dedicated consoles also added shooting games that used light gun controllers to their mix to increase the variety of built-in games. In the price guide later in this chapter, the shooting game consoles are listed along with the other *Pong*-type systems, since most of them had a number of built-in *Pong* games as well.

As a general rule, *Pong*-clone console systems today are quite inexpensive. Many of them sell in online auctions and at conventions for $25 or less. There are exceptions to this rule, however. Because it was the first system of its kind, *Pong*—both the Atari and Sears version—has a considerably higher value in the collectors' marketplace. A number of the later Atari and Sears systems also tend to fetch higher prices than the lesser-known dedicated consoles.

Dedicated consoles are easier to find in a complete state than cartridge-based systems because their controllers are not generally detachable and few of them included accessories other than the antenna/game switchbox and cable, an instruction manual, and (in some cases) an AC adaptor.

The simplicity of most dedicated *Pong*-clones ensures that many of them are still in working order. The biggest problems you're likely to encounter are broken controllers, missing antenna/game switchboxes, and in the case of battery-operated consoles, internal damage caused by battery corrosion. Consoles that include light guns and/or detachable controllers are more likely to have missing or broken parts.

Notable *Pong* Consoles

With over 50 companies churning out *Pong*-clone systems in the mid-1970s, the home video game marketplace at the time offered a confusing array of choices. Most of the consoles play the same basic *Pong*-like games and are essentially interchangeable with one another as far as gameplay is concerned. There are, however, a number of *Pong*-type consoles that stand out from a collector's standpoint.

Atari/Tele-Games *Pong* (1975)

Tele-Games *Pong* has the distinction of being the first dedicated console to hit the market after the Magnavox Odyssey was discontinued. Atari, new to the consumer marketplace at the time, contacted many toy companies and other retail outlets searching for someone who was interested in selling the console, but there was little interest in a game that retailed for $100, far more than the price of the average toy at the time.

One of the companies Atari contacted was Sears and Roebuck. Like other toy retailers, the Sears toy department wasn't interested. However, Tom Quinn, the sporting goods buyer for Sears, was *very* interested in the product. He placed an order for 150,000 *Pong* consoles, with the stipulation that Sears would initially have exclusive distribution rights for the game. Atari jumped at the deal, and obtained the necessary venture capital required to fill this huge order. The entire 150,000 run of Tele-Games *Pong* consoles sold out during the 1975 Christmas season.

In 1976, Atari re-released the system under its own label, and they went on to produce a large number of variations on their original *Pong* theme over the next two years. Like the original *Pong*, most of these consoles were also marketed under the Sears Tele-Games label.

Because of its historical significance, *Pong* generally is the highest-priced dedicated console (with the exception of the original Magnavox Odyssey). Boxed, complete Atari *Pong* systems can fetch up to $150 in an online auction. The Sears Tele-Games version tends to be slightly less expensive.

The Magnavox Odyssey Series (1975–1977)

After a two-year hiatus from the video game business, Magnavox reentered the marketplace with a new series of dedicated Odyssey consoles. Starting with the **Odyssey 100** in 1975, these systems eliminated the huge number of overlays and accessories required by Magnavox's original Odyssey. These simplified game systems also offered fewer game choices, but added features like sound and scoring.

The Odyssey 100 was primitive compared to Tele-Games *Pong* in that it didn't feature on-screen scoring. Score was kept manually using plastic sliders on the console. It wasn't until the

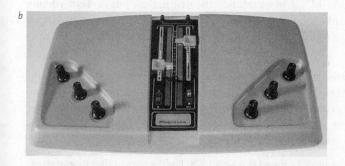

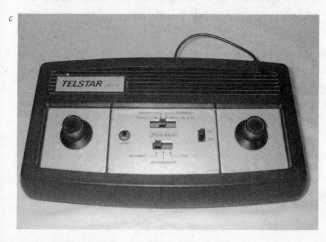

a **Atari Pong.** Atari entered the home video game market with Pong, a home version of their hit arcade game. This console was originally sold exclusively through Sears stores under the Tele-Games label.

b **Odyssey 100,** released in 1975, eliminated the game choices (and the huge number of associated accessories) of the original Magnavox Odyssey. Magnavox opted instead for features like sound and manual scoring for their new Pong-clone console.

c **Telstar Alpha.** Coleco's Telstar line was a low-priced alternative to Atari's Pong consoles. The first game in the Telstar series sold nearly a million units in 1976.

Odyssey 400 (1976) that Magnavox introduced on-screen scoring to its consoles. Also in 1976, Magnavox released its first color game system, the Odyssey 500, which also replaced the typical on-screen paddles with simple game characters—tennis players for Tennis, squash players for Squash, and hockey players for Hockey.

The Odyssey series continued through 1977. All of the Magnavox consoles stuck to the basic *Pong* game formula, adding very little gameplay innovation. Nevertheless, this series of consoles was one of the more popular product lines at the time.

The Coleco Telstar Series (1976–1978)

One of the most successful early competitors in the fledgling video game industry was a small New England–based company that had originally been a leather goods firm. The Connecticut Leather Company got into the toy industry in the 1950s, selling wading pools and other plastic toys. As their focus shifted into this new market, the company shortened its name to Coleco.

As the *Pong* craze ramped up in 1976, Coleco released the first in their line of **Telstar home video games**. The first Telstar, like most of the games on the market, only played *Pong*. It was, however, about half the price of Atari's *Pong* console and hence a popular alternative for families on a tight budget.

Coleco's early success also benefited from a lucky turn of fate. The glut of new video game manufacturers had caused a severe chip shortage. Most companies got only a fraction of the General Instruments microchips they needed to complete their game consoles. Coleco, on the other hand, got their entire allotment. As a result of this and their budget-friendly pricing, Coleco sold nearly a million Telstar consoles during the first year.

The Telstar line continued to grow and expand through 1978. Unlike many other manufacturers, Coleco introduced a variety of non-*Pong* games in their dedicated consoles, including a number of target shooting games.

Although many of the early *Pong*-console companies dropped out of the market in the mid- to late-'70s, Coleco maintained a video game presence well into the cartridge-based console era. Although their first cartridge-based system, the Telstar Arcade was never a huge hit, the ColecoVision, introduced in the early '80s, briefly set the graphics and gameplay standard for the industry. (See Chapter 6 for details on the ColecoVision console.)

Dedicated Console Price Guide
Pong Systems

ADVERSARY
Manufacturer: National Semiconductor
Year: ?
Rarity: 5
Loose: $3–5
Complete: $7–12
Notes: 2-player; includes 4 games; wired joystick controllers

COMPUVISION
Manufacturer: Bentley
Year: 1978
Rarity: 2
Loose: $3–5
Complete: $7–12
Notes: 2-player; includes 4 games; wired paddle controllers

GAMEROOM TELE-PONG

Manufacturer: Entex
Year: 1976
Rarity: 7
Loose: $8–10*
Complete: $15–20

GUNSLINGER

Manufacturer: Sears
Year: ?
Rarity: 9
Loose: $30–35*
Complete: $45–60*

GUNSLINGER II

Manufacturer: Sears
Year: ?
Rarity: 9
Loose: $30–35*
Complete: $45–60*

HANIMEX 777

Manufacturer: Hanimex
Year: ?
Rarity: 5
Loose: $3–7
Complete: $8–15
Notes: 2-player; includes 4 games and 2 wired paddle controllers

ODYSSEY 100

Manufacturer: Magnavox
Year: 1975
Rarity: 4
Loose: $9–12
Complete: $18–30
Notes: 2-player; includes 2 games (*Tennis* and *Hockey*); black and white with manual scoring and no sound

ODYSSEY 200

Manufacturer: Magnavox
Year: 1975
Rarity: 4
Loose: $8–10*
Complete: $15–25*
Notes: 4-player; includes 3 games (*Tennis, Hockey,* and *Smash*)

ODYSSEY 2000

Manufacturer: Magnavox
Year: 1977
Rarity: 3
Loose: $5–9
Complete: $12–18
Notes: 2-player; includes 4 games

ODYSSEY 300

Manufacturer: Magnavox
Year: 1976
Rarity: 3
Loose: $5–9
Complete: $10–15
Notes: Virtually identical to the Odyssey 200

ODYSSEY 3000

Manufacturer: Magnavox
Year: 1977
Rarity: 3
Loose: $5–9
Complete: $10–15
Notes: Newly styled version of the Odyssey 2000 with wired controllers

ODYSSEY 400

Manufacturer: Magnavox
Year: 1976
Rarity: 4
Loose: $8–10
Complete: $15–30
Notes: Virtually identical to the Odyssey 200 except that it featured on-screen digital scoring

ODYSSEY 4000

Manufacturer: Magnavox
Year: 1977
Rarity: 3
Loose: $5–9
Complete: $10–15
Notes: 2-player; includes 8 games; used detachable joysticks (as opposed to paddles) that were styled like those later found on the Magnavox Odyssey[2]

ODYSSEY 500

Manufacturer: Magnavox
Year: 1976
Rarity: 4
Loose: $8–10*
Complete: $15–25*
Notes: Includes 4 games; first Odyssey system with color graphics; quite advanced for its time—the normal paddles were replaced by simple player graphics

PONG

Manufacturer: Atari
Year: 1976
Rarity: 2
Loose: $25–65
Complete: $50–150
Notes: Model C-100; 2-player

PONG

Manufacturer: Gemini
Year: 1976
Rarity: 8
Loose: $10–12*
Complete: $15–20*
Notes: 2-player; wired paddle controllers; case was wood, not plastic

PONG DOUBLES

Manufacturer: Atari
Year: 1976
Rarity: 4
Loose: $10–15*
Complete: $20–30*
Notes: Model C-160; 4-player

Q-376

Manufacturer: Quadtronics
Year: ?
Rarity: 7
Loose: $10–15
Complete: $20–30*

Q-476

Manufacturer: Quadtronics
Year: ?
Rarity: 7
Loose: $10–15*
Complete: $20–30*

RALLY IV

Manufacturer: Roberts
Year: 1977
Rarity: 4
Loose: $5–10
Complete: $12–18
Notes: 2-player; includes 4 games

S FOUR THOUSAND

Manufacturer: K-Mart
Year: 1977
Rarity: 3
Loose: $5–10
Complete: $15–20
Notes: 2-player; includes 4 games and 2 wired controllers; controllers used vertical sliders rather than the paddle controllers used on most other systems

S EIGHT THOUSAND

Manufacturer: K-Mart
Year: 1977
Rarity: 4
Loose: $5–10*
Complete: $15–20*
Notes: 4-player; includes 8 games, 4 wired controllers, and a light gun

SUPER PONG

Manufacturer: Atari
Year: 1976
Rarity: 2
Loose: $12–20
Complete: $25–45
Notes: Model C-140; 2-player; includes 4 games

SUPER PONG TEN

Manufacturer: Atari
Year: 1976
Rarity: 4
Loose: $10–20*
Complete: $25–40
Notes: Model C-180; 4-player; includes 10 games

SUPER PONG PRO-AM

Manufacturer: Atari
Year: 1977
Rarity: 6
Loose: $10–20*
Complete: $25–40*
Notes: Model C-200; 2-player; includes 4 games

SUPER PONG PRO-AM TEN

Manufacturer: Atari
Year: 1977
Rarity: 6
Loose: $10–20*
Complete: $25–40*
Notes: Model C-202; 4-player; includes 10 games

TELE-ACTION MINI TV GAME

Manufacturer: DMS
Year: ?
Rarity: 3
Loose: $4–8
Complete: $9–12
Notes: 2-player; includes 4 games; unique design with 2 independent controllers and no actual base console (the console functions are on the controllers themselves)

TELE-GAMES HOCKEY-PONG

Manufacturer: Sears
Year: 1976
Rarity: 3
Loose: $7–12*
Complete: $15–20*
Notes: 2-player; includes 4 games

TELE-GAMES HOCKEY-TENNIS II

Manufacturer: Sears
Year: 1977
Rarity: 4
Loose: $7–12
Complete: $15–20*
Notes: 2-player; includes 4 games

TELE-GAMES HOCKEY-TENNIS III

Manufacturer: Sears
Year: 1977
Rarity: 5
Loose: $8–12
Complete: $15–20
Notes: 2-player; includes 4 games

TELE-GAMES PONG

Manufacturer: Sears
Year: 1975
Rarity: 2
Loose: $25–40
Complete: $45–60
Notes: Sears version of Atari's *Pong*

TELE-GAMES PONG IV

Manufacturer: Sears
Year: 1976
Rarity: 4
Loose: $5–8
Complete: $10–15
Notes: Sears version of Atari's *Pong Doubles*

TELE-GAMES PONG SPORTS II

Manufacturer: Sears
Year: 1977
Rarity: 4
Loose: $5–8
Complete: $10–15
Notes: Sears version of Atari's *Ultra Pong*

TELE-GAMES PONG SPORTS IV
Manufacturer: Sears
Year: 1977
Rarity: 3
Loose: $8–10
Complete: $15–25
Notes: Sears version of Atari's *Ultra Pong Doubles*

TELE-GAMES SPEEDWAY IV
Manufacturer: Sears
Year: 1976
Rarity: 6
Loose: $10–15*
Complete: $18–25*

TELE-GAMES SUPER PONG
Manufacturer: Sears
Year: 1976
Rarity: 2
Loose: $8–10*
Complete: $15–20*
Notes: Sears version of Atari's *Super Pong*

TELE-GAMES SUPER PONG IV
Manufacturer: Sears
Year: 1976
Rarity: 3
Loose: $7–12
Complete: $15–25
Notes: 4-player; includes 4 games

TELSTAR
Manufacturer: Coleco
Year: 1976
Rarity: 2
Loose: $5–10
Complete: $10–20
Notes: 2-player; includes 3 games; also sold under the Montgomery Ward brand name (Montgomery Ward model value is about 10% higher)

TELSTAR ALPHA
Manufacturer: Coleco
Year: 1977
Rarity: 3
Loose: $5–10
Complete: $20–35
Notes: 2-player; includes 4 games

TELSTAR CLASSIC
Manufacturer: Coleco
Year: 1976
Rarity: 5
Loose: $10–15*
Complete: $20–30*
Notes: Identical to the Telstar, but in a deluxe wood case

TELSTAR COLORMATIC
Manufacturer: Coleco
Year: 1977
Rarity: 5
Loose: $9–12*
Complete: $15–20*
Notes: Identical to the Telstar Alpha except that the controllers are wired and it has a color display

TELSTAR COLORTRON
Manufacturer: Coleco
Year: 1978
Rarity: 4
Loose: $7–10
Complete: $10–15
Notes: 2-player; includes 4 games; color display

TELSTAR DELUXE
Manufacturer: Coleco
Year: 1976
Rarity: 6
Loose: $9–12*
Complete: $15–20*
Notes: Identical to the Telstar, but on a plastic pedestal; also marketed by Montgomery Ward stores as *Coleco Video World of Sports*

TELSTAR GALAXY
Manufacturer: Coleco
Year: 1977
Rarity: 6
Loose: $9–12*
Complete: $15–20*
Notes: 2-player; includes 48 Pong-variants; had 2 paddle controllers mounted on the console and 2 wired joysticks

TELSTAR GEMINI
Manufacturer: Coleco
Year: ?
Rarity: 5
Loose: $9–12*
Complete: $15–20*
Notes: Includes 6 games and a light gun pistol (2 games were target games and the others were Pong variants); color display

TELSTAR MARKSMAN
Manufacturer: Coleco
Year: 1978
Rarity: 4
Loose: $10–15
Complete: $18–25
Notes: Includes 6 games and a unique 3-in-1 light gun that could be converted from a pistol to a target pistol or a rifle (2 games were shooting games, the others were Pong variants)

TELSTAR RANGER
Manufacturer: Coleco
Year: 1977
Rarity: 3
Loose: $7–10*
Complete: $10–20
Notes: Includes 6 games and a light gun pistol (2 games were shooting games, the others were variants of Pong); has 2 wired paddle controllers

TELSTAR REGENT
Manufacturer: Coleco
Year: 1977
Rarity: 7
Loose: $7–10*
Complete: $10–20
Notes: Identical to the Telstar Colormatic but with a black-and-white display and a slightly different case and controller style

CLASSIC VIDEO GAMES

TELSTAR SPORTSMAN
Manufacturer: Coleco
Year: ?
Rarity: 6
Loose: $9–12*
Complete: $15–25*
Notes: Includes 2 wired paddles and a light gun pistol

TELSTAR VIDEO WORLD OF SPORTS
Manufacturer: Coleco
Year: 1976
Rarity: 6
Loose: $9–12*
Complete: $15–20*
Notes: Identical to the Telstar Deluxe; this version was marketed by Montgomery Ward stores

TV FUN 401
Manufacturer: APF
Year: 1976
Rarity: 3
Loose: $5–10
Complete: $10–15
Notes: 2-player; includes 4 games

TV FUN 402
Manufacturer: APF
Year: ?
Rarity: 4
Loose: $8–12
Complete: $12–20
Notes: 4-player; includes 5 games, 2 wired bat controllers (in addition to the fixed paddles) and a light gun pistol; color display

TV FUN 405
Manufacturer: APF
Year: 1977
Rarity: 5
Loose: $8–12*
Complete: $12–20*
Notes: 2-player; includes 4 games; had wired paddle controllers

TV FUN 406
Manufacturer: APF
Year: ?
Rarity: 7
Loose: $9–14*
Complete: $17–22*

TV FUN 442
Manufacturer: APF
Year: ?
Rarity: 7
Loose: $9–14*
Complete: $17–22*

TV FUN 444
Manufacturer: APF
Year: ?
Rarity: 7
Loose: $9–14*
Complete: $17–22*

TV FUN 500
Manufacturer: APF
Year: ?
Rarity: 7
Loose: $9–14*
Complete: $17–22*

TV FUN SPORTSARAMA
Manufacturer: APF
Year: ?
Rarity: 3
Loose: $5–10*
Complete: $10–15*
Notes: Similar to the TV Fun 402, but with 8 games instead of 5

TV GAME (EP-500)
Manufacturer: Granada
Year: ?
Rarity: 8
Loose: $9–12*
Complete: $15–20*
Notes: 2-player; includes 2 detachable paddle controllers

TV GAME 2 (EP-800)
Manufacturer: Granada
Year: ?
Rarity: 8
Loose: $9–12*
Complete: $15–20*
Notes: 4-player; includes 4 games and 4 detachable paddle controllers; box is simply labeled "Granada"

TV SCOREBOARD (MODEL 60-3050)
Manufacturer: Radio Shack
Year: 1976
Rarity: 3
Loose: $6–9*
Complete: $10–15*

TV SCOREBOARD (MODEL 60-3051)
Manufacturer: Radio Shack
Year: 1976
Rarity: 2
Loose: $5–7*
Complete: $9–12*
Notes: 2-player; includes 4 games and 2 wired paddle controllers

TV SCOREBOARD (MODEL 60-3052)
Manufacturer: Radio Shack
Year: 1976
Rarity: 2
Loose: $5–7*
Complete: $9–12*
Notes: 2-player; includes 4 games; detachable controllers are a unique lever-style 2-way joystick

TV SCOREBOARD (MODEL 60-3054)
Manufacturer: Radio Shack
Year: 1976
Rarity: 4
Loose: $7–10*
Complete: $12–18*

TV SCOREBOARD (MODEL 60-3055)
Manufacturer: Radio Shack
Year: 1977
Rarity: 2
Loose: $5–7*
Complete: $9–12*

TV SCOREBOARD (MODEL 60-3056)
Manufacturer: Radio Shack
Year: 1977
Rarity: 3
Loose: $6–9*
Complete: $10–15*

TV SCOREBOARD (MODEL 60-3057)
Manufacturer: Radio Shack
Year: 1977
Rarity: 2
Loose: $5–7*
Complete: $9–12*
Notes: 4-player; includes 6 games and a light gun pistol that could be converted to a rifle; slider-style wired controllers

TV SCOREBOARD (MODEL 60-3060)
Manufacturer: Radio Shack
Year: 1977
Rarity: 2
Loose: $5–7*
Complete: $9–12*

TV SCOREBOARD (MODEL 60-3061)
Manufacturer: Radio Shack
Year: 1977
Rarity: 2
Loose: $5–7*
Complete: $9–12*
Notes: 2-player; includes 6 games and a light gun pistol; the console controls were built into the right paddle controller and the left paddle controller was detachable

ULTRA PONG
Manufacturer: Atari
Year: 1977
Rarity: 5
Loose: $10–12
Complete: $15–20
Notes: Model C-402(S); 2-player; includes 16 games

ULTRA PONG DOUBLES
Manufacturer: Atari
Year: 1977
Rarity: 5
Loose: $15–20*
Complete: $25–40
Notes: Model C-402(D); 4-player; includes 16 games

VIDEO SPORTS
Manufacturer: JC Penny
Year: ?
Rarity: 6
Loose: $7–9*
Complete: $10–15*

VIDEO SPORTS
Manufacturer: Venture
Year: 1977
Rarity: 5
Loose: $6–8*
Complete: $10–14*
Notes: 2-player; includes 4 games

WONDER WIZARD BULLS EYE
Manufacturer: General Home Products
Year: 1976
Rarity: 6
Loose: $5–7*
Complete: $8–14*
Notes: 2-player; includes multiple games and a light gun pistol; portable console design with 2 wired pistol grip paddle controllers

WONDER WIZARD SCORE BOARD
Manufacturer: General Home Products
Year: 1976
Rarity: 6
Loose: $5–7
Complete: $8–14
Notes: 2-player; includes 4 games (*Hockey, Jai-alai, Tennis,* and *Handball*); wired controllers

WONDER WIZARD SHARP SHOOTER
Manufacturer: General Home Products
Year: 1976
Rarity: 6
Loose: $5–7*
Complete: $8–14*
Notes: 2-player; includes 6 games (*Hockey, Tennis, Handball, Jai-alai, Target,* and *Skeet*), wired controllers, and a light gun pistol; color

WONDER WIZARD TELEVISION SPORTS GAME
Manufacturer: General Home Products
Year: 1976
Rarity: 5
Loose: $5–7
Complete: $8–14
Notes: 2-player; includes 3 games; proprietary antenna/game switchbox

WONDER WIZARD TRIPLE CHALLENGE
Manufacturer: General Home Products
Year: 1976
Rarity: 7
Loose: $6–9*
Complete: $10–20
Notes: 2-player; includes 3 games (*Hockey, Tennis,* and *Handball*)

a

a **Coleco's Telstar Combat *console*** *is one of the more interesting examples of a non-*Pong *dedicated console. Many companies released dedicated consoles that played games other than* Pong.

Other Dedicated Consoles

While most companies in the mid-1970s stuck to the basic *Pong* theme, some were trying to boost home console sales by introducing dedicated video games that deviated from the basic *Pong* theme. Atari introduced dedicated home console versions of their arcade hits *Stunt Cycle* and *Video Pinball* (which also included *Breakout,* another of their arcade hits) in 1977. In the same year, Coleco released **Telstar *Combat***, a tank battle game with unique controllers, which was obviously based on *Tank*, an arcade game released by Kee Games in 1974.

Compared to the number of *Pong*-clone dedicated consoles, there are a mere handful of dedicated consoles based on other game themes. Due to their unique controls and gameplay, these consoles tend to be more collectible than most of their more common TV tennis counterparts. Most were produced in smaller quantities than *Pong* systems, so they are a bit harder to find.

Like *Pong*-clone consoles, unique dedicated systems are easier to find in complete, working condition than are most cartridge-based systems. Once again, the major things to look out for are missing antenna/game switchboxes, and missing AC adaptors (where applicable). Damaged controllers are quite prevalent in non-*Pong* dedicated systems, especially on games with unique controllers like *Stunt Cycle* and Telstar *Combat*.

Dedicated Console Price Guide
Non-*Pong* Systems Price Guide

STUNT CYCLE
Manufacturer: Atari
Year: 1977
Rarity: 6
Loose: $15–25
Complete: $30–50
Notes: 1-player; includes 4 games; unique handlebar controller; one of the most collectible dedicated consoles

**TELE-GAMES MOTOCROSS/
PONG SPORTS IV**
Manufacturer: Sears
Year: 1977
Rarity: 8
Loose: $40–60
Complete: $65–75*
Notes: Sears version of Atari's *Stunt Cycle* combined with *Pong Sports IV*; includes 4 paddle controllers

TELE-GAMES PINBALL BREAKAWAY
Manufacturer: Sears
Year: 1977
Rarity: 5
Loose: $10–14
Complete: $15–25
Notes: Sears version of Atari's *Video Pinball*

TELSTAR COMBAT
Manufacturer: Coleco
Year: 1977
Rarity: 6
Loose: $20–35
Complete: $45–55*
Notes: Unique console with 2 dual-grip tank controllers; includes 4 tank game variants

VIDEO PINBALL
Manufacturer: Atari
Year: 1977
Rarity: 4
Loose: $10–14
Complete: $15–35
Notes: 1-player; includes 7 games including *Breakout;* sold in both wood grain (the original version) and white

4 The Atari VCS (2600)

Of all the classic video game consoles, the Atari Video Computer System (VCS)—which eventually came to be known as **the Atari 2600**—is easily the best known. During the classic era, the name Atari was synonymous with home video games in the same way that Kleenex and Jell-O have become generic terms describing facial tissues and wiggly gelatin desserts, respectively. "Have you played Atari today?" was Atari's advertising tag line at the height of the console's popularity, and as a result, playing home video games was "playing Atari," regardless of what game system you were *actually* playing.

The Atari VCS was introduced in 1977 and was produced in one form or another through 1991—the longest production run for any video game console in history. During this time, more than 25 million Atari VCSs were sold worldwide.

History of the VCS

In the mid-1970s, Atari's home video game business was booming. They had branched out from their basic *Pong*-derivative consoles into conversions of their other arcade hits such as *Video Pinball* and *Stunt Cycle*, and saw a continuing opportunity for further conversions of their arcade hits to home consoles. Unfortunately, the expense of developing a new dedicated console for every title was extremely high.

Following the example of Fairchild Camera and Instrument's Channel F video game console, Atari set out to design a programmable video game system that could play an unlimited number of games by simply plugging in new cartridges.

Their first attempt was called **Game Brain**. This console looked a lot like the *Pong* systems of the time, with two paddle controllers and a pair of four-way directional pads built into the console. Five prototype cartridges, all based on existing Atari stand-alone home consoles, were produced. The Game Brain never saw the light of day, however, since it lacked the versatility and capabilities of another Atari cartridge-based system that was also in development at the time.

That other system, nicknamed "Stella" during its development (after the bicycle of its chief designer, Joe Decuir), was the Atari Video Computer System. The console itself contained only a meager amount of memory, a 1 MHz processor chip and a graphics chip. The game programs were built into the cartridges that plugged into the console.

The VCS debuted in 1977. The $200 console came packaged with a pair of paddle controllers, two joysticks (a new type of controller in the home market at the time), and *Combat*, a tank battle game. At the time of release, there were eight additional cartridges available.

The VCS wasn't an instant hit. In fact, after a dismal Christmas season, Nolan Bushnell was ready to pull the plug on the console. Warner Communications, which had recently purchased Atari, had other ideas. They bought out Bushnell and took control of the company he had founded. Their first mission: set about trying to sell the huge number of VCS consoles they had on hand.

The key to the eventual success of the VCS, like Atari's initial success in the home video game market, can be attributed to the wild popularity of a video game that was taking arcades by storm. In 1980, Atari secured the home video game rights to Taito's **Space Invaders** and released it as a cartridge for the VCS. Suddenly, people were buying the VCS specifically to play *Space Invaders*. Sales went through the roof, and Atari's profits suddenly doubled. Thanks to VCS sales, Atari was on its way to becoming the fastest growing company in the history of the United States.

The conversion of arcade hits to VCS cartridges became the foundation of Atari's home console business, and they enjoyed great success as a result. With a huge stable of their own arcade hits to choose from, Atari introduced the exclusive home versions of games like *Missile Command*, *Centipede*, and *Asteroids*. They also bought the home console rights to many of the most popular non-Atari arcade games of the time, leaving their competitors to fight over the more obscure titles.

Between their arcade titles and growing library of original games, Atari was flourishing. Several groups of Atari's best game programmers split off from the company to form their own companies dedicated to the manufacture of games for the VCS. Activision and Imagic set the stage for a huge number of independent game manufacturers, and paved the way for the video game industry business model that still exists to this day. (See Chapter 1 for more details on the emergence of these new companies.) The immediate result was a flood of new VCS game cartridges, which eventually gave the VCS the largest library of games available for any classic game system.

When the video game industry began its rapid decline in 1983, the VCS (by then known as the 2600) was at the epicenter of the fall. Even so, the console lived on. When video games regained some popularity in the mid-'80s as a result of the introduction of the Nintendo Entertainment System in the United States, Atari continued to manufacture new 2600 consoles. In 1991, after 14 years on the market, the console was finally discontinued.

Atari 2600 Collecting

The Atari 2600 is easily the most collected classic video game console. The reason for this is simple—with over 25 million consoles sold worldwide, the system itself is easy to find, as are the vast majority of the cartridges and peripherals that were manufactured for it. On any given day, there are several thousand Atari 2600-related online auctions in progress. Many of the console

NOTE **

Throughout the text, **BOLD** indicates that an item appears in a picture.

a **The Atari 2600,** *the most popular video game console of the classic era, found its way into more than 25 million homes worldwide during its 14 years in production.*

b **The Game Brain,** *Atari's first attempt at a cartridge-based home video game console, never made it past the prototype stage.*

c **Space Invaders** *home version. The Atari 2600 enjoyed only moderate success until the release of the Space Invaders cartridge. Since this was the only home version of Space Invaders available, a huge number of people purchased the 2600 specifically to play this game. (Photo courtesy of Dan Cage.)*

variations sell for $20 to $50, and the most common cartridges, of which millions were produced, commonly sell for a mere $1 to $2 apiece. It is, therefore, very easy and fairly inexpensive to start an Atari 2600 collection.

On the other hand, the incredible popularity of the 2600 in the classic era led to the release of such a vast library of games and peripherals, compiling a *complete* collection of 2600 items can become a lifelong task. Not that such a task would deter most collectors. In fact, to most collectors, this is the type of challenge that fuels their ongoing fervor for the hobby.

The Atari 2600 has more unique considerations for collectors than most other classic video game systems. There are numerous console variations, some of which are considered more collectible than others. Some games were released multiple times, sometimes by different manufacturers, and the variation in cartridge and label styles are often significant in determining the collectibility of a game. Some games were available only as promotional items, or only through mail order, and are therefore much rarer than their commercially released counterparts. On top of all of these considerations, there are still cartridges being produced for the system to this day, adding to the already vast library of games available.

The general considerations for 2600 collecting are the same as those for other classic game consoles. The console itself should be in good working order—all switches functioning, solid connections, and so on. The controllers should be solid and responsive. The paddle controllers especially have a tendency to produce "jittery" movement when they become worn. Luckily, replacement controllers are relatively easy to find, and for the most part, fairly inexpensive. For collectors with some technical savvy, repair kits and materials are available to revive ailing consoles and components.

The power adaptor for most 2600 consoles is standard, as is the antenna/game switch used to connect the console to the television, so if these are missing they can be replaced with inexpensive modern equivalents.

As with any classic system, boxed and complete systems (or new systems on the rare occasion that you find one) command a higher price than their loose counterparts.

When purchasing cartridges, make sure the cases are in good shape and not cracked. The condition of the cartridge face and spine labels (where applicable) is very important if resale value is a consideration. The boxes for some cartridges are extremely hard to come by and, in some cases, are more expensive than the games themselves.

The primary concern with the cartridges themselves is that they be in good working order. A nonworking cartridge, even if its labels are in pristine condition, is little more than a worthless plastic box. Note that cartridges might require cleaning in order to work. You can easily clean Atari cartridge contacts (the gold strips visible on the board at the open end of the cartridge) by rubbing them lightly with a pencil eraser.

Console Variations

Over the 14-year history of the Atari 2600, numerous console variations were produced. Atari released many of these consoles over the years, while others were released by other manufacturers.

There are many distinguishing features that set the various versions apart from one another, but the primary difference (prior to the release of the redesigned Atari 2600 Jr. in 1986) is the number of switches that appear on the front of the console. Prior to 1980, every VCS console had six silver toggle switches on the front:

- Power

- Color/BW (to set the output for a black-and-white or color television set)

- Game Select

- Game Reset

- Game Difficulty (2)

Starting with the VCS 2600A in 1980, the Game Difficulty switches were changed to black slider switches and moved to the upper back edge of the console, leaving only four silver toggles on the front. For this reason, pre-2600 Jr. consoles are frequently identified as either "6-switch" or "4-switch" models.

The following sections describe the major Atari 2600 variants released in the United States between 1977 and 1991.

VCS CX2600 (1977–1979)

There are two versions of the **original Atari VCS**, both of which carry the same model number: CX2600. The original version, which was manufactured only during the first year of production, is a 6-switch model with a wood grain front panel and rounded corners. This VCS model is much heavier than the versions that followed it. The number of switches and the console's weight prompted collectors to nickname the original VCS the "Heavy Sixer."

Other than the weight and rounded corners, the one other major identifying mark of the original VCS is its production label, located on the bottom of the unit. The Heavy Sixer was manufactured in Sunnyvale, California, whereas its successors were built in Hong Kong.

Starting in 1978, the "Heavy Sixer" was replaced by the **second-generation CX2600**. This 6-switch model, which remained on the market through 1979, retains the same basic look of its predecessor, but is much lighter. The case is slightly thinner on the sides and bottom, and the front corners are more angular than those on the original version.

Both CX2600 models were packaged with two joysticks, two paddle controllers, and the *Combat* game cartridge.

VCS CX2600A (1980–1981)

The **CX2600A**, which was on the market for two years, is very similar in appearance to the second-generation CX2600 console. The only real difference is the number of switches on the front—four, instead of six. The wood grain front panel is still present, and the included accessories are identical to those present in the earlier packages.

A **promotional version of the CX2600A** was also produced. This console, which was available only to retailers for display purposes, is nearly identical to the production model. The identifying marks on the unit itself are the yellow striping around the front panel and switches (as opposed to the orange striping on production models), an imprint on the bottom identifying the console as a promotional unit, and the manufacturing label identifying Sunnyvale, California, as the place of manufacture. The box is clearly marked "For Promotional Purposes Only."

Atari 2600 (1982)

In 1982, the VCS went through yet another redesign. While this version retains the shape and 4-switch design of its immediate predecessor, the wood grain front panel was dropped in favor

a

b

c

d

a *The original Atari VCS console,* known by collectors as the "Heavy Sixer." (Photo courtesy of Albert Yaruso, http://www.atariage.com.)

b *The second version of the Atari VCS* was identical to the first except for its lighter weight and the more angular appearance of the front panel. (Photo courtesy of Albert Yaruso, http://www.atariage.com.)

c *The CX2600A* features only four option switches on the front panel as opposed to the six switches present on earlier models. (Photo courtesy of Albert Yaruso, http://www.atariage.com.)

d *The promotional version of the CX2600A* is distinguishable from the production version by the promotional stamp on the box and on the bottom of the console. (Photo courtesy of Cassidy Nolen.)

of an all-black case. This design decision has earned this version of the console the nickname "Darth Vader" among collectors. The new front panel also sports the console's new official name: **Atari 2600**.

The box and accessories for the new 2600 also changed. Two versions were available during the console's lifetime:

- A version in a large silver box, packaged with two joysticks (but no paddles) and two games: *Combat* and *Pac-Man*.

- A version in a smaller silver box, packaged with only one joystick and no paddles or games.

Atari 2600 Jr. (1986)

Three years after the video game market crashed and one year after its rebirth (thanks to the new Nintendo Entertainment System introduced in 1985), Atari continued to keep the 2600 line alive.

Atari reintroduced the 2600 in the form of the completely redesigned, compact **2600 Jr**. This inexpensive console was sold in two different boxes—one silver, the other red—and was packaged with a single joystick and no game cartridges. Two slight **cosmetic variations of the 2600 Jr**. exist. The earlier model has an Atari 2600 logo and a small rainbow logo centered in the silver strip that runs along the top of the unit. Collectors call this the "short rainbow" version. The later model has Atari written in large letters and a rainbow stripe that stretches the entire width of the console.

Sears Tele-Games Video Arcade Systems

After their successful collaboration on the original *Pong* system, Atari and Sears continued their marketing partnership for years to come. As a result, the Atari 2600 line was also marketed through Sears stores under the Tele-Games label.

Through 1981, the **Sears Tele-Games Video Arcade** consoles mirrored the design and configuration of their Atari-labeled counterparts, with the only major differences being the labeling and packaging. All of the early Sears systems were packaged with two joysticks, two paddle controllers, and *Tank Plus* (the Sears version of Atari's *Combat* cartridge).

In the late '80s, Sears produced a unique Atari 2600 clone called **the Tele-Games Video Arcade II**. This console looked very much like the Atari 7800 system, but was only capable of playing Atari 2600 games. It was packaged with two paddle/joystick combination controllers and a *Space Invaders* cartridge. This system is among the rarest Atari 2600 console variants, and complete units often sell for more than $200. An unopened Video Arcade II system sold for $450 on eBay in late 2003.

Notable Atari 2600 Clones

Not long after third-party companies won the right to create software for the Atari 2600, Atari's rivals decided to take a crack at producing their own versions of the Atari 2600 hardware as well. Atari's major competitors, Mattel and Coleco, released adaptors that allowed owners of the Intellivision and ColecoVision systems to play Atari 2600 cartridges in addition to their own game cartridges.

A number of competing companies also produced standalone Atari 2600 consoles. While many of the 2600 clones were only released outside the United States, a couple went head-to-head with Atari on their own turf.

a **The Atari 2600.** *The first VCS model officially known as the Atari 2600 was released in 1982. It has been nicknamed "Darth Vader" among collectors because of its all-black case design. (Photo courtesy of Albert Yaruso, http:// www.atariage.com.)*

b **Atari 2600 Jr.** *Trying to cash in on the success of video games in the wake of the Nintendo boom, Atari introduced the completely re-designed 2600 Jr. in 1986. (Photo courtesy of Albert Yaruso, http:// www.atariage.com.)*

c **A cosmetic variation of the 2600 Jr.** *This later model has a larger rainbow logo than the original 2600 Jr. variant, but is otherwise pretty much identical. (Photo courtesy of Albert Yaruso, http://www. atariage.com.)*

d *The Sears Tele-Games Video Arcade. These consoles are identical to the Atari VCS/2600 except for their labeling and packaging. Like the Atari-branded consoles, the Sears models are available in both 4- and 6-switch versions. (Photo courtesy of Albert Yaruso, http://www.atariage.com.)*

In 1983, Coleco released the **Gemini**, a sleek, compact Atari 2600 clone. The system, which retailed for less than the Atari 2600, was fully compatible with the hundreds of 2600 games on the market. The system included two joystick/paddle combination controllers, and used a standard power adaptor and antenna/game switch. Two packaging variations were available, each of which included a different 2600 cartridge from Coleco's lineup—one variation shipped with *Donkey Kong*, the other with *Mouse Trap*. This system was fairly common, and is relatively easy to find today.

One of the rarest Atari 2600-compatible systems is the **Columbia Home Arcade**. Other than its markings, this console is identical to the Coleco Gemini. This is not surprising, since Columbia House licensed the system from Coleco. The Columbia Home Arcade was available only through Columbia House's short-lived video game club, a mail-order organization based on Columbia House's successful record and tape club. Although the price of the Columbia Home Arcade was about half that of the Atari 2600 at the time, the home video game club was never very successful. Hence, only a small number of Columbia Home Arcade systems were sold.

Atari VCS Cartridges

The biggest component of any Atari 2600 collection is the library of game cartridges. All told, there are well over 700 U.S. titles (including all variants) available for this console, and the number continues to grow every year as new prototype games from the classic era are uncovered and published, and as hobbyists continue to program brand new games for the system.

Atari 2600 cartridge collecting presents some unique challenges. The following sections provide you with a crash course on some of the most important considerations for Atari cartridge collectors.

Cartridge Style

Because so many companies released cartridges for the 2600, it was inevitable that stylistic differences would exist in the cases themselves. While most case variations simply serve to identify a game's manufacturer, there are some occasions where a game is available in more than one cartridge style. To complicate things further, some companies used cases from other companies for some of their cartridges. In some instances, the case style can be a determining factor in a game's rarity and value.

When the VCS was first introduced, Atari produced all of the cartridges. As such, the cartridge cases were identical to one another. Atari stuck with the same cartridge shape for their games throughout the entire life of the 2600. **Sears** also used the standard Atari cartridge style exclusively, and many other companies used this style as well. Some companies, like CBS and Coleco, used standard-style cartridges molded in different colors like white and gray. CommaVid used standard-style cases that were slightly longer than other 2600 carts.

As other software companies started producing games for the 2600, new cartridge styles were introduced to set these games apart from the standard Atari fare. Some, like the cartridges used by Activision and Sega, exhibit only slight modifications. **Activision's cartridges** had notches on the sides near the spine on either side. Sega used a similar design, but with more pronounced finger grips on each side. Parker Brothers carts featured a sleeker, angular design.

Other manufacturers were more imaginative with their cartridge cases. **Imagic cartridges** were tapered and sleek, with the company logo embossed on the case. Spectravision's carts also had the company name on the carts themselves, and featured a unique rounded shape and different colors of plastic for each game.

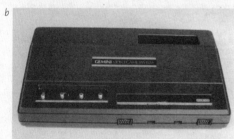

a **The Tele-Games Video Arcade II.** *Although it looked like an Atari 7800, this system was actually just the last of Sears' Atari 2600-compatible game consoles. This is one of the rarest and most collectible 2600 console variants.*

b **Coleco's Gemini system,** *released in 1983, is the best known of the third-party Atari 2600-compatible video game consoles. (Photo courtesy of Albert Yaruso, http://www.atariage.com.)*

c **The Columbia Home Arcade,** *a licensed version of the Coleco Gemini system that was available only through mail order, is rare and very collectible. (Photo courtesy of Albert Yaruso, http://www.atariage.com.)*

a **Atari and Sears cartridges.** *The black, rectangular cartridge design was the standard for both Atari and Sears. Many other manufacturers used this cartridge type as well. (Photo courtesy of Dan Cage.)*

b **Activision's cartridges** *(right) were similar to the Atari standard, but featured grooved grips near the top end of the cartridge.* **Sega's "grip case"** *cartridges (left) featured more prominent finger grips. (Photo courtesy of Dan Cage.)*

A company called **Xonox** had two unique cartridge designs: a sleek tapered cart that flared out at the spine and a double-length design that housed two games in a single cart. Playaround, a company that manufactured adult-themed games, also had a double-game cartridge, although theirs was smaller than the Xonox double-enders. **Playaround double-end cartridges** also included covers with spine labels that could be snapped into place on the exposed end of the cartridge while the other end was plugged into the console.

M-Network (which later became INTV) was a branch of Mattel Electronics that made Atari 2600 versions of popular Intellivision games. **M-Network/INTV** carts sported the familiar Intellivision wedge shape, with a flared end that was designed to fit in the 2600's wider cartridge slot.

Some manufacturers built **game cartridges with handles** to make them easier to remove from the 2600. Telesys molded a simple handle into the spine, while US Games opted for a beveled cartridge on some of their titles. MenAvision, who manufactured a single game—*Air Raid*—used a cartridge with a unique T-shaped grip. A similar T-grip design was used by both K-Tel and Ultravision on their titles.

a

b

c

a **Spectravision rounded cartridge style** (left) and **Imagic's carts** (right). stood out from the plainer Atari design. (Photo courtesy of Dan Cage.)

b **Xonox cartridges.** Xonox, a company that manufactured only a handful of games, used unique cartridge styles for both their single- and double-game releases. (Photo courtesy of Dan Cage.)

c **Playaround cartridges.** Adult game manufacturer Playaround sold many of their titles in double-cartridges. These cartridges featured plastic covers with the game titles imprinted on them that could be snapped into the exposed end of the cart while the other game was in use. (Photo courtesy of Albert Yaruso, http://www.atariage.com.)

Perhaps the most unique cartridge style is one that isn't a cartridge at all. Starpath released a product called the Supercharger, a cartridge that provides an interface between the Atari 2600 and a cassette tape player. The games are loaded into the Supercharger cartridge through this interface. Twelve games were released for the **Starpath Supercharger**, all on standard audiocassette tapes.

Label Variations

One of the more subtle aspects of collecting Atari 2600 cartridges is becoming aware of and gaining the ability to recognize variations in cartridge labels. Many of the games produced for the 2600 over the years were released multiple times, and in many cases, the re-released versions of the cartridges featured a different label style. In some instances, label variations are merely a means of identifying when a cartridge was produced. In other cases, the label type signals the cartridge's rarity and collectibility.

For example, Atari's *Gravitar* cartridge was originally released with a silver label only through the Atari Club (an organization that offered special games and merchandise exclusively to club members), and later re-released commercially with a red label. Because the **original silver label** version was produced in limited quantities and was available primarily through mail order, it is much more collectible (and worth a great deal more money) than the more common red label version.

Many of the label variations noted in the price guide at the end of this chapter are self-explanatory. For example, some of 20th Century Fox's cartridges were produced with "picture" labels, which feature stylish artwork depicting the theme of the game, while others were produced with plainer "red" labels with white text and an artist's rendering of a game screen.

Other companies had more subtle label variations. **Atari's label legacy**, for example, used no less than six different label styles over the years. The earliest cartridges had black text-only labels with the game name and description on their face, and a numbered spine label denoting the order of the game's release. When it became clear that there would be a large number of game cartridges, Atari dropped the numbering scheme and switched to unnumbered text labels. In 1981, Atari again changed its label style, replacing the plain black labels with labels featuring a glossy picture on a black background.

Sears' Tele-Games cartridges also followed these standards. The original releases featured text-only labels, while the later releases featured picture labels. In many cases, the Tele-Games picture labels featured the same artwork as their Atari counterparts.

From 1981 on, Atari stuck with **picture labels**, but varied the background color. Silver label cartridges were sold from 1982 through 1985, and the background color was changed to red from 1986 to 1990. The labels for Atari's children's cartridges varied in color from game to game, but all featured pictures.

Activision's cartridge labels are generally identified by color. Most of their games were originally released with standard labels depicting a rendering of a game screen and white text on a colored background. The label colors ranged from dark blue to bright pink depending on the game. A few of Activision's games were released with more stylish picture labels. Later, as budgets became tighter, Activision switched to plain dark blue labels with white text. White labels with black text, and black labels with white text were also used for the company's later games. The black-and-white label variations were generally found on European releases.

a **M-Network and INTV games** were Atari 2600 versions of Intellivision titles. The cartridges that housed them were designed to resemble the cartridges for Mattel's console. (Photo courtesy of Dan Cage.)

b **Game cartridges with handles.** Some game manufacturers incorporated handles into their cartridge designs, like US Games (left) and Telesys (right). (Photo courtesy of Dan Cage.)

c **Games that played through Starpath's Supercharger** were stored on cassette tapes rather than cartridges. (Photo courtesy of Dan Cage.)

a **The original silver label Gravitar cartridge** (pictured) typically sells for 40 to 70 times as much as the common red label version. A difference in label style and color can mean a huge difference in value. (Photo courtesy of Dan Cage.)

b **Atari's early label legacy.** From left to right: the numbered text, text, and picture label versions of Combat. (Photo courtesy of Albert Yaruso, http://www.atariage.com.)

c **Atari picture labels.** Later labels featured red (center) and silver (right) backgrounds. The children's cartridges (left) also featured pictures on brightly colored backgrounds. (Photo courtesy of Dan Cage.)

Like Activision, Imagic changed their label style over time to cut costs. The original **Imagic labels** featured interesting pictures depicting stylized action scenes on a silver foil background. Later releases featured the same flashy silver label, but dropped the picture.

Other companies stuck to a fairly standard labeling scheme, unique to the company but standard across all of the company's cartridges. The price guide at the end of this chapter notes label variations and the effect that the various label styles have on cartridge value and rarity where applicable.

Because the Atari 2600's cartridge library is so vast, new label variations are being discovered all the time as collectors unearth rare versions of cartridges that have yet to be recorded. If you encounter a label variation other than those listed in this book, you are encouraged to share this information with the collecting community through AtariAge (http://www.atariage.com) or one of the many other Atari 2600 Web sites.

Boxes

As mentioned in Chapter 2, boxed, complete games are generally more valuable than loose cartridges. For more common titles, boxes are fairly common. For rare titles, the boxes are sometimes more difficult to come by than the games themselves. Often, the boxes for rare games actually sell for a higher price than the cartridge.

Depending on your collecting goals, boxed games might or might not be important to you. If you are a stickler for boxed games, however, here are a few of the games that will present a challenge when it comes to locating boxes:

- *Chase the Chuck Wagon* (Spectravision)

- *Glib* (**Selchow & Righter**)

- Sears Tele-Games cartridges

A number of the earliest Atari 2600 titles originally shipped in "clamshell boxes" (boxes that opened like books from the front). These boxes are much harder to find than the standard box style, so boxed copies of these games might command a slightly higher price than the standard-box versions of the same games.

Note that there are some games—most notably many of the newer homebrew titles—that do not include boxes. If a box doesn't exist for a game, this fact is noted in the price guide at the end of this chapter.

Sears Cartridges

In addition to marketing their own versions of Atari's 2600 consoles, Sears produced their own line of Atari cartridges under their **Tele-Games** label. (This is not to be confused with "Telegames," a company that also sold games for the 2600.) With the exception of three original titles (***Steeplechase, Stellar Track,*** and ***Submarine Commander***), the Tele-Games cartridges are exact copies of games released by Atari. In nearly every instance, Sears changed the title of the games, but gameplay was identical to the Atari counterparts.

Because they were sold only in Sears stores, Sears Tele-Games titles were produced in smaller quantities and are therefore not as common. Even so, in most cases, Sears carts do not generally fetch significantly more in today's marketplace than their Atari counterparts. For some reason, the boxes for Sears games are particularly hard to find today, so boxed versions are more collectible.

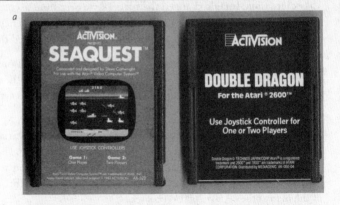

a **Examples of Activison label styles**—standard (left) and black. (Photo courtesy of Dan Cage.)

b **Imagic label styles.** To save money in later production runs, Imagic switched to simple foil text labels (left) rather than continuing to use the original graphic label style (right). (Photo courtesy of Dan Cage.)

Of all of the Sears Tele-Games cartridges, the three original titles are the most coveted among collectors. These games are fairly rare and generally priced higher than other Sears-branded cartridges.

The Atari Club

During the height of the Atari 2600's popularity, Atari established the **Atari Club**. For a mere dollar a year, players could join the club and receive a subscription to *Atari Age*, the club's bi-monthly magazine, which provided inside information on Atari products and sneak-peeks at upcoming games and other products. The magazine also hosted game contests for club members.

The primary purpose of the club and the magazine was merchandising. Every issue included extensive mail-order shopping opportunities for Atari-related products and offered discounts for cartridges.

The most notable benefit of Atari Club membership was the opportunity to purchase games that were manufactured exclusively for club members. These cartridges are among the most coveted Atari 2600 collectibles today. Because they were produced in limited quantities, they can be a challenge to find.

a **Selchow & Righter's Glib game box.** *Boxes for some games are extremely difficult to find and can add greatly to the game's value. A boxed version of Selchow & Righter's Glib is considerably more valuable than the cartridge alone. (Photo courtesy of Dan Cage.)*

b **Tele-Games cartridges.** *Most of the Atari 2600 games marketed by Sears under the Tele-Games label were simply renamed and repackaged versions of Atari titles. (Photos courtesy of Albert Yaruso, http://www.atariage.com and Dan Cage.)*

Five cartridges were released as Atari Club exclusives:

- *Atari Video Cube* (also known as *Rubik's Cube*)
- *Crazy Climber*
- *Gravitar* (silver label version)
- *Quadrun*
- *Swordquest: Waterworld*

While all five games are quite rare and were originally sold only through mail order, four were eventually sold in stores in limited quantities. In fact, *Gravitar* was repackaged and re-released to the general public after its initial run. (The Atari Club version of *Gravitar*, which is much more valuable, has a silver label—the re-release has a red label.)

Of the five Atari Club games, *Quadrun* is the rarest and most sought-after. Reportedly, only about 10,000 were produced. Although it is possible that this game, too, was eventually sold in limited quantities through retail stores, the small number of cartridges produced makes this doubtful.

a

"JOIN THE ATARI CLUB!"

Membership in The Atari Club means inside information about Atari video games—all the details on hot new releases, and "Sneak Peeks" at upcoming games and systems months before they're released.

It means Atari Club exclusives—special games not found at any store, available only to Club members!

It means terrific special offers—everything from money-saving cartridge prices to T-shirts, duffel bags, and other valuable bonuses.

It means members-only contests, with fantastic prizes.

And The Atari Club excitement is growing, with more members, greater benefits, a bigger Club magazine, nationwide high-scoring video-game competitions, and lots more!

The best news of all is that every Atari video game player is invited to join the Club, and it only costs $1.00!

That's right, just $1.00 brings you a year's membership in The Atari Club, complete with a one-year subscription to Atari Age, the Club's full-color bimonthly magazine, and all other Atari Club benefits and privileges.

To join, fill in the coupon at right (or write your name, address, age, and telephone number on a piece of paper)

and send it along with $1.00 to The Atari Club, P.O. Box 14064, Baltimore, MD 21203.

We make Atari fun even *more* fun— The Atari Club.

$1

YES! I want to join The Atari Club. Please start my 1-year membership. I am enclosing $1.00.

Name _____
Address _____
City _____ State _____ Zip _____
Age _____ Telephone # _____

13

a **Steeplechase, Stellar Track, and Submarine Commander** *were the only three original Sears Tele-Games titles. As such, they are considered the most collectible games in the Sears Tele-Games line. (Photo courtesy of Dan Cage.)*

b **Atari Club.** *Members of the Atari Club had the opportunity to purchase a number of games that were not released in stores. (Scan courtesy of Dan Cage.)*

Recordable Cartridges

Some companies came up with a number of unique marketing schemes to deliver Atari 2600 games to customers. One of the most interesting involved placing game kiosks in stores where a customer could choose from a variety of games and have the selected game copied to a blank cartridge on the spot. The cartridge, once recorded, was labeled with a simple typewritten (or handwritten) sticker and sold in a generic box with a simple instruction sheet.

A number of companies placed game kiosks in select test markets across the country. Two of the better-known kiosk manufacturers were Romox and Xante. Both cartridge types are extremely rare today since the test markets for the kiosk systems at the time were very limited. A number of game companies licensed games for these kiosks, most notably 20th Century Fox and Imagic.

Prototypes and Reproductions

When the video game crash of 1983–1984 hit, it came without much warning at a time when cartridge sales had been at an all-time high. As a result, when the reality of the crisis finally hit the industry, there were a large number of games that were in production—and in some cases completed—sitting in game development companies across the country. These prototype games slipped into obscurity and disappeared. Most of them, anyway.

From time to time over the years, collectors have found these prototypes, usually in the form of unlabeled cartridges or bare circuit boards with attached game chips. Collectors covet **original prototype cartridges** as they are extremely rare. Very few collectors can boast of owning an actual prototype—and those who do are unlikely to part with them.

Classic console collectors are always in search of new games, and the unearthing of a previously unknown prototype is always the cause for excitement. For many years, collectors with the equipment to do so have copied the ROM images of prototype games and distributed them to other collectors, either as an online ROM image or as a homemade cartridge. Until relatively recently, home-burned prototype copies were generally distributed in plain cartridge cases that were, to the untrained eye, very similar to the original prototypes themselves. A lot of these **prototype reproductions** are still floating around, so when you go shopping for a prototype, insist on some sort of proof that the prototype is real and not a reproduction. The prototype prices included in the price lists in this book (in the rare cases that such prices are available) are based on the actual prototypes. Reproductions are listed as such.

Over the past several years, the reproduction of prototype cartridges has become more organized. Prototype games are acquired by companies or individuals with the means to turn them into finished products: cartridges with labels, manuals, and (often) boxes that are professionally designed to look like the labeling and packaging used by the company that was slated to produce the game back in the classic era.

Most prototype reproductions are introduced at classic gaming conventions and shows. Generally, the reproductions are produced in limited quantities—usually 50 to 200 copies, depending on the resources of the individual or company producing the game. The asking price is usually in the $30 to $50 range at the time of release, and the cartridges usually sell out quickly. Many find their way onto Internet auction sites shortly thereafter, where they are often considerably more expensive.

If you miss the opportunity to attend a show where prototypes are being sold, check the Web site of the company that introduced the prototype at the show before you resort to online auctions. Some titles don't sell out or are produced in larger quantities and remain on sale at the company

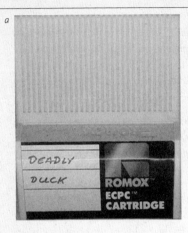

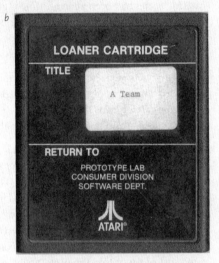

a **Recordable cartridge games.** *Several companies briefly attempted to distribute their games through kiosks that copied the game programs onto generic blank cartridges. These cartridges are extremely rare today. Two of the better-known manufacturers of recordable cartridges were Romox (left) and Xante (right). (Photo courtesy of Albert Yaruso, http:// www.atariage.com.)*

b **Original prototype cartridges—** *ones bearing actual evidence that they came directly from a software lab—are extremely rare and generally very collectible. (Photo courtesy of Albert Yaruso, http://www. atariage.com.)*

c **Prototype reproduction of sequel to Atari's Combat.** *Today, many previously unreleased prototypes are reproduced, professionally packaged, and released for sale at gaming conventions each year. (Photo courtesy of Dan Cage.)*

Web site for their original show/convention prices for some time after the event. Both AtariAge (http://www.atariage.com) and Atari2600.com (http://www.atari2600.com) are good sources for recently released prototype reproductions.

Nonprototype Reproductions

Recently, there has been a trend to acquire the rights to extremely rare Atari 2600 cartridges for the purpose of reproducing them in larger quantities. This allows collectors who want every game available for the system but who *don't* want to pay huge prices for the rarer titles to acquire some of the more difficult-to-find cartridges at reasonable prices.

This is a relatively new trend in the hobby, but a number of titles have already received this treatment. For example, Sunmark (http://www.sunmark.com) sells reproductions of the difficult to find *MagiCard* and *Video Life* cartridges by CommaVid, games that were originally available only through mail order and are, thus, extremely rare. The reproductions sell for considerably less than the originals.

If your intention is to collect only original games, it is important to be aware that reproductions exist. Although reproductions are generally labeled as such, it is not unheard of for unscrupulous sellers (especially in online auctions) to attempt to pass off currently available reproductions as "rare originals."

"Homebrew" and "Hack" Games

A testament to the continuing popularity of classic video game systems is the number of new games that are being produced for them today. Every year, enterprising hobbyists release several new Atari 2600 games. These are not prototype reproductions or repackaged versions of existing games, but new, original games.

The growing popularity of classic video game collecting has led to the release of several new Atari 2600 games every year. Like prototype reproductions, new original games—known among hobbyists as **"homebrew" games**—are generally released to the public at large game conventions like the Austin Gaming Expo (http://www.austingamingexpo.com), Philly Classic (http://www.phillyclassic.com), and the Classic Gaming Expo (http://www.cgexpo.com).

Homebrew games often include professional labeling and manuals. Some are sold without packaging, but others include boxes or totally original packages in keeping with the game's theme.

Because private individuals usually produce homebrew games, quantities are generally very limited. Most sell out quickly at the shows where they are introduced. Many are re-released afterward depending on their popularity. In many cases, the first cartridges produced are special "limited edition" versions that are labeled differently from the cartridges produced after the game's initial release and might contain additional game or title screens. Depending on the game, the limited edition "show" versions of homebrew games might garner a higher price on the collectors' market than subsequent versions of the same game.

While some homebrew cartridges are difficult to find after their initial release, many remain available for some time through collector sites. AtariAge usually has a wide variety of homebrew titles for sale through their online store.

Some present-day Atari 2600 programmers don't choose to create their own games. Instead, they take original games released in the classic era and modify them, adding improved graphics and sound, new themes, and even new levels and screens. These games are known to collectors as "hacks."

Quite a number of games have gotten the hack treatment with impressive results. For example *Pac-Man*, a game that was a huge disappointment in its original Atari 2600 incarnation, was updated with graphics and gameplay closer to the original arcade version and re-released in hack form as *Pac-Man Arcade*. **Space Invaders** received a similar arcade update.

Other games have been updated to use different controllers that make their game play closer to that of the arcade games upon which they were based. *Asteroids DC+* uses the Atari Driving Controller to turn the ship, and *Missile Command: Trak-Ball* allows the use of a trackball controller instead of the standard Atari joystick. Still other games have been updated with additional levels, like *Adventure Plus*.

Hack titles were originally available only as ROM images or homemade cartridges passed from person to person in the game collecting community. Now, many of these hack cartridges have been professionally reproduced, labeled, and sold through game collecting sites like AtariAge and Packrat Video Games (http://www.packgratvg.com).

"Holy Grail" Cartridges for the VCS

While the subject of which cartridges are considered the most collectible is always a topic of debate among serious collectors, there are some titles that everyone agrees are extremely valuable additions to any Atari 2600 collection.

Rare and valuable games like these are typically known as "Holy Grails" among collectors. The following sections describe just a few of the Holy Grail cartridges for the Atari 2600.

MagiCard (CommaVid)

MagiCard is generally considered to be one of the holiest of Holy Grail cartridges for the 2600. This cartridge is not a game, it is a programming utility that allows you to create your own games using the Atari's keyboard controllers.

Available only through mail order directly from CommaVid, the *MagiCard* had very limited distribution. The cartridge was shipped with a rather extensive manual but no box. Some *MagiCard* labels list the manufacturer as "Computer Magic," which was CommaVid's original name.

This cartridge is seldom seen for sale through any venue, but when one does become available, it fetches an extremely high price. One *MagiCard* is rumored to have sold on eBay for as much as $1,800, although that price is not necessarily indicative of the average price. At any rate, it is unlikely that the cartridge would ever sell for under $700.

Video Life (CommaVid)

Also produced by CommaVid, **Video Life** was only available through mail order to customers who owned the *MagiCard* cartridge. Because *MagiCard* itself is so rare, it only stands to reason that *Video Life* is even more so. It is rumored that only about 20 copies of this game were produced. If that is the case, it is certainly one of the rarest 2600 titles in existence.

The value of *Video Life* is debated among collectors. It is rumored that collectors have paid as much as $3,000 for a complete *Video Life*. This is difficult to confirm, since this title is seldom, if ever, available on the open market.

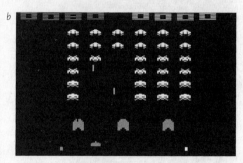

a **SCSIcide *by Pixels Past,*** *a homebrew game where you control the read head of a hard drive as you attempt to collect data bits, is sold in an antistatic bag like those used to package computer components. (Photo courtesy of Albert Yaruso, http://www.atariage.com.)*

b **Space Invaders *Arcade*** *replaces the original Atari graphics with graphics that more closely match those of the arcade game. (Photo courtesy of Albert Yaruso, http://www.atariage.com.)*

c **MagiCard *by CommaVid*** *is generally considered to be among the most collectible of all Atari 2600 cartridges. (Photo courtesy of Dan Cage.)*

d **CommaVid's Video Life cartridge,** *which was available only to those who purchased MagiCard, is easily one of the rarest of all Atari 2600 games. Only 20 are known to exist. (Photo courtesy of Dan Cage.)*

a **Ikari Warriors** *and* **Motorodeo**— *these NTSC versions were thought to be rumors until both were proven to exist in 2003. (Photo courtesy of Dan Cage.)*

b ***Menavision's* Air Raid** *is an oddly shaped cartridge that is high on most collectors' lists. Very few are known to exist. (Photo courtesy of Albert Yaruso, http://www. atariage.com.)*

c **Quadrun** *is the rarest and most sought-after of the five games that were originally produced exclusively for Atari Club members. (Photo courtesy of Dan Cage.)*

Ikari Warriors and Motorodeo (Atari)

These two Atari titles are grouped together because they share a common history: they are both recently discovered Holy Grail cartridges.

The video game crash that so profoundly impacted the industry in the United States didn't have the same effect in other parts of the world. As the market for new cartridges fell off domestically, companies released some of their games exclusively in Europe and in other parts of the world. For this reason, many games that are considered common abroad are extremely rare in the United States—if they were released here at all.

Until recently, it was thought that both *Ikari Warriors* and *Motorodeo* were only released in PAL format for overseas markets. Rumors of NTSC versions released in the United States were thought to be false until a collector produced the conclusive evidence of their existence: pristine, boxed copies of both games.

The fact that the existence of the U.S. versions of these games wasn't confirmed until 2003 indicates that NTSC versions of these games are probably extremely rare indeed. They are so new to the collector's market that accurate pricing is difficult to determine at this time.

Air Raid (MenAvision)

Not much information is available about MenAvision, other than that they were one of the myriad of companies producing games for the 2600 back in the classic era. They were also one of the least successful since *Air Raid* was the only game they ever released.

The production statistics for this game are not known, but supplies and distribution were apparently very limited. According to collector sources, fewer than 10 confirmed copies of this game exist today. To date, no one has a box or manual for the game. As such, this is one of the most sought-after cartridges, and would probably fetch quite a high price on the open market—assuming that anyone would be willing to part with it.

Quadrun (Atari)

The five games designed to be sold exclusively by mail through the Atari Club can all arguably be considered Holy Grail cartridges due to their rarity. Of the five, four of them eventually made it to store shelves in limited quantities, and so are slightly more common. The only one that most likely did not make it into stores was *Quadrun*.

Quadrun is valued for its gameplay as much as for its rarity. The game is very original and challenging, and it was the first Atari 2600 game to feature synthesized speech—no small feat for the technology available at the time.

Atari reportedly produced only around 10,000 *Quadrun* cartridges, so the game is rather hard to come by. If you're lucky enough to find one, you can expect to pay upward of $300 for the cartridge alone (without the box and instructions).

Atari VCS (2600) Price Guides
2600 Hardware Price Guide

CONSOLES

ATARI VCS CX2600 CONSOLE
Manufacturer: Atari
Rarity: 5
Loose: $40–50
Boxed/Complete: $90–250
Notes: 1977; 6-switch model; heavier than later models (known to collectors as the "Heavy Sixer"); complete package includes 2 paddles, 2 joysticks, and *Combat* cartridge

ATARI VCS CX2600 CONSOLE
Manufacturer: Atari
Rarity: 1
Loose: $25–35
Boxed/Complete: $45–90
Notes: 1978–1979; 6-switch model; complete package includes 2 paddles, 2 joysticks, and *Combat* cartridge

ATARI VCS CX2600A CONSOLE
Manufacturer: Atari
Rarity: 3
Loose: $20–35
Boxed/Complete: $50–100
Notes: 1980–1981; 4-switch, wood grain model; complete package includes 2 paddles, 2 joysticks, and *Combat* cartridge

ATARI VCS CX2600A PROMOTIONAL CONSOLE
Manufacturer: Atari
Rarity: 8
Loose: $60–80*
Boxed/Complete: $100–200*
Notes: Promotional version of the CX2600A; distinguishable by the "Promotional Use Only" stamp on the box and on the bottom of the unit

ATARI 2600 CONSOLE
Manufacturer: Atari
Rarity: 3
Loose: $20–35
Boxed/Complete: $50–100
Notes: 1982; 4-switch black ("Darth Vader") model; originally packaged with 2 joysticks, *Pac-Man* and *Combat;* later packaged with a single joystick and no games

ATARI 2600 JUNIOR CONSOLE
Manufacturer: Atari
Rarity: 2
Loose: $15–25
Boxed/Complete: $30–40
Notes: 1986; smaller, streamlined console with short rainbow logo; available in both silver and red boxes (console identical regardless of box); includes one joystick

ATARI 2600 JUNIOR REV. A CONSOLE
Manufacturer: Atari
Rarity: 2
Loose: $15–25
Boxed/Complete: $30–40
Notes: 1986; similar to the 2600 Junior but with a rainbow logo that spans the entire console width; includes one joystick

COLECO GEMINI CONSOLE
Manufacturer: Coleco
Rarity: 3
Loose: $15–25
Boxed/Complete: $30–40
Notes: Coleco Atari 2600-compatible system; includes 2 combination paddle/joystick controllers and a *Donkey Kong* cartridge

COLUMBIA HOME ARCADE CONSOLE
Manufacturer: CBS Games
Rarity: 8
Loose: $40–50
Boxed/Complete: $60–75
Notes: Nearly identical to the Coleco Gemini; available only through the Columbia House Video Game club; very rare

SEARS TELE-GAMES VIDEO ARCADE REV. A CONSOLE
Manufacturer: Sears
Rarity: 6
Loose: $20–40
Boxed/Complete: $50–100
Notes: Sears version of the 1977; 6-switch Atari VCS CX2600 "Heavy Sixer"

SEARS TELE-GAMES VIDEO ARCADE REV. A CONSOLE
Manufacturer: Sears
Rarity: 2
Loose: $20–40
Boxed/Complete: $45–80
Notes: Sears version of the 1978; 6-switch Atari VCS CX2600

SEARS TELE-GAMES VIDEO ARCADE REV. B CONSOLE
Manufacturer: Sears
Rarity: 3
Loose: $20–40
Boxed/Complete: $45–80
Notes: Sears version of the 1980–1981; Atari 4-switch CX2600A

SEARS TELE-GAMES VIDEO ARCADE II CONSOLE
Manufacturer: Sears
Rarity: 8
Loose: $60–100
Boxed/Complete: $200–400
Notes: Sears 2600-compatible console, styled like the Atari 7800; includes 2 combination paddle/joystick controllers; packaged with *Space Invaders*

ACCESSORIES

COSMIC COMMAND JOYSTICK

Manufacturer: Milton Bradley
Rarity: 8
Loose: $30–40
Boxed/Complete: $50–70
Notes: Originally packaged with the game *Survival Run;* difficult to find in working condition

DRIVING CONTROLLERS (PAIR)

Manufacturer: Atari
Rarity: 1
Loose: $5–10
Boxed/Complete: $10–15
Notes: Not to be confused with the Paddle Controllers included with the original system

FLIGHT COMMANDER JOYSTICK

Manufacturer: Milton Bradley
Rarity: 8
Loose: $30–40
Boxed/Complete: $50–70
Notes: Originally packaged with the game *Spitfire Attack;* difficult to find in working condition

FOOT CRAZ CONTROLLER

Manufacturer: Exus
Rarity: 7
Loose: $80–100
Boxed/Complete: $150–250*
Notes: Originally packaged with the games *Video Jogger* and *Video Reflex*

GAMELINE MASTER MODULE

Manufacturer: CVC
Rarity: 8
Loose: $40–50
Boxed/Complete: $80–100
Notes: Modem/cartridge used to download 2600 games from an online service; complete version includes cart, cables, and documentation

IMAGIC GAME SELECTOR

Manufacturer: Imagic
Rarity: 9
Loose: $400–500*
Boxed/Complete: N/A
Notes: Point of sale demo unit that allows up to 38 cartridges to be plugged in to a 2600 console and selected by number, very rare

JOYBOARD CONTROLLER

Manufacturer: Amiga
Rarity: 6
Loose: $30–45
Boxed/Complete: $45–55
Notes: Originally packaged with the game *Mogul Maniac*

JOYSTICK (CX-40)

Manufacturer: Atari
Rarity: 1
Loose: $10–15
Boxed/Complete: $15–20
Notes: The standard Atari 2600 joystick

JOYSTICK (GAME MATE II REMOTE, PAIR)

Manufacturer: Atari
Rarity: 5
Loose: $20–30
Boxed/Complete: $40–50
Notes: Pair of wireless joysticks with base unit

KEYBOARD CONTROLLERS (PAIR)

Manufacturer: Atari
Rarity: 1
Loose: $5–7
Boxed/Complete: $7–25
Notes: Keypads used for a number of Atari cartridges and games, including *Basic Programming*

KID'S CONTROLLER

Manufacturer: Atari
Rarity: 2
Loose: $4–10
Boxed/Complete: $10–15
Notes: Used with several of Atari's children's games (including the *Sesame Street* series)

KID VID CONTROLLER

Manufacturer: Coleco
Rarity: 10
Loose: $150–200
Boxed/Complete: $250–300
Notes: Cassette player with an interface cable; packaged with *Smurfs Save the Day;* the only other game that uses the controller is *Berenstain Bears*

PADDLE CONTROLLERS (PAIR)

Manufacturer: Atari
Rarity: 1
Loose: $3–12
Boxed/Complete: $15–17
Notes: Same as the paddles packaged with the original system

SUPERCHARGER

Manufacturer: Starpath
Rarity: 3
Loose: $15–20
Boxed/Complete: $20–30
Notes: Cartridge with a cassette tape interface used to play all Starpath and Arcadia cassette games

TOUCH PAD CONTROLLER (FOR *STAR RAIDERS*)

Manufacturer: Atari
Rarity: 3
Loose: $3–4
Boxed/Complete: N/A
Notes: Loose Keypad Controller (originally packaged with the *Star Raiders* game)

TRACK & FIELD CONTROLLER

Manufacturer: Atari
Rarity: 5
Loose: $10–15
Boxed/Complete: $30–40
Notes: Blue, 3-button controller for use with the *Track & Field* cartridge

2600 Cartridge Price Guide

TRACKBALL CONTROLLER
Manufacturer: Atari
Rarity: 2
Loose: $10–12
Boxed/Complete: $15–25

3D TIC-TAC-TOE
Manufacturer: Atari
Label: Text; Picture
Rarity: 2
Game Only: $1–4
Complete: $3–6

3D TIC-TAC-TOE
Manufacturer: Sears
Label: Text
Rarity: 3
Game Only: $2–5
Complete: $4–8
Notes: Sears version of the Atari game of the same title

A-TEAM
Manufacturer: Atari
Label: Prototype
Rarity: Prototype
Game Only: ?
Complete: N/A
Notes: 2 versions exist; game is nearly identical to *Saboteur;* price unavailable; for more info, see http://www.atariprotos.com

ACTION PACK
Manufacturer: Atari
Label: N/A
Rarity: 6
Game Only: N/A
Complete: $30–40
Notes: 3-pack including *Breakout, Dodge 'Em,* and *Othello;* must include all packaging to be considered complete

THE ACTIVISION DECATHLON
Manufacturer: Activision
Label: All
Rarity: 3
Game Only: $1–3
Complete: $5–10

AD&D: TOWER OF MYSTERY
Manufacturer: M Network
Label: Prototype
Rarity: Prototype
Game Only: ?
Complete: N/A
Notes: Price unavailable; for more info, see http://www.atariprotos.com

AD&D: TREASURE OF TARMIN
Manufacturer: M Network
Label: Prototype
Rarity: Prototype
Game Only: ?
Complete: N/A
Notes: Price unavailable; for more info, see http://www.atariprotos.com

ADVENTURE
Manufacturer: Atari
Label: Text; Picture
Rarity: 2
Game Only: $1–4
Complete: $6–10

ADVENTURE
Manufacturer: Sears
Label: Text
Rarity: 3
Game Only: $2–6
Complete: $10–20
Notes: Sears version of the Atari game of the same title

ADVENTURE
Manufacturer: Sears
Label: Picture
Rarity: 4
Game Only: $2–7
Complete: $10–25

ADVENTURE PLUS
Manufacturer: AtariAge
Label: Picture
Rarity: Hack
Game Only: $15
Complete: N/A
Notes: Updated version of the Atari game *Adventure;* available at the AtariAge store (http://www.atariage.com); no box or manual

ADVENTURES OF TRON
Manufacturer: INTV
Label: White
Rarity: 3
Game Only: $2–4
Complete: $5–7

ADVENTURES OF TRON
Manufacturer: M Network
Label: Black
Rarity: 3
Game Only: $2–4
Complete: $5–7

AIR RAID
Manufacturer: Menavision
Label: Unique
Rarity: 10
Game Only: $1,000+*
Complete: $3,000+*
Notes: One of the rarest games for the 2600; blue cartridge with a t-shaped handle on top

AIR RAIDERS
Manufacturer: INTV
Label: White
Rarity: 3
Game Only: $2–5
Complete: $5–7

AIR RAIDERS
Manufacturer: M Network
Label: Black
Rarity: 2
Game Only: $1–3
Complete: $4–6

AIR-SEA BATTLE
Manufacturer: Atari
Label: Numbered Text
Rarity: 3
Game Only: $1–2
Complete: $2–5
Notes: Original numbered label (reads: *"02 Air-Sea Battle"* on end)

AIR-SEA BATTLE
Manufacturer: Atari
Label: Text; Picture
Rarity: 2
Game Only: $1–2
Complete: $3–6

AIRLOCK
Manufacturer: Data Age
Label: Silver
Rarity: 3
Game Only: $1–4
Complete: $8–12

ALFRED CHALLENGE
Manufacturer: Ebivision
Label: Unique
Rarity: Homebrew
Game Only: $25
Complete: $25
Notes: No box available—"complete" is the game plus the manual

ALIEN
Manufacturer: 20th Century Fox
Label: Picture
Rarity: 4
Game Only: $2–5
Complete: $10–20

ALLIA QUEST
Manufacturer: Ebivision
Label: Unique
Rarity: Homebrew
Game Only: $20–30
Complete: $30–40
Notes: Released at the 2001 Classic Gaming Expo; includes box and manual; price refers to an original version; reproductions are also available for around $20

ALLIGATOR PEOPLE
Manufacturer: 20th Century Fox
Label: Unique
Rarity: Prototype
Game Only: ?
Complete: N/A
Notes: Price unavailable; for more info, see http://www.atariprotos.com

ALLIGATOR PEOPLE
Manufacturer: Sunmark
Label: Picture
Rarity: Homebrew
Game Only: N/A
Complete: $25
Notes: Released at the 2003 Philly Classic; no box; available at AtariAge (http://www.atariage.com)

ALPHA BEAM WITH ERNIE
Manufacturer: Atari
Label: Picture
Rarity: 4
Game Only: $4–8
Complete: $15–20
Notes: Requires the Atari Kid's Controller; not considered complete without the controller overlay

AMIDAR
Manufacturer: Parker Brothers
Label: Picture
Rarity: 2
Game Only: $1–4
Complete: $4–7

ANTEATER
Manufacturer: M Network
Label: Unique
Rarity: Prototype
Game Only: ?
Complete: N/A
Notes: Price unavailable; for more info, see http://www.atariprotos.com

AQUAVENTURE
Manufacturer: Atari
Label: Unique
Rarity: Prototype
Game Only: ?
Complete: N/A
Notes: Price unavailable; for more info, see http://www.atariprotos.com

ARCADE GOLF
Manufacturer: Sears
Label: Text
Rarity: 3
Game Only: $2–5
Complete: $5–7
Notes: Sears version of the Atari game *Miniature Golf*

ARCADE PINBALL
Manufacturer: Sears
Label: Text; Picture
Rarity: 3
Game Only: $2–4
Complete: $10–15
Notes: Sears version of the Atari game *Video Pinball*

ARMOR AMBUSH
Manufacturer: INTV
Label: White
Rarity: 4
Game Only: $2–5
Complete: $5–7
Notes: 2600 version of the Intellivision game *Armor Battle*

ARMOR AMBUSH

Manufacturer: M Network
Label: Black
Rarity: 3
Game Only: $1–4
Complete: $4–6
Notes: 2600 version of the Intellivision game *Armor Battle*

ARTILLERY DUEL

Manufacturer: Xonox
Label: Picture
Rarity: 5
Game Only: $8–11
Complete: $15–25

ARTILLERY DUEL/CHUCK NORRIS SUPER-KICKS

Manufacturer: Xonox
Label: Double
Rarity: 5
Game Only: $5–12
Complete: $14–20

ARTILLERY DUEL/GHOST MANOR

Manufacturer: Xonox
Label: Double
Rarity: 5
Game Only: $10–15
Complete: $25–30

ARTILLERY DUEL/SPIKE'S PEAK

Manufacturer: Xonox
Label: Double
Rarity: 6
Game Only: $11–20
Complete: $30–40

ASSAULT

Manufacturer: Bomb
Label: Text
Rarity: 9
Game Only: $50–60
Complete: $70–90

ASTERIX

Manufacturer: Atari
Label: Red
Rarity: 4
Game Only: $10–15
Complete: $20–30
Notes: Easier to find in European (PAL) format

ASTEROIDS

Manufacturer: Atari
Label: Picture
Rarity: 1
Game Only: $1–2
Complete: $3–5

ASTEROIDS

Manufacturer: Atari
Label: Silver
Rarity: 3
Game Only: $2–3
Complete: $4–6

ASTEROIDS

Manufacturer: Sears
Label: Text; Picture
Rarity: 2
Game Only: $2–3
Complete: $4–6
Notes: There are 2 text label versions—one marked "66 Games," the other marked "64 Games"

ASTEROIDS DC

Manufacturer: AtariAge
Label: Picture
Rarity: Hack
Game Only: $20
Complete: N/A
Notes: Updated version of the Atari game *Asteroids;* available at the AtariAge store (http://www.atariage.com); no box or manual

ASTROBLAST

Manufacturer: M Network
Label: Black
Rarity: 2
Game Only: $1–2
Complete: $3–5
Notes: 2600 version of the Intellivision game *Astrosmash*

ASTROBLAST

Manufacturer: Telegames
Label: Silver
Rarity: 3
Game Only: $2–3
Complete: $5–6
Notes: 2600 version of the Intellivision game *Astrosmash*

ATARI VIDEO CUBE

Manufacturer: Atari
Label: Silver
Rarity: 7
Game Only: $30–40
Complete: $60–120

ATLANTIS

Manufacturer: Imagic
Label: Text; Picture
Rarity: 2
Game Only: $1–2
Complete: $3–4
Notes: There are 2 picture label versions—one with a night picture, the other with a day picture

ATLANTIS

Manufacturer: Activision
Label: Blue
Rarity: 3
Game Only: $5–8
Complete: $9–12
Notes: Blue label version released after Activision acquired rights to the game from Imagic

ATLANTIS II

Manufacturer: Imagic
Label: Picture
Rarity: 10
Game Only: $300*
Complete: $800*
Notes: Special version of *Atlantis* produced for a contest, sent directly to players by Imagic; label shows the "night" picture; box is the same as *Atlantis* with a sticker that says "Atlantis II" pasted on.

BACHELOR PARTY

Manufacturer: Mystique
Label: Picture
Rarity: 5
Game Only: $25–50
Complete: $51–65
Notes: Adult game

BACHELOR PARTY/GIGOLO

Manufacturer: Playaround
Label: Double
Rarity: 5
Game Only: $30–45
Complete: $35–65
Notes: 2 adult games on one double-ended cartridge

BACHELORETTE PARTY/BURNING DESIRE

Manufacturer: Playaround
Label: Double
Rarity: 5
Game Only: $30–45
Complete: $45–55
Notes: Repackaged version of *Bachelor Party/Gigolo* with the graphics changed to cater to female players

BACK TO SCHOOL PAK

Manufacturer: Atari
Label: N/A
Rarity: 6
Game Only: N/A
Complete: $30–40
Notes: *Basic Programming* and *Brain Games* packaged together with a set of Keyboard Controllers; must include all packaging to be considered complete

BACKGAMMON

Manufacturer: Atari
Label: Text; Picture
Rarity: 2
Game Only: $2–4
Complete: $4–6

BACKGAMMON

Manufacturer: Sears
Label: Text
Rarity: 3
Game Only: $3–5
Complete: $5–7
Notes: Sears version of the Atari game of the same title

BACKFIRE

Manufacturer: Self-Published
Label: Picture
Rarity: Homebrew
Game Only: N/A
Complete: $20
Notes: Available at the AtariAge store (http://www.atariage.com); no box

BANK HEIST

Manufacturer: 20th Century Fox
Label: Picture
Rarity: 5
Game Only: $13–15
Complete: $20–30

BARNSTORMING

Manufacturer: Activision
Label: Picture
Rarity: 2
Game Only: $2–4
Complete: $7–12

BASEBALL

Manufacturer: Sears
Label: Text
Rarity: 2
Game Only: $2–4
Complete: $5–7
Notes: Sears version of the Atari game *Home Run;* there are 2 text label versions—one numbered "49-75108," the other numbered "6-99819"

BASEBALL

Manufacturer: Sears
Label: Picture
Rarity: 5
Game Only: $4–10
Complete: $10–12
Notes: Sears version of the Atari game *Home Run;* the picture used on the label is different from the one used on the Atari label

BASIC MATH

Manufacturer: Atari
Label: Numbered Text
Rarity: 4
Game Only: $3–7
Complete: $7–12
Notes: Original numbered label (reads: "61 Basic Math" on end)

BASIC MATH

Manufacturer: Atari
Label: Text
Rarity: 3
Game Only: $3–5
Complete: $6–8

BASIC PROGRAMMING

Manufacturer: Atari
Label: Text; Picture
Rarity: 3
Game Only: $3–5
Complete: $10–15
Notes: Requires Keyboard Controller; original (color box) version includes controller overlays, the re-release (gray box) version does not

BASKETBALL

Manufacturer: Atari
Label: Text; Picture
Rarity: 2
Game Only: $1–3
Complete: $3–5
Notes: 2 boxes available—color (original) and black and white (re-release)

BASKETBALL
Manufacturer: Sears
Label: Text; Picture
Rarity: 3
Game Only: $2–4
Complete: $4–6
Notes: Sears version of the Atari game of the same title; there are 2 text label versions—one numbered "6-99826," the other numbered "49-75113"

BATTLEZONE
Manufacturer: Atari
Label: Silver
Rarity: 2
Game Only: $1–3
Complete: $3–5

BEAMRIDER
Manufacturer: Activision
Label: Picture
Rarity: 5
Game Only: $8–11
Complete: $12–15

BEANY BOPPER
Manufacturer: 20th Century Fox
Label: Red
Rarity: 4
Game Only: $2–3
Complete: $7–9
Notes: 2 label variations—one shows 6 levels of play and the other 8 levels of play; both are equally common

BEAT 'EM & EAT 'EM
Manufacturer: Mystique
Label: Picture
Rarity: 5
Game Only: $20–50
Complete: $42–61
Notes: Adult game

BEAT 'EM & EAT 'EM/LADY IN WADING
Manufacturer: Playaround
Label: Double
Rarity: 5
Game Only: $30–40
Complete: $45–60
Notes: 2 adult games on one double-ended cartridge

BERENSTEIN BEARS
Manufacturer: Coleco
Label: Picture
Rarity: 9
Game Only: $80–100
Complete: $100–150
Notes: Requires the KidVid Controller; must include the 3 audio tapes originally packaged with the game to be considered complete (and playable)

BERMUDA TRIANGLE
Manufacturer: Data Age
Label: Picture
Rarity: 4
Game Only: $2–3
Complete: $5–7

BERZERK
Manufacturer: Atari
Label: Picture
Rarity: 1
Game Only: $1–2
Complete: $3–4

BERZERK
Manufacturer: Sears
Label: Picture
Rarity: 3
Game Only: $2–3
Complete: $4–5
Notes: Sears version of the Atari game by the same name

BERZERK VOICE ENHANCED
Manufacturer: AtariAge
Label: Red
Rarity: Hack
Game Only: N/A
Complete: $25
Notes: Updated version of the Atari game *Berzerk;* available at the AtariAge store (http://www.atariage.com); manual but no box

BIG BIRD'S EGG CATCH
Manufacturer: Atari
Label: Picture
Rarity: 4
Game Only: $5–10
Complete: $11–15
Notes: Requires the Atari Kid's Controller; not considered complete without the controller overlay

BIONIC BREAKTHROUGH
Manufacturer: Atari
Label: Unique
Rarity: Prototype
Game Only: ?
Complete: N/A
Notes: Playable only with the (unreleased) Atari Mindlink Controller; price unavailable; for more info, see http://www.atariprotos.com

BLACKJACK
Manufacturer: Atari
Label: Numbered Text
Rarity: 3
Game Only: $1–3
Complete: $7–12
Notes: Original numbered label (reads: "51 Blackjack" on the end)

BLACKJACK
Manufacturer: Atari
Label: Text; Picture
Rarity: 2
Game Only: $1–2
Complete: $5–7

BLACKJACK
Manufacturer: Sears
Label: Text
Rarity: 2
Game Only: $1–3
Complete: $6–8
Notes: Sears version of the Atari game by the same name

BLACKJACK
Manufacturer: Sears
Label: Picture
Rarity: 4
Game Only: $2–4
Complete: $7–12
Notes: Sears version of the Atari game by the same name

BLUE PRINT
Manufacturer: CBS Electronics
Label: Text
Rarity: 3
Game Only: $1–4
Complete: $5–7

BMX AIRMASTER
Manufacturer: Atari
Label: Picture
Rarity: 10
Game Only: $150–250*
Complete: $300–400*
Notes: Atari-branded version of the TNT game by the same name; extremely rare

BMX AIRMASTER
Manufacturer: TNT Games
Label: Red; White
Rarity: 4
Game Only: $8–10
Complete: $15–20
Notes: Both label variations have the same rarity

BOING!
Manufacturer: First Star Software
Label: All
Rarity: 8
Game Only: $45–60
Complete: $70–90
Notes: There are 2 cartridge styles—Xonox (with flared sides) and standard; rarity is identical for each

BORGWARS ASTEROIDS
Manufacturer: Self-Published
Label: Picture
Rarity: Hack
Game Only: N/A
Complete: $22
Notes: Hacked version of Atari's *Asteroids* with a *Star Trek* theme; released at the 2003 Classic Gaming Expo; includes manual (no box); available at http://www.packratvg.com

BOWLING
Manufacturer: Atari
Label: Text; Picture
Rarity: 2
Game Only: $1–3
Complete: $4–6

BOWLING
Manufacturer: Sears
Label: Text
Rarity: 2
Game Only: $2–4
Complete: $5–7

BOXING
Manufacturer: Activision
Label: Red
Rarity: 2
Game Only: $1–3
Complete: $4–7

BOXING
Manufacturer: Activision
Label: Blue
Rarity: 3
Game Only: $5–10
Complete: $10–15

BRAIN GAMES
Manufacturer: Atari
Label: Text; Picture
Rarity: 3
Game Only: $2–4
Complete: $5–7
Notes: Requires Keyboard Controller

BRAIN GAMES
Manufacturer: Sears
Label: Text
Rarity: 3
Game Only: $2–4
Complete: $5–7
Notes: Requires Keyboard Controller

BREAKAWAY IV
Manufacturer: Sears
Label: Text; Picture
Rarity: 3
Game Only: $1–7
Complete: $7–9
Notes: Sears version of the Atari game *Breakout*

BREAKOUT
Manufacturer: Atari
Label: Text; Picture
Rarity: 2
Game Only: $1–3
Complete: $4–5

BRIDGE
Manufacturer: Activision
Label: Green
Rarity: 4
Game Only: $1–3
Complete: $9–12

BUCK ROGERS: PLANET OF ZOOM
Manufacturer: Sega
Label: Picture
Rarity: 4
Game Only: $4–6
Complete: $7–10

BUGS
Manufacturer: Data Age
Label: Picture
Rarity: 3
Game Only: $3–9
Complete: $10–15

BUGS BUNNY
Manufacturer: Atari
Label: Unique
Rarity: Prototype
Game Only: ?
Complete: N/A
Notes: Price unavailable; for more info, see
http://www.atariprotos.com

BUGS BUNNY
Manufacturer: Self-Published
Label: Picture
Rarity: Reproduction
Game Only: N/A
Complete: $45
Notes: Self-published version of the Atari prototype;
available from Atari2600.com
(http://www.atari2600.com); signed copies slightly
more expensive

BUMP 'N JUMP
Manufacturer: INTV
Label: White
Rarity: 5
Game Only: $9–12
Complete: $14–20

BUMP 'N JUMP
Manufacturer: M Network
Label: Black
Rarity: 4
Game Only: $3–6
Complete: $7–9

BUMP 'N JUMP
Manufacturer: Telegames
Label: Silver
Rarity: 5
Game Only: $9–12
Complete: $14–20

BUMPER BASH
Manufacturer: Spectravision
Label: Text
Rarity: 9
Game Only: $80–100
Complete: $150–200*
Notes: Manual alone often sells for over $20

BURGERTIME
Manufacturer: INTV
Label: White
Rarity: 4
Game Only: $5–10
Complete: $15–20*

BURGERTIME
Manufacturer: M Network
Label: Black
Rarity: 3
Game Only: $4–8
Complete: $12–15

BUSY POLICE
Manufacturer: Zellers
Label: Picture
Rarity: 5
Game Only: $15–20
Complete: $20–30*

CAKEWALK
Manufacturer: CommaVid
Label: Picture
Rarity: 9
Game Only: $125–180
Complete: $200–300*
Notes: Available only by mail order in the U.S.; European (PAL) version is more common

CALIFORNIA GAMES
Manufacturer: Epyx
Label: Text
Rarity: 4
Game Only: $2–5
Complete: $8–12

CANNON MAN
Manufacturer: Sears
Label: Text
Rarity: 6
Game Only: $15–20
Complete: $20–30*
Notes: Sears version of the Atari game *Human Cannonball*

CANYON BOMBER
Manufacturer: Atari
Label: Text; Picture
Rarity: 2
Game Only: $1–2
Complete: $3–5

CANYON BOMBER
Manufacturer: Sears
Label: Text; Picture
Rarity: 2
Game Only: $1–3
Complete: $4–6
Notes: Sears version of the Atari game by the same name

CAPTURE
Manufacturer: Sears
Label: Text
Rarity: 3
Game Only: $3–5
Complete: $15–30
Notes: Sears version of the Atari game *Flag Capture*

CARNIVAL
Manufacturer: Coleco
Label: Text
Rarity: 2
Game Only: $1–3
Complete: $4–6

CASINO
Manufacturer: Atari
Label: Text; Picture
Rarity: 1
Game Only: $1–3
Complete: $4–6

CAT TRAX

Manufacturer: UA Limited
Label: Unique
Rarity: Prototype
Game Only: ?
Complete: N/A
Notes: Price unavailable; for more info, see
http://www.atariprotos.com

CAT TRAX

Manufacturer: Self-Published
Label: Picture
Rarity: Reproduction
Game Only: $25
Complete: $35
Notes: Recently released reproduction of the proto-
type; available from the AtariAge store
(http://www.atariage.com)

CENTIPEDE

Manufacturer: Atari
Label: Silver
Rarity: 2
Game Only: $1–3
Complete: $5–10

CHALLENGE

Manufacturer: Zellers
Label: Picture
Rarity: 4
Game Only: $10–15
Complete: $20–25*

CHALLENGE OF NEXAR

Manufacturer: Spectravision
Label: Text
Rarity: 4
Game Only: $3–6
Complete: $7–12
Notes: Often referred to simply as *Nexar*

CHAMPIONSHIP SOCCER

Manufacturer: Atari
Label: Text
Rarity: 2
Game Only: $1–3
Complete: $7–9
Notes: Later renamed *Pele's Soccer*

CHASE

Manufacturer: Sears
Label: Text
Rarity: 3
Game Only: $3–5
Complete: $6–10
Notes: Sears version of the Atari game *Surround*

CHASE

Manufacturer: Sears
Label: Picture
Rarity: 5
Game Only: $4–6
Complete: $8–12
Notes: Sears version of the Atari game *Surround*

CHASE THE CHUCK WAGON

Manufacturer: Spectravision
Label: Picture
Rarity: 8
Game Only: $85–125
Complete: $450–550
Notes: Originally available only via mail order from
the Ralston-Purina company; box and manual are ex-
tremely rare

CHECKERS

Manufacturer: Activision
Label: Green
Rarity: 4
Game Only: $1–7
Complete: $8–10

CHECKERS

Manufacturer: Sears
Label: Text
Rarity: 3
Game Only: $2–4
Complete: $5–7
Notes: Sears version of the Atari game *Video Checkers*

CHINA SYNDROME

Manufacturer: Spectravision
Label: Text
Rarity: 5
Game Only: $6–9
Complete: $25–30

CHOPPER COMMAND

Manufacturer: Activision
Label: Orange
Rarity: 2
Game Only: $1–3
Complete: $5–10

CHOPPER COMMAND

Manufacturer: Activision
Label: Blue
Rarity: 3
Game Only: $6–9
Complete: $9–12

CHUCK NORRIS SUPERKICKS

Manufacturer: Xonox
Label: Picture
Rarity: 5
Game Only: $10–15
Complete: $20–25

CHUCK NORRIS SUPERKICKS/GHOST MANOR

Manufacturer: Xonox
Label: Double
Rarity: 7
Game Only: $25–35*
Complete: $35–45*

CHUCK NORRIS SUPERKICKS/SPIKE'S PEAK

Manufacturer: Xonox
Label: Double
Rarity: 6
Game Only: $20–30*
Complete: $30–40*

CIRCUS

Manufacturer: Sears
Label: Text
Rarity: 3
Game Only: $2–4
Complete: $5–7
Notes: Sears version of the Atari game *Circus Atari*

CIRCUS

Manufacturer: Zellers
Label: Picture
Rarity: 4
Game Only: $12–17
Complete: $18–25*

CIRCUS ATARI

Manufacturer: Atari
Label: Text; Picture
Rarity: 2
Game Only: $1–3
Complete: $4–6

COCONUTS

Manufacturer: Telesys
Label: Picture
Rarity: 4
Game Only: $2–5
Complete: $7–9
Notes: Available in 2 cartridge styles, both of which
are equally common

CODEBREAKER

Manufacturer: Atari
Label: Text; Picture
Rarity: 3
Game Only: $1–4
Complete: $5–7
Notes: Requires Keyboard Controller

CODEBREAKER

Manufacturer: Sears
Label: Text
Rarity: 4
Game Only: $2–5
Complete: $6–8
Notes: Sears version of the Atari game by the same
name; requires Keyboard Controller

COLOR BAR GENERATOR

Manufacturer: Videosoft
Label: Text
Rarity: 9
Game Only: $100–200*
Complete: N/A
Notes: Videosoft's only cartridge is a service tool to
generate color bars (used for fixing TVs and VCRs);
very hard to find

COMBAT

Manufacturer: Atari
Label: Numbered Text
Rarity: 2
Game Only: $1–2
Complete: $3–5
Notes: Original numbered label (reads: "01 Combat"
on end)

COMBAT

Manufacturer: Atari
Label: Text; Picture
Rarity: 1
Game Only: $1
Complete: $2–3

COMBAT ROCK

Manufacturer: AtariAge
Label: Picture
Rarity: Hack
Game Only: $15
Complete: N/A
Notes: Updated version of the Atari game *Combat*;
available at the AtariAge store
(http://www.atariage.com); no manual or box

COMBAT TWO

Manufacturer: Atari
Label: Unique
Rarity: Prototype
Game Only: ?
Complete: N/A
Notes: Price unavailable; for more info, see
http://www.atariprotos.com

COMBAT TWO

Manufacturer: Self-Published
Label: Picture
Rarity: Reproduction
Game Only: $20–30*
Complete: $90–125
Notes: Released commercially at the 2001 Classic
Gaming Expo; originally priced at $30 each

COMMANDO

Manufacturer: Activision
Label: White
Rarity: 3
Game Only: $4–8
Complete: $12–20

COMMANDO RAID

Manufacturer: US Games
Label: Picture
Rarity: 2
Game Only: $2–3
Complete: $5–7

COMMUNIST MUTANTS FROM SPACE

Manufacturer: Starpath
Label: Cassette
Rarity: 4
Game Only: $3–6
Complete: $4–8
Notes: Cassette game; requires the Supercharger and
a cassette tape player

COMPUTER CHESS

Manufacturer: Atari
Label: Unique
Rarity: Prototype
Game Only: ?
Complete: N/A
Notes: Price unavailable; for more info, see
http://www.atariprotos.com

CONDOR ATTACK

Manufacturer: Ultravision
Label: Picture
Rarity: 9
Game Only: $100–150
Complete: $160–200*
Notes: U.S. version difficult to find; more commonly seen in overseas (PAL) or pirated form

CONFRONTATION

Manufacturer: Answer
Label: Unique
Rarity: Prototype
Game Only: ?
Complete: N/A
Notes: Price unavailable; for more info, see http://www.atariprotos.com

CONGO BONGO

Manufacturer: Sega
Label: Picture
Rarity: 4
Game Only: $3–5
Complete: $7–10

COOKIE MONSTER MUNCH

Manufacturer: Atari
Label: Picture
Rarity: 4
Game Only: $4–10
Complete: $10–15
Notes: Requires the Atari Kid's Controller; not considered complete without the controller overlay

COPY CART

Manufacturer: VidCo
Label: Unique
Rarity: 10
Game Only: $75–90*
Complete: $95–125*

COSMIC ARK

Manufacturer: Imagic
Label: Text; Picture
Rarity: 2
Game Only: $1–2
Complete: $6–8

COSMIC COMMUTER

Manufacturer: Activision
Label: Blue
Rarity: 5
Game Only: $15–18
Complete: $25–30

COSMIC CORRIDOR

Manufacturer: Zimag
Label: Picture
Rarity: 6
Game Only: $7–15
Complete: $20–30

COSMIC CREEPS

Manufacturer: Telesys
Label: Picture
Rarity: 4
Game Only: $3–6
Complete: $22–26
Notes: Applies to both cartridge versions; complete version includes a mail-off coupon for a *Fast Food* t-shirt

COSMIC SWARM

Manufacturer: CommaVid
Label: Picture
Rarity: 6
Game Only: $11–26
Complete: $19–30

CRACK'ED

Manufacturer: Atari
Label: Unique
Rarity: Prototype
Game Only: ?
Complete: N/A
Notes: Released for the Atari 7800 but not for the 2600; price unavailable; for more info, see http://www.atariprotos.com

CRACK'ED

Manufacturer: Self-Published
Label: Picture
Rarity: Reproduction
Game Only: N/A
Complete: $40
Notes: Released at the 2002 Classic Gaming Expo complete with box and instructions; limited quantity available at the CGE web site (http://www.cgecpo.com)

CRACKPOTS

Manufacturer: Activision
Label: Purple
Rarity: 4
Game Only: $3–7
Complete: $5–10

CRASH DIVE

Manufacturer: 20th Century Fox
Label: Picture
Rarity: 5
Game Only: $6–14
Complete: $15–20

CRAZY CLIMBER

Manufacturer: Atari
Label: Silver
Rarity: 8
Game Only: $95–125
Complete: $150–250*
Notes: Originally available only through the Atari Club; very collectable

CRAZY VALET

Manufacturer: Self-Published
Label: Unique
Rarity: Homebrew
Game Only: $30
Complete: $30
Notes: Limited edition signed version; no box

81

CRAZY VALET

Manufacturer: Self-Published
Label: Unique
Rarity: Homebrew
Game Only: $30
Complete: $30
Notes: CGE 2001 version (has a CGE title screen and extra levels); no box

CRAZY VALET

Manufacturer: Self-Published
Label: Unique
Rarity: Homebrew
Game Only: $20
Complete: $20
Notes: Standard version; no box; available from the AtariAge store (http://www.atariage.com)

CROSS FORCE

Manufacturer: Spectravision
Label: Text
Rarity: 5
Game Only: $6–10
Complete: $12–20

CROSSBOW

Manufacturer: Atari
Label: Red
Rarity: 2
Game Only: $2–5
Complete: $6–8

CRUISE MISSILE

Manufacturer: Froggo
Label: White
Rarity: 4
Game Only: $3–5
Complete: $7–9

CRYPTS OF CHAOS

Manufacturer: 20th Century Fox
Label: Picture
Rarity: 5
Game Only: $10–14
Complete: $15–25*

CRYSTAL CASTLES

Manufacturer: Atari
Label: Silver
Rarity: 2
Game Only: $2–5
Complete: $6–9

CUBICOLOR

Manufacturer: Imagic
Label: Unique
Rarity: Prototype
Game Only: $300–500*
Complete: N/A
Notes: Approximately 60 were sold via mail order by the programmer, Rob Fulop, in the '80s and '90s; original price was $100; for more info, see http://www.atariprotos.com

CUBICOLOR

Manufacturer: Self-Published
Label: Unique
Rarity: Reproduction
Game Only: $20
Complete: N/A
Notes: Reproduction of the Atari prototype; previously available at Atari2600.com (http://www.atari2600.com), though apparently sold out

CUSTER'S REVENGE

Manufacturer: Mystique
Label: Picture
Rarity: 5
Game Only: $35–50
Complete: $55–65
Notes: Adult game

CUTTLE CART

Manufacturer: Schell's Electronics
Label: Unique
Rarity: Homebrew
Game Only: N/A
Complete: $275–375*
Notes: Cartridge with an audio input that allows you to load game ROM files from a CD; originally sold for $100 (now discontinued); no box

DARE DIVER

Manufacturer: Sears
Label: Text
Rarity: 5
Game Only: $4–8
Complete: $9–12
Notes: Sears version of the Atari game *Sky Diver*

DARK CAVERN

Manufacturer: M Network
Label: Black
Rarity: 2
Game Only: $1–4
Complete: $5–7
Notes: 2600 version of the Intellivision game *Night Stalker*

DARK CHAMBERS

Manufacturer: Atari
Label: Red
Rarity: 4
Game Only: $3–5
Complete: $7–9
Notes: Based on the Atari *Gauntlet* arcade game

DARK MAGE

Manufacturer: Self-Published
Label: N/A
Rarity: Homebrew
Game Only: $15
Complete: N/A
Notes: Text adventure game

DEADLY DUCK

Manufacturer: 20th Century Fox
Label: Red
Rarity: 4
Game Only: $6–10
Complete: $10–12

DEATH TRAP
Manufacturer: Avalon Hill
Label: Picture
Rarity: 8
Game Only: $45–60
Complete: $70–150

DEFENDER
Manufacturer: Atari
Label: Picture
Rarity: 1
Game Only: $1–2
Complete: $3–5

DEFENDER
Manufacturer: Sears
Label: Picture
Rarity: 2
Game Only: $2–4
Complete: $4–6
Notes: Sears version of the Atari game by the same name

DEFENDER II
Manufacturer: Atari
Label: Red
Rarity: 4
Game Only: $3–5
Complete: $5–8

DEMOLITION HERBY
Manufacturer: Telesys
Label: Color
Rarity: 7
Game Only: $30–50
Complete: $55–70*

DEMOLITION HERBY
Manufacturer: Telesys
Label: Black and White
Rarity: 6
Game Only: $30–50*
Complete: $55–70*

DEMON ATTACK
Manufacturer: Imagic
Label: Text; Picture
Rarity: 2
Game Only: $1–3
Complete: $4–7
Notes: Applies to the foil text label and the picture label versions

DEMON ATTACK
Manufacturer: Activision
Label: Blue
Rarity: 5
Game Only: $2–5
Complete: $6–9
Notes: Blue label version released after Activision acquired rights to the game from Imagic

DEMONS TO DIAMONDS
Manufacturer: Atari
Label: Picture
Rarity: 2
Game Only: $1–4
Complete: $3–5

DEMONS TO DIAMONDS
Manufacturer: Sears
Label: Picture
Rarity: 3
Game Only: $2–5
Complete: $5–8
Notes: Sears version of the Atari game by the same name

DESERT FALCON
Manufacturer: Atari
Label: Red
Rarity: 4
Game Only: $2–3
Complete: $4–7

DIAGNOSTIC CARTRIDGE
Manufacturer: Atari
Label: Text
Rarity: 8
Game Only: $100–200*
Complete: N/A
Notes: Not to be confused with *Testcart*, the diagnostic cart released by AtariAge—this one is manufactured by Atari

DICE PUZZLE
Manufacturer: Panda
Label: End Only
Rarity: 6
Game Only: $15–20
Complete: $60–100
Notes: Only has a label on the end

DIG DUG
Manufacturer: Atari
Label: Silver
Rarity: 2
Game Only: $2–4
Complete: $5–7

DISHASTER
Manufacturer: Zimag
Label: Picture
Rarity: 5
Game Only: $5–15
Complete: $17–25

DODGE 'EM
Manufacturer: Atari
Label: All
Rarity: 2
Game Only: $1–3
Complete: $5–8

DODGER CARS
Manufacturer: Sears
Label: Text
Rarity: 3
Game Only: $2–4
Complete: $5–7
Notes: Sears version of the Atari game *Dodge 'Em*

DODGER CARS

Manufacturer: Sears
Label: Picture
Rarity: 4
Game Only: $3–5
Complete: $6–8
Notes: Sears version of the Atari game *Dodge 'Em*

DOLPHIN

Manufacturer: Activision
Label: Pink
Rarity: 3
Game Only: $2–4
Complete: $5–7

DONALD DUCK'S SPEEDBOAT

Manufacturer: Atari
Label: N/A
Rarity: Prototype
Game Only: $50*
Complete: N/A
Notes: For more info, see http://www.atariprotos.com

DONKEY KONG

Manufacturer: Atari
Label: Red
Rarity: 3
Game Only: $4–6
Complete: $7–12
Notes: Re-release of the Coleco *Donkey Kong* cartridge; cartridge is black with a red Atari label

DONKEY KONG

Manufacturer: Coleco
Label: Text
Rarity: 1
Game Only: $1–4
Complete: $5–10
Notes: White cartridge with Coleco label

DONKEY KONG JUNIOR

Manufacturer: Atari
Label: Red
Rarity: 4
Game Only: $5–9
Complete: $10–12
Notes: Re-release of the Coleco *Donkey Kong Junior* cartridge; cartridge is black with a red Atari label

DONKEY KONG JUNIOR

Manufacturer: Coleco
Label: Text
Rarity: 4
Game Only: $3–7
Complete: $8–10
Notes: White cartridge with Coleco label

DOUBLE DRAGON

Manufacturer: Activision
Label: Black
Rarity: 5
Game Only: $10–16
Complete: $18–20

DOUBLE DUNK

Manufacturer: Atari
Label: Red
Rarity: 4
Game Only: $3–6
Complete: $7–12

DRAGON TREASURE

Manufacturer: Zellers
Label: Picture
Rarity: 5
Game Only: $6–10
Complete: $12–20*

DRAGONFIRE

Manufacturer: Imagic
Label: Picture
Rarity: 2
Game Only: $1–4
Complete: $5–7

DRAGONSTOMPER

Manufacturer: Starpath
Label: Cassette
Rarity: 5
Game Only: $12–15
Complete: $18–20
Notes: Cassette game; requires the Supercharger and a cassette tape player

DRAGSTER

Manufacturer: Activision
Label: Purple
Rarity: 2
Game Only: $2–5
Complete: $3–7

DUKES OF HAZZARD

Manufacturer: Atari
Label: Unique
Rarity: Prototype
Game Only: $30–40
Complete: N/A
Notes: Never officially released, but it was sold by Best Electronics for $12 at one point

DUKES OF HAZZARD VERSION 2

Manufacturer: Atari
Label: Unique
Rarity: Prototype
Game Only: ?
Complete: N/A
Notes: Similar in gameplay to *Stunt Cycle;* price unavailable; for more info, see http://www.atariprotos.com

DUMBO'S FLYING CIRCUS

Manufacturer: Atari
Label: N/A
Rarity: Prototype
Game Only: ?
Complete: N/A
Notes: Price unavailable; for more info, see http://www.atariprotos.com

DUNE
Manufacturer: Atari
Label: N/A
Rarity: Prototype
Game Only: ?
Complete: N/A
Notes: Recently discovered prototype; price unavailable; for more info, see http://www.atariprotos.com

E.T. THE EXTRA-TERRESTRIAL
Manufacturer: Atari
Label: Silver
Rarity: 1
Game Only: $1–2
Complete: $3–7
Notes: Millions of these cartridges went unsold and were buried in the New Mexico desert in the late '80s

EARTH ATTACK
Manufacturer: Zellers
Label: Picture
Rarity: 5
Game Only: $5–10
Complete: $15–20

EARTH DIES SCREAMING
Manufacturer: 20th Century Fox
Label: Picture
Rarity: 5
Game Only: $6–16
Complete: $20–25*

EDTRIS 2600
Manufacturer: Self-Published
Label: Unique
Rarity: Homebrew
Game Only: N/A
Complete: $30*
Notes: Homebrew version of *Tetris;* no box

EGGOMANIA
Manufacturer: US Games
Label: Picture
Rarity: 4
Game Only: $4–9
Complete: $9–12
Notes: Applies to both the beveled and standard cartridge case versions

ELEVATOR ACTION
Manufacturer: Atari
Label: N/A
Rarity: Prototype
Game Only: ?
Complete: N/A
Notes: Price unavailable; for more info, see http://www.atariprotos.com

ELEVATOR ACTION
Manufacturer: Self-Published
Label: Silver
Rarity: Reproduction
Game Only: $20–30*
Complete: $30–50*
Notes: Approximately 200 copies were sold at the 2001 Classic Gaming Expo

ELI'S LADDER
Manufacturer: Simage
Label: Unique
Rarity: 10
Game Only: $900–1,100
Complete: $1,200+*
Notes: A religious educational game; one of the most difficult 2600 titles to locate

ELK ATTACK
Manufacturer: Atari
Label: N/A
Rarity: Prototype
Game Only: $15*
Complete: N/A

ENCOUNTER AT L-5
Manufacturer: Data Age
Label: Picture
Rarity: 3
Game Only: $2–4
Complete: $6–8

ENDURO
Manufacturer: Activision
Label: Green
Rarity: 2
Game Only: $1–2
Complete: $3–5

ENDURO
Manufacturer: Activision
Label: Blue
Rarity: 3
Game Only: $2–3
Complete: $4–5

THE ENTITY
Manufacturer: 20th Century Fox
Label: N/A
Rarity: Prototype
Game Only: ?
Complete: N/A
Notes: Based on the '80s horror film by the same name; price unavailable; for more info, see http://www.atariprotos.com

THE ENTITY
Manufacturer: CGE Services Corp.
Label: Picture
Rarity: Reproduction
Game Only: N/A
Complete: $40
Notes: Reproduction of the 20th Century Fox prototype; released at the 2003 Classic Gaming Expo; includes box and instructions; limited quantities available at the CGE web site (http://www.cgexpo.com)

ENTOMBED
Manufacturer: US Games
Label: Picture
Rarity: 4
Game Only: $2–7
Complete: $10–12

ESCAPE FROM THE MINDMASTER
Manufacturer: Starpath
Label: Cassette
Rarity: 4
Game Only: $6–9
Complete: $10–12
Notes: Cassette game; requires the Supercharger and a cassette tape player

ESPIAL
Manufacturer: Tigervision
Label: Picture
Rarity: 6
Game Only: $30–40
Complete: $40–50*

EUCHRE
Manufacturer: Self-Published
Label: Picture
Rarity: Homebrew
Game Only: N/A
Complete: $20
Notes: Released in 2002; available at AtariAge (http://www.atariage.com); no box

EXOCET
Manufacturer: Panda
Label: End Only
Rarity: 6
Game Only: $25–35
Complete: $40–80
Notes: Only has a label on the end

FANTASTIC VOYAGE
Manufacturer: 20th Century Fox
Label: Picture
Rarity: 4
Game Only: $2–5
Complete: $6–10

FARMER DAN
Manufacturer: Zellers
Label: Picture
Rarity: 5
Game Only: $10–15*
Complete: $15–20*

FAST EDDIE
Manufacturer: 20th Century Fox
Label: Red
Rarity: 4
Game Only: $3–7
Complete: $8–10

FAST FOOD
Manufacturer: Telesys
Label: Picture
Rarity: 4
Game Only: $4–6
Complete: $7–14
Notes: "Handle" style cartridge

FAST FOOD
Manufacturer: Telesys
Label: Picture
Rarity: 3
Game Only: $4–6
Complete: $7–14
Notes: Standard style cartridge

FATHOM
Manufacturer: Imagic
Label: Text
Rarity: 4
Game Only: $2–6
Complete: $8–12

FINAL APPROACH
Manufacturer: Apollo
Label: Picture
Rarity: 4
Game Only: $4–8
Complete: $12–23

FIRE FIGHTER
Manufacturer: Imagic
Label: Picture
Rarity: 3
Game Only: $2–4
Complete: $6–8

FIRE FLY
Manufacturer: Mythicon
Label: Picture
Rarity: 4
Game Only: $4–7
Complete: $8–10

FIREBALL
Manufacturer: Starpath
Label: Cassette
Rarity: 4
Game Only: $5–7
Complete: $7–10
Notes: Cassette game; requires the Supercharger and a cassette tape player

FISHING DERBY
Manufacturer: Activision
Label: Blue
Rarity: 2
Game Only: $1–3
Complete: $4–6

FLAG CAPTURE
Manufacturer: Atari
Label: Text
Rarity: 4
Game Only: $1–4
Complete: $5–7

FLAG CAPTURE
Manufacturer: Atari
Label: Picture
Rarity: 5
Game Only: $2–5
Complete: $6–8

FLASH GORDON
Manufacturer: 20th Century Fox
Label: Picture
Rarity: 4
Game Only: $3–8
Complete: $9–12

FOOTBALL

Manufacturer: Atari
Label: Text; Picture
Rarity: 1
Game Only: $1–2
Complete: $3–4

FOOTBALL

Manufacturer: Sears
Label: Text
Rarity: 2
Game Only: $1–2
Complete: $3–5
Notes: Sears version of the Atari game by the same name

FOOTBALL—REALSPORTS SOCCER

Manufacturer: Atari
Label: Silver
Rarity: 4
Game Only: $2–4
Complete: $4–5

FRANKENSTEIN'S MONSTER

Manufacturer: Data Age
Label: Picture
Rarity: 5
Game Only: $9–11
Complete: $12–15

FREEWAY

Manufacturer: Activision
Label: Red
Rarity: 2
Game Only: $1–3
Complete: $4–5

FREEWAY

Manufacturer: Activision
Label: Blue
Rarity: 3
Game Only: $2–4
Complete: $5–6

FREEWAY

Manufacturer: Zellers
Label: Picture
Rarity: 4
Game Only: $10–15
Complete: $20–25

FROG POND

Manufacturer: Atari
Label: N/A
Rarity: Prototype
Game Only: ?
Complete: N/A
Notes: Price unavailable; for more info, see
http://www.atariprotos.com

FROGGER

Manufacturer: Parker Brothers
Label: Picture
Rarity: 1
Game Only: $2–6
Complete: $8–12

FROGGER II: THREEDEEP

Manufacturer: Parker Brothers
Label: Text
Rarity: 6
Game Only: $15–18
Complete: $20–25

FROGGER, THE OFFICIAL

Manufacturer: Starpath
Label: Cassette
Rarity: 6
Game Only: $20–30*
Complete: $30–40*
Notes: Cassette game; requires the Supercharger and a cassette tape player

FROGS AND FLIES

Manufacturer: INTV
Label: White
Rarity: 5
Game Only: $2–3
Complete: $4–5
Notes: 2600 version of the Intellivision game *Frog Bog*

FROGS AND FLIES

Manufacturer: M Network
Label: Black
Rarity: 2
Game Only: $1–2
Complete: $3–4
Notes: 2600 version of the Intellivision game *Frog Bog*

FRONT LINE

Manufacturer: Coleco
Label: Text
Rarity: 4
Game Only: $7–10
Complete: $12–15

FRONTLINE

Manufacturer: Zellers
Label: Picture
Rarity: 4
Game Only: $5–8
Complete: $15–20

FROSTBITE

Manufacturer: Activision
Label: Green
Rarity: 4
Game Only: $3–5
Complete: $10–30

FUN WITH NUMBERS

Manufacturer: Atari
Label: Text; Picture
Rarity: 3
Game Only: $3–7
Complete: $8–10
Notes: Retitled version of *Basic Math*

FUNKY FISH

Manufacturer: UA Limited
Label: N/A
Rarity: Prototype
Game Only: ?
Complete: N/A
Notes: Price unavailable; for more info, see
http://www.atariprotos.com

FUNKY FISH

Manufacturer: Self-Published
Label: Picture
Rarity: Reproduction
Game Only: N/A
Complete: $35
Notes: Available at the AtariAge store
(http://www.atariage.com)

GALAXIAN

Manufacturer: Atari
Label: Silver
Rarity: 2
Game Only: $1–3
Complete: $4–6

GALAXIAN ARCADE

Manufacturer: AtariAge
Label: Silver
Rarity: Hack
Game Only: $20
Complete: N/A
Notes: Updated version of the Atari game Galaxian;
available at the AtariAge store
(http://www.atariage.com); no manual or box

A GAME OF CONCENTRATION

Manufacturer: Atari
Label: Text; Picture
Rarity: 3
Game Only: $3–5
Complete: $6–8
Notes: Requires Atari Keyboard Controller; origi-
nally released as *Hunt & Score*

GANGSTER ALLEY

Manufacturer: Spectravision
Label: Text
Rarity: 4
Game Only: $2–5
Complete: $9–12

GARFIELD

Manufacturer: Atari
Label: Picture
Rarity: Prototype
Game Only: ?
Complete: N/A
Notes: Price unavailable; for more info, see
http://www.atariprotos.com

GAS HOG

Manufacturer: Spectravision
Label: Text
Rarity: 8
Game Only: $65–75
Complete: $80–100*
Notes: European (PAL) version is more common (and
a lot cheaper); manual alone sells for $20 or more

GAUNTLET

Manufacturer: Answer
Label: Text
Rarity: 10
Game Only: $1,000+*
Complete: N/A
Notes: Originally available only via mail order from
Answer; no box; has nothing to do with the Atari
Gauntlet arcade game

GHOST MANOR

Manufacturer: Xonox
Label: Picture
Rarity: 6
Game Only: $12–15
Complete: $20–25

GHOST MANOR/SPIKE'S PEAK

Manufacturer: Xonox
Label: Double
Rarity: 4
Game Only: $11–15
Complete: $15–20

GHOSTBUSTERS

Manufacturer: Activision
Label: Picture; Blue
Rarity: 4
Game Only: $2–6
Complete: $10–15

GHOSTBUSTERS II

Manufacturer: Self-Published
Label: Picture
Rarity: Homebrew
Game Only: N/A
Complete: $30*
Notes: Available in both NTSC and PAL (NTSC ver-
sion has picture label, PAL version is text); complete
with manual and box

G.I. JOE—COBRA STRIKE

Manufacturer: Parker Brothers
Label: Color
Rarity: 4
Game Only: $3–5
Complete: $10–12

G.I. JOE—COBRA STRIKE

Manufacturer: Parker Brothers
Label: Gray
Rarity: 3
Game Only: $3–5
Complete: $10–12

GLACIER PATROL

Manufacturer: Telegames
Label: Silver
Rarity: 4
Complete: $25–30

GLIB

Manufacturer: Selchow & Righter/QDI
Label: Picture
Rarity: 9
Game Only: $40–90
Complete: $400–600
Notes: Box and manual are much rarer than the car-
tridge (hence the high price for a complete version)

GOLF

Manufacturer: Atari
Label: Text; Picture
Rarity: 2
Game Only: $1–2
Complete: $3–5

GOLF
Manufacturer: Sears
Label: Text
Rarity: 3
Game Only: $1–2
Complete: $3–5

GOOD LUCK, CHARLIE BROWN
Manufacturer: Atari
Label: N/A
Rarity: Prototype
Game Only: ?
Complete: N/A
Notes: Prototype cartridge was found at a flea market in Wisconsin; price unavailable; for more info, see http://www.atariprotos.com

GOPHER
Manufacturer: US Games
Label: Picture
Rarity: 4
Game Only: $2–6
Complete: $8–15
Notes: Applies to both the beveled and standard cartridge case versions

GORF
Manufacturer: CBS Electronics
Label: Text
Rarity: 3
Game Only: $2–6
Complete: $7–9

GRAND PRIX
Manufacturer: Activision
Label: Purple
Rarity: 2
Game Only: $1–3
Complete: $5–10

GRAND PRIX
Manufacturer: Activision
Label: Blue
Rarity: 3
Game Only: $2–4
Complete: $6–10

GRAND PRIX
Manufacturer: Activision
Label: White
Rarity: 3
Game Only: $2–4
Complete: $6–10

GRAVITAR
Manufacturer: Atari
Label: Silver
Rarity: 8
Game Only: $45–65
Complete: $100–200*
Notes: Originally available only through the Atari Club; very collectable

GRAVITAR
Manufacturer: Atari
Label: Red
Rarity: 2
Game Only: $1–2
Complete: $3–5
Notes: Mass-released, red label version

GREAT ESCAPE
Manufacturer: Bomb
Label: Text
Rarity: 9
Game Only: $65–80*
Complete: $100–150*
Notes: European (PAL) version is more common (and a lot cheaper)

GREMLINS
Manufacturer: Atari
Label: Silver
Rarity: 6
Game Only: $7–17
Complete: $100–200

GROVER'S MUSIC MAKER
Manufacturer: Atari
Label: N/A
Rarity: Prototype
Game Only: ?
Complete: N/A
Notes: Requires Atari Kid's Controller; price unavailable; for more info, see http://www.atariprotos.com

GUARDIAN
Manufacturer: Apollo
Label: Blue
Rarity: 8
Game Only: $50–90
Complete: $95–125*

GUNFIGHT
Manufacturer: XYPE
Label: Picture
Rarity: Homebrew
Game Only: N/A
Complete: $20
Notes: Released in 2001; available at the AtariAge store (http://www.atariage.com)

GUNSLINGER
Manufacturer: Sears
Label: Text
Rarity: 3
Game Only: $2–4
Complete: $5–7
Notes: Sears version of the Atari game *Outlaw;* there are 2 text label versions—one numbered "49-75109," the other numbered "6-99822"

GUNSLINGER
Manufacturer: Sears
Label: Picture
Rarity: 5
Game Only: $3–5
Complete: $6–8
Notes: Sears version of the Atari game *Outlaw*

GYRUSS
Manufacturer: Parker Brothers
Label: Text
Rarity: 4
Game Only: $3–8
Complete: $9–12

H.E.R.O.
Manufacturer: Activision
Label: Picture
Rarity: 5
Game Only: $5–14
Complete: $15–17

HALLOWEEN
Manufacturer: Wizard Video
Label: Red
Rarity: 7
Game Only: $100–150
Complete: $175–250

HALLOWEEN
Manufacturer: Wizard Video
Label: N/A
Rarity: 8
Game Only: $80–100
Complete: $125–200*
Notes: Handwritten label; possibly rarer, but not as popular with collectors

HANGMAN
Manufacturer: Atari
Label: Text; Picture
Rarity: 2
Game Only: $2–4
Complete: $5–7

HARBOR ESCAPE
Manufacturer: Panda
Label: Picture
Rarity: 6
Game Only: $20–30
Complete: $40–50*

HAUNTED HOUSE
Manufacturer: Atari
Label: Picture
Rarity: 2
Game Only: $2–5
Complete: $6–10

HAUNTED HOUSE
Manufacturer: Sears
Label: Picture
Rarity: 2
Game Only: $3–6
Complete: $8–10
Notes: Sears version of the Atari game by the same name

HOLEY MOLEY
Manufacturer: Atari
Label: N/A
Rarity: Prototype
Game Only: $15
Complete: N/A

HOLEY MOLEY
Manufacturer: Self-Published
Label: Unique
Rarity: Reproduction
Game Only: $30–35
Complete: $45
Notes: Released at the 2002 Classic Gaming Expo; available from http://www.atari2600.com; requires Atari Kid's Controller, and includes overlay

HOME RUN
Manufacturer: Atari
Label: Text; Picture
Rarity: 2
Game Only: $1–2
Complete: $3–4

HUMAN CANNONBALL
Manufacturer: Atari
Label: Text; Picture
Rarity: 2
Game Only: $1–2
Complete: $3–4

HUNT & SCORE
Manufacturer: Atari
Label: Text
Rarity: 3
Game Only: $2–4
Complete: $5–7
Notes: Requires Atari Keyboard Controller; later re-released as *A Game of Concentration*

I WANT MY MOMMY
Manufacturer: Zimag
Label: Picture
Rarity: 5
Game Only: $9–15
Complete: $20–25

ICE HOCKEY
Manufacturer: Activision
Label: Blue
Rarity: 2
Game Only: $1–3
Complete: $4–7
Notes: Original label (with screen shot)

ICE HOCKEY
Manufacturer: Activision
Label: Blue
Rarity: 3
Game Only: $2–4
Complete: $5–8
Notes: Re-release text-only label

IKARI WARRIORS
Manufacturer: Atari
Label: Red
Rarity: 9
Game Only: $50–75*
Complete: $80–150*
Notes: European (PAL) version is more common (and a lot cheaper)

IN SEARCH OF THE GOLDEN SKULL

Manufacturer: M Network
Label: N/A
Rarity: Prototype
Game Only: ?
Complete: N/A
Notes: Price unavailable; for more info, see
http://www.atariprotos.com

INCA GOLD

Manufacturer: Zellers
Label: Picture
Rarity: 6
Game Only: $8–12
Complete: $15–20

INDY 500

Manufacturer: Atari
Label: Numbered Text
Rarity: 3
Game Only: $1–3
Complete: $20–30
Notes: Original numbered label (reads: "11 Indy 500"
on end); complete version price reflects package in-
cluding Atari Driving Controllers

INDY 500

Manufacturer: Atari
Label: Text; Picture
Rarity: 2
Game Only: $1–3
Complete: $20–30
Notes: Complete version price reflects package in-
cluding Atari Driving Controllers

INFILTRATE

Manufacturer: Apollo
Label: Red; Blue
Rarity: 3
Game Only: $2–4
Complete: $10–12

INTERNATIONAL SOCCER

Manufacturer: M Network
Label: Black
Rarity: 2
Game Only: $2–4
Complete: $5–7

INTERNATIONAL SOCCER

Manufacturer: Telegames
Label: Silver
Rarity: 4
Game Only: $5–7
Complete: $8–10

INV

Manufacturer: Self-Published
Label: Picture
Rarity: Homebrew
Game Only: N/A
Complete: $20
Notes: Available at the AtariAge store
(http://www.atariage.com); no box

JAMES BOND 007

Manufacturer: Parker Brothers
Label: Text
Rarity: 6
Game Only: $10–18
Complete: $30–50

JAMMED

Manufacturer: XYPE
Label: Picture
Rarity: Homebrew
Game Only: N/A
Complete: $20
Notes: Available at the AtariAge store
(http://www.atariage.com); no box

JAWBREAKER

Manufacturer: Tigervision
Label: Picture
Rarity: 5
Game Only: $8–11
Complete: $15–25

JOURNEY ESCAPE

Manufacturer: Data Age
Label: Picture
Rarity: 2
Game Only: $1–5
Complete: $10–13

JOUST

Manufacturer: Atari
Label: Silver
Rarity: 2
Game Only: $2–4
Complete: $5–7

JR. PAC-MAN

Manufacturer: Atari
Label: Red
Rarity: 2
Game Only: $2–5
Complete: $5–13

JUNGLE FEVER/KNIGHT ON THE TOWN

Manufacturer: Playaround
Label: Double
Rarity: 7
Game Only: $30–40*
Complete: $50–70*
Notes: 2 adult games on one double-ended cartridge

JUNGLE HUNT

Manufacturer: Atari
Label: Silver
Rarity: 2
Game Only: $1–3
Complete: $5–9

KABOBBER

Manufacturer: Activision
Label: N/A
Rarity: Prototype
Game Only: ?
Complete: N/A
Notes: Price unavailable; for more info, see
http://www.atariprotos.com

KABOOM!
Manufacturer: Activision
Label: Pink
Rarity: 2
Game Only: $2–4
Complete: $6–14

KABOOM!
Manufacturer: Activision
Label: Blue
Rarity: 3
Game Only: $4–6
Complete: $6–14

KAMIKAZE SAUCERS
Manufacturer: Syncro
Label: N/A
Rarity: Prototype
Game Only: ?
Complete: N/A
Notes: Price unavailable; for more info, see
http://www.atariprotos.com

KANGAROO
Manufacturer: Atari
Label: Silver
Rarity: 2
Game Only: $1–3
Complete: $4–6

KARATE
Manufacturer: Froggo
Label: White
Rarity: 4
Game Only: $4–7
Complete: $7–10
Notes: Re-release of the Ultravision game of the same
title; much more common than the Ultravision version

KARATE
Manufacturer: Ultravision
Label: Picture
Rarity: 10
Game Only: $100–150*
Complete: $200–250*

KEYSTONE KAPERS
Manufacturer: Activision
Label: Pink
Rarity: 2
Game Only: $2–3
Complete: $6–10

KEYSTONE KAPERS
Manufacturer: Activision
Label: Blue
Rarity: 3
Game Only: $3–4
Complete: $7–12

KILLER SATELLITES
Manufacturer: Starpath
Label: Cassette
Rarity: 4
Game Only: $3–5
Complete: $6–8
Notes: Cassette game; requires the Supercharger and
a cassette tape player

KING KONG
Manufacturer: Tigervision
Label: Picture
Rarity: 5
Game Only: $9–11
Complete: $15–20

KLAX
Manufacturer: Atari
Label: N/A
Rarity: Prototype
Game Only: ?
Complete: N/A
Notes: Never released in the U.S.; European (PAL)
versions are fairly common, and usually sell for
around $7–10 complete; for more info, go to
http://www.atariprotos.com

KOOL-AID MAN
Manufacturer: M Network
Label: Black
Rarity: 4
Game Only: $6–10
Complete: $12–15
Notes: Originally offered as an exclusive from Kool-
Aid, but fairly easy to find

KRULL
Manufacturer: Atari
Label: Silver
Rarity: 4
Game Only: $4–6
Complete: $10–16

KUNG-FU MASTER
Manufacturer: Activision
Label: Black
Rarity: 4
Game Only: $3–5
Complete: $7–10

KUNG FU SUPERKICKS
Manufacturer: Telegames
Label: White
Rarity: 5
Game Only: $3–5
Complete: $6–10
Notes: Originally released as *Chuck Norris Superkicks*

LASER BLAST
Manufacturer: Activision
Label: Orange
Rarity: 2
Game Only: $1–2
Complete: $4–7

LASER GATES
Manufacturer: Imagic
Label: Text
Rarity: 5
Game Only: $9–15
Complete: $18–25

LASER VOLLEY
Manufacturer: Zellers
Label: Picture
Rarity: 4
Game Only: $10–17
Complete: $18–20

THE LAST STARFIGHTER
Manufacturer: Atari
Label: N/A
Rarity: Prototype
Game Only: ?
Complete: N/A
Notes: Price unavailable; for more info, see http://www.atariprotos.com

THE LAST STARFIGHTER
Manufacturer: Self-Published
Label: Picture
Rarity: Reproduction
Game Only: $25
Complete: N/A
Notes: Reproduction of the Atari prototype; available at Atari2600.com (http://www.atari2600.com)

LOCHJAW
Manufacturer: Apollo
Label: Picture
Rarity: 9
Game Only: $200–300*
Complete: $350–450*
Notes: Re-released as *Shark Attack* due to copyright issues; *Shark Attack* is slightly different (and much more common)

LOCK 'N' CHASE
Manufacturer: INTV
Label: White
Rarity: 3
Game Only: $2–3
Complete: $5–10

LOCK 'N' CHASE
Manufacturer: M Network
Label: Black
Rarity: 2
Game Only: $2–3
Complete: $5–10

LOCK 'N' CHASE
Manufacturer: Telegames
Label: Silver
Rarity: 3
Game Only: $3–4
Complete: $5–10

LOCO-MOTION
Manufacturer: M Network
Label: N/A
Rarity: Prototype
Game Only: ?
Complete: N/A
Notes: Based on the Centuri arcade game by the same name; price unavailable; for more info, see http://www.atariprotos.com

LONDON BLITZ
Manufacturer: Avalon Hill
Label: Picture
Rarity: 5
Game Only: $10–15
Complete: $18–30

LOOPING
Manufacturer: Coleco
Label: N/A
Rarity: Prototype
Game Only: ?
Complete: N/A
Notes: Based on the Venture Line arcade game by the same title; price unavailable; for more info, see http://www.atariprotos.com

LOOPING
Manufacturer: CGE Services Corp.
Label: Picture
Rarity: Reproduction
Game Only: N/A
Complete: $40
Notes: Reproduction of the Coleco prototype; released at the 2003 Classic Gaming Expo; includes box and instructions; limited number available at the CGE web site (http://www.cgexpo.com)

LORD OF THE RINGS: FELLOWSHIP OF THE RING
Manufacturer: Self-Published
Label: Picture
Rarity: Homebrew
Game Only: N/A
Complete: $19
Notes: A text adventure game that uses the *Dark Mage* game engine; available at http://www.packratvg.com

LORD OF THE RINGS: JOURNEY TO RIVENDELL
Manufacturer: Parker Brothers
Label: Unique
Rarity: Prototype
Game Only: ?
Complete: N/A
Notes: Prototype discovered in 2001; a prototype box also exists; price unavailable; for more info, see http://www.atariprotos.com

LOST LUGGAGE
Manufacturer: Apollo
Label: Green; Blue
Rarity: 4
Game Only: $2–6
Complete: $7–10
Notes: The blue-label version includes an opening screen not found in the green-label version

M*A*S*H
Manufacturer: 20th Century Fox
Label: Picture
Rarity: 3
Game Only: $2–6
Complete: $7–10
Notes: Some packages included a free t-shirt ("complete" price reflects the package *without* the t-shirt)

M.A.D.
Manufacturer: US Games
Label: Picture
Rarity: 4
Game Only: $3–5
Complete: $6–9
Notes: Applies to both the beveled and standard cartridge case versions

MAGICARD

Manufacturer: CommaVid
Label: Text
Rarity: 10
Game Only: $400–600
Complete: $800–1,500
Notes: Programming cartridge available only through mail order; no box; this is one of the most collectable 2600 cartridges that exists; includes Keyboard controller overlays

MAGICARD

Manufacturer: Sunmark
Label: None
Rarity: Reproduction
Game Only: $80
Complete: N/A
Notes: Reproduction of the original *MagiCard* cartridge with no case; available at http://www.sunmark.com

MALAGAI

Manufacturer: Answer
Label: Text
Rarity: 9
Game Only: $375–550
Complete: $675–1,000*
Notes: Beware of reproductions! Reproductions typically sell for $50 or less

MANGIA

Manufacturer: Spectravision
Label: Text
Rarity: 10
Game Only: $140–300
Complete: $350–500*

MARAUDER

Manufacturer: Tigervision
Label: Picture
Rarity: 6
Game Only: $25–30
Complete: $35–40*

MARBLE CRAZE

Manufacturer: XYPE
Label: Picture
Rarity: Homebrew
Game Only: N/A
Complete: $25
Notes: Released at the 2002 Classic Gaming Expo; "complete" price reflects version available at AtariAge.com; original version was sold in a tin box

MARINE WARS

Manufacturer: Konami
Label: Picture
Rarity: 5
Game Only: $10–30
Complete: $35–40*

MARIO BROS.

Manufacturer: Atari
Label: Silver
Rarity: 4
Game Only: $3–12
Complete: $12–19

MASTER BUILDER

Manufacturer: Spectravision
Label: Text
Rarity: 8
Game Only: $15–60
Complete: $50–75*
Notes: Originally available only through the Columbia House Videogame Club; difficult to find

MASTERS OF THE UNIVERSE: THE POWER OF HE MAN

Manufacturer: INTV
Label: White
Rarity: 4
Game Only: $7–10
Complete: $12–15

MASTERS OF THE UNIVERSE: THE POWER OF HE MAN

Manufacturer: M Network
Label: Black
Rarity: 4
Game Only: $7–10
Complete: $12–15

MATH

Manufacturer: Sears
Label: Text
Rarity: 4
Game Only: $1–4
Complete: $5–7
Notes: Sears version of the Atari game *Basic Math/Fun with Numbers*

MATH GRAN PRIX

Manufacturer: Atari
Label: Picture
Rarity: 3
Game Only: $1–3
Complete: $4–6

MATH GRAN PRIX

Manufacturer: Sears
Label: Picture
Rarity: 4
Game Only: $2–4
Complete: $5–7
Notes: Sears version of the Atari game by the same name

MAZE

Manufacturer: Sears
Label: Text
Rarity: 3
Game Only: $2–4
Complete: $6–10
Notes: Sears version of the Atari game *Slot Racers*; there are 2 text label versions—one numbered "49-75112," and the other numbered "6-99825"

MAZE

Manufacturer: Sears
Label: Picture
Rarity: 2
Game Only: $2–4
Complete: $6–10
Notes: Sears version of the Atari game *Slot Racers*

MAZE CRAZE

Manufacturer: Atari
Label: Text; Picture
Rarity: 2
Game Only: $2–4
Complete: $4–6
Notes: Full title of the game is *Maze Craze: A Game of Cops 'n Robbers*

MAZE MANIA

Manufacturer: Sears
Label: Text
Rarity: 2
Game Only: $2–4
Complete: $5–7
Notes: Sears version of the Atari game *Maze Craze*

MCDONALD'S

Manufacturer: Parker Brothers
Label: N/A
Rarity: Prototype
Game Only: ?
Complete: N/A
Notes: Nonplayable prototype that displays the famous McDonald's Golden Arches; price unavailable; for more info, see http://www.atariprotos.com

MEGA FORCE

Manufacturer: 20th Century Fox
Label: Black
Rarity: 2
Game Only: $2–4
Complete: $15–20

MEGAMANIA

Manufacturer: Activision
Label: Red
Rarity: 2
Game Only: $2–4
Complete: $5–7

MEGAMANIA

Manufacturer: Activision
Label: Blue
Rarity: 5
Game Only: $3–7
Complete: $10–15

MEMORY MATCH

Manufacturer: Sears
Label: Text
Rarity: 4
Game Only: $3–4
Complete: $5–7
Notes: Sears version of the Atari game *A Game of Concentration/Hunt & Score;* requires Atari Keyboard controller

MENTAL KOMBAT

Manufacturer: Simon Quernhorst
Label: Picture
Rarity: Homebrew
Game Only: N/A
Complete: $20
Notes: Standard edition; released at the 2002 Classic Gaming Expo; available in the AtariAge store (http://www.atariage.com)

MENTAL KOMBAT—LIMITED EDITION

Manufacturer: Simon Quernhorst
Label: Limited Edition
Rarity: Homebrew
Game Only: N/A
Complete: $55
Notes: Signed/numbered limited edition; released at the 2002 Classic Gaming Expo; available in the AtariAge store (http://www.atariage.com)

MERLIN'S WALLS

Manufacturer: Ebivision
Label: Picture
Rarity: Homebrew
Game Only: $20–30*
Complete: N/A

MIDNIGHT MAGIC

Manufacturer: Atari
Label: Red
Rarity: 3
Game Only: $2–4
Complete: $12–15

MILLIPEDE

Manufacturer: Atari
Label: Silver
Rarity: 3
Game Only: $2–5
Complete: $6–9

MINE SWEEPER

Manufacturer: Self-Published
Label: N/A
Rarity: Homebrew
Game Only: $15
Complete: N/A

MINER 2049ER

Manufacturer: Tigervision
Label: Picture
Rarity: 5
Game Only: $7–15
Complete: $18–25

MINER 2049ER VOLUME II

Manufacturer: Tigervision
Label: Picture
Rarity: 7
Game Only: $45–55
Complete: $60–80

MINES OF MINOS

Manufacturer: CommaVid
Label: Picture
Rarity: 6
Game Only: $15–25
Complete: $30–40*

MINIATURE GOLF

Manufacturer: Atari
Label: Text
Rarity: 3
Game Only: $2–5
Complete: $4–10

MISS PIGGY'S WEDDING

Manufacturer: Atari
Label: N/A
Rarity: Prototype
Game Only: ?
Complete: N/A
Notes: Price unavailable; for more info, see
http://www.atariprotos.com

MISSILE COMMAND

Manufacturer: Atari
Label: Picture
Rarity: 1
Game Only: $1–2
Complete: $2–3

MISSILE COMMAND

Manufacturer: Sears
Label: Text
Rarity: 2
Game Only: $1–2
Complete: $2–3

MISSILE COMMAND

Manufacturer: Sears
Label: Picture
Rarity: 5
Game Only: $2–4
Complete: $4–6
Notes: Sears version of the Atari game by the same
name

MISSILE COMMAND: TRAK-BALL (TB)

Manufacturer: AtariAge
Label: Picture
Rarity: Hack
Game Only: $15
Complete: N/A
Notes: Updated version of the Atari game *Missile
Command;* available at the AtariAge store
(http://www.atariage.com); no manual or box

MISSION 3000 A.D.

Manufacturer: Bit Corp.
Label: N/A
Rarity: Prototype
Game Only: ?
Complete: N/A
Notes: Price unavailable; for more info, see
http://www.atariprotos.com

MISSION 3000 A.D.

Manufacturer: Self-Published
Label: Picture
Rarity: Reproduction
Game Only: $20
Complete: N/A
Notes: Reproduction of the Bit Corp. prototype; available at Atari2600.com (http://www.atari2600.com)

MOGUL MANIAC

Manufacturer: Amiga
Label: Picture
Rarity: 4
Game Only: $6–20
Complete: $45–55
Notes: Must include the Joyboard Controller to be
considered complete

MONDO PONG

Manufacturer: Self-Published
Label: N/A
Rarity: Homebrew
Game Only: $15–20*
Complete: N/A

MONSTERCISE

Manufacturer: Atari
Label: N/A
Rarity: Prototype
Game Only: $15–20*
Complete: N/A
Notes: Requires Atari Kid's Controller

MONTEZUMA'S REVENGE

Manufacturer: Parker Brothers
Label: Text
Rarity: 5
Game Only: $18–30
Complete: $35–40*

MOON PATROL

Manufacturer: Atari
Label: Silver
Rarity: 2
Game Only: $2–4
Complete: $4–6

MOONSWEEPER

Manufacturer: Imagic
Label: Text
Rarity: 4
Game Only: $2–7
Complete: $8–10

MOONSWEEPER

Manufacturer: Activision
Label: Blue
Rarity: 4
Game Only: $2–7
Complete: $8–10
Notes: Blue label version released after Activision acquired rights to the game from Imagic

MOTOCROSS RACER

Manufacturer: Xonox
Label: Picture
Rarity: 7
Game Only: $35–40
Complete: $60–70*
Notes: European (PAL) version is more common (and
a lot cheaper)

MOTORODEO

Manufacturer: Atari
Label: Red
Rarity: 10
Game Only: $100–150*
Complete: $175–225*
Notes: Until recently, the existence of an NTSC version was disputed. It *does* exist, but was only available
via mail order. Very rare.

MOUNTAIN KING
Manufacturer: CBS Electronics
Label: Text
Rarity: 4
Game Only: $2–3
Complete: $5–17

MOUSE TRAP
Manufacturer: Atari
Label: Red
Rarity: 3
Game Only: $3–5
Complete: $7–9
Notes: Black cartridge with red Atari label

MOUSE TRAP
Manufacturer: Coleco
Label: Text
Rarity: 2
Game Only: $2–3
Complete: $5–7
Notes: White cartridge with black Coleco label

MR. DO!
Manufacturer: Coleco
Label: Text
Rarity: 5
Game Only: $3–7
Complete: $9–12

MR. DO!'S CASTLE
Manufacturer: Parker Brothers
Label: Text
Rarity: 8
Game Only: $33–65
Complete: $75–90*

MR. ROBOTO
Manufacturer: AtariAge
Label: Picture
Rarity: Hack
Game Only: $20
Complete: N/A
Notes: Updated version of the Atari game Berzerk; available at the AtariAge store (http://www.atariage.com); no manual or box

MS. PAC-MAN
Manufacturer: Atari
Label: Silver
Rarity: 2
Game Only: $2–4
Complete: $4–6

MULTI-CART
Manufacturer: Sean Kelly
Label: Unique
Rarity: Homebrew
Game Only: $125
Complete: N/A
Notes: Menu-driven cartridge that contains 255 Atari 2600 titles; typically available only at shows and conventions directly from Digital Press

MUSIC MACHINE
Manufacturer: Sparrow
Label: Picture
Rarity: 10
Game Only: $200–300
Complete: $350–450*
Notes: Originally available only in religious bookstores

NAME THIS GAME
Manufacturer: US Games
Label: Picture
Rarity: 4
Game Only: $3–5
Complete: $7–10
Notes: Beveled case version; released in Europe as *Octopus*

NAME THIS GAME
Manufacturer: US Games
Label: Picture
Rarity: 3
Game Only: $2–4
Complete: $5–7
Notes: Standard case version

NIGHT DRIVER
Manufacturer: Atari
Label: Text; Picture
Rarity: 1
Game Only: $1–3
Complete: $3–5

NIGHT DRIVER
Manufacturer: Sears
Label: Text
Rarity: 2
Game Only: $1–3
Complete: $3–5
Notes: Sears version of the Atari game by the same name

NIGHT DRIVER
Manufacturer: Sears
Label: Picture
Rarity: 6
Game Only: $2–5
Complete: $7–9
Notes: Sears version of the Atari game by the same name

NIGHT STALKER
Manufacturer: Telegames
Label: Silver
Rarity: 5
Game Only: $8–10
Complete: $12–15

NO ESCAPE!
Manufacturer: Imagic
Label: Picture
Rarity: 4
Game Only: $2–5
Complete: $25–30

NWCGE INVADERS

Manufacturer: ResQsoft
Label: Unique
Rarity: Homebrew
Game Only: N/A
Complete: $20
Notes: Available from ResQsoft (http://home.earth-link.net/~resqsoft/products.htm)

OBELIX

Manufacturer: Atari
Label: Silver
Rarity: 10
Game Only: $70–150
Complete: $140–175
Notes: The European (PAL) version is much more common (and a lot cheaper)

OCEAN CITY DEFENDER

Manufacturer: Zellers
Label: Picture
Rarity: 4
Game Only: $7–16
Complete: $16–20

OFF THE WALL

Manufacturer: Atari
Label: Red
Rarity: 5
Game Only: $8–10
Complete: $18–22

OFF YOUR ROCKER

Manufacturer: Amiga
Label: Unique
Rarity: Prototype
Game Only: ?
Complete: N/A
Notes: A number of these cartridges were sold to the public with handwritten labels in 1983; price unavailable; for more info, see http://www.atariprotos.com

OINK!

Manufacturer: Activision
Label: Blue
Rarity: 3
Game Only: $2–4
Complete: $12–15

OKIE DOKIE

Manufacturer: Retroware
Label: Text
Rarity: Homebrew
Game Only: N/A
Complete: $20
Notes: Available at the AtariAge store (http://www.atariage.com); limited edition also exists (only 100 were produced); no box

OMEGA RACE

Manufacturer: CBS Electronics
Label: Text
Rarity: 3
Game Only: $2–6
Complete: $15–25*
Notes: Complete version includes the Booster Grip Controller, a hand grip that slips over the standard joystick

OSCAR'S TRASH RACE

Manufacturer: Atari
Label: Picture
Rarity: 4
Game Only: $10–12
Complete: $15–18
Notes: Requires Atari Kid's Controller; overlay adds to value (even if otherwise incomplete)

OTHELLO

Manufacturer: Atari
Label: All
Rarity: 2
Game Only: $1–2
Complete: $3–4

OTHELLO

Manufacturer: Sears
Label: Text
Rarity: 4
Game Only: $2–4
Complete: $5–6

OUT OF CONTROL

Manufacturer: Avalon Hill
Label: Picture
Rarity: 9
Game Only: $150–200*
Complete: $500–650
Notes: Last 2600 game released by Avalon Hill

OUTER SPACE

Manufacturer: Sears
Label: Text
Rarity: 3
Game Only: $4–6
Complete: $7–9
Notes: Sears version of the Atari game *Star Ship*

OUTER SPACE

Manufacturer: Sears
Label: Picture
Rarity: 4
Game Only: $4–6
Complete: $7–9
Notes: Sears version of the Atari game *Star Ship*

OUTLAW

Manufacturer: Atari
Label: Text; Picture
Rarity: 2
Game Only: $1–3
Complete: $4–6

OYSTRON

Manufacturer: XYPE
Label: Picture
Rarity: Homebrew
Game Only: N/A
Complete: $20
Notes: Available at the AtariAge store (http://www.atariage.com); no box

PAC-MAN

Manufacturer: Atari
Label: Picture
Rarity: 1
Game Only: $1
Complete: $3–5

PAC-MAN
Manufacturer: Sears
Label: Picture
Rarity: 3
Game Only: $1–2
Complete: $3–5
Notes: Sears version of the Atari game by the same name

PAC-MAN ARCADE
Manufacturer: AtariAge
Label: Silver
Rarity: Hack
Game Only: $20
Complete: N/A
Notes: Updated version of the Atari game *Pac-Man;* available at the AtariAge store (http://www.atariage.com); no box or manual

PARTY MIX
Manufacturer: Starpath
Label: Cassette
Rarity: 7
Game Only: $50–60
Complete: $70–150
Notes: Cassette game; requires the Supercharger and a cassette tape player

PEEK-A-BOO
Manufacturer: Atari
Label: N/A
Rarity: Prototype
Game Only: $15–20*
Complete: N/A
Notes: For more info, see http://www.atariprotos.com

PELE'S SOCCER
Manufacturer: Atari
Label: Picture
Rarity: 2
Game Only: $1–3
Complete: $5–9
Notes: *Championship Soccer* with a celebrity endorsement—games are identical

PENGO
Manufacturer: Atari
Label: Silver
Rarity: 6
Game Only: $10–14
Complete: $50–100
Notes: A prototype version with different graphics also exists

PEPSI INVADERS
Manufacturer: Atari
Label: N/A
Rarity: 10
Game Only: $400–500*
Complete: N/A
Notes: Only 125 copies exist—there is no box; given away as a promotional item to Coca-Cola employees; also (incorrectly) known as *Coke Wins*

PESCO
Manufacturer: Ebivision
Label: Picture
Rarity: Homebrew
Game Only: $25–35*
Complete: N/A

PETE ROSE BASEBALL
Manufacturer: Absolute Entertainment
Label: Text
Rarity: 5
Game Only: $5–7
Complete: $10–15

PHASER PATROL
Manufacturer: Starpath
Label: Cassette
Rarity: 4
Game Only: $5–8
Complete: $20–30
Notes: Originally packaged with the Starpath Supercharger; complete price reflects the inclusion of the Supercharger and all documentation

PHILLY FLASHER/CATHOUSE BLUES
Manufacturer: Playaround
Label: Double
Rarity: 5
Game Only: $30–40
Complete: $50–60
Notes: 2 adult games on one double-ended cartridge

PHOENIX
Manufacturer: Atari
Label: Silver
Rarity: 2
Game Only: $1–2
Complete: $3–5

PICK UP
Manufacturer: 20th Century Fox
Label: N/A
Rarity: Prototype
Game Only: ?
Complete: N/A
Notes: Adult game prototype; price unavailable; for more info, see http://www.atariprotos.com

PICK UP
Manufacturer: Self-Published
Label: Picture
Rarity: Reproduction
Game Only: N/A
Complete: $40
Notes: Adult game; commercially released at the 2002 Classic Gaming Expo; a limited number of copies are available at the CGE web site (http://www.cgexpo.com)

PICNIC
Manufacturer: US Games
Label: Picture
Rarity: 5
Game Only: $3–10
Complete: $12–15

PIECE O' CAKE
Manufacturer: US Games
Label: Picture
Rarity: 5
Game Only: $4–9
Complete: $12–15

PIGS IN SPACE
Manufacturer: Atari
Label: Picture
Rarity: 5
Game Only: $6–8
Complete: $12–15

PINBALL
Manufacturer: Zellers
Label: Picture
Rarity: 4
Game Only: $8–12*
Complete: $15–20

PINK PANTHER
Manufacturer: Probe 2000
Label: N/A
Rarity: Prototype
Game Only: ?
Complete: N/A
Notes: Price unavailable; for more info, see
http://www.atariprotos.com

PITFALL II: LOST CAVERNS
Manufacturer: Activision
Label: Brown
Rarity: 4
Game Only: $7–15
Complete: $25–40

PITFALL!
Manufacturer: Activision
Label: Green
Rarity: 2
Game Only: $1–5
Complete: $12–15

PITFALL!
Manufacturer: Activision
Label: Blue
Rarity: 3
Game Only: $1–5
Complete: $12–15

PLANET OF THE APES
Manufacturer: 20th Century Fox
Label: N/A
Rarity: Prototype
Game Only: ?
Complete: N/A
Notes: Price unavailable; for more info, see
http://www.atariprotos.com

PLANET PATROL
Manufacturer: Spectravision
Label: Text
Rarity: 3
Game Only: $2–4
Complete: $8–10

PLAQUE ATTACK
Manufacturer: Activision
Label: Pink
Rarity: 4
Game Only: $1–4
Complete: $12–18

PLEIADES
Manufacturer: UA Limited
Label: N/A
Rarity: Prototype
Game Only: ?
Complete: N/A
Notes: Price unavailable; for more info, see
http://www.atariprotos.com

PLEIADES
Manufacturer: Self-Published
Label: Picture
Rarity: Reproduction
Game Only: N/A
Complete: $35
Notes: Available at the AtariAge store
(http://www.atariage.com)

POKER PLUS
Manufacturer: Sears
Label: Text; Picture
Rarity: 3
Game Only: $1–3
Complete: $4–6
Notes: Sears version of the Atari game *Casino*

POLARIS
Manufacturer: Tigervision
Label: Picture
Rarity: 6
Game Only: $15–20
Complete: $25–30
Notes: Blue end label

POLARIS
Manufacturer: Tigervision
Label: Picture
Rarity: 7
Game Only: $15–20
Complete: $25–30
Notes: Green end label

POLE POSITION
Manufacturer: Atari
Label: Silver
Rarity: 4
Game Only: $2–4
Complete: $5–7
Notes: End label says "Pole Position"

POLE POSITION
Manufacturer: Atari
Label: Silver
Rarity: 2
Game Only: $1–3
Complete: $4–5
Notes: End label says "Pole Position"; a misprinted
end label version ("Ploe Position") also exists, but is
very rare

POLO

Manufacturer: Atari
Label: N/A
Rarity: Prototype
Game Only: ?
Complete: N/A
Notes: Only 2 copies exist; price unavailable; for more info, see http://www.atariprotos.com

POLO

Manufacturer: Self-Published
Label: Picture
Rarity: Reproduction
Game Only: N/A
Complete: $40–50
Notes: Released at the 2003 Philly Classic; only 50 copies were produced; complete with (red) box and manual

POLO (RALPH LAUREN POLO)

Manufacturer: Self-Published
Label: Text
Rarity: Reproduction
Game Only: N/A
Complete: $45–55
Notes: Released at the 2002 Philly Classic; label reads "Ralph Lauren Polo"; complete with (green) box and manual

POMPEII

Manufacturer: Apollo
Label: N/A
Rarity: Prototype
Game Only: ?
Complete: N/A
Notes: A prototype box also exists; price unavailable; for more info, see http://www.atariprotos.com

PONG SPORTS

Manufacturer: Sears
Label: Text
Rarity: 3
Game Only: $4–10
Complete: $10–15
Notes: Sears version of the Atari game *Video Olympics*

PONG SPORTS

Manufacturer: Sears
Label: Picture
Rarity: 5
Game Only: $4–10
Complete: $10–15
Notes: Sears version of the Atari game *Video Olympics*

POOYAN

Manufacturer: Konami
Label: Picture
Rarity: 5
Game Only: $7–15
Complete: $20–25

POPEYE

Manufacturer: Parker Brothers
Label: Picture
Rarity: 2
Game Only: $2–6
Complete: $9–12

PORKY'S

Manufacturer: 20th Century Fox
Label: Picture
Rarity: 4
Game Only: $3–7
Complete: $8–10

PRESSURE COOKER

Manufacturer: Activision
Label: Red
Rarity: 4
Game Only: $2–8
Complete: $9–12

PRESSURE GAUGE

Manufacturer: Self-Published
Label: Picture
Rarity: Homebrew
Game Only: $15
Complete: N/A

PRIVATE EYE

Manufacturer: Activision
Label: Picture
Rarity: 5
Game Only: $9–13
Complete: $15–25

Q*BERT

Manufacturer: Atari
Label: Red
Rarity: 3
Game Only: $4–8
Complete: $7–10
Notes: Standard cartridge with red Atari label

Q*BERT

Manufacturer: Parker Brothers
Label: Picture
Rarity: 2
Game Only: $3–8
Complete: $10–12
Notes: Beveled cartridge with silver Parker Brothers picture label

Q*BERT'S QUBES

Manufacturer: Parker Brothers
Label: Text
Rarity: 9
Game Only: $60–125
Complete: $200–300*

QB

Manufacturer: XYPE
Label: Unique
Rarity: Homebrew
Game Only: N/A
Complete: $20
Notes: Standard version is available from the AtariAge store (http://www.atariage.com); a limited, numbered edition also exists; no box

QUADRUN

Manufacturer: Atari
Label: Silver
Rarity: 9
Game Only: $250–400
Complete: $450–600*
Notes: Originally available only through the Atari Club; 1 of only 2 Atari 2600 games to feature speech; beware of reproductions

QUEST FOR QUINTANA ROO

Manufacturer: Sunrise
Label: Text
Rarity: 8
Game Only: $25–50
Complete: $75–90*
Notes: Original Sunrise version is rare—especially complete; instructions are a typed sheet

QUEST FOR QUINTANA ROO

Manufacturer: Telegames
Label: Silver
Rarity: 3
Game Only: $8–10
Complete: $10–25
Notes: Much more common than the Sunrise version

QUICK STEP!

Manufacturer: Imagic
Label: Text
Rarity: 5
Game Only: $6–8
Complete: $10–12

RABBIT TRANSIT

Manufacturer: Atari
Label: N/A
Rarity: Prototype
Game Only: ?
Complete: N/A
Notes: Price unavailable; for more info, see http://www.atariprotos.com

RABBIT TRANSIT

Manufacturer: Self-Published
Label: Picture
Rarity: Reproduction
Game Only: $25
Complete: N/A
Notes: Cartridge reproduction of the Atari prototype; available at Atari2600.com (http://www.atari2600.com)

RABBIT TRANSIT

Manufacturer: Starpath
Label: Cassette
Rarity: 6
Game Only: $30–40*
Complete: $90–125
Notes: Cassette game; requires the Supercharger and a cassette tape player

RACE

Manufacturer: Sears
Label: Text
Rarity: 3
Game Only: $2–3
Complete: $5–8
Notes: Sears version of the Atari game *Indy 500*; requires Atari Driving Controller

RACE

Manufacturer: Sears
Label: Picture
Rarity: 4
Game Only: $2–3
Complete: $5–8
Notes: Sears version of the Atari game *Indy 500*; requires Atari Driving Controller

RACING PAK

Manufacturer: Atari
Label: Picture
Rarity: 6
Game Only: N/A
Complete: $30–50*
Notes: Package containing *Indy 500* and *Slot Racer,* along with an Atari Driving Controller; must include all packaging to be considered complete

RACQUETBALL

Manufacturer: Apollo
Label: Picture
Rarity: 4
Game Only: $3–7
Complete: $9–12

RADAR

Manufacturer: Zellers
Label: Picture
Rarity: 5
Game Only: $7–15
Complete: $10–16

RADAR LOCK

Manufacturer: Atari
Label: Red
Rarity: 5
Game Only: $10–12
Complete: $15–20

RAFT RIDER

Manufacturer: US Games
Label: Picture
Rarity: 5
Game Only: $6–16
Complete: $18–22*

RAIDERS OF THE LOST ARK

Manufacturer: Atari
Label: Silver
Rarity: 2
Game Only: $1–4
Complete: $3–5
Notes: End label reads "Raiders of the Lost Ark"

RAIDERS OF THE LOST ARK
Manufacturer: Atari
Label: Silver
Rarity: 5
Game Only: $2–6
Complete: $8–12
Notes: End label reads "Raiders Lost Ark"

RAM IT
Manufacturer: Telesys
Label: Color
Rarity: 7
Game Only: $30–42
Complete: $40–50

RAM IT
Manufacturer: Telesys
Label: Black and White
Rarity: 6
Game Only: $20–30
Complete: $35–45*

RAMPAGE
Manufacturer: Activision
Label: Black
Rarity: 5
Game Only: $6–9
Complete: $10–12

REACTOR
Manufacturer: Parker Brothers
Label: Picture
Rarity: 2
Game Only: $2–3
Complete: $3–5

REALSPORTS BASEBALL
Manufacturer: Atari
Label: Silver
Rarity: 2
Game Only: $1–2
Complete: $3–5

REALSPORTS BASKETBALL
Manufacturer: Atari
Label: N/A
Rarity: Prototype
Game Only: ?
Complete: N/A
Notes: Price unavailable; for more info, see
http://www.atariprotos.com

REALSPORTS BASKETBALL
Manufacturer: Self-Published
Label: Silver
Rarity: Reproduction
Game Only: N/A
Complete: $45
Notes: Released commercially at the 2002 Classic
Gaming Expo; available at the AtariAge store
(http://www.atariage.com)

REALSPORTS BOXING
Manufacturer: Atari
Label: Red
Rarity: 3
Game Only: $2–3
Complete: $4–5

REALSPORTS FOOTBALL
Manufacturer: Atari
Label: Silver
Rarity: 2
Game Only: $1–2
Complete: $3–4

REALSPORTS SOCCER
Manufacturer: Atari
Label: Silver
Rarity: 3
Game Only: $1–2
Complete: $3–4

REALSPORTS TENNIS
Manufacturer: Atari
Label: Silver
Rarity: 3
Game Only: $1–2
Complete: $3–4

REALSPORTS VOLLEYBALL
Manufacturer: Atari
Label: Silver
Rarity: 3
Game Only: $1–3
Complete: $3–4

RESCUE TERRA I
Manufacturer: VentureVision
Label: Picture
Rarity: 9
Game Only: $60–80*
Complete: $150–450
Notes: VentureVision's only game

RETURN OF MARIO BROS.
Manufacturer: AtariAge
Label: Picture
Rarity: Hack
Game Only: $20
Complete: N/A
Notes: Updated version of the Atari game *Mario
Bros.;* available at the AtariAge store
(http://www.atariage.com); no box

REVENGE OF THE APES
Manufacturer: Self-Published
Label: Picture
Rarity: Reproduction
Game Only: N/A
Complete: $45
Notes: Released at the 2003 Philly Classic, complete
with box and manual

REVENGE OF THE BEEFSTEAK TOMATOES
Manufacturer: 20th Century Fox
Label: Picture
Rarity: 4
Game Only: $3–7
Complete: $9–12

RIDDLE OF THE SPHINX
Manufacturer: Imagic
Label: Picture
Rarity: 2
Game Only: $2–3
Complete: $8–10

RIVER PATROL

Manufacturer: Tigervision
Label: Picture
Rarity: 9
Game Only: $200–300*
Complete: $350–450*
Notes: Based on the Kersten arcade game by the same name; very rare

RIVER RAID

Manufacturer: Activision
Label: Red
Rarity: 2
Game Only: $2–7
Complete: $8–10

RIVER RAID

Manufacturer: Activision
Label: Blue
Rarity: 3
Game Only: $4–8
Complete: $8–10

RIVER RAID II

Manufacturer: Activision
Label: Black; White
Rarity: 6
Game Only: $12–15
Complete: $20–25

ROAD RUNNER

Manufacturer: Atari
Label: Red
Rarity: 6
Game Only: $10–16
Complete: $18–25
Notes: Signed copies have sold for up to $70, but such prices are uncommon to say the least

ROBIN HOOD

Manufacturer: Xonox
Label: Picture
Rarity: 8
Game Only: $25–50
Complete: $50–60*

ROBIN HOOD/SIR LANCELOT

Manufacturer: Xonox
Label: Double
Rarity: 8
Game Only: $30–50
Complete: $60–75*

ROBOT TANK

Manufacturer: Activision
Label: Gray
Rarity: 3
Game Only: $2–3
Complete: $5–8

ROBOT TANK

Manufacturer: Activision
Label: Blue
Rarity: 4
Game Only: $2–3
Complete: $5–8

ROC N ROPE

Manufacturer: Coleco
Label: Text
Rarity: 5
Game Only: $3–10
Complete: $12–15
Notes: Based on the Konami arcade game by the same name

ROCKY AND BULLWINKLE

Manufacturer: M Network
Label: N/A
Rarity: Prototype
Game Only: ?
Complete: N/A
Notes: Price unavailable; for more info, see http://www.atariprotos.com

ROOM OF DOOM

Manufacturer: CommaVid
Label: Picture
Rarity: 6
Game Only: $13–18
Complete: $55–65

RUBIK'S CUBE

Manufacturer: Atari
Label: Silver
Rarity: 8
Game Only: $40–70
Complete: $80–100*
Notes: Originally available only through the Atari Club; identical to *Atari Video Cube,* but rarer

RUBIK'S CUBE 3D

Manufacturer: Atari
Label: N/A
Rarity: Prototype
Game Only: ?
Complete: N/A
Notes: Price unavailable; for more info, see http://www.atariprotos.com

RUBIK'S CUBE 3D

Manufacturer: Self-Published
Label: Silver
Rarity: Reproduction
Game Only: N/A
Complete: $50
Notes: Released at the 2003 Philly Classic, complete with box and manual; available at the AtariAge store (http://www.atariage.com); numbered editions can sell for as much as 100% more

RUSH HOUR

Manufacturer: CommaVid
Label: N/A
Rarity: Prototype
Game Only: ?
Complete: N/A
Notes: Price unavailable; for more info, see http://www.atariprotos.com

RUSH HOUR
Manufacturer: CGE Services Corp.
Label: Picture
Rarity: Reproduction
Game Only: N/A
Complete: $40
Notes: Reproduction of the CommaVid prototype; released at the 2003 Classic Gaming Expo; includes box and instructions; a limited number are still available on the CGE web site (http://www.cgexpo.com)

SABOTEUR
Manufacturer: Atari
Label: N/A
Rarity: Prototype
Game Only: ?
Complete: N/A
Notes: Price unavailable; for more info, see http://www.atariprotos.com

SAVE MARY
Manufacturer: Atari
Label: N/A
Rarity: Prototype
Game Only: ?
Complete: N/A
Notes: Price unavailable; for more info, see http://www.atariprotos.com

SAVE THE WHALES
Manufacturer: 20th Century Fox
Label: N/A
Rarity: Prototype
Game Only: ?
Complete: N/A
Notes: Price unavailable; for more info, see http://www.atariprotos.com

SAVE THE WHALES
Manufacturer: Self-Published
Label: Picture
Rarity: Reproduction
Game Only: N/A
Complete: $40
Notes: Released commercially at the 2002 Classic Gaming Expo; a limited number of copies are still available on the CGE web site (http://www.cgexpo.com)

SCSLCIDE
Manufacturer: Pixels Past
Label: CGE
Rarity: Homebrew
Game Only: $30–50*
Complete: $30–50*
Notes: Numbered CGE2K1 special release version; only 50 copies produced and sold at the 2001 Classic Gaming Expo; packaged in an antistatic bag (no box)

SCSLCIDE
Manufacturer: Pixels Past
Label: PhillyClassic
Rarity: Homebrew
Game Only: $30–50*
Complete: $30–50*
Notes: Numbered Philly Classic 3 version; only 50 copies produced; label looks like a PC hard drive; packaged in an antistatic bag (no box)

SCSLCIDE
Manufacturer: Pixels Past
Label: Picture
Rarity: Homebrew
Game Only: N/A
Complete: $25
Notes: Wide release version; available at the AtariAge store (http://www.atariage.com); packaged in an anti-static bag (no box)

SCUBA DIVER
Manufacturer: Panda
Label: End Only
Rarity: 6
Game Only: $20–40
Complete: $80–100

SEA BATTLE
Manufacturer: Intellivision Productions
Label: Picture
Rarity: Reproduction
Game Only: N/A
Complete: $25
Notes: 2600 version of the Intellivision game of the same name; available at the AtariAge store (http://www.atariage.com); no box

SEA HAWK
Manufacturer: Froggo
Label: White
Rarity: 4
Game Only: $4–7
Complete: $8–15

SEA HAWK
Manufacturer: Panda
Label: End Only
Rarity: 6
Game Only: $12–18
Complete: $25–35*
Notes: Panda version of the Froggo game by the same name

SEA HUNT
Manufacturer: Froggo
Label: White
Rarity: 4
Game Only: $2–7
Complete: $8–15

SEAQUEST
Manufacturer: Activision
Label: Light Blue
Rarity: 2
Game Only: $2–4
Complete: $6–10

SECRET AGENT
Manufacturer: Data Age
Label: Unique
Rarity: Prototype
Game Only: ?
Complete: N/A
Notes: Price unavailable; for more info, see http://www.atariprotos.com

SECRET AGENT

Manufacturer: Self-Published
Label: Unique
Rarity: Reproduction
Game Only: N/A
Complete: $35
Notes: 50 copies were released at the 2001 Classic
Gaming Expo for $30 each; no box; available at
Atari2600.com (http://www.atari2600.com)

SECRET QUEST

Manufacturer: Atari
Label: Red
Rarity: 4
Game Only: $4–8
Complete: $7–10

SENTINEL

Manufacturer: Atari
Label: Red
Rarity: 5
Game Only: $8–10
Complete: $15–20
Notes: Requires the Atari XE Light Gun Controller

SHARK ATTACK

Manufacturer: Apollo
Label: Picture
Rarity: 3
Game Only: $3–6
Complete: $10–15
Notes: End label has the game name written in white
letters that appear to be torn apart by a shark's teeth

SHARK ATTACK

Manufacturer: Apollo
Label: Picture
Rarity: 4
Game Only: $4–7
Complete: $11–16
Notes: End label has the game name written in plain
white letters with a yellow line above and below the
title

SHOOTIN' GALLERY

Manufacturer: Imagic
Label: Picture
Rarity: 5
Game Only: $3–10
Complete: $15–20

SHOOTING ARCADE

Manufacturer: Atari
Label: N/A
Rarity: Prototype
Game Only: ?
Complete: N/A
Notes: Requires the Atari XE Light Gun Controller;
price unavailable; for more info, see
http://www.atariprotos.com

SHUTTLE ORBITER

Manufacturer: Avalon Hill
Label: Picture
Rarity: 7
Game Only: $45–55
Complete: $80–150

SINISTAR

Manufacturer: Atari
Label: N/A
Rarity: Prototype
Game Only: ?
Complete: N/A
Notes: Price unavailable; for more info, see
http://www.atariprotos.com

SIR LANCELOT

Manufacturer: Xonox
Label: Picture
Rarity: 7
Game Only: $20–45
Complete: $50–60*

SKATE BOARDIN'

Manufacturer: Absolute Entertainment
Label: Picture
Rarity: 4
Game Only: $2–6
Complete: $10–15

SKEET SHOOT

Manufacturer: Apollo
Label: Orange
Rarity: 5
Game Only: $7–13
Complete: $15–20

SKELETON

Manufacturer: Self-Published
Label: Picture
Rarity: Homebrew
Game Only: N/A
Complete: $20
Notes: Includes manual (no box)

SKELETON +

Manufacturer: Self-Published
Label: Picture
Rarity: Homebrew
Game Only: N/A
Complete: $20
Notes: Improved version of *Skeleton;* released at the
2003 Classic Gaming Expo; includes manual (no box);
available at http://www.packratvg.com

SKIING

Manufacturer: Activision
Label: Blue
Rarity: 2
Game Only: $1–3
Complete: $4–10
Notes: Standard Activision blue label (with game
screen shot)

SKIING

Manufacturer: Activision
Label: Blue
Rarity: 3
Game Only: $1–3
Complete: $4–10
Notes: Dark blue re-release label (text only)

SKY DIVER

Manufacturer: Atari
Label: Text; Picture
Rarity: 2
Game Only: $1–3
Complete: $4–6

SKY JINKS

Manufacturer: Activision
Label: Blue
Rarity: 2
Game Only: $1–3
Complete: $6–9

SKY PATROL

Manufacturer: Imagic
Label: Picture
Rarity: Prototype
Game Only: ?
Complete: N/A
Notes: Both a labeled cartridge and a box exist for this prototype; price unavailable; for more info, see http://www.atariprotos.com

SKY SKIPPER

Manufacturer: Parker Brothers
Label: Picture
Rarity: 3
Game Only: $5–8
Complete: $9–12

SLOT MACHINE

Manufacturer: Atari
Label: Text
Rarity: 3
Game Only: $2–6
Complete: $8–12

SLOT RACERS

Manufacturer: Atari
Label: Text; Picture
Rarity: 2
Game Only: $1–2
Complete: $4–6

SLOTS

Manufacturer: Sears
Label: Text
Rarity: 4
Game Only: $4–6
Complete: $8–12
Notes: Sears version of the Atari game *Slot Machine*

SMURFS: RESCUE IN GARGAMEL'S CASTLE

Manufacturer: Coleco
Label: Text
Rarity: 4
Game Only: $4–15
Complete: $15–26

SMURFS SAVE THE DAY

Manufacturer: Coleco
Label: Picture
Rarity: 8
Game Only: $40–60
Complete: $250–300
Notes: Requires the KidVid Controller; must include the 3 audio tapes originally packaged with the game to be considered complete (and playable)

SNEAK N' PEEK

Manufacturer: US Games
Label: Black
Rarity: 2
Game Only: $1–3
Complete: $3–6

SNOOPY AND THE RED BARON

Manufacturer: Atari
Label: Picture
Rarity: 5
Game Only: $9–14
Complete: $15–20*

SNOW WHITE

Manufacturer: Atari
Label: N/A
Rarity: Prototype
Game Only: ?
Complete: N/A
Notes: Price unavailable; for more info, see http://www.atariprotos.com

SNOW WHITE

Manufacturer: Self-Published
Label: Picture
Rarity: Reproduction
Game Only: N/A
Complete: $40–50
Notes: Commercially released at the 2002 Classic Gaming Expo

SOCCER

Manufacturer: Sears
Label: Text
Rarity: 3
Game Only: $3–5
Complete: $6–8
Notes: Sears version of the Atari games *Championship Soccer* and *Pele's Championship Soccer*

SOLAR FOX

Manufacturer: CBS Electronics
Label: Text
Rarity: 3
Game Only: $1–5
Complete: $6–8

SOLAR STORM

Manufacturer: Imagic
Label: Text
Rarity: 4
Game Only: $6–9
Complete: $10–14

SOLARIS

Manufacturer: Atari
Label: Red
Rarity: 2
Game Only: $1–2
Complete: $2–4

SORCERER

Manufacturer: Mythicon
Label: Picture
Rarity: 4
Game Only: $2–8
Complete: $9–11

SORCERER'S APPRENTICE
Manufacturer: Atari
Label: Picture
Rarity: 4
Game Only: $2–7
Complete: $8–12

SPACE ADVENTURE
Manufacturer: Zellers
Label: Picture
Rarity: 6
Game Only: $10–12
Complete: $15–20*

SPACE ATTACK
Manufacturer: M Network
Label: Black
Rarity: 2
Game Only: $1–2
Complete: $3–4
Notes: Based on the Intellivision game *Space Battle*

SPACE ATTACK
Manufacturer: Telegames
Label: Silver
Rarity: 3
Game Only: $1–2
Complete: $3–4
Notes: Based on the Intellivision game *Space Battle*

SPACE CANYON
Manufacturer: Panda
Label: White
Rarity: 6
Game Only: $10–30
Complete: $40–100
Notes: Identical to the Apollo game *Space Cavern*

SPACE CAVERN
Manufacturer: Apollo
Label: All
Rarity: 3
Game Only: $2–6
Complete: $8–12

SPACE COMBAT
Manufacturer: Sears
Label: Text
Rarity: 3
Game Only: $1–3
Complete: $4–6
Notes: Sears version of the Atari game *Space War*

SPACE INSTIGATORS
Manufacturer: XYPE
Label: Picture
Rarity: Homebrew
Game Only: N/A
Complete: $25
Notes: A version of *Space Invaders* that's much closer to the arcade version; available from the AtariAge store (http://www.atariage.com)

SPACE INVADERS
Manufacturer: Atari
Label: Text; Picture
Rarity: 1
Game Only: $1–3
Complete: $4–7

SPACE INVADERS
Manufacturer: Atari
Label: Silver; Red
Rarity: 2
Game Only: $2–4
Complete: $5–10

SPACE INVADERS
Manufacturer: Sears
Label: Text; Picture
Rarity: 2
Game Only: $1–3
Complete: $4–7
Notes: Sears version of the Atari game by the same name

SPACE INVADERS ARCADE
Manufacturer: AtariAge
Label: Silver
Rarity: Hack
Game Only: N/A
Complete: $15
Notes: Updated version of the Atari game *Space Invaders;* available at the AtariAge store (http://www.atariage.com)

SPACE JOCKEY
Manufacturer: US Games
Label: Black
Rarity: 2
Game Only: $1–2
Complete: $4–8

SPACE SHUTTLE
Manufacturer: Activision
Label: Blue
Rarity: 3
Game Only: $2–4
Complete: $10–17
Notes: Standard Activision blue label (with game screen shot); console overlay must be included to be considered complete

SPACE SHUTTLE
Manufacturer: Activision
Label: Blue
Rarity: 4
Game Only: $5–8
Complete: $10–17
Notes: Dark blue re-release label (text only); console overlay must be included to be considered complete

SPACE SHUTTLE
Manufacturer: Activision
Label: White
Rarity: 6
Game Only: $8–10
Complete: $12–18
Notes: Console overlay must be included to be considered complete

SPACE TREAT
Manufacturer: Self-Published
Label: Picture
Rarity: Homebrew
Game Only: $20–30*
Complete: $20–30*
Notes: Released at the 2002 Classic Gaming Expo

SPACE WAR

Manufacturer: Atari
Label: Text; Picture
Rarity: 2
Game Only: $1–2
Complete: $3–4

SPACECHASE

Manufacturer: Apollo
Label: All
Rarity: 3
Game Only: $2–8
Complete: $9–12
Notes: A superrare "monogrammed" version—where the owner's initials replace the ship explosion when your ship is killed—reportedly exists

SPACEMASTER X-7

Manufacturer: 20th Century Fox
Label: Picture
Rarity: 6
Game Only: $10–16
Complete: $25–100

SPEEDWAY II

Manufacturer: Sears
Label: Text; Picture
Rarity: 3
Game Only: $2–6
Complete: $7–9
Notes: Sears version of the Atari game *Street Racer*

SPELLING

Manufacturer: Sears
Label: Text
Rarity: 4
Game Only: $4–8
Complete: $9–12*
Notes: Sears version of the Atari game *Hangman*

SPIDER FIGHTER

Manufacturer: Activision
Label: Orange
Rarity: 2
Game Only: $2–4
Complete: $5–7

SPIDER MAZE

Manufacturer: K-Tel Vision
Label: Picture
Rarity: 9
Game Only: $50–60*
Complete: $75–90*
Notes: NTSC version was sold exclusively in Canada; much more common (and less expensive) in European (PAL) format

SPIDER-MAN

Manufacturer: Parker Brothers
Label: Picture
Rarity: 3
Game Only: $2–6
Complete: $10–14

SPIDERDROID

Manufacturer: Froggo
Label: White
Rarity: 3
Game Only: $2–5
Complete: $8–12

SPIKE'S PEAK

Manufacturer: Xonox
Label: Picture
Rarity: 9
Game Only: $25–50
Complete: $55–65*

SPITFIRE ATTACK

Manufacturer: Milton Bradley
Label: Picture
Rarity: 4
Game Only: $3–12
Complete: $50–70
Notes: Complete version (which includes the Flight Command joystick) is very difficult to find

SPRINGER

Manufacturer: Tigervision
Label: Picture
Rarity: 7
Game Only: $40–50
Complete: $90–110

SPRINTMASTER

Manufacturer: Atari
Label: Red
Rarity: 4
Game Only: $2–6
Complete: $7–10

SPY HUNTER

Manufacturer: Sega
Label: Picture
Rarity: 6
Game Only: $11–15
Complete: $20–30
Notes: Originally packaged with a joystick coupler that held 2 joysticks together—not considered complete without this item

SQUEEZE BOX

Manufacturer: US Games
Label: Picture
Rarity: 4
Game Only: $3–6
Complete: $10–12

SQUOOSH

Manufacturer: Apollo
Label: N/A
Rarity: Prototype
Game Only: ?
Complete: N/A
Notes: Price unavailable; for more info, see http://www.atariprotos.com

SSSNAKE

Manufacturer: Data Age
Label: Picture
Rarity: 4
Game Only: $2–7
Complete: $8–10

STAMPEDE
Manufacturer: Activision
Label: Brown
Rarity: 2
Game Only: $1–4
Complete: $4–6

STAR FOX
Manufacturer: Mythicon
Label: Picture
Rarity: 4
Game Only: $2–6
Complete: $8–12

STAR RAIDERS
Manufacturer: Atari
Label: Picture
Rarity: 1
Game Only: $1–3
Complete: $8–10
Notes: Complete version price reflects package including the *Star Raiders* Touchpad and comic book

STAR RAIDERS
Manufacturer: Sears
Label: Picture
Rarity: 3
Game Only: $2–4
Complete: $9–12
Notes: Sears version of the Atari game by the same name; complete version price reflects package including the *Star Raiders* Touchpad and comic book

STAR SHIP
Manufacturer: Atari
Label: All
Rarity: 3
Game Only: $3–5
Complete: $8–15

STAR STRIKE
Manufacturer: INTV
Label: White
Rarity: 5
Game Only: $4–8
Complete: $9–12
Notes: Based on the Intellivision game by the same name

STAR STRIKE
Manufacturer: M Network
Label: Black
Rarity: 5
Game Only: $4–8
Complete: $9–12
Notes: Based on the Intellivision game by the same name

STAR TREK: STRATEGIC OPERATIONS SIMULATOR
Manufacturer: Sega
Label: Picture
Rarity: 4
Game Only: $5–10
Complete: $25–30
Notes: Complete game includes joystick command overlays

STAR VOYAGER
Manufacturer: Imagic
Label: Text; Picture
Rarity: 2
Game Only: $1–2
Complete: $4–8

STAR WARS: THE ARCADE GAME
Manufacturer: Parker Brothers
Label: Text
Rarity: 5
Game Only: $21–25
Complete: $35–45

STAR WARS: THE EMPIRE STRIKES BACK
Manufacturer: Parker Brothers
Label: Picture
Rarity: 2
Game Only: $2–4
Complete: $10–14

STAR WARS: EWOK ADVENTURE
Manufacturer: Parker Brothers
Label: N/A
Rarity: Prototype
Game Only: ?
Complete: N/A
Notes: Price unavailable; for more info, see http://www.atariprotos.com

STAR WARS: JEDI ARENA
Manufacturer: Parker Brothers
Label: Picture
Rarity: 3
Game Only: $4–9
Complete: $18–25

STAR WARS: RETURN OF THE JEDI DEATH STAR BATTLE
Manufacturer: Parker Brothers
Label: Picture
Rarity: 4
Game Only: $7–11
Complete: $12–15
Notes: Often referred to as *Return of the Jedi*

STARGATE
Manufacturer: Atari
Label: Silver
Rarity: 4
Game Only: $2–7
Complete: $10–15
Notes: Later re-released as *Defender II*

STARGUNNER
Manufacturer: Telesys
Label: Color
Rarity: 7
Game Only: $18–26
Complete: $30–45*

STARGUNNER
Manufacturer: Telesys
Label: Black and White
Rarity: 6
Game Only: $18–26
Complete: $30–45*

STARMASTER
Manufacturer: Activision
Label: Blue
Rarity: 2
Game Only: $1–3
Complete: $4–6

STEEPLECHASE
Manufacturer: Sears
Label: Text
Rarity: 4
Game Only: $3–6
Complete: $15–20
Notes: One of only 3 Atari 2600 games exclusively released by Sears

STELL-A-SKETCH/OKIE DOKIE
Manufacturer: Retroware
Label: CD-ROM
Rarity: Homebrew
Game Only: $30–40*
Complete: $30–40*
Notes: CD title for use with the Supercharger; no longer produced due to copyright problems with Ohio Art, makers of Etch-a-Sketch

STELL-A-SKETCH/OKIE DOKIE
Manufacturer: Retroware
Label: Cassette
Rarity: Homebrew
Game Only: $30–40*
Complete: $30–40*
Notes: Cassette title for use with the Supercharger; no longer produced due to copyright problems with Ohio Art, makers of Etch-a-Sketch

STELLAR TRACK
Manufacturer: Sears
Label: Text; Picture
Rarity: 4
Game Only: $5–8
Complete: $8–12
Notes: One of only 3 Atari 2600 games exclusively released by Sears

STRATEGY X
Manufacturer: Konami
Label: Picture
Rarity: 5
Game Only: $5–10
Complete: $15–20*

STRAWBERRY SHORTCAKE MUSICAL MATCHUPS
Manufacturer: Parker Brothers
Label: Picture
Rarity: 4
Game Only: $6–10
Complete: $12–20

STREET RACER
Manufacturer: Atari
Label: Numbered Text
Rarity: 3
Game Only: $1–2
Complete: $3–5
Notes: Original numbered label (reads: "12 Street Racer" on the end)

STREET RACER
Manufacturer: Atari
Label: Text; Picture
Rarity: 2
Game Only: $1–2
Complete: $3–5

STRONGHOLD
Manufacturer: CommaVid
Label: Picture
Rarity: 9
Game Only: $90–120
Complete: $150–200*
Notes: Never sold in stores—available through the Columbia House Video Club and directly from CommaVid only

STUNT CYCLE
Manufacturer: Atari
Label: N/A
Rarity: Prototype
Game Only: ?
Complete: N/A
Notes: Price unavailable; for more info, see http://www.atariprotos.com

STUNT CYCLE
Manufacturer: Self-Published
Label: Numbered
Rarity: Reproduction
Game Only: N/A
Complete: $45–125
Notes: Released at the 2003 Philly Classic; only 50 serial numbered copies were produced; complete with box and manual

STUNT CYCLE
Manufacturer: Self-Published
Label: Unnumbered
Rarity: Reproduction
Game Only: N/A
Complete: $45
Notes: Same as the 2003 Philly Classic version, but without serial number; available from Atari2600.com (http://atari2600.com)

STUNTMAN
Manufacturer: Panda
Label: End Only
Rarity: 6
Game Only: $30–40
Complete: $45–100

SUB SCAN
Manufacturer: Sega
Label: Picture
Rarity: 4
Game Only: $1–6
Complete: $8–12*

SUBMARINE COMMANDER
Manufacturer: Sears
Label: Picture
Rarity: 5
Game Only: $10–15
Complete: $20–30*
Notes: One of only 3 Atari 2600 games exclusively released by Sears

SUBTERRANEA
Manufacturer: Imagic
Label: Text
Rarity: 6
Game Only: $35–50
Complete: $50–60*

SUICIDE MISSION
Manufacturer: Starpath
Label: Cassette
Rarity: 4
Game Only: $5–8
Complete: $9–12
Notes: Cassette game; requires the Supercharger and a cassette tape player

SUMMER GAMES
Manufacturer: Epyx
Label: White
Rarity: 4
Game Only: $2–3
Complete: $6–12

SUPER BASEBALL
Manufacturer: Atari
Label: Red
Rarity: 2
Game Only: $2–4
Complete: $8–10
Notes: Slightly updated version of *RealSports Baseball*

SUPER BREAKOUT
Manufacturer: Atari
Label: Picture
Rarity: 2
Game Only: $1–3
Complete: $2–6

SUPER BREAKOUT
Manufacturer: Sears
Label: Text
Rarity: 3
Game Only: $2–3
Complete: $3–7
Notes: Sears version of the Atari game by the same name

SUPER CHALLENGE BASEBALL
Manufacturer: INTV
Label: White
Rarity: 3
Game Only: $1–3
Complete: $4–6
Notes: End label shows the title as *Baseball;* 2600 version of the Intellivision game *Major League Baseball*

SUPER CHALLENGE BASEBALL
Manufacturer: M Network
Label: Black
Rarity: 3
Game Only: $2–5
Complete: $6–10
Notes: 2600 version of the Intellivision game *Major League Baseball*

SUPER CHALLENGE BASEBALL
Manufacturer: Telegames
Label: Silver
Rarity: 3
Game Only: $1–3
Complete: $4–6
Notes: Label shows the title as *Baseball;* 2600 version of the Intellivision game *Major League Baseball*

SUPER CHALLENGE FOOTBALL
Manufacturer: INTV
Label: White
Rarity: 3
Game Only: $1–3
Complete: $5–8
Notes: End label shows the title as *Football;* 2600 version of the Intellivision game *NFL Football*

SUPER CHALLENGE FOOTBALL
Manufacturer: M Network
Label: Black
Rarity: 3
Game Only: $1–3
Complete: $5–8
Notes: 2600 version of the Intellivision game *NFL Football*

SUPER CHALLENGE FOOTBALL
Manufacturer: Telegames
Label: Silver
Rarity: 3
Game Only: $2–5
Complete: $6–10
Notes: Label shows the title as *Football;* 2600 version of the Intellivision game *NFL Football*

SUPER COBRA
Manufacturer: Parker Brothers
Label: Picture
Rarity: 3
Game Only: $4–10
Complete: $12–15

SUPER FOOTBALL
Manufacturer: Atari
Label: Red
Rarity: 2
Game Only: $1–2
Complete: $3–5

SUPERMAN
Manufacturer: Atari
Label: Text; Picture
Rarity: 2
Game Only: $2–5
Complete: $6–10

SUPERMAN
Manufacturer: Sears
Label: Text
Rarity: 4
Game Only: $5–8
Complete: $10–15
Notes: Sears version of the Atari game by the same name

SURF'S UP

Manufacturer: Amiga
Label: Unique
Rarity: Prototype
Game Only: ?
Complete: N/A
Notes: Price unavailable; for more info, see
http://www.atariprotos.com

SURROUND

Manufacturer: Atari
Label: Numbered Text
Rarity: 3
Game Only: $2–3
Complete: $8–10
Notes: Original numbered label (reads: "41 Surround" on the end)

SURROUND

Manufacturer: Atari
Label: Text; Picture
Rarity: 2
Game Only: $1–2
Complete: $6–8

SURVIVAL ISLAND

Manufacturer: Starpath
Label: Cassette
Rarity: 8
Game Only: $40–60
Complete: $55–75
Notes: Cassette game; requires the Supercharger and
a cassette tape player; originally available only directly
from Starpath; no box

SURVIVAL RUN

Manufacturer: Milton Bradley
Label: Picture
Rarity: 4
Game Only: $2–6
Complete: $50–70
Notes: Complete version (which includes the Cosmic
Command joystick) is very difficult to find

SWEAT: THE DECATHLON GAME

Manufacturer: Starpath
Label: N/A
Rarity: Prototype
Game Only: ?
Complete: N/A
Notes: Price unavailable; for more info, see
http://www.atariprotos.com

SWORD FIGHT

Manufacturer: M Network
Label: N/A
Rarity: Prototype
Game Only: ?
Complete: N/A
Notes: Price unavailable; for more info, see
http://www.atariprotos.com

SWORD FIGHT

Manufacturer: Intellivision Productions
Label: Picture
Rarity: Reproduction
Game Only: N/A
Complete: $25
Notes: Available at the AtariAge store
(http://www.atariage.com); no box

SWORD OF SAROS

Manufacturer: Starpath
Label: Cassette
Rarity: 8
Game Only: $40–60
Complete: $55–75
Notes: Cassette game; requires the Supercharger and
a cassette tape player; originally available only directly
from Starpath; no box

SWORDQUEST: EARTHWORLD

Manufacturer: Atari
Label: Silver
Rarity: 2
Game Only: $1–2
Complete: $4–6

SWORDQUEST: FIREWORLD

Manufacturer: Atari
Label: Silver
Rarity: 3
Game Only: $1–3
Complete: $5–8

SWORDQUEST: WATERWORLD

Manufacturer: Atari
Label: Silver
Rarity: 9
Game Only: $80–160
Complete: $200–275
Notes: Originally available only through the Atari
Club

SYNTHCART

Manufacturer: Self-Published
Label: Green
Rarity: Homebrew
Game Only: N/A
Complete: $25
Notes: Requires 2 Atari Keyboard Controllers; available from the AtariAge store
(http://www.atariage.com)

TAC-SCAN

Manufacturer: Sega
Label: Picture
Rarity: 3
Game Only: $3–5
Complete: $15–23

TANK BRIGADE

Manufacturer: Panda
Label: White
Rarity: 6
Game Only: $30–40
Complete: $50–125
Notes: Panda version of the Zimag game *Tanks But
No Tanks*

TANK PLUS

Manufacturer: Sears
Label: Text
Rarity: 2
Game Only: $1–2
Complete: $3–5
Notes: Sears version of the Atari game *Combat*

TANKS BUT NO TANKS

Manufacturer: Zimag
Label: Picture
Rarity: 5
Game Only: $15–30
Complete: $35–45*

TAPE WORM

Manufacturer: Spectravision
Label: Text
Rarity: 3
Game Only: $3–5
Complete: $15–20

TAPPER

Manufacturer: Sega
Label: Picture
Rarity: 6
Game Only: $10–20
Complete: $25–35*

TARGET FUN

Manufacturer: Sears
Label: Text
Rarity: 2
Game Only: $1–2
Complete: $3–5
Notes: Sears version of the Atari game *Air-Sea Battle;* there are 4 text label versions (different part numbers), all of which are equally common

TASK FORCE

Manufacturer: Froggo
Label: White
Rarity: 4
Game Only: $4–6
Complete: $7–10

TAX AVOIDERS

Manufacturer: American Videogame
Label: Red
Rarity: 5
Game Only: $8–12
Complete: $15–25

TAZ

Manufacturer: Atari
Label: Silver
Rarity: 4
Game Only: $3–8
Complete: $14–21

TELEPATHY

Manufacturer: Atari
Label: N/A
Rarity: Prototype
Game Only: ?
Complete: N/A
Notes: Price unavailable; for more info, see http://www.atariprotos.com

TEMPEST

Manufacturer: Atari
Label: Picture
Rarity: Prototype
Game Only: ?
Complete: N/A
Notes: Price unavailable; for more info, see http://www.atariprotos.com

TENNIS

Manufacturer: Activision
Label: Green
Rarity: 2
Game Only: $2–3
Complete: $5–7

TESTCART

Manufacturer: Self-Published
Label: Picture
Rarity: Homebrew
Game Only: N/A
Complete: $20
Notes: Available at the AtariAge store (http://www.atariage.com)

TETRIS 26

Manufacturer: Self-Published
Label: N/A
Rarity: Homebrew
Game Only: $15–20*
Complete: N/A

TEXAS CHAINSAW MASSACRE

Manufacturer: Wizard Video
Label: Red
Rarity: 7
Game Only: $50–100
Complete: $110–250

TEXAS CHAINSAW MASSACRE

Manufacturer: Wizard Video
Label: Hand-Lettered
Rarity: 7
Game Only: $60–70
Complete: $100–200*

THIS PLANET SUCKS

Manufacturer: Self-Published
Label: Picture
Rarity: Homebrew
Game Only: N/A
Complete: $20
Notes: Includes manual (no box); available at http://www.packratvg.com

THRESHOLD

Manufacturer: Tigervision
Label: Picture
Rarity: 6
Game Only: $14–18
Complete: $20–25*

THRUST

Manufacturer: XYPE
Label: Picture
Rarity: Homebrew
Game Only: N/A
Complete: $20–35*

THRUST +: DC EDITION
Manufacturer: XYPE
Label: Picture
Rarity: Homebrew
Game Only: N/A
Complete: $35
Notes: Uses both joystick and driving controllers; can also use a custom foot pedal controller

THRUST + PLATINUM
Manufacturer: XYPE
Label: Picture
Rarity: Homebrew
Game Only: N/A
Complete: $35
Notes: Uses both joystick and driving controllers; can also use a custom foot pedal controller; available at AtariAge (http://www.atariage.com)

THUNDERGROUND
Manufacturer: Sega
Label: Picture
Rarity: 4
Game Only: $3–10
Complete: $12–15*

THWOCKER
Manufacturer: Activision
Label: Unique
Rarity: Prototype
Game Only: ?
Complete: N/A
Notes: Price unavailable; for more info, see http://www.atariprotos.com

TIME PILOT
Manufacturer: Coleco
Label: Text
Rarity: 5
Game Only: $3–8
Complete: $30–50

TIME WARP
Manufacturer: Zellers
Label: Picture
Rarity: 5
Game Only: $2–10
Complete: $12–15

TITLE MATCH PRO WRESTLING
Manufacturer: Absolute Entertainment
Label: Black
Rarity: 4
Game Only: $5–8
Complete: $12–15

TOMARC THE BARBARIAN
Manufacturer: Xonox
Label: Picture
Rarity: 7
Game Only: $40–70
Complete: $80–100*

TOMARC THE BARBARIAN/MOTOCROSS RACER
Manufacturer: Xonox
Label: Double
Rarity: 9
Game Only: $60–130
Complete: $140–175*

TOMCAT: THE F-14 FIGHTER SIMULATOR
Manufacturer: Absolute Entertainment
Label: All
Rarity: 4
Game Only: $3–12
Complete: $14–16

TOOTH PROTECTORS
Manufacturer: DSD/Camelot
Label: Picture
Rarity: 9
Game Only: $100–150
Complete: N/A
Notes: Promotional cartridge originally available only through mail order from Johnson & Johnson; no box

TOWERING INFERNO
Manufacturer: US Games
Label: Black
Rarity: 3
Game Only: $2–4
Complete: $5–8

TRACK & FIELD
Manufacturer: Atari
Label: Silver
Rarity: 6
Game Only: $14–20
Complete: $50–70*
Notes: Complete version includes the *Track & Field* controller

TRICK SHOT
Manufacturer: Imagic
Label: Text; Picture
Rarity: 3
Game Only: $2–4
Complete: $6–8

TRON: DEADLY DISCS
Manufacturer: INTV
Label: White
Rarity: 3
Game Only: $2–5
Complete: $14–18
Notes: Based on the Intellivision game by the same name

TRON: DEADLY DISCS
Manufacturer: M Network
Label: Black
Rarity: 3
Game Only: $2–5
Complete: $14–18
Notes: Based on the Intellivision game by the same name

TUNNEL RUNNER
Manufacturer: CBS Electronics
Label: Text
Rarity: 4
Game Only: $7–9
Complete: $15–20

TURMOIL
Manufacturer: 20th Century Fox
Label: Black
Rarity: 3
Game Only: $3–7
Complete: $13–20

TURMOIL
Manufacturer: Zellers
Label: Picture
Rarity: 5
Game Only: $7–10*
Complete: $14–16

TUTANKHAM
Manufacturer: Parker Brothers
Label: Picture
Rarity: 3
Game Only: $2–5
Complete: $5–10

UNIVERSAL CHAOS
Manufacturer: Telegames
Label: Silver
Rarity: 5
Game Only: $18–23
Complete: $25–35

UP N' DOWN
Manufacturer: Sega
Label: Picture
Rarity: 7
Game Only: $30–60
Complete: $65–80*

VANGUARD
Manufacturer: Atari
Label: Silver
Rarity: 2
Game Only: $1–2
Complete: $2–4

VAULT ASSAULT
Manufacturer: Self-Published
Label: Blue
Rarity: Homebrew
Game Only: N/A
Complete: $25–35*
Notes: Released at the 2001 Classic Gaming Expo; no box

VAULT ASSAULT
Manufacturer: Self-Published
Label: Picture
Rarity: Homebrew
Game Only: N/A
Complete: $20
Notes: Wide release version; available at the AtariAge store (http://www.atariage.com); no box

VAULT ASSAULT TOURNAMENT EDITION
Manufacturer: Self-Published
Label: PhillyClassic
Rarity: Homebrew
Game Only: N/A
Complete: $25–35*
Notes: Version released at the 2002 Philly Classic; no box

VENTURE
Manufacturer: Atari
Label: Red
Rarity: 2
Game Only: $1–2
Complete: $3–5
Notes: Black cartridge with red Atari label

VENTURE
Manufacturer: Coleco
Label: Text
Rarity: 2
Game Only: $1–2
Complete: $3–5
Notes: White cartridge with black Coleco label

VENTURE II
Manufacturer: Self-Published
Label: CGE
Rarity: Homebrew
Game Only: N/A
Complete: $35–55*
Notes: Only 24 exist, distributed in a wooden treasure chest at the 2001 Classic Gaming Expo (at prices up to $200)

VENTURE II
Manufacturer: Self-Published
Label: Unique
Rarity: Homebrew
Game Only: N/A
Complete: $20
Notes: Available at the AtariAge store (http://www.atariage.com); no box

VIDEO CHECKERS
Manufacturer: Atari
Label: Text; Picture
Rarity: 2
Game Only: $1–3
Complete: $4–6

VIDEO CHESS
Manufacturer: Atari
Label: Text; Picture
Rarity: 3
Game Only: $1–3
Complete: $5–7

VIDEO CHESS
Manufacturer: Sears
Label: Text
Rarity: 3
Game Only: $1–3
Complete: $5–7
Notes: Sears version of the Atari game by the same name

VIDEO JOGGER
Manufacturer: Exus
Label: Text
Rarity: 9
Game Only: $30–90
Complete: $150–250*
Notes: Requires the Foot Craz Controller; "complete" package includes both the Foot Craz Controller and the game *Reflex*

VIDEO LIFE
Manufacturer: CommaVid
Label: Picture
Rarity: 10
Game Only: $1,000–1,500*
Complete: $2,000–3,000*
Notes: Originally available directly from Commavid only to owners of *MagiCard* (which is quite rare as well); only 20 copies are known to have been manufactured

VIDEO LIFE
Manufacturer: Sunmark
Label: Picture
Rarity: Reproduction
Game Only: N/A
Complete: $130
Notes: A reproduction of the original *Video Life* cartridge that looks like the original in every detail, except that it is marked as a reproduction; available from Sunmark (http://www.sunmark.com)

VIDEO LIFE/MAGICARD
Manufacturer: Sunmark
Label: Picture
Rarity: Reproduction
Game Only: N/A
Complete: $50
Notes: A reproduction cartridge that contains 2 of the rarest 2600 carts; available from Sunmark (http://www.sunmark.com); no box

VIDEO OLYMPICS
Manufacturer: Atari
Label: Numbered Text
Rarity: 3
Game Only: $1–2
Complete: $5–7
Notes: Original numbered label (reads: "21 Video Olympics" on the end)

VIDEO OLYMPICS
Manufacturer: Atari
Label: Text; Picture
Rarity: 2
Game Only: $1–2
Complete: $5–7

VIDEO PINBALL
Manufacturer: Atari
Label: Picture
Rarity: 1
Game Only: $1–2
Complete: $3–5

VIDEO REFLEX
Manufacturer: Exus
Label: Text
Rarity: 9
Game Only: $30–50
Complete: $150–250*
Notes: Requires the Foot Craz Controller; "complete" package includes both the Foot Craz Controller and the game *Video Jogger*

VIDEO SIMON
Manufacturer: Self-Published
Label: N/A
Rarity: Homebrew
Game Only: $20–30*
Complete: N/A

VULTURE ATTACK
Manufacturer: K-Tel Vision
Label: Picture
Rarity: 9
Game Only: $80–100
Complete: $150–200*
Notes: NTSC version was sold exclusively in Canada

WABBIT
Manufacturer: Apollo
Label: Picture
Rarity: 4
Game Only: $5–11
Complete: $25–35

WALL BALL
Manufacturer: Avalon Hill
Label: Picture
Rarity: 7
Game Only: $30–50
Complete: $60–130

WALL DEFENDER
Manufacturer: Bomb
Label: Text
Rarity: 9
Game Only: $35–75
Complete: $100–150*

WARLORDS
Manufacturer: Atari
Label: Picture
Rarity: 1
Game Only: $1–2
Complete: $3–4

WARLORDS
Manufacturer: Atari
Label: Text
Rarity: 2
Game Only: $1–3
Complete: $4–5

WARLORDS
Manufacturer: Sears
Label: Picture
Rarity: 2
Game Only: $1–3
Complete: $4–5
Notes: Sears version of the Atari game by the same name

WARPLOCK

Manufacturer: Data Age
Label: Picture
Rarity: 3
Game Only: $4–6
Complete: $10–14

WARRING WORMS

Manufacturer: Baroque Gaming
Label: Unique
Rarity: Homebrew
Game Only: N/A
Complete: $25
Notes: Available at the AtariAge store
(http://www.atariage.com); no box

WINTER GAMES

Manufacturer: Epyx
Label: White
Rarity: 4
Game Only: $3–8
Complete: $10–14

WIZARD

Manufacturer: Atari
Label: N/A
Rarity: Prototype
Game Only: ?
Complete: N/A
Notes: Price unavailable; for more info, see
http://www.atariprotos.com

WIZARD

Manufacturer: Self-Published
Label: Picture
Rarity: Reproduction
Game Only: $20
Complete: N/A
Notes: Reproduction of the Atari prototype; available
at Atari2600.com (http://www.atari2600.com)

WIZARD OF WOR

Manufacturer: CBS Electronics
Label: Text
Rarity: 3
Game Only: $2–6
Complete: $7–10

WORD ZAPPER

Manufacturer: US Games
Label: Black
Rarity: 3
Game Only: $2–4
Complete: $5–7

WORM WAR I

Manufacturer: 20th Century Fox
Label: Red
Rarity: 3
Game Only: $2–5
Complete: $10–20

X3VOLUX

Manufacturer: ResQsoft
Label: Unique
Rarity: Homebrew
Game Only: $25–35*
Complete: N/A

X-MAN

Manufacturer: Universal Gamex
Label: Text
Rarity: 9
Game Only: $300–400
Complete: $400–600
Notes: Adult game, one of the rarest 2600 titles; more
common (and less expensive) in European (PAL) for-
mat

XENOPHOBE

Manufacturer: Atari
Label: Red
Rarity: 7
Game Only: $12–20
Complete: $30–50
Notes: Easier to find in European (PAL) format

XEVIOUS

Manufacturer: Atari
Label: N/A
Rarity: Prototype
Game Only: ?
Complete: N/A
Notes: Price unavailable; for more info, see
http://www.atariprotos.com

YAHTZEE

Manufacturer: Self-Published
Label: N/A
Rarity: Homebrew
Game Only: $20–25*
Complete: N/A

YAR'S REVENGE

Manufacturer: Atari
Label: Picture
Rarity: 2
Game Only: $1–3
Complete: $6–9
Notes: Must include minicomic book to be considered
complete

YAR'S REVENGE

Manufacturer: Sears
Label: Picture
Rarity: 4
Game Only: $2–4
Complete: $7–10
Notes: Must include minicomic book to be considered
complete

Z-TACK

Manufacturer: Bomb
Label: Text
Rarity: 9
Game Only: $50–75
Complete: $80–100*

ZAXXON

Manufacturer: Coleco
Label: Text
Rarity: 3
Game Only: $3–7
Complete: $10–15

5 The Atari 5200 and 7800

Atari became a household name in the 1970s and 1980s largely due to the success of the Atari 2600, but the 2600 wasn't the only cartridge-based video game console that Atari released. As the advanced capabilities of competitors' game consoles started to outshine the aging 2600, Atari fought back by releasing advanced systems of their own.

While neither of the Atari systems released in the 1980s came close to the popularity of the 2600, both the Atari 5200 and the Atari 7800 have found a niche in the classic console collectors' market.

Atari 5200 (1982)

The Atari 5200 debuted in 1982. The console shipped with two controllers—joysticks with built-in numeric keypads—and a *Pac-Man* cartridge. This version of *Pac-Man* was very close to the arcade game both graphically and in terms of gameplay, a vast improvement over the dis-appointing 2600 version. Atari continued their strategy of releasing cartridges based on arcade hits—*Centipede, Missile Command, Galaxian,* and *Defender* were among the initial games re-leased for the new system.

Because the 5200 was based on the same technology found in the heart of Atari's home com-puter, the Atari 400, the graphics on the new system were a vast improvement over those of the 2600. The 5200 was easily on par graphically with the ColecoVision, and most of the initial press response to the new console was quite favorable.

There were several problems that kept the 5200 from becoming a success. First, the library of games for the console was extremely limited. The Atari 5200 was incompatible with existing 2600 games, and the software developers at Atari found their energy split between continued game development for the 2600 and development for the new system. Third-party software manufacturers put most of their energy into 2600 development as well because of the huge in-stalled base for the older system.

Another problem with the 5200 was that it was expensive. With an initial rollout price tag of $250, the Atari 5200 was $50 more expensive than the ColecoVision, which was already developing a following at the time.

Perhaps the biggest complaint people had about the 5200, however, concerned the controllers. The 5200's joysticks were not self-centering—when you moved the stick to the side, it stayed there unless you moved it back. This made playing games that required precise control very difficult. On top of that, the controllers tended to break easily.

The Atari 5200 had a fairly short run in the marketplace. Like most of the other systems of the era, it disappeared when the video game market crashed. Atari stopped manufacturing the system in 1984.

Atari 5200 Consoles

There are two versions of the Atari 5200 console. The two console variations are easy to distinguish at a glance due to the number of joystick ports with which they are equipped. From a collector's perspective, each version has advantages and disadvantages.

The original Atari 5200 console, released in 1982, had four joystick ports and is, as a result, now referred to as the "4-port" model. The antenna/game switchbox for this version of the console (which also houses a connector for the power supply) is proprietary—the console can only function via this piece of hardware. This is a major disadvantage, especially for collectors today, since replacement switchboxes are very difficult to find. When purchasing a 4-port 5200, make sure that the switchbox is functional. The console is useless without it.

It is important to note that the Atari 2600 adaptor later released for the 5200 is incompatible with some 4-port 5200 consoles.

Atari redesigned the 5200 about a year after its initial release. The newer model eliminated two of the four joystick ports, and as a result, is known as the **"2-port" version**. This console also eliminated the proprietary power/antenna/game switchbox. This is a great boon to collectors, since a modern-day replacement for a defective antenna/game switchbox can be found at any electronics store.

The downside of the 2-port model is that some (but apparently not all) 2-port 5200s are incompatible with two Atari 5200 cartridges: *Pitfall!* and *Mountain King*.

The 4- and 2-port versions of the Atari 5200 fetch about the same price in the marketplace today. The 2-port model is slightly more popular among collectors who intend to play with the console extensively due to the ready availability of replacement antenna/game switchboxes.

Atari 5200 Cartridges

With a grand total of just over 100 cartridges (including homebrews, reproductions, and prototypes), **the Atari 5200 cartridge** library is a lot less intimidating than that of the 2600 for collectors who are trying to amass a complete collection of games for the system.

The bulk of the Atari 5200's game library was released under Atari's label, although many of the Atari games were actually developed by a third-party software company called General Computer. Most of the Atari-branded cartridges are quite common and inexpensive.

The continued popularity of the 2600 at the time the 5200 was released, combined with the short retail life of the 5200, severely limited the number of third-party cartridges released for the system. Only seven third-party software companies released games for the 5200:

a *The original Atari 5200 "4-port" console.* (Photo courtesy of Albert Yaruso, http://www.atariage.com.)

b *The updated "2-port" version of the Atari 5200.* (Photo courtesy of Albert Yaruso, http://www.atariage.com.)

- Activision (13 titles)

- Big Five Software (2 titles)

- CBS Electronics (5 titles)

- Electra Concepts (1 title)

- Parker Brothers (12 titles)

- Sega (4 titles)

- Sunrise (1 title)

Like the Atari 2600, there were a number of prototype games for the 5200 that never made it into production. Some of these titles are now being reproduced and sold by collector sites like AtariAge (http://www.atariage.com). There are also a handful of homebrew titles available in the marketplace today.

a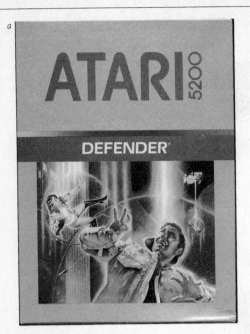

b

a **Atari 5200 game cartridge.** *Many of the titles released for the 5200 were released directly by Atari. These cartridges, many of which are based on popular classic arcade games, are fairly common and inexpensive today. (Photo courtesy of Albert Yaruso, http://www.atariage.com.)*

b **Bounty Bob Strikes Back** *is one of the rarest and most sought-after Atari 5200 cartridges. The box (pictured here) is far more difficult to find than the cartridge itself. (Photo courtesy of Albert Yaruso, http://www.atariage.com.)*

Despite the relatively small number of cartridges available for the console and the ease with which most of these games can be found today, there are a few coveted "Holy Grail" titles for the Atari 5200. For the most part, these titles are among those produced by the third-party software manufacturers listed earlier. The following are a few of the more sought-after titles for the system.

Bounty Bob Strikes Back (Big Five Software)

Bounty Bob Strikes Back is the sequel to *Miner 2049'er*, a game that was popular on many console systems and home computers in the early 1980s. This cartridge was produced in fairly limited quantities, making it extremely difficult to find today. The box and the poster that were originally packaged with the game are much harder to locate than the cartridge itself. This is one of the few Atari 5200 cartridges for which you can expect to spend over $100 for the cartridge alone, and considerably more for a boxed, complete copy.

This game is a 5200 Holy Grail not only because of its rarity, but because it is also considered by many to be one of the most enjoyable classic home video games of all time.

a **Meteorites** *was the only game released by Electra Concepts for the Atari 5200, and it is extremely rare. (Photo courtesy of Albert Yaruso, http://www.atariage.com.)*

b ***Parker Brothers'* Return of the Jedi.** Star Wars *games were popular on all home consoles for which they were produced. Death Star Battle is the rarest of the two Star Wars titles for the 5200. (Photo courtesy of Albert Yaruso, http://www.atariage.com.)*

Meteorites (Electra Concepts)

Electra Concepts is probably best known for their Masterplay Interface—a hardware add-on that allows the use of Atari 2600 controllers with the 5200. This device is something of a hardware Holy Grail for the system. However, the company also produced a single game—*Meteorites*.

Meteorites was similar in concept to *Asteroids*. In fact, the original title of the game was slated to be *Disasteroids* until Atari threatened legal action. The game apparently saw very limited distribution or was produced in small numbers because it is very difficult to locate today. Like many rare cartridges, the box is even harder to find than the game itself.

Star Wars: Return of the Jedi Death Star Battle (Parker Brothers)

Parker Brothers marketed *Star Wars* video games for just about every major classic console, and all were extremely popular. Two of these titles found their way to the 5200: *Star Wars: The Arcade Game* and ***Star Wars: Return of the Jedi Death Star Battle***. While both games are popular collectibles, *Death Star Battle* is by far the rarer of the two. The cartridge itself is quite uncommon, and the box is rarer still.

123

Atari 5200 Price Guides

5200 Hardware Price Guide

CONSOLES

ATARI 5200 CONSOLE (4-PORT)
Manufacturer: Atari
Rarity: 3
Loose: $20–30
Boxed/Complete: $40–60
Notes: Original version with 4 joystick ports; uses a proprietary RF/power switchbox (won't work without it); incompatible with the 2600 (VCS) Adaptor

ATARI 5200 CONSOLE (2-PORT)
Manufacturer: Atari
Rarity: 3
Loose: $25–30
Boxed/Complete: $40–60
Notes: Updated version with 2 joystick ports and standard RF and power switchboxes

ACCESSORIES

2600 (VCS) ADAPTOR
Manufacturer: Atari
Rarity: 3
Loose: $14–16
Boxed/Complete: $25–30
Notes: Allows Atari 2600 games to be played on the 5200

CARRYING CASE
Manufacturer: Atari
Rarity: 4
Loose: $45–55
Boxed/Complete: $65–75*

CONTROLLER/JOYSTICK COUPLER
Manufacturer: Atari
Rarity: 4
Loose: $10–25
Boxed/Complete: N/A
Notes: Controller/Joystick coupler originally included with *Robotron: 2084* and *Space Dungeon*

JOYSTICK, ATARI 5200
Manufacturer: Atari
Rarity: 3
Loose: $10–25
Boxed/Complete: $30–40
Notes: The standard joystick included with the console; inaccurate control and prone to malfunctions

JOYSTICK, COMPETITION PRO
Manufacturer: Coin Control
Rarity: 7
Loose: $30–50
Boxed/Complete: $50–60*
Notes: Requires a Y-adaptor to access control pad and start functions on the standard 5200 controller; incomplete without the Y-adaptor

JOYSTICK, FIRE COMMAND
Manufacturer: GIM Electronics
Rarity: 7
Loose: $30–40
Boxed/Complete: $45–55*
Notes: Requires a Y-adaptor to access control pad and start functions on the standard 5200 controller; incomplete without the Y-adaptor

JOYSTICK, WICO COMMAND CONTROL
Manufacturer: Wico
Rarity: 5
Loose: $18–25
Boxed/Complete: $30–40
Notes: Requires a Y-adaptor to access control pad and start functions on the standard 5200 controller; incomplete without the Y-adaptor

KEYPAD, WICO COMMAND CONTROL
Manufacturer: Wico
Rarity: 7
Loose: $25–30
Boxed/Complete: $45–55

MASTERPLAY INTERFACE
Manufacturer: Electra Concepts
Rarity: 8
Loose: $50–80
Boxed/Complete: $100–200*
Notes: Allows 2600 controllers to be used on the 5200

NEWPORT CONTROL GUIDE
Manufacturer: Newport
Rarity: 8
Loose: $15–20
Boxed/Complete: $25–35*
Notes: Controller overlay that makes the 5200 controllers more precise in games that require only 4-way movement (*Pac-Man, Ms. Pac-Man*, etc.)

POWER SUPPLY
Manufacturer: Atari
Rarity: 2
Loose: $3–6
Boxed/Complete: $8–10
Notes: Works with both 5200 consoles

RF/POWER SWITCHBOX
Manufacturer: Atari
Rarity: 3
Loose: $8–12
Boxed/Complete: $15–20
Notes: The proprietary RF/power switchbox for the Atari 5200 4-port console

TRAK-BALL CONTROLLER
Manufacturer: Atari
Rarity: 3
Loose: $12–15
Boxed/Complete: $30–50

5200 Cartridge Price Guide

A.E.
Manufacturer: Atari
Label: N/A
Rarity: Prototype
Game Only: ?
Complete: N/A
Notes: Price not available; for more info, see
http://www.atariprotos.com

THE ACTIVISION DECATHLON
Manufacturer: Activision
Label: Blue
Rarity: 3
Game Only: $7–10
Complete: $18–25
Notes: Usually referred to simply as *Decathlon*

ASTEROIDS
Manufacturer: Atari
Label: N/A
Rarity: Prototype
Game Only: ?
Complete: N/A
Notes: Price not available; for more info, see
http://www.atariprotos.com

ASTEROIDS
Manufacturer: AtariAge
Label: Silver
Rarity: Reproduction
Game Only: $25
Complete: N/A
Notes: Available from the AtariAge store
(http://www.atariage.com); no box or manual

ASTROCHASE
Manufacturer: Parker Brothers
Label: Text
Rarity: 3
Game Only: $6–10
Complete: $15–45

BALLBLAZER
Manufacturer: Atari
Label: Silver (No Title)
Rarity: 3
Game Only: $8–12
Complete: $15–18
Notes: The name of the game does not appear on the
cartridge label

BARROOM BASEBALL
Manufacturer: Atari
Label: N/A
Rarity: Prototype
Game Only: ?
Complete: N/A
Notes: Price not available; for more info, see
http://www.atariprotos.com

BATTLEZONE
Manufacturer: Atari
Label: N/A
Rarity: Prototype
Game Only: ?
Complete: N/A
Notes: Price not available; for more info, see
http://www.atariprotos.com

BEAMRIDER
Manufacturer: Activision
Label: Blue
Rarity: 5
Game Only: $12–15
Complete: $25–60
Notes: Must include keypad overlays to be considered
complete

BERZERK
Manufacturer: Atari
Label: Silver
Rarity: 2
Game Only: $5–8
Complete: $10–15

BLACK BELT
Manufacturer: Atari
Label: N/A
Rarity: Prototype
Game Only: ?
Complete: N/A
Notes: Price not available; for more info, see
http://www.atariprotos.com

BLUE PRINT
Manufacturer: CBS Electronics
Label: Black
Rarity: 3
Game Only: $4–6
Complete: $8–10

BOOGIE DEMO
Manufacturer: Atari
Label: N/A
Rarity: Prototype
Game Only: ?
Complete: N/A
Notes: Price not available; for more info, see
http://www.atariprotos.com

BOUNTY BOB STRIKES BACK
Manufacturer: Big Five Software
Label: Green
Rarity: 9
Game Only: $90–150
Complete: $500–750
Notes: One of the rarest 5200 titles; the box is very dif-
ficult to find; must include the poster originally
packed with the game to be considered complete

BUCK ROGERS: PLANET OF ZOOM
Manufacturer: Sega
Label: Picture
Rarity: 3
Game Only: $5–8
Complete: $9–12

CASTLE BLAST
Manufacturer: Self-Published
Label: Silver
Rarity: Homebrew
Game Only: N/A
Complete: $35
Notes: Released at the 2002 Classic Gaming Expo; available at the AtariAge Store (http://www.atariage.com); autographed copies worth slightly more

CENTIPEDE
Manufacturer: Atari
Label: Silver
Rarity: 1
Game Only: $2–4
Complete: $5–8

CHOPLIFTER!
Manufacturer: Atari
Label: Silver
Rarity: 3
Game Only: $4–6
Complete: $15–18

COMBAT II ADVANCED
Manufacturer: Self-Published
Label: Gold
Rarity: Homebrew
Game Only: $45–50*
Complete: N/A
Notes: 100 copies were produced with a special gold reflective label

COMBAT II ADVANCED
Manufacturer: Self-Published
Label: Silver
Rarity: Homebrew
Game Only: $30
Complete: N/A
Notes: Available from the AtariAge store (http://www.atariage.com); no box

CONGO BONGO
Manufacturer: Sega
Label: Picture
Rarity: 3
Game Only: $4–9
Complete: $10–12

COUNTERMEASURE
Manufacturer: Atari
Label: Silver
Rarity: 2
Game Only: $2–5
Complete: $6–8

DEFENDER
Manufacturer: Atari
Label: Silver
Rarity: 1
Game Only: $2–3
Complete: $4–6

DIAGNOSTIC CARTRIDGE
Manufacturer: Atari
Label: White
Rarity: 9
Game Only: $45–60*
Complete: N/A

DIG DUG
Manufacturer: Atari
Label: Silver
Rarity: 1
Game Only: $1–3
Complete: $4–6

THE DREADNAUGHT FACTOR
Manufacturer: Activision
Label: Picture
Rarity: 3
Game Only: $4–6
Complete: $10–15

FINAL LEGACY
Manufacturer: Atari
Label: N/A
Rarity: Prototype
Game Only: ?
Complete: N/A
Notes: Price not available; for more info, see http://www.atariprotos.com

FINAL LEGACY
Manufacturer: AtariAge
Label: Silver
Rarity: Reproduction
Game Only: $25
Complete: N/A
Notes: Available from the AtariAge store (http://www.atariage.com); no box or manual

FRISKY TOM
Manufacturer: Atari
Label: N/A
Rarity: Prototype
Game Only: ?
Complete: N/A
Notes: Price not available; for more info, see http://www.atariprotos.com

FROGGER
Manufacturer: Parker Brothers
Label: Picture
Rarity: 2
Game Only: $2–5
Complete: $7–9

FROGGER II: THREEEDEEP!
Manufacturer: Parker Brothers
Label: Text
Rarity: 6
Game Only: $20–30
Complete: $50–75

GALAXIAN
Manufacturer: Atari
Label: Silver
Rarity: 1
Game Only: $1–3
Complete: $4–6

GORF

Manufacturer: CBS Electronics
Label: Black
Rarity: 3
Game Only: $5–8
Complete: $12–16

GREMLINS

Manufacturer: Atari
Label: Silver
Rarity: 4
Game Only: $12–18
Complete: $30–50

GYRUSS

Manufacturer: Parker Brothers
Label: Text
Rarity: 4
Game Only: $8–14
Complete: $40–60

HAUNTED HOUSE II 3-D

Manufacturer: Self-Published
Label: Picture
Rarity: Homebrew
Game Only: N/A
Complete: $30
Notes: Released at the 2002 Classic Gaming Expo;
previously available from the AtariAge store
(http://www.atariage.com); no box; possibly discontinued

H.E.R.O.

Manufacturer: Activision
Label: Picture
Rarity: 3
Game Only: $10–12
Complete: $15–20*

JAMES BOND 007

Manufacturer: Parker Brothers
Label: Text
Rarity: 5
Game Only: $8–15
Complete: $25–50

JOUST

Manufacturer: Atari
Label: Silver
Rarity: 1
Game Only: $2–4
Complete: $8–10

JR. PAC-MAN

Manufacturer: Atari
Label: N/A
Rarity: Prototype
Game Only: ?
Complete: N/A
Notes: Price not available; for more info, see
http://www.atariprotos.com

JR. PAC-MAN

Manufacturer: AtariAge
Label: Silver
Rarity: Reproduction
Game Only: $25
Complete: N/A
Notes: Currently available from the AtariAge store
(http://www.atariage.com); no box or manual

JUNGLE HUNT

Manufacturer: Atari
Label: Silver
Rarity: 1
Game Only: $3–5
Complete: $6–9

K-RAZY SHOOT-OUT

Manufacturer: CBS Electronics
Label: Black
Rarity: 4
Game Only: $30–35
Complete: $60–120
Notes: Box is particularly difficult to find

KABOOM!

Manufacturer: Activision
Label: Picture
Rarity: 3
Game Only: $2–4
Complete: $5–10

KANGAROO

Manufacturer: Atari
Label: Silver
Rarity: 1
Game Only: $1–3
Complete: $4–6

KEYSTONE KAPERS

Manufacturer: Activision
Label: Picture
Rarity: 3
Game Only: $3–5
Complete: $8–25

KLAX

Manufacturer: Mean Hamster Software
Label: Picture
Rarity: Homebrew
Game Only: N/A
Complete: $45
Notes: Based on the Atari arcade game by the same
name; available from AtariAge
(http://www.atariage.com); complete with box and
manual

KOFFI: YELLOW KOPTER

Manufacturer: Self-Published
Label: Silver
Rarity: Homebrew
Game Only: N/A
Complete: $30
Notes: Available from the AtariAge store
(http://www.atariage.com); no box

THE LAST STARFIGHTER

Manufacturer: Atari
Label: N/A
Rarity: Prototype
Game Only: ?
Complete: N/A
Notes: Based on the movie by the same name; price not available; for more info, see http://www.atariprotos.com

LOONEY TOONS HOTEL

Manufacturer: Atari
Label: N/A
Rarity: Prototype
Game Only: ?
Complete: N/A
Notes: Price not available; for more info, see http://www.atariprotos.com

MARIO BROS.

Manufacturer: Atari
Label: Silver
Rarity: 3
Game Only: $4–7
Complete: $8–10

MEEBZORK

Manufacturer: Atari
Label: N/A
Rarity: Prototype
Game Only: ?
Complete: N/A
Notes: Price not available; for more info, see http://www.atariprotos.com

MEGAMANIA

Manufacturer: Activision
Label: Picture
Rarity: 3
Game Only: $4–6
Complete: $7–12

METEORITES

Manufacturer: Electra Concepts
Label: Picture
Rarity: 8
Game Only: $85–95
Complete: $150–300
Notes: One of the rarest 5200 titles; box is difficult to find

MICRO-GAMMON SB

Manufacturer: Atari
Label: N/A
Rarity: Prototype
Game Only: ?
Complete: N/A
Notes: Price not available; for more info, see http://www.atariprotos.com

MILLIPEDE

Manufacturer: Atari
Label: N/A
Rarity: Prototype
Game Only: ?
Complete: N/A
Notes: Price not available; for more info, see http://www.atariprotos.com

MILLIPEDE

Manufacturer: AtariAge
Label: Silver
Rarity: Reproduction
Game Only: $25
Complete: N/A
Notes: Available from the AtariAge store (http://www.atariage.com); no box or manual

MINER 2049ER

Manufacturer: Big Five Software
Label: Red
Rarity: 3
Game Only: $14–20
Complete: $25–35*

MINER 2049ER

Manufacturer: Big Five Software
Label: Gold
Rarity: 4
Game Only: $14–20
Complete: $25–35*

MINIATURE GOLF

Manufacturer: Atari
Label: N/A
Rarity: Prototype
Game Only: ?
Complete: N/A
Notes: Price not available; for more info, see http://www.atariprotos.com

MISSILE COMMAND

Manufacturer: Atari
Label: Silver
Rarity: 2
Game Only: $2–3
Complete: $4–6

MONTEZUMA'S REVENGE

Manufacturer: Parker Brothers
Label: Text
Rarity: 4
Game Only: $10–20
Complete: $25–50

MOON PATROL

Manufacturer: Atari
Label: Silver
Rarity: 2
Game Only: $3–5
Complete: $14–16

MOUNTAIN KING

Manufacturer: CBS Electronics
Label: Black
Rarity: 3
Game Only: $8–12
Complete: $15–20

MR. DO!'S CASTLE

Manufacturer: Parker Brothers
Label: Text
Rarity: 6
Game Only: $25–35
Complete: $50–70

MS. PAC-MAN

Manufacturer: Atari
Label: Silver
Rarity: 2
Game Only: $2–5
Complete: $12–15

PAC-MAN

Manufacturer: Atari
Label: Silver
Rarity: 1
Game Only: $1–2
Complete: $5–7
Notes: *Pac-Man* was included with later Atari 5200 consoles (replacing *Super Breakout*)

PENGO

Manufacturer: Atari
Label: Silver
Rarity: 3
Game Only: $2–5
Complete: $10–15

PETE'S TEST CARTRIDGE

Manufacturer: Self-Published
Label: Silver
Rarity: Reproduction
Game Only: $25
Complete: N/A
Notes: Available from the AtariAge store (http://www.atariage.com); no box or manual

PITFALL II: LOST CAVERNS

Manufacturer: Activision
Label: Brown
Rarity: 3
Game Only: $5–8
Complete: $12–15

PITFALL!

Manufacturer: Activision
Label: Blue
Rarity: 2
Game Only: $3–5
Complete: $6–8

POLE POSITION

Manufacturer: Atari
Label: Silver
Rarity: 1
Game Only: $2–3
Complete: $5–7

POPEYE

Manufacturer: Parker Brothers
Label: Picture
Rarity: 2
Game Only: $1–3
Complete: $4–6

Q*BERT

Manufacturer: Parker Brothers
Label: Picture
Rarity: 2
Game Only: $3–5
Complete: $8–12

QIX

Manufacturer: Atari
Label: Silver
Rarity: 2
Game Only: $2–4
Complete: $6–8
Notes: Must include keypad overlays to be considered complete

QUEST FOR QUINTANA ROO

Manufacturer: Sunrise
Label: Text
Rarity: 5
Game Only: $12–15
Complete: $20–25*

REALSPORTS BASEBALL

Manufacturer: Atari
Label: Silver
Rarity: 2
Game Only: $2–4
Complete: $5–7

REALSPORTS BASKETBALL

Manufacturer: Atari
Label: N/A
Rarity: Prototype
Game Only: ?
Complete: N/A
Notes: Price not available; for more info, see http://www.atariprotos.com

REALSPORTS FOOTBALL

Manufacturer: Atari
Label: Silver
Rarity: 2
Game Only: $1–3
Complete: $4–6
Notes: Originally simply titled *Football* (there are two label variations, one with and one without the "RealSports" branding)

REALSPORTS SOCCER

Manufacturer: Atari
Label: Silver
Rarity: 2
Game Only: $1–3
Complete: $6–9
Notes: Originally simply titled *Soccer* (there are two label variations, one with and one without the "RealSports" branding)

REALSPORTS TENNIS

Manufacturer: Atari
Label: Silver
Rarity: 3
Game Only: $1–5
Complete: $6–9

RESCUE ON FRACTALUS

Manufacturer: Atari
Label: Silver (No Title)
Rarity: 4
Game Only: $15–20
Complete: $30–35
Notes: The name of the game doesn't appear on the cartridge label

RIVER RAID

Manufacturer: Activision
Label: Picture
Rarity: 2
Game Only: $2–4
Complete: $8–10

ROADRUNNER

Manufacturer: Atari
Label: N/A
Rarity: Prototype
Game Only: ?
Complete: N/A
Notes: Price not available; for more info, see
http://www.atariprotos.com

ROBOTRON: 2084

Manufacturer: Atari
Label: Silver
Rarity: 2
Game Only: $4–8
Complete: $25–50
Notes: Included a controller coupler that allowed the
use of both controllers simultaneously; must include
this coupler to be considered complete

SPACE DUNGEON

Manufacturer: Atari
Label: Silver
Rarity: 2
Game Only: $4–8
Complete: $30–60
Notes: Included a controller coupler that allowed the
use of both controllers simultaneously; must include
this coupler to be considered complete

SPACE INVADERS

Manufacturer: Atari
Label: Silver
Rarity: 1
Game Only: $1–3
Complete: $5–7

SPACE SHUTTLE

Manufacturer: Activision
Label: Picture
Rarity: 3
Game Only: $3–6
Complete: $10–25

SPITFIRE

Manufacturer: Atari
Label: N/A
Rarity: Prototype
Game Only: ?
Complete: N/A
Notes: Price not available; for more info, see
http://www.atariprotos.com

SPORT GOOFY

Manufacturer: Atari
Label: N/A
Rarity: Prototype
Game Only: ?
Complete: N/A
Notes: Price not available; for more info, see
http://www.atariprotos.com

STAR RAIDERS

Manufacturer: Atari
Label: Silver
Rarity: 1
Game Only: $1–3
Complete: $4–6
Notes: Must include keypad overlays to be considered
complete

STAR TREK: STRATEGIC OPERATIONS SIMU-LATOR

Manufacturer: Sega
Label: Picture
Rarity: 3
Game Only: $2–5
Complete: $10–12

STAR WARS: RETURN OF THE JEDI DEATH STAR BATTLE

Manufacturer: Parker Brothers
Label: Text
Rarity: 7
Game Only: $30–40
Complete: $50–100
Notes: Box is particularly difficult to find

STAR WARS: THE ARCADE GAME

Manufacturer: Parker Brothers
Label: Text
Rarity: 5
Game Only: $7–15
Complete: $15–35
Notes: Box is particularly difficult to find

STARGATE

Manufacturer: Atari
Label: N/A
Rarity: Prototype
Game Only: ?
Complete: N/A
Notes: Price not available; for more info, see
http://www.atariprotos.com

SUPER BREAKOUT

Manufacturer: Atari
Label: Silver
Rarity: 1
Game Only: $1–2
Complete: $4–7
Notes: Packaged with early versions of the Atari 5200
console (later replaced by *Pac-Man*)

SUPER COBRA

Manufacturer: Parker Brothers
Label: Picture
Rarity: 4
Game Only: $5–7
Complete: $15–30

SUPER PAC-MAN

Manufacturer: Atari
Label: N/A
Rarity: Prototype
Game Only: ?
Complete: N/A
Notes: Price not available; for more info, see
http://www.atariprotos.com

SUPER PAC-MAN
Manufacturer: AtariAge
Label: Silver
Rarity: Reproduction
Game Only: $25
Complete: N/A
Notes: Available from the AtariAge store
(http://www.atariage.com); no box or manual

TEMPEST
Manufacturer: Atari
Label: Silver
Rarity: Prototype
Game Only: ?
Complete: N/A
Notes: Price not available; for more info, see
http://www.atariprotos.com

TRACK AND FIELD
Manufacturer: Atari
Label: N/A
Rarity: Prototype
Game Only: ?
Complete: N/A
Notes: Price not available; for more info, see
http://www.atariprotos.com

VANGUARD
Manufacturer: Atari
Label: Silver
Rarity: 2
Game Only: $3–6
Complete: $9–16

WIZARD OF WOR
Manufacturer: CBS Electronics
Label: Black
Rarity: 3
Game Only: $4–8
Complete: $10–25
Notes: Must include keypad overlays to be considered
complete

XARI ARENA
Manufacturer: Atari
Label: N/A
Rarity: Prototype
Game Only: ?
Complete: N/A
Notes: Price not available; for more info, see
http://www.atariprotos.com

XEVIOUS
Manufacturer: Atari
Label: N/A
Rarity: Prototype
Game Only: ?
Complete: N/A
Notes: Price not available; for more info, see
http://www.atariprotos.com

XEVIOUS
Manufacturer: AtariAge
Label: Silver
Rarity: Reproduction
Game Only: $25
Complete: N/A
Notes: Currently available from the AtariAge store
(http://www.atariage.com); no box or manual

YELLOW SUBMARINE
Manufacturer: Atari
Label: N/A
Rarity: Prototype
Game Only: ?
Complete: N/A
Notes: Price not available; for more info, see
http://www.atariprotos.com

ZAXXON
Manufacturer: Sega
Label: Picture
Rarity: 6
Game Only: $30–35
Complete: $50–75
Notes: Box is particularly difficult to find

ZENJI
Manufacturer: Activision
Label: Black
Rarity: 5
Game Only: $15–30
Complete: $35–45*

ZONE RANGER
Manufacturer: Activision
Label: Silver; Black
Rarity: 5
Game Only: $8–10
Complete: $15–20
Notes: The silver label (Telegames) release of this
game is slightly more common

Atari 7800 (1986)

Because it wasn't released until 1986, the Atari 7800 *technically* falls outside the stated timeframe for this book. There are, however, several compelling reasons to include it.

The 7800 was actually fully designed and ready to go into production in 1984, but the crash of the video game industry made its release at that time unviable. It wasn't until Nintendo proved in 1985 that the video game market in the United States wasn't dead that Atari released the 7800 to try and regain a share of the industry it had essentially created.

Designed by General Computer, the company that had programmed many of the game cartridges for the Atari 5200, the 7800 was the best of both worlds for Atari. It was capable of producing graphics that rivaled any system on the market at the time. It was also designed to be compatible with existing 2600 cartridges, which gave the system an instant library of hundreds of titles. In addition to software compatibility, the 7800 was compatible with Atari 2600 controllers. The system came packaged with two Proline joystick controllers and the *Pole Position II* game cartridge.

Unfortunately, Atari was past its prime by the time the 7800 hit the shelves. Most third-party companies had given up on Atari in favor of developing for Nintendo, or were pursuing the more lucrative home computer game market. As a result, the library of new game titles for the 7800 was extremely small and remained that way throughout the lifetime of the console. Despite this, the Atari 7800 remained on the market well into 1991.

Although the Atari 7800 is far from the most popular system among serious collectors, it is ideal for those new to the hobby due to its small cartridge library. It is a great system for those interested in collecting and playing Atari 2600 games as well.

Atari 7800 Consoles
Despite the fact that it was on the market longer than the Atari 5200, the 7800 went through few design changes over the years. The only difference between the original consoles and those produced later is the presence of an **expansion slot** on the left side of the console in later models. This expansion slot, which was to be used for add-on accessories that were never produced, serves no function. This subtle difference is worth noting, however, because the earlier models (without the expansion slot) are incompatible with a small number of Atari 2600 cartridges. There is no difference in value or collectibility between the nonexpansion port model and the later version, and the packaging for the system remained the same throughout the console's run.

Atari 7800 Cartridges
If the cartridge library for the Atari 5200 is small compared to that of the 2600, the cartridge library for the Atari 7800 is downright miniscule. Fewer than 70 cartridges were released for the system and, unlike the 2600 and 5200, very little in the way of new homebrew development or prototype reproduction has taken place for this system.

Physically, Atari 7800 cartridges are nearly identical to 2600 cartridges. Some games were produced for both the 2600 and the 7800, so make sure that you look closely at the label to make sure you're purchasing the version you want. Label variations don't play a huge role in 7800 collecting, but there are a few games—most notably *Ball Blazer*—where variations in label style can affect collectibility and price.

Like the 5200, most of the titles released for the 7800 system were released by Atari. Only three outside companies developed games for the 7800:

- Absolute Entertainment (6 titles)
- Activision (2 titles)
- **Froggo** (2 titles)

The lack of new games for the system was one of the primary reasons for the Atari 7800's failure. The upside of the small library from a collector's standpoint is that it is fairly easy to amass

a

b

a   **Atari 7800 expansion slot.** *The only difference between early and later model Atari 7800 consoles is the presence of an expansion slot located on the left side in the later models. (Photo courtesy of Albert Yaruso, http://www.atariage.com.)*

b   **Froggo games.** *The two Atari 7800 games released by Froggo are among the most difficult cartridges to find for the system today. (Photo courtesy of Albert Yaruso, http://www.atariage.com.)*

a complete library of titles. In fact, many Atari 7800 cartridges are still available *brand new* for as little as $5 online at AtariAge (http://www.atariage.com) and O'Shea, Ltd. (http://www.os-healtd.com).

There are no cartridges that are really considered Holy Grail games for the Atari 7800, since most titles are inexpensive and easy to find. Even the rarest 7800 games don't approach the astronomical prices of the rarest Atari 2600 carts. Nevertheless, there are a few games for the system that are fairly elusive.

Tank Command and *Water Ski* (Froggo)

Froggo's games for the Atari 2600 are widely considered to be rather disappointing and cheesy. Considering this, it is interesting that the two games this company produced for the Atari 7800 are actually quite good. Both *Tank Command* and *Water Ski* featured decent graphics and good game play.

The two Froggo titles had very limited distribution and, as a result, these cartridges are among the most difficult Atari 7800 games to locate today.

a **Double Dragon *for the Atari
7800.*** *Despite their strong support
of the Atari 2600, Activision
produced only two cartridges for
the 7800. Double Dragon is the
rarer of the two. (Photo courtesy of
Albert Yaruso, http://www.
atariage.com.)*

b **Atari's Fatal Run.** *Released late in
the 7800's lifetime, Fatal Run is
one of the more difficult Atari-
produced titles to locate. (Photo
courtesy of Albert Yaruso,
http://www.atariage.com.)*

Double Dragon (Activision)

By the time the Atari 7800 was released, Activision had turned most of their attention to the
burgeoning home computer game market. They only produced two titles for the 7800, both
based on popular classic arcade games.

Double Dragon is reportedly quite buggy, but is a reasonably faithful translation of the arcade
game. For some reason, this cartridge is harder to find than *Rampage*, the other Activision title
for the system.

Fatal Run (Atari)

Games released later in the Atari 7800's history were generally harder to find than the early titles. *Fatal Run* falls into this category.

An automobile combat game set in a postapocalyptic world, *Fatal Run* is an enjoyable game
with decent graphics that takes advantage of the 7800's advanced capabilities. Because it is a lot
of fun to play *and* fairly hard to come by (as Atari 7800 games go), *Fatal Run* is considered to be
among the more collectible cartridges for the system.

Atari 7800 Price Guides

7800 Hardware Price Guide

CONSOLE

ATARI 7800 CONSOLE
Manufacturer: Atari
Rarity: 2
Loose: $25–35
Boxed/Complete: $40–50
Notes: Earlier versions (those with expansion ports) were incompatible with a few 2600 games; originally packaged with 2 Proline joysticks and *Pole Position II*

ACCESSORIES

JOYPAD, ATARI
Manufacturer: Atari
Rarity: 3
Loose: $10–15
Boxed/Complete: $17–25*
Notes: Packaged with European versions of the 7800 console; fairly easy to find loose, but very rare with complete packaging

JOYSTICK, ATARI PROLINE (ATARI DELUXE JOYSTICK)
Manufacturer: Atari
Rarity: 2
Loose: $4–8
Boxed/Complete: $10–15
Notes: Original joystick packaged with the 7800 system

JOYSTICK, BEST
Manufacturer: Best Electronics
Rarity: 3
Loose: $10–15
Boxed/Complete: $15–20*

JOYSTICK, SUPER DELUXE
Manufacturer: Telegames
Rarity: 4
Loose: $10–15
Boxed/Complete: $15–20*

LIGHT GUN, ATARI XE
Manufacturer: Atari
Rarity: 3
Loose: $12–15
Boxed/Complete: $17–25*

LIGHT GUN, BEST
Manufacturer: Best Electronics
Rarity: 3
Loose: $18–20
Boxed/Complete: $25–30*

7800 Cartridge Price Guide

GAMES

3D ASTEROIDS
Manufacturer: Atari
Label: N/A
Rarity: Prototype
Game Only: ?
Complete: N/A
Notes: Prerelease, working title of *Asteroids* for the 7800; price not available; for more info, see http://www.atariprotos.com

ACE OF ACES
Manufacturer: Atari
Label: Color
Rarity: 2
Game Only: $3–5
Complete: $8–10

ALIEN BRIGADE
Manufacturer: Atari
Label: Color
Rarity: 2
Game Only: $10–15
Complete: $35–40
Notes: Currently very pricey despite being rather common; Light Gun compatible

ASTEROIDS
Manufacturer: Atari
Label: Gray
Rarity: 1
Game Only: $1–2
Complete: $3–5

135

BALLBLAZER

Manufacturer: Atari
Label: Color
Rarity: 1
Game Only: $1–3
Complete: $4–6
Notes: Prices and rarity reflect the silver end label version; cartridges with red end label are rarer and slightly more expensive

BARNYARD BLASTER

Manufacturer: Atari
Label: Color
Rarity: 1
Game Only: $1–2
Complete: $4–6
Notes: Requires the Atari XE Light Gun

BASKETBRAWL

Manufacturer: Atari
Label: Color
Rarity: 4
Game Only: $10–12
Complete: $30–40

CENTIPEDE

Manufacturer: Atari
Label: Gray
Rarity: 1
Game Only: $1–2
Complete: $3–5

CHOPLIFTER!

Manufacturer: Atari
Label: Color
Rarity: 2
Game Only: $1–3
Complete: $4–6

COMMANDO

Manufacturer: Atari
Label: Color
Rarity: 4
Game Only: $8–10
Complete: $28–32

CRACK'ED

Manufacturer: Atari
Label: Color
Rarity: 2
Game Only: $3–5
Complete: $7–10

CROSSBOW

Manufacturer: Atari
Label: Color
Rarity: 2
Game Only: $1–3
Complete: $4–7

DARK CHAMBERS

Manufacturer: Atari
Label: Color
Rarity: 1
Game Only: $1–4
Complete: $7–9

DESERT FALCON

Manufacturer: Atari
Label: Color
Rarity: 1
Game Only: $1–2
Complete: $3–5

DIAGNOSTIC TEST CARTRIDGE

Manufacturer: Atari
Label: White
Rarity: 6
Game Only: $35–45
Complete: N/A

DIG DUG

Manufacturer: Atari
Label: Gray
Rarity: 1
Game Only: $1–2
Complete: $3–5

DONKEY KONG

Manufacturer: Atari
Label: Color
Rarity: 1
Game Only: $1–2
Complete: $3–5

DONKEY KONG JUNIOR

Manufacturer: Atari
Label: Color
Rarity: 1
Game Only: $1–3
Complete: $5–7

DOUBLE DRAGON

Manufacturer: Activision
Label: White
Rarity: 5
Game Only: $8–10
Complete: $25–30

F-18 HORNET

Manufacturer: Absolute Entertainment
Label: Black
Rarity: 3
Game Only: $3–8
Complete: $10–15

FATAL RUN

Manufacturer: Atari
Label: Color
Rarity: 5
Game Only: $10–12
Complete: $35–40

FIGHT NIGHT

Manufacturer: Atari
Label: Color
Rarity: 3
Game Only: $3–5
Complete: $8–16

FOOD FIGHT
Manufacturer: Atari
Label: Gray
Rarity: 3
Game Only: $2–4
Complete: $8–10

GALAGA
Manufacturer: Atari
Label: Gray
Rarity: 1
Game Only: $1–2
Complete: $3–5

HAT TRICK
Manufacturer: Atari
Label: Color
Rarity: 1
Game Only: $1–2
Complete: $4–6

HIGH SCORE CARTRIDGE
Manufacturer: Atari
Label: Color
Rarity: Homebrew
Game Only: $30–40*
Complete: N/A
Notes: Announced by Atari in 1984, but not published until it was sold (in limited quantities) in 2000; incompatible with some cartridges

IKARI WARRIORS
Manufacturer: Atari
Label: Color
Rarity: 4
Game Only: $10–12
Complete: $20–25

IMPOSSIBLE MISSION
Manufacturer: Atari
Label: Color
Rarity: 4
Game Only: $10–15
Complete: $15–20*

JINKS
Manufacturer: Atari
Label: Color
Rarity: 1
Game Only: $1–2
Complete: $3–5

JOUST
Manufacturer: Atari
Label: Gray
Rarity: 1
Game Only: $1–2
Complete: $3–5

KARATEKA
Manufacturer: Atari
Label: Color
Rarity: 2
Game Only: $1–3
Complete: $5–7

KLAX
Manufacturer: Atari
Label: N/A
Rarity: Prototype
Game Only: ?
Complete: N/A
Notes: Completed, but never released by Atari; price not available; for more info, see http://www.atariprotos.com

KLAX
Manufacturer: ResQsoft
Label: Color
Rarity: Reproduction
Game Only: N/A
Complete: $30–45

KUNG-FU MASTER
Manufacturer: Absolute Entertainment
Label: Black
Rarity: 3
Game Only: $10–15
Complete: $16–21

MARIO BROS.
Manufacturer: Atari
Label: Color
Rarity: 2
Game Only: $6–8
Complete: $12–15

MAT MANIA CHALLENGE
Manufacturer: Atari
Label: Color
Rarity: 3
Game Only: $4–6
Complete: $8–12

MEAN 18 ULTIMATE GOLF
Manufacturer: Atari
Label: Color
Rarity: 5
Game Only: $40–50
Complete: $55–70*

MELTDOWN
Manufacturer: Atari
Label: Color
Rarity: 3
Game Only: $3–5
Complete: $5–10
Notes: Requires the Atari XE Light Gun

MIDNIGHT MUTANTS
Manufacturer: Atari
Label: Color
Rarity: 3
Game Only: $5–7
Complete: $10–20

MONITOR CARTRIDGE

Manufacturer: Harry Dodgson/Video 61
Label: Text
Rarity: Current
Game Only: N/A
Complete: $100
Notes: Cartridge that allows the programming of 2600 and 7800 games; requires Keyboard Controllers; currently available at http://www.atarisales.com

MOTOR PSYCHO

Manufacturer: Atari
Label: Color
Rarity: 4
Game Only: $5–8
Complete: $25–35

MS. PAC-MAN

Manufacturer: Atari
Label: Gray
Rarity: 1
Game Only: $1–2
Complete: $3–5

NINJA GOLF

Manufacturer: Atari
Label: Color
Rarity: 3
Game Only: $5–7
Complete: $12–16

ONE-ON-ONE BASKETBALL

Manufacturer: Atari
Label: Color
Rarity: 1
Game Only: $1–2
Complete: $3–5

PETE ROSE BASEBALL

Manufacturer: Absolute Entertainment
Label: Black
Rarity: 3
Game Only: $5–15
Complete: $13–18

PIT FIGHTER

Manufacturer: Atari
Label: N/A
Rarity: Prototype
Game Only: ?
Complete: N/A
Notes: Price not available; for more info, see http://www.atariprotos.com

PLANET SMASHERS

Manufacturer: Atari
Label: Color
Rarity: 4
Game Only: $8–10
Complete: $20–30

POLE POSITION II

Manufacturer: Atari
Label: White; Color
Rarity: 1
Game Only: $1–2
Complete: $3–5
Notes: The most common game because it was packed with the system (but also sold separately); both labels are equally common

RAMPAGE

Manufacturer: Activision
Label: White and Black
Rarity: 4
Game Only: $10–15
Complete: $18–25

REALSPORTS BASEBALL

Manufacturer: Atari
Label: Color
Rarity: 1
Game Only: $1–2
Complete: $3–5

ROBOTRON: 2084

Manufacturer: Atari
Label: Gray
Rarity: 1
Game Only: $1–3
Complete: $10–12

SCRAPYARD DOG

Manufacturer: Atari
Label: Color
Rarity: 2
Game Only: $1–2
Complete: $8–11

SENTINEL

Manufacturer: ResQsoft
Label: Color
Rarity: Reproduction
Game Only: N/A
Complete: $25–35*
Notes: Released by Atari only in PAL format; was at one time available in NTSC from ResQsoft Productions (http://home.earthlink.net/~resqsoft/products.htm)

SUMMER GAMES

Manufacturer: Atari
Label: Color
Rarity: 2
Game Only: $5–7
Complete: $10–14

SUPER HUEY UH-1X

Manufacturer: Atari
Label: Color
Rarity: 2
Game Only: $3–5
Complete: $8–12

SUPER SKATEBOARDIN'
Manufacturer: Absolute Entertainment
Label: Black
Rarity: 3
Game Only: $7–10
Complete: $18–21

TANK COMMAND
Manufacturer: Froggo
Label: White
Rarity: 6
Game Only: $45–55
Complete: $50–70

TITLE MATCH PRO WRESTLING
Manufacturer: Absolute Entertainment
Label: Black
Rarity: 3
Game Only: $8–12
Complete: $15–20*

TOMCAT: THE F-14 FIGHTER SIMULATOR
Manufacturer: Absolute Entertainment
Label: Black
Rarity: 3
Game Only: $3–7
Complete: $10–15*
Notes: Some 7800 versions are incorrectly labeled as 2600 versions

TOUCHDOWN FOOTBALL
Manufacturer: Atari
Label: Color
Rarity: 2
Game Only: $3–5
Complete: $5–7

TOWER TOPPLER
Manufacturer: Atari
Label: Color
Rarity: 1
Game Only: $1–3
Complete: $4–6

WATER SKI
Manufacturer: Froggo
Label: White
Rarity: 6
Game Only: $15–18
Complete: $20–30

WINTER GAMES
Manufacturer: Atari
Label: Color
Rarity: 1
Game Only: $1–2
Complete: $3–5

XENOPHOBE
Manufacturer: Atari
Label: Color
Rarity: 3
Game Only: $8–10
Complete: $11–20

XEVIOUS
Manufacturer: Atari
Label: Gray
Rarity: 1
Game Only: $1–2
Complete: $3–5

6 ColecoVision

For most of the golden age of home video games, two companies, Atari and Mattel, vied for dominance. Although there were many challengers along the way (see Chapter 9 for details), no console seemed able to make any headway against Atari 2600 and Intellivision. None, that is, until one of the earliest players in the video game industry introduced a console that made everyone sit up and take notice.

ColecoVision History

Coleco first tested the waters of the video game marketplace in 1976 when they introduced Telstar, one of the earliest home *Pong* consoles. The company enjoyed a great deal of success in the fledgling market, and released a number of different Telstar-dedicated consoles through the late 1970s.

When the home video game market started shifting from dedicated consoles to cartridge-based programmable systems, Coleco released the Telstar Arcade, a triangular game console that featured different controllers on each side and interchangeable game cartridges that provided a variety of shooting and driving games as well as the obligatory *Pong*-clone games. This console, which debuted in 1977, was short-lived, and proved to be one of the last consoles in Coleco's Telstar line. (For more information on the Telstar Arcade, see Chapter 9.) For the remainder of the late '70s and early '80s, Coleco abandoned the game console business and concentrated on handheld and tabletop electronic games. (For more information on Coleco's handheld and tabletop games, see Chapter 10.)

When Coleco finally reentered the video game market in 1982, they did so in a big way. The ColecoVision was easily superior to any video game console available at the time. Atari's biggest selling point for the aging 2600 was the availability of home versions of hit arcade games. This was indeed the case, but the Atari versions of these games sometimes bore only passing resemblance to their arcade counterparts. ColecoVision games actually looked and sounded like the real thing.

Atari had sewn up most of the home console rights to the big arcade hits of the time, but Coleco managed the small coup of grabbing the console rights to *Donkey Kong*, which they packaged with the ColecoVision console. Many of the other arcade titles in the early ColecoVision lineup were lesser-known arcade games like *Pepper II*, *Time Pilot*, and *Mr. Do!*, but the translations of these games to the console were masterfully done.

In addition to the *Donkey Kong* cartridge, ColecoVision shipped with two controllers equipped with joysticks and a full numeric keypad. Many games made use of the keypad for additional game controls. Rounding out the console's list of features was an expansion slot on the front that accommodated a variety of add-on components, including a driving controller and an adaptor that allowed the ColecoVision to play Atari 2600 games.

The ColecoVision's expansion slot also provided an interface to ADAM, an expansion that turned the ColecoVision into a full-featured home computer. ADAM was also available separately as a self-contained computer system. The ADAM computer, which had at first seemed very promising, was plagued with problems after its release and disappeared along with the ColecoVision in 1985.

Despite its relatively short run in the video game market, ColecoVision left an indelible mark on the industry. The games for the system still look good and play well even by today's standards. This makes the ColecoVision popular among classic console collectors.

ColecoVision Collecting

Just as it was the third most popular console during the classic era, ColecoVision is arguably the third most collected console today.

From a collector's standpoint, there are a number of advantages to collecting for ColecoVision. There was really only one version of the ColecoVision console (not counting ADAM and the one ColecoVision clone that was released after the original console was discontinued), as opposed to the numerous console variations for the Atari 2600. The peripherals—controllers, add-ons, and so on—produced for the system are relatively limited in number and are still easy to come by for the most part. The game library isn't huge, and many of the games are easy to find and relatively inexpensive.

Telegames (http://www.telegames.com) is a good source for ColecoVision cartridges. Before you buy any cartridge used, check Telegames first. They stock many brand new copies of common and semicommon ColecoVision games at fairly competitive prices.

ColecoVision Consoles

Unlike some classic video game consoles, ColecoVision had few hardware variations. Coleco stuck to the same design throughout the life of the console, the only variant being the ADAM computer itself (which has a slot that accepts ColecoVision game cartridges). A number of ColecoVision clones were released overseas, but only one was released in the United States.

ColecoVision

The **basic ColecoVision game console** is a bit larger and less sleek than the Atari 2600. It features two very functional joystick controllers, which are housed in slots on the top of the console when not in use. The console connects to the television via a standard antenna/game switchbox of the type that is readily available in electronics stores today.

a **The basic ColecoVision console**
*shipped with two controllers and
the Donkey Kong game cartridge.
(Photo courtesy of Cassidy Nolen.)*

b **ADAM computer.** *The ill-fated
ADAM never found a niche in the
home computer market due to its
unreliability. On the other hand,
it worked fairly well as a
ColecoVision console.*

The only drawback to the ColecoVision from a collector's standpoint is its bulky, proprietary power supply. The huge transformer takes up the lion's share of any power strip, and due to its unique connector at the console end, it cannot be replaced by a modern generic AC power supply. Luckily, replacement original power supplies are fairly easy to find.

One interesting thing to note about the power supply is that, when defective, it can cause the game graphics to behave strangely. I went through several apparently defective ColecoVision consoles before realizing that the consoles themselves were fine but the power supply I was using was malfunctioning.

ColecoVision's controllers are detachable, so they are easy to replace when they malfunction. Replacement controllers are fairly common. Although they don't coordinate color-wise with the console, the white controllers designed for the ADAM computer can be used as replacement ColecoVision controllers as well.

ADAM

ADAM is a home computer, and as such, doesn't really belong in this book. However, since the ADAM was capable of playing ColecoVision cartridges, it can technically be considered a console variation in the ColecoVision line.

When it was first announced, the ADAM sounded like an excellent home computer system. It included everything a user would need in one huge package: a computer with a built-in tape drive for saving and loading programs; three built-in applications (a word processor, spreadsheet, and database); and a printer. On top of all of that, it included two ColecoVision-style controllers, and was fully compatible with all ColecoVision game cartridges. In fact, there was even a version of ADAM that could plug into an existing ColecoVision console and turn the console into a full-featured home computer.

Unfortunately, ADAM never lived up to expectations. The system was prone to hardware failures and wasn't very reliable. There was an initial surge of sales when ADAM was released, but most of the units were returned defective. Coleco had been counting on the ADAM to transition their home electronics business into the burgeoning home computer market. Instead, the computer drove the company to the brink of financial ruin.

The ADAM computer is an interesting conversation piece in any classic electronics collection, but it isn't overly collectible in and of itself. Boxed, complete ADAM systems generally sell for little more than complete ColecoVision systems. From a playability standpoint, the more reliable (and much smaller) ColecoVision console is a much better way to enjoy your ColecoVision games.

Telegames Personal Arcade (DINA 2-in-1)

In 1988, Telegames introduced a console that was compatible with both the ColecoVision and with the Sega SG-1000 (a game system that was never sold in the United States). This console is compatible with nearly all ColecoVision games. The only exceptions to this rule are those games requiring special controllers (the Super Action controllers, Roller Controller, or Driving Controller).

The two controllers included with the system are joypads with two buttons each, very similar to the gamepads used on the original Nintendo Entertainment System. The gamepads don't include numeric keypads (which are necessary for ColecoVision games), but there is a keypad built into the front of the console itself. There is one game (*Meteoric Shower*) built into the console.

Two versions of this console exist: the Telegames Personal Arcade and the DINA 2-in-1. The only difference between the two is the name on the box and on the console. The Telegames version is more common than the DINA version and is usually a bit less expensive.

Telegames still manufactures a version of this console, which is now known simply as the DINA System. This new system is virtually identical to the systems released in 1988, and still ships with the same controllers and built-in game. It is currently available for $150 directly from Telegames (http://www.telegames.com).

ColecoVision Cartridges

Because ColecoVision was introduced shortly before the video game crash, the console's life cycle was fairly short. The game library for this system totals fewer than 200 cartridges including homebrew games, prototypes, and reproductions. Even so, amassing a complete ColecoVision cartridge collection is challenging since some of the games are fairly rare.

A factor that further adds to the challenge of collecting for this system is that the demand for **ColecoVision cartridges** remains fairly high. The quality of most ColecoVision games is quite

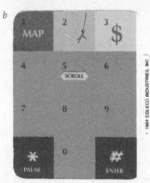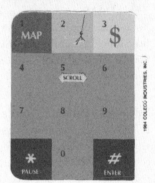

a **ColecoVision cartridges.** *The primary label variation is evidenced in the ColecoVision label (left) versus the ADAM label (right). This variation generally has little effect on the game's value.*

b **ColecoVision keypad overlays.** *A number of ColecoVision games utilized the numeric keypad on the controller for in-game functions and commands. These games were shipped with overlays that illustrated the keypad functions.*

high, and the games remain enjoyable even today. This contributes to the scarcity of some ColecoVision titles.

Label Variations

Label variation plays a fairly small role in ColecoVision cartridge value. Most games were released with standard Coleco labels: black labels with the game title and ColecoVision logos on the face and on the spine. After the release of the ADAM, many cartridges were relabeled to indicate their compatibility with the computer. These labels note that the cartridge is "for Coleco-Vision & ADAM Family Computer System." For the most part, there is no difference in value between cartridges with the standard and the "ADAM" label variants.

Overlays

ColecoVision's controllers have built-in keypads that allow players to select pregame options and to reset the game. This is the only function the keypad serves in most games, but in some cases, ColecoVision games took advantage of the keypad for in-game controls. Games that used the **controller keypads** in this manner were packaged with overlays that show the function of each button.

Some of the ColecoVision games packaged with overlays include:

- *2010: The Action Game*

- *Cabbage Patch Kids: Picture Show*

- *Dam Busters*

- *Dr. Seuss' Fix-Up the Mix-Up Puzzler*

- *Facemaker*

- *Fortune Builder*

- *Front Line*

- *Ken Uston's Blackjack/Poker*

- *Mouse Trap*

- *Rocky Super Action Boxing*

- *Smurf: Paint 'N Play Workshop*

- *Spy Hunter*

- *Star Trek: Strategic Operations Simulator*

- *Super Action Baseball*

- *Super Action Football*

- *Super Action Soccer*

- *War Games*

- *War Room*

Some of these games were packaged with overlays for both the standard ColecoVision controllers and for Coleco's Super Action controllers.

While these games are playable without the overlay (assuming you can memorize the functions of each button on the keypad), most are much easier to play if you have the overlay. When purchasing a cartridge that uses overlays, try to find one that includes the overlays. You can expect to pay a bit more if the overlays are included, but chances are that the added enjoyment you get out of the game as a result of not having to guess what the keypad controls do is worth the extra money.

If you cannot find a copy of the game with the overlays included, you might be able to find reproduction overlays on the Internet. Many collectors have scanned their ColecoVision overlays and made them available for download from their web sites. A copied overlay doesn't add to the value of the game, but it does make it a lot more enjoyable to play.

Note that games that originally shipped with controller overlays are not considered "complete" from a collecting standpoint unless the overlays are present.

Games Requiring Special Controllers

Nearly all ColecoVision games are playable with the standard controllers included with the console. However, a number of games were specifically designed to function only with specialized controllers that were available separately.

The Super Action Controllers are add-on joysticks that plug into the standard controller ports. These well-designed pistol-grip controllers feature numeric keypads and joysticks on top, and four action buttons on the grip. While most standard ColecoVision games work well with the Super Action Controllers, four games are specifically designed for them and do not function with the standard controllers:

- *Rocky Super Action Boxing*
- *Super Action Baseball*
- *Super Action Football*
- *Super Action Soccer*

Coleco's Roller Controller is a trackball that was designed to enhance gameplay on some cartridges. A handful of ColecoVision titles are compatible with the Roller Controller, but there are only two games that cannot be played without it:

- *Slither* (originally packaged with the Roller Controller)
- *Victory*

Expansion Module #2, **the Driving Controller**, provides a unique driving interface for the ColecoVision, complete with a gas pedal and steering wheel. The Driving Controller *only* works with the games that were designed specifically for it:

- *Destructor*
- *Dukes of Hazzard*
- *Turbo* (originally packaged with the Driving Controller)

Like the other games designed exclusively for specialized controllers, you cannot play the three driving games without the Driving Controller.

Homebrews, Reproductions, and Prototypes

Present-day hobbyists have been inspired to produce more new, original games for the ColecoVision than for any other classic game system with the exception of the Atari 2600. Like the homebrew games for other consoles, these cartridges often debut at classic game conventions and are produced in limited numbers. This makes some of the homebrew games rather difficult to find. Other games are available from their creators' web sites for download as ROM images or, occasionally, for sale in cartridge form.

Like the Atari 2600, companies producing cartridges for the ColecoVision planned and developed more titles than were actually released commercially. A number of previously unreleased titles have been reproduced in limited quantities and sold over the past several years. For exam-

a

b

c

a **The Super Action Controllers** were designed for use with Coleco's Super Action line of games, but work well with most ColecoVision titles. (Photo courtesy of Cassidy Nolen.)

b **Coleco's Roller Controller** is required in order to play the games Slither and Victory. (Photo courtesy of Cassidy Nolen.)

c **ColecoVision Driving Controller.** Several games were designed to function exclusively with the Driving Controller (ColecoVision Expansion Module #2). (Photo courtesy of Cassidy Nolen.)

ple, CGE Services reproduced several Atarisoft prototype titles including *Pac-Man*, *Joust*, and *Dig Dug* and released them at the 2001 Classic Gaming Expo in Las Vegas.

There are not as many prototype cartridges for ColecoVision floating around as there are for the Atari 2600, but some do exist. As is true when buying prototype cartridges for any system, insist on some form of authentication from the seller before paying high prototype prices. True prototypes are extremely rare.

ColecoVision Boxes

One of the oddities about collecting for the ColecoVision is that the boxes for the games seem to be in far shorter supply than the cartridges themselves. While loose cartridges are more common than boxed games for *any* classic console system, it appears that ColecoVision owners were particularly fond of discarding their game boxes.

This trend is so prevalent, that many of the rarer games' boxes are often worth as much as the cartridges themselves. In some cases, you can expect a bigger discrepancy between loose and complete game prices for most ColecoVision games than for cartridges for other classic consoles.

ColecoVision Holy Grail Cartridges

The majority of cartridges in the ColecoVision library are fairly easy to find. As is true with most classic game systems, certain games were very popular and were produced in huge quantities. These games typically sell for only a few dollars loose. Other cartridges were produced in smaller numbers and are extremely difficult to find. Among these are several that could be considered Holy Grail cartridges by ColecoVision collectors.

It should be noted that, despite the popularity of the ColecoVision among collectors, few ColecoVision cartridges command the stratospheric prices of some of their Atari 2600 counterparts. Even the rarest loose ColecoVision cartridges seldom sell for more than $100 or so.

Motocross Racer/Tomarc the Barbarian (Xonox)

Xonox produced a number of games for both the ColecoVision and the Atari 2600. They are probably best known for their double-ended cartridges, which included two games in a single, double-long cartridge case.

While most of the Xonox games for ColecoVision are somewhat difficult to find, the *Motocross Racer/Tomarc the Barbarian* double cartridge is easily the rarest of the lot. The NTSC version of the game is particularly hard to find, since it was never released in the United States. The game was only released in NTSC form in Canada.

Q*Bert's Qubes (Parker Brothers)

Parker Brothers released *Q*Bert's Qubes* for both the Atari 2600 and the ColecoVision, but apparently not many of either version made it into the stores—it is a rare cartridge for both systems.

Although not as rare as some of the Xonox titles, *Q*Bert's Qubes* is extremely difficult to find. You can expect to pay $50 or more for a loose copy in good condition—if you're lucky enough to come across one.

Super Sketch (Personal Peripheral)

Super Sketch is actually more than a cartridge—it's a complete electronic drawing system for the ColecoVision. It consists of a drawing tablet with an attached stylus that plugs into the cartridge port. Using the tablet and stylus, you can draw pictures on the screen.

a **Fortune Builder,** *while not particularly rare, is a particularly fascinating and deep strategy game that plays very much like the original* Sim City, *a popular computer strategy game that was released about five years later.*

Since it's not a game, some collectors might not be particularly interested in *Super Sketch*. However, it is an interesting and unique addition to any collection. You can expect to pay over $100 for a complete package.

Fortune Builder (Coleco)

Although it isn't exactly rare, **Fortune Builder** bears mentioning because it is rather unique. It is a strategy/economics simulation game—a very uncommon game type for modern-day consoles much less for video game systems in the classic era.

The object of this game is to build a functioning city and control its growth and economy. Fans of computer strategy games will find *Fortune Builder* to be very similar in gameplay to *Sim City*, the popular city management simulation released by Maxis in 1989. What's fascinating is that *Fortune Builder* predates *Sim City* by five years. Even more amazing is that *Fortune Builder* runs on a game console with only 8 kilobytes of memory. *Sim City* required a personal computer with 64 times as much memory.

Fortune Builder was sold in a plastic clamshell-style box rather than the normal cardboard boxes used for most ColecoVision cartridges. Perhaps more than any other game in the ColecoVision library this game requires the accompanying documentation and controller overlays. Without them, it's next to impossible to figure out what you're supposed to be doing.

ColecoVision Price Guides
ColecoVision Hardware Price

CONSOLES

COLECO ADAM COMPUTER
Manufacturer: Coleco
Rarity: 4
Loose: $40–50
Boxed/Complete: $50–120
Notes: Coleco's stand-alone computer system; packaged with 2 controllers, a keyboard, and a printer; plays ColecoVision cartridges and ADAM games on cassette

COLECOVISION CONSOLE
Manufacturer: Coleco
Rarity: 2
Loose: $25–35
Boxed/Complete: $60–100
Notes: Originally packaged with 2 controllers and *Donkey Kong;* factory sealed new units can fetch $400 or more

DINA SYSTEM
Manufacturer: Telegames
Rarity: 1
Loose: N/A
Boxed/Complete: $$150
Notes: A ColecoVision-compatible system (current version of the Telegames Personal Arcade); currently available from Telegames (http://www.telegames.com)

TELEGAMES PERSONAL ARCADE
Manufacturer: Telegames/BIT Corp
Rarity: 6
Loose: $30–40
Boxed/Complete: $70–100
Notes: ColecoVision-compatible system, also known as "Dina 2-in-1"; also compatible with Sega SG-1000 game cartridges; Dina 2-in-1 version is much rarer

DUST COVER
Manufacturer: Coleco
Rarity: 6
Loose: $10–15
Boxed/Complete: $20–25*
Notes: Vinyl dust cover for the ColecoVision console; emblazoned with the ColecoVision logo

EXPANSION MODULE 1: ATARI 2600 CONVERTER
Manufacturer: Coleco
Rarity: 3
Loose: $10–20
Boxed/Complete: $25–35
Notes: Allows Atari 2600 games to be played on the ColecoVision

EXPANSION MODULE 2: DRIVING CONTROLLER
Manufacturer: Coleco
Rarity: 3
Loose: $15–20
Boxed/Complete: $40–50
Notes: Originally packaged with *Turbo;* includes steering wheel and gas pedal

EXPANSION MODULE 3: ADAM
Manufacturer: Coleco
Rarity: 8
Loose: $40–50
Boxed/Complete: $55–65*
Notes: Add-on that turns the ColecoVision console into an ADAM computer

JOYSTICK, COLECOVISION
Manufacturer: Coleco
Rarity: 3
Loose: $5–12
Boxed/Complete: $15–20*
Notes: The standard ColecoVision controller

JOYSTICK, COLECOVISION ADAM
Manufacturer: Coleco
Rarity: 3
Loose: $5–12
Boxed/Complete: $15–20*
Notes: The standard controller for the Coleco ADAM computer; identical to the standard ColecoVision controller, only white instead of black

JOYSTICK, SUPER ACTION CONTROLLERS (PAIR)
Manufacturer: Coleco
Rarity: 5
Loose: $20–30
Boxed/Complete: $35–45

JOYSTICK, WICO COMMAND CONTROL
Manufacturer: Wico
Rarity: 6
Loose: $10–15
Boxed/Complete: $20–30*
Notes: Third-party joystick with a built-in keypad

MODEM, ADAMLINK
Manufacturer: Coleco
Rarity: 6
Loose: $5–10
Boxed/Complete: $10–20
Notes: 300 baud modem for the ADAM computer

POWER SUPPLY
Manufacturer: Coleco
Rarity: 2
Loose: $8–12
Boxed/Complete: $15–20
Notes: Dedicated ColecoVision power supply; after-market units were sold in a white box

ROLLER CONTROLLER
Manufacturer: Coleco
Rarity: 3
Loose: $10–15
Boxed/Complete: $21–35
Notes: The ColecoVision's trackball controller; originally packaged with the game *Slither*

ColecoVision Cartridge Price Guide

421
Manufacturer: Self-Published
Rarity: Homebrew
Game Only: N/A
Complete: $20–30

2010: THE ACTION GAME
Manufacturer: Coleco
Rarity: 6
Game Only: $10–15
Complete: $12–20
Notes: Must include controller overlays to be considered complete

THE ACTIVISION DECATHLON
Manufacturer: Activision
Rarity: 4
Game Only: $7–10
Complete: $12–15*

ALCAZAR: THE FORGOTTEN FORTRESS
Manufacturer: Telegames
Rarity: 8
Game Only: $25–30
Complete: $35–45*

ALPHABET ZOO
Manufacturer: Spinnaker
Rarity: 7
Game Only: $6–12
Complete: $14–17

AMAZING BUMPMAN
Manufacturer: Telegames
Rarity: 8
Game Only: $15–20
Complete: $25–35*

AMAZING SNAKE
Manufacturer: Self-Published
Rarity: Homebrew
Game Only: N/A
Complete: $20–30

ANTARCTIC ADVENTURE
Manufacturer: Coleco
Rarity: 6
Game Only: $8–12
Complete: $15–20

ACCESSORIES

SUPER SKETCH
Manufacturer: Personal Peripheral
Rarity: 10
Loose: N/A
Boxed/Complete: $125–160
Notes: A tablet controller with a cartridge input and plastic stylus that allows you to create on-screen computer art with the ColecoVision; very rare

AQUATTACK
Manufacturer: Interphase
Rarity: 8
Game Only: $35–45
Complete: $50–60*

ARTILLERY DUEL
Manufacturer: Xonox
Rarity: 7
Game Only: $12–20
Complete: $25–35*

ARTILLERY DUEL/CHUCK NORRIS
Manufacturer: Xonox
Rarity: 9
Game Only: $40–60
Complete: $70–90*
Notes: Combo cartridge released only in Canada and Europe

B.C. II: GROG'S REVENGE
Manufacturer: Coleco
Rarity: 4
Game Only: $5–10
Complete: $15–25

B.C.'S QUEST FOR TIRES
Manufacturer: Sierra
Rarity: 3
Game Only: $8–10
Complete: $9–15
Notes: Applies to both the picture and white label versions

BEAMRIDER
Manufacturer: Activision
Rarity: 4
Game Only: $6–8
Complete: $10–16

BEJEWELED
Manufacturer: Self-Published
Rarity: Homebrew
Game Only: N/A
Complete: $20–30
Notes: Based on the PC game by the same title

BLOCKADE RUNNER
Manufacturer: Interphase
Rarity: 6
Game Only: $18–22
Complete: $25–35*

BOULDER DASH
Manufacturer: Telegames
Rarity: 8
Game Only: $25–30
Complete: $35–45*

BRAIN STRAINERS
Manufacturer: Coleco
Rarity: 5
Game Only: $6–12
Complete: $15–20*

BUCK ROGERS: PLANET OF ZOOM
Manufacturer: Coleco
Rarity: 2
Game Only: $5–8
Complete: $10–15

BUMP 'N JUMP
Manufacturer: Coleco
Rarity: 4
Game Only: $10–15
Complete: $20–25*

BURGERTIME
Manufacturer: Coleco
Rarity: 3
Game Only: $6–10
Complete: $12–17

BUSTIN OUT VOL. I
Manufacturer: Self-Published
Rarity: Homebrew
Game Only: N/A
Complete: $20–30

BUSTIN OUT VOL. II
Manufacturer: Self-Published
Rarity: Homebrew
Game Only: N/A
Complete: $20–30

CABBAGE PATCH KIDS: ADVENTURES IN THE PARK
Manufacturer: Coleco
Rarity: 3
Game Only: $4–8
Complete: $12–17

CABBAGE PATCH KIDS: PICTURE SHOW
Manufacturer: Coleco
Rarity: 5
Game Only: $12–20
Complete: $25–30

CAMPAIGN '84
Manufacturer: Sunrise
Rarity: 7
Game Only: $20–30
Complete: $35–40

CARNIVAL
Manufacturer: Coleco
Rarity: 1
Game Only: $1–3
Complete: $3–7

CVDRUM
Manufacturer: E-Mancanics
Rarity: Homebrew
Game Only: N/A
Complete: $25
Notes: Cartridge that turns your ColecoVision into a drum synthesizer; avaialable at AtariAge (http://www.atariage.com)

CENTIPEDE
Manufacturer: Atarisoft
Rarity: 3
Game Only: $2–5
Complete: $6–10

CHOPLIFTER!
Manufacturer: Coleco
Rarity: 6
Game Only: $10–15
Complete: $40–60

CHUCK NORRIS SUPERKICKS
Manufacturer: Xonox
Rarity: 6
Game Only: $10–20
Complete: $25–35*
Notes: Later re-released as *Kung Fu Superkicks*

COLECOVISION CREATIONS
Manufacturer: Self-Published
Rarity: Homebrew
Game Only: N/A
Complete: $20–30

COLECOVISION MULTICART SET
Manufacturer: Self-Published
Rarity: Homebrew
Game Only: N/A
Complete: $140
Notes: 155 ColecoVision games on 7 cartridges; games selectable via DIP switches; available at Atari2600.com (http://www.atari200.com)

CONGO BONGO
Manufacturer: Coleco
Rarity: 5
Game Only: $14–16
Complete: $18–20

COSMIC AVENGER
Manufacturer: Coleco
Rarity: 1
Game Only: $1–3
Complete: $8–10

COSMIC CRISIS
Manufacturer: Telegames
Rarity: 2
Game Only: $10–15
Complete: $20–25*
Notes: Although the NTSC version is very rare, the PAL version is still sold online by Telegames (http://www.telegames.co.uk)

COSMO FIGHTER 3

Manufacturer: Good Deal Games
Rarity: Homebrew
Game Only: N/A
Complete: $20–30

DAC-MAN V1.0

Manufacturer: Self-Published
Rarity: Homebrew
Game Only: N/A
Complete: $20–30
Notes: Released at the 2000 Classic Gaming Expo; it is likely that fewer than 20 exist

DAC-MAN V1.3

Manufacturer: Self-Published
Rarity: Homebrew
Game Only: N/A
Complete: $20–30

DAM BUSTERS

Manufacturer: Coleco
Rarity: 5
Game Only: $15–20
Complete: $25–28
Notes: Must include controller overlays to be considered complete

DANCE FANTASY

Manufacturer: Fisher Price
Rarity: 7
Game Only: $15–20
Complete: $25–35*

DEFENDER

Manufacturer: Atarisoft
Rarity: 3
Game Only: $2–6
Complete: $5–10

DESTRUCTOR

Manufacturer: Coleco
Rarity: 4
Game Only: $2–7
Complete: $12–15
Notes: Requires Driving Controller

DIG DUG

Manufacturer: CGE Services
Rarity: Reproduction
Game Only: $20–35*
Complete: N/A
Notes: Based on the Atarisoft prototype; released commercially at the 2001 Classic Gaming Expo

DONKEY KONG

Manufacturer: Coleco
Rarity: 1
Game Only: $1–2
Complete: $15–20
Notes: Cartridge is very common (packaged with the console); box is very rare, and worth more than the cartridge itself

DONKEY KONG JUNIOR

Manufacturer: Coleco
Rarity: 2
Game Only: $3–6
Complete: $8–10*

DR. SEUSS' FIX-UP THE MIX-UP PUZZLER

Manufacturer: Coleco
Rarity: 5
Game Only: $15–18
Complete: $15–25

DRAGONFIRE

Manufacturer: Imagic
Rarity: 6
Game Only: $12–15
Complete: $20–25*

DUKES OF HAZZARD

Manufacturer: Coleco
Rarity: 5
Game Only: $12–15
Complete: $20–30
Notes: Requires Driving Controller

EVOLUTION

Manufacturer: Sydney
Rarity: 5
Game Only: $9–20
Complete: $20–25

FACEMAKER

Manufacturer: Spinnaker
Rarity: 6
Game Only: $8–12
Complete: $10–20
Notes: Also known as *Make-a-Face;* must include controller overlays to be considered complete

FALL GUY

Manufacturer: Coleco
Rarity: Prototype
Game Only: $15
Complete: N/A

FATHOM

Manufacturer: Imagic
Rarity: 6
Game Only: $10–15
Complete: $20–25
Notes: New copies are generally available from Telegames (http://www.telegames.com)

FINAL TEST CARTRIDGE

Manufacturer: Coleco
Rarity: 10
Game Only: $75–100*
Complete: N/A
Notes: A cartridge used for testing ColecoVision and controller functions

FINAL TEST CARTRIDGE

Manufacturer: Self-Published
Rarity: Reproduction
Game Only: $20
Complete: N/A
Notes: Reproduction of the original Coleco cartridge

FLIPPER SLIPPER

Manufacturer: Spectravision
Rarity: 3
Game Only: $8–10
Complete: $15–20
Notes: New copies are generally available from Telegames (http://www.telegames.com)

FORTUNE BUILDER

Manufacturer: Coleco
Rarity: 5
Game Only: $5–15
Complete: $20–30
Notes: Must include controller overlays to be considered complete; new copies are generally available from Telegames (http://www.telegames.com)

FRACTION FEVER

Manufacturer: Spinnaker
Rarity: 5
Game Only: $7–12
Complete: $15–25
Notes: New copies are generally available from Telegames (http://www.telegames.com)

FRANTIC FREDDY

Manufacturer: Spectravision
Rarity: 6
Game Only: $10–15
Complete: $20–25*

FRENZY

Manufacturer: Coleco
Rarity: 3
Game Only: $5–12
Complete: $14–25
Notes: New copies are generally available from Telegames (http://www.telegames.com)

FROGGER

Manufacturer: Parker Brothers
Rarity: 2
Game Only: $3–7
Complete: $10–15

FROGGER II: THREEEDEEP

Manufacturer: Parker Brothers
Rarity: 6
Game Only: $10–20
Complete: $25–50
Notes: New copies are generally available from Telegames (http://www.telegames.com)

FRONT LINE

Manufacturer: Coleco
Rarity: 3
Game Only: $2–8
Complete: $10–12
Notes: Must include controller overlays to be considered complete

GALAXIAN

Manufacturer: Atarisoft
Rarity: 6
Game Only: $10–15
Complete: $20–25*

GATEWAY TO APSHAI

Manufacturer: Epyx
Rarity: 5
Game Only: $8–12
Complete: $20–30

GORF

Manufacturer: Coleco
Rarity: 3
Game Only: $3–8
Complete: $10–12

GUST BUSTER

Manufacturer: Sunrise
Rarity: 7
Game Only: $14–20
Complete: $30–40

GYRUSS

Manufacturer: Parker Brothers
Rarity: 5
Game Only: $4–10
Complete: $18–20

H.E.R.O.

Manufacturer: Activision
Rarity: 5
Game Only: $6–11
Complete: $15–20

THE HEIST

Manufacturer: Micro Fun
Rarity: 4
Game Only: $3–6
Complete: $10–15*

ILLUSIONS

Manufacturer: Coleco
Rarity: 6
Game Only: $7–15
Complete: $20–30

IT'S ONLY ROCK 'N ROLL

Manufacturer: Xonox
Rarity: 8
Game Only: $20–30
Complete: $30–40
Notes: New copies are generally available from Telegames (http://www.telegames.com)

JAMES BOND 007

Manufacturer: Parker Brothers
Rarity: 6
Game Only: $10–15
Complete: $18–25*

JOUST

Manufacturer: CGE Services
Rarity: Reproduction
Game Only: $20–35*
Complete: N/A
Notes: Based on the Atarisoft prototype; released commercially at the 2001 Classic Gaming Expo

JUKEBOX

Manufacturer: Spinnaker
Rarity: 7
Game Only: $15–20
Complete: $30–40

JUMPMAN JR.

Manufacturer: Epyx
Rarity: 5
Game Only: $8–10
Complete: $12–15

JUNGLE HUNT

Manufacturer: Atarisoft
Rarity: 6
Game Only: $20–30
Complete: $30–55
Notes: New copies are generally available from Telegames (http://www.telegames.com)

KEN USTON'S BLACKJACK/POKER

Manufacturer: Coleco
Rarity: 3
Game Only: $1–4
Complete: $8–12
Notes: Must include controller overlays to be considered complete

KEVTRIS

Manufacturer: Self-Published
Rarity: Homebrew
Game Only: N/A
Complete: $50–75
Notes: Based on the game *Tetris;* only 100 were produced; very collectable

KEYSTONE KAPERS

Manufacturer: Activision
Rarity: 5
Game Only: $5–10
Complete: $15–20

KUNG FU SUPERKICKS

Manufacturer: Telegames
Rarity: 7
Game Only: $15–20
Complete: $25–30

LADY BUG

Manufacturer: Coleco
Rarity: 2
Game Only: $3–5
Complete: $7–10

LEARNING WITH LEEPER

Manufacturer: Sierra
Rarity: 6
Game Only: $15–18
Complete: $20–30*

LINKING LOGIC

Manufacturer: Fisher Price
Rarity: 7
Game Only: $17–20
Complete: $25–35*

LOGIC LEVELS

Manufacturer: Fisher Price
Rarity: 7
Game Only: $17–20
Complete: $25–35

LOOPING

Manufacturer: Coleco
Rarity: 2
Game Only: $2–4
Complete: $7–10

LORD OF THE DUNGEON

Manufacturer: NAP
Rarity: Reproduction
Game Only: $40–60
Complete: N/A
Notes: Commercial release of the Coleco prototype *Creatures & Caverns;* released at the 2000 Classic Gaming Expo; only 70 were produced

MAKE-A-FACE

Manufacturer: Spinnaker
Rarity: 7
Game Only: $30–40
Complete: $40–50*
Notes: Also known as *Facemaker;* must include controller overlays to be considered complete

MEMORY MANOR

Manufacturer: Spinnaker
Rarity: 6
Game Only: $10–15
Complete: $15–25*

MINER 2049'ER

Manufacturer: Micro Fun
Rarity: 3
Game Only: $3–12
Complete: $25–30

MONKEY ACADEMY

Manufacturer: Coleco
Rarity: 5
Game Only: $12–15
Complete: $14–25

MONTEZUMA'S REVENGE

Manufacturer: Parker Brothers
Rarity: 6
Game Only: $10–20
Complete: $30–40

MOONSWEEPER

Manufacturer: Imagic
Rarity: 5
Game Only: $8–12
Complete: $18–25

MOTOCROSS RACER

Manufacturer: Telegames
Rarity: 1
Game Only: N/A
Complete: $20
Notes: New copies are generally available from Telegames (http://www.telegames.com)

MOTOCROSS RACER

Manufacturer: Xonox
Rarity: 7
Game Only: $25–30
Complete: $35–45*

MOTOCROSS RACER/ TOMARC THE BARBARIAN

Manufacturer: Xonox
Rarity: 10
Game Only: $90–120
Complete: $140–180*
Notes: Combo cartridge released in only in Canada and Europe; one of the rarest ColecoVision titles

155

MOUNTAIN KING
Manufacturer: Sunrise
Rarity: 6
Game Only: $25–30
Complete: $40–50

MOUSE TRAP
Manufacturer: Coleco
Rarity: 1
Game Only: $2–5
Complete: $8–10
Notes: Must include controller overlays to be considered complete

MR. DO!
Manufacturer: Coleco
Rarity: 2
Game Only: $2–7
Complete: $10–15

MR. DO!'S CASTLE
Manufacturer: Parker Brothers
Rarity: 7
Game Only: $25–35
Complete: $45–55
Notes: The European (PAL) version is currently available from Telegames (http://www.telegame.co.uk) for about $15 (complete in box)

MS. SPACE FURY
Manufacturer: Digital Press
Rarity: Homebrew
Game Only: N/A
Complete: $40–50
Notes: Released at the 2001 Classic Gaming Expo; only 75 copies were produced; manual, but no box

MUSIC BOX DEMO
Manufacturer: Coleco
Rarity: 10
Game Only: $25–35
Complete: N/A
Notes: Point of sale demo cartridge that plays music from various ColecoVision games

NOVA BLAST
Manufacturer: Imagic
Rarity: 4
Game Only: $4–12
Complete: $15–20

OIL'S WELL
Manufacturer: Sierra
Rarity: 6
Game Only: $20–25
Complete: $30–35*

OMEGA RACE
Manufacturer: Coleco
Rarity: 3
Game Only: $2–8
Complete: $9–12

ONE ON ONE BASKETBALL
Manufacturer: Micro Fun
Rarity: 7
Game Only: $15–20
Complete: $22–25

PAC-MAN
Manufacturer: CGE Services
Rarity: Reproduction
Game Only: $25–35*
Complete: N/A
Notes: Based on the Atarisoft prototype; released commercially at the 2001 Classic Gaming Expo

PEPPER II
Manufacturer: Coleco
Rarity: 1
Game Only: $1–3
Complete: $8–10

PITFALL II: LOST CAVERNS
Manufacturer: Activision
Rarity: 5
Game Only: $5–10
Complete: $15–25
Notes: New copies are generally available from Telegames (http://www.telegames.com)

PITFALL!
Manufacturer: Activision
Rarity: 3
Game Only: $5–7
Complete: $15–20

PITSTOP
Manufacturer: Epyx
Rarity: 5
Game Only: $4–7
Complete: $10–15

POPEYE
Manufacturer: Parker Brothers
Rarity: 3
Game Only: $3–5
Complete: $8–10

POWER LORDS
Manufacturer: Probe 2000
Rarity: Reproduction
Game Only: $25–40
Complete: N/A
Notes: Released at the 2000 Classic Gaming Expo; enhanced version of the Magnavox Odyssey^2 game by the same name

PURPLE DINOSAUR MASSACRE DEMO
Manufacturer: Classic Game Creations
Rarity: Homebrew
Game Only: N/A
Complete: $20
Notes: Currently available for download from the Classic Game Creations Web site (http://www.classicgamecreations.com); no box or manual

Q*BERT
Manufacturer: Parker Brothers
Rarity: 2
Game Only: $3–7
Complete: $10–15

Q*BERT'S QUBES
Manufacturer: Parker Brothers
Rarity: 9
Game Only: $30–60
Complete: $80–250

Q*BERT'S QUBES

Manufacturer: Self-Published
Rarity: Reproduction
Game Only: $20
Complete: N/A
Notes: Reproduction of the original Parker Brothers cartridge with a black-and-white label; available at Atari2600.com (http://www.atari2600.com)

QUEST FOR QUINTANA ROO

Manufacturer: Sunrise
Rarity: 6
Game Only: $18–36
Complete: $35–40

RIVER RAID

Manufacturer: Activision
Rarity: 4
Game Only: $5–7
Complete: $15–18

ROBIN HOOD

Manufacturer: Xonox
Rarity: 6
Game Only: $16–35
Complete: $40–60*

ROBIN HOOD/SIR LANCELOT

Manufacturer: Xonox
Rarity: 9
Game Only: $60–80
Complete: $100–150*
Notes: Combo cartridge released only in Canada and Europe; one of the rarest ColecoVision titles

ROCK 'N BOLT

Manufacturer: Telegames
Rarity: 2
Game Only: $10–12
Complete: $20–30
Notes: New copies are generally available from Telegames (http://www.telegames.com)

ROC 'N ROPE

Manufacturer: Coleco
Rarity: 4
Game Only: $6–8
Complete: $10–15

ROCKY SUPER ACTION BOXING

Manufacturer: Coleco
Rarity: 4
Game Only: $3–5
Complete: $8–10
Notes: Requires the Super Action Controller; must include controller overlays to be considered complete

ROLLOVERTURE

Manufacturer: Sunrise
Rarity: 4
Game Only: $15–20
Complete: $20–30
Notes: New copies are generally available from Telegames (http://www.telegames.com) at considerably less than the going auction rates

ROOT BEER TAPPER

Manufacturer: Coleco
Rarity: 5
Game Only: $12–16
Complete: $20–30
Notes: New copies are generally available from Telegames (http://www.telegames.com)

SAMMY LIGHTFOOT

Manufacturer: Sierra
Rarity: 8
Game Only: $20–30
Complete: $35–45*

SECTOR ALPHA

Manufacturer: Spectravision
Rarity: 8
Game Only: $50–60
Complete: $60–70*

SEWER SAM

Manufacturer: Interphase
Rarity: 7
Game Only: $18–25
Complete: $25–50
Notes: New copies are generally available from Telegames (http://www.telegames.com)

SIR LANCELOT

Manufacturer: Xonox
Rarity: 7
Game Only: $10–30
Complete: $40–50

SLITHER

Manufacturer: Coleco
Rarity: 2
Game Only: $2–5
Complete: $25–35
Notes: Originally packaged with the Coleco Roller Controller; requires the Roller Controller

SLURPY

Manufacturer: Xonox
Rarity: 8
Game Only: $20–30
Complete: $40–50
Notes: The European (PAL) version is currently available from Telegames (http://www.telegame.co.uk) for about $43 (complete in box)

SMURF: PAINT 'N PLAY WORKSHOP

Manufacturer: Coleco
Rarity: 5
Game Only: $3–5
Complete: $5–7
Notes: Typically sells for much less than its rarity would indicate; must include controller overlays to be considered complete

SMURF: RESCUE IN GARGAMEL'S CASTLE

Manufacturer: Coleco
Rarity: 1
Game Only: $3–4
Complete: $5–7

SPACE FURY

Manufacturer: Coleco
Rarity: 2
Game Only: $4–6
Complete: $8–12

SPACE INVADERS COLLECTION

Manufacturer: Opcode Games
Rarity: Homebrew
Game Only: N/A
Complete: $25
Notes: Includes faithful reproductions of *Space Invaders* and *Space Invaders Part II;* available at Opcode Games (http://www.opcodegames.com); complete with box and manual

SPACE INVASION

Manufacturer: Classic Game Creations
Rarity: Homebrew
Game Only: N/A
Complete: $20
Notes: Based on *Space Invaders;* currently available for download from the Classic Game Creations web site (http://www.classicgamecreations.com)

SPACE PANIC

Manufacturer: Coleco
Rarity: 2
Game Only: $2–4
Complete: $8–10

SPECTRON

Manufacturer: Spectravision
Rarity: 7
Game Only: $25–30
Complete: $50–60

SPY HUNTER

Manufacturer: Coleco
Rarity: 6
Game Only: $15–25
Complete: $40–50
Notes: Must include controller overlays to be considered complete

SQUISH 'EM FEATURING SAM

Manufacturer: Interphase
Rarity: 5
Game Only: $6–10
Complete: $17–23

STAR FORTRESS

Manufacturer: Classic Game Creations
Rarity: Homebrew
Game Only: N/A
Complete: $20–30*
Notes: Based on *Star Castle;* currently available for download from the Classic Game Creations web site (http://www.classicgamecreations.com)

STAR TREK: STRATEGIC OPERATIONS SIMULATOR

Manufacturer: Coleco
Rarity: 5
Game Only: $8–15
Complete: $18–25*

STAR WARS: THE ARCADE GAME

Manufacturer: Parker Brothers
Rarity: 4
Game Only: $10–15
Complete: $25–40

STEAMROLLER

Manufacturer: Retrotopia
Rarity: 2
Game Only: N/A
Complete: $25–35
Notes: Released at the 2000 Classic Gaming Expo

STRIKE IT

Manufacturer: Telegames
Rarity: 2
Game Only: N/A
Complete: $15–25
Notes: New copies are generally available from Telegames (http://www.telegames.com)

SUBROC

Manufacturer: Coleco
Rarity: 3
Game Only: $2–5
Complete: $10–14

SUPER ACTION BASEBALL

Manufacturer: Coleco
Rarity: 2
Game Only: $1–4
Complete: $6–10
Notes: Requires the Super Action Controller

SUPER ACTION FOOTBALL

Manufacturer: Coleco
Rarity: 3
Game Only: $2–5
Complete: $10–25
Notes: Requires the Super Action Controller

SUPER ACTION SOCCER

Manufacturer: Coleco
Rarity: 8
Game Only: $20–25*
Complete: $30–40
Notes: Requires the Super Action Controller

SUPER COBRA

Manufacturer: Parker Brothers
Rarity: 6
Game Only: $5–10
Complete: $14–25

SUPER CROSS FORCE

Manufacturer: Spectravision
Rarity: 7
Game Only: $20–30
Complete: $45–55

SUPER DONKEY KONG

Manufacturer: Coleco
Rarity: Prototype
Game Only: ?
Complete: N/A
Notes: Bootleg, improved edition of the Coleco ADAM version of *Donkey Kong*

SUPER DONKEY KONG JUNIOR
Manufacturer: Coleco
Rarity: Prototype
Game Only: ?
Complete: N/A
Notes: Bootleg, improved edition of the Coleco
ADAM version of *Donkey Kong Junior*

SUPER SKETCH
Manufacturer: Personal Peripheral
Rarity: 10
Game Only: $80–100*
Complete: $125–160
Notes: Utilizes a tablet controller with a cartridge
input and plastic stylus; very rare; cartridge is useless
without the drawing tablet

TANK WARS
Manufacturer: Telegames
Rarity: 2
Game Only: N/A
Complete: $15–25
Notes: New copies are generally available from Tel-
egames (http://www.telegames.com)

TARZAN
Manufacturer: Coleco
Rarity: 4
Game Only: $10–20
Complete: $25–30
Notes: New copies are generally available from Tel-
egames (http://www.telegames.com)

TELLY TURTLE
Manufacturer: Coleco
Rarity: 6
Game Only: $10–15
Complete: $11–25

THRESHOLD
Manufacturer: Sierra
Rarity: 6
Game Only: $10–25
Complete: $45–55

TIME PILOT
Manufacturer: Coleco
Rarity: 3
Game Only: $3–8
Complete: $10–12

TOMARC THE BARBARIAN
Manufacturer: Xonox
Rarity: 6
Game Only: $12–30
Complete: $30–40
Notes: New copies are generally available from Tel-
egames (http://www.telegames.com)

TOURNAMENT TENNIS
Manufacturer: Imagic
Rarity: 8
Game Only: $30–40
Complete: $45–55*

TOURNAMENT TENNIS
Manufacturer: Telegames
Rarity: 1
Game Only: N/A
Complete: $15–20
Notes: New copies are generally available from Tel-
egames (http://www.telegames.com)

TURBO
Manufacturer: Coleco
Rarity: 2
Game Only: $1–3
Complete: $40–50
Notes: Originally packaged with the Driving Con-
troller; requires the Driving Controller

TUTANKHAM
Manufacturer: Parker Brothers
Rarity: 5
Game Only: $10–15
Complete: $25–35

UP 'N DOWN
Manufacturer: Sega
Rarity: 8
Game Only: $15–35
Complete: $40–50*

VENTURE
Manufacturer: Coleco
Rarity: 1
Game Only: $1–3
Complete: $5–7

VIDEO HUSTLER
Manufacturer: Coleco
Rarity: Prototype
Game Only: $20–30*
Complete: N/A

VICTORY
Manufacturer: Coleco
Rarity: 3
Game Only: $3–6
Complete: $13–15
Notes: Requires the Roller Controller

WAR GAMES
Manufacturer: Coleco
Rarity: 4
Game Only: $8–10
Complete: $12–15
Notes: Must include controller overlays to be consid-
ered complete

WAR ROOM
Manufacturer: Probe 2000
Rarity: 4
Game Only: $4–8
Complete: $15–20
Notes: Must include controller overlays to be consid-
ered complete

WING WAR
Manufacturer: Imagic
Rarity: 6
Game Only: $9–15
Complete: $25–30

THE WIZARD OF ID'S WIZ MATH

Manufacturer: Sierra
Rarity: 7
Game Only: $10–20
Complete: $25–30*

WORD FEUD

Manufacturer: Xonox
Rarity: 7
Game Only: $15–20
Complete: $25–35
Notes: New copies are generally available from Telegames (http://www.telegames.com)

ZAXXON

Manufacturer: Coleco
Rarity: 1
Game Only: $1–3
Complete: $8–12

ZENJI

Manufacturer: Activision
Rarity: 6
Game Only: $15–17
Complete: $20–30
Notes: New copies are generally available from Telegames (http://www.telegames.com)

7 Intellivision

By the 1970s, Mattel was well established as one of the biggest toy manufacturers in the world. With their high-profile name and huge distribution network, it is interesting that the company shied away from the burgeoning video game industry for as long as they did. When they finally *did* get involved in 1980, they quickly rose to be the number-two player in the home video game market.

Intellivision History

In the mid- to late-1970s, when just about every imaginable company was diving headfirst into the home video game market, Mattel elected to take a "wait and see" stance on video games. Meanwhile, they created a whole new game market: handheld electronic games.

Mattel's first handheld game, *Auto Race*, was introduced in 1976. Mattel followed up over the next couple of years with a line of sports titles including *Football*, *Baseball*, and *Basketball* among others. These simple, calculator-sized LED games did a booming business during a time when interest in the first wave of home video game consoles was declining. (For more information on the handheld games by Mattel and other companies, see Chapter 10.)

When it became apparent that the Atari 2600 was going to be a success, Mattel finally decided to develop a console of their own. Intellivision (a contraction of "Intelligent Television") was originally engineered to be part of a modular home computer system. When the console was introduced in 1980, the eventual computer upgrade was the primary marketing focus.

As it became apparent that there was money to be made in the video game market, however, Mattel quickly shifted its focus to games. Starting in 1981, Mattel spent millions of dollars on an advertising campaign that went head-to-head with the Atari 2600. This ad campaign touched off the first "console war" as the two biggest players in the industry battled for supremacy in the home marketplace. Direct comparison advertising was a totally new concept in the '80s, though it became commonplace in the video game industry from that point on.

There was no doubt that the Intellivision's graphics and gameplay were superior to those of the 2600. Side-by-side comparisons of the two systems made the Atari look primitive by comparison. Because Atari had the market cornered on home versions of popular arcade games, Mattel focused their attention on primarily on sports titles. In this area, the Intellivision shined. Mattel's sports games were the most realistic available at the time.

By the end of 1981, Mattel had sold 850,000 Intellivisions worldwide, making the console second only to the Atari 2600 in popularity. The cartridge library grew. Along with their successful sports titles, Mattel introduced a number of very popular original games.

In 1982, as the system continued to gain popularity, third-party companies like Activision and Imagic began releasing some of their more popular titles for both Atari 2600 and Intellivision. At the same time, Mattel started releasing some Intellivision cartridges for the Atari 2600 under the M Network label.

In 1983, Mattel replaced the original Intellivision console with the more compact Intellivision II, and announced the Entertainment Computer System (ECS) peripheral, the long-awaited computer upgrade. Mattel also released the System Changer module, which allowed Intellivision consoles to play Atari 2600 games.

The following year, as a result of the video game industry crash, Mattel closed its electronics division, but the Intellivision lived on. A number of Mattel employees formed a new company, INTV, and bought the rights to the system.

INTV continued to sell the remaining stock of Intellivision consoles and games through the end of 1984. In 1985, the company started building its own Intellivision consoles, starting with the INTV System III and, a year later, INTV began releasing new titles—games that had been completed by Mattel but never released.

As newer, flashier video game systems like the Nintendo Entertainment System and the Sega Master System gained popularity, the demand for Intellivision dropped rapidly. By 1988, INTV was selling games and systems strictly by mail order. Finally, in 1991, INTV closed its doors, and Intellivision faded into video game history. By this time, over 3 million Intellivision consoles had been sold.

Intellivision Collecting

Intellivision is probably the second most collected classic game system behind the Atari 2600. Because it sold well during its 11-year history, finding and securing an Intellivision system and a collection of the more common cartridges is relatively easy and inexpensive today.

The number of unique cartridges released for the system in the United States stands at around 125 (not including label and brand variations of individual games and prototypes). Like most classic consoles, the common cartridges for Intellivision are *very* common and can be found just about anywhere for rock-bottom prices. With a few standout exceptions, building a complete or near-complete Intellivision game library isn't too difficult.

Hardware, on the other hand, presents something of a challenge. With the exception of widely released peripherals like the IntelliVoice, add-on components for Intellivision can be hard to come by. The ECS computer module and ECS music synthesizer are fairly rare, as is the System Changer. Third-party joysticks and controllers for Intellivision are almost nonexistent, primarily because the original console didn't have detachable controllers.

Intellivision Consoles

Mattel only released two variants of the Intellivision themselves, but they licensed the game system to several other companies who produced clones of the console. Add these to the INTV variants that were manufactured starting in 1985 and you get quite a variety of available Intellivision consoles in today's marketplace.

Intellivision

The original Intellivision console (known at the time as the Intellivision Master Component) was introduced in 1980. The system has brown wood grain trim on the front and back panels and gold trim on the top. The two included controllers fit in slots in the top of the unit for storage purposes. The earliest consoles shipped with the *Las Vegas Poker & Blackjack* cartridge. Later consoles were packaged with *Astrosmash*.

Intellivision uses a standard antenna/game switchbox, which makes replacements easy to find today. Unlike most classic consoles, the original Intellivision has an internal power supply/transformer. This is a definite advantage over the bulky external power supplies used by other video games that tend to cover an entire wall outlet or half of a surge protector. On the other hand, Intellivision's power supply is notorious for overheating.

The controllers on this console present several potential problems for the collector. The numeric keypad built into each controller is covered by a thin plastic membrane that tends to crack and tear with extended use. On most other classic consoles, a broken controller is no problem. Not so on the Intellivision. The original console's controllers are hard-wired into the unit, and cannot be removed without opening the console case.

Replacement controllers don't exist for this console, so the only remedies available for broken controllers are to repair the existing controllers or replace them with controllers from another unit. If you intend to play your Intellivision extensively, you should probably invest in an Intellivision II, which has detachable controllers. Play on the Intellivision II and keep the original console primarily for display purposes.

Note that the System Changer peripheral that allows Atari 2600 games to play on Intellivision does *not* work with the original Intellivision or its clones (Sylvania/GTE Intellivision, Sears Super Video Arcade, and Tandyvision One).

Intellivision II

The Intellivision II incorporates a number of design improvements over its predecessor (in addition to its smaller footprint). First and foremost, Intellivision II has detachable controllers that can be easily replaced if they break. The numeric keypad on the controllers abandons the bubble-type membrane buttons of the original in favor of a sturdier plastic membrane with flat buttons. Also gone is the internal power supply (which accounts for the Intellivision II's smaller size) and its associated overheating problems.

The one downside to the Intellivision II is its incompatibility with certain games. Most notable among these titles are three cartridges manufactured by Coleco (*Carnival, Donkey Kong,* and *Mouse Trap*), which are clearly marked on their boxes to indicate their incompatibility with the system. Most of the games affected by this incompatibility problem are third-party titles, but a few Mattel games are affected as well. The problems range from minor sound flaws to complete incompatibility.

NOTE ✵✵

Throughout the text,
BOLD indicates that an
item appears in a picture.

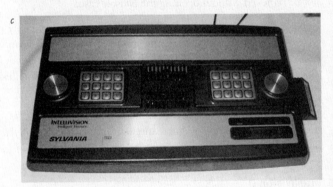

a   ***The original Intellivision console,***
released in 1980 by Mattel.

b   ***Mattel's Intellivision II*** *replaced
the original Intellivision in 1983.*

c   ***The GTE/Sylvania version of
Intellivision*** *was basically the
same as the original Intellivision
with a few cosmetic changes and
a different label.*

Since fewer Intellivision IIs were manufactured than the original console, collectors' prices for this variant tend to be slightly higher.

Intellivision (Sylvania/GTE)

At about the same time the original Intellivision was released, Mattel set up marketing arrangements with several retailers who sold the Intellivision under their own brand labels.

GTE sold the console through their phone stores as the GTE Intellivision. Although the GTE/Sylvania version of the console is virtually identical to the Mattel version, there are some cosmetic differences. The trim on the top of the unit is silver instead of gold, and there is no faux wood grain on the front and back.

This Intellivision variant was produced in smaller numbers than the Mattel version. In fact, this is the least common Intellivision console variant and, as such, it commands a higher price in the collectors' marketplace than most other versions of the system.

Sears Tele-Games Super Video Arcade

Mattel manufactured the **Tele-Games Super Video Arcade** exclusively for Sears stores. Unlike Atari, who simply changed the brand markings on its 2600 to create the Sears version of the console, Mattel crafted a console with a completely different look that set it apart from the Intellivision itself.

The Super Video Arcade is off-white with black trim. The controllers are nearly the same as the original Intellivision's controllers with one important difference: they are detachable and, therefore, easy to replace if they malfunction (provided, of course, that you can find replacement controllers). The one other notable difference is that, when a game starts, the "Mattel Electronics Presents" text doesn't appear on the screen. The Super Video Arcade was packaged with the Sears version of *Las Vegas Poker & Blackjack*.

Other than these differences and, of course, Sears-exclusive packaging, the Tele-Games Super Video Arcade is electronically identical to the original Intellivision. It is compatible with all Intellivision cartridges and peripherals except for the peripherals that are only compatible with Intellivision II (like the System Changer).

Tandyvision One

Tandyvision One was yet another variant of the original Intellivision console that was released in 1980. This console is identical to the original Mattel version in every respect except for cosmetic variations and packaging. Tandyvision One features an all-black case, with wood grain panels on the top. Like the Mattel system, Tandyvision One was packaged with the *Las Vegas Poker & Blackjack* cartridge.

Despite the fact that the Tandyvision One is rarer than the Mattel version, collector prices for this system tend to be about the same as those for the original Intellivision console.

INTV System III and Super Pro System

The INTV System III, which was later sold as the **Intellivision Super Pro System,** copies the style of the original Intellivision, right down to the internal power supply and (unfortunately) the hard-wired controllers. Also present in the INTV System III is the original console's incompatibility with the System Changer peripheral.

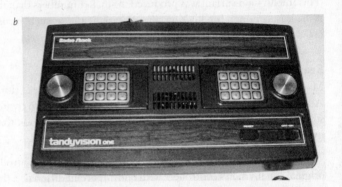

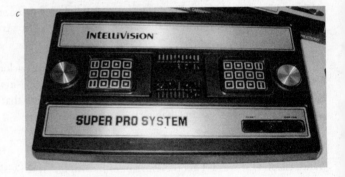

a **Tele-Games Super Video Arcade.** Like Atari, Mattel made a version of their game console that was marketed exclusively through Sears department stores. Although it had a different look, it was essentially the same as the original Intellivision console.

b **Tandyvision One.** Mattel manufactured this Intellivision console that was sold exclusively through Radio Shack stores.

c **Intellivision Super Pro System.** Starting in 1986, INTV began manufacturing the INTV System III console, which was later sold as the Intellivision Super Pro System.

The differences between this console and the original Intellivision are purely cosmetic. The System III is all black (no wood grain panels) with silver panels on the top and silver trim and thumb pads on the controllers. INTV also added an LED next to the power switch to indicate whether the unit was switched on or off (a detail that was overlooked in the original Intellivision's design).

At some point in the five-year history of this console, INTV changed the name of the system to the Intellivision Super Pro System. Other than the name change and the cartridges included (the Super Pro System included several of INTV's sports titles), the System III and Super Pro System are identical.

The Intellivision Keyboard Component and ECS

If one were to identify a single Intellivision item that was considered the Holy Grail of Intellivision collectibles, The **Keyboard Component** would be that item.

When the Intellivision was introduced, Mattel wanted to set their new console apart from the Atari 2600. In an effort to do so, they announced the Keyboard Component when the Intellivision was first introduced. Scheduled for release in 1981, this peripheral was a huge piece of hardware with a built-in computer keyboard and cassette tape drive. On the top of the Keyboard Component was a rectangular slot big enough to house the entire Intellivision console.

The Keyboard Component was released in limited test markets and made available through mail order. (A printer designed to go with the unit was also available.) About 4,000 Keyboard Components were produced during this test run, and a number of programs were developed for the system.

The high price of production for the Keyboard Component ultimately made it impractical for widespread release. Mattel stopped production and offered refunds to consumers who had purchased the unit. Any customers who chose to keep the Keyboard Component were forced to sign a waiver that absolved Mattel of any responsibility to provide support for the unit.

Because of the buy back offer, it is unknown how many Keyboard Components remain in circulation today. This is not an item that is likely to come on the open market very often and, if one should ever surface, the going price would likely be astronomical. The Keyboard Component is one of the rarest classic video game collectibles in existence.

The Keyboard Component is not to be confused with the **Entertainment Computer System (ECS)** that was released by Mattel in 1983. This less bulky, less powerful computer add-on was released to appease the Federal Trade Commission, which had imposed an ongoing fine on Mattel for their failure to deliver the promised computer upgrade for the original Intellivision. A number of cartridges were released to take advantage of the ECS. A musical keyboard component was also released, although only one cartridge (*Melody Blaster*) was designed to take advantage of it.

Intellivision Cartridges

Because the Intellivision's cartridge library is small compared to that of the Atari 2600, amassing a near-complete collection is not that difficult. Although there was some third-party software produced for the console, most of the cartridges were published under the Mattel (and later, the INTV) label.

Even so, within this relatively small collection of cartridges there are a number of variations, re-releases, and oddities that are worth noting.

a **The Intellivision Keyboard Component** is the rarest piece of hardware built for the console. It is unknown how many of these units still exist. A working model would certainly fetch an astronomical price today. (Photo courtesy of Steve Orth, http://intvfunhouse. com.)

b **The Entertainment Computer System (ECS)** was released in 1983, in part to ease legal sanctions that were placed on Mattel for their failure to release the Keyboard Component promised in 1981. This add-on computer (and its optional musical keyboard) are much more common than the Keyboard Component.

c **Sears game cartridges.** Many Mattel titles were also released by Sears under the Tele-Games brand label (right). The Sears games had different packaging, and usually, white cartridge labels (as opposed to the varying colors of the Mattel labels).

Label and Packaging Variations

Learning about the label and box variations among Intellivision cartridges isn't nearly as difficult as accomplishing the same task in the Atari 2600 realm. Most of the label variations evidenced in the Intellivision library are manufacturer or brand-oriented.

For example, because of Mattel's distribution agreement with Sears, many Mattel cartridges were also released under the Sears Tele-Games brand. The packaging for these games is different, but the cartridges are identical *except* for the label color. Most **Sears game cartridges** have white labels whereas the Mattel versions have label colors that vary from game to game.

Sears also dropped most of the official licensing affiliations from their versions of Mattel's games. For example, Mattel's *NFL Football* was released by Sears as **Super Pro Football**. Generally speaking, there is little or no difference in value between Mattel and Sears cartridge versions.

The other primary label and packaging differences in the Intellivision library are between Mattel and INTV titles. INTV re-released some of the Mattel sports titles under slightly different names and with new gameplay additions. They also re-released a number of nonsports cartridges and new titles. (See "INTV Titles" for more details.) INTV cartridges have white labels with plain black text.

INTV Titles

In 1986, the year after they purchased the Intellivision rights from Mattel, INTV began releasing new games into the marketplace. The first batch of cartridges were games that Mattel had completed but never released. When these titles proved to be popular, INTV hired programmers to complete unfinished Mattel prototypes.

In addition to completing unreleased prototype titles, INTV programmers enhanced several of Mattel's existing sports games by adding a single-player option, greatly increasing their playability.

The remainder of the INTV releases were a handful of original titles and re-releases of existing titles from companies like Atarisoft (the branch of Atari that produced cartridges for competing console systems).

Most INTV cartridges were produced in quantities of 20,000 or less, and are therefore harder to find than most Intellivision games. The later cartridges, like *Spiker! Super Pro Volleyball* and *Stadium Mud Buggies,* are particularly difficult to locate.

In all, there are 31 INTV titles, including INTV's version of the Intellivision Test Cartridge.

IntelliVoice Games

In 1982, at the height of the Intellivision's popularity, Mattel released **the IntelliVoice add-on**, a peripheral that added speech synthesis to the console's already impressive array of features.

Despite IntelliVoice's popularity, only five games were produced to take advantage of its capabilities:

- *B-17 Bomber*

- *Bomb Squad*

a **Super Pro Football** *cartridge.* INTV's cartridges have plain white labels with black text. Because some of the re-released INTV titles (especially the sports games) are different than their Mattel counterparts, it is important to learn the labeling distinction between the two. (*Photo courtesy of Steve Orth, http://intvfunhouse. com.*)

b **Mountain Madness Super Pro Skiing.** *INTV re-released a number of Mattel's sports titles with the added feature of a single-player option (in the case of two-player-only games) and other new features. This game, for example, adds a course builder and randomizer to Mattel's U.S. Ski Team Skiing. (Photo courtesy of Steve Orth, http:// intvfunhouse.com.)*

- *Space Spartans*

- *Tron Solar Sailor*

- *World Series Major League Baseball*

These five games cannot be played without the IntelliVoice. (*World Series Baseball* also requires the ECS computer module.)

IntelliVoice was extremely popular in its day, and is very easy to find in today's collector's market. This peripheral is compatible with all Intellivision console variants.

ECS Titles

As mentioned earlier in this chapter, Mattel was forced to make good on its promise to release a computer add-on for the Intellivision to avoid ongoing legal costs following their failure to deliver the original Keyboard Component. The peripheral they eventually introduced was the Entertainment Computer System (ECS).

The ECS was styled to match the Intellivision II. It and its companion musical keyboard were released in both white (in the United States) and brown (in Europe and other countries). It is compatible with all versions of the Intellivision.

Because the ECS was released just before the video game crash, few titles were produced to take advantage of it:

- *Conversational French*

- *Crosswords* (prototype—never released)

- *Family Budgeting* (prototype—never released)

- *The Jetsons' Way with Words*

- *Melody Blaster* (the only cartridge produced for the ECS Music Synthesizer)

- *Mind Strike*

- *World Series Major League Baseball* (also requires IntelliVoice)

The ECS cartridges that actually made it into commercial release are fairly difficult to find and command moderately high prices in today's collectors' market. The prototypes are, of course, much harder to locate.

Overlays

Most Intellivision cartridges were packaged with a pair of plastic overlays that slip into the faces of the controllers, covering the keypad buttons and illustrating their functions within the game. Although all games can be played without the aid of the **controller overlays**, many cartridges are difficult to master without them.

It was apparently felt that players expected their Intellivision cartridges to include controller overlays, since many games that didn't even use the keypad nevertheless included overlays. Only a handful of cartridges—most notably the titles produced by Coleco—were packaged without overlays.

a **The Intellivoice add-on.** *Although only five cartridges took advantage of its capabilities, this accessory was extremely popular, and is very common today.*

b **Loco-Motion** *controller overlays. Most Intellivision games were packaged with controller overlays. While many games don't require the overlays in order to play the game, collectors do not consider a game that was originally packaged with overlays complete without them.*

c **4-Tris** *by Joe Zbiciak is the only homebrew (fan-produced) game that has been commercially released for the Intellivision.*

Because overlays are almost essential to some of the more complicated games, you can expect to pay a couple dollars more for a cartridge that includes one or both overlays than you would for the cartridge alone. When buying a "complete" game, remember to make sure that the overlays are included.

Homebrews, Reproductions, and Prototypes

Despite the popularity of Intellivision among collectors, only one known homebrew game has been produced for Intellivision. *4-Tris*, a clone of the popular game *Tetris*, was released in very limited quantities (30 cartridges) at the 2001 PhillyClassic video game convention, and another limited run was produced shortly thereafter. The game was packaged in a homemade box and included two controller overlays. Needless to say, this one and only Intellivision homebrew is fairly difficult to locate.

The only other homebrew product that has been produced is the Intellicart, an interface cartridge that allows Intellivision game ROMs to be downloaded from a PC and played on the Intellivision. The cartridge was designed and built by Chad Schell, the designer of the Atari 2600 Cuttle Cart and the Atari 7800 Cuttle Cart 2. Only 234 Intellicarts were produced, and all of them were sold by the end of 2002. Intellicarts still occasionally appear on eBay and at classic game conventions, but they are fairly difficult to find. Details on the Intellicart and the Atari Cuttle Carts can be found at http://www.schells.com.

Perhaps INTV's continued support of the Intellivision into the 1990s accounts in some part for the lack of homebrew games. Certainly, INTV's effort in this area explains the relatively small number of prototypes and reproductions in the Intellivision library. Most of the games that were incomplete when Mattel stopped producing products were eventually completed and released by INTV. There are no known reproductions of Intellivision prototypes, and very few actual prototype cartridges that have been uncovered to date.

Intellivision Holy Grail Cartridges

Most Intellivision titles are very common. This, combined with the relatively small number of total games (especially compared to the library for the Atari 2600) makes amassing a near-complete Intellivision cartridge collection fairly easy and inexpensive.

Like other systems, however, there are some Intellivision games that are difficult to locate in the marketplace today. Most of the hard-to-find titles are third-party games manufactured in relatively small quantities near the end of the classic era and INTV titles that saw limited distribution shortly before the company closed up shop in the early '90s.

Although some of the rarer titles can reach prices of several hundred dollars (especially for complete, packaged games), none of the Intellivision games are valued as high as the rarest Atari 2600 titles.

Congo Bongo (Sega)

Sega produced a number of titles for the Atari 2600, but only a single game for Intellivision. *Congo Bongo*, based on the Sega arcade game by the same name, was released in 1984, the same year that Mattel Electronics closed up shop. It is speculated that the distribution of the cartridge was extremely limited, and the game's rarity seems to confirm this. The box is even rarer than the game, so complete copies of *Congo Bongo*—on the rare occasion that they turn up—fetch a premium price among collectors.

a **Congo Bongo,** *the only cartridge that Sega made for the Intellivision, is extremely difficult to find. (Photo courtesy of Steve Orth, http://intvfunhouse.com.)*

b **Spiker! Super Pro Volleyball** *was one of the last two new games released for Intellivision before INTV went out of business. (Photo courtesy of Steve Orth, http://intvfunhouse.com.)*

c **Turbo for Intellivision.** *Of the many arcade conversions that Coleco released for Intellivision, this is the rarest. (Photo courtesy of Steve Orth, http://intvfunhouse.com.)*

Spiker! Super Pro Volleyball

As INTV ran into financial troubles during the last year of their existence, the production runs of their games became smaller and smaller. The last two games they released, *Stadium Mud Buggies* and *Spiker! Super Pro Volleyball,* were produced in extremely limited quantities.

Although both of these games are rare, *Spiker!* is the less common of the two. It is one of the most difficult Intellivision titles to locate, and usually commands a high price.

Turbo (Coleco)

Coleco released a number of arcade conversions for both the Atari 2600 and Intellivision. *Turbo* was one of Coleco's last titles for Intellivison and is among the hardest cartridges to locate in today's collector's market. Like so many games, the box is even more difficult to locate than the cartridge, and thus adds a great deal to the value of the game.

Intellivision Price Guides

Intellivision Hardware Price Guide

CONSOLES

INTELLIVISION CONSOLE
Manufacturer: Mattel
Rarity: 1
Loose: $15–20
Boxed/Complete: $40–80*
Notes: The original console with hard-wired controllers; packaged with *Las Vegas Poker and Blackjack;* early boxes advertise the Keyboard Component on the back

INTELLIVISION CONSOLE
Manufacturer: Sylvania/GTE
Rarity: 7
Loose: $35–45*
Boxed/Complete: $70–90*
Notes: Identical to the original Intellivision, but with the Sylvania and GTE logos printed below the Intellivision logo

INTELLIVISION II CONSOLE
Manufacturer: Mattel
Rarity: 1
Loose: $20–25
Boxed/Complete: $40–60
Notes: A smaller, white console with detachable controllers; incompatible with several cartridges

INTV SYSTEM III CONSOLE
Manufacturer: INTV
Rarity: 5
Loose: $25–35
Boxed/Complete: $45–65*
Notes: Similar in appearance to the original console except for the color scheme (no wood grain) and the addition of a power LED

INTV SUPER PRO SYSTEM CONSOLE
Manufacturer: INTV
Rarity: 5
Loose: $25–35
Boxed/Complete: $45–65*
Notes: Identical to the INTV System III except for the "Superpro" logo; packaged with several INTV sports titles

TELE-GAMES SUPER VIDEO ARCADE CONS
Manufacturer: Sears
Rarity: 5
Loose: $25–45
Boxed/Complete: $50–60*
Notes: Sears version of the original console, white with detachable controllers; packaged with the Sears version of *Las Vegas Poker and Blackjack*

TANDYVISION ONE
Manufacturer: Radio Shack
Rarity: 5
Loose: $20–30
Boxed/Complete: $35–55*
Notes: Radio Shack version of the original console; cosmetically different, but very similar to the first Intellivision

ACCESSORIES

CONTROLLER, INTELLIVISION II
Manufacturer: Mattel
Rarity: 5
Loose: $10–15
Boxed/Complete: $15–20*

CONTROLLER, WICO COMMAND CONTROL
Manufacturer: Wico
Rarity: 9
Loose: $45–60*
Boxed/Complete: $90–110
Notes: A rare third-party joystick (with built-in keypad) for Intellivision; very hard to find

COVER, INTELLIVISION II
Manufacturer: Mattel
Rarity: 2
Loose: $8–10
Boxed/Complete: $12–15
Notes: Soft cover for the Intellivision II system

ECS COMPUTER MODULE
Manufacturer: Mattel
Rarity: 6
Loose: $15–30
Boxed/Complete: $35–125
Notes: Large plug-in module and computer keyboard add-on; most commonly seen in white (matching the Intellivision II), but also available in brown and black

ECS MUSIC SYNTHESIZER
Manufacturer: Mattel
Rarity: 7
Loose: $16–30
Boxed/Complete: $50–80
Notes: Musical keyboard for use with the ECS Computer Module; boxed version with the ECS Computer Module can sell for over $300

INTELLIVISION KEYBOARD COMPONENT
Manufacturer: Mattel
Rarity: 10
Loose: $1,500–2,000
Boxed/Complete: $3,000+*
Notes: The original computer component from 1982; 4,000 were sold through mail order and in test markets, but it was never released comercially; extremely rare

INTELLIVOICE
Manufacturer: Mattel
Rarity: 1
Loose: $5–10
Boxed/Complete: $12–20

PLAYCABLE MODULE
Manufacturer: Mattel
Rarity: 10
Loose: $500+*
Boxed/Complete: $1,000+*
Notes: Module that allowed the download of games through cable television systems; very limited release, and available for rental only from the cable operator

SYSTEM CHANGER
Manufacturer: Mattel
Rarity: 6
Loose: $20–40
Boxed/Complete: $45–60
Notes: Allows Atari 2600 games to be played on the Intellivision

Intellivision Cartridge Price Guide

4-TRIS
Manufacturer: Self-Published
Label: Philly Class
Rarity: Homebrew
Game Only: N/A
Complete: $60–80*
Notes: Philly Classic special edition; only 30 were produced; includes box and 2 overlays

4-TRIS
Manufacturer: Self-Published
Label: Standard
Rarity: Homebrew
Game Only: N/A
Complete: $45–60*
Notes: Standard edition; includes box and 2 overlays

APBA BACKGAMMON
Manufacturer: Mattel
Rarity: 3
Game Only: $2–3
Complete: $5–7

ADVANCED DUNGEONS & DRAGONS
Manufacturer: Mattel
Rarity: 1
Game Only: $2–3
Complete: $5–10

ADVANCED DUNGEONS & DRAGONS: TREASURE OF TARMIN
Manufacturer: Mattel
Rarity: 4
Game Only: $5–7
Complete: $7–11

ARMOR BATTLE
Manufacturer: Mattel
Label: Red
Rarity: 1
Game Only: $1–2
Complete: $3–8

ARMOR BATTLE
Manufacturer: Sears
Label: White
Rarity: 2
Game Only: $2–3
Complete: $5–9

ASTROSMASH
Manufacturer: Mattel
Label: Red
Rarity: 1
Game Only: $1–2
Complete: $3–5

ASTROSMASH
Manufacturer: Sears
Label: White
Rarity: 2
Game Only: $2–3
Complete: $4–6
Notes: Sears version of the Mattel game by the same name

ATLANTIS
Manufacturer: Imagic
Rarity: 2
Game Only: $2–3
Complete: $4–8

AUTO RACING
Manufacturer: Mattel
Label: Blue
Rarity: 1
Game Only: $1–2
Complete: $2–3

AUTO RACING
Manufacturer: Sears
Label: White
Rarity: 3
Game Only: $2–4
Complete: $5–6
Notes: Sears version of the Mattel game by the same name

B-17 BOMBER
Manufacturer: Mattel
Rarity: 3
Game Only: $2–3
Complete: $4–10
Notes: Compatible with the IntelliVoice voice module

BACKGAMMON
Manufacturer: Sears
Rarity: 3
Game Only: $3–4
Complete: $6–8
Notes: Sears version of the Mattel game *APBA Backgammon*

BASEBALL
Manufacturer: Sears
Rarity: 3
Game Only: $1–2
Complete: $3–5
Notes: Sears version of the Mattel game *Major League Baseball*

BASKETBALL
Manufacturer: Sears
Rarity: 3
Game Only: $2–3
Complete: $5–7
Notes: Sears version of the Mattel game *NBA Basketball*

BEAMRIDER
Manufacturer: Activision
Rarity: 5
Game Only: $6–8
Complete: $12–15

BEAUTY AND THE BEAST
Manufacturer: Imagic
Rarity: 2
Game Only: $1–2
Complete: $3–5

BIG LEAGUE BASEBALL
Manufacturer: INTV
Rarity: 6
Game Only: $10–14
Complete: $15–20*
Notes: INTV version of the Mattel game *Major League Baseball;* label reads simply "Baseball"

BLOCKADE RUNNER
Manufacturer: Interphase
Label: All
Rarity: 5
Game Only: $5–7
Complete: $9–12
Notes: 2 different labels, both equally common

BODY SLAM SUPER PRO WRESTLING
Manufacturer: INTV
Rarity: 7
Game Only: $25–50
Complete: $80–150

BOMB SQUAD
Manufacturer: Mattel
Rarity: 2
Game Only: $2–3
Complete: $5–8
Notes: Compatible with the IntelliVoice voice module

BOWLING
Manufacturer: Sears
Rarity: 2
Game Only: $2–3
Complete: $5–8
Notes: Sears version of the Mattel game *PBA Bowling*

BOXING
Manufacturer: Mattel
Label: Blue
Rarity: 1
Game Only: $1–2
Complete: $3–5

BOXING
Manufacturer: Sears
Label: White
Rarity: 1
Game Only: $1–2
Complete: $3–5

BUMP 'N JUMP
Manufacturer: Mattel
Rarity: 4
Game Only: $3–5
Complete: $6–20

BURGERTIME
Manufacturer: Mattel
Rarity: 3
Game Only: $2–4
Complete: $5–16

BUZZ BOMBERS
Manufacturer: Mattel
Rarity: 5
Game Only: $3–5
Complete: $5–12

CARNIVAL
Manufacturer: Coleco
Rarity: 3
Game Only: $1–3
Complete: $5–11
Notes: Incompatible with Intellivision II; no overlays

CENTIPEDE
Manufacturer: Atarisoft
Rarity: 4
Game Only: $3–5
Complete: $12–17

CHAMPIONSHIP TENNIS
Manufacturer: INTV
Rarity: 7
Game Only: $10–12
Complete: $30–45

CHECKERS
Manufacturer: Mattel
Rarity: 2
Game Only: $1–3
Complete: $4–8
Notes: Released in England as *Draughts*

CHECKERS
Manufacturer: Sears
Rarity: 3
Game Only: $1–3
Complete: $4–8
Notes: Sears version of the Mattel game by the same name

CHESS
Manufacturer: INTV
Rarity: 6
Game Only: $12–15
Complete: $20–25*
Notes: INTV version of the Mattel game *USCF Chess*

CHIP SHOT SUPER PRO GOLF
Manufacturer: INTV
Rarity: 6
Game Only: $12–15
Complete: $30–50

COMMANDO
Manufacturer: INTV
Rarity: 7
Game Only: $8–12
Complete: $20–40

CONGO BONGO
Manufacturer: Sega
Rarity: 9
Game Only: $50–130
Complete: $250–400
Notes: The only game released for Intellivision by Sega; one of the rarest Intellivision titles

CONVERSATIONAL FRENCH
Manufacturer: Mattel
Rarity: 10
Game Only: $80–150
Complete: $200–250*
Notes: Requires the ECS Computer Module

CROSSWORDS
Manufacturer: Mattel
Label: N/A
Rarity: Prototype
Game Only: ?
Complete: N/A
Notes: Requires the ECS Computer Module

DEEP POCKETS SUPER PRO POOL AND BILLIARDS
Manufacturer: INTV
Label: N/A
Rarity: Prototype
Game Only: ?
Complete: N/A
Notes: Only one copy is known to exist

DEFENDER
Manufacturer: Atarisoft
Rarity: 6
Game Only: $10–15
Complete: $12–20
Notes: No overlays

DEMON ATTACK
Manufacturer: Imagic
Rarity: 1
Game Only: $1–2
Complete: $5–8

DEMONSTRATION CARTRIDGE (1978)
Manufacturer: Mattel
Label: White
Rarity: 8
Game Only: $40–50*
Complete: $100–150*
Notes: Nonplayable Intellivision demo; includes mention of the Keyboard Component (a computer add-on that was never released)

DEMONSTRATION CARTRIDGE (1978 REVISED)
Manufacturer: Mattel
Label: White
Rarity: 9
Game Only: $50–100*
Complete: $150–250*
Notes: Nonplayable Intellivision demo; identical to the 1978 Demonstration Cartridge except that it omits mention of the Keyboard Component

DEMONSTRATION CARTRIDGE (1982 INTERNATIONAL)
Manufacturer: Mattel
Label: Red
Rarity: 9
Game Only: $50–100*
Complete: $150–350*
Notes: Nonplayable Intellivision demo

DEMONSTRATION CARTRIDGE (1983)
Manufacturer: Mattel
Label: Green
Rarity: 9
Game Only: $50–100*
Complete: $150–250*
Notes: Nonplayable Intellivision demo

DIG DUG
Manufacturer: INTV
Rarity: 7
Game Only: $15–25*
Complete: $30–50

DINER
Manufacturer: INTV
Rarity: 7
Game Only: $9–14
Complete: $30–60

DONKEY KONG
Manufacturer: Coleco
Rarity: 2
Game Only: $2–3
Complete: $5–10
Notes: Incompatible with Intellivision II; no overlays

DONKEY KONG JUNIOR
Manufacturer: Coleco
Rarity: 5
Game Only: $7–9
Complete: $15–17
Notes: No overlays

DRACULA
Manufacturer: Imagic
Rarity: 5
Game Only: $8–10
Complete: $20–42

DRAGONFIRE
Manufacturer: Imagic
Rarity: 3
Game Only: $3–4
Complete: $8–10

THE DREADNOUGHT FACTOR
Manufacturer: Activision
Rarity: 4
Game Only: $5–7
Complete: $18–20

FAMILY BUDGETING
Manufacturer: Mattel
Label: N/A
Rarity: Prototype
Game Only: ?
Complete: N/A
Notes: Requires the ECS Computer Module

FATHOM
Manufacturer: Imagic
Rarity: 8
Game Only: $22–46
Complete: $70–80*

FOOTBALL
Manufacturer: Sears
Rarity: 2
Game Only: $1–2
Complete: $2–5
Notes: Sears version of the Mattel game *NFL Football*

FROG BOG
Manufacturer: Mattel
Rarity: 3
Game Only: $2–3
Complete: $5–8

FROGGER
Manufacturer: Parker Brothers
Rarity: 2
Game Only: $2–4
Complete: $6–12

GOLF
Manufacturer: Sears
Rarity: 2
Game Only: $1–2
Complete: $3–4
Notes: Sears version of the Mattel game *PGA Golf*

HAPPY TRAILS
Manufacturer: Activision
Rarity: 4
Game Only: $4–7
Complete: $9–18

HOCKEY
Manufacturer: Sears
Rarity: 2
Game Only: $1–2
Complete: $3–4
Notes: Sears version of the Mattel game *NHL Hockey*

HORSE RACING
Manufacturer: Mattel
Rarity: 3
Game Only: $2–3
Complete: $6–8

HOVER FORCE
Manufacturer: INTV
Rarity: 6
Game Only: $10–15
Complete: $20–30

ICE TREK
Manufacturer: Imagic
Rarity: 4
Game Only: $5–7
Complete: $6–14

INTELLICART
Manufacturer: Schell's Electronics
Label: Unique
Rarity: Homebrew
Game Only: $100–150
Complete: $150–200
Notes: Cartridge with an input that allows you to load game ROM files from a PC; originally sold for $100 (now discontinued—only 234 were produced); no box

THE JETSONS' WAY with WORDS

Manufacturer: Mattel
Rarity: 7
Game Only: $18–20
Complete: $45–55
Notes: Requires the ECS Computer Module

KOOL-AID MAN

Manufacturer: Mattel
Rarity: 5
Game Only: $8–12
Complete: $30–40

LADY BUG

Manufacturer: Coleco
Rarity: 5
Game Only: $3–5
Complete: $10–14

LAS VEGAS POKER & BLACKJACK

Manufacturer: Mattel
Rarity: 1
Game Only: $1–2
Complete: $2–3
Notes: Also seen labeled simply as *Poker;* value is the same regardless of the label

LAS VEGAS POKER & BLACKJACK

Manufacturer: Sears
Rarity: 2
Game Only: $1–2
Complete: $2–3
Notes: Sears version of the Mattel game by the same name

LAS VEGAS ROULETTE

Manufacturer: Mattel
Rarity: 2
Game Only: $1–3
Complete: $4–7

LAS VEGAS ROULETTE

Manufacturer: Sears
Rarity: 3
Game Only: $1–3
Complete: $4–7
Notes: Sears version of the Mattel game by the same name

LEAGUE OF LIGHT

Manufacturer: Activision
Rarity: Prototype
Game Only: ?
Complete: N/A
Notes: Only one copy is known to exist

LEARNING FUN I

Manufacturer: INTV
Rarity: 7
Game Only: $15–20
Complete: $70–120

LEARNING FUN II

Manufacturer: INTV
Rarity: 6
Game Only: $12–18
Complete: $70–120

LOCK 'N CHASE

Manufacturer: Mattel
Rarity: 1
Game Only: $1–3
Complete: $4–7

LOCO-MOTION

Manufacturer: Mattel
Rarity: 3
Game Only: $2–4
Complete: $4–8

MAJOR LEAGUE BASEBALL

Manufacturer: Mattel
Rarity: 1
Game Only: $1–2
Complete: $3–6

MASTERS OF THE UNIVERSE: THE POWER OF H

Manufacturer: Mattel
Rarity: 3
Game Only: $5–8
Complete: $12–20
Notes: Often referred to simply as *He-Man*

MATH FUN, THE ELECTRIC COMPANY

Manufacturer: Mattel
Rarity: 4
Game Only: $2–4
Complete: $12–18

MELODY BLASTER

Manufacturer: Mattel
Rarity: 7
Game Only: $15–18
Complete: $25–35
Notes: Only title produced for the Music Keyboard; requires the ECS Computer Module and the Music Keyboard

MICROSURGEON

Manufacturer: Imagic
Rarity: 2
Game Only: $2–5
Complete: $8–12

MIND STRIKE

Manufacturer: Mattel
Rarity: 7
Game Only: $15–18
Complete: $18–25
Notes: Requires the ECS Computer Module

MISSION X

Manufacturer: Mattel
Rarity: 3
Game Only: $2–4
Complete: $5–8

MOTOCROSS

Manufacturer: Mattel
Rarity: 4
Game Only: $5–7
Complete: $10–20

MOUNTAIN MADNESS SUPER PRO SKIING
Manufacturer: INTV
Rarity: 7
Game Only: $15–25
Complete: $50–130

MOUSE TRAP
Manufacturer: Coleco
Rarity: 3
Game Only: $4–6
Complete: $6–20
Notes: Incompatible with Intellivision II

MR. BASIC MEETS BITS 'N BYTES
Manufacturer: Mattel
Rarity: 6
Game Only: $12–15
Complete: $15–25
Notes: Must include all 6 overlays to be considered complete; requires the ECS Computer Module

NASL SOCCER
Manufacturer: Mattel
Rarity: 1
Game Only: $1–2
Complete: $3–5

NBA BASKETBALL
Manufacturer: Mattel
Rarity: 1
Game Only: $1–2
Complete: $3–7

NFL FOOTBALL
Manufacturer: Mattel
Rarity: 1
Game Only: $1–2
Complete: $3–6

NHL HOCKEY
Manufacturer: Mattel
Rarity: 1
Game Only: $1–2
Complete: $3–5

NIGHT STALKER
Manufacturer: Mattel
Label: Red
Rarity: 1
Game Only: $1–2
Complete: $2–5

NIGHT STALKER
Manufacturer: Mattel
Label: White
Rarity: 2
Game Only: $2–3
Complete: $3–6

NOVA BLAST
Manufacturer: Imagic
Rarity: 4
Game Only: $3–5
Complete: $15–20

PAC-MAN
Manufacturer: Atarisoft
Label: Color
Rarity: 6
Game Only: $6–9
Complete: $10–17
Notes: Cartridge has a pink and white label with Pac-Man pictured on it

PAC-MAN
Manufacturer: INTV
Label: White
Rarity: 5
Game Only: $6–9
Complete: $10–17
Notes: INTV version of the Atarisoft game by the same title; cartridge has a plain white end label that reads "Pac-Man"

PBA BOWLING
Manufacturer: Mattel
Rarity: 2
Game Only: $1–2
Complete: $3–5

PGA GOLF
Manufacturer: Mattel
Rarity: 1
Game Only: $1–2
Complete: $3–5

PINBALL
Manufacturer: Mattel
Rarity: 4
Game Only: $5–7
Complete: $9–25

PITFALL!
Manufacturer: Activision
Rarity: 2
Game Only: $3–5
Complete: $8–14

POLE POSITION
Manufacturer: INTV
Rarity: 7
Game Only: $10–15
Complete: $20–30*

POPEYE
Manufacturer: Parker Brothers
Rarity: 3
Game Only: $5–8
Complete: $30–45

Q*BERT
Manufacturer: Parker Brothers
Rarity: 4
Game Only: $5–10
Complete: $12–20

REVERSI
Manufacturer: Mattel
Rarity: 3
Game Only: $2–6
Complete: $6–10

RIVER RAID
Manufacturer: Activision
Rarity: 4
Game Only: $4–6
Complete: $14–18

ROBOT RUBBLE
Manufacturer: Activision
Rarity: Prototype
Game Only: ?
Complete: N/A

ROYAL DEALER
Manufacturer: Mattel
Rarity: 3
Game Only: $2–3
Complete: $5–8

SAFECRACKER
Manufacturer: Imagic
Rarity: 6
Game Only: $5–8
Complete: $19–35

SCOOBY DOO MAZE CHASE
Manufacturer: Mattel
Rarity: 7
Game Only: $15–20
Complete: $40–50

SEA BATTLE
Manufacturer: Mattel
Rarity: 1
Game Only: $1–2
Complete: $3–5

SEA BATTLE
Manufacturer: Sears
Rarity: 2
Game Only: $2–3
Complete: $4–6

SEWER SAM
Manufacturer: Interphase
Rarity: 5
Game Only: $2–6
Complete: $10–50
Notes: Despite its apparent rarity, the online auction prices for this game are usually quite low

SHARK! SHARK!
Manufacturer: Mattel
Rarity: 4
Game Only: $3–6
Complete: $9–12

SHARP SHOT
Manufacturer: Mattel
Rarity: 4
Game Only: $3–5
Complete: $7–10

SKIING
Manufacturer: Sears
Label: White
Rarity: 2
Game Only: $2–3
Complete: $7–10
Notes: Sears version of the Mattel game *US Ski Team Skiing*

SLAM DUNK SUPER PRO BASKETBALL
Manufacturer: INTV
Rarity: 7
Game Only: $10–20
Complete: $25–30*

SLAP SHOT SUPER PRO HOCKEY
Manufacturer: INTV
Rarity: 7
Game Only: $8–15
Complete: $17–25

SNAFU
Manufacturer: Mattel
Rarity: 1
Game Only: $1–2
Complete: $3–5

SOCCER
Manufacturer: Sears
Rarity: 2
Game Only: $3–4
Complete: $7–9
Notes: Sears version of the Mattel game *NASL Soccer*

SPACE ARMADA
Manufacturer: Mattel
Label: Red
Rarity: 1
Game Only: $1–2
Complete: $3–5

SPACE ARMADA
Manufacturer: Sears
Label: White
Rarity: 1
Game Only: $1–2
Complete: $2–4
Notes: Sears version of the Mattel game by the same name

SPACE BATTLE
Manufacturer: Mattel
Label: Red
Rarity: 2
Game Only: $2–3
Complete: $4–6
Notes: Red box version; easier to play (and less common) than the blue box version; cartridge and label identical to blue box version

SPACE BATTLE
Manufacturer: Mattel
Label: Red
Rarity: 1
Game Only: $1–2
Complete: $3–5
Notes: Blue box version; cartridge and label identical to red box version

SPACE BATTLE
Manufacturer: Sears
Label: White
Rarity: 1
Game Only: $1–2
Complete: $3–5
Notes: Sears version of the Mattel game by the same name

SPACE HAWK
Manufacturer: Mattel
Label: Red
Rarity: 1
Game Only: $1–2
Complete: $3–5

SPACE HAWK
Manufacturer: Sears
Label: White
Rarity: 2
Game Only: $2–3
Complete: $4–7
Notes: Sears version of the Mattel game by the same name

SPACE SPARTANS
Manufacturer: Mattel
Rarity: 2
Game Only: $2–3
Complete: $4–10
Notes: Compatible with the IntelliVoice voice module

SPIKER! SUPER PRO VOLLEYBALL
Manufacturer: INTV
Rarity: 9
Game Only: $45–60
Complete: $140–170
Notes: One of the last games commercially produced for Intellivision; extremely rare

STADIUM MUD BUGGIES
Manufacturer: INTV
Rarity: 8
Game Only: $25–35
Complete: $60–120
Notes: One of the last games commercially produced for Intellivision; extremely rare; occasionally, the cartridge alone can sell for $75 or more

STAMPEDE
Manufacturer: Activision
Rarity: 2
Game Only: $3–5
Complete: $4–12

STAR STRIKE
Manufacturer: Mattel
Label: Red
Rarity: 1
Game Only: $1–2
Complete: $3–4

STAR STRIKE
Manufacturer: Sears
Label: White
Rarity: 2
Game Only: $1–3
Complete: $3–5
Notes: Sears version of the Mattel game by the same name

STAR WARS: THE EMPIRE STRIKES BACK
Manufacturer: Parker Brothers
Rarity: 3
Game Only: $3–5
Complete: $18–30

SUB HUNT
Manufacturer: Mattel
Label: Red
Rarity: 1
Game Only: $1–2
Complete: $3–5

SUB HUNT
Manufacturer: Sears
Label: Red
Rarity: 2
Game Only: $2–3
Complete: $4–6
Notes: Sears version of the Mattel game by the same name

SUPER PRO DECATHLON
Manufacturer: INTV
Rarity: 8
Game Only: $11–20
Complete: $30–50*

SUPER PRO FOOTBALL
Manufacturer: INTV
Rarity: 6
Game Only: $5–10
Complete: $15–36
Notes: Has some compatibility problems with Intellivision II

SWORDS & SERPENTS
Manufacturer: Imagic
Rarity: 5
Game Only: $3–6
Complete: $15–30

TENNIS
Manufacturer: Mattel
Label: Blue
Rarity: 1
Game Only: $1–2
Complete: $4–6

TENNIS
Manufacturer: Sears
Label: White
Rarity: 2
Game Only: $2–3
Complete: $5–7
Notes: Sears version of the Mattel game by the same name

TEST CARTRIDGE IMI

Manufacturer: Mattel
Rarity: 9
Game Only: $80–100*
Complete: N/A
Notes: First version of the Mattel test cartridge

TEST CARTRIDGE IMI (VERSION 4.1)

Manufacturer: Mattel
Rarity: 9
Game Only: $80–100*
Complete: N/A
Notes: Intellivision II test cartridge

TEST CARTRIDGE IMI (VERSION 4.1.2)

Manufacturer: INTV
Rarity: 9
Game Only: $80–100*
Complete: N/A
Notes: Same as the 4.2 version, but with a built-in game (*Night Stalker*)

TEST CARTRIDGE MTE-201 (VERSION 3)

Manufacturer: Mattel
Label: Red; Blue
Rarity: 9
Game Only: $80–100*
Complete: N/A
Notes: Test cartridge compatible with all Intellivision consoles; includes a partially playable version of *Baseball*

TEST CARTRIDGE MTE-201 (VERSION 3.3)

Manufacturer: Mattel
Rarity: Prototype
Game Only: ?
Complete: N/A

THIN ICE

Manufacturer: INTV
Rarity: 7
Game Only: $10–15
Complete: $20–30*

THUNDER CASTLE

Manufacturer: Mattel
Rarity: 7
Game Only: $5–9
Complete: $16–46

TOWER OF DOOM

Manufacturer: INTV
Rarity: 6
Game Only: $8–15
Complete: $30–40

TRIPLE ACTION

Manufacturer: Mattel
Label: Red
Rarity: 1
Game Only: $1–2
Complete: $3–5
Notes: 3-game cartridge that includes *Racing Cars*, *Battle Tanks*, and *Biplanes*

TRIPLE ACTION

Manufacturer: Sears
Label: White
Rarity: 2
Game Only: $2–3
Complete: $4–6
Notes: Sears version of the Mattel game by the same name

TRIPLE CHALLENGE

Manufacturer: INTV
Label: White
Rarity: 4
Game Only: $8–15
Complete: $25–40*
Notes: 3-game cartridge that includes *Checkers*, *Chess*, and *Backgammon*

TRON DEADLY DISCS

Manufacturer: Mattel
Rarity: 2
Game Only: $1–2
Complete: $3–10

TRON MAZE-A-TRON

Manufacturer: Mattel
Rarity: 2
Game Only: $1–2
Complete: $3–5

TRON SOLAR SAILOR

Manufacturer: Mattel
Rarity: 4
Game Only: $3–6
Complete: $9–14
Notes: Compatible with the IntelliVoice voice module

TROPICAL TROUBLE

Manufacturer: Imagic
Rarity: 5
Game Only: $9–14
Complete: $10–20

TRUCKIN'

Manufacturer: Imagic
Rarity: 5
Game Only: $10–15
Complete: $15–30

TURBO

Manufacturer: Coleco
Rarity: 8
Game Only: $25–35
Complete: $75–90
Notes: Box is particularly hard to find

US SKI TEAM SKIING

Manufacturer: Mattel
Rarity: 1
Game Only: $1–2
Complete: $5–10

USCF CHESS

Manufacturer: Mattel
Rarity: 5
Game Only: $4–8
Complete: $6–23

UTOPIA

Manufacturer: Mattel
Label: Purple
Rarity: 1
Game Only: $2–3
Complete: $4–8

UTOPIA

Manufacturer: Sears
Label: White
Rarity: 2
Game Only: $2–3
Complete: $4–8
Notes: Sears version of the Mattel game by the same name

VECTRON

Manufacturer: Mattel
Rarity: 2
Game Only: $2–3
Complete: $4–10

VENTURE

Manufacturer: Coleco
Rarity: 4
Game Only: $4–8
Complete: $15–20

WHITE WATER!

Manufacturer: Imagic
Rarity: 6
Game Only: $8–12
Complete: $15–40

WORD FUN, THE ELECTRIC COMPANY

Manufacturer: Mattel
Rarity: 2
Game Only: $2–3
Complete: $5–8

WORLD CHAMPIONSHIP BASEBALL

Manufacturer: INTV
Rarity: 5
Game Only: $8–12
Complete: $14–25

WORLD CUP SOCCER

Manufacturer: INTV
Rarity: 7
Game Only: $10–15
Complete: $30–50

WORLD SERIES MAJOR LEAGUE BASEBALL

Manufacturer: Mattel
Rarity: 7
Game Only: $12–18
Complete: $50–75
Notes: Requires the ECS Computer Module and In-telliVoice

WORM WHOMPER

Manufacturer: Activision
Rarity: 3
Game Only: $6–8
Complete: $9–12

YOGI'S FRUSTRATION

Manufacturer: Mattel
Rarity: Prototype
Game Only: ?
Complete: N/A
Notes: Only one copy is known to exist

ZAXXON

Manufacturer: Coleco
Rarity: 4
Game Only: $8–12
Complete: $12–18

8 Odyssey²

By the time 1981 rolled around, the first big video game console war was in full swing. Atari and Mattel were at each other's throats as "Have you played Atari today" commercials went head-to-head against the reserved British demeanor of author George Plimpton as he hawked the superior graphics and gameplay of Intellivision.

Every once in a while, another video game spokesperson appeared on the small screen. A magical fellow known as the Wizard of Odyssey advertised the wondrous worlds that awaited players on a third video game system, the Magnavox Odyssey². Although this console was a distant third in the race for video game dominance in the classic era (prior to the release of ColecoVision, anyway), the Odyssey² managed to carve a small niche in the market.

Odyssey² History

Magnavox's Odyssey line started with the very first video game console in 1972, and continued through a number of *Pong*-clone systems that were released throughout the mid-1970s. (See Chapter 3 for details on the early games in the Odyssey series.)

Like the other companies of the era, Magnavox abandoned dedicated consoles in favor of a programmable, cartridge-based system. In 1978, they released Odyssey², a game console that combined "The excitement of a game!" and "The mind of a computer!" according to Magnavox's advertising campaign.

At first glance, the Odyssey² was quite different than the other game systems on the market. The major distinction was the plastic membrane keyboard built into the top of the unit. This made the console look more like a computer than a game system. In fact, Magnavox's original plan was to emphasize the console's usefulness as an educational tool as well as a game system. Although the built-in keyboard was a step in the right direction, like nearly every other classic game system that promised home computer functionality, the Odyssey² never delivered.

The console's potential as a game system was far superior to that of the Atari 2600, its major competition at the time of release. Unfortunately, the Odyssey²'s games seldom lived up to the potential of the hardware. Half of the original 50 games released for the system were designed by a single game developer at Magnavox (Ed Averett), which probably accounts for the lack of gameplay variety. Outside the United States, support for the Odyssey² was much more widespread, and a number of European titles show off the system's abilities to a much greater extent than any of the games released in the United States.

Unlike Atari, Magnavox wasn't able to bolster its original game library with licensed arcade titles. This further reduced the appeal of the console. Games like *Alien Invaders—Plus!* and *K.C. Munchkin!* copied gameplay elements of popular arcade games, but they were unable to attract the attention of the official home translations of popular arcade games that Atari was pumping out. Although a handful of enjoyable titles were available for this system, many of the games were bland and featured blocky graphics. Even the inclusion of an exclamation mark after each and every cartridge title didn't help to add excitement to the games.

Although the Odyssey² keyboard was never fully utilized in the educational capacity for which it was originally designed, several games did take advantage of it to provide uniquely immersive adventure and strategy game experiences that were impossible to recreate on other console systems at the time. *Quest for the Rings!*, for example, was a *Dungeons and Dragons*-style adventure game that combined video and board game elements, and used a keyboard overlay to add additional controls beyond the joystick and fire button. This flagship game, part of Magnavox's Master Strategy Series, was one of the primary selling points for the Odyssey².

In 1982, Magnavox released The Voice!, a speech synthesizer that plugged into the Odyssey²'s cartridge port. Although few games took advantage of the speech capabilities of this peripheral, the voice synthesis was very good for the time.

The Odyssey² stood little chance of becoming a hit in the United States with the Atari 2600 and Intellivision dominating the marketplace. Even so, Magnavox stuck it out to the bitter end. As new consoles like ColecoVision and the Atari 5200 made their way into the marketplace, Magnavox planned to release a competitive system of their own: the Odyssey³. This system never saw the light of day (although a prototype is rumored to exist). When the video game market crashed in 1983, it took Odyssey², the last video game system produced by the company that had pioneered home video games, down with it.

Odyssey² Collecting

Odyssey² has many advantages when it comes to collecting. Although the system was never as popular as the Atari 2600 or the Intellivision, a *lot* of Odyssey² consoles were produced. It is, therefore, very easy to find a system in today's marketplace. The cartridges are also very common (not to mention inexpensive), and the relatively small number of games produced for the console (and the low prices of most of these cartridges) makes a complete cartridge collection for Odyssey² a very attainable goal.

There are a few things to keep in mind when collecting Odyssey² hardware. Some console variations include two joysticks that are hardwired to the console. Although these joysticks can be replaced if you are willing to take the console apart (and if you can actually find replacement joysticks), the models that include detachable joysticks are preferable. Detachable joysticks are easy to spot—most are silver (although there *are* some black detachable joysticks as well). Hardwired joysticks are always black. Joysticks for the detachable joystick version of the console are readily available.

The Odyssey^2 AC power adaptor also varies from console to console. There are three different AC adaptor types: one with a male tip on the console end, one with a female tip, and one with both male *and* female tips. The male-tipped adaptor is compatible with the power adaptor for the Nintendo Entertainment System (NES), and is therefore very easy to replace. The female-tipped version is *not* NES compatible. If you buy a console without a power adaptor, check the power connection on the back to see which adaptor you need. If you cannot find a Magnavox or NES replacement, you can also use a generic 12v AC adaptor that you can find at any electronics store.

One other feature that Magnavox changed over the years is the antenna/game switchbox. Some Odyssey^2 consoles have standard RCA jacks on the cable that connects the console to the antenna/game switchbox. For these consoles, the switchbox is a standard design and can be replaced with an antenna/game switchbox available from any electronics store.

Other models feature a nonstandard connector and, hence, use a nonstandard switchbox. The switchbox for these Odyssey^2 units is difficult to find, so if you need a replacement there is no solution readily available. If possible, it is best to find a console that uses a standard switchbox. If you do purchase the nonstandard variety, make sure the switchbox is included and functional.

One conundrum that collectors face when deciding which Odyssey^2 model to purchase is that all the models with the more-desirable detachable joysticks feature the nonstandard antenna/game switchbox. Luckily, there is a solution to the switchbox problem.

If you are willing to open up the console, it is fairly simple to replace the nonstandard RF cable with a standard RCA-style cable. When the unit is opened, you will note that the nonstandard cable actually connects to a standard RCA female jack inside the console itself. Simply remove the existing cable and replace it with a new cable with male RCA connectors on each end. After doing so, you can use a standard antenna/game switchbox with your Odyssey^2.

One other feature that varies from model to model is the keyboard. Some Odyssey^2 consoles feature keyboards with a rough finish rather than the smooth, shiny finish found on most units. While there is functionally no difference between the two versions, the lettering on the rough-keyboard version tends to wear off under heavy use.

Odyssey^2 Consoles

Magnavox released a number of Odyssey^2 console variants in the United States. Unlike the variants for other systems, it isn't always easy to spot the differences between models at a glance. The only difference between some units is the model number. Regardless of the model number and minor feature differences, all Odyssey^2 consoles were packaged with two joysticks and the *Speedway!/Spinout!/Crypto-Logic!* game cartridge.

Odyssey^2 (Hardwired Joysticks)

The majority of **Odyssey^2** console models released in North America feature black, hardwired joysticks. All of these consoles also feature a standard antenna/game switchbox and NES-compatible AC adaptors.

There are some minor variations between models within this category. Two models (BC7600 GY02 and CC7600 GY02) feature a raised Odyssey^2 logo and do not have the Magnavox logo printed above the power switch. These models also feature rough-textured keyboards, as does model number BC7600 GT02. All of the other models in this category feature smooth keyboards and flat Odyssey^2 logos.

a

b

a Some **Odyssey²** models used hard-wired joysticks that could not be removed without opening the console. Some models in this category can be identified by the raised Odyssey2 logo in the upper left corner and the lack of a Magnavox logo printed above the power switch. (Photo courtesy of Cassidy Nolen.)

b **Odyssey² consoles** with detachable joysticks are rarer than the hardwired variety, and fetch a slightly higher price today.

Because Odyssey² consoles with hardwired joysticks are more common than those with detachable joysticks (and because the detachable joystick version tends to be more popular among collectors due to the easy replaceability of the controllers), the hardwired version is usually less expensive in today's collectors' market.

Odyssey² (Detachable Joysticks)

Only about a third of the Odyssey² models released in North America feature detachable joysticks. Although the **consoles with detachable joysticks** are definitely preferable to the hardwired models, there is a drawback: these models are also saddled with nonstandard antenna/game switches. Whether the convenience of easily replaceable joysticks outweighs the difficulty of locating Magnavox's proprietary switchbox is a matter of personal choice. Two of the three variants in this group share the same model number (BJ7600 GY02). Originally, this model was packaged with black joysticks, although later packages included silver joysticks. Regardless of color, the joysticks are interchangeable among all detachable-stick models.

All detachable joystick Odyssey² models feature flat logos and smooth-finish keyboards. Model number BJ7600 GY02 (both the black and the silver joystick version) uses the power supply with the female connector that is not NES compatible. Model number BK7600 GY02 uses the male-connector, NES-compatible model.

Odyssey^2 consoles with detachable controllers are rarer than the hardwired variety, and therefore garner a slightly higher price.

Odyssey^2 Cartridges

Because the library of game titles is so small, Odyssey^2 is one of the easiest systems for which to collect. The prices for most cartridges are extremely low, and it is not unusual to find some common titles selling for under a dollar in online auctions. The supply of Odyssey^2 games is much smaller than that of the more popular classic console systems, however, so it might take a while to locate all of the titles you need to complete your collection.

As mentioned earlier, most of the North American games for this system were released by Magnavox. Only two games were released by a third-party manufacturer in the United States: *Atlantis* and *Demon Attack* by Imagic. These two games are among the rarer and more expensive Odyssey^2 cartridges today.

Most Odyssey^2 games are packaged in gatefold boxes (boxes that open like books), with the instruction booklets and other game literature tucked into the front cover. Unlike boxes for other classic console systems, Odyssey^2 boxes aren't terribly difficult to find.

There is generally little difference in price between loose cartridges and complete games. The exceptions to this rule are the three games in the Master Strategy Series: *Quest for the Rings!*, *Conquest of the World!*, and *The Great Wall Street Fortune Hunt!* These games were packaged in oversized boxes that housed not only the cartridge and the game literature, but also game boards, keyboard overlays, playing pieces, and other accessories. These games are among the most coveted among Odyssey^2 collectors and command higher prices, especially for complete, boxed versions. Complete Master Strategy games are difficult to come by because they include so many pieces.

Odyssey^2 is one of a handful of classic consoles for which the number of games released overseas significantly exceeds the number of games released in North America. Odyssey^2 was particularly well received in Europe and South America (where it was sold by Philips as the "Videopac"). All of the U.S. titles were duplicated overseas, but many original titles that did not make it to the U.S. market were also produced. New hardware and accessories, including an upgraded "plus" version of the Videopac console, were released overseas long after the Odyssey^2 disappeared from North American stores. Some of the overseas games occasionally trickle into the U.S. collectors' market.

Homebrews, Reproductions, and Prototypes

There are a handful of homebrew games available for the Odyssey^2. Two of these are multicarts that include a large number of games on a single cartridge. Multicarts are available for many systems, and they are an excellent way to amass an instant game collection. The Odyssey^2 multicarts are particularly nice in that they include foreign releases as well as all of the games released in North America. The 128-game multicart, which is available from Video Game Connections (http://www.videogameconnections.com), includes most commercially released US, European, and South American games, as well as a large number of homebrews, hacks, and enhanced games that aren't available anywhere else.

The two other homebrews for the system are *Amok!* (a game based on the arcade video game *Berzerk*) and *Pinball!*, a demo game written by Ralph Baer, the creator of the original Magnavox Odyssey. *Amok!* is still readily available, but *Pinball!* is extremely difficult to find.

There are a number of known (or suspected) prototype games for the Odyssey², though most of them are European titles not covered in this book. Prototype cartridges for Odyssey² are very rare and almost never come up for sale in any venue.

Odyssey² Holy Grail Cartridges

One of the features that makes Odyssey² an easy system to collect is that most of the titles available for the system are very common and quite inexpensive. Typical prices for loose Odyssey² cartridges run from $1 to $6.

Like any other classic console, however, there are a few elusive titles that stand out in both rarity and price.

Power Lords! (Magnavox)

Power Lords! is easily the holiest of Holy Grail cartridges for the Odyssey². Released at the end of the console's North American lifetime, this game apparently saw very limited distribution. It is, therefore, very difficulty to find.

Based on a line of toy action figures and a series of comic books released by DC Comics, *Power Lords!* is consistently rated among collectors as one of the most engaging and fun games for the Odyssey². Unfortunately for collectors who are anxious to play the game, it is also one of the most *expensive* games for the console. Loose copies fetch as much as $100 and boxed/complete versions can sell for considerably more.

Atlantis and *Demon Attack* (Imagic)

Because there was virtually no third-party support for Odyssey² in the United States, it isn't surprising that the two games produced by Imagic are among the hardest cartridges to locate: *Atlantis* and *Demon Attack*. Of the two games, *Atlantis* is the most popular among collectors since it takes full advantage of the Odyssey²'s graphics and sound capabilities. *Demon Attack* is more or less a straight conversion from the other classic consoles for which it was released.

One of the reasons these games are relatively rare is that they were released in 1983, making them among the last handful of games produced for the Odyssey² before the console's demise in the United States. While neither game comes close in value to the ultrarare *Power Lords!* cartridge, complete copies of the Imagic titles typically sell for around $25.

The Master Strategy Series (Magnavox)

The three games in the **Odyssey² Master Strategy Series**—*Conquest of the World!, The Great Wall Street Fortune Hunt!,* and *Quest for the Rings!*—are widely considered to be the signature games for the system. They have the type of gameplay depth that was all but impossible to achieve on the other console systems at the time.

The game depth comes in part from the ancillary game accessories packaged with each title. The Master Strategy Series combines video games with board games, an idea that originated with the first Magnavox Odyssey. But, whereas the original Odyssey used board game elements out of necessity (to augment the extremely simple gameplay that was available onscreen in 1972), the Odyssey² Master Strategy titles meshed these elements to add new dimensions to gameplay.

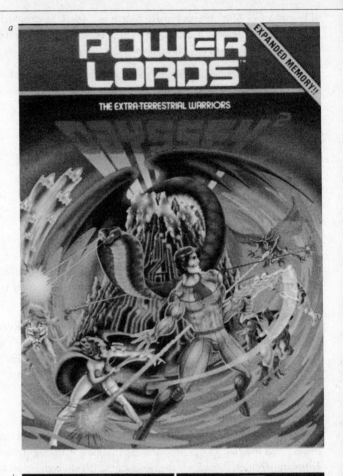

a **Power Lords!** *is the rarest Odyssey² title that was commercially released in North America. A boxed copy of this game is likely to cost you more than your Odyssey² console and all of the other cartridges for the system combined. (Photo courtesy of William Cassidy, http://www. classicgaming.com/o2home/.)*

b **Atlantis** *and* **Demon Attack** *were the only third-party cartridges produced for Odyssey² in the U.S. (Photo courtesy of William Cassidy, http://www. classicgaming.com/o2home/.)*

a

a **Odyssey² Master Strategy Series.**
These three games remain some of the most sought-after Odyssey² titles among collectors. It is particularly difficult to find the games with all of their accessories and pieces intact. (Photo courtesy of William Cassidy, http://www. classicgaming.com/o2home/.)

The rarity listed for the Master Strategy games reflects the rarity for complete packaged versions. Because the accessories packaged with these games are essential to gameplay, loose Master Strategy cartridges are all but useless. Make sure all of the accessories are present before you purchase the game. The contents for each game are as follows:

Conquest of the World! accessories:

- 6 sets of magnetic markers (30 Conquest/Alliance markers, 1 Homeland marker)—one set each in blue, green, yellow, red, black, and white

- Power Base Unit (PBU) chips, in denominations of 100, 500, and 1,000 PBUs (100 chips total)

- Game Board Map (1)

The Great Wall Street Fortune Hunt! accessories:

- Investment record pads/option-pricing calculators (2)

- Master Strategy Game Board (1)

a   **The Pinball!** *demo cartridge—*
    programmed by Ralph Baer, the
    creator of the original Magnavox
    Odyssey—is a highly sought-after
    collectible. Only 30 were produced.
    (Photo courtesy of William
    Cassidy, http://www.
    classicgaming.com/o2home/.)

- Green Share/Margin tokens (14)

- Gold Share/Margin tokens (14)

- Prime Rate tokens (2)

- Time Frame token (1)

  Quest for the Rings! accessories:

- Keyboard Overlay (1)

- Game Board Map (1)

- Castle tokens (23)

- Dragon Monster tokens (3)

- Nightmare Monster tokens (3)

- Ring tokens (10)

- Quest token (1)

- Hourglass token (1)

- "Possessions" tokens (8)

Quest for the Rings! was the most widely distributed of the three games, and tends to be easier to find and slightly less expensive than the other two Master Strategy titles.

Pinball!

Ralph Baer more or less left the home video game industry shortly after he created the original Odyssey game system for Magnavox. Although he remained involved in entertainment electronics, he was a relatively low-profile figure throughout most of the late classic era.

When the Odyssey² was released, Baer decided to see how the new system worked. He created the *Pinball!* demo as a learning exercise. The Odyssey² proved to be a difficult system to program, so Baer never took this game beyond the demo stage.

Ralph Baer sold 30 signed copies of his one and only Odyssey² cartridge, *Pinball!*, at the 2000 Classic Gaming Expo in Las Vegas. These are the only copies in existence and they are extremely rare. Should one actually appear on the open market, it is likely that it would sell for far more than the $25 price for which it was sold in 2000.

Odyssey² Price Guides
Odyssey² Hardware Price Guide

CONSOLES

ODYSSEY² CONSOLE (HARDWIRED CONTROLLERS)
Manufacturer: Philips/Magnavox
Rarity: 3
Loose: $10–15
Boxed/Complete: $20–30
Notes: The original release of the console, which had 2 controllers hardwired into the unit; packaged with *Speedway!/Spinout!/Crypto-Logic!*

ODYSSEY² CONSOLE (DETACHABLE CONTROLLERS)
Manufacturer: Philips/Magnavox
Rarity: 5
Loose: $15–20
Boxed/Complete: $25–35
Notes: The later release of the console, packaged with 2 removable controllers and *Speedway!/Spinout!/Crypto-Logic!*

ACCESSORIES

HOME COMPUTER MODULE
Manufacturer: Philips/Magnavox
Rarity: 9
Loose: $100–150*
Boxed/Complete: $175–225*
Notes: BASIC programming module

JOYSTICK
Manufacturer: Philips/Magnavox
Rarity: 6
Loose: $5–10
Boxed/Complete: $20–30
Notes: The standard joystick compatible with later release Odyssey² consoles with detachable controllers

RF SWITCHBOX
Manufacturer: Philips/Magnavox
Rarity: 8
Loose: $15–25*
Boxed/Complete: N/A
Notes: Many Odyssey² consoles used a nonstandard RF cable and required a proprietary RF switchbox; hard to come by, so don't buy an Odyssey² without it

TRACKBALL CONTROLLER

Manufacturer: Wico
Rarity: 10
Loose: $50–60*
Boxed/Complete: $75–90*
Notes: Compatible only with the later release
Odyssey² consoles with detachable controllers

THE VOICE!

Manufacturer: Philips/Magnavox
Rarity: 4
Loose: $20–40
Boxed/Complete: $45–55*
Notes: Voice synthesis module that adds voice to
voice-enhanced games

Odyssey² Cartridge Price Guide

72 IN 1

Manufacturer: Classic Game Creations
Rarity: Homebrew
Game Only: $30
Complete: N/A
Notes: 72 Odyssey² games on a single cartridge; no
longer produced by fairly common (price reflects the
original retail price)

128 IN 1

Manufacturer: Classic Game Creations
Rarity: Homebrew
Game Only: $50
Complete: N/A
Notes: 128 Odyssey² games on a single cartridge (in-
cludes foreign releases); currently available from
Video Game Connections (http://www.videogamecra-
tions.com)

ALIEN INVADERS—PLUS!

Manufacturer: Magnavox/Philips
Rarity: 1
Game Only: $1–2
Complete: $3–4

ALPINE SKIING!

Manufacturer: Magnavox/Philips
Rarity: 2
Game Only: $1–2
Complete: $3–4

AMOK!

Manufacturer: Classic Game Creations
Rarity: Homebrew
Game Only: $20
Complete: N/A
Notes: Based on the Stern arcade game *Berserk;* cur-
rently available from Video Game Connections
(http://www.videogamecrations.com)

ARMORED ENCOUNTER!/SUB CHASE!

Manufacturer: Magnavox/Philips
Rarity: 1
Game Only: $1–2
Complete: $2–3

ATLANTIS

Manufacturer: Imagic
Rarity: 5
Game Only: $12–15
Complete: $16–25
Notes: One of only 2 third-party games released in the
U.S.; foreign versions are much more common

ATTACK OF THE TIMELORD!

Manufacturer: Magnavox/Philips
Rarity: 4
Game Only: $3–5
Complete: $8–12

BASEBALL!

Manufacturer: Magnavox/Philips
Rarity: 1
Game Only: $1–2
Complete: $2–3

BLOCKOUT!/BREAKDOWN!

Manufacturer: Magnavox/Philips
Rarity: 1
Game Only: $1–2
Complete: $2–3

BOWLING!/BASKETBALL!

Manufacturer: Magnavox/Philips
Rarity: 1
Game Only: $1–2
Complete: $2–3

CASINO SLOT MACHINE!

Manufacturer: Magnavox/Philips
Rarity: 3
Game Only: $3–4
Complete: $6–8

COMPUTER GOLF!

Manufacturer: Magnavox/Philips
Rarity: 2
Game Only: $1–3
Complete: $4–6

COMPUTER INTRO!

Manufacturer: Magnavox/Philips
Rarity: 3
Game Only: $3–5
Complete: $6–8

CONQUEST OF THE WORLD!

Manufacturer: Magnavox/Philips
Rarity: 5
Game Only: $6–8
Complete: $18–40
Notes: Packaged in a large box with a game board,
keyboard overlay, and many game pieces (all must be
present to be considered complete)

COSMIC CONFLICT!

Manufacturer: Magnavox/Philips
Rarity: 1
Game Only: $1–2
Complete: $3–5

DEMON ATTACK
Manufacturer: Imagic
Rarity: 5
Game Only: $12–15
Complete: $16–25
Notes: One of only 2 third-party games released in the U.S.; foreign versions are much more common

DYNASTY!
Manufacturer: Magnavox/Philips
Rarity: 1
Game Only: $1–2
Complete: $2–3

ELECTRONIC TABLE SOCCER!
Manufacturer: Magnavox/Philips
Rarity: 3
Game Only: $2–3
Complete: $4–7

FOOTBALL!
Manufacturer: Magnavox/Philips
Rarity: 1
Game Only: $1–2
Complete: $3–4

FREEDOM FIGHTERS!
Manufacturer: Magnavox/Philips
Rarity: 1
Game Only: $1–2
Complete: $2–3
Notes: Odyssey²'s answer to *Defender*

THE GREAT WALL STREET FORTUNE
Manufacturer: Magnavox/Philips
Rarity: 6
Game Only: $6–8
Complete: $18–40
Notes: Packaged in a large box with a game board, keyboard overlay, and many game pieces (all must be present to be considered complete)

HOCKEY!/SOCCER!
Manufacturer: Magnavox/Philips
Rarity: 1
Game Only: $1–2
Complete: $2–3

INVADERS FROM HYPERSPACE!
Manufacturer: Magnavox/Philips
Rarity: 1
Game Only: $1–2
Complete: $2–3

I'VE GOT YOUR NUMBER!
Manufacturer: Magnavox/Philips
Rarity: 2
Game Only: $2–3
Complete: $4–7

K.C. MUNCHKIN!
Manufacturer: Magnavox/Philips
Rarity: 1
Game Only: $1–2
Complete: $2–3

K.C.'S KRAZY CHASE!
Manufacturer: Magnavox/Philips
Rarity: 3
Game Only: $3–5
Complete: $6–8

KEYBOARD CREATIONS!
Manufacturer: Magnavox/Philips
Rarity: 3
Game Only: $2–4
Complete: $5–7

KILLER BEES!
Manufacturer: Magnavox/Philips
Rarity: 4
Game Only: $3–10
Complete: $12–15*
Notes: The wide range in price represents the difference between typical auction and dealer prices

LAS VEGAS BLACKJACK!
Manufacturer: Magnavox/Philips
Rarity: 1
Game Only: $1–2
Complete: $2–3

MATCHMAKER!/BUZZWORD!/LOGIX
Manufacturer: Magnavox/Philips
Rarity: 2
Game Only: $1–3
Complete: $4–5

MATH A MAGIC!/ECHO!
Manufacturer: Magnavox/Philips
Rarity: 2
Game Only: $1–3
Complete: $4–5

MONKEYSHINES!
Manufacturer: Magnavox/Philips
Rarity: 2
Game Only: $1–3
Complete: $4–6

NIMBLE NUMBERS NED!
Manufacturer: Magnavox/Philips
Rarity: 2
Game Only: $1–3
Complete: $4–5

OUT OF THIS WORLD!/HELICOPTER R
Manufacturer: Magnavox/Philips
Rarity: 2
Game Only: $1–3
Complete: $4–5

P.T. BARNUM'S ACROBATS!
Manufacturer: Magnavox/Philips
Rarity: 3
Game Only: $3–5
Complete: $6–8

PACHINKO!
Manufacturer: Magnavox/Philips
Rarity: 3
Game Only: $2–4
Complete: $5–7

PICK AXE PETE!

Manufacturer: Magnavox/Philips
Rarity: 3
Game Only: $2–3
Complete: $3–5

PINBALL! (DEMO)

Manufacturer: Self-Published
Rarity: Homebrew
Game Only: $150–250*
Complete: N/A
Notes: Only 30 of these cartridges exist; programmed by Ralph Baer and sold at the 2000 Classic Gaming Expo; no box or manual; very rare and collectible

POCKET BILLIARDS!

Manufacturer: Magnavox/Philips
Rarity: 2
Game Only: $2–3
Complete: $4–7

POWER LORDS!

Manufacturer: Magnavox/Philips
Rarity: 8
Game Only: $80–100
Complete: $110–150
Notes: The rarest Odyssey² title

QUEST FOR THE RINGS!

Manufacturer: Magnavox/Philips
Rarity: 5
Game Only: $5–7
Complete: $15–30
Notes: Packaged in a large box with a game board, keyboard overlay, and many game pieces (all must be present to be considered complete)

S.I.D. THE SPELLBINDER!

Manufacturer: Magnavox/Philips
Rarity: 3
Game Only: $4–6
Complete: $7–10

SHOWDOWN IN 2100 A.D.!

Manufacturer: Magnavox/Philips
Rarity: 1
Game Only: $1–2
Complete: $3–5

SMITHEREENS!

Manufacturer: Magnavox/Philips
Rarity: 3
Game Only: $2–4
Complete: $5–7

SPEEDWAY!/SPINOUT!/CRYPTO-LO

Manufacturer: Magnavox/Philips
Rarity: 1
Game Only: $1
Complete: $2
Notes: This cartridge was included with the Odyssey² console

TAKE THE MONEY AND RUN!

Manufacturer: Magnavox/Philips
Rarity: 2
Game Only: $1–3
Complete: $4–5

THUNDERBALL!

Manufacturer: Magnavox/Philips
Rarity: 2
Game Only: $1–3
Complete: $3–4
Notes: A pinball game (not in any way associated with the James Bond film by the same name)

TURTLES!

Manufacturer: Magnavox/Philips
Rarity: 4
Game Only: $3–10
Complete: $14–16*
Notes: Based on the Stern arcade game by the same name; the wide range in price represents the difference between typical auction and dealer prices

TYPE AND TELL!

Manufacturer: Magnavox/Philips
Rarity: 3
Game Only: $3–4
Complete: $5–10

UFO!

Manufacturer: Magnavox/Philips
Rarity: 2
Game Only: $1–3
Complete: $4–5

VOLLEYBALL!

Manufacturer: Magnavox/Philips
Rarity: 2
Game Only: $1–3
Complete: $3–4

WAR OF NERVES!

Manufacturer: Magnavox/Philips
Rarity: 2
Game Only: $1–3
Complete: $4–5

9 Other Notable Classic Consoles

After Atari's original home *Pong* console took off in the mid-1970s, a huge number of companies entered the home video game market and created a glut of dedicated home consoles. After a few years, the number of manufacturers dwindled considerably as it became obvious that a few key players would dominate the marketplace as the new decade approached.

Not everyone dropped out of the race, however. As dedicated home consoles became a thing of the past, a number of companies tried their hand at the emerging programmable (cartridge-based) console market. These companies included pioneers in the cartridge-based field like Fairchild Camera and Instrument, Coleco, and RCA (whose programmable consoles preceded the Atari 2600) and companies like Emerson and Bally who entered the race during the height of the video game craze to grab a piece of the ever-growing market.

Compared to the rampant success of consoles like the 2600, Intellivision, and ColecoVision, the consoles described in this chapter hardly made a dent in the classic home video game market. Even so, these systems are considered collectible—*very* collectible in some cases—today.

APF M1000/MP1000 (APF, 1978)

Many early cartridge-based video game consoles were designed to be the central component of a home computer system. Atari promised a computer upgrade for the 2600, but never delivered. Mattel also promised a computer upgrade for the Intellivision. The ambitious Keyboard Component never saw the light of day (at least not in any widespread way) and the ECS Computer Module took years to develop and was a huge disappointment.

Interestingly enough, the one company that managed to release its game console and the promised computer upgrade within a year of one another was a relatively obscure company called APF Electronics, Inc.

APF, known primarily for manufacturing calculators, first entered the video game market in the mid-1970s with the TV Fun series of *Pong*-clone consoles. When the market turned to cartridge-based systems, APF responded by releasing the M1000 and MP1000 consoles in 1978.

a

a **APF M1000**—*APF actually
delivered on its promised computer
component, the Imagination
Machine, within a year of the
console's release.*

These systems had graphics and gameplay similar to the Atari 2600.

The following year, APF released the Imagination Machine, a large keyboard component with an integrated cassette tape drive and a rectangular bay in the top to house the game console. The Imagination Machine included a BASIC programming cartridge and had a built-in music synthesizer. APF also released the Expander Box, which allowed the user to add-on a mini-floppy drive controller and extra memory. The cost of the Imagination machine itself was a whopping $600, with the Expander Box and Mini-floppy Controller weighing in at $200 each. Add-on 8K memory cards were an additional $100 each. A very pricy system to be sure—but it was actually *available*, which was more than APF's competitors could say of their promised computer upgrades at the time.

The **APF M1000** and MP1000 systems are virtually identical. Each was packaged with two hardwired controllers (similar in style to the controllers ColecoVision eventually used, but smaller) and a built-in game called *Rocket Patrol*.

A total of 13 cartridges were produced for the system. This does not include *Rocket Patrol*, which was never released in cartridge form. One of the cartridges, the BASIC Interpreter, was shipped with the Imagination Machine.

The games are all original titles, although one (*Space Destroyers*) was an obvious attempt to imitate *Space Invaders*. Several APF titles included multiple games on a single cartridge.

Because APF consoles and cartridges saw fairly limited distribution in their time, they are among the most difficult classic game collectibles to find in today's market. Even more difficult to find are the Imagination Machine and its components. Despite the relatively small number of actual components and cartridges in the APF category, you can expect to pay quite a bit for a complete collection.

APF M1000/MP1000 Price Guide
APF Price Guide

CONSOLES

APF M1000 CONSOLE
Manufacturer: APF
Rarity: 9
Loose: $70–80*
Complete: $100–150*
Notes: Console with 2 hardwired controllers; comes with one built-in game (*Rocket Patrol*)

APF MP1000 CONSOLE
Manufacturer: APF
Rarity: 9
Loose: $70–80
Complete: $150–250
Notes: Same as the M1000, but compatible with the Imagination Machine

ACCESSORIES

EXPANSION CARTRIDGE
Manufacturer: APF
Rarity: 10
Loose: $40–60*
Complete: $80–90*
Notes: Memory expansion cartridge for the Imagination Machine

IMAGINATION MACHINE
Manufacturer: APF
Rarity: 10
Loose: $150–250*
Complete: $250–300*
Notes: Computer add-on for the APF MP1000, including keyboard and a built-in cassette drive

IMAGINATION MACHINE EXPANDER
Manufacturer: APF
Rarity: 10
Loose: $200–250*
Complete: $250–350*
Notes: Adds 3 expansion slots and 2 cartridge ports to the Imagination Machine

MINI-FLOPPY CONTROLLER
Manufacturer: APF
Rarity: 10
Loose: $60–80*
Complete: $90–120*
Notes: Disk drive controller for the Imagination Machine

SERIAL INTERFACE
Manufacturer: APF
Rarity: 10
Loose: $55–75*
Complete: $80–100*
Notes: Serial port interface for the Imagination Machine

GAMES

BACKGAMMON
Manufacturer: APF
Rarity: 7
Loose: $6–10*
Complete: $15–20*

BASEBALL
Manufacturer: APF
Rarity: 6
Loose: $5–8
Complete: $12–15*

BASIC INTERPRETER
Manufacturer: APF
Rarity: 8
Loose: $6–10*
Complete: $15–25*

BLACKJACK
Manufacturer: APF
Rarity: 8
Loose: $6–10
Complete: $15–25*

BOWLING/MICRO MATCH
Manufacturer: APF
Rarity: 6
Loose: $5–8
Complete: $12–15*

BOXING

Manufacturer: APF
Rarity: 7
Loose: $6–10*
Complete: $15–20*

BRICKDOWN/SHOOTING GALLERY

Manufacturer: APF
Rarity: 6
Loose: $5–8
Complete: $12–15*

CASINO 1: ROULETTE/KENO/SLOTS

Manufacturer: APF
Rarity: 6
Loose: $5–8*
Complete: $12–15*

CATENA

Manufacturer: APF
Rarity: 6
Loose: $5–8
Complete: $12–15*

HANGMAN/TIC-TAC-TOE/DOODLE

Manufacturer: APF
Rarity: 6
Loose: $5–8
Complete: $12–15*

PINBALL/DUNGEON HUNT/BLOCKOUT

Manufacturer: APF
Rarity: 6
Loose: $5–8*
Complete: $12–15*

SPACE DESTROYERS

Manufacturer: APF
Rarity: 8
Loose: $6–10*
Complete: $15–25*

UFO/SEA MONSTER/BREAK IT DOWN/RE-BUILD/SHOOT

Manufacturer: APF
Rarity: 7
Loose: $6–10*
Complete: $15–20*

Arcadia 2001 (Emerson, 1982)

If most casual fans of classic home video games were asked to list as many classic console systems that they could remember, chances are that the **Emerson Arcadia 2001** wouldn't make it to the list. The Arcadia 2001 was released at a time when the Atari 2600 and Intellivision were firmly entrenched as the top two competitors in the marketplace and ColecoVision was taking the world by storm with its state-of-the-art graphics and sound, so the system came and went without making much of an impact on the industry.

It wasn't that the Arcadia 2001 didn't have the technical specifications to compete—quite the opposite, actually. It had more memory than any of the systems on the market at the time (apart from the ColecoVision), and featured controllers with built-in numeric keypads (very similar to Intellivision controllers) that could be used to add additional controls to its games. On top of all this, the console was introduced with a $100 price tag, which made it the least expensive new console available at the time.

Unfortunately, the potential of the console was never fully realized, at least not in North America. Like the Magnavox Odyssey², Arcadia 2001 enjoyed far more success overseas than it did in the United States. That means that most of the games for this system were never made available to the handful of Arcadia 2001 owners in this country. A number of Arcadia 2001–compatible consoles and console variants were released overseas as well.

The games are a mix of original titles and clones of popular arcade games of the time, like *Breakaway* (*Breakout*), *Missile War* (*Missile Command*), and *Escape* (*Berzerk*). There were also licensed versions of a couple of obscure arcade titles like *Jungler* and *Red Clash*.

The Arcadia 2001 was difficult to find in its time, and is even more difficult to find today. The console commands a slightly higher price than many classic consoles due to its rarity and relative obscurity. It is particularly rare to find a boxed/complete system, so expect to pay a premium if you come across one. The console was packaged with two detachable controllers, each of which was equipped with a small joystick that screwed into the center of the control disk. No game cartridge was packaged with the console.

a   **The Emerson Arcadia 2001** *hit the video game marketplace in 1982 and vanished into history virtually unnoticed. It is probably one of the least-known classic console systems. (Photo courtesy of Cassidy Nolen.)*

The U.S. game catalog for Arcadia 2001 is very small—only 20 games. Thus, a complete collection of titles isn't hard to accumulate if you manage to actually find the games. For the most part, the cartridges are generally quite inexpensive, and even boxed/complete versions often sell for under $20. As always, you can expect to pay a bit more for the rarer titles. (See the price guide for details.)

Arcadia 2001 cartridges are roughly the size and shape of Atari 2600 cartridges, though some games were housed in longer cartridge cases. Boxes for Arcadia 2001 games seem to be fairly easy to find for the most part, so there is not a huge difference in price between loose and boxed games. Like most Intellivision games, Arcadia 2001 titles shipped with controller overlays that identified the functions of the keypad buttons. A game is not considered complete unless the overlays are present.

One difficulty facing Arcadia 2001 collectors who decide to collect the overseas game releases in addition to the U.S. titles is the wide array of name and packaging variations that exist among many of the foreign titles. If you intend to branch out beyond the North American titles, prepare for a challenging collecting experience.

Arcadia 2001 Price Guide
Arcadia Price Guide

ARCADIA 2001 CONSOLE
Manufacturer: Emerson
Rarity: 8
Loose: $30–60
Complete: $80–120*

3D BOWLING
Manufacturer: Emerson
Rarity: 3
Loose: $2–6
Complete: $6–8
Notes: Must include keypad overlays to be considered complete

ALIEN INVADERS
Manufacturer: Emerson
Rarity: 2
Loose: $3–5
Complete: $6–8
Notes: Must include keypad overlays to be considered complete

AMERICAN FOOTBALL
Manufacturer: Emerson
Rarity: 2
Loose: $3–5
Complete: $6–8
Notes: Must include keypad overlays to be considered complete

BASEBALL
Manufacturer: Emerson
Rarity: 2
Loose: $3–5
Complete: $6–8
Notes: Must include keypad overlays to be considered complete

BRAIN QUIZ
Manufacturer: Emerson
Rarity: 2
Loose: $3–5
Complete: $10–15
Notes: Must include keypad overlays to be considered complete

CAPTURE
Manufacturer: Emerson
Rarity: 2
Loose: $3–5
Complete: $6–8
Notes: Must include keypad overlays to be considered complete

CAT TRAX
Manufacturer: Emerson
Rarity: 2
Loose: $3–5
Complete: $4–6
Notes: Must include keypad overlays to be considered complete

ESCAPE
Manufacturer: Emerson
Rarity: 2
Loose: $3–5
Complete: $4–6
Notes: Must include keypad overlays to be considered complete

GRAND SLAM TENNIS
Manufacturer: Emerson
Rarity: 6
Loose: $12–16
Complete: $17–30
Notes: Must include keypad overlays to be considered complete

JUNGLER
Manufacturer: Emerson
Rarity: 2
Loose: $4–6
Complete: $7–8
Notes: Based on the 1981 Konami arcade game by the same name; must include keypad overlays to be considered complete

MISSILE WAR
Manufacturer: Emerson
Rarity: 5
Loose: $8–10
Complete: $10–15
Notes: Must include keypad overlays to be considered complete

OCEAN BATTLE
Manufacturer: Emerson
Rarity: 5
Loose: $10–15
Complete: $16–20
Notes: Must include keypad overlays to be considered complete

RED CLASH
Manufacturer: Emerson
Rarity: 8
Loose: $10–20
Complete: $25–35
Notes: Based on the 1982 Kaneko arcade game by the same name; must include keypad overlays to be considered complete

SOCCER
Manufacturer: Emerson
Rarity: 2
Loose: $3–5
Complete: $6–8
Notes: Must include keypad overlays to be considered complete

SPACE ATTACK
Manufacturer: Emerson
Rarity: 2
Loose: $3–5
Complete: $6–8
Notes: Must include keypad overlays to be considered complete

SPACE MISSION

Manufacturer: Emerson
Rarity: 3
Loose: $4–6
Complete: $7–9
Notes: Must include keypad overlays to be considered complete

SPACE RAIDERS

Manufacturer: Emerson
Rarity: 2
Loose: $3–5
Complete: $6–8
Notes: Must include keypad overlays to be considered complete

SPACE VULTURES

Manufacturer: Emerson
Rarity: 4
Loose: $3–15
Complete: $16–20
Notes: Must include keypad overlays to be considered complete

SPIDERS

Manufacturer: Emerson
Rarity: 6
Loose: $12–18
Complete: $20–25
Notes: Based on the 1981 Venture Line/Sigma arcade game by the same name; must include keypad overlays to be considered complete

STAR CHESS

Manufacturer: Emerson
Rarity: 5
Loose: $10–15
Complete: $16–20
Notes: Must include keypad overlays to be considered complete

TANKS A LOT

Manufacturer: Emerson
Rarity: 2
Loose: $3–5
Complete: $6–8
Notes: Must include keypad overlays to be considered complete

Bally Professional Arcade (Bally, 1977)

One distinction held by Bally's entry into the home video game market is the "classic console system with the most names" award. Originally released in 1978 as the **Bally Professional Arcade**, the console's name was changed to the Bally Computer System when Bally sold the rights to the console to Astrovision in 1981. Astrovision then rechristened the system Astrocade shortly before discontinuing it in 1984.

Regardless of the name on the console and the packaging, the Bally Professional Arcade was a rather impressive game system for its time. Unlike other classic consoles, the Bally Professional Arcade was powered by a Z-80 microprocessor, the same chip that Bally's arcade division, Midway, used in their coin-operated video games. As a result, the console's graphics and speed were superior to the Atari 2600 and other home systems that were on the market at the time. Like most console manufacturers, Bally promised an eventual upgrade that would turn the Professional Arcade into a full-fledged home computer. Bally never released such an upgrade, but a third-party developer called Viper Systems did produce a memory expansion module that included a 64-key keyboard. This rare, highly collectible peripheral resembles the equally rare Intellivision Keyboard Component. The console sits on top of the keyboard unit and connects to the unit via the interface port.

Even without a keyboard, the Professional Arcade was user-programmable. The console had a 24-key keypad and a built-in BASIC computer language interpreter that allowed players to write simple programs—though the basic console lacked a method for *saving* the programs. A BASIC cartridge with a cassette interface was later released. This cartridge greatly enhanced the programmability of the system. Professional Arcade owners all over the world soon started exchanging homemade games, creating a small cult following for the console.

The Bally Professional Arcade shipped with four built-in games and two detachable controllers. Bally's controllers are quite unique. The handle is a pistol grip with a trigger fire but-

a **The Bally Professional Arcade** *was a programmable game system that was, in many ways, ahead of its time. Though it sold well to a small niche audience, the console never gained widespread appeal. Pictured: the rare Montgomery Ward version of the console. (Photo courtesy of Cassidy Nolen.)*

ton and a small joystick/knob mounted on top. The console has ports to accommodate up to four controllers. A covered compartment on top of the console provides storage for game cartridges. An interface port on the back of the unit provides a connection point for peripherals such as memory expansions.

Bally's entry into the consumer video game marketplace was not a financially successful one. Rather than marketing their console through high-profile department store chains, Bally chose to sell the Professional Arcade through computer and television stores. The Professional Arcade was also priced higher than the competition—$100 more than the Atari 2600—another factor that severely limited sales. The systems that *did* sell were often defective. Early Professional Arcades had numerous flaws and many were returned.

Bally stopped selling the Professional Arcade in 1980. A year later, they sold the rights to Astrovision, who continued to produce the console (under various names) until 1984.

There are several console variations, all of which are electronically identical and packaged with the same controllers and built-in games. The differences are the packaging, nameplates, and small cosmetic variations:

- Bally Professional Arcade has a black case with wood grain highlights and a black nameplate. An alternate version, sold through Montgomery Ward department stores, sports a red nameplate and a Montgomery Ward logo, but is otherwise identical.

- The Bally Computer System can be found in the same black and wood grain motif as the Bally Professional Arcade. It is also available in a rarer white-case version.

- The Astrocade was exclusively produced in black and wood grain.

Cartridges for the Professional Arcade resemble cassette tapes (they are sometimes called "cassetridges" by collectors). The library of commercially released titles for the system is relatively small, and many titles are relatively inexpensive and easy to find. Most of the titles are original while some, like *Seawolf/Bombardier* and *Galaxian*, are based on Bally Midway arcade games. In addition to the commercial releases, there are a number of homebrew cartridges. Homebrew titles are generally harder to locate, and their prices reflect this.

A number of cartridges were packaged with overlays for the Professional Arcade's keypad. They include:

- *Bally BASIC*

- *Machine Language Manager*

- *Scribbling* (one of the built-in games)

These overlays must be included if the game is to be considered complete.

The easy programmability of the Professional Arcade might have inadvertently led to its lack of commercial success. The profit model of the console video game industry is based on selling the console itself at a loss and making profit from the games cartridges. Since the community most dedicated to the Professional Arcade console tended to program their own games—especially after the *Bally BASIC* cartridge and its cassette interface made saving games practical—a lot of games for this system were homemade titles traded among enthusiasts on cassettes. Some of these homebrew games were released for sale in limited numbers, but cassette-based Professional Arcade games are very difficult to find today. Since no complete list of titles is available, these games are not included in the price guide in this book.

Bally Professional Arcade Price Guide
Bally Price Guide

CONSOLE

ASTROCADE
Manufacturer: Astrocade, Inc.
Rarity: 5
Loose: $30–50
Complete: $70–100*
Notes: Renamed version of the Bally Computer System; packaged with 2 controllers; *Gunfight/ Checkmate/Calculator/Scribbling* multigame is built into the console

BALLY COMPUTER SYSTEM (WHITE)
Manufacturer: Astrovision
Rarity: 7
Loose: $45–75*
Complete: $90–120*
Notes: A limited number of consoles were housed in white cases—this version is rarer than the wood grain version; packaged with 2 controllers; *Gunfight/ Checkmate/Calculator/Scribbling* multigame is built into the console

BALLY COMPUTER SYSTEM (WOOD GRAIN)

Manufacturer: Astrovision
Rarity: 6
Loose: $35–70
Complete: $80–120*
Notes: Renamed version of the Bally Professional Arcade; packaged with 2 controllers; *Gunfight/Checkmate/Calculator/Scribbling* multigame is built into the console

BALLY PROFESSIONAL ARCADE CONSOLE (MONTGOMERY WARD)

Manufacturer: Bally
Rarity: 6
Loose: $45–75*
Complete: $90–120*
Notes: Version of the console manufactured for the Montgomery Ward department store chain; red label (instead of black); packaged with 2 controllers; *Gunfight/Checkmate/Calculator/Scribbling* multigame is built into the console

BALLY PROFESSIONAL ARCADE CONSOLE (WOOD GRAIN)

Manufacturer: Bally
Rarity: 5
Loose: $35–70
Complete: $80–120
Notes: Packaged with 2 controllers; *Gunfight/Checkmate/Calculator/Scribbling* multigame is built into the console

ACCESSORIES

64K RAM BOARD

Manufacturer: R&L Enterprises
Rarity: 10
Loose: $100–150*
Complete: $150–200*
Notes: Memory upgrade available from 1982–1984; originally sold for around $220

ARCADE DISPLAY CABINET

Manufacturer: Santa Cruz Wire and Mfg.
Rarity: 10
Loose: $500–1,000*
Complete: N/A
Notes: Cabinet designed as a store display; looks very much like a coin-operated arcade game; has a built-in cartridge selector that can house up to 10 cartridges

BASIC AUDIO CASSETTE INTERFACE

Manufacturer: Bally
Rarity: 9
Loose: $10–15*
Complete: $15–20*
Notes: Cable that connects the console to a cassette recorder (used for saving programs); not the same as the interface sold with the Bally BASIC cartridge

BLUE RAM

Manufacturer: Perkins Engineering
Rarity: 10
Loose: $100–150*
Complete: $150–200*
Notes: A unit that plugs into the interface port on the back of the console to expand the console's programming abilities; very rare

CONTROLLER, *I.C.B.M. ATTACK*

Manufacturer: Spectre Systems
Rarity: 10
Loose: $20–40*
Complete: $250–500*
Notes: Controller for the game *I.C.B.M. Attack*; originally shipped with the game, which is unplayable without it; complete version includes game

CONTROLLER, STANDARD

Manufacturer: Bally
Rarity: 6
Loose: $5–7
Complete: $12–17*
Notes: The standard controller included with the system

VIPER SYSTEM 1

Manufacturer: Viper Systems
Rarity: 10
Loose: $200–400*
Complete: $300–500*
Notes: 64-key keyboard and 16K memory expansion for the Professional Arcade; also available without the keyboard; very rare

VIPER SYSTEM 5

Manufacturer: Viper Systems
Rarity: 10
Loose: $200–400*
Complete: $300–500*
Notes: 64-key keyboard and memory expansion (16K or 32K) for the Professional Arcade; also available without the keyboard; very rare

GAMES

280 ZZZAP/DODGEM

Manufacturer: Bally
Rarity: 5
Loose: $5–8
Complete: $9–12

AMAZIN' MAZE/TIC-TAC-TOE

Manufacturer: Bally
Rarity: 6
Loose: $5–8
Complete: $9–12

ARTILLERY DUEL

Manufacturer: Astrocade, Inc.
Rarity: 6
Loose: $5–9
Complete: $10–14

ASTRO BATTLE

Manufacturer: Astrovision, Inc.
Rarity: 6
Loose: $5–8
Complete: $9–12
Notes: Originally released as *Space Invaders*

ASTROCADE PINBALL

Manufacturer: Astrovision, Inc.
Rarity: 7
Loose: $10–15
Complete: $18–25*
Notes: Originally released as *Bally Pin,* which is more common

BALLY BASIC

Manufacturer: Bally
Rarity: 6
Loose: $17–20
Complete: $20–30
Notes: Originally available both with and without a cassette tape interface; interface version is more common; includes a keypad overlay

BALLY BASIC DEMO

Manufacturer: Bally
Rarity: 8
Loose: $45–55
Complete: N/A
Notes: Demo distributed to dealers; difficult to find

BALLY PIN

Manufacturer: Bally
Rarity: 6
Loose: $5–8
Complete: $9–12
Notes: Later re-released as *Astrocade Pinball*

BINGO MATH/SPEED MATH

Manufacturer: Astrovision, Inc.
Rarity: 6
Loose: $5–8
Complete: $9–12

BIORHYTHM

Manufacturer: Astrovision, Inc.
Rarity: 5
Loose: $4–6
Complete: $8–10

BLACKJACK/POKER/ACEY-DEUCEY

Manufacturer: Bally
Rarity: 6
Loose: $5–8
Complete: $9–12

BLAST DROIDS

Manufacturer: Esoterica
Rarity: 8
Loose: $20–30
Complete: $45–60

BLUE RAM BASIC 1.1

Manufacturer: Perkins Engineering
Rarity: 8
Loose: $25–35
Complete: $40–50*
Notes: Requires at least 4K of expanded memory

CLOWNS/BRICKYARD

Manufacturer: Bally
Rarity: 5
Loose: $4–6
Complete: $8–10

COSMIC RAIDERS

Manufacturer: Astrocade, Inc.
Rarity: 7
Loose: $15–20
Complete: $25–35

DEALER DEMO

Manufacturer: Bally
Rarity: 8
Loose: $30–60
Complete: N/A
Notes: Demo distributed to dealers; difficult to find

DOGPATCH

Manufacturer: Astrovision, Inc.
Rarity: 7
Loose: $8–10
Complete: $12–16

ELEMENTARY MATH/BINGO MATH

Manufacturer: Bally
Rarity: 6
Loose: $5–8
Complete: $9–12

FOOTBALL

Manufacturer: Bally
Rarity: 5
Loose: $4–6
Complete: $8–10

GALACTIC INVASION

Manufacturer: Astrovision, Inc.
Rarity: 4
Loose: $4–5
Complete: $5–7
Notes: Originally released as *Galaxian*

GALAXIAN

Manufacturer: Astrovision, Inc.
Rarity: 6
Loose: $5–9
Complete: $10–14
Notes: Later re-released as *Galactic Invasion*

GRAND PRIX

Manufacturer: Astrovision, Inc.
Rarity: 6
Loose: $5–8
Complete: $9–12
Notes: Cartridge also includes *Demolition Derby*

I.C.B.M. ATTACK

Manufacturer: Spectre Systems
Rarity: 9
Loose: $65–80
Complete: $250–500
Notes: Requires a custom-built hand controller to play (controller was distributed with the game); various sources say that only 50–125 were made

THE INCREDIBLE WIZARD

Manufacturer: Astrocade, Inc.
Rarity: 5
Loose: $5–8
Complete: $10–14

LETTER MATCH/SPELL 'N SCORE/CROSSWORDS

Manufacturer: Bally
Rarity: 5
Loose: $4–6
Complete: $8–10

LIFE

Manufacturer: Conway
Rarity: 10
Loose: N/A
Complete: $440
Notes: Purportedly, the only copy in existence was available as of October 12, 2003, at Atari2600.com (http://www.atari2600.com)

MACHINE LANGUAGE MANAGER

Manufacturer: Bit Fiddlers
Rarity: 9
Loose: $45–60
Complete: $65–75*
Notes: Includes a keypad overlay

MAZEMAN

Manufacturer: Dave Carson
Rarity: Homebrew
Loose: $20–30
Complete: $55–65
Notes: Includes box

MS. CANDYMAN

Manufacturer: L&M Software
Rarity: 8
Loose: $25–35
Complete: $55–65

MULTI-CART

Manufacturer: Self-Published
Rarity: Homebrew
Loose: $100
Complete: N/A
Notes: Single cartridge that includes nearly all titles available for the system; fewer than 30 of these hand-made cartridges exist

MUNCHER

Manufacturer: Esoterica
Rarity: Prototype
Loose: $100–160
Complete: N/A
Notes: Cartridge label reads either "Test Programme" or "Demo" (never "Muncher"); *Pac-Man* clone

MUNCHER

Manufacturer: Esoterica
Rarity: Reproduction
Loose: N/A
Complete: $20–30

MUSIC MAKER

Manufacturer: Astrocade, Inc.
Rarity: Prototype
Loose: $85
Complete: N/A
Notes: A keypad overlay exists for this cartridge

PANZER ATTACK/RED BARON

Manufacturer: Bally
Rarity: 6
Loose: $5–8
Complete: $10–14

PIRATE'S CHASE

Manufacturer: Astrocade, Inc.
Rarity: 7
Loose: $8–12
Complete: $15–20

SEA DEVIL

Manufacturer: L&M Software
Rarity: 8
Loose: $25–35
Complete: $55–65

SEAWOLF/BOMBARDIER

Manufacturer: Bally
Rarity: 8
Loose: $15–25
Complete: $25–30*
Notes: Also known as *Seawolf/Missile;* this version is the rarer of the two

SEAWOLF/MISSILE

Manufacturer: Bally
Rarity: 5
Loose: $5–8
Complete: $9–12

SNEAKY SNAKE

Manufacturer: New Image
Rarity: Homebrew
Loose: N/A
Complete: $380
Notes: Atari2600.com (http://atari2600.com) asserts that they have the only known copy of this cartridge (for $380); other sources claim that many exist

SOCCER/SHOOT OUT

Manufacturer: Unknown
Rarity: 10
Loose: N/A
Complete: $360
Notes: Purportedly, the only copy in existence was available as of October 12, 2003, at Atari2600.com (http://www.atari2600.com)

SOLAR CONQUEROR

Manufacturer: Astrocade, Inc.
Rarity: 7
Loose: $8–15
Complete: $17–25

SPACE FORTRESS

Manufacturer: Astrovision, Inc.
Rarity: 5
Loose: $5–8
Complete: $10–15

SPACE INVADERS

Manufacturer: Bally
Rarity: 7
Loose: $10–15
Complete: $20–25*
Notes: Later re-released as *Astro Battle*

STAR BATTLE

Manufacturer: Bally
Rarity: 5
Loose: $5–8
Complete: $10–15

**TORNADO
BASEBALL/TENNIS/HOCKEY/HANDBALL**
Manufacturer: Bally
Rarity: 5
Loose: $5–8
Complete: $9–11

TREASURE COVE
Manufacturer: Esoterica
Rarity: 8
Loose: $20–30
Complete: $50–70

Fairchild Video Entertainment System/Channel F
(Fairchild Camera and Instrument, 1976)

At the 2003 Classic Gaming Expo, Nolan Bushnell (founder of Atari) commented that the development of programmable cartridge-based game consoles evolved out of necessity. Although companies had enjoyed great success with dedicated consoles, he said, "there are only so many of those things a person can pile in their closet."

While Atari was working on their solution to the programmable console equation, a newcomer to the video game business beat Atari to the punch. Fairchild Camera and Instrument released the **Fairchild Video Entertainment System** (better known by its later name, the Fairchild Channel F) in August 1976. This console was the first cartridge-based video game system, beating the Atari 2600 to the shelves by nearly a year. (Although some consider the original Magnavox Odyssey the first programmable system, the "cartridges" for the Odyssey were actually simple circuit boards that acted as switches—not game cartridges.)

The original Fairchild Video Entertainment System shipped with a built-in hockey/tennis game and two hardwired controllers. The controllers are unique, with triangular heads that mimic both joysticks and paddles. There is no fire button. To fire, you push down on the controller head. A covered compartment on the top of the unit acts as a storage area for the controllers. Sound is generated by the console itself rather than through the TV speaker.

The Fairchild Video Entertainment System did not fare well in the marketplace and was pulled from the shelves in 1977. As the video game industry continued to flourish and grow, the console resurfaced in a slightly altered form. Zircon International purchased the rights to the console from Fairchild and introduced the **Channel F System II** in 1982.

This console, which had been designed by Fairchild but never released, is slightly smaller than the original system. It shipped with the same built-in games as the original and two detachable controllers. The Channel F System II has no storage compartment on top—instead, it sports a small open storage area in the back that houses the controllers when not in use. Unlike the original console, the System II channels game sounds through the television speaker.

Zircon was fighting a losing battle. The Channel F's primitive graphics and small game library couldn't compete with the likes of the Atari 2600 and Intellivision. After a short comeback, the Channel F disappeared into video game history.

Both the Fairchild Video Entertainment System and the Channel F System II are somewhat difficult to find compared to the more popular systems of the time (though quite common when compared to the consoles released by APF and Arcadia described earlier in this chapter). Both models are nearly identical electronically (apart from the internal sound on the original console). The System II is slightly less common than the original.

a **Fairchild Video Entertainment System.** *Fairchild Camera and Instrument has the distinction of releasing the first cartridge-based home video game console (later renamed the Fairchild Channel F). The console was eclipsed in popularity by the Atari 2600 and other systems available at the time. (Photo courtesy of Cassidy Nolen.)*

b **Channel F System II.** *Zircon International bought the rights to all of the Channel F hardware and software from Fairchild and reintroduced the product line in 1982. In addition to a slightly redesigned console, Zircon released several new game cartridges. (Photo courtesy of Cassidy Nolen.)*

The Channel F software library consists of only 28 cartridges. Fairchild cartridges are bright yellow and are about the size and shape of an eight-track tape. Every game is prominently numbered. On some of the labels and packaging, it is difficult to find the actual name of the game(s), but the number is always obvious. For this reason, the Channel F price guide in this book lists the cartridges in numerical order rather than alphabetically by title.

Most Channel F cartridges are inexpensive and fairly easy to find considering the relative obscurity of the system. The most collectible of the lot are the games released by Zircon after the reintroduction of the console in 1982, and the two demonstration cartridges that Fairchild shipped to dealers to show off the features of the system.

Channel F is certainly not the most exciting classic game system, but it has great historical significance since it was the first of the cartridge-based consoles. Many collectors consider this reason enough to add the Channel F to their collections.

Channel F Price Guide
Fairchild Price Guide

CONSOLES

FAIRCHILD VIDEO ENTERTAINMENT SYSTEM
Manufacturer: Fairchild
Rarity: 5
Loose: $20–30
Complete: $35–65
Notes: Original release with hardwired controllers and RF cord; controllers are stored in a covered compartment; *Tennis/Hockey* game built-in; originally packaged as the Fairchild Video Entertainment System, later renamed as Fairchild Channel F

FAIRCHILD CHANNEL F SYSTEM II CONSOLE
Manufacturer: Fairchild
Rarity: 6
Loose: $25–40
Complete: $40–60
Notes: Updated (System II) version with removable controllers and a smaller controller compartment; *Tennis/Hockey* game built-in

ITT TELE-MATCH CONSOLE
Manufacturer: ITT Family Games
Rarity: 7
Loose: $50–80*
Complete: $90–125*
Notes: Compact Fairchild-compatible console with removable controllers and no controller compartment; *Tennis/Hockey* game built-in

ACCESSORIES

JOYSTICK, FAIRCHILD
Manufacturer: Fairchild
Rarity: 4
Loose: $3–5
Complete: $8–12*
Notes: Standard joystick for the updated Channel F console

JOYSTICK, ITT
Manufacturer: ITT Family Games
Rarity: 5
Loose: $10–12*
Complete: $15–20*
Notes: Standard joystick for the ITT Tele-Match console

GAMES

1: TIC-TAC-TOE/SHOOTING GALLERY/ DOODLE/QUADRADOODLE
Manufacturer: Fairchild
Rarity: 3
Loose: $1–3
Complete: $3–6

2: DESERT FOX/SHOOTING GALLERY
Manufacturer: Fairchild
Rarity: 3
Loose: $1–3
Complete: $3–6

3: VIDEO BLACKJACK
Manufacturer: Fairchild
Rarity: 3
Loose: $1–3
Complete: $3–6

4: SPITFIRE
Manufacturer: Fairchild
Rarity: 4
Loose: $3–6
Complete: $6–9

5: SPACE WAR
Manufacturer: Fairchild
Rarity: 3
Loose: $1–3
Complete: $3–6

6: MATH QUIZ I
Manufacturer: Fairchild
Rarity: 4
Loose: $4–6
Complete: $6–9

7: MATH QUIZ II
Manufacturer: Fairchild
Rarity: 4
Loose: $4–6
Complete: $6–9

8: MAGIC NUMBERS
Manufacturer: Fairchild
Rarity: 3
Loose: $1–3
Complete: $3–6

9: DRAG STRIP
Manufacturer: Fairchild
Rarity: 3
Loose: $1–3
Complete: $3–6

10: MAZE
Manufacturer: Fairchild
Rarity: 3
Loose: $1–3
Complete: $3–6

11: BACKGAMMON/ACEY-DEUCEY
Manufacturer: Fairchild
Rarity: 3
Loose: $1–3
Complete: $3–6

12: BASEBALL

Manufacturer: Fairchild
Rarity: 3
Loose: $1–3
Complete: $3–6

13: ROBOT WAR/TORPEDO ALLEY

Manufacturer: Fairchild
Rarity: 3
Loose: $1–3
Complete: $3–6

14: SONAR SEARCH

Manufacturer: Fairchild
Rarity: 3
Loose: $1–3
Complete: $3–6

15: MEMORY MATCH 1 & 2

Manufacturer: Fairchild
Rarity: 4
Loose: $4–6
Complete: $6–9

16: DODGE IT

Manufacturer: Fairchild
Rarity: 3
Loose: $1–3
Complete: $3–6

17: PINBALL CHALLENGE

Manufacturer: Fairchild
Rarity: 3
Loose: $1–3
Complete: $3–6

18: HANGMAN

Manufacturer: Fairchild
Rarity: 5
Loose: $5–8
Complete: $9–12

19: CHECKERS

Manufacturer: Zircon
Rarity: 6
Loose: $8–12
Complete: $15–20

20: VIDEO WHIZBALL

Manufacturer: Fairchild
Rarity: 4
Loose: $4–6
Complete: $6–9

21: BOWLING

Manufacturer: Fairchild
Rarity: 5
Loose: $3–6
Complete: $7–9

22: SLOT MACHINE

Manufacturer: Fairchild
Rarity: 6
Loose: $8–12
Complete: $15–20

23: GALACTIC SPACE WARS

Manufacturer: Zircon
Rarity: 6
Loose: $9–15
Complete: $18–25

24: PRO FOOTBALL

Manufacturer: Fairchild
Rarity: 6
Loose: $9–15
Complete: $18–25

25: CASINO POKER

Manufacturer: Zircon
Rarity: 8
Loose: $20–30*
Complete: $40–50*
Notes: Originally available only through mail order; very rare

26: ALIEN INVASION

Manufacturer: Zircon
Rarity: 8
Loose: $20–30*
Complete: $40–50*
Notes: Originally available only through mail order; very rare

DEMOCART 1

Manufacturer: Fairchild
Rarity: 9
Loose: $45–50*
Complete: $60–70*
Notes: Controller demonstration with a playable *Hockey* demo

DEMOCART 2

Manufacturer: Fairchild
Rarity: 9
Loose: $45–50*
Complete: $60–70
Notes: Noninteractive, multiproduct demo

RDI Halcyon (RDI, 1984)

The video game crash of 1983–1984 hit the home market a lot harder than it hit the arcade market at first. For a couple of years, the arcades continued to do fairly well thanks in large part to innovations in graphics and gameplay. One arcade innovation that made everyone sit up and take notice was the introduction of laser disc games.

In 1983, *Dragon's Lair* took the arcades by storm. The jaw-dropping game graphics looked like a beautifully animated cartoon. In fact, the game *was* a beautifully animated cartoon designed as a series of disjointed scenes that, together, formed a simple adventure story. The player con-

a   **The RDI Halycon** was one of the most ambitious—and most expensive—home video game systems of all time. It was the only console that brought laser disk arcade games into the home.

trolled the path of the story by guiding the actions of the game's main character. When the character performed an action, the laser disc accessed a new scene and displayed the result.

The reaction to *Dragon's Lair* was phenomenal, leading to the creation of a numerous laser disc arcade games. Although these games were initially thought to be the new path that video games would take in the future, they quickly lost their appeal. The graphics were second-to-none, but the gameplay of most of the games was simple and repetitive.

While the laser disc genre was at the height of its brief popularity, RDI Video Systems (founded by Rick Dyer, who had produced *Dragon's Lair*) designed the first—and only—home video game system designed to play laser disc games.

The Halcyon was a huge system that consisted of a laser disc player, the game unit (which was also sold as a stand-alone computer), and a keyboard. The system was packaged with *Thayer's Quest*, an adventure game that also appeared in arcades at the time. One other game, *NFL Football*—a simple football game that used live NFL game footage—was released concurrently with the system. Action in the games is controlled through keyboard input and vocally through a headset/microphone that was included with the system. The built-in voice recognition was part of a grand design to make Halcyon a central home computer that would eventually be capable of performing a myriad of simple household tasks.

Halcyon was introduced in a limited number of markets in early 1985. With a price tag of around $2,500 and a price of nearly $100 for the one additional game title available at launch, Halcyon's popularity was understandably limited. Although a number of game titles were promised for the system, only *Thayer's Quest* and *NFL Football* were actually completed before the console disappeared from store shelves less than a year later.

Very few Halcyon systems were sold during its brief lifetime, so the console is exceedingly rare today. It seldom, if ever, appears in the collectors' market, and it is therefore difficult to determine an accurate price range. It is likely that the rarity of the system and its historical significance would make it very pricey indeed should one ever surface.

RDI Halcyon Price Guide
RDI Price Guide

CONSOLES

RDI HALCYON CONSOLE
Manufacturer: RDI
Rarity: 10
Loose: $1,000–2,000*
Complete: $2,500–3,500*
Notes: Laser disc home game console released by the company that created the *Dragon's Lair* arcade game; originally cost $2,500; very rare

THAYER'S QUEST
Manufacturer: RDI
Rarity: 10
Loose: $100–200*
Complete: $200–300*
Notes: Laser disc originally packaged with the Halcyon system

GAMES

NFL FOOTBALL
Manufacturer: RDI
Rarity: 10
Loose: $75–90*
Complete: $95–150*
Notes: Other than *Thayer's Quest* (which was packaged with the system), this is the only game available for the RDI Halcyon console

Studio II (RCA, 1976)

RCA has the distinction of releasing the second cartridge-based video game console. The **RCA Studio II** Home TV Programmer was released in late 1976, not long after the Fairchild Video Entertainment System.

Studio II had several strikes against it from the start. At a time when even dedicated consoles generated color graphics, RCA chose to saddle Studio II with a primitive black-and-white display capability. In addition, RCA chose a rather nontraditional control method. Instead of knobs or joysticks, the Studio II uses two built-in calculator-style keypads for player input. Directional control in Studio II games is similar to using a computer keyboard's cursor keys to control PC action games.

Another drawback to this console, especially for collectors today, is its dedicated game/antenna/power switchbox. There is no present-day equivalent to replace this unique item, so Studio II units without the switchbox are completely useless.

a

a **The RCA Studio II** *was a very
basic cartridge-based system with
black-and-white graphics and no
controllers other than two built-in
keypads. (Photo courtesy of
Cassidy Nolen.)*

Not surprisingly, the Studio II didn't make a dent in the video game marketplace. Even so, despite being severely outclassed by the competition, the Studio II remained on the market until 1979.

The Studio II has five built-in games: *Doodle, Patterns, Bowling, Freeway*, and *Addition*. The game library consists of a mere 11 cartridges. Only one of these titles, *Bingo*, consistently commands a high price among collectors. The rarest game in the Studio II library, *Bingo*, included 150 marker chips and was packaged in a box larger than those of the rest of the RCA library. A complete version of this game (with all of the markers) is very difficult to find.

Most collectors consider Studio II one of the least collectible of the classic game consoles. If you are creating a timeline of classic systems, however, Studio II is certainly a necessary link in the chain.

One important thing to be aware of with regard to the Studio II is that this system, more than any other classic console, can cause severe screen burn-in on your television when playing for extended periods of time. If you intend to use the system, you should hook it up to a television or monitor that you don't mind the possibility of messing up.

Studio II Price Guide
RCA Price Guide

CONSOLES & ACCESSORIES

RCA STUDIO II HOME TV PROGRAMMER CONSOLE
Manufacturer: RCA
Rarity: 5
Loose: $25–35
Complete: $40–55
Notes: *Doodles/Patterns/Bowling/Freeway/Addition* multigame built in; uses a proprietary power/RF switch box (don't buy it if the switchbox isn't included or is malfunctioning)

POWER SUPPLY/RF SWITCHBOX
Manufacturer: RCA
Rarity: 8
Loose: $15–20
Complete: N/A*

GAMES

BASEBALL
Manufacturer: RCA
Rarity: 5
Loose: $3–5
Complete: $6–8

BINGO
Manufacturer: RCA
Rarity: 9
Loose: $20–30*
Complete: $45–55*
Notes: Packaged with 20 bingo cards and 150 marker chips (must include these items to be considered complete)

BIORHYTHM
Manufacturer: RCA
Rarity: 6
Loose: $6–9
Complete: $10–15

BLACKJACK
Manufacturer: RCA
Rarity: 3
Loose: $2–3
Complete: $4–6

FUN WITH NUMBERS
Manufacturer: RCA
Rarity: 5
Loose: $3–4
Complete: $5–7

GUNFIGHTER/MOONSHIP BATTLE
Manufacturer: RCA
Rarity: 6
Loose: $6–9
Complete: $10–15

SPACE WAR
Manufacturer: RCA
Rarity: 6
Loose: $6–9
Complete: $10–16

SPEEDWAY/TAG
Manufacturer: RCA
Rarity: 5
Loose: $3–4
Complete: $5–7

TENNIS/SQUASH
Manufacturer: RCA
Rarity: 4
Loose: $2–3
Complete: $4–6

TV SCHOOLHOUSE I
Manufacturer: RCA
Rarity: 6
Loose: $6–9*
Complete: $10–15*

TV SCHOOLHOUSE II
Manufacturer: RCA
Rarity: 6
Loose: $6–9*
Complete: $10–15*

Telstar Arcade (Coleco, 1978)

Depending on one's point of view, the **Telstar Arcade** is either a basic attempt at a cartridge-based video game console or the ultimate *Pong* system. As the home market became saturated with *Pong* clones in the mid-1970s, many companies (Coleco included) started adding new game types to their dedicated consoles to increase their replay value. As discussed in Chapter 3, it was not uncommon for dedicated systems to include target shooting games as well as the usual TV tennis variants.

With Telstar Arcade, Coleco took the idea of *Pong* system augmentation two steps beyond dedicated systems. The unique triangular console has a different set of controls built into each side.

a

a **Telstar Arcade,** *Coleco's first attempt at a cartridge-based game console, met with only limited success. It was Coleco's last console until ColecoVision in 1982. (Photo courtesy of Cassidy Nolen.)*

Side one has standard rotary knobs for *Pong*-style games, side two has a gearshift and steering wheel for driving games, and side three has a light gun for shooting games.

Telstar Arcade's other upgrade from the dedicated console crowd was the ability to use interchangeable cartridges to increase the variety of games available for the system. This wasn't a new idea at the time—several cartridge-based systems were available by the time Telstar Arcade hit the shelves—but the programmability combined with the unique control options made this system stand out from the rest of the crowd, at least from a design perspective.

Unfortunately for Coleco, the unique design of the unit wasn't enough to make the console a serious competitor. Had the Telstar Arcade shipped on time (in 1977), it would have stood a fighting chance against systems like Fairchild Channel F and RCA Studio II. As it was, the system didn't hit store shelves until 1978, and by that time the Atari 2600 had already become the console of choice. Compared to the 2600, Telstar Arcade was a primitive and much less versatile system. As a result, the console's shelf life was quite short. After the failure of Telstar Arcade, Coleco dropped out of the video game console market for four years and instead set their sights on the growing handheld electronic game market.

Telstar Arcade cartridges are as unique as the system itself. Like the console, the cartridges are triangular. Another unique visual feature of the cartridges is their silver color. This was developed out of necessity. During testing, the cartridges put out a great deal of electronic interference. To block the interference, the carts were coated in aluminum.

Only four cartridges were produced for the Telstar Arcade. The first, which includes three games—*Road Race, Tennis*, and *Quick Draw*, one game for each controller type—was packaged with the console. The other three games were available separately. Because each cartridge includes up to four games, the cartridges are identified by number rather than by game titles.

Although a complete Telstar Arcade collection consists of a mere six items, two of these items are very difficult to find today. Telstar Cartridge 4 is the rarest of the three additional cartridges, and you can expect to pay more for it than you do for the console itself.

The other rare item is the set of remote paddle controllers available for the system. These are so rare, in fact, that most collector web sites and books don't even list them. They were designed for use with Telstar Cartridge 2, which includes four-player versions of *Hockey* and *Tennis*. The Paddle Controllers plug into the Remote port above the connector for the light gun.

Telstar Arcade uses a standard antenna/game switch and is packaged with an AC adaptor. Like the original Fairchild Video Entertainment System, sound is generated through the console itself rather than through the television speaker.

Because it is a unique system that is fairly easy (if not inexpensive) to collect, Telstar Arcade is popular among collectors. This short-lived, odd-looking console is a great addition to any classic video game collection.

Telstar Arcade Price Guide
Telstar Price Guide

CONSOLE & ACCESSORIES

TELSTAR ARCADE CONSOLE
Manufacturer: Coleco
Rarity: 6
Loose: $30–50
Complete: $60–100
Notes: Box and instructions are rare; instructions alone often sell for $20 or more

PADDLE CONTROLLERS
Manufacturer: Coleco
Rarity: 10
Loose: $15–20*
Complete: $25–35*
Notes: A pair of paddle controllers that allowed 4-players to play *Hockey* and *Tennis* on Telstar Cartridge 2; very rare

GAMES

TELSTAR ARCADE CARTRIDGE 1
Manufacturer: Coleco
Rarity: 6
Loose: $10–15
Complete: N/A
Notes: 3 games: *Road Race, Quick Draw*, and *Tennis*; packaged with the Telstar Arcade console

TELSTAR ARCADE CARTRIDGE 2
Manufacturer: Coleco
Rarity: 7
Loose: $15–20
Complete: $30–45*
Notes: 4 games: *Hockey, Tennis, Handball*, and *Target*; *Hockey* and *Tennis* have a 4-player option that requires the add-on Paddle Controllers

TELSTAR ARCADE CARTRIDGE 3
Manufacturer: Coleco
Rarity: 7
Loose: $15–20
Complete: $30–45*
Notes: 4 games: *Bonus Pinball, Deluxe Pinball, Shooting Gallery*, and *Shoot the Bear*

TELSTAR ARCADE CARTRIDGE 4
Manufacturer: Coleco
Rarity: 9
Loose: $50–60*
Complete: $75–85*
Notes: 3 games: *Naval Battle, Blast-away*, and *Speed Ball*; difficult to find

a

a **Vectrex** *was Milton Bradley's first and only entry into the home video game console market. It is a unique and highly collectible system that stands out as one of the most advanced and ambitious consoles of the classic era.*

Vectrex (GCE/Milton Bradley, 1982)

In the early days of arcade video games, one of the major obstacles that programmers faced was graphic resolution. Video game hardware at the time was capable of generating only blocky images at the time on a standard raster (TV-style) monitor.

In the late 1970s, Larry Rosenthal, an engineer and programmer at Cinematronics, developed a system for displaying game graphics on a vector monitor (a monitor like those used on scientific equipment like oscilloscopes). Vector graphics had the advantage of being able to produce crisp images and thin, straight lines. Cinematronics and several other arcade game manufacturers released a number of vector games that were very popular in the arcades. (For more information on raster and vector graphics in arcade games, see Chapter 12.)

Although several console systems had introduced home versions of popular vector arcade games like *Asteroids*, these games lost a great deal of graphic detail when converted to the raster graphics used in the home consoles. Unfortunately, there was no alternative—at least, not until 1982 when GCE, a company known for its wristwatch-sized LCD games, designed a new home console that incorporated a nine-inch vector monitor.

The **Vectrex** was (and still is) a totally unique video game console. Originally selling for $200, this stand-alone console was able to produce true arcade-style graphics—something that no other console on the market at the time could achieve. The game library for the Vectrex included home versions of popular vector arcade games such as *Armor Attack*, *Rip-Off*, and *Space Wars*. Some conversions of raster arcade games were also released for the Vectrex, including *Pole Position* and *Berzerk*, which are rather interesting to see in vector form.

Players were drawn to the Vectrex by the great graphics. Parents loved it because it didn't need to be hooked to the television. It seemed the console had the makings of a hit.

Unfortunately, the video game crash was just around the corner and Vectrex fell on the same hard times as all other video game systems. GCE was shut down, and after a brief period of marketing the system directly, Milton Bradley (which had purchased the rights to the system) ceased production on the Vectrex in late 1984.

By comparison to other classic consoles, Vectrex sales were rather modest. The system did garner a strong cult following at the time, however, and the cult continues to grow today. Vectrex is currently one of the most collected classic console systems.

Vectrex shipped with a single controller that snaps into a slot below the screen. Replacement and additional controllers are difficult to come by and rather expensive. Several hobbyist-produced replacements, including one that uses a converted Sega Genesis controller, are occasionally available at classic game events and online.

The Vectrex has one built-in game—an *Asteroids*-like game called *Mine Storm*. The vector monitor is black and white, since color vector monitors were more expensive and less reliable. One color Vectrex prototype exists, but it is unlikely that it would ever show up in the collectors' market—it is owned by Jay Smith, the founder of GCE.

There were 27 cartridges commercially released for the Vectrex in the United States during its short lifespan. Most of the cartridges include plastic full-screen overlays that fit onto the monitor to add color and, in some cases, graphic elements to the games. Although these overlays are not vital to gameplay, they do add to the experience and are prized by collectors. Expect to pay more for cartridges that include overlays. Other than the few titles that didn't use overlays, no Vectrex game is considered complete unless the overlay is included. Note that *Mine Storm*, the built-in game, also has an overlay. The console itself is not considered complete without the *Mine Storm* overlay.

The Vectrex is second only to the Atari 2600 when it comes to homebrew titles. New fan-produced Vectrex cartridges are being produced on a semiregular basis. One or two new titles seem to surface every year at classic game conventions and shows.

One of the most convenient ways to amass a near-complete Vectrex game collection is to purchase a Vectrex Multi-Cart. A number of Multi-Cart variants have been produced over the years, but the best of the bunch is the one manufactured by collector Sean Kelly. Sean's menu-driven cartridge includes all of the commercially released Vectrex titles and a huge number of the homebrew games and demos. Although some purists might not consider such a game collection "official," it certainly saves space and money. The main drawback is the lack of screen overlays.

Kelly's Vectrex Multi-Cart is usually available at the Classic Gaming Expo. Multi-Carts occasionally show up in online auctions as well. Details on the Vectrex Multi-Cart (and multicarts for other systems as well) can be found on Sean Kelly's Web site (http://home.xnet.com/~skelly/multis.htm).

Two notable hardware add-ons were produced for the Vectrex: the Light Pen and the 3D Imager. The Light Pen plugs into the controller port and allows you to draw and interact with objects directly on the screen. Only three cartridges support the Light Pen:

- *Art Master* (packaged with the Light Pen)

- *Animaction*

- *Melody Master*

The Light Pen titles do not function without the pen peripheral and do not include screen overlays. The cartridges themselves are easier to find than the Light Pen. The Light Pen is very collectible and can cost quite a bit, especially complete/boxed.

The 3D Imager is one of the most collectible Vectrex items and is extremely rare. It is a bulky headset with special eyepieces that rectify the screen image from supported games into 3-D images. Three 3-D cartridges were produced:

- *3D Mine Storm* (packaged with the 3D Imager)

- *3D Crazy Coaster*

- *3D Narrow Escape*

Like the Light Pen games, the 3-D games do not include screen overlays. Another similarity to the Light Pen games is that the 3-D titles are much easier to find than the peripheral they require in order to function. Without the 3D Imager, the 3-D cartridges do not function. The 3D Imager includes two color wheels that are necessary for the unit to function. Don't bother buying the 3D Imager if the color wheels are missing.

The 3D Imager is one of the Holy Grails among Vectrex collectors, and it isn't uncommon for this item to sell for far more than the Vectrex system itself, especially for a boxed, complete version.

Other noncartridge Vectrex Holy Grails are the extremely rare store display stand ($500–$1,200) and the carrying case for the console.

Cartridges vary widely in cost and rarity. As is true with many systems, the games that were released late in the console's life tend to be the rarest. The hardest-to-find title for Vectrex is *Polar Rescue*, the price of which can get into the triple digits.

Prices on some of the more common Vectrex titles can also be relatively high due to their popularity among collectors. *Star Castle* is an excellent example. Although this game isn't terribly hard to find, it is the *only* version of *Star Castle* produced for any home console system. For this reason, the prices for complete copies of this title tend to be high.

Vectrex arguably stands the test of time better than any other classic console system. The unique nature of the console, combined with the excellent gameplay value of the games, make the Vectrex one of the most sought-after classic video game collectibles.

Vectrex Price Guide
Vectrex Price Guide

CONSOLE

VECTREX
Manufacturer: GCE
Rarity: 5
Loose: $50–80
Complete: $90–150
Notes: Complete version includes 1 controller and the overlay and instructions for the built-in game (*Mine Storm*)

ACCESSORIES

3D IMAGER
Manufacturer: GCE
Rarity: 8
Loose: $200–275
Complete: $300–425
Notes: Complete version includes *3D Mine Storm* and a color wheel (required to play the three 3D games)

CARRYING CASE
Manufacturer: GCE
Rarity: 10
Loose: $100–150*
Complete: $150–200*
Notes: Originally available only through mail order from GCE; very rare; cheaper reproductions can also be found

CONTROLLER, MODIFIED SEGA GENESIS
Manufacturer: Classic Game Creations
Rarity: Homebrew
Loose: $20
Complete: N/A
Notes: A Sega Genesis controller modified for use with the Vectrex; available from Classic Game Creations (http://www.classicgamecreations.com)

CONTROL PANEL (JOYSTICK)
Manufacturer: GCE
Rarity: 6
Loose: $25–40
Complete: $50–60
Notes: The standard controller for the Vectrex

DUST COVER
Manufacturer: GCE
Rarity: 10
Loose: $60–90*
Complete: $90–125*
Notes: Originally available only through mail order from GCE; very rare

LIGHT PEN
Manufacturer: GCE
Rarity: 7
Loose: $50–90
Complete: $140–160
Notes: Complete version includes *Art Master* cartridge

VECTREX STORE DISPLAY STAND
Manufacturer: GCE
Rarity: 10
Loose: N/A
Complete: $500–1,200
Notes: A store display stand that holds the Vectrex and controller, and houses 50 or so cartridges; very rare, very big, and very expensive

GAMES

3D CRAZY COASTER
Manufacturer: GCE
Rarity: 8
Loose: $50–60
Complete: $65–70*
Notes: Requires the 3D Imager; no overlay

3D MINE STORM
Manufacturer: GCE
Rarity: 8
Loose: $40–50
Complete: N/A
Notes: Originally packaged with the 3D Imager; requires the 3D Imager; no overlay

3D NARROW ESCAPE
Manufacturer: GCE
Rarity: 8
Loose: $25–35
Complete: $40–50
Notes: Requires the 3D Imager; no overlay

ALL GOOD THINGS
Manufacturer: Classic Game Creations
Rarity: Homebrew
Loose: N/A
Complete: $20
Notes: Several games on a single cartridge; currently available from Classic Game Creations (http://www.classicgamecreations.com); no manual

ANIMACTION
Manufacturer: GCE
Rarity: 7
Loose: $8–15
Complete: $40–50
Notes: Requires the Light Pen; no overlay

ARMOR ATTACK
Manufacturer: GCE
Rarity: 2
Loose: $5–10
Complete: $15–25

ART MASTER
Manufacturer: GCE
Rarity: 6
Loose: $10–20
Complete: N/A
Notes: Originally packaged with the Light Pen; requires the Light Pen; no overlay

BEDLAM
Manufacturer: GCE
Rarity: 4
Loose: $10–15
Complete: $20–30

BERZERK
Manufacturer: GCE
Rarity: 3
Loose: $5–9
Complete: $10–20

BERZERK DEBUGGED
Manufacturer: Self-Published
Rarity: Hack
Loose: N/A
Complete: $10
Notes: Available from Mark's Video Game Manufacturing (http://www.vectrexcarts.com)

BLITZ!
Manufacturer: GCE
Rarity: 4
Loose: $7–10
Complete: $12–22

CLEAN SWEEP
Manufacturer: GCE
Rarity: 3
Loose: $7–12
Complete: $15–25

COSMIC CHASM
Manufacturer: GCE
Rarity: 3
Loose: $7–10
Complete: $15–25

FORTRESS OF NARZOD
Manufacturer: GCE
Rarity: 4
Loose: $10–15
Complete: $20–45

GCE'S TOUR DE FRANCE
Manufacturer: Self-Published
Rarity: Homebrew
Loose: N/A
Complete: $10
Notes: Available from Mark's Video Game Manufacturing (http://www.vectrexcarts.com)

GRAVITREX
Manufacturer: Classic Game Creations
Rarity: Homebrew
Loose: N/A
Complete: $20
Notes: Based on the Atari arcade game *Gravitar;* currently available from Classic Game Creations (http://www.classicgamecreations.com); no manual

HEADS UP ACTION SOCCER
Manufacturer: GCE
Rarity: 6
Loose: $15–25
Complete: $30–40

HYPERCHASE
Manufacturer: GCE
Rarity: 3
Loose: $5–9
Complete: $10–20

MELODY MASTER
Manufacturer: GCE
Rarity: 8
Loose: $10–30
Complete: $40–70
Notes: Requires the Light Pen; no overlay

MINE STORM (II)
Manufacturer: GCE
Rarity: 10
Loose: $100–200*
Complete: ?
Notes: Cartridge version of the built-in *Mine Storm* game that fixed a bug in the original; originally available directly from GCE; very rare

MINE STORM (II)
Manufacturer: Self-Published
Rarity: Reproduction
Loose: N/A
Complete: $10
Notes: Reproduction of GCE's *Mine Storm II;* currently available from Mark's Video Game Manufacturing (http://www.vectrexcarts.com)

MOON LANDER
Manufacturer: Clay Cowgill
Rarity: Homebrew
Loose: N/A
Complete: $10
Notes: Based on the Atari arcade game *Lunar Lander;* currently available from Mark's Video Game Manufacturing (http://www.vectrexcarts.com)

MULTI-CART
Manufacturer: Sean Kelly
Rarity: Homebrew
Loose: $70–125
Complete: N/A
Notes: Includes nearly all of Vectrex games and demos on a single cartridge, menu-selectable; no box or manual; currently available

MULTI-CART
Manufacturer: Mark Woodward
Rarity: Homebrew
Loose: $70–125*
Complete: N/A
Notes: Rarer multigame cartridge with fewer games

OMEGA CHASE DELUXE
Manufacturer: Self-Published
Rarity: Homebrew
Loose: $50–60*
Complete: $20–30
Notes: Complete version includes a box and rule sheet, fairly easy to find; a collectors' edition also exists, but is rarer and more expensive

PATRIOTS

Manufacturer: Classic Game Creations
Rarity: Homebrew
Loose: N/A
Complete: $20
Notes: Based on the Atari arcade game *Missile Command;* currently available from Classic Game Creations (http://www.classicgamecreations.com); no manual

POLAR RESCUE (PROTOTYPE)

Manufacturer: Self-Published
Rarity: Reproduction
Loose: N/A
Complete: $10
Notes: Reproduction of GCE's prototype; currently available from Mark's Video Game Manufacturing (http://www.vectrexcarts.com); no overlay

POLAR RESCUE

Manufacturer: GCE
Rarity: 8
Loose: $50–60*
Complete: $90–100

POLE POSITION

Manufacturer: GCE
Rarity: 8
Loose: $15–25
Complete: $45–60

RIP-OFF

Manufacturer: GCE
Rarity: 3
Loose: $5–9
Complete: $10–15

ROCKAROIDS REMIX

Manufacturer: John Dondzila
Rarity: Homebrew
Loose: N/A
Complete: $10
Notes: Based on the Atari arcade game *Asteroids;* currently available from Mark's Video Game Manufacturing (http://www.vectrexcarts.com)

RONEN'S GAME CART

Manufacturer: Ronen Habot
Rarity: Homebrew
Loose: N/A
Complete: $10
Notes: Includes the games *VectRace* and *Vaboom!;* currently available from Mark's Video Game Manufacturing (http://www.vectrexcarts.com)

SCRAMBLE

Manufacturer: GCE
Rarity: 2
Loose: $3–6
Complete: $12–20

SOLAR QUEST

Manufacturer: GCE
Rarity: 4
Loose: $4–8
Complete: $10–15

SPACE WARS

Manufacturer: GCE
Rarity: 4
Loose: $9–12
Complete: $30–35

SPIKE!

Manufacturer: GCE
Rarity: 4
Loose: $8–10
Complete: $11–20

SPIKE HOPPIN'

Manufacturer: Classic Game Creations
Rarity: Homebrew
Loose: N/A
Complete: $20
Notes: Based on the arcade game *Q*Bert;* currently available from Classic Game Creations (http://www.classicgamecreations.com); no manual

SPIKE'S WATER BALLOONS ANALOG

Manufacturer: John Dondzila
Rarity: Homebrew
Loose: N/A
Complete: $10
Notes: Available from Mark's Video Game Manufacturing (http://www.vectrexcarts.com)

SPINBALL

Manufacturer: GCE
Rarity: 4
Loose: $9–12
Complete: $20–30
Notes: Also known as *Flipper Pinball*

SPINNERAMA

Manufacturer: Self-Published
Rarity: Homebrew
Loose: ?
Complete: $20–30
Notes: Versions of 11 Vectrex games updated to use an Atari 2600 Driving Controller for input; must include box and controller to be complete

STAR CASTLE

Manufacturer: GCE
Rarity: 6
Loose: $12–20
Complete: $45–55

STAR TREK DEBUGGED

Manufacturer: Self-Published
Rarity: Hack
Loose: N/A
Complete: $10
Notes: *Star Trek: The Motion Picture* with updated graphics and a pause feature; available from Mark's Video Game Manufacturing (http://www.vectrexgames.com)

STAR TREK: THE MOTION PICTURE

Manufacturer: GCE
Rarity: 2
Loose: $4–8
Complete: $10–15
Notes: Not in any way related to the Sega *Star Trek* arcade game; also known as *Star Ship*

STARHAWK
Manufacturer: GCE
Rarity: 4
Loose: $9–12
Complete: $20–30

V-FROGGER
Manufacturer: Chris Salomon
Rarity: Homebrew
Loose: N/A
Complete: $10
Notes: Based on the arcade game *Frogger;* currently available from Mark's Video Game Manufacturing (http://www.vectrexcarts.com)

VEC SPORTS BOXING
Manufacturer: Good Deal Games
Rarity: Homebrew
Loose: N/A
Complete: $25
Notes: Available from Good Deal Games (http://www.gooddealgames.com); no overlay

VECMAINIA
Manufacturer: Classic Game Creations
Rarity: Homebrew
Loose: N/A
Complete: $20
Notes: Several games and demos on a single cartridge; currently available from Classic Game Creations (http://www.classicgamecreations.com); no manual

VECTOPIA
Manufacturer: Classic Game Creations
Rarity: Homebrew
Loose: N/A
Complete: $20
Notes: Several games and demos on a single cartridge; currently available from Classic Game Creations (http://www.classicgamecreations.com); no manual

VECTOR VADERS
Manufacturer: Classic Game Creations
Rarity: Homebrew
Loose: N/A
Complete: $20
Notes: Based on the arcade game *Space Invaders;* currently available from Classic Game Creations (http://www.classicgamecreations.com); no manual

VECTRACE
Manufacturer: Ronen Habot
Rarity: Homebrew
Loose: $15–25*
Complete: N/A
Notes: An updated version of this game is included on the *All Good Things* cartridge

WEBWARS
Manufacturer: GCE
Rarity: 5
Loose: $7–15
Complete: $15–25
Notes: Also known as *Web Warp*

10 Classic Handheld and Tabletop Games

Video games and electronic handheld games share a parallel evolutionary path. Both were introduced at nearly the same time (the 1970s), and both grew increasingly complex as the components used to build them became more compact and more sophisticated.

The earliest handheld electronic games that appeared on toy store shelves in the early 1970s were "electronic" only in that they used batteries to power simple lighting effects. Often, lights were combined with electric or wind-up motors that moved the lights around. Tomy's *Blip*, for example, used a light-emitting diode (LED) mounted on a motorized moving arm to produce a *Pong*-like electromechanical tennis game.

As home video games began to gain popularity in the mid-'70s, some companies ignored the trend and instead threw their development efforts into electronic handheld games. One of the most prominent companies in this category was Mattel, who stayed out of the home video game market until 1980. Mattel produced the first 100% electronic handheld game, *Auto Race*, in 1976. Shortly thereafter, they followed up with a series of handheld sports games that became extremely popular. Other prominent companies in the early handheld market included Coleco, Entex, Bandai, Tomy, and Milton Bradley.

Many of these companies also produced successful lines of tabletop games. Similar in most respects to handheld games, tabletop games have larger screens and often include more complex controls or multiple sets of controls that allow two players to play simultaneously.

Early handheld and tabletop games use one of three different display types:

- Light-emitting diode (LED): The simplest display type, LED games generate static lights or simple moving blips, usually in red, on the game screen. Examples of typical LED games include the popular handheld sports games by Mattel and Coleco.

- Liquid crystal display (LCD): LCD displays began to appear early in the handheld era, and continue to be used in many of today's handheld games. These black-and-white displays are

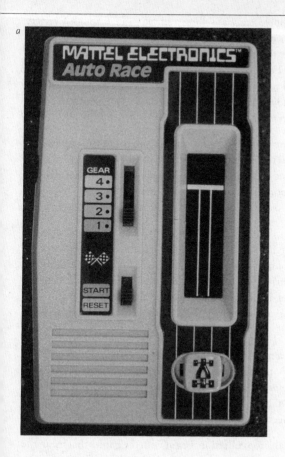

NOTE **

Throughout the text,
BOLD indicates that an
item appears in a picture.

a **Mattel's Auto Race** *was the first fully electronic handheld game ever produced. (Photo courtesy of Rik Morgan, http://www. handheldmuseum.com.)*

capable of displaying more complex objects and action. Classic examples include most of the pocket-sized handhelds produced by Radio Shack/Tandy.

- Vacuum fluorescent display (VFD): A bright, full-color display that is used in many tabletop games. Examples include Coleco's tabletop arcade series.

As was true in the home video game market, early successes by the pioneers in the handheld and tabletop game field induced dozens of other companies to try their hand at handheld game development. For example, there were more than a dozen handheld LED football games, all of which bear a striking resemblance to Mattel's 1978 LED *Football* game, released in the late '70s and early '80s.

Next to sports games, classic arcade hits were the most popular subject of classic handheld and tabletop games. A myriad of *Space Invaders* and *Pac-Man* clones were produced with just-different-enough-to-avoid-lawsuit titles like *Space Attack* and *Packri Monster*. Licensed reproductions of arcade games also made it into the handheld and tabletop world. Perhaps the most collectible examples of these are the tabletop arcade games by Coleco.

A popular practice during the classic handheld era was selling a single game through a variety of distributors. In some cases, the appearance and name of the game was changed when another company distributed it, while in other cases the game was identical to the original version except for new packaging and the brand name. For example, Sears department stores sold a line of LED sports games under the Sears brand name, but most of the games were simply relabeled versions of Coleco and Entex products. Radio Shack/Tandy also primarily sold handheld games that were licensed from other manufacturers.

In most cases, classic handheld and tabletop games were limited to a single built-in game. This began to change over time as handheld and tabletop manufacturers, like their home video game counterparts, realized that consumers could only buy so many games before their closets began to overflow. Most of the early attempts at portable multigame machines used switches to change between multiple built-in games (usually sports titles with similar gameplay), and plastic overlays to change the playing field.

Prior to the release of the Nintendo Game Boy in 1989, few portable games had a library of interchangeable cartridges. There were a couple of exceptions, however. Milton Bradley's Micro-Vision, released in 1979, was the first cartridge-based handheld game. Several classic tabletop games were also cartridge-based. Most notable among these was the innovative Adventure Vision by Entex. Other entries in this category include Sears' *7-in-1 Sports*, Coleco's *Total Control 4,* and Entex's *Select-A-Game Machine*.

Classic handheld and tabletop games are a mixed lot when it comes to collectibility. Some, like Mattel's LED sports games and Coleco's tabletop arcade series, generally fetch high prices among collectors today, and Entex's *Adventure Vision* is one of the highest-priced and most coveted classic game systems of *any* type. Other handhelds, especially those released by obscure manufacturers, are all but ignored by collectors.

When starting a classic handheld and/or tabletop collection, begin with the games that mean the most to you personally and continue from there. Because there were literally hundreds of handheld and tabletop games released in the classic era, this branch of classic game collecting is one of the most demanding in terms of time and effort, and is likely to be a lifetime pursuit if you intend to collect every classic handheld game ever made.

The subject of classic handheld games is huge and could easily warrant a dedicated price guide. As such, it is necessary to narrow the field somewhat for this book. This chapter covers only fully electronic games (no electromechanical games) released in North America between 1976 and 1985, with occasional exceptions for particularly collectible titles and classic game titles released in the late '80s.

For the most part, only games that fall into the general gameplay pattern of video games—games with displays/screens that react to user input—are covered here. The exceptions to this rule are popular electronic games like *Simon* that are considered classic among today's collectors.

Because there are so many games and manufacturers in this category, full information (such as release dates) for all of the listed games is not available. Unavailable data is indicated by a question mark in the price lists.

The following sections describe some of the top manufacturers and some of the better-known classic handheld and tabletop games they produced. For more information on handheld and tabletop game companies and the games they produced, check out the Handheld Game Mu-

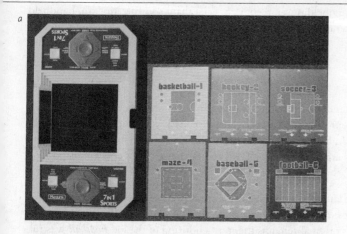

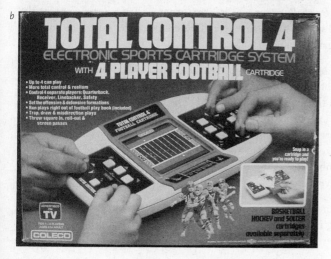

a **Sears' 7-in-1 Sports** *is an example of an early handheld that was able to play more than one game. (Photo courtesy of Rik Morgan, http://www.handheldmuseum. com.)*

b **Coleco's Total Control 4** *was one of a handful of early portable games that played multiple games that were available on interchangeable cartridges. (Photo courtesy of Rik Morgan, http:// www.handheldmuseum.com.)*

seum web site (http://www.handheldmuseum.com). Special thanks to Rik Morgan, handheld game enthusiast and webmaster of the Handheld Game Museum, who provided photos and information for this chapter.

Mattel

Mattel kicked off the classic handheld era with *Auto Race* in 1976. The object of this calculator-sized game is to maneuver your racecar (a player-controlled LED blip) through traffic (computer-controlled LED blips) on a three-lane racetrack as you raced endlessly toward the top of the screen. The only controls are a slider that allows you to change lanes and a four-position gearshift switch.

This simple game became the launch title for an entire line of handheld sports games by Mattel. The second game in the series, **Football,** was an instant hit and spawned dozens of clones by other manufacturers. Mattel's original remains the most enduring of the lot. *Football* was followed by *Football 2, Basketball, Baseball, Soccer,* and *Hockey* (to name a few). Some games in the Mattel sports line were reissued several times, so several different box styles exist. The box style doesn't significantly affect the game's value.

With classic video game collecting on the rise today, Mattel recently cashed in on its former success by re-releasing a number of its LED sports titles for nostalgia buffs. *Football, Football 2, Baseball,* and a number of other titles were released in 2001. The re-released versions of Mattel's classic games are a great way to experience the games firsthand without paying collectors' prices for them. If you are searching for the originals, however, make sure that they *are* original. Without the packaging, the newly released reproductions can pass for their original counterparts rather easily. The rule of thumb is that if the word "Classic" appears above the name on the front of the game, it's the 2001 version.

Mattel's success did more than dominate the classic handheld electronic game market—it *created* the market. Following in Mattel's footsteps, other companies jumped on the handheld game bandwagon to get their chunk of what would become a half-billion-dollar business.

Coleco

Coleco jumped into the handheld game industry after a brief foray into video game consoles. When their first cartridge-based console, the Telstar Arcade, failed to achieve a significant following, Coleco almost went under. Handheld and tabletop games provided much-needed revenue that kept the company alive into the early '80s.

Coleco LED Sports Games

Coleco's first handhelds were designed to compete with Mattel's popular LED sports line. *Electronic Quarterback* was nearly identical in gameplay to Mattel's *Football*, but added a passing option and the ability to run backward as well as forward.

While Mattel stuck with single-player sports games, Coleco introduced their *Head to Head* series. These LED sports games gave players the option of competing against a human opponent rather than the computer, such as **Coleco *Head to Head Baseball*.** For much of the classic era, Coleco battled Mattel for dominance of the LED handheld sports game category.

a **Mattel's LED** Football *was copied by dozens of companies after its initial release, but remains the best-remembered game of its type. The game has remained so popular over the years that Mattel re-released it in 2001. (Photo courtesy of Rik Morgan, http://www.handheldmuseum.com.)*

b **Coleco** Head to Head Baseball. *Coleco became well known for its Head to Head series of two-player LED sports games. (Photo courtesy of Rik Morgan, http://www.handheldmuseum.com.)*

a **Coleco tabletop** Donkey Kong. *Coleco's line of tabletop miniature arcade games emulated classic video games right down to the game cabinet side art. These portable games are among the most collectible tabletop games today. (Photo courtesy of Rik Morgan, http://www.handheldmuseum.com.)*

233

Coleco Tabletop Arcade Games

The portable games for which Coleco is probably best remembered are the tabletop arcade games that they released in the early 1980s. These games modeled not only the gameplay of popular arcade games, but the cabinets as well. Each game was designed to look like a miniature version of the arcade cabinet of the game it emulated. Their clever design made this line of games very popular at the time, and Coleco's tabletop arcade games are still counted among the most collectible tabletop games in today's market.

The following games were available in Coleco's tabletop arcade series:

- *Donkey Kong*

- *Donkey Kong Junior*

- *Frogger*

- *Galaxian*

- *Ms. Pac-Man*

- *Pac-Man*

- *Zaxxon*

Several other titles, including *Berzerk* and *Omega Race*, were announced (and even shown in 1982 sales brochures), but were never released.

Most of the Coleco miniarcade games show up regularly in online auctions. The hardest to find of the bunch seems to be *Zaxxon*, and the most valuable (those that garner the highest prices) are *Donkey Kong* and *Ms. Pac-Man*.

Donkey Kong Junior is the only game of the bunch that doesn't match the others stylistically. This game was the last in the series, and Coleco licensed Nintendo's tabletop version of the game rather than building it themselves. The game has an LCD screen as opposed to the VFD screens used in the other games in the series. Even though it doesn't match the other games in the series, it is still quite popular among collectors today. Nintendo made several games in the style of *Donkey Kong Junior*, including *Mario's Cement Factory*, *Popeye*, and *Snoopy*, all of which can be quite valuable.

Milton Bradley

Milton Bradley will probably go down in history as being one of the top board game manufacturers of all time, a reputation that is indeed well deserved. When compared to the number of board games the company has produced over the years, their involvement in the video and electronic game industry is a mere footnote.

Among classic video and electronic game collectors, however, Milton Bradley is an important name. Aside from being the company that (indirectly) introduced the unique Vectrex video game console to the world (see Chapter 9), Milton Bradley made two lasting electronic game contributions during the classic era: the best-known musical game and the handheld game that was a harbinger of the popular cartridge-based handhelds that hit the market nearly a decade later.

Simon

Milton Bradley's best-known electronic game is a simple musical game where players repeat increasingly fast and complex musical sequences by pressing the appropriate lighted buttons in the right order. The game is called *Simon*, and it was a huge hit in 1978.

Simon doesn't really fit into the category of games defined for this guide, but it bears mentioning both for its enduring quality (it is still sold in stores today, after being on the market for 25 years) and for its connections to classic video games.

Simon is nearly identical to *Touch Me*, a 1974 Atari arcade game that was turned into Atari's one and only handheld game in early 1978. The classic video game connection doesn't end there, though. *Simon* was designed by Ralph Baer, creator of the Magnavox Odyssey.

A simple, fun to play game, *Simon* went on to inspire a myriad of sequels and clones. In the classic game era, nearly every electronic game manufacturer marketed some sort of *Simon* knock-off. In June 2003, Hasbro (the company that currently owns Milton Bradley and *Simon*) promoted the 25th anniversary of the game by releasing commemorative editions of the game that were sold on eBay to benefit charity. A number of these games were signed by famous Simons, including singer/songwriter Paul Simon, playwright Neil Simon, and *American Idol* judge Simon Cowell.

So many versions of *Simon* have been released over the years (and throughout the world) that it's difficult to keep track of the subtle changes through which the game has gone. The primary difference between modern versions and the original is that the original game's colored buttons were translucent, while later versions feature clear buttons with colored lights beneath them. Today, *Simon* is available in its original tabletop size as well as in handheld and keychain size.

The value of *Simon* in today's market lies simply in its fun gameplay. Because the game has been continually available since its original release, vintage *Simon* games often sell for less than the brand new models you can buy in toy stores.

MicroVision

The Milton Bradley product that was arguably the most influential on the handheld electronic game industry was **MicroVision**. MicroVision was the first handheld system designed around the idea of interchangeable game cartridges.

MicroVision is primitive—its tiny LCD screen has a resolution of only 16x16 pixels (as compared to the Nintendo Game Boy released ten years later, which has a resolution of 160x144). Nevertheless, the idea behind the system was way ahead of its time. Cartridge-based home consoles were just starting to gain momentum in the marketplace, and translating this idea to handheld form was nothing short of genius. It is telling that the designer of this innovative handheld game, Jay Smith, went on to design the most innovative classic video game console: the Vectrex.

The MicroVision console itself is little more than an LCD screen, a control knob, and some simple interface circuitry. The game cartridges, which are nearly the same size as the unit itself, house the microprocessor for the game as well as pushbutton controls for game functions. On U.S. MicroVision units, the buttons are thin plastic membranes that tend to wear out, crack, or fall off entirely with repeated use. European MicroVision cartridges use actual raised plastic buttons that *look* more durable, but these have a tendency to break easily as well. Always con-

PROGRAMMABLE ELECTRONIC GAME SYSTEM
microvision

INCLUDES THE FAST ACTION GAME
CARTRIDGE OF BLOCK BUSTER

MB ELECTRONICS
MILTON BRADLEY

Ages 8-Adult
For 1 or more
players

microvision
BLOCK
BUSTER

BALLS   SPEED   PADDLE

Easy-to-insert, interchangeable game cartridges
snap into the console. To change games, simply
remove one cartridge and drop in another.

**A new concept in
electronic game systems—
a hand-held console
with interchangeable
cartridges.
A wide variety of
game cartridges available,
see back.**

Two 9-volt batteries required, not included.

a **Milton Bradley's MicroVision**
*was the first handheld that
hinted at the potential for cartridge-based handheld game systems. This game was the
forerunner of popular handheld
systems like the Nintendo Game
Boy that wouldn't appear in the
marketplace for another decade.
(Photo courtesy of Rik Morgan,
http://www.handheldmuseum.
com.)*

firm that the control buttons on the cartridges are intact and undamaged before making a purchase.

Another problem that plagues MicroVision units is the LCD screen itself. The screen tends to grow dim with age. Many MicroVision games today are totally useless because of this. When purchasing a unit, be sure to test it or inquire about the condition of the screen.

Two versions of the MicroVision unit exist. Early versions have two battery compartments. After the game had been on the market for some time, Milton Bradley eventually discovered what players already knew—that the game operated just as well with a single battery as it did with two. Later versions of the unit had a single battery compartment and an empty bay labeled "battery storage." Both MicroVision versions are equally common today, and both are relatively inexpensive.

Only 11 MicroVision game cartridges were released in the United States during the game's two-year retail lifespan. (Several additional titles were released in Europe.) One of these, *Block Buster*, was packaged with the game unit. Most of the cartridges are fairly common and inexpensive today, although those released near the end of MicroVision's run—*Alien Raiders, Cosmic*

Hunter, and *Sea Duel*—are rarer and command higher prices. One game, *Star Trek Phaser Strike* was re-released after its initial run under a different title (*Phaser Strike*).

After a brief period of popularity immediately following its release, MicroVision quickly faded into obscurity. The idea of a cartridge-based handheld system was obviously ahead of its time. Because the system and its games are quite inexpensive in today's collectors' market, MicroVision is an excellent starter system for collectors who are new to the classic game collecting hobby.

Parker Brothers

The late '70s and early '80s was a time when every company on Earth seemed to be getting into the video game or electronic handheld/tabletop game industry. Like Milton Bradley, Parker Brothers is best known for its board and card games. Although the company did release quite a number of video game cartridges, its entries in the handheld and tabletop field were limited.

One notable exception was Parker Brothers' excellent tabletop version of the arcade game *Q*Bert*. Styled similarly to Coleco's tabletop arcade games, *Q*Bert* faithfully reproduces the gameplay of its arcade namesake on a tiny color VFD screen. This game is coveted by collectors just as most of the Coleco arcade series are, so you can expect to pay top dollar when you're lucky enough to find one on the market.

Other noteworthy Parker Brothers electronic games include *Bank Shot* (an LED billiards game) and *Merlin*, a handheld that plays a number of pattern and sound recognition games similar to *Simon*. *Merlin*, easily the most popular of Parker Brothers' electronic games at the time, went on to spawn two sequels, the most recent of which was released in 1996.

Entex

Entex was one of the most prominent players in the classic handheld and tabletop game market in the United States. They produced a lot of the standard fare of the time: LED sports games and handheld and tabletop arcade reproductions. But among collectors today, Entex is probably best remembered for the most unique cartridge-based tabletop system ever made: Adventure Vision.

Handhelds and Tabletops

After Mattel and Coleco, Entex was easily the biggest competitor in the LED handheld and tabletop sports game market. They offered the standard fare in this field: numerous variations on baseball, basketball, football, hockey, and soccer. Many of these games were licensed to companies that didn't produce their own games, like Sears department stores.

In addition to their sports games, Entex dabbled quite heavily in the handheld and tabletop arcade game market. The company reproduced several popular arcade games, including *Crazy Climber, Defender, Galaxian,* and *Pac-Man* (which was released as *Pac-Man2*). Some of these games were released in handheld form, others in tabletop form, and still others in both tabletop and handheld versions. Most of the games were very faithful to their namesakes in gameplay.

One interesting Entex tabletop is the ***Select-A-Game Machine***. This two-player console used interchangeable cartridges to play a number of games on a built-in VFD display. All eight of the games available for the system are based on Entex's handheld line. Each cartridge comes with a plastic overlay that fits over the screen.

a **Q*Bert, *a* VFD *tabletop*** game
that is reminiscent of Coleco's
tabletop arcade series, is the most
collectible of the Parker Brothers'
electronic games. (Photo courtesy
of Rik Morgan, http://www.
handheldmuseum.com.)

b **Crazy Climber** is one Entex's arcade titles, which tend to be fairly
popular among collectors today.
(Photo courtesy of Rik Morgan,
http://www.handheldmuseum.
com.)

Among collectors, Entex handheld and tabletop games (especially those styled after popular arcade titles) tend to be popular. They are also fairly easy to find in today's market because most of them were produced in large quantities at the time. The sports games, which are also fairly easy to find, tend to garner lower prices. Like the LED sports games by most other manufacturers (with the exception of Mattel), the nostalgia for these games is moderate at best.

Adventure Vision

Adventure Vision is the most collectible tabletop game from the classic era. This system, released in 1982, is a little larger than Coleco's tabletop arcade games, and is unique in many ways.

Adventure Vision is a cartridge-based system. It was packaged with *Defender* (a licensed version of the Williams arcade game), and three other cartridges—*Super Cobra, Turtles,* and *Space Force*—were available when the system was released. These were the only Adventure Vision cartridges ever produced.

Perhaps the most unique feature of Adventure Vision is its display. The built-in screen projects a red dot matrix display using a row of 40 LEDs and a rapidly spinning mirror. The result is a surprisingly clear 150X40 resolution picture. The downside is that there is quite a bit of flicker due to the relatively slow screen refresh rate. Because of the moving parts, Adventure Vision consoles can easily become inoperable with extended use.

If there is a "Holy Grail" among handheld and tabletop classic games, Adventure Vision is definitely it. This odd tabletop system is in huge demand among collectors today, and it is extremely rare. Loose, working models generally sell for at least $500, and boxed complete versions can fetch up to three times as much. The tiny cartridges for the system are also very rare and very expensive.

Bandai

Bandai is a Japanese electronic game company that got its start in the classic era and continues to make pocket and handheld games today. The majority of Bandai's titles were (and continue to be) released overseas, but many of Bandai's classic-era titles made it to North America.

Bandai's first LED games, released in 1978, were little more than random number generators. Five early games—**Bandai *Baseball**, Basketball, Football, Hockey,* and *Space Shot,* feature pretty much the same gameplay: press the play button, and a random labeled LED lights up to show you a result. Score is kept manually on a rotary wheel. Compared to the LED sports games that Mattel was producing at the same time, Bandai's offerings were primitive at best.

Some of Bandai's later games were a lot more creative (and a lot more fun). Their tabletop air traffic controller game, *TC-7*, features a unique radar screen display and complex controls, and *Vampire* is an interesting twist on *Donkey Kong*–style gameplay, where you jump tumbling bats instead of barrels.

Bandai also released a number of arcade game reproductions. Like Entex, Bandai produced a good version of *Crazy Climber*. They also produced *Packri Monster*, a poorly disguised *Pac-Man* clone, which was fairly interesting.

Bandai's better games—especially the arcade titles—tend to be fairly popular among collectors. Because Bandai is such a diverse and long-lived company, it can be difficult to sort through online auction listings to find the classic-era products.

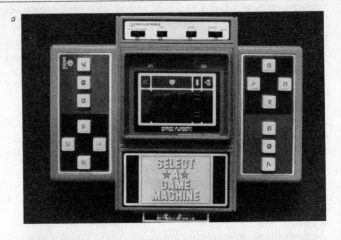

a **The Entex** **Select-A-Game Machine** *used interchangeable cartridges to play recreations of a number of Entex's dedicated handheld games. (Photo courtesy of Rik Morgan, http://www. handheldmuseum.com.)*

b **Adventure Vision** *is one of the most unique—and most collectible—LED tabletop games ever produced.*

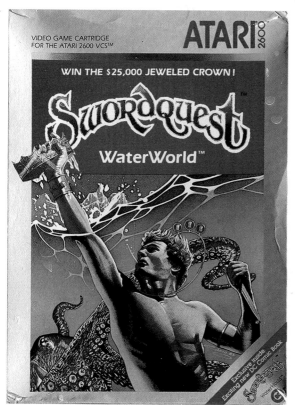

A Adventure Vision by Entex is easily the most valuable tabletop classic game. Boxed units consistently
sell for more than $1,000.

B Parker Brothers' tabletop version
of Q*Bert is similar in design to
the popular tabletop arcade
games by Coleco. (Photo courtesy
of Rik Morgan, http://www.hand-
heldmuseum.com)

C Swordquest: Waterworld is one of
the hard-to-find Atari 2600 cartridges that was originally available exclusively to Atari Club
members. (Photo courtesy of Dan
Cage.)

D CommaVid's Video Life is one of the rarest and most coveted Atari 2600 cartridges. A boxed copy can easily sell for as much as $3,000. (Photo courtesy of Dan Cage.)

E Pac-Man is one of the most widely recognizable classic arcade video games, and is very popular among collectors. (Photo courtesy of James Bright, http://www.quarterarcade.com.)

F Coleco's Telstar Combat!—a dedicated console alternative to the Pong-clones of the late 1970s.

G

H

I

G The Intellivision keyboard component (shown here in its original
packaging) is one of the rarest
Intellivision accessories. (On display
at the 2003 Classic Gaming Expo.)

H Donkey Kong, one of the popular
tabletop arcade games released by
Coleco in the 1980s. (Photo courtesy
of Rik Morgan, http://www.hand-
heldmuseum.com.)

I Atari's Tempest is among the most
collected arcade video games today.
(Photo courtesy of James Bright,
http://www.quarterarcade.com.)

J

K

L

J The Game Brain, which was created by Atari before the 2600,
was a console designed to play
cartridge-based versions many of
the dedicated games that Atari
had released up to that point.
The system was never released.
(On display at the 2003 Classic
Gaming Expo.)

K Stadium Mud Buggies, one of
the rarest Intellivision titles was
one of the last two games
released by INTV before they
went out of business in 1991.
(Photo courtesy of Steve Orth,
http://intvfunhouse.com.)

L Lunar Lander was Atari's first
vector graphics video game. It is
difficult to find today because it
was produced in relatively small
numbers, and many Lunar
Lander cabinets were converted
into Asteroids machines to meet
the high demand for that game.
(Photo courtesy of James Bright,
http://www.quarterarcade.com.)

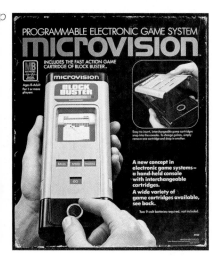

M A rare prototype of the Atari Cosmos, a
holographic tabletop game system that
was never released. (On display at the
2003 Classic Gaming Expo.)

N Tron is popular among collectors not
only for its ties to the Disney movie
that helped to pioneer computer animation in films, but also for its stylish
cabinet and excellent game play.
(Photo courtesy of James Bright,
http://www.quarterarcade.com.)

O Milton Bradley's Microvision handheld
is one of the earliest ancestors of modern cartridge-based handheld games
like Nintendo's Game Boy. (Photo
courtesy of Rik Morgan,
http://www.handheldmuseum.com.)

P

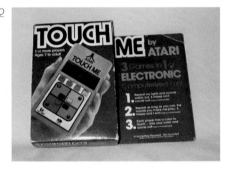

Q

R

P Atari's Puppy Pong is a rare
   arcade video game that was
   designed for use in Chuck E.
   Cheese restaurants. This machine,
   signed by Nolan Bushnell, founder
   of Atari, was displayed at the 2003
   Classic Gaming Expo.

Q Touch Me was Atari's only handheld electronic game. It is based
   on an early Atari arcade video
   game, and was (by many
   accounts) the inspiration for
   Milton Bradley's Simon. (Photo
   courtesy of Cassidy Nolen.)

R Entex Crazy Climber. Entex was
   one of the most successful handheld game manufacturers in the
   classic era. In addition to tabletop
   and handheld arcade game conversions, they produced an extensive line of LED sports games.
   (Photo courtesy of Rik Morgan,
   http://www.handheldmuseum.com.)

S   Pong is the arcade game that
    started it all. Its success in the
    arcades paved the way for a
    multi-billion dollar industry.
    (Photo courtesy of James Bright,
    http://www.quarterarcade.com.)

T   The Atari 2600 is the undisputed
    king of classic video game
    consoles. (Photo courtesy
    of Albert Yaruso,
    http://www.atariage.com.)

U   The Intellivision PlayCable
    modem. This rare Intellivison
    add-on was only available in
    select test markets, and is quite
    rare today. This example was on
    display at the 2003 Classic
    Gaming Expo.

V

W

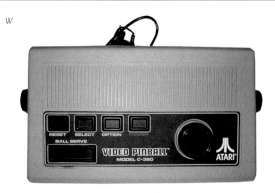

X

V Space Ace. *Laser disc games enjoyed a brief period of popularity in the mid-1980s. Space Ace, one of the most popular of the genre, was one of several games that featured animation by former Disney animator Don Bluth. (Photo courtesy of James Bright, http://www.quarterarcade.com.)*

W Video Pinball. *Following their success with home* Pong, *Atari released dedicated console versions of some of their other arcade games.* Video Pinball *included versions of both the title game and* Breakout.

X *Three Williams games in rare Duramold cabinets. (Photo courtesy of Duramold.com, http://www.duramold.com.)*

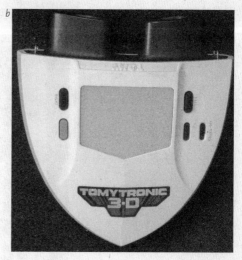

a *Bandai* **Baseball,** *one of the company's earliest releases in the U.S., featured extremely primitive gameplay. (Photo courtesy of Rik Morgan, http://www. handheldmuseum.com.)*

b **Tomytronic 3-D** *games were released in the early '80s. These games are among the more unique classic handheld game collectibles. (Photo courtesy of Rik Morgan, http://www.handheldmuseum. com.)*

Tomy

Like so many other companies, Tomy (a company that had entered the handheld game market with a number of electromechanical games, including *Blip*, a *Pong*-like LED game) introduced a line of LED sports games to compete with Mattel and Coleco. These games were moderately successful at the time, but are not overly popular among collectors today.

Tomy also produced its share of arcade game conversions. Besides the obligatory *Pac-Man* game, Tomy released handheld or tabletop versions of *Scramble*, *Space Attack* (a *Space Invaders* clone), and *Break Up* (a *Breakout* clone).

Among Tomy's more interesting offerings is the **Tomytronic 3-D** series. These handheld games, shaped like binoculars, produced the illusion of 3-D images on their tiny internal LCD screens. Seven games were released in this series: *Jungle Fighter, Planet Zeon, Shark Attack, Sky Attack, Sky Duel, Sky Fighters,* and *Thundering Turbo*. While these games are not particularly valuable in today's market (except for *Planet Zeon*, which seems to be in greater demand than the others), they do make unique and interesting collectibles.

a **Star Castle** *was the only licensed arcade game conversion for Tiger's Electronic Mini Arcade line. Tiger produced a number of their arcade-style games in both tabletop and handheld versions. (Photo courtesy of Rik Morgan, http://www. handheldmuseum.com.)*

b **Tiger's After Burner** *is an example of the some of the elaborate table-top games released in the late '80s. Based on the Sega arcade game, the tabletop version is presented as a miniature cockpit complete with flight-style controls. (Photo courtesy of Rik Morgan, http://www. handheldmuseum.com.)*

Tiger

Tiger manufactured a huge number of handheld and tabletop games in the classic era, and continues to manufacture handheld games today.

It seems that every handheld game company followed similar marketing paths in the late '70s and early '80s, and Tiger is no exception. They created a number of LED sports games, some of which were licensed to large chains like Sears and Radio Shack and distributed under different names. One such example is Tiger's *7 in 1 Sports Stadium*, which was sold in Sears stores as *7 in 1 Sports*.

Tiger also got into the arcade game conversion market. Their handheld lineup included licensed LCD conversions of *Space Invaders*, *Ms. Pac-Man*, and *Star Castle*. Other games, like *King Kong* and *Monster Maze* were obvious clones of other popular arcade hits.

A number of Tiger's handheld LCD games were converted to tabletop color LCD versions. This line of games, known as the Tiger Electronic Mini Arcade, was obviously designed to compete with the miniarcade games released by other companies (most notably Coleco). One of these games, *Jawbreaker*, is based on the Atari 2600 game cartridge published by Tigervision, a branch of Tiger that manufactured video game cartridges.

Tiger continued to release handheld and tabletop games based on classic arcade titles, including *Gauntlet, Marble Madness,* and *Paperboy*, well into the late '80s. Because of their classic video game connections, these games are listed in this price guide.

A couple of the tabletop games from the late '80s are particularly interesting. Tiger's LCD tabletop version of Sega's **After Burner** arcade game is extremely elaborate, with a flight stick and throttle control and a small screen set into a miniature jet fighter cockpit. *Outrun*, another Sega arcade classic, received similar treatment—a steering wheel controller mounted on a miniature car dashboard that houses the game screen.

Most Tiger handheld games are relatively inexpensive to acquire in today's collectors' market. The most valuable and hardest to find Tiger products are their unique tabletop arcade-style games.

Classic Handheld and Tabletop Price Guide

HANDHELD CLASSIC GAME PRICE GUIDE

2 GAMES IN 1 SAFARI & DARTS
Manufacturer: Tiger
Year: 1981
Rarity: 9
Loose: $5–8*
Complete: $9–12*
Notes: Simple LED "shooting" game that lets you shoot at animals or a dart board depending on the overlay you use; manual scoring

2 GAMES IN 1 SPACE INVADER & GONE FISHIN'
Manufacturer: Tiger
Year: 1981
Rarity: 9
Loose: $5–8*
Complete: $9–12*
Notes: Another LED "shooting" game with manual scoring; this one has alien and fishing overlays

2-PLAYER BASEBALL
Manufacturer: Tandy
Year: 1981
Rarity: 8
Loose: $3–5*
Complete: $6–9
Notes: 2-player LED baseball game

3D GALAXX

Manufacturer: Tiger
Year: 1984
Rarity: 9
Loose: $8–10*
Complete: $15–17*
Notes: LCD game shaped like a pair of binoculars with an internal screen

3-D SKY DUEL

Manufacturer: Tandy
Year: 1985
Rarity: 9
Loose: $8–10*
Complete: $15–17*
Notes: LCD air battle game; game case is styled like a pair of binoculars with the screen inside

3 IN 1 SPORTS

Manufacturer: Tandy
Year: 1984
Rarity: 9
Loose: $6–8*
Complete: $8–12*
Notes: 2-player LED game with 2 built-in game options (football, hockey, and basketball); each game has a plastic overlay for the screen

4-IN-1 ELECTRONIC SPORTS

Manufacturer: Regency Electronics
Year: 1979
Rarity: 9
Loose: $6–8*
Complete: $8–12*
Notes: LED sports game that plays baseball, basketball, football, and hockey

7 IN 1 SPORTS

Manufacturer: Sears
Year: ?
Rarity: 8
Loose: $8–10
Complete: $12–15*
Notes: 2-player LED game with 7 built-in games (basketball, hockey, soccer, maze, baseball, football, and racquetball); each game has a plastic overlay; overlays stored in the bottom of the unit; licensed version of Tiger's *7-in-1 Sports Stadium*

7-IN-1 SPORTS STADIUM

Manufacturer: Tiger
Year: ?
Rarity: 7
Loose: $8–10
Complete: $12–15*
Notes: 2-player LED game with 7 built-in games (basketball, hockey, soccer, maze, baseball, football, and racquetball); each game has a plastic overlay; overlays stored in the bottom of the unit

ADVANCED FOOTBALL III

Manufacturer: NIT
Year: ?
Rarity: 9
Loose: $4–6*
Complete: $7–10*
Notes: One of the many LED football games of the late '70s; similar in gameplay to Mattel's *Football 2*

AIR BOMBER

Manufacturer: Tandy
Year: ?
Rarity: 9
Loose: $5–7*
Complete: $8–12*
Notes: LCD air combat game in a case shaped like a futuristic white airplane

AIR WAR

Manufacturer: Radio Shack
Year: ?
Rarity: 9
Loose: $2–4*
Complete: $5–7*
Notes: Pocket LCD air combat game

AIRPORT PANIC

Manufacturer: Bandai
Year: 1982
Rarity: 9
Loose: $4–6*
Complete: $7–9*
Notes: Solar powered LCD game

ALIEN ATTACK

Manufacturer: Coleco
Year: 1982
Rarity: 5
Loose: $5–10
Complete: $15–20
Notes: Space battle game with a VFD

ARCADE TIME

Manufacturer: GCE
Year: ?
Rarity: 9
Loose: $3–5*
Complete: $7–9*
Notes: LCD watch-sized game developed by the company that went on to design the Vectrex game console

ARMOR ATTACK

Manufacturer: Mattel
Year: 1982
Rarity: 9
Loose: $4–6*
Complete: $7–10*
Notes: LCD game based on the Cinematronics arcade game by the same name; released in Japan as *Combat* under the Bandai label

ARMOR BATTLE

Manufacturer: Mattel
Year: 1978
Rarity: 7
Loose: $5–7
Complete: $8–12*
Notes: LED tank battle game

AUTO RACE
Manufacturer: Mattel
Year: 1976
Rarity: 5
Loose: $5–7
Complete: $8–15
Notes: The first handheld computer game ever made; simple LED auto racing game

AUTO RACE
Manufacturer: Sears
Year: 1978
Rarity: 8
Loose: $4–6*
Complete: $7–12*
Notes: LED auto race game; virtually identical to Mattel's *Auto Race*

AUTO RACE
Manufacturer: Sears
Year: ?
Rarity: 9
Loose: $3–5*
Complete: $6–10*
Notes: LED auto race game; Sears' version of Tiger's *Raceway*

AUTORACE
Manufacturer: Electronic Readout Systems
Year: ?
Rarity: 9
Loose: $4–6*
Complete: $7–12*
Notes: LED racing game shaped like a car; almost identical in gameplay to Mattel's *Auto Race*

BACKGAMMON
Manufacturer: Mattel
Year: 1980
Rarity: 8
Loose: $3–5*
Complete: $6–8*
Notes: LCD display

BACKGAMMON
Manufacturer: Tandy
Year: 1984
Rarity: 9
Loose: $4–6*
Complete: $7–9*
Notes: LCD Backgammon game; licensed from Gakken; packaged with dice (stored in a compartment on the underside of the game)

BANANA
Manufacturer: Vtech
Year: 1981
Rarity: 9
Loose: $2–4*
Complete: $5–7*
Notes: Pocket-sized LCD game in the "Time and Fun" series

BANK SHOT
Manufacturer: Parker Brothers
Year: 1980
Rarity: 7
Loose: $5–7
Complete: $9–12
Notes: LED pool (pocket billiards) game; released in the UK as *Cue Ball*

BASEBALL
Manufacturer: Acer
Year: ?
Rarity: 9
Loose: $3–5*
Complete: $7–9*
Notes: LED baseball game

BASEBALL
Manufacturer: Bandai
Year: 1978
Rarity: 9
Loose: $3–5*
Complete: $7–9*
Notes: Early LED baseball game with manual scoring; virtually identical in gameplay to Bandai's *Basketball, Football, Hockey,* and *Space Shot*

BASEBALL
Manufacturer: Entex
Year: 1979
Rarity: 7
Loose: $4–8*
Complete: $9–12*
Notes: LED baseball game that is a bit more sophisticated version of Entex's *Hip Pocket Baseball;* 2-player with separate batting and pitching controls

BASEBALL
Manufacturer: Fonas
Year: 1979
Rarity: 9
Loose: $3–5*
Complete: $7–9*
Notes: 2-player LED baseball game

BASEBALL
Manufacturer: Mattel
Year: 1977
Rarity: 6
Loose: $12–15
Complete: $20–30
Notes: Popular LED baseball game; 2 box styles—large with Styrofoam inserts (original) and a smaller version

BASEBALL
Manufacturer: Micro Electronics
Year: 1981
Rarity: 9
Loose: $3–6*
Complete: $7–9*
Notes: LED baseball game; also released by Radio Shack as *Championship Baseball*

BASEBALL

Manufacturer: Sears
Year: 1978
Rarity: 9
Loose: $3–5*
Complete: $7–9*
Notes: LED baseball game; licensed version of
Bandai's *Baseball*

BASEBALL

Manufacturer: Tomy
Year: ?
Rarity: 9
Loose: $3–5*
Complete: $7–9*
Notes: LED baseball game

BASEBALL 2

Manufacturer: Entex
Year: 1979
Rarity: 5
Loose: $6–8
Complete: $9–15
Notes: Second of 3 very similar LED baseball games
by Entex

BASEBALL 2

Manufacturer: Sears
Year: 1979
Rarity: 9
Loose: $5–7*
Complete: $8–12*
Notes: LED baseball game; licensed version of Entex's
Baseball 2

BASEBALL 3

Manufacturer: Entex
Year: 1979
Rarity: 5
Loose: $3–10
Complete: $12–20
Notes: LED baseball game; similar gameplay to Entex
Baseball, but slightly more compact

BASKETBALL

Manufacturer: Bandai
Year: 1978
Rarity: 8
Loose: $5–7
Complete: $8–10*
Notes: Early LED sports game with manual scoring;
virtually identical in gameplay to Bandai's *Baseball,
Football, Hockey,* and *Space Shot*

BASKETBALL

Manufacturer: Mattel
Year: 1978
Rarity: 5
Loose: $12–15
Complete: $20–30
Notes: One of the popular Mattel LED sports games;
2 box styles—large with Styrofoam inserts (original)
and a smaller version

BASKETBALL

Manufacturer: Tomy
Year: ?
Rarity: 9
Loose: $3–5*
Complete: $7–9*
Notes: 2-player LED basketball game

BASKETBALL

Manufacturer: US Games
Year: ?
Rarity: 9
Loose: $3–5*
Complete: $7–9*
Notes: LED basketball game

BASKETBALL (DRIBBLE AWAY)

Manufacturer: Bambino
Year: 1979
Rarity: 9
Loose: $5–7*
Complete: $9–12*
Notes: Uniquely-shaped VFD basketball game; or-
ange case with blue and orange control buttons

BASKETBALL 2

Manufacturer: Entex
Year: 1980
Rarity: 9
Loose: $4–6*
Complete: $8–10*
Notes: Head-to-head LED basketball game

BASKETBALL 2

Manufacturer: Mattel
Year: 1979
Rarity: 7
Loose: $8–20
Complete: $40–80
Notes: LED sequel to the original Mattel *Basketball;*
this version allows passing and had several defensive
options

BATTLESTAR GALACTICA SPACE ALERT

Manufacturer: Mattel
Year: 1978
Rarity: 8
Loose: $25–55
Complete: $65–80*
Notes: Previously released as *Missile Attack;* same
game repackaged with box and game case graphics
taken from the *Battlestar Galactica* TV series.

BLACK KNIGHT PINBALL

Manufacturer: Entex
Year: 1982
Rarity: 8
Loose: $5–7*
Complete: $8–10*
Notes: LED pinball game; a redesigned version of
Raise the Devil Pinball (Entex, 1980) based loosely on
the *Black Knight* pinball machine by Williams; very
rare

BLAST IT

Manufacturer: Entex
Year: 1980
Rarity: 9
Loose: $5–7*
Complete: $12–17*
Notes: LED *Breakout* clone; box is difficult to find; released in Japan as *DIGIT-COM Block*

BLAST IT

Manufacturer: Sears
Year: 1980
Rarity: 9
Loose: $5–7*
Complete: $8–10*
Notes: Licensed version of Entex's *Blast It*

BLOCK ATTACK

Manufacturer: Tomy
Year: ?
Rarity: 9
Loose: $3–5*
Complete: $7–9*
Notes: LED *Breakout* clone; renamed version of Tomy's *Break Up*

BLOCK OUT

Manufacturer: Bandai
Year: 1980
Rarity: 9
Loose: $4–6*
Complete: $8–10*
Notes: *Breakout* clone with a VFD; included options for paddle size

BRAIN DRAIN

Manufacturer: Tandy
Year: ?
Rarity: 9
Loose: $3–5*
Complete: $7–9*
Notes: LED game identical to Sears' *Numbers Game*

BREAK IN

Manufacturer: Tomy
Year: ?
Rarity: 9
Loose: $3–5*
Complete: $7–9*
Notes: LED *Breakout* clone; renamed version of Tomy's *Break Up* with a white case (as opposed to black)

BREAK UP

Manufacturer: Tomy
Year: ?
Rarity: 9
Loose: $3–5*
Complete: $7–9*
Notes: LED *Breakout* clone; also known as *Break In* and *Block Attack*

BURGERTIME

Manufacturer: Mattel
Year: 1982
Rarity: 9
Loose: $3–5*
Complete: $8–12*
Notes: Small LCD game based on the arcade game by the same name; originally packaged with stickers and a coupon book; versions were also released by Radio Shack and Bandai

CHAMPION RACER

Manufacturer: Bandai
Year: 1980
Rarity: 8
Loose: $6–8
Complete: $10–12*
Notes: LED car racing game; also sold by Radio Shack as *Cycle Race*

CHAMPIONSHIP BASEBALL

Manufacturer: Tandy
Year: 1981
Rarity: 9
Loose: $3–6*
Complete: $7–9*
Notes: LED baseball game; licensed version of Micro Electronics' *Baseball*

CHAMPIONSHIP ELECTRONIC BASEBALL

Manufacturer: Tandy
Year: ?
Rarity: 9
Loose: $3–6*
Complete: $7–9*
Notes: 2-player LED baseball game

CHAMPIONSHIP ELECTRONIC FOOTBALL

Manufacturer: Tandy
Year: 1981
Rarity: 8
Loose: $3–6
Complete: $7–9
Notes: LED football game similar in gameplay to Mattel's *Football 2;* green case with yellow and red buttons

CHAMPIONSHIP ELECTRONIC GOLF

Manufacturer: Tandy
Year: ?
Rarity: 8
Loose: $3–6
Complete: $7–9*
Notes: LED golf game; licensed version of Mego's *Pulsonic Golf*

CHASE-N-COUNTER

Manufacturer: GCE
Year: ?
Rarity: 9
Loose: $3–5*
Complete: $7–9*
Notes: LCD calculator/game combo created by the company that went on to design the Vectrex console

CHESS MASTER
Manufacturer: Vtech
Year: ?
Rarity: 9
Loose: $5–7*
Complete: $8–12*
Notes: LCD chess game

CHICKY WOGGY
Manufacturer: Vtech
Year: 1981
Rarity: 9
Loose: $3–5*
Complete: $7–9*
Notes: LCD maze game; also released in a tabletop version

CLASSIC BASEBALL
Manufacturer: Mattel
Year: 2001
Rarity: 1
Loose: $5–10
Complete: $12–20
Notes: 2001 re-release of the popular Mattel LED *Baseball* game; identical gameplay to the original

CLASSIC BASKETBALL
Manufacturer: Mattel
Year: 2002
Rarity: 1
Loose: $5–10
Complete: $15–25
Notes: 2001 re-release of the popular Mattel LED *Basketball* game

CLASSIC FOOTBALL
Manufacturer: Mattel
Year: 2001
Rarity: 1
Loose: $5–10
Complete: $12–20
Notes: 2001 re-release of the popular Mattel *Football* game; identical gameplay to the original

CLASSIC FOOTBALL/CLASSIC BASEBALL 2-PACK
Manufacturer: Mattel
Year: 2001
Rarity: 1
Loose: N/A
Complete: $25–45
Notes: The re-released versions of Mattel *Football* and *Baseball* packaged together.

CLASSIC FOOTBALL 2
Manufacturer: Mattel
Year: 2002
Rarity: 1
Loose: $5–10
Complete: $12–20
Notes: 2002 re-release of the popular Mattel LED *Football 2* game; identical gameplay to the original

COCO TO THE RESCUE GAME
Manufacturer: Kelloggs
Year: ?
Rarity: 9
Loose: $3–5*
Complete: $7–9*
Notes: LCD promotional game available only through mail order from Kelloggs

COMPETITION FOOTBALL
Manufacturer: Mattel
Year: 1982
Rarity: 9
Loose: $4–6*
Complete: $8–10*
Notes: Pocket-sized LCD football game; could be played by 2 players

COMPUTER BASEBALL
Manufacturer: Regency Electronics
Year: 1978
Rarity: 9
Loose: $4–6*
Complete: $8–10*
Notes: LED baseball game with a case shaped like a baseball

COMPUTER BASEBALL
Manufacturer: Tiger
Year: 1979
Rarity: 9
Loose: $3–5*
Complete: $7–9*
Notes: Simple 2-player LED baseball game

COMPUTER CHESS
Manufacturer: Mattel
Year: 1980
Rarity: 8
Loose: $35–45
Complete: $50–60*
Notes: Early LCD computer chess game

COMPUTER GIN
Manufacturer: Mattel
Year: 1979
Rarity: 9
Loose: $5–10*
Complete: $10–15*
Notes: LCD gin rummy game

COMPUTER GIN II
Manufacturer: Mattel
Year: 1980
Rarity: Prototype
Loose: ?
Complete: N/A
Notes: Sequel to the 1979 *Computer Gin,* with better gameplay; never released; only one prototype is known to exist; no pricing information available due to extreme rarity

COMPUTERIZED ARCADE
Manufacturer: Tandy
Year: ?
Rarity: 7
Loose: $3–5*
Complete: $7–9*
Notes: Music and lights game with 12 lighted buttons; basically a clone of *Simon,* but with 12 built-in games

COMPUTERIZED FOOTBALL
Manufacturer: Tandy
Year: ?
Rarity: 9
Loose: $3–5*
Complete: $7–9*
Notes: Early LED football game, similar in gameplay to Mattel's *Football;* blue case with red and yellow buttons

COMPUTERIZED FOOTBALL/BASKETBALL/SOCCER
Manufacturer: Fonas
Year: ?
Rarity: 9
Loose: $6–8*
Complete: $8–12*
Notes: 3-in-1 LED game with overlays for each of the 3 games

COPYCAT
Manufacturer: Tiger
Year: 1988
Rarity: 5
Loose: $2–5
Complete: $6–9*
Notes: LED *Simon* clone

COSMIC COMBAT
Manufacturer: Tomy
Year: 1980
Rarity: 7
Loose: $10–15
Complete: $15–20*
Notes: *Space Invaders* clone with a VFD

COSMIC FIRE AWAY 1000
Manufacturer: Tandy
Year: 1982
Rarity: 8
Loose: $10–20*
Complete: $40–70*
Notes: Second in Tandy's *Fire Away* series; yellow case with a square red fire button; VFD

COSMIC FIRE AWAY 3000
Manufacturer: Tandy
Year: 1984
Rarity: 8
Loose: $3–5
Complete: $8–12*
Notes: Fourth in Tandy's *Fire Away* series; orange case with a square black fire button; VFD

COSMIC FIRE-AWAY GAME WATCH
Manufacturer: Tandy
Year: 1983
Rarity: 9
Loose: $3–5*
Complete: $7–12*
Notes: LCD wristwatch version of Tandy's *Fire Away* game

COSMIC INVADER
Manufacturer: Grandstand
Year: 1981
Rarity: 9
Loose: $3–5*
Complete: $7–12*
Notes: VFD *Space Invaders* clone

COSMIC PINBALL
Manufacturer: Sears
Year: ?
Rarity: 9
Loose: $4–6*
Complete: $7–10*
Notes: LED pinball game; licensed version of Tiger's *Rocket Pinball*

DALLAS
Manufacturer: Mattel
Year: 198?
Rarity: 9
Loose: $5–8*
Complete: $10–15*
Notes: Actually a board game with a handheld computer component that looks a lot like a green calculator; the computer component is useless without the rest of the game

DEFENDER
Manufacturer: Entex
Year: 1982
Rarity: 6
Loose: $10–20
Complete: $30–65
Notes: Based on the arcade game by the same name; VFD

DIGITAL DIAMOND
Manufacturer: Tomy
Year: 1978
Rarity: 7
Loose: $4–6
Complete: $7–10*
Notes: LED baseball game; U.S. version is black, Japanese version is white

DRAGON CASTLE
Manufacturer: Vtech
Year: 1982
Rarity: 9
Loose: $3–5*
Complete: $7–9*
Notes: LCD calculator/game combo; also available as a game-only tabletop

DUNK 'N SUNK
Manufacturer: K-Mart
Year: ?
Rarity: 8
Loose: $4–6*
Complete: $8–10*
Notes: LED game that plays both basketball and a submarine battle game

DR. DUNK BASKETBALL
Manufacturer: Bandai
Year: ?
Rarity: 9
Loose: $4–6*
Complete: $8–10*
Notes: LED basketball game

DUNGEONS AND DRAGONS
Manufacturer: Mattel
Year: 1981
Rarity: 8
Loose: $4–7*
Complete: $10–12
Notes: Pocket-sized LCD game based on the popular TSR role playing game of the same name

ELECTRON BLASTER
Manufacturer: Vanity Fair
Year: ?
Rarity: 9
Loose: $3–5*
Complete: $8–12*
Notes: VFD space game identical to Radio Shack's *Fire Away*

ELECTRONIC 2-PLAYER FOOTBALL
Manufacturer: Tandy
Year: 1981
Rarity: 9
Loose: $3–6*
Complete: $7–9*
Notes: 2-player LED football game; licensed version of US Games' *Football*

ELECTRONIC BASEBALL
Manufacturer: Sears
Year: 1979
Rarity: 8
Loose: $1–4
Complete: $6–8*
Notes: LED baseball game; similar to Entex's *Baseball 2*

ELECTRONIC BASEBALL 3
Manufacturer: Four Star
Year: 1980
Rarity: 9
Loose: $3–5*
Complete: $7–9*
Notes: 2-player LED baseball game

ELECTRONIC BASKETBALL
Manufacturer: Cardinal
Year: ?
Rarity: 9
Loose: $3–5*
Complete: $7–9*
Notes: Simple LED basketball game

ELECTRONIC BASKETBALL
Manufacturer: Electronic Readout Systems
Year: ?
Rarity: 9
Loose: $3–5*
Complete: $7–9*
Notes: LED basketball game, similar to Mattel's *Basketball;* red case

ELECTRONIC BASKETBALL
Manufacturer: Sears
Year: ?
Rarity: 8
Loose: $2–4*
Complete: $6–9
Notes: LED basketball game; licensed version of Tiger's *Half Court Basketball*

ELECTRONIC BASKETBALL
Manufacturer: Tandy
Year: ?
Rarity: 8
Loose: $5–7*
Complete: $9–14
Notes: LED basketball game; licensed version of US Games' *Basketball*

ELECTRONIC FOOTBALL
Manufacturer: Cardinal
Year: ?
Rarity: 8
Loose: $4–6
Complete: $7–10
Notes: LED football game

ELECTRONIC FOOTBALL
Manufacturer: Straco
Year: ?
Rarity: 9
Loose: $3–5*
Complete: $7–9*
Notes: LED football game, similar to most of the LED football games of the time

ELECTRONIC FOOTBALL II
Manufacturer: Tandy
Year: 1983
Rarity: 8
Loose: $3–5*
Complete: $7–9
Notes: Another LED football game from Tandy; dark green case with red arrow buttons and yellow action buttons

ELECTRONIC POKER
Manufacturer: Entex
Year: 1979
Rarity: 7
Loose: $2–5*
Complete: $6–12*
Notes: Early LED poker game

ELECTRONIC QUARTERBACK

Manufacturer: Coleco
Year: 1978; 1980
Rarity: 3
Loose: $10–20
Complete: $30–60
Notes: Originally released in 1978; re-released in 1980; also released by Sears as *Electronic Touchdown*

ELECTRONIC REPEAT

Manufacturer: Tandy
Year: 1988
Rarity: 7
Loose: $2–4
Complete: $5–7*
Notes: LED Simon clone; licensed version of Tiger's *Copycat*

ELECTRONIC TOUCHDOWN

Manufacturer: Sears
Year: 1978
Rarity: 7
Loose: $5–9
Complete: $12–16
Notes: LED football game; licensed version of Coleco's *Electronic Quarterback*

ENCORE

Manufacturer: Toytronic
Year: ?
Rarity: 9
Loose: $3–5*
Complete: $8–10*
Notes: *Simon* clone, with 8 buttons instead of 4

ESCAPE

Manufacturer: Vtech
Year: 1981
Rarity: 9
Loose: $2–4*
Complete: $5–7*
Notes: Pocket-sized LCD game in the "Time and Fun" series

ESCAPE FROM THE DEVIL'S DOOM

Manufacturer: Bandai
Year: 1981
Rarity: 9
Loose: $4–6*
Complete: $7–9*
Notes: Solar powered LCD game

FIRE AWAY

Manufacturer: Tandy
Year: 1981
Rarity: 8
Loose: $3–5*
Complete: $7–12*
Notes: First in the series of VFD games that are similar in play to *Space Invaders;* there were a total of 6 in the series; this one is in a blue case with a round red fire button

FLIGHT TIME

Manufacturer: Bandai
Year: 1980
Rarity: 9
Loose: $3–5*
Complete: $7–12*
Notes: VFD game with gameplay similar to *Galaxian*

FOLLOW ME

Manufacturer: Sears
Year: 1988
Notes: LED Simon clone; licensed version of Tiger's *Copycat*

FOOTBALL

Manufacturer: Bandai
Year: 1978
Rarity: 9
Loose: $3–5*
Complete: $7–10*
Notes: Early LED sports game with manual scoring; simple gameplay that is nearly identical to Bandai's *Baseball, Basketball, Hockey,* and *Space Shot* games

FOOTBALL

Manufacturer: Electronic Readout Systems
Year: ?
Rarity: 9
Loose: $4–6*
Complete: $8–10*
Notes: 2-player LED football game; very similar in design to the US Games' *Football* game

FOOTBALL

Manufacturer: Mattel
Year: 1977
Rarity: 3
Loose: $15–20
Complete: $50–60
Notes: The most popular of the LED handheld football games of the era; second LED game released by Mattel (after Auto Race); renamed *Football I* after the release of Mattel's *Football 2*

FOOTBALL

Manufacturer: Sears
Year: 1978
Rarity: 9
Loose: $3–5*
Complete: $7–10*
Notes: Simple LED football game with mechanical scoring; licensed version of Bandai's *Football*

FOOTBALL

Manufacturer: Toytronic
Year: ?
Rarity: 9
Loose: $3–5*
Complete: $7–9*
Notes: LED football game; 3 case styles, one of which is very similar in shape to Mattel's *Football*

FOOTBALL

Manufacturer: US Games
Year: 1981
Rarity: 9
Loose: $4–6*
Complete: $8–10*
Notes: LED 2-player football game; also released under the Radio Shack brand name

FOOTBALL CLASSIC

Manufacturer: Bambino
Year: 1982
Rarity: 7
Loose: $5–7
Complete: $10–15
Notes: Black case styled like the case for *Basketball Dribble Away*

FOOTBALL 2

Manufacturer: Mattel
Year: 1978
Rarity: 4
Loose: $12–20
Complete: $20–30
Notes: Similar to the original Mattel LED *Football* but with additional gameplay functionality like passing, kicking, and backward movement; also known as *Football II*

FOOTBALL 3

Manufacturer: Entex
Year: 1980
Rarity: 8
Loose: $6–8
Complete: $9–12*
Notes: Head-to-head LED football game; black case

FOOTBALL 4

Manufacturer: Entex
Year: 1980
Rarity: 9
Loose: $6–8*
Complete: $9–12*
Notes: Head-to-head LED football game; white case; slimmer design than *Football 3*

FRANKENSTEIN

Manufacturer: Bandai
Year: ?
Rarity: 9
Loose: $4–6*
Complete: $7–9*
Notes: Solar powered LCD game

FRISKY TOM

Manufacturer: Bandai
Year: 1982
Rarity: 9
Loose: $2–4*
Complete: $5–7*
Notes: LCD game based on the Nichibutsu arcade game by the same name

FRISKY TOM

Manufacturer: Bandai
Year: 1982
Rarity: 9
Loose: $5–7*
Complete: $8–12*
Notes: VFD game based on the Nichibutsu arcade game by the same name

FUNTRONICS DRAG RACE

Manufacturer: Mattel
Year: 1979
Rarity: 9
Loose: $2–4*
Complete: $5–7*
Notes: Primitive pocket-sized LED drag race game; game is emblazoned with the Hot Wheels logo

FUNTRONICS JACKS

Manufacturer: Mattel
Year: 1979
Rarity: 9
Loose: $1–3*
Complete: $4–6*
Notes: Primitive pocket-sized LED game

FUNTRONICS TAG

Manufacturer: Mattel
Year: 1979
Rarity: 9
Loose: $1–3*
Complete: $4–6*
Notes: Primitive pocket-sized LED game with gameplay akin to Whack-A-Mole

FUNTRONICS RED LIGHT GREEN LIGHT

Manufacturer: Mattel
Year: 1979
Rarity: 9
Loose: $1–3*
Complete: $4–6*
Notes: Primitive pocket-sized LED drag race game; identical to *Funtronics Drag Race,* but without the Hot Wheels logo

GALACTIC INVADER

Manufacturer: Prinztronic
Year: 1981
Rarity: 9
Loose: $4–6*
Complete: $7–12*
Notes: VFD *Space Invaders* style game; box graphics include spaceships that look suspiciously like a Y-Wing fighter from *Star Wars* and the Cygnus from Disney's *The Black Hole;* nearly identical to Grandstand's *Cosmic Invader*

GALAXIAN

Manufacturer: Bandai
Year: 1980
Rarity: 8
Loose: $4–6
Complete: $7–12*
Notes: VFD *Galaxian* clone

GALAXIAN2
Manufacturer: Entex
Year: 1981
Rarity: 7
Loose: $5–15
Complete: $16–20
Notes: Entex's try at a *Galaxian* clone; VFD

GAME TIME
Manufacturer: GCE
Year: ?
Rarity: 9
Loose: $3–5*
Complete: $7–9*
Notes: LCD watch-sized game developed by the company that went on to design the Vectrex game console

GAUNTLET
Manufacturer: Tiger
Year: 1988
Rarity: 8
Loose: $3–5*
Complete: $7–9*
Notes: LCD game based on the Atari arcade classic by the same name

GIN RUMMY & BLACKJACK (JACKPOT)
Manufacturer: Entex
Year: 1980
Rarity: 8
Loose: $6–8*
Complete: $9–12*
Notes: LED 2-in-1 card game handheld

GRAVITY
Manufacturer: Mattel
Year: 1980
Rarity: 8
Loose: $4–6*
Complete: $7–12*
Notes: LED game where you deflect incoming projectiles; originally called *Catastrophe*, but never released under that name

GUNFIGHTER
Manufacturer: Bandai
Year: 1980
Rarity: 8
Loose: $3–5
Complete: $7–10*
Notes: Roughly based on Midway's *Gun Fight;* VFD; also known as *Duel*

HALF COURT BASKETBALL
Manufacturer: Tiger
Year: ?
Rarity: 9
Loose: $3–5*
Complete: $7–9*
Notes: LED basketball game

HARLEM GLOBETROTTERS ELECTRONIC BA
Manufacturer: Regency Electronics
Year: 1979
Rarity: 8
Loose: $15–30
Complete: $35–45*
Notes: LED basketball game with a case shaped like a basketball

HEAD CHASER
Manufacturer: Bandai
Year: 1980
Rarity: 9
Loose: $3–5*
Complete: $7–9*
Notes: LCD auto racing game

HEAD TO HEAD BASEBALL
Manufacturer: Coleco
Year: 1982
Rarity: 5
Loose: $6–10
Complete: $12–25
Notes: LED baseball game for 2 players

HEAD TO HEAD BASKETBALL
Manufacturer: Coleco
Year: 1979
Rarity: 8
Loose: $6–10*
Complete: $12–25*
Notes: LED basketball game for 2 players; 3 slight case variations exist, but the gameplay is identical in all versions

HEAD TO HEAD BOXING
Manufacturer: Coleco
Year: 1980
Rarity: 7
Loose: $5–15
Complete: $16–25*
Notes: LED boxing game

HEAD TO HEAD FOOTBALL
Manufacturer: Coleco
Year: 1980
Rarity: 6
Loose: $5–12
Complete: $15–25
Notes: LED football game for 2 players; also released by Sears as *Team Play Football*

HEAD TO HEAD HOCKEY
Manufacturer: Coleco
Year: 1980
Rarity: 7
Loose: $5–8
Complete: $7–15
Notes: LED ice hockey game for 2 players; 3 slight case variations exist, but the gameplay is identical in all versions

HEAD TO HEAD SOCCER

Manufacturer: Coleco
Year: 1980
Rarity: 8
Loose: $5–8*
Complete: $7–15*
Notes: LED soccer game for 2 players; 2 slight case variations exist, but the gameplay is identical in both versions

HIP POCKET BASEBALL

Manufacturer: Entex
Year: 1979
Rarity: 9
Loose: $4–6*
Complete: $7–10*
Notes: Early LED game with manual scoring

HOCKEY

Manufacturer: Bandai
Year: 1978
Rarity: 8
Loose: $4–6*
Complete: $7–10
Notes: LED hockey game with manual scoring; the gameplay is virtually identical to Bandai's *Baseball, Basketball, Football,* and *Space Shot* games

HOCKEY

Manufacturer: Entex
Year: 1979
Rarity: 9
Loose: $5–6*
Complete: $7–12*
Notes: LED ice hockey game

HOCKEY

Manufacturer: Mattel
Year: 1978
Rarity: 7
Loose: $6–15
Complete: $15–30
Notes: Popular LED hockey game in the Mattel sports line

HOCKEY

Manufacturer: Sears
Year: 1978
Rarity: 9
Loose: $3–5*
Complete: $7–9*
Notes: Simple LED hockey game with manual scoring; licensed version of Bandai's *Hockey*

HOLD UP

Manufacturer: Tandy
Year: 1983
Rarity: 8
Loose: $8–12
Complete: $15–18
Notes: LCD game where you are a bank robber who is trying to keep uncooperative bank tellers in line (and people wonder why video games have a bad reputation . . .)

HUNGRY MONSTER

Manufacturer: Tandy
Year: 1983
Rarity: 8
Loose: $5–8
Complete: $15–25*
Notes: *Pac-Man* clone with a VFD; licensed version of Bandai's *Packri Monster;* also known as *Ogre Eater*

THE INCREDIBLE HULK ESCAPES

Manufacturer: Bandai
Year: 1978
Rarity: 9
Loose: $3–5*
Complete: $7–9*
Notes: LED game with a superhero theme (and shape); gameplay is identical to *Spider-Man Rescue*

ICE HOCKEY (LUCKY PUCK)

Manufacturer: Bambino
Year: 1979
Rarity: 9
Loose: $3–5*
Complete: $7–9*
Notes: White case with black control buttons and a blue screen

INVADERS

Manufacturer: Vtech
Year: 1981
Rarity: 9
Loose: $4–6*
Complete: $7–12*
Notes: *Space Invaders* clone with a VFD; nearly identical to Grandstand's *Cosmic Invader*

INVADERS OF THE MUMMY'S TOMB

Manufacturer: Bandai
Year: 1982
Rarity: 9
Loose: $4–6*
Complete: $7–9*
Notes: Solar-powered LCD game

JAWBREAKER

Manufacturer: Tiger
Year: 1984
Rarity: 9
Loose: $5–7*
Complete: $8–10*
Notes: Pocket LCD game based on Tigervision's *Jawbreaker* cartridge for the Atari 2600; also available as a tabletop game

JUNGLE FIGHTER

Manufacturer: Tomy
Year: 1983
Rarity: 9
Loose: $8–10*
Complete: $12–18*
Notes: One of the Tomytronic 3D series—an LCD game shaped like a pair of binoculars with an internal screen; this is the rarest of the 6 games in the series

KING KONG

Manufacturer: Tiger
Year: ?
Rarity: 9
Loose: $3–5*
Complete: $7–9*
Notes: Pocket LCD *Donkey Kong* clone; also available as a tabletop game

KING MAN

Manufacturer: Tandy
Year: 1984
Rarity: 9
Loose: $4–6*
Complete: $8–10*
Notes: VFD game; gameplay is very similar to *Donkey Kong*

L.C.D. BOWLING

Manufacturer: Vtech
Year: 1981
Rarity: 9
Loose: $3–5*
Complete: $7–9*
Notes: LCD bowling game

LCD FIRE-AWAY

Manufacturer: Tandy
Year: 1989
Rarity: 9
Loose: $3–5*
Complete: $7–9*
Notes: Another game in the Tandy *Fire Away* series; this one is smaller with a red case, yellow fire button, and an LCD display; later repackaged and sold as *LCD Invasion Force* and *Jet Fighter*

LCD MIRACLE BASEBALL

Manufacturer: Bandai
Year: 1980
Rarity: 9
Loose: $5–8*
Complete: $9–12*
Notes: LCD *Baseball* game

LIVE ACTION FOOTBALL

Manufacturer: Kenner
Year: 1980
Rarity: 9
Loose: $5–8*
Complete: $9–12*
Notes: 2-player LED football game; different than the competing games of the time in that it featured actual animated LED players instead of blips

LONG BEACH GRAND PRIX

Manufacturer: Kenner
Year: 1981
Rarity: 9
Loose: $5–9*
Complete: $10–12*
Notes: LED car racing game in a unique steering wheel-shaped case

LONG BOMB FOOTBALL

Manufacturer: Mattel
Year: 198?
Rarity: 9
Loose: $4–6*
Complete: $8–10*
Notes: Pocket-sized LCD football game; part of the *Arcade Action* series

LOOK ALIVE FOOTBALL

Manufacturer: Mattel
Year: 1980
Rarity: 9
Loose: $4–6*
Complete: $8–10*
Notes: Football game from a first-person perspective; *Look Alive Baseball* and *Look Alive Basketball* were planned but never released

LUCKY LUKE

Manufacturer: Tiger
Year: 1984
Rarity: 9
Loose: $3–5*
Complete: $7–9*
Notes: Pocket LCD game with a Western theme

LUCKY LUKE

Manufacturer: Tiger
Year: 1984
Rarity: 9
Loose: $5–7*
Complete: $8–10*
Notes: Flip-top 2-screen LCD western game

MARBLE MADNESS

Manufacturer: Tiger
Year: 1989
Rarity: 7
Loose: $3–6
Complete: $7–12*
Notes: LCD handheld game based on Atari Games' classic arcade game by the same name

MARINE SHARK

Manufacturer: Bandai
Year: ?
Rarity: 9
Loose: $4–6*
Complete: $8–10*
Notes: LED submarine battle game

MASTER MERLIN

Manufacturer: Parker Brothers
Year: 1981
Rarity: 9
Loose: $5–7*
Complete: $10–20*
Notes: LED game with 9 game variations, most of which are variations on *Simon*-like musical matching games; sequel to *Merlin*

MASTERS OF THE UNIVERSE
Manufacturer: Mattel
Year: 1982
Rarity: 9
Loose: $3–5*
Complete: $7–9*
Notes: Pocket-sized LCD game based on the TV series by the same name; originally packaged with stickers and product coupons

MEMORY MATCH
Manufacturer: Tandy
Year: 1981
Rarity: 9
Loose: $3–5*
Complete: $7–8*
Notes: LED *Concentration*-like matching game

MERLIN
Manufacturer: Parker Brothers
Year: 1978
Rarity: 3
Loose: $5–7
Complete: $10–30
Notes: LED game with 6 game variations, most of which are variations on the *Simon* theme

MICKEY MOUSE
Manufacturer: Tiger
Year: 1984
Rarity: 9
Loose: $5–7*
Complete: $8–10*
Notes: Flip-top 2-screen LCD game with a Mickey Mouse theme

MIND BOGGLER
Manufacturer: Mattel
Year: 1978
Rarity: 8
Loose: $3–5*
Complete: $5–8
Notes: LED code-breaking game that looks more like a calculator than a game; packaged with a *Mind Boggler* pad and pencil

MINER 2049ER
Manufacturer: Tiger
Year: 1984
Rarity: 9
Loose: $5–7*
Complete: $8–10*
Notes: Flip-top 2-screen LCD game based on the popular computer and console game by the same name

MINI WIZARD
Manufacturer: Vtech
Year: 1977
Rarity: 8
Loose: $3–5*
Complete: $7–9
Notes: *Simon* clone

MISSILE ATTACK
Manufacturer: Mattel
Year: 1977
Rarity: 8
Loose: $4–6
Complete: $8–10*
Notes: Missile defense game (a sort of primitive precursor to *Missile Command*); withdrawn from distribution and re-released a year later as *Battlestar Galactica Space Alert*

MISSILE INVADER
Manufacturer: Bandai
Year: 1980
Rarity: 7
Loose: $5–7
Complete: $8–12
Notes: LED game with gameplay similar to *Space Invaders;* also available in a larger size (*Super Galaxy Invader*)

MISSILE INVADER
Manufacturer: Sears
Year: 1980
Rarity: 8
Loose: $3–5*
Complete: $5–10
Notes: Licensed version of Bandai's *Missile Invader*

MOLE PATROL
Manufacturer: Bandai
Year: ?
Rarity: 9
Loose: $6–8*
Complete: $10–15*
Notes: VFD game of valiant combat versus a horde of moles

MONKEY
Manufacturer: Vtech
Year: ?
Rarity: 9
Loose: $2–4*
Complete: $5–7*
Notes: Pocket-sized LCD game in the "Time and Fun" series

MONKEY JUMP
Manufacturer: Vtech
Year: ?
Rarity: 9
Loose: $3–5*
Complete: $6–8*
Notes: LCD *Donkey Kong* clone; also available in a tabletop version called *Wild Man Jump*

MONSTER MAZE
Manufacturer: Tiger
Year: 1982
Rarity: 9
Loose: $6–9*
Complete: $10–15*
Notes: LCD *Pac-Man* clone; also available in a tabletop version

MR. BULLFROG
Manufacturer: Tiger
Year: 1982
Rarity: 9
Loose: $2–4*
Complete: $5–7*
Notes: Tiny pocket-sized LCD game; gameplay is similar to the *Frog Bog* cartridge for the Intellivision

MS. PAC-MAN
Manufacturer: Tiger
Year: 1984
Rarity: 9
Loose: $5–7*
Complete: $8–12*
Notes: Pink LCD game with Ms. Pac-Man herself featured on the case; loosely based on the arcade game

MUSICAL MARVIN
Manufacturer: Entex
Year: ?
Rarity: 9
Loose: $3–5*
Complete: $7–9*
Notes: LED game similar to Milton Bradley's *Simon,* but with 8 colored buttons instead of 4; plays 6 musical games

NFL DELUXE ELECTRONIC FOOTBALL
Manufacturer: Tudor
Year: ?
Rarity: 9
Loose: $4–6*
Complete: $8–10*
Notes: LED football game similar to Mattel's *Football 2*

NFL ELECTRONIC FOOTBALL
Manufacturer: Tudor
Year: ?
Rarity: 9
Loose: $4–6*
Complete: $8–10*
Notes: LED football game similar to Mattel's *Football*

NUMBERS GAME
Manufacturer: Sears
Year: ?
Rarity: 9
Loose: $3–5*
Complete: $8–10*
Notes: LED game with gameplay similar to the board game *Mastermind;* packaged with a score sheet

OFFENSE/DEFENSE ELECTRONIC BASKETBALL
Manufacturer: Sears
Year: ?
Rarity: 9
Loose: $4–6*
Complete: $8–10*
Notes: 2-player LED basketball game; licensed version of Entex's *Basketball 2*

OFFENSE/DEFENSE ELECTRONIC FOOTBALL
Manufacturer: Sears
Year: 1980
Rarity: 9
Loose: $4–6*
Complete: $8–10*
Notes: 2-player LED football game; licensed version of Entex's *Football 3*

OFFENSE/DEFENSE ELECTRONIC SOCCER
Manufacturer: Sears
Year: 1979
Rarity: 9
Loose: $4–6*
Complete: $8–10*
Notes: 2-player LED soccer game; licensed version of Entex's *Soccer*

PACIII
Manufacturer: Ecstoy/Spica
Year: ?
Rarity: 9
Loose: $6–8*
Complete: $9–12*
Notes: LCD *Pac-Man* clone with a tiny joystick controller; rare

PACKRI MONSTER
Manufacturer: Bandai
Year: 1981
Rarity: 5
Loose: $8–10
Complete: $20–50
Notes: VFD game based on *Pac-Man;* also sold by Radio Shack as *Hungry Monster*

PAC-MAN
Manufacturer: Tiger
Year: 1984
Rarity: 9
Loose: $3–5*
Complete: $7–9*
Notes: Flip-top 2-screen LCD game based on the arcade game

PAC-MAN
Manufacturer: Tiger
Year: 1984
Rarity: 9
Loose: $3–5*
Complete: $7–9*
Notes: Pocket LCD "large screen" game based on the arcade game

PACMAN2
Manufacturer: Entex
Year: 1980
Rarity: 8
Loose: $7–12
Complete: $15–20*
Notes: *Pac-Man* clone with a VFD; allowed 2 players to play simultaneously (hence the title)

PANCAKE
Manufacturer: Vtech
Year: ?
Rarity: 9
Loose: $2–4*
Complete: $5–7*
Notes: Pocket-sized LCD game in the "Time and Fun" series

PAPERBOY
Manufacturer: Tiger
Year: 1988
Rarity: 7
Loose: $3–6
Complete: $7–12*
Notes: LCD game based on the classic Atari arcade game by the same name

PAPERBOY 2
Manufacturer: Tiger
Year: 1988
Rarity: 7
Loose: $3–6*
Complete: $7–12*
Notes: LCD game base don the classic Atari arcade game *Paperboy*

THE PINK PANTHER
Manufacturer: Tiger
Year: 1983
Rarity: 9
Loose: $2–4*
Complete: $5–7*
Notes: Pocket LCD "large screen" game based on the *Pink Panther* cartoon series

PIRATE
Manufacturer: Vtech
Year: ?
Rarity: 9
Loose: $2–4*
Complete: $5–7*
Notes: Pocket-sized LCD game in the "Time and Fun" series

PLANET ZEON
Manufacturer: Tomy
Year: 1983
Rarity: 9
Loose: $20–30
Complete: $35–55*
Notes: One of the Tomytronic 3D series—an LCD game shaped like a pair of binoculars with an internal screen; this one has a space battle theme

PLAY MAKER BASKETBALL/HOCKEY/SOCCER
Manufacturer: Tiger
Year: ?
Rarity: 9
Loose: $4–6*
Complete: $8–10*
Notes: 2-player LED game that plays hockey, basketball, and soccer; comes with 3 notched plastic overlays—the overlay notches are the means by which the unit knows which game to play

PLAY MAKER FOOTBALL
Manufacturer: Tiger
Year: ?
Rarity: 9
Loose: $4–6*
Complete: $8–10*
Notes: 2-player LED football game similar in design to *Play Maker Basketball/Hockey/Soccer;* unique among the LED football clones in that it has an instant replay feature

POCKET KING KONG
Manufacturer: Tandy
Year: 1984
Rarity: 9
Loose: $3–5*
Complete: $7–9*
Notes: LCD game; sort of like *Donkey Kong* from an isometric top-down perspective

POCKET REPEAT
Manufacturer: Tandy
Year: 1981
Rarity: 8
Loose: $2–4
Complete: $5–7*
Notes: Pocket-sized LED *Simon* clone

POWER PIGSKIN ELECTRONIC FOOTBALL
Manufacturer: Regency Electronics
Year: 1979
Rarity: 8
Loose: $9–12
Complete: $15–20*
Notes: 2-player LED football game with a case shaped like a football

POWERHOUSE PINBALL
Manufacturer: Tomy
Year: ?
Rarity: 9
Loose: $4–6*
Complete: $8–10*
Notes: LED pinball game; released in Europe as *Flipper Pinball*

PRO ACTION BASEBALL
Manufacturer: Caprice
Year: ?
Rarity: 9
Loose: $3–5*
Complete: $7–9*
Notes: 2-player LED baseball game

PRO ACTION SOCCER
Manufacturer: Caprice
Year: ?
Rarity: 9
Loose: $3–5*
Complete: $7–9*
Notes: LED soccer game

PRO-TENNIS

Manufacturer: Tomy
Year: 1979
Rarity: 9
Loose: $4–6*
Complete: $8–9*
Notes: VFD tennis game

PULSONIC BASEBALL

Manufacturer: Mego
Year: 1979
Rarity: 8
Loose: $5–7
Complete: $8–10*
Notes: 2-player LED baseball game

PULSONIC BASEBALL II

Manufacturer: Mego
Year: 1979
Rarity: 9
Loose: $5–7*
Complete: $8–10*
Notes: 2-player LED baseball game; slightly more advanced than the original *Pulsonic Baseball;* green case with hidden controls for the second player

PULSONIC GOLF

Manufacturer: Mego
Year: ?
Rarity: 9
Loose: $4–6*
Complete: $7–10*
Notes: LED golf game

RACE 'N CHASE

Manufacturer: Bambino
Year: 1982
Rarity: 9
Loose: $4–6*
Complete: $8–10*
Notes: Racing game with a VFD

RACE TIME

Manufacturer: Bandai
Year: 1980
Rarity: 9
Loose: $3–5*
Complete: $7–12*
Notes: LED racing game, similar in design to *Flight Time*

RACETRACK

Manufacturer: Toytronic
Year: ?
Rarity: 9
Loose: $3–5*
Complete: $6–10*
Notes: LED car race game similar to Mattel's *Auto Race;* uses a miniature steering wheel controller

RACEWAY

Manufacturer: Tiger
Year: 1978
Rarity: 9
Loose: $3–5*
Complete: $6–10*
Notes: LED care race game with a tiny steering wheel controller

RAISE THE DEVIL PINBALL

Manufacturer: Entex
Year: 1980
Rarity: 8
Loose: $2–6
Complete: $7–10
Notes: LED pinball game

RAISE THE DEVIL PINBALL

Manufacturer: Sears
Year: 1980
Rarity: 8
Loose: $2–6
Complete: $7–10
Notes: Licensed version of the Entex game by the same name

RED LINE

Manufacturer: Kenner
Year: 1980
Rarity: 9
Loose: $4–6*
Complete: $8–10*
Notes: Simple LED drag racing game with a red dual grip case and thumb control buttons; featured a jack that allowed you to connect two *Red Line* games together for head-to-head play

ROCKET PINBALL

Manufacturer: Tandy
Year: ?
Rarity: 9
Loose: $2–4*
Complete: $5–7*
Notes: Simple LED pinball game; licensed version of Tiger's *Rocket Pinball*

ROCKET PINBALL

Manufacturer: Tiger
Year: ?
Rarity: 9
Loose: $2–4*
Complete: $5–7*
Notes: Simple LED pinball game

SKI SLALOM

Manufacturer: Mattel
Year: 1980
Rarity: 9
Loose: $4–6*
Complete: $7–12*
Notes: LED skiing game that is little more than a repackaged version of *Auto Race,* the only difference being that you race from top to bottom instead of vice-versa

SAFARI

Manufacturer: Bambino
Year: 1981
Rarity: 8
Loose: $5–10
Complete: $15–25
Notes: VFD

SAFARI

Manufacturer: Vtech
Year: ?
Rarity: 9
Loose: $2–4*
Complete: $5–7*
Notes: Pocket-sized LCD game in the "Time and Fun" series

SHARK ATTACK

Manufacturer: Tomy
Year: 1983
Rarity: 7
Loose: $9–15
Complete: $20–25
Notes: One of the Tomytronic 3-D series—an LCD game shaped like a pair of binoculars with an internal screen; released in Japan as *Jaws 3-D*

SHARK ISLAND

Manufacturer: Bandai
Year: ?
Rarity: 9
Loose: $4–6*
Complete: $7–9*
Notes: Solar powered LCD game

SHARK ISLAND

Manufacturer: Tandy
Year: 1984
Rarity: 9
Loose: $2–4*
Complete: $5–7*
Notes: LCD game; not related to the Bandai game of the same name

SHOOTING GALLERY

Manufacturer: Tandy
Year: 1981
Rarity: 8
Loose: $2–5
Complete: $5–6
Notes: Simple LED shooting game with manual scoring; had overlays that "changed" the game between darts, safari, and spaceships; licensed version of Tiger's *2 Games in 1 Safari & Darts*

SKY ATTACK

Manufacturer: Tomy
Year: 1983
Rarity: 8
Loose: $5–10
Complete: $12–18*
Notes: One of the Tomytronic 3D series—an LCD game shaped like a pair of binoculars with an internal screen; you control a tank shooting at futuristic flying vessels

SKYFIGHTERS

Manufacturer: Tomy
Year: 1983
Rarity: 9
Loose: $5–10*
Complete: $12–18*
Notes: One of the Tomytronic 3D series—an LCD game shaped like a pair of binoculars with an internal screen; World War I air combat game

SLEEP WALKER

Manufacturer: Vtech
Year: 1981
Rarity: 9
Loose: $2–4*
Complete: $5–7*
Notes: Pocket-sized LCD game in the "Time and Fun" series

SLIMLINE SPEEDWAY

Manufacturer: Tomy
Year: 1980
Rarity: 8
Loose: $5–8
Complete: $8–18
Notes: LCD car race game with 5 game variations; comes with a folding plastic storage case similar to a calculator case

SMURF

Manufacturer: Tiger
Year: 1984
Rarity: 9
Loose: $3–5*
Complete: $7–9*
Notes: LCD 2-screen flip-top game based on the *Smurfs* cartoon

SOCCER

Manufacturer: Entex
Year: 1979
Rarity: 8
Loose: $5–8
Complete: $9–15*
Notes: Head-to-head LED soccer game

SOCCER

Manufacturer: Interstate
Year: ?
Rarity: 9
Loose: $3–5*
Complete: $7–9*
Notes: LED soccer game

SOCCER

Manufacturer: Mattel
Year: 1978
Rarity: 6
Loose: $8–12
Complete: $15–30
Notes: One of the least common of the Mattel LED sports games; 2 box versions—one large with Styrofoam inserts (original) and a smaller version

SOCCER

Manufacturer: NIT
Year: 1979
Rarity: 9
Loose: $3–5*
Complete: $7–9*
Notes: LED soccer game

SOCCER 2

Manufacturer: Mattel
Year: 1979
Rarity: 8
Loose: $15–20
Complete: $25–45
Notes: Sequel to the 1978 version; least common of the Mattel LED sports games

SOCCER (KICK THE GOAL)

Manufacturer: Bambino
Year: 1979
Rarity: 9
Loose: $3–5*
Complete: $7–9*
Notes: Case is styled like *Hockey* (*Lucky Puck*)—with black control buttons and a green screen

SONIC INVADER

Manufacturer: Vtech
Year: 1981
Rarity: 9
Loose: $4–6*
Complete: $7–12
Notes: Renamed version of Vtech's *Invaders*

SPACE ATTACK

Manufacturer: Tomy
Year: ?
Rarity: 9
Loose: $7–9*
Complete: $10–15*
Notes: *Space Invaders* clone with a VFD; very similar to *Cosmic Combat*

SPACE BATTLE

Manufacturer: Entex
Year: 1979
Rarity: 9
Loose: $4–6*
Complete: $8–10*
Notes: Head-to-head LED space combat game

SPACE CRUISER

Manufacturer: US Games
Year: ?
Rarity: 9
Loose: $4–6*
Complete: $8–12*
Notes: Oval LED game that plays both *Space Cruiser* and a football game; each game has its own overlay

SPACE HARRIER

Manufacturer: Tiger
Year: 1988
Rarity: 9
Loose: $3–5*
Complete: $7–9*
Notes: LCD game based on the classic Sega arcade game by the same name

SPACE INVADER

Manufacturer: Entex
Year: 1980
Rarity: 8
Loose: $6–8*
Complete: $10–15
Notes: LED *Space Invaders* clone; available with both black and gray cases

SPACE INVADERS

Manufacturer: Tiger
Year: 1982
Rarity: 9
Loose: $3–5*
Complete: $7–9*
Notes: Pocket LCD game based on the arcade game by the same name; silver case with controls at the bottom

SPACE INVADERS

Manufacturer: Tiger
Year: 1984
Rarity: 9
Loose: $3–5*
Complete: $7–9*
Notes: Pocket LCD "large screen" game based on the arcade game

SPACE INVADERS CALCULATOR

Manufacturer: Tiger
Year: 1982
Rarity: 9
Loose: $3–5*
Complete: $7–9*
Notes: LCD game built into a calculator; based on the arcade game

SPACE-N-COUNTER

Manufacturer: GCE
Year: ?
Rarity: 9
Loose: $3–5*
Complete: $7–9*
Notes: LCD calculator/game combo created by the company that went on to design the Vectrex console

SPACE SHOT

Manufacturer: Bandai
Year: 1978
Rarity: 9
Loose: $3–5*
Complete: $7–9*
Notes: Early LED space battle game; little more than a few LEDs and a fire button; gameplay is virtually identical to that of Bandai's *Baseball, Basketball, Football,* and *Hockey* games

SPACE SHUTTLE

Manufacturer: Wing Group
Year: ?
Rarity: 9
Loose: $5–7*
Complete: $8–12*
Notes: VFD space flying game in a case shaped like the space shuttle

SPACESHIP PINBALL

Manufacturer: Toytronic
Year: 1980
Rarity: 9
Loose: $2–4*
Complete: $6–9*
Notes: LED pinball game

SPEED FREAK

Manufacturer: Mattel
Year: 1982
Rarity: 9
Loose: $2–4*
Complete: $5–7*
Notes: Pocket-sized LCD auto racing game

SPIDER-MAN RESCUE

Manufacturer: Bandai
Year: 1978
Rarity: 9
Loose: $3–5*
Complete: $7–9*
Notes: Early superhero LED game by Bandai with a Spider-Man-shaped case; gameplay is identical to *The Incredible Hulk Escapes*

SPLIT SECOND

Manufacturer: Parker Brothers
Year: 1980
Rarity: 8
Loose: $5–8*
Complete: $10–12
Notes: LED handheld with 5 built-in action games

SPORTS ARENA

Manufacturer: Tandy
Year: 1981
Rarity: 9
Loose: $5–8*
Complete: $10–15*
Notes: LED sports game that plays hockey, soccer, and basketball; includes plastic overlays for each game

SPORTS CENTER

Manufacturer: House of Games
Year: 1980
Rarity: 9
Loose: $5–8*
Complete: $10–15*
Notes: LED sports game that plays baseball, basketball, and football; plastic overlay included for each game

SPORTS TIME

Manufacturer: GCE
Year: ?
Rarity: 9
Loose: $3–5*
Complete: $7–9*
Notes: LCD watch-sized game developed by the company that went on to design the Vectrex game console

STAR CASTLE

Manufacturer: Tiger
Year: 1982
Rarity: 9
Loose: $5–8*
Complete: $9–12*
Notes: Pocket-sized LCD game based on the arcade game by the same name; also available as a tabletop game

STAR HAWK

Manufacturer: Mattel
Year: 1978
Rarity: 9
Loose: $4–6*
Complete: $8–10*
Notes: VFD space battle game; not related to the Cinematronics arcade game by the same name

STAR TREK

Manufacturer: Coleco
Year: 1979
Rarity: 9
Loose: $5–7*
Complete: $8–12*
Notes: Unique LED game shaped like the starship *Enterprise;* marketed to coincide with the release of the first *Star Trek* feature film

SUB CHASE

Manufacturer: Mattel
Year: 1978
Rarity: 7
Loose: $6–10*
Complete: $12–18*
Notes: LED naval battle game with radar-like display screen; also released by Bandai as *Submarine*

SUB ATTACK

Manufacturer: Bandai
Year: 1982
Rarity: 9
Loose: $4–6*
Complete: $7–9*
Notes: Solar powered LCD game

SUB WARS

Manufacturer: Tiger
Year: 1980
Rarity: 9
Loose: $5–7*
Complete: $8–10*
Notes: LED submarine battle game; case is shaped like the handles and viewer of a periscope; Tiger released a pocket-sized LCD *Sub Wars* game in 1988

SUBMARINE
Manufacturer: Bandai
Year: 1978
Rarity: 9
Loose: $6–10*
Complete: $12–15*
Notes: LED naval battle game with radar-like display screen; also released by Mattel as *Sub Chase*

SUBMARINE BASKETBALL
Manufacturer: Tandy
Year: ?
Rarity: 9
Loose: $4–6*
Complete: $8–10*
Notes: LED game that plays both basketball and a submarine battle game; very similar to K-Mart's *Dunk 'N Sunk*

SUPER ALIEN INVADER2
Manufacturer: Entex
Year: 1982
Rarity: 9
Loose: $7–9*
Complete: $10–15*
Notes: Renamed version of *Super Space Invader2;* case styled like that of *Galaxian2*

SUPER COBRA
Manufacturer: Entex
Year: 1982
Rarity: 8
Loose: $10–15*
Complete: $25–50*
Notes: Based on the arcade game by the same name; VFD

SUPER GALAXY INVADER
Manufacturer: Bandai
Year: 1980
Rarity: 8
Loose: $8–12
Complete: $15–18*
Notes: "Deluxe" version of Bandai's *Galaxy Invader;* identical gameplay to its non-deluxe counterpart

SUPER SPACE INVADER2
Manufacturer: Entex
Year: 1981
Rarity: 9
Loose: $8–10*
Complete: $12–15*
Notes: First release, with a sleek case styled like the Entex *Defender* game; VFD; based on *Space Invaders*

SUPER SPACE INVADER2
Manufacturer: Entex
Year: 1982
Rarity: 9
Loose: $8–10*
Complete: $12–15*
Notes: Second release, with a chunkier case styled like then Entex *Galaxian2* game; VFD; same exact gameplay as the 1981 release by the same name

SUPER SPACE JACK
Manufacturer: Onko
Year: ?
Rarity: 9
Loose: $3–5*
Complete: $7–9*
Notes: LED game with a case shaped more or less like the starship *Enterprise* from *Star Trek;* not a *Star Trek* game, however

SUPER SPORTS-4
Manufacturer: US Games
Year: ?
Rarity: 9
Loose: $6–8*
Complete: $8–12*
Notes: LED 2-player sports game that played soccer, football, hockey, and basketball; each game had its own overlay

SUPERSTAR FOOTBALL
Manufacturer: Bambino
Year: 1979
Rarity: 8
Loose: $3–5
Complete: $7–9*
Notes: Nearly identical to *Football Classic,* but with a white case

TANDY CYCLE RACE
Manufacturer: Tandy
Year: 1981
Rarity: 8
Loose: $3–5
Complete: $7–9*
Notes: LED racing game; licensed version of Bandai's *Championship Racer*

TEAM PLAY BASKETBALL
Manufacturer: Sears
Year: 1982
Rarity: 8
Loose: $3–5
Complete: $7–9*
Notes: 2-player LED basketball game; licensed version of Coleco's *Head to Head Basketball*

TEAM PLAY FOOTBALL
Manufacturer: Sears
Year: 1980
Rarity: 8
Loose: $3–5
Complete: $7–9*
Notes: 2-player LED football game; licensed version of Coleco's *Head to Head Football*

TEAM PLAY HOCKEY
Manufacturer: Sears
Year: 1980
Rarity: 9
Loose: $3–5*
Complete: $7–9*
Notes: 2-player LED hockey game; licensed version of Coleco's *Head to Head Hockey*

TEAM PLAY SOCCER
Manufacturer: Sears
Year: 1980
Rarity: 9
Loose: $3–5*
Complete: $7–9*
Notes: 2-player LED soccer game; licensed version of Coleco's *Head to Head Soccer*

TENNIS
Manufacturer: Entex
Year: ?
Rarity: 8
Loose: $4–6*
Complete: $8–10*
Notes: LED tennis game that can be played solo or head-to-head with a second player

TENNIS
Manufacturer: Tomy
Year: 1980
Rarity: 9
Loose: $4–6*
Complete: $8–9*
Notes: VFD tennis game; nearly identical to Tomy's *Pro-Tennis*

TENNIS MENACE
Manufacturer: Vtech
Year: ?
Rarity: 9
Loose: $2–4*
Complete: $5–7*
Notes: LCD tennis game; one of the "Mini Time and Fun" series

THUNDERING TURBO
Manufacturer: Tomy
Year: 1983
Rarity: 6
Loose: $5–10
Complete: $12–20
Notes: One of the Tomytronic 3-D series—an LCD game shaped like a pair of binoculars with an internal screen; 3-D auto race game

TORPEDO SHOOT
Manufacturer: Bandai
Year: 1980
Rarity: 8
Loose: $3–5
Complete: $7–9*
Notes: LED submarine battle game

TOUCH ME
Manufacturer: Atari
Year: 1978
Rarity: 5
Loose: $6–10
Complete: $12–15*
Notes: Gameplay similar to Milton Bradley's *Simon,* which was released later the same year; 3 Atari handheld games were designed, but this was the only one released

TRACK STAR
Manufacturer: Tandy
Year: 1985
Rarity: 9
Loose: $3–5*
Complete: $6–8*
Notes: LCD track and field running/hurdling game

TREASURE
Manufacturer: Tiger
Year: 1982
Rarity: 9
Loose: $2–4*
Complete: $5–7*
Notes: LCD pocket-sized game with a scuba diving/treasure hunting theme

TRI-1
Manufacturer: Fonas
Year: 1979
Rarity: 9
Loose: $3–5*
Complete: $7–9*
Notes: LED 3-in-1 game; plays 3 baseball-oriented games

TRICK SHOT BASKETBALL
Manufacturer: Tandy
Year: ?
Rarity: 9
Loose: $3–5*
Complete: $7–9*
Notes: LED basketball game; very similar to US Games' *Basketball*

TURTLES
Manufacturer: Entex
Year: 1982
Rarity: 9
Loose: $8–10*
Complete: $12–15*
Notes: Based on the arcade game by the same name; VFD

UFO ATTACK
Manufacturer: Tomy
Year: ?
Rarity: 9
Loose: $6–8*
Complete: $10–12*
Notes: VFD Space Invaders clone; very similar to Tomy's *Cosmic Combat*

UFO MASTER BLASTER
Manufacturer: Bambino
Year: 1979
Rarity: 8
Loose: $6–8
Complete: $10–20
Notes: VFD action game vaguely similar to *Galaxian*

VARIETY

Manufacturer: Vtech
Year: 1983
Rarity: 9
Loose: $40–50*
Complete: $70–80
Notes: A cartridge-based LCD game system; the "system" is just a housing for self-contained LCD games; number of games released is unknown; packaged with a cartridge called *Past Invasions*

VOLLEYBALL

Manufacturer: Tomy
Year: ?
Rarity: 9
Loose: $8–10*
Complete: $12–15*
Notes: 2-player LED volleyball game; each player position has a button for hitting the "ball"
a unique game amidst the other LED sports clones of the time

WILDFIRE

Manufacturer: Parker Brothers
Year: 1979
Rarity: 7
Loose: $3–5
Complete: $7–10
Notes: LED handheld pinball game

WORLD CHAMPIONSHIP BASEBALL

Manufacturer: Mattel
Year: 1980
Rarity: 9
Loose: $5–7*
Complete: $8–12*
Notes: Baseball game with a VFD; the last of Mattel's handheld baseball games

WORLD CHAMPIONSHIP FOOTBALL

Manufacturer: Mattel
Year: 1980
Rarity: 8
Loose: $5–7
Complete: $8–12*
Notes: Football game with a VFD; the last of Mattel's handheld football games

WORLD CUP SOCCER

Manufacturer: Tomy
Year: ?
Rarity: 9
Loose: $3–5*
Complete: $7–9*
Notes: 2-player LED soccer game

ZAP!

Manufacturer: Coleco
Year: 1979
Rarity: 8
Loose: $3–5
Complete: $7–9
Notes: LED game where you bounce the LED back and forth between 2 players; not as much like *Pong* as it sounds . . .

ZAP

Manufacturer: Tandy
Year: 1985
Rarity: 9
Loose: $2–4*
Complete: $5–7*
Notes: Pocket LCD game with a space alien–zapping theme

ZINGO

Manufacturer: Tandy
Year: 1981
Rarity: 9
Loose: $3–5*
Complete: $7–9*
Notes: LED game; sort of a cross between pachinko and *Connect 4;* try to line up 4 bouncing blips

TABLETOP CLASSIC GAME PRICE GUIDE

3-D ESCAPE!

Manufacturer: Entex
Year: 1981
Rarity: 9
Loose: $8–12*
Complete: $15–20*
Notes: One of 2 LCD games made by Entex

3-D GRAND PRIX

Manufacturer: Entex
Year: 1981
Rarity: 9
Loose: $8–12*
Complete: $15–20*
Notes: Entex's second LCD game; has a tiny steering wheel controller

AFTER BURNER

Manufacturer: Tiger
Year: 1989
Rarity: 8
Loose: $7–10*
Complete: $12–15*
Notes: Extremely interesting LCD tabletop version of Sega's *After Burner* arcade game; large joystick control and cockpit-like appearance

ALIEN CHASE

Manufacturer: Tandy
Year: 1984
Rarity: 7
Loose: $6–8
Complete: $10–12
Notes: 2-player space combat game with a VFD; licensed version of Tomy's Alien Chase

ALIEN CHASE

Manufacturer: Tomy
Year: 1984
Rarity: 9
Loose: $7–10*
Complete: $12–15*
Notes: 2-player space combat game with a 2-sided VFD

ALIEN INVADERS
Manufacturer: Ramtex
Year: ?
Rarity: 9
Loose: $6–9*
Complete: $10–12*
Notes: LED *Space Invaders* clone; prequel to Ramtex *Space Invaders/Block Buster,* with an identical case style; sold by a number of other companies as well

BOWLATRONIC
Manufacturer: Coleco
Year: 1979
Rarity: 6
Loose: $6–12
Complete: $15–18*
Notes: Tabletop LED bowling game

BOWLING
Manufacturer: Mattel
Year: 1980
Rarity: 9
Loose: $8–12*
Complete: $15–20*
Notes: Rare bowling game that combines LED and electromechanical elements

BOXING (KNOCK EM OUT)
Manufacturer: Bambino
Year: 1979
Rarity: 7
Loose: $5–7
Complete: $9–12
Notes: Released in 2 versions—yellow case with a green screen, and white case with a blue screen

CAVEMAN
Manufacturer: Tandy
Year: 1983
Rarity: 8
Loose: $10–12*
Complete: $15–25*
Notes: VFD game; licensed version of Tomy's *Caveman*

CAVEMAN
Manufacturer: Tomy
Year: 1983
Rarity: 7
Loose: $10–12*
Complete: $15–25*
Notes: VFD game with a prehistoric theme; available with both red and white cases

CHICKY WOGGY
Manufacturer: Vtech
Year: 1981
Rarity: 9
Loose: $7–10*
Complete: $12–15*
Notes: LCD maze game; also released in a handheld version

COBRA SUPER COPTER
Manufacturer: Tandy
Year: 1985
Rarity: 8
Loose: $10–15
Complete: $18–25
Notes: VFD game; licensed version of Tomy's *Super Cobra*

COMPUTER PERFECTION
Manufacturer: Lakeside
Year: 1979
Rarity: 6
Loose: $5–10
Complete: $15–20
Notes: LED version of the board game by the same name

COSMIC FIRE AWAY 2000
Manufacturer: Tandy
Year: 1983
Rarity: 8
Loose: $15–25*
Complete: $40–70*
Notes: The third game in Tandy's *Fire Away* series is a tabletop model, blue with a VFD

COSMOS
Manufacturer: Atari
Year: 1981
Rarity: Prototype
Loose: ?
Complete: N/A
Notes: 2-D game system with holographic backgrounds that was introduced at trade shows but never produced in quantity; 2 working prototypes and 8 cartridges are known to exist; pricing information unavailable due to extreme rarity

CRAZY CLIMBER
Manufacturer: Bandai
Year: 1982
Rarity: 7
Loose: $25–40
Complete: $50–60*
Notes: Based on the arcade game by the same name; 2 thumb joysticks and a VFD; rare

CRAZY CLIMBER
Manufacturer: Entex
Year: 1982
Rarity: 9
Loose: $15–30*
Complete: $35–45*
Notes: Based on the arcade game by the same name; 2 thumb joysticks and a VFD; rare

DONKEY KONG
Manufacturer: Coleco
Year: 1982
Rarity: 3
Loose: $30–70
Complete: $90–170
Notes: One of the Coleco miniarcade game series

DONKEY KONG JUNIOR

Manufacturer: Coleco
Year: 1983
Rarity: 7
Loose: $30–50
Complete: $55–70
Notes: One of the Coleco miniarcade game series, though differently styled with an LCD display; manufactured by Nintendo; not as collectable as the Coleco-made miniarcade games

DRAGON CASTLE

Manufacturer: Vtech
Year: 1981
Rarity: 9
Loose: $7–10*
Complete: $12–15*
Notes: LCD game of medieval combat; also released as a handheld game/calculator

FROGGER

Manufacturer: Coleco
Year: 1981
Rarity: 4
Loose: $30–90
Complete: $100–150
Notes: One of the Coleco miniarcade game series

GALAXIAN

Manufacturer: Coleco
Year: 1981
Rarity: 4
Loose: $25–75
Complete: $90–140
Notes: One of the Coleco miniarcade game series

HOME SWEET HOME

Manufacturer: Vtech
Year: 1981
Rarity: 9
Loose: $7–10*
Complete: $12–15*
Notes: One of Vtech's tabletop LCD games

JAWBREAKER

Manufacturer: Tiger
Year: 1984
Rarity: 9
Loose: $8–12*
Complete: $15–20*
Notes: LCD tabletop version of the Atari 2600 cartridge *Jawbreaker* by Tigervision; also available as a handheld

KING KONG

Manufacturer: Tiger
Year: 1981
Rarity: 9
Loose: $8–12*
Complete: $15–20*
Notes: LCD tabletop version of Tiger's handheld King Kong; gameplay is nearly identical to *Donkey Kong*

KINGMAN

Manufacturer: Tomy
Year: 1982
Rarity: 8
Loose: $15–20*
Complete: $25–35*
Notes: Gameplay similar to *Donkey Kong*

LUPIN

Manufacturer: Tomy
Year: ?
Rarity: 8
Loose: $15–20
Complete: $25–30
Notes: VFD game based on the Japanese cartoon character Lupin III

MARIO'S CEMENT FACTORY

Manufacturer: Nintendo
Year: 1983
Rarity: 8
Loose: $20–35
Complete: $45–55*
Notes: LCD game, styled like Coleco's *Donkey Kong Junior*

MINI-VID BREAKFREE

Manufacturer: Mego
Year: 1979
Rarity: 8
Loose: $8–10
Complete: $15–25
Notes: 2-player Breakout clone with a VFD

MINI-VID DODGE CITY

Manufacturer: Mego
Year: 1979
Rarity: 8
Loose: $8–10
Complete: $15–25
Notes: 2-player gunfight game with a VFD

MINI-VID SEA BATTLE

Manufacturer: Mego
Year: 1979
Rarity: 9
Loose: $8–10*
Complete: $15–25*
Notes: LCD 2-player sea battle game

MINI-VID SPACEWAR

Manufacturer: Mego
Year: 1979
Rarity: 9
Loose: $8–10*
Complete: $15–25*
Notes: LCD 2-player space combat game

MONSTER CHASE

Manufacturer: Vtech
Year: 1982
Rarity: 9
Loose: $9–12*
Complete: $15–20*
Notes: LCD *Pac-Man* clone; very similar to Tiger's *Monster Maze*

MONSTER MAZE

Manufacturer: Tiger
Year: 1982
Rarity: 9
Loose: $9–12*
Complete: $15–20*
Notes: LCD *Pac-Man* clone; tabletop version of the Tiger handheld by the same name

MS. PAC-MAN

Manufacturer: Coleco
Year: 1981
Rarity: 5
Loose: $50–100
Complete: $20–180
Notes: One of the Coleco miniarcade game series

OUT-RUN

Manufacturer: Tiger
Year: 1988
Rarity: 9
Loose: $7–10*
Complete: $12–15*
Notes: LCD tabletop version of the Sega arcade game by the same name; has an elaborate dashboard/steering wheel controller, with the game screen built into the dashboard

PAC-MAN

Manufacturer: Coleco
Year: 1981
Rarity: 3
Loose: $20–80
Complete: $60–120
Notes: One of the Coleco miniarcade game series

PAC MAN

Manufacturer: Tomy
Year: 1981
Rarity: 4
Loose: $5–20
Complete: $30–40
Notes: Round yellow unit with touch pad controls and a VFD; also released under the names *Puck Man* and *Munchman*

PAC MAN-1

Manufacturer: Futuretronics
Year: 1981
Rarity: 9
Loose: $5–20*
Complete: $30–40*
Notes: Identical to Tomy's *Pac Man*

POPEYE

Manufacturer: Nintendo
Year: 1983
Rarity: 6
Loose: $30–45
Complete: $60–70
Notes: LCD game based on the Nintendo arcade game by the same name; styled like Coleco's *Donkey Kong Junior*

Q*BERT

Manufacturer: Parker Brothers
Year: 1983
Rarity: 6
Loose: $30–80
Complete: $60–100
Notes: Tabletop miniature arcade game with a VFD; somewhat similar in style to the popular Coleco series of miniarcade tabletops

SCRAMBLE

Manufacturer: Tomy
Year: 1982
Rarity: 7
Loose: $10–25
Complete: $30–45*
Notes: VFD tabletop version of the arcade game by the same name

SIMON

Manufacturer: Milton Bradley
Year: 1978
Rarity: 2
Loose: $6–15
Complete: $16–30
Notes: The most popular "follow the sequence" lights and music game; invented by Ralph Baer, creator of the original Magnavox Odyssey; still sold in stores today, though the style is slightly different from the original; prices are for the original 1978 version

SNOOPY

Manufacturer: Nintendo
Year: 1983
Rarity: 8
Loose: $40–60
Complete: $100–200
Notes: LCD game starring Charlie Brown's dog; styled like Coleco's *Donkey Kong Junior*

SPACE CHASER

Manufacturer: Bandai
Year: 1980
Rarity: 9
Loose: $5–8*
Complete: $10–12*
Notes: LED air combat game

SPACE INVADERS/BLOCK BUSTER

Manufacturer: Ramtex
Year: ?
Rarity: 9
Loose: $7–10*
Complete: $12–15*
Notes: LED game that plays both *Space Invaders* and a *Breakout* clone; directional buttons are on the sides, and the fire button is on top, just below the screen; the same game was also sold under several other names by several other companies

SPACE LASER FIGHT

Manufacturer: Bambino
Year: 1980
Rarity: 7
Loose: $5–8
Complete: $10–35
Notes: Head-to-head shootout game with a VFD; two versions—one has a green screen, the other blue

SPACE SHOT

Manufacturer: Tandy
Year: ?
Rarity: 9
Loose: $5–8*
Complete: $10–12
Notes: LED space shooter game

SPIDERS

Manufacturer: Entex
Year: 1982
Rarity: 8
Loose: $15–25
Complete: $35–50
Notes: Based on the arcade game by the same name; VFD

STAR CASTLE

Manufacturer: Tiger
Year: 1982
Rarity: 9
Loose: $10–20*
Complete: $30–40*
Notes: LCD tabletop game based on the arcade game by the same name; also available as a handheld

STAR TREK PHASER BATTLE

Manufacturer: Mego
Year: 1976
Rarity: 9
Loose: $20–35
Complete: $45–60*
Notes: Simple space battle game with a cool black case and small joystick with thumb trigger; LED score readout, but the game screen actually used lights

STAR WARS BATTLE COMMAND

Manufacturer: Kenner
Year: 1979
Rarity: 7
Loose: $4–8
Complete: $10–12
Notes: LED space battle game with a fairly involved keypad controller

STAR WARS ELECTRONIC LASER BATTLE

Manufacturer: Kenner
Year: 1979
Rarity: 9
Loose: $4–7
Complete: $8–10
Notes: Head-to-head LED space battle game with two control buttons on each end of the board; players race to be the first to win seven battles and reach the Death Star at the center

STARGATE

Manufacturer: Entex
Year: 1982
Rarity: 8
Loose: $15–20
Complete: $25–45
Notes: Based on the arcade game by the same name; VFD

SUPER SIMON

Manufacturer: Milton Bradley
Year: 1980
Rarity: 6
Loose: $7–10
Complete: $10–30
Notes: 2-player sequel to *Simon*

TC-7 AIR TRAFFIC CONTROL

Manufacturer: Bandai
Year: 1981
Rarity: 9
Loose: $7–10*
Complete: $10–15*
Notes: LED air traffic controller game with a unique radar screen display; complex controls consisted of a 16-button membrane keypad

TRON

Manufacturer: Tomy
Year: 1981
Rarity: 7
Loose: $15–30
Complete: $45–90
Notes: VFD game based on the movie by the same name

VAMPIRE

Manufacturer: Bandai
Year: 1982
Rarity: 9
Loose: $8–12*
Complete: $15–20*
Notes: VFD game with a vampire theme; gameplay is similar to *Donkey Kong*

WILD MAN JUMP

Manufacturer: Vtech
Year: 1981
Rarity: 9
Loose: $7–10*
Complete: $12–15*
Notes: LCD *Donkey Kong* clone; tabletop version of Vtech's *Monkey Jump* handheld

ZACKMAN

Manufacturer: Tandy
Year: 1984
Rarity: 8
Loose: $7–10
Complete: $12–20
Notes: VFD game with a space theme

ZAXXON

Manufacturer: Coleco
Year: 1982
Rarity: 6
Loose: $20–60
Complete: $70–100*
Notes: One of the Coleco miniarcade game series; uses two VFDs and a mirror to create a 3D effect

ADVENTURE VISION PRICE GUIDE

ADVENTURE VISION CONSOLE

Manufacturer: Entex
Year: 1982
Rarity: 10
Loose: $600–800
Complete: $900–1,500
Notes: Unique tabletop LED game console that used interchangeable cartridges; packaged with the *Defender* cartridge

GAMES

DEFENDER

Manufacturer: Entex
Year: 1982
Rarity: 9
Loose: $35–45
Complete: N/A
Notes: Based on the arcade game by the same name; included with the Adventure Vision console

SPACE FORCE

Manufacturer: Entex
Year: 1982
Rarity: 10
Loose: $40–50
Complete: $55–65
Notes: Based on the arcade game by the same name

SUPER COBRA

Manufacturer: Entex
Year: 1982
Rarity: 10
Loose: $40–50*
Complete: $55–65*
Notes: Based on the arcade game by the same name

TURTLES

Manufacturer: Entex
Year: 1982
Rarity: 10
Loose: $40–50*
Complete: $55–65*
Notes: Based on the arcade game by the same name

ENTEX SELECT-A-GAME MACHINE GUIDE

SELECT-A-GAME MACHINE

Manufacturer: Entex
Year: 1982
Rarity: 10
Loose: $20–30*
Complete: $40–50*
Notes: Tabletop 2-player system with a VFD; had a total of 6 interchangeable cartridges available; cartridges came packaged with screen overlays; came packaged with the *Space Invader 2* cartridge

GAMES

BASEBALL4

Manufacturer: Entex
Year: 1982
Rarity: 9
Loose: $5–7*
Complete: $8–12*
Notes: Baseball cartridge with overlay

BASKETBALL3

Manufacturer: Entex
Year: 1982
Rarity: 9
Loose: $5–7*
Complete: $8–12*
Notes: Basketball cartridge with overlay

FOOTBALL4

Manufacturer: Entex
Year: 1982
Rarity: 9
Loose: $5–7*
Complete: $8–12*
Notes: Football cartridge with overlay

PACMAN2

Manufacturer: Entex
Year: 1982
Rarity: 9
Loose: $5–7*
Complete: $8–12*
Notes: *Pac-Man* clone game with overlay

PINBALL

Manufacturer: Entex
Year: 1982
Rarity: 9
Loose: $5–7*
Complete: $8–12*
Notes: Pinball cartridge with overlay

SPACE INVADER 2

Manufacturer: Entex
Year: 1982
Rarity: 9
Loose: $5–7*
Complete: N/A
Notes: *Space Invaders* clone; included with the game system

TOTAL CONTROL 4 PRICE GUIDE

TOTAL CONTROL IV CONSOLE
Manufacturer: Coleco
Year: 1981
Rarity: 9
Loose: $15–20*
Complete: $25–35*
Notes: 4-player LED sports handheld that accepted game cartridges (in the form of interchangeable faceplates); shipped with *Football*

GAMES

BASKETBALL, HOCKEY, AND SOCCER
Manufacturer: Coleco
Year: 1981
Rarity: 8
Loose: N/A
Complete: $15–20
Notes: 3-pack of cartridges for Total Control 4; the cartridges were not sold separately

BASKETBALL
Manufacturer: Coleco
Year: 1981
Rarity: 8
Loose: $4–6*
Complete: N/A
Notes: Faceplate/cartridge for Total Control 4; originally sold as part of a set of 3 along with *Hockey* and *Soccer*

HOCKEY
Manufacturer: Coleco
Year: 1981
Rarity: 8
Loose: $4–6*
Complete: N/A
Notes: Faceplate/cartridge for Total Control 4; originally sold as part of a set of 3 along with *Basketball* and *Soccer*

SOCCER
Manufacturer: Coleco
Year: 1981
Rarity: 8
Loose: $4–6*
Complete: N/A
Notes: Faceplate/cartridge for Total Control 4; originally sold as part of a set of 3 along with Basketball and Hockey

MICROVISION PRICE GUIDE

MICROVISION CONSOLE
Manufacturer: Milton Bradley
Year: 1979
Rarity: 3
Loose: $10–15
Complete: $15–30
Notes: LCD handheld game system that uses interchangeable cartridges; simple paddle controller on the console, but additional control buttons were built into the cartridges themselves; packaged with *Block Buster,* a *Breakout* clone

GAMES

ALIEN RAIDERS
Manufacturer: Milton Bradley
Year: 1981
Rarity: 6
Loose: $8–12*
Complete: $15–20*
Notes: *Space Invaders* clone; one of the last games made for the MicroVision in the US

BASEBALL
Manufacturer: Milton Bradley
Year: 1980
Rarity: 3
Loose: $3–5
Complete: $5–7

BLOCK BUSTER
Manufacturer: Milton Bradley
Year: 1979
Rarity: 3
Loose: $1–3
Complete: N/A
Notes: Cartridge originally packaged with the MicroVision console

BOWLING
Manufacturer: Milton Bradley
Year: 1979
Rarity: 3
Loose: $3–5
Complete: $5–7

CONNECT FOUR
Manufacturer: Milton Bradley
Year: 1979
Rarity: 3
Loose: $3–5
Complete: $5–7
Notes: Micro vision version of the board game by the same name

COSMIC HUNTER
Manufacturer: Milton Bradley
Year: 1981
Rarity: 6
Loose: $8–12*
Complete: $15–20*
Notes: Space battle game; one of the last games made for the MicroVision in the US

MINDBUSTER
Manufacturer: Milton Bradley
Year: 1979
Rarity: 5
Loose: $8–12
Complete: $15–20

PHASER STRIKE
Manufacturer: Milton Bradley
Year: 1980
Rarity: 4
Loose: $3–5
Complete: $5–7
Notes: Re-release of *Star Trek Phaser Strike* without the *Star Trek* name

PINBALL
Manufacturer: Milton Bradley
Year: 1979
Rarity: 3
Loose: $3–5
Complete: $5–7

SEA DUEL
Manufacturer: Milton Bradley
Year: 1980
Rarity: 3
Loose: $3–5
Complete: $5–7

STAR TREK PHASER STRIKE
Manufacturer: Milton Bradley
Year: 1979
Rarity: 3
Loose: $3–5
Complete: $5–7
Notes: Space battle game in which you shoot Klingon warships

VEGAS SLOTS
Manufacturer: Milton Bradley
Year: 1979
Rarity: 4
Loose: $3–5
Complete: $5–7

11 The Future of Console Collecting

Among classic video game collectors, the hobbyists most envied are those people who have been collecting since the games were originally on the market in the 1970s and 1980s. These collectors got in on the ground floor of the hobby, and have amassed huge and impressive game collections over the last several decades for a mere fraction of what it would cost to put together similar collections today.

Video and electronic games are based on technology, and technology goes through periodic cycles of change. The first such change in the video game industry was in the late '70s, when dedicated video game consoles gave way to cartridge-based systems. As consoles like the Atari 2600 and Intellivision took off, *Pong* and its clones dropped dramatically in price as retailers rushed to dump old inventory in favor of the latest technology. People who bought dedicated consoles at that time got some excellent bargains. When the video game crash of 1983–1984 hit the industry, almost everyone in the United States thought that the video game market was dead. Stores were once again rushing to get rid of inventory, and they dumped their consoles and games at extremely low prices.

These lulls in the industry are the ideal time for collector speculation in the video and electronic game market. In 1985, a potential Atari 2600 collector could stock up on games for about a dollar per cartridge. A collection that cost $500 to accumulate in 1985 could easily be worth $5,000 to $10,000 at today's collector prices.

Even video game items purchased at full-price at the height of their original popularity can turn into valuable collectibles if you're willing to hold onto them for a couple of decades or so. How many of you are kicking yourselves for throwing out the Entex Adventure Vision you bought for $70 back in the 1980s now that you know it's worth as much as $1,500?

The point is that, in the relatively new hobby of video game collecting, you never know what will be considered collectible in the future. Collectors are beginning to consider some of the video game consoles released shortly after the classic era in the late '80s, like the Nintendo Entertainment System (NES) and the Sega Master System, collectible. These systems are getting more and more table space at classic gaming events and conventions every year. Can the newer systems be far behind?

This chapter takes a brief look at the major video game consoles and handhelds that have been released from 1985 to the present with an eye toward evaluating their potential collectibility.

Nintendo Consoles and Handhelds

From 1975 to 1984, "video game" and "Atari" were interchangeable words. Even after the video game market in the United States was for all intents and purposes dead, Atari continued to be the name that represented the industry.

In 1985, the age of Atari came to an end when a new player entered the seemingly defunct U.S. video game market. It was the dawn of the Nintendo dynasty.

Nintendo Entertainment System (1985)

In 1985, when just about every American company had given up on the video game industry, Japanese game company Nintendo made a gutsy move and released a new video game system in a limited test market. The response to the Nintendo Entertainment System (NES), was good enough to warrant wide release in the following year. By the end of 1986, Nintendo had sold over a million NES units, proving once and for all that the video game market was still very much alive.

The NES was the first video game system to exceed the Atari 2600 in popularity and in the size of its game library. By 1990, Nintendo had sold over 50 million NES units worldwide. During the console's lifespan, over 700 game cartridges were produced, and the best-selling titles sold millions of copies apiece.

The NES is gaining popularity among classic video game collectors. Because of the huge number of consoles sold during the console's history, NESs are readily available at reasonable prices today. Loose NES consoles with controllers generally sell for around $30. Boxed consoles sell for slightly more. A boxed original NES with R.O.B. (a small robot that was packaged with the system during the first year or so) is perhaps the most collectible version of the system available.

Most NES games are also readily available at reasonable prices. Common titles generally sell for under $10 (many for under $5). A few of the rarer titles are beginning to creep up into the $20 range.

At this point in time, there are few cartridges that collectors would consider Holy Grails in the NES market. One possible exception is the version of *Tetris* released by Tengen, a division of Atari that made a number of games for the NES. Because of licensing issues, the cartridge was pulled from the shelves when Nintendo released their own version of the game. Boxed copies of Tengen's *Tetris* often sell for as much as $60.

Because interest in the NES is gaining momentum, now is a good time to start collecting for this system if you're interested in doing so. Be prepared for a daunting task, however. The system's huge game and accessory library make amassing a complete NES collection a challenge.

Super Nintendo (1991)

Nintendo released the 16-bit **Super Nintendo Entertainment System (SNES)** console in 1991 at the height of the company's popularity and, not surprisingly, the console was an instant hit. Its graphics and animation capabilities were far superior to those of the NES, and the console fea-

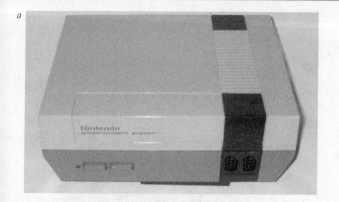

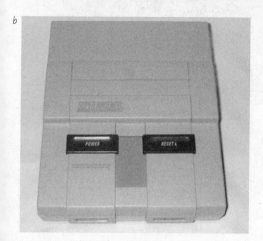

a *The Nintendo Entertainment
System (NES) is making its way
into the classic console realm as
the 20th anniversary of its release
approaches. (Photo courtesy of
Cassidy Nolen.)*

b *The Super Nintendo Entertainment System (SNES) featured
improved graphics and stereo
sound. Upon its release, Nintendo
once again set the standard by
which other game consoles were
judged. (Photo courtesy of Cassidy
Nolen.)*

tured true stereo sound. The SNES's sales numbers were nearly as impressive as those of its
predecessor, with over 20 million systems sold in the United States (46 million worldwide) during the console's lifetime. The game library for the system is about the same size as that of the
NES—around 700 cartridges.

The SNES hasn't yet achieved the neoclassic status of the NES among collectors. The prices for
both the console itself and most of the game cartridges are currently running at about the same
level as those of the NES—$20 to $40 for the console (without a box) and under $10 for most
cartridges. There are some rare SNES titles that are currently selling for over $50, so the popu-
larity of the system is definitely growing. Even so, now is a good time to start collecting SNES
items before the market really takes off.

Game Boy (1989)

Popularity of a video game system can make it a collectible commodity. The Atari 2600 is an excellent example. Despite the fact that it was on the market for about 14 years and that millions
of consoles and cartridges were released, collectors find the system appealing, in part, because it
was so popular and because it holds a special significance to them. On the other hand, wide-

a **Nintendo Game Boy** is not only the most popular handheld video game system; it is the most popular video game system of any type ever produced.

spread popularity and long shelf life can also *delay* the elevation of a video game system to collectible status.

The **Nintendo Game Boy** is something of an anomaly in the video game industry. When it was introduced in 1989, it was already inferior in many ways to the other handheld game systems that were on the market at the time. Even so, the black and white handheld sold by the millions and remains the top-selling handheld video game system to this day. The Game Boy remained virtually unchanged until 1996, when Nintendo released a smaller version, the Pocket Game Boy. Other handhelds with superior color graphics and more sophisticated games came and went, but Game Boy remained strong. Nearly a decade after the original unit was released in 1998, Nintendo finally introduced Game Boy Color. The original Game Boy and Game Boy Color remained so popular, that Nintendo delayed the release of its new system, Game Boy Advance (GBA) until 2000, even though it was ready for an earlier release.

Game Boy holds the record as the most popular video game system of all time. Over 110 million Game Boys have been sold worldwide (not including Game Boy Advance and Game Boy Advance SP). There are currently over 700 Game Boy cartridges (once again, not including Game Boy Advance titles).

Even though it was introduced fifteen years ago, Game Boy has not yet attained collectible status. The reason for this is that Nintendo has been careful to make all of its Game Boy systems backward compatible with older cartridges. That means that you can play all of the cartridges you bought for your black and white Game Boy on your new Game Boy Advance SP. Collectible value in video games depends a great deal on the obsolescence of the technology upon which the games are based. While older Game Boy units might be obsolete, the cartridges themselves are not.

Original black-and-white Game Boy units generally sell for between $10 and $20, slightly more for complete boxed units (which include the *Tetris* cartridge, which was originally included with the system). Pocket Game Boy units run about 50% higher on average, and Game Boy Color systems are slightly higher still.

Older Game Boy cartridges are usually available for around $5 (sometimes much less), with newer Game Boy Color cartridges and popular titles running to a maximum of about $20 or so. Keep in mind that many Game Boy Color games are still on the market, and most of these sell for $20 to $30 new.

Because of the volume of cartridges and ongoing production, Game Boy is a challenging system to collect. The continuing popularity of the system in its newer forms means that it could be some time before Game Boy attains a true collectible status that is on par with other video game systems that were introduced in the late 1980s.

Virtual Boy (1995)

Every company is entitled to make mistakes, and after a decade of dominating the home video game market, Nintendo made a huge one. The name of the mistake was **Virtual Boy**.

This portable, tabletop game system uses an array of light emitting diodes (LEDs) and several mirrors to produce 3-D "virtual reality" graphics. The entire game system is contained in a small binocular-shaped viewfinder that sits on a short tabletop tripod.

Virtual Boy was doomed from the start. Despite its 3-D imaging capabilities, the graphics were dull. Red-on-black images couldn't compete with the amazing color graphics produced by all of the other game consoles at the time. On top of all this, the graphics caused eyestrain and headaches in players who played for extended periods of time.

Despite Nintendo's considerable marketing power, Virtual Boy never caught on and was selling for under $100 (less than half of its introductory price) within a year. Only 14 game cartridges were released in the United States before Nintendo discontinued support for the system in 1996. The magnitude of the failure of Virtual Boy is evidenced in the fact that the Nintendo web site (http://www.nintendo.com) doesn't include Virtual Boy on the page that lists every other video game console they have ever released in the United States. Even an in-depth search on the site reveals only a few references to the system.

Virtual Boy is a good example of how a video game that was unpopular in its time can quickly attain collectible status. Hundreds of Virtual Boy items are regularly listed on eBay. Boxed Virtual Boy systems are already selling for more than they did when they were discontinued in 1996, with average prices running anywhere from about $50 (for just the unit) to as much as $250 (for a boxed system with multiple game cartridges and accessories included). Individual game cartridges sell for as little as $5 or less.

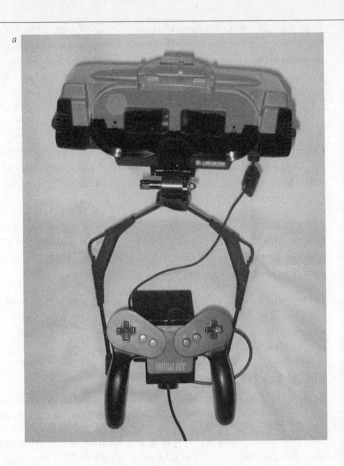

a **Virtual Boy,** *an attempt at a portable virtual reality game system, stands out as one of Nintendo's biggest failures. (Photo courtesy of Cassidy Nolen.)*

As far as video game collectibles go, Virtual Boy is bound to retain a cult following as the collecting hobby continues to grow. Like the Entex Adventure Vision and the GCE/Milton Bradley Vectrex, Virtual Boy is a truly unique game system that has some historical significance in the video game industry. Whether it will ever be considered as collectible as either of these classic systems remains to be seen.

If nothing else, Virtual Boy serves as evidence that even a corporate video game giant on top of its game can produce a lemon from time to time.

Nintendo[64] (1996)

Nintendo's fall from the top position in the video game industry came gradually. While the company relied on the huge fan base for the Super Nintendo and the public's trust in, and awe of, the Nintendo name to carry the company forward, their competitors were developing game systems that made the aging Super Nintendo's games obsolete.

In 1996, a year after Sony and Sega had released their new 32-bit game systems (the PlayStation and the Saturn, respectively), Nintendo finally released the new game system they had been promising for years.

278

a **The Nintendo⁶⁴** *was technologically superior to Nintendo's previous systems and other consoles on the market at the time, but was unable to make significant headway against the Sony PlayStation. (Photo courtesy of Cassidy Nolen.)*

Although the **Nintendo⁶⁴** was in some ways superior to both the PlayStation and the Saturn, it had a number of drawbacks. Primary among these was the fact that, while their competitors were distributing games on CD-ROM, Nintendo continued producing games on cartridges. Cartridges have the advantage of loading games faster, but they lack the massive data storage space of CDs. In addition, cartridges cost more to produce, and the added cost was passed on to the consumer. While typical PlayStation games retailed for $30 to $50, **Nintendo⁶⁴** cartridges sold for as much as $75.

Although Nintendo was able to retain some of its fan base, consumer loyalty shifted to Sony. The **Nintendo⁶⁴** was discontinued in 2001, shortly after the release of the GameCube, Nintendo's current console. During its retail lifetime, about 200 game titles were produced for the **Nintendo⁶⁴**.

Because it is a very recent system, the **Nintendo⁶⁴** is not considered a collectible—but that's not to say that it won't become a collectible at some point. **Nintendo⁶⁴** is the last cartridge-based home console, and that piece of trivia could make it historically significant, just as the Fairchild Channel F is significant for being the *first* cartridge-based console.

If you are interested in starting a **Nintendo⁶⁴** collection, now is a good time to begin. Consoles are still readily available, and often sell for $30 or less. In fact, you can obtain a console with controllers and a number of games for around $50 to $100 in a typical online auction. Cartridges themselves sell for from as little as a few dollars for common/less popular titles, to $15–$30 for rare/popular games.

Sega Consoles and Handhelds

Sega was founded in 1965 by the merger of two American-owned companies based in Japan, Service Games and Rosen Enterprises, Ltd. Sega was a major force in the coin-operated amusement industry, so when video games became the rage in the 1970s, they moved from electromechanical games to video games.

Although they had produced a number of cartridges for various home video game systems during the classic era, Sega never released a game system of their own until after the success of the NES ushered in the video game renaissance of the late '80s.

For a short time, Sega was Nintendo's only serious competition. The battle between Sega's and Nintendo's game consoles in the late '80s was the first major console war since Intellivision vs. Atari 2600 nearly a decade earlier. Sega targeted an older audience than Nintendo, with edgy advertising that introduced the now-famous Sega scream ("SEGA!") and, later, the advertising tagline "Genesis does what Nintendon't."

Sega continued to compete in the console market until 2001 when, after discontinuing production of the Dreamcast, the company announced that they were leaving the home video game hardware business for good. Today, Sega continues to produce arcade games and software for consoles and PCs.

Sega Master System (1986)

The Sega Master System was the primary competition for the NES in the mid-'80s. The Master System was technologically superior to the NES, but Nintendo had such a hold on the video game marketplace both in the United States and in Japan that Sega's console was a definite underdog. At the time of the Master System's release, Nintendo controlled 90% of the home video game marketplace—not an easy lead to overcome. Nintendo ensured its continued dominance by forcing the companies that developed software for the NES into exclusive contracts that implied that they could not develop software for Sega's console (or any other consoles on the market, for that matter). This made it difficult for Sega to find game developers for its new system.

The Master System was interesting in that it accepted two different types of game media: cartridges (which had twice the memory capacity of their Nintendo counterparts) and cards (credit card–sized miniature game cartridges that had less memory but cost less). Relatively few games were produced on the card media.

Nintendo's strong market presence combined with Sega's lack of consumer product marketing strategy and small library of games resulted in small sales numbers for the Master System. Just over 100 games were released for the console during its three years on the market. Some, like *Phantasy Star*, are among the most memorable home video games ever produced and spawned ongoing game series that continue to this day. Others came and went relatively unnoticed.

Two versions of the Sega Master System console were produced. The biggest difference between the two is that the original has a slot for the card-style games and the redesigned version (released in 1990) does not.

Like the NES, the Sega Master System is beginning to work its way into the classic console category, although the collector's market for this console is nowhere near as active as that of the NES at present. It is not uncommon to find a Sega Master System with a number of games and peripherals for $50 to $75 in an online auction.

The games for the Master System are, as a general rule, equally common and inexpensive. Only the most popular titles sell for more than $15. Even the harder to find card-style games seldom sell for more than $10.

The combination of easy availability, low prices, and a relatively small library of games and peripherals make the Sega Master System one of the easiest systems to collect for those interested in neoclassic (post-1985) game systems.

a

b

a **The Sega Master System,** *the only serious competition for the Nintendo Entertainment System in the late 1980s, hardly made a dent in Nintendo's home console business. (Photo courtesy of Cassidy Nolen.)*

b **Sega Genesis** *established Sega's reputation as the console for an older generation of gamers. (Photo courtesy of Cassidy Nolen.)*

Genesis (1989)

The Sega Genesis was the first video game console that actually made a significant dent in Nintendo's hold on the home video game marketplace in the postclassic era. Two factors contributed to the Genesis's success: timing and image.

Nintendo, still enjoying brisk sales, was in no rush to release a new console to replace the successful NES. While Nintendo rested on their laurels, Sega released the Genesis to rave reviews. Compared to the NES, Genesis was a technological marvel, with graphics and sound far superior to those of Nintendo's four-year-old console. With no new Nintendo console in sight for at least another year, Genesis was the primary choice for consumers who wanted the latest in gaming technology.

Sega established an image for the Genesis that set it apart from the NES (and from the Super Nintendo when it was finally released). Sega targeted an older audience with its games, establishing the system as being "cooler" than Nintendo through a combination of edgy advertising and the introduction of a line of sophisticated sports games endorsed by well-known athletes. Starting in 1991, the Genesis was packaged with *Sonic the Hedgehog*, a fast-paced game with a central character that was created specifically to compete with Nintendo's Mario.

When Nintendo finally released their 16-bit Super Nintendo system, the numbers told the story of Sega's success. In the first year that the two consoles were in competition, Sega had grabbed over 50% of the 16-bit console market. For the first time in years, Nintendo was the underdog.

Sega went on to release tons of peripherals and add-ons for the Genesis, including a module that allowed Sega Master System games to play on the Genesis, Sega CD (a CD-ROM drive), and 32X (an upgrade that turned Genesis into a 32-bit game system—sort of).

Like most consoles released in the last decade or so, Genesis has not yet achieved classic status and is, therefore, not yet thought of as a true collectible. There are thousands of Genesis items listed on online auction sites on any given day. At this point, it is not uncommon to find a Genesis with peripherals (CD, 32X, and so on) and a number of games packaged together at a price of around $100. Game cartridges and CDs range in price from under $5 for the majority of the common titles to around $20 or so for rare titles like *Shining Force* and *Shining Force II*.

Game Gear (1991) and Nomad (1995)

After the success of the Game Boy, it wasn't surprising that Nintendo's number-one rival would enter the handheld game market. Sega actually released two handhelds: **Game Gear**, a standalone system with its own game library, and Nomad, a portable version of the Sega Genesis.

Game Gear debuted in 1991, two years after Game Boy took the handheld market by storm. Based on the same eight-bit technology used in the Sega Master System, Game Gear was technologically superior to Game Boy and had a large backlit screen that displayed 4,096 colors.

Although Game Gear had a fairly decent following, its popularity never approached that of Game Boy. One of the main factors contributing to the system's lack of popularity was that its battery life was much shorter than that of Game Boy.

The cartridge library for Game Gear comprises approximately 240 titles. The cartridges include handheld versions of some of Sega's most popular games like *Sonic the Hedgehog*, *Shinobi*, and *Golden Axe*. A number of interesting accessories are available for the unit, including a TV tuner.

Game Gear is currently quite inexpensive and easy to find, as are the accessories and games. Game Gear packages including numerous games and accessories are sometimes found in online auctions for under $75. Individual games often sell for under a dollar.

Although Game Gear might never attain significant collectible status, it is a solid game system with a number of fun and enjoyable games.

Sega Nomad is an interesting handheld system in that it doesn't have its own game library. Instead, it is designed to play the same cartridges as the Sega Genesis. Essentially it *is* a portable Genesis.

Released in 1995, the Nomad was less than successful in its time. It was bulkier than other handheld games (it had to be large in order to accommodate the Genesis cartridges), and it burned through batteries at an alarming rate. Even so, this handheld offers a single-console solution for Genesis lovers since it can be connected to a television as well as used as a portable.

Because it is a multipurpose console, Nomad tends to be more collectible than Game Gear. Typical Nomad prices run in the $75 to $150 range today. If you are planning to start a Genesis collection, consider adding a Nomad to your list of "must have" items.

a

b

a **Game Gear,** *Sega's first portable system, was released in 1991. Although superior to Game Boy in many ways, the Game Gear never attained the following of Nintendo's handheld. (Photo courtesy of Cassidy Nolen.)*

b **Sega Saturn,** *introduced at about the same time as the Sony PlayStation in 1995, failed to catch on with American gamers due to high price and a lack of game titles at release. (Photo courtesy of Cassidy Nolen.)*

Saturn (1995)

By the mid-1990s, the buzzwords in the video game industry were "32-bit processor" and "3-D polygonal graphics." Sony's PlayStation, which was awash in techno-buzzword features like these, was due to hit the shelves in 1995, and Sega wanted to beat them to the punch with the **Saturn**.

Saturn was plagued with a number of problems from the time it was launched in May 1995. Its initial $399 price tag was $100 higher than that of the PlayStation. To make matters worse, the unique combination of 2-D and 3-D arcade hardware upon which the Saturn's technology was based made it very difficult to program games for the console. As a result, only one title, *Virtua Fighter*, was available when the console was introduced.

Saturn was a hit in Japan, but after a strong start, never garnered much of an audience in the United States. Despite the introduction of a number of excellent software titles (many based on Sega's arcade hits of the mid-'90s) and frequent price drops, the popularity of the system continued to drop until Sega stopped supporting it in 1998. (Sega continued supporting the Saturn in Japan until 1999.)

Although certainly too new to be considered a collectible system, interest in the Saturn seems to be fairly strong. The console itself typically sells for around $100 or so. The games are a mixed lot, with some of the more popular titles (*Shining Force III*, for example) selling for nearly as much as the system itself, while the common titles sell for as little as a dollar. Japanese import titles are particularly popular among Saturn owners today, since many games released in Japan were never available in the United States.

Dreamcast (1999)

Dreamcast had a lot going for it from the start. The first 128-bit game system, it was released in 1999, a full year before the scheduled release of Sony's highly anticipated PlayStation 2 (PS2). With 15 game titles available at launch, a built-in modem for online gameplay, and memory units that could be used not only to save games but also as data displays and handheld mini-games, Dreamcast was extremely impressive. Nearly a million consoles were sold in the United States during the first three months.

Unfortunately, the public anticipation for the PS2 was impossible to overcome, even with the continued release of excellent, cutting-edge games for the Dreamcast. Sales leveled off and began to drop as the 2000 release date of the PS2 approached. Many of Dreamcast's third-party game developers shifted their focus to the PS2. Price cuts by Sega and a shortage of PS2 consoles during the 2000 holiday season weren't enough to increase Dreamcast sales. After a brief retail run of less than two years, with only around 2 million consoles sold in the United States and a software library of 248 game titles, the Dreamcast was discontinued in February 2001.

Because it was discontinued so recently, Dreamcast consoles and games are still readily available. In fact, some retail stores still carry games, peripherals, and used Dreamcast consoles. Used consoles with a single controller run around $40, and games sell for anywhere between $1 and $20. Online auction sites often feature the console with a number of games and accessories included for around $100.

Today's Dreamcast market is very much like the Atari 2600 market was in 1984, just after the video game market crashed. For a relatively small investment, you can amass a huge Dreamcast collection. The future status of the Dreamcast as a collectible video game system is unknown, but now is definitely the time to make speculative purchases.

Since this console is purportedly the last one that Sega will produce, it is possible that the Dreamcast will be considered an important milestone in video game history. If the system turns out to be a collectible 20 years from now, you'll be glad you started your Dreamcast collection when the prices were low.

Atari Systems

Although the Nintendo video game renaissance in the mid-'80s all but eclipsed the company that first put home video games on the map, Atari remained active in the industry. The company had shifted most of its hardware focus to its home computer line, but they continued to release video game systems well into the early 1990s.

Atari XE Video Game System (1987)

At about the same time that Atari debuted the 7800, they introduced a second new game console based on their line of Atari XE computers. The Atari XE Video Game System was nearly identical to the Atari 65XE computer, and was shipped with a keyboard, a light gun, and a joystick. The system's game library consisted of cartridge translations of many of the disk-based games that were available for full-fledged XE computers.

Out of all of Atari's consoles, the XE Video Game System is easily the least known. It is also the most difficult to find in today's collectors' market. Despite this, the system is not considered particularly collectible, and usually sells for a fairly low price on the rare occasion that one becomes available.

Atari Lynx

Atari released their **Lynx** handheld at about the same time that Nintendo released the Game Boy in 1989. The cartridge-based Lynx, the first handheld game system with a color display, sported a backlit screen with a resolution of 160x102, and 64K of memory. Like the Sega Game Gear that would be released two years later, the Lynx was technologically superior to Nintendo's handheld, but had a number of problems. Chief among Atari's woes were short battery life and short supply of Lynx units at launch. The Lynx sold out early, leaving consumers with the choice of waiting for new stock or buying a Game Boy.

Atari addressed the battery issue by releasing the Lynx II, a smaller, more energy efficient version of the handheld, in 1991. Unfortunately, by this time, Nintendo had a huge established base of Game Boys, and the Sega Game Gear had been released, creating additional competition.

By the time it was discontinued, the Lynx had a library of around 100 games. Many of these are excellent handheld versions of classic arcade games like *Robotron: 2084*, *Joust*, and *Ms. Pac-Man*. A handful of hobbyists and companies like Songbird Productions (http://www.songbird-productions.com) continue to produce new games for the Lynx today.

Like most relatively recent systems, the Lynx has not yet attained a huge collector base. That means that both the console itself and most game cartridges are available at reasonable prices, both at online auction sites and at classic gaming shows and events. A few of the later commercially released games are becoming a bit scarce, but many common titles are still available new from various sources.

Because of its relatively low price at the moment and the small size of its cartridge library, the Lynx is a prime opportunity for new collectors to build a complete collection for an Atari-produced game system. Even if the Lynx never becomes a valuable collectible, it is an excellent handheld system with some very good games.

Atari Jaguar (1993)

Atari's last attempt at a game system ultimately proved to be anticlimactic. The **Atari Jaguar** was billed as the world's first 64-bit game console, an assertion that was disputed by Atari's competitors at the time. The cartridge-based system was released in 1993 at a price of $250, considerably less than the 3DO game system which was released in the same year, but still fairly pricey. Although Atari announced that a huge number of third-party software developers had signed on to produce games for the system, only five games were available when the console hit the shelves.

Even though several decent games were eventually released for the system, the number of games available was always a problem compared to the competition. Despite aggressive marketing and a lineup of peripherals including a CD-ROM unit, the Jaguar's sales slipped steadily

a **Dreamcast** *was Sega's last home video game console. After the last Dreamcast was built, Sega announced that they were leaving the video game hardware business. (Photo courtesy of Cassidy Nolen.)*

b **Atari's Lynx** *was the first color handheld game system on the market. Two versions were released—the original in 1989 and the smaller, more common Lynx II in 1991 (pictured). (Photo courtesy of Cassidy Nolen.)*

over the years until it was discontinued in 1996. During its three-year retail run, fewer than 100 Jaguar games saw the light of day.

In a manner of speaking, the Jaguar lives on today. Hasbro Interactive, the company that purchased the rights to most of Atari's consumer line in the late '90s, released the rights to the Jaguar into the public domain in 1999. Since that time, a number of individuals and companies have produced new games for the system.

For collectors, the Jaguar can be a bit puzzling. The console, its peripherals, and many game titles are readily available for a reasonable price at online auction sites, just as one would expect from such a recent system. On the other hand, there are a couple of game titles that still regularly sell for $50 or more, and many online vendors still charge nearly full retail price for Jaguar games and accessories.

Since it is likely the last game system that will bear the Atari name, Jaguar might well become quite collectible some day. If this is the case, now is the time to start collecting. It doesn't look like the prices are likely to get any lower than they are at present.

a

b

a **Atari Jaguar** was the first 64-bit home game console. Unfortunately, like so many of Atari's later products, the Jaguar had little support and only a small fan following. (Photo courtesy of Cassidy Nolen.)

b **PlayStation** marked the third major turning point in the video game console industry by putting Sony in the lead of the ever-changing video game race. (Photo courtesy of Cassidy Nolen.)

Sony PlayStation (1995)

In 1975, Atari was the company name synonymous with video games, and the rapid growth of the company's game business seemed unstoppable. Ten years later, in 1985, the torch was passed to Nintendo, and it looked like Nintendo's position at the top of the heap was unassailable. Then, exactly ten years later, Nintendo was unseated by a new challenger as Sony took the reigns of home video game development as the industry entered its third decade.

Interestingly enough, it was Nintendo that drove Sony to develop a game system. Nintendo had made a deal with Sony to develop a CD-ROM drive (called the PlayStation) for the Super Nintendo. After the deal was made, Nintendo secretly made a deal with another company for a less expensive drive, and dumped the deal with Sony. In the end, Nintendo never released a CD-ROM drive for the SNES, and Sony ended up producing the **PlayStation** as a stand-alone game system.

After eight years on the market and the release of the PlayStation 2 (PS2) in 2000, the PlayStation remains one of the most popular video game consoles ever made. A redesigned version of the original console, dubbed the PSOne, is still sold for around $50 (used units sell for about

$30), and hundreds of game titles are still available through retail stores. The continued sale of games designed for the original PlayStation is fueled by the fact that the PS2 is compatible with the nearly 1,000 games in the PlayStation's vast software library.

Obviously, since it is still a current console, the PlayStation is not considered a collectible and is not likely to enter that realm for some time. Historically speaking (as historically as possible, given the short amount of time that video games have existed), it has taken about 20 years for game consoles to attain collectible status. Since Sony is currently the leader in the video game industry, it is impossible to say when PlayStation will become obsolete. But, since a big change in the direction of the video game industry has taken place every ten years since 1975, it is entirely possible that the next big shift in power at the top of the electronic entertainment industry food chain is just around the corner.

Now is probably as good a time as ever to start your PlayStation collection, although amassing a complete collection of PlayStation games and accessories is a truly daunting task—not to mention quite expensive. If you already own a PlayStation, the best advice is to hold on to what you have in your collection at present and keep your eyes open for bargains.

Other Notable Systems

During the classic video game era, companies like Bally, APF, and Arcadia tried their hand at competing with industry leaders Atari, Mattel, and Coleco for their share of the video game market. As the video game industry entered its second decade and Nintendo and Sega battled for the top position in the marketplace, other companies continued to fight for their piece of the multibillion dollar action.

NEC TurboGrafx-16 (1989), TurboExpress (1990), and TurboDuo (1992)

In 1988, NEC released a video game system called the PC Engine in Japan. It was an instant hit and actually made headway against the Famicom (the Japanese version of the Nintendo Entertainment System). U.S. video game enthusiasts were actually importing PC Engine consoles for as much as $500 apiece.

A year later, NEC released the console in the United States, redubbing it the **TurboGrafx-16**. The system was technologically superior to both the Nintendo Entertainment System and the Sega Master System. Peripherals included a CD-ROM drive (the TurboGrafix-CD) and a multiplayer adaptor (the TurboTap) that allowed simultaneous play for up to five players. In 1995, a new consolidated version of the console that integrated the CD-ROM drive (the TurboDuo) was released.

Unfortunately, a lack of compelling game software and limited marketing kept the console from becoming a hit. Although many excellent games were released for the system in Japan, only a handful of these titles made it to the United States This is especially true of the CD-ROM games—many of the hundreds of Japanese titles were never translated for the U.S. market. The TurboGrafx-16 disappeared from store shelves in 1994.

One of the peripherals for the TurboGrafx-16 wasn't a peripheral at all, but a full-fledged portable version of the console. The **TurboExpress**, released in 1990, was similar to Sega's Nomad in that it was designed to play the same games as the full-sized system it was modeled to emulate. While unable to play the CD-ROM titles, the TurboExpress was fully compatible with all of the TurboGrafx-16 cartridges.

Since they are relatively recent systems, the NEC consoles and handhelds have not yet gained a significant following of collectors. These systems are, however, beginning to show up with greater frequency at classic game gatherings and events and, like the NES and Sega Master System, are on the verge of being considered classic.

Currently, the NEC consoles themselves are available at reasonable prices at online auction sites. Typically, the TurboGrafx-16 console sells for around $40, with the TurboExpress and Turbo-Duo selling for significantly more. Common game cartridges sell for between $2 and $10, and U.S.-released CD-ROM titles start at around $10.

Like the NES and Sega Master system, now is probably a good time to start a TurboGrafx collection if you're so inclined. Because its classic status is just around the corner, you can expect the demand and price of the hardware and software for this system to start increasing over the next couple of years.

Neo-Geo (1990)

One of the goals of every classic video game console was to accurately reproduce arcade graphics in the home. In 1990, SNK, a manufacturer of arcade games, finally accomplished this daunting task.

The **Neo-Geo** home console essentially replicated the hardware used in SNK's arcade game cabinets, which allowed arcade owners to change games quickly and easily by using interchangeable cartridges. The home console used the same cartridges as the arcade machines, so the graphics and gameplay of the home games were identical to those of the arcade versions.

Although the Neo-Geo system remained on the market for over six years, it never competed directly with the most popular game systems of the early '90s. The primary reason for this was price. The basic Neo-Geo (with a single controller and no game) sold for $399, and the deluxe system (with an extra controller and one game cartridge) sold for $599. Additional game cartridges retailed for $199 apiece. These prices put Neo-Geo out of the running for the average video game consumer. Eventually, SNK released a new version of the console with a CD-ROM player, which reduced the price of software considerably.

The Neo-Geo home consoles have always had a cult following of sorts, and that continues today. The console itself still regularly sells for $150 or more, and the cartridges sell for $20 to $150 each. CD games range from a mere $2 to as much as $80 apiece. Japanese import systems and software often sell for considerably more than U.S. titles.

Of all of the newer consoles discussed in this price guide, the Neo-Geo is the most difficult and expensive system to collect. It is safe to say that very few hobbyists will ever count a complete set of Neo-Geo hardware and software as part of their personal collections.

CD-i (1991)

Philips introduced its CD-i multimedia system in 1991. When it hit the market, it was billed as an educational tool, but store displays for the CD-i usually showed off the handful of games that were available. Although it got a great deal of attention, mostly because "multimedia" was the technological buzzword at the time, CD-i players didn't exactly fly off the shelves at $1,400 apiece.

A number of different CD-i players were introduced over the years and, in the mid-'90s, Philips started playing up the gaming aspects of the system. By 1994, the system was down to $300. The

a **NEC TurboGrafx-16** *developed a strong cult following among U.S. video game players, but never achieved the success of the Nintendo and Sega consoles with which it was competing. This unit is shown in a carrying case with the optional CD-ROM drive. (Photo courtesy of Cassidy Nolen.)*

b **TurboExpress,** *the portable version of the NEC TurboGrafx-16, is compatible with all of its larger counterpart's cartridges. (Photo courtesy of Cassidy Nolen.)*

shift in focus and the price drop did nothing to bolster sales, and Philips discontinued CD-i production and support in 1996.

For the most part, video game collectors have ignored the CD-i since it never was meant to be a dedicated video game system. CD-i players (depending on the model) typically sell for $100 or less, and software is generally quite inexpensive.

One interesting piece of information for would-be collectors, however, is that several games based on Nintendo's *Legend of Zelda* franchise were released for the CD-i. These games, which were the only three *Zelda* games produced for non-Nintendo systems, are probably the most collectible CD-i items. It is not uncommon for these games—*Link: Faces of Evil, Zelda: Wand of Gamelon,* and *Zelda's Adventure*—to to sell for as much as $200.

3DO (1993)

In the early '90s Trip Hawkins—the founder of Electronic Arts, one of the biggest computer game companies in the early years of home computers—announced that he was starting a new company and jumping into the home video game hardware business. His new system, 3DO (the console's name was the same as that of the company), was a game console that was also designed to be an expandable educational tool and a viewer for Kodak photo-CDs. Hawkins's marketing approach was unique, to say the least. 3DO designed the system, but licensed the manufacture of the unit to a number of different electronics companies including Panasonic, Sanyo, Samsung, and Goldstar.

Although the initial response from game developers was enthusiastic, there was little software available for the 3DO when the system was introduced in 1993. The dearth of software continued as the public reacted poorly to the price of the 3DO unit—a whopping $700! The lack of marketing focus for the product didn't help either. Even 3DO didn't seem sure whether their console was a game machine, an educational tool, a general home entertainment system, or some new hybrid of all three.

By 1996, the price of the 3DO had been slashed to around $200. 3DO sold the rights to a new 3DO system called "M2" to Matsushita, but the new system never materialized. The 3DO console slowly faded away in the late '90s. It is unclear how much software was produced for the system, but the catalog certainly includes more than 60 titles, ranging from games to children's software to multimedia reference products. There were a variety of 3DO players produced. The most common in the United States seems to be the **Panasonic Real 3DO** system.

Because it was available in stores as recently as the late 1990s, 3DO has not achieved collectible status. Currently, you can typically pick up a console with dozens of software titles for under $200. Consoles alone seldom sell for more than $40 or so.

Because it was such an ill-defined product—sort of a video game system but not quite—it is unknown whether the 3DO will ever be more than a curiosity among video game collectors.

The "Next Generation" Consoles

One interesting thing about the video game industry is that it never stops. Even in 1984 when it looked like the industry was dead, someone came along and proved that video games are here to stay.

The first few years of the 21st century have seen the introduction of three new game consoles from Nintendo (GameCube, Game Boy Advance, and Game Boy Advance SP) and a new con-

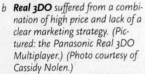

a   **Neo-Geo** was the first video game
    console to literally bring arcade-
    quality gameplay and graphics
    into the home. This expensive sys-
    tem actually plays the same game
    cartridges used in SNK's arcade
    video game cabinets. (Photo cour-
    tesy of Cassidy Nolen.)

b   **Real 3DO** suffered from a combi-
    nation of high price and lack of a
    clear marketing strategy. (Pic-
    tured: the Panasonic Real 3DO
    Multiplayer.) (Photo courtesy of
    Cassidy Nolen.)

sole from the current king of the video game hill, Sony (the PlayStation 2). And, just as it has always been in the past, a new player has entered the fray in the ongoing console wars. This time, however, the new contender is a huge company with a bankroll big enough keep them in the race for some time should they choose to stick it out. Microsoft's Xbox, introduced in 2001, is the most technologically advanced home video game console ever created, and is slowly but surely gaining popularity.

Will any of these new systems ever become collectible? Only time will tell. In the short history of video games, pivotal game consoles—the first video game system for a company or one that introduces some new or unique technology—have typically become collectible. By that standard, the Nintendo GameCube (the first noncartridge Nintendo system—and, according to rumor, possibly the *last* Nintendo nonhandheld system) could be considered a historical milestone by future collectors. Xbox, the first game system by Microsoft, could similarly be viewed as a milestone in video game history.

The best advice that veteran video game collectors can offer to would-be collectors who are just starting to accumulate video games today is this: *keep everything*! Hold onto every game, every accessory, and every box that you have for the next 20 years or so.

Also, when your current game console of choice becomes obsolete—and it will, possibly by the time you read this—don't throw it away or trade it in. Store it in a nice safe, dry, climate-controlled place for a couple of decades. Who knows? That PlayStation 2 you were originally planning to trade in for a $50 credit on a PlayStation 3 in 2005 might be worth $200 to a collector in 2025.

12 Insert Coin to Begin—The Basics of Arcade Collecting

"You want to collect *what?*"

The moment you decide to collect arcade video games, you're bound to hear that from someone. Collectors whose classic video game interests lie in the realm of consoles and handheld games hardly ever have to deal with this question (at least not at first), because consoles and handhelds share a common characteristic with more commonplace collectibles like shot glasses, books, or stamps: they're *small*. You can usually display them on a shelf in the corner somewhere where they are relatively unobtrusive and won't readily invoke the ire of significant others.

Coin-operated (coin-op) arcade video games are a different story. These things are *big*—upright models are about the size and weight of a small refrigerator, and cockpit versions are even more massive. They require a significant amount of effort to move into your house, and a significant amount of dedicated space once inside. Most arcade games also have the disadvantage of not quite matching any existing home décor. In other words, unlike more conventional collectibles, arcade games are decidedly *not* unobtrusive. Add to this the fact that, like any other hobby, coin-op video game collecting is addictive—read: you're likely to have a *lot* of these things in your house eventually—and it's easy to understand why this branch of the classic video game collecting hobby comes under such close scrutiny by those with whom you cohabitate.

Why Collect Classic Arcade Video Games?

In most cases, the reasons for collecting coin-op classic video games are the same as the reasons for collecting classic console and handheld games (see Chapter 2). Nostalgia, a longing for simpler gameplay, and a desire to turn a profit, are all valid reasons for getting into classic coin-op collecting. There are a couple of additional reasons that some classic video game collectors take that extra step and plunge headlong into the arcade realm.

One of these reasons is artistic appeal—not just for the games themselves, but for the cabinets that house them as well. In their own way, arcade video game cabinets are works of art. You might never see the side art from a *Donkey Kong* machine hanging in the Louvre museum, but the art of video games is quite appealing in its own way. Many arcade collectors choose to collect only machines that have all of their original artwork intact. The aesthetic appeal alone is reason enough for some hobbyists to amass their own arcades. In fact, some collectors ignore the machines entirely and collect only the side art and marquees from classic games.

Classic arcade collectors also see this hobby as a way to preserve the past. Most of the arcade video games covered in this guide are officially antiques since they are over 20 years old. Unlike other antiques—like cars, for example—there are no official museums dedicated to the preservation and display of arcade games. This is slowly changing as nostalgia for classic video games continues to grow, but until recently the only way that these games were preserved was through the efforts of collectors. Many of the classic coin-op video games of the '70s and '80s were demolished or piled in dank, dusty warehouses after the popularity of the arcades passed. If it had not been for collectors who felt strongly about preserving these technological relics, there would be few remaining in the world today.

Finally, and most importantly to many collectors (myself included), the *feel* of playing an actual arcade game is a strong motivator. Most of the classic arcade hits of the '70s and '80s were reproduced on the classic consoles of the era like Atari 2600, Intellivision, and ColecoVision, and are now available on modern consoles from the Nintendo Entertainment System to the Xbox. The Multiple Arcade Machine Emulator (MAME), which is available for download from dozens of web sites worldwide, even allows nostalgia buffs to play classic arcade games from images of the original game ROMS on a home computer. In other words, classic arcade games are available in many forms that don't take up nearly as much space as the actual cabinets themselves.

The problem is that many arcade games simply don't feel right when played on a PC or a home game console. Driving the car in *Spy Hunter* isn't the same when using cursor keys instead of a steering wheel. Moving your marble through the maze in *Marble Madness* isn't as fun with a mouse as it is with a big, colorful trackball. And who wants to play *Robotron: 2084* with a single thumb pad on a PlayStation controller when the game was meant to be played with two joysticks? Some arcade games simply don't feel right unless you play them in their original form.

The Arcade Game Collecting Community

As discussed in Chapter 2, one of the driving forces behind classic video game console collecting is a strong community of hobbyists who share a passion for the pastime. The same is true of the coin-op arcade branch of classic video game collecting.

Arcade game collectors are a very close-knit bunch, and most are very active in promoting the hobby. Many arcade game collectors maintain web sites with pictures of their games, stories of their coin-op acquisitions, and advice on buying, selling, and restoring arcade games. There are a number of informal organizations dedicated to the preservation of classic arcade games. One of the most active of these groups is the Video Arcade Preservation Society (VAPS). By logging onto http://www.vaps.org, you can find contact information for hundreds of collectors all over the world and details on the games in their collections.

The arcade newsgroup rec.games.video.arcade.collecting (RGVAC) is host to many very active collectors who are always ready to provide helpful information about collecting and restoring games. This is also a good place to visit if you want to locate restoration materials or a particular game for purchase, although (technically), games and parts that are offered for sale are supposed to be listed on the rec.games.video.arcade.marketplace newsgroup.

Experienced arcade game collectors are invaluable to those new to the hobby. Classic arcade video games are bound to break down from time to time. If you are not familiar enough with electronics to fix a game yourself, with a little searching, chances are that you can find a fellow collector in your area who might be willing to lend a hand.

Appendix B at the back of this book provides a list of web sites and events related to collecting classic arcade video games.

Deciding What to Collect

If setting goals is important when starting a collection of classic console and handheld games, it is absolutely *imperative* when you set out to create a classic coin-op collection. Ten video game consoles fill a good-sized bookshelf or entertainment center. Ten arcade games fill the better part of a one-car garage.

There are a number of schools of thought on deciding what arcade games to collect. You could collect only games that are historically significant in some way—games like *Pong*, *Space Invaders*, *Pac-Man*, and *Dragon's Lair*, for example, are all pivotal in arcade video game history. A collection like this makes quite an impressive display, but it can also cost you a fortune. Historically significant games are often among the most expensive.

You can also set out to collect games built by specific manufacturers. Many coin-op video game collectors are very brand conscious. Collections consisting exclusively of Atari or Williams games (for example) are not at all uncommon.

Still other hobbyists collect games based on potential resale value. As is true with classic console and handheld video games, buying classic arcade games specifically to resell them is a speculative business, and you need to remember that there is always a chance that you won't get enough money to recoup your purchase price much less turn a profit. The secret of amassing a collection of this type is to buy cheap and restore the games yourself. Only then are you (almost) guaranteed a profitable return on your investment.

In the end, you need to be true to yourself when building your personal arcade. Stick to the games that mean something to you. Some of the games you like might be historically significant, and if that is the case you could end up paying a premium price to add these games to your collection. On the other hand, some of your personal favorites might be among the more obscure classic titles. Games that had low commercial popularity in their time are often quite inexpensive in today's market.

Remember, it's *your* collection. When you're talking about the commitment in space and (potentially) maintenance involved in an arcade game collection, you should collect what you *want*—not what people expect you to have in your arcade.

One helpful piece of advice: games that have unlimited continuation ("add coin to continue") aren't as much fun when you're not paying by the game. In an arcade, where it costs money to continue, you're motivated to do well and probably won't play all the way through the game in one session. When it's free to continue, there's no need to stop, which means you'll play through the game quickly and will likely tire of it rapidly.

Similarly, games that cannot be played as single-player games tend not to be as fun to have around as games that you can play alone. Unless you always have an opponent handy, games like *Pong* and *Space Wars* tend to sit idle in your arcade most of the time.

Keep these tips in mind as you compile your wish list.

Where Can You Find These Things?

If you had the means to start collecting classic arcade games back in the late '80s, you're one of the lucky ones. Back then, arcade owners were leaving the business in droves. There are stories of games being hauled to the dump and destroyed by the hundreds. Other stories tell of warehouses full of games, locked up, forgotten, and gathering dust. Often, lucky players could purchase their favorite games for a couple hundred dollars or less—if they were in the right place at the right time.

All of the games that weren't destroyed or dumped in a warehouse either remained in arcades (usually tucked away in some dark corner while the new fighting and driving games were displayed prominently in the front) or sold off to private individuals. One way or another, most classic arcade games disappeared off the face of the planet along with most of the arcades that originally housed them.

As the Internet became commonplace in the mid-1990s, one of the results was that arcade game aficionados all over the world found a way to communicate with one another quickly and easily. This increased the awareness of the arcade game collecting hobby and provided venues for collectors to buy, sell, and trade games. It also served as virtual word of mouth for local game auctions, which are not particularly easy for private individuals to find since they cater to arcade owners and amusement operators.

Today, there are lots of places where you can purchase arcade video games for your collection.

Live Auctions

There are companies all over the country that regularly hold arcade game auctions. Although these auctions are still primarily attended by arcade owners and operators, they are open to the public.

Live auctions are often home to the best arcade game bargains you're ever likely to find—but there's a catch. At a live auction, you're buying equipment that is essentially in unknown condition. While some games purchased at an auction are in perfect working condition and provide years of trouble-free operation, this is not always the case. Auction games usually require at least some cosmetic work. At worst, games purchased at a live auction can require a great deal of electronic work to get them up and running. The upside of being there in person is that you have the opportunity to inspect and test the game before placing a bid.

If you're getting into the hobby with the intention of restoring and repairing games, live auctions are ideal. If, on the other hand, you're just interested in getting a game that you can play without having to worry about repair and restoration, live auctions are probably not the route to go.

That said, arcade game auctions are an exciting and fun experience, and everyone interested in the hobby of collecting coin-op video games should attend at least one such event. For a look inside the activities that take place at a typical arcade auction and for tips on how to make a purchase in such a venue, see Chapter 13.

Online Auctions

Online auctions are another way in which the Internet provides a valuable service for classic arcade collectors. Depending on who you talk to, online auctions are either the lifeblood of the hobby or an evil force that drives the prices of collectible arcade video games into ranges that only the richest collectors can afford.

No matter what your view on the subject, there is one undeniable fact: online auctions are convenient search tools. Whereas finding a particular arcade video game used to be a tedious, drawn-out affair that involved long, laborious searches, you can now go online, surf to your auction venue of choice, and type the name of the game you want in the site's search engine. Most of the popular classic coin-op collectibles are available on any given day in online auctions, and even the rarest games show up once or twice a year.

There are several disadvantages of buying coin-op arcade games through an online auction. First, you're buying the game without ever having seen it in person. You're relying on a few small pictures and the honesty of the seller to convey the condition of the machine. Most sellers are honest, but not all of them are. Use the seller's feedback rating as a gauge of how trustworthy he or she is, and don't be afraid to ask plenty of questions before you place a bid. You can also check the RGVAC newsgroup for references to a particular seller. Honest sellers are often praised by RGVAC members, and warnings about dishonest sellers are posted to caution other members from dealing with these people.

Price is also a consideration in an online auction. While it is occasionally possible to get remarkable deals, more often than not prices tend to be higher in an online auction than they are at a live auction. Part of this is due to the typical auction fever that sets in when people get caught up in the excitement of the bidding. Unfortunately, dishonesty can also play a part in bid prices. Some sellers "shill" their auctions—that is, they place bids themselves (through friends or through other auction accounts) to artificially inflate the price. The best way to avoid paying too much in an online auction is to set a limit for yourself and stick to it.

Finally, and perhaps most decisively, shipping is a huge drawback in online auctions. It costs about $200 to ship an upright arcade video game across the United States. When you're deciding how much to bid in an online auction, you have to figure the shipping cost to your final total. The $200 game "bargain" you find on eBay could actually cost you as much as $400 when all is said and done. To avoid shipping costs, look for sellers that are within driving distance of your area. Often, you can find a seller who is willing to personally deliver the game to your house for a nominal fee or is willing to let you pick up the game yourself.

The most popular online auction site is, of course, eBay (http://www.ebay.com). This site has categories specifically dedicated to coin-op video games, as well as categories for parts and accessories.

The best thing to remember about online auctions is that just about any item that is listed will be listed again at some point. Prices go through high and low trends. If the game you're looking for is currently selling for more than your set budget, hold off and keep watching. Eventually, you might just get a bargain when interest in the game dies out. You've lived without the game for 20 years or more, so you needn't be in a hurry to buy the first one you see.

Dealers

Because classic arcade video game collecting has become very popular over the last several years, many dealers who cater specifically to the home market have appeared on the scene. Some are local antique dealers who also dabble in games, while others are full-fledged video game dealers.

Not all dealers operate physical store locations. Many have set up shop on the Internet. These dealers tend to have a larger inventory than storefront dealers, with searchable databases of titles and pictures of the games they have in stock. Many dealers also offer a service where they will locate a specific game for you.

Dealers provide services that are not available when you purchase games through other sources. They generally "shop" their games—completely check them for physical and electronic defects, repair or replace monitors, and make sure that the game is fully functional before it is sold. Some dealers even offer warranties on the games they sell and perform on-site service and repair work on machines that are sold locally. This is ideal for collectors who don't want to deal with restoration and maintenance. Buying a shopped game from an arcade game dealer is like buying a 1965 Mustang from a knowledgeable auto dealer who has lovingly restored it to like-new condition, whereas buying a used game from an auction is the equivalent of buying a junker car and fixing it up yourself.

Of course, all of these services come at a price. Dealer prices are generally higher than those that you find through most other sources. You get what you pay for. There is also the matter of shipping. Unless the dealer is local, you can expect to pay the same shipping charges for dealer games as you do for games purchased through an online auction. Note that the price ranges on the arcade price list in Chapter 14 do *not* reflect dealer prices. You can expect to pay considerably more than the prices listed in this guide for most fully restored games from a dealer. This is only fair, considering the amount of time and money that dealers spend fixing up the games.

Several online classic coin-op dealers are listed in Appendix B.

Fellow Collectors

Another good source for arcade video games is fellow hobbyists. As we've already discussed, finding space for a large collection of arcade video games is a challenge, and most collectors, at one time or another, amass a collection that is so large that they are forced to sell some of their existing games to make room for new ones.

Often, to avoid the hassles of shipping a game or to give fellow collectors in their area an opportunity to provide a good home for a prized collectible, hobbyists offer their games for sale locally before attempting to sell them through other venues. This is often a great opportunity to purchase a quality game at a reasonable price.

If the game is in your area, the owner is usually amenable to letting you examine and play the game before you buy it. Even if you have to drive a couple of hours, it's worthwhile to put the game through its paces before you part with your money. Collectors tend to take very good care of their games and usually have details on the game's performance and repair history (at least from the time that they purchased it themselves). Although there are always a few dishonest people in any crowd, most collectors are very forthcoming with this type of information. They also tend to be pretty fair when setting a price. You can expect a fair collector price to fall somewhere between a live auction price and an eBay/dealer price.

Ease of transportation is another advantage of buying locally. If you don't have a vehicle that can transport the game, you can rent an inexpensive truck or trailer to move the game to your home. Often, collectors who have the means to do so will be happy to deliver the game for you within a reasonable distance for a nominal fee.

The best places to look for collector games that are offered for sale are the big hobbyist news-groups like RGVAC and local arcade collector's newsgroups if there are any in your area. You can also check the newspaper classifieds.

Thrift Shops and Yard Sales

Admittedly, discount consignment shops and yard sales that feature coin-op arcade games are few and far between. It is much more common to find classic console and handheld video games in such venues. Even so, there are still occasional stories of collectors running across arcade games at a thrift store or at a yard sale. It pays to keep your eyes open. Some collectors have even spotted classic arcade game cabinets on the street awaiting pickup by trash collectors! (If you come across such a find, make sure you get permission from the owner before you throw the game in the back of your truck and drive off.)

Some collectors have also reported getting deals on video games that are being discarded by local bowling alleys and similar recreational facilities. If you know of such a place that might be going out of business, check with the owners to see if they have any coin-op machines they want to unload.

Even more so than live auctions, you must be wary of the condition of games you find in these locations. More often than not, these games are being discarded for a reason. Even so, if the game is offered at a bargain price (or for free), it might be worth the effort to repair it.

Warehouse Raids

If you had to choose two words that would send shivers of joy up and down a classic arcade video game collector's spine, those words would be "warehouse raid."

By the end of the '80s, thousands of **video arcade games** were socked away in huge warehouses (and barns and other storage facilities) where their future remained uncertain. Over the last two decades, many such warehouses have been located by collectors. The owners of these ware-houses were, more often than not, willing to sell the entire contents of the building for a bargain price just to avoid ongoing storage fees.

Although these mythical warehouses are far less common today than they once were, lucky col-lectors with lots of perseverance (and more than a little luck) still occasionally manage to un-earth one of these treasure troves.

Most of the warehouses that are revealed today belong to operators (professional video game owners) who decide it's finally time to let go of their old stock. In some cases, these ware-houses provide poor protection from the elements, and many of the games inside are dam-aged beyond repair. Even so, such a place is the arcade game collector's equivalent of discovering King Tut's tomb. One might find dozens—even *hundreds*—of working or nearly working games in a single location. If the collector's luck holds, the owner might be so anx-ious to get rid of his stock that he'll sell everything cheap. Admittedly, this is increasingly un-likely now that the popularity of collecting classic arcade games is growing. Warehouses full of games are now sometimes listed on eBay, and the games sell for a lot more today than they would have five- to 10-years ago.

If you're lucky enough to find such an arcade collector's dream in your area, you'd be wise to jump at the opportunity to plunder it. Find fellow collectors in your area to share the cost of the haul, keep the games you want and sell the rest as either complete games or as parts. If you do your research and figure out how much all of the games are worth individually *and* you pay a

NOTE **

Throughout the text, **BOLD** indicates that an item appears in a picture.

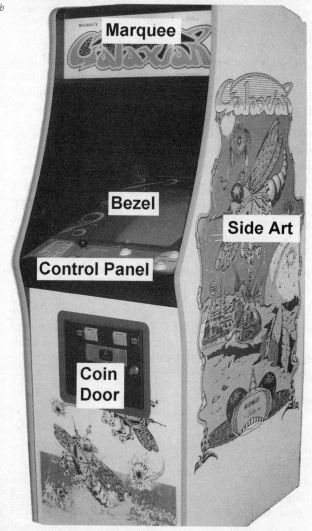

Marquee

Bezel

Side Art

Control Panel

Coin Door

a   *A warehouse full of classic video arcade games. Although they are becoming scarcer as time goes on, such warehouses are still out there waiting to be found by some lucky collector. (Photo courtesy of James Bright, http://www. quarterarcade.com.)*

b   *The parts of a typical coin-operated arcade video game. (Photo Courtesy of James Bright, http://www.quarterarcade.com.)*

price for the lot that is significantly below the games' combined value, you're bound to come out ahead financially—and you might possibly pick up a few games that you want in the process.

What to Look for When Collecting

When you have decided which games you are looking for, your next task is to become familiar with the basics of coin-op arcade video games.

The Anatomy of an Arcade Video Game

Before you can assess the condition of a game, it helps to get a handle on the terminology associated with the basic parts of the game. The labels on the *Galaxian* game on the previous page point out the **major exterior parts of a typical coin-operated arcade video game**. For more information on the various parts, see the Glossary of Terms in Appendix A.

Cabinet Types

Video games are available in a variety of shapes and sizes. In some cases, a single game might exist in three or more cabinet styles.

Cabinet style has significance for collectors for a number of reasons. First, some cabinet styles are significantly smaller than others. The style of cabinet that you choose determines how much space the game will take up in your personal arcade. For example, you can typically fit three cabaret-style cabinets in the space it takes to display two upright cabinets.

Different cabinet styles also offer different levels of aesthetic appeal. For example, cockpit/sitdown cabinets often offer more elaborate art and controls than their upright counterparts. In other words, some game cabinet styles look nicer than others.

For collectors who also want to restore games, certain cabinet types present a greater challenge. There is an abundance of replacement hardware and reproduction artwork available for most well-known upright classic video games. This is not the case for other cabinet types. While some artwork is produced for some popular cocktail cabinets, most cocktail-style games are completely ignored. It is even harder to locate parts and artwork for cabaret machines, and very few manufacturers today attempt to market reproduction art for cockpit cabinets.

Finally, in most cases, the cabinet style of a game affects its price. Collectors are generally willing to pay more for a game in a particular cabinet style if fewer of that style were produced. Smaller cabinet styles (cocktails and cabarets) also often command a higher price because they take up less space. On the other hand, cockpit-style machines almost always command higher prices because they are bigger and more impressive.

The various cabinet styles are illustrated and explained in the following sections.

Upright Cabinets

Upright cabinets are the most common cabinet type among classic arcade games. Although uprights vary greatly in size and shape, they typically stand 5 to 6 feet tall, are approximately 24 to 30 inches wide, and are 30 to 36 inches deep. The average weight of an upright game is around 300 pounds, so it is difficult to move an upright cabinet without the aid of a hand truck or a willing (or blissfully unaware) friend. Most classic upright video games feature either 19-inch or 25-inch monitors.

Upright games are often among the most aesthetically pleasing of the cabinet types. Their artwork ranges from fairly ordinary cabinets with simple side art stickers to elaborate cabinets that are specifically designed and decorated to suit the theme of the game.

Duramold Cabinets

While there were a number of upright arcade games with intricately designed cabinets, one cabinet type in particular warrants its own category.

Williams, the manufacturer of such arcade classics as *Defender* and *Robotron: 2084*, produced some of their games in molded plastic upright cabinets in addition to the more common cabinet styles. Games housed in these cabinets, known as Duramold cabinets, are coveted by collectors. **Williams Duramold** games are rare, and almost always fetch higher prices than their standard upright counterparts. The cabinets were produced in several colors including black, red, and blue.

While the subject of what Duramold games actually exist is constantly in dispute among collectors, Williams definitely produced Duramold versions of the following games:

* *Blaster*

* *Bubbles*

* *Sinistar*

According to some collectors, Duramold cabinets were designed as multigame machines that could be changed to different game titles simply by switching control panels, marquees, and circuit boards. If this is the case, it is possible that a number of additional Williams games might exist in Duramold form.

Although all of the Duramold games are rare, *Sinistar* seems to be the rarest of the lot. (It is claimed by some that only two have been discovered.)

Cocktail Cabinets

Cocktail cabinets were designed for use in bars and restaurants. They are considerably smaller and lighter than upright cabinets—about 36 inches wide, 24 inches deep, and (usually) about 36 inches tall. Most cocktail cabinets have 19-inch monitors, though a few were produced with 13-inch screens.

Because cocktail cabinets generally require that both sides remain accessible (the controls for two players are generally mounted on the opposite sides or ends of the cabinet, and players must sit down to play), they potentially take up more space than uprights. Even so, they are popular among collectors because they are generally less obtrusive than any other cabinet style. Some collectors actually use cocktail-cabinet games as coffee tables.

There are some exceptions to the sit-down rule in cocktail-cabinet design. Some cabinets are taller and allow players to stand at the controls. For the purposes of this book, stand-up games with tabletop displays like Atari's *Football* and *Warlords*, are considered cocktail cabinets.

Although there are rare exceptions to the rule, manufacturers generally produced far fewer cocktail-style cabinets than uprights. In some cases, this makes cocktail versions of some popular classic arcade games quite rare and pricey.

a

b

a **An upright arcade cabinet.**
     (Photo Courtesy of James Bright,
     http://www.quarterarcade.com.)

b **A Williams Duramold upright ar-**
     cade cabinet. *(Photo courtesy of*
     Duramold.com, http://www.
     duramold.com.)

Joust (Williams, 1982)

Compared to companies like Atari and Bally Midway, Williams—a company known primarily as a pinball manufacturer—produced only a handful of video games. They proved, however, that quality often triumphs over quantity. Almost every Williams video game was a hit in the arcades, and three of Williams's titles are among the top 20 most collected classic arcade games today.

Joust is an example of something that is all too rare in the industry today—a totally unique and innovative video game. If a designer were to pitch a concept that pits ostrich-mounted players against buzzard-mounted enemies in a mid air jousting tournament to a video game publisher today, the designer would probably be fired on the spot. But, in the early '80s, Williams designer John Newcomer proved that such a game was not only feasible but fun.

Joust was released in both upright and cocktail form. The upright version is among the more common Williams machines. It can regularly be found both online and at live game auctions, and is often available through dealers. The cocktail version of the game, which features side-by-side controls rather than controls on opposing sides of the table (the typical control layout for most cocktail cabinets), is one of the rarest and most collectible classic arcade video games. Some estimates place the number of cocktail cabinets produced as low as 250, although it is generally believed that more exist. At any rate, the cocktail version is much rarer than the upright, and generally sells for considerably more.

Like all Williams uprights, *Joust* features side art that is stenciled onto the cabinet. Restoration materials available for this game include both stencils and side art that is reproduced in sticker form.

One of the most common electronic problems that plagues *Joust* (and a number of other Williams machines) is failure of the battery pack that allows the machine to save high scores and game settings. The original battery pack holds three standard AA batteries, and often has loose connections. The batteries also have a tendency to leak and damage the game board. A modern-day replacement battery connector that uses a flat Ni-Cad battery is available for under $10 and can be installed with a minimum of soldering skill.

A conversion kit exists to upgrade *Joust* and a number of other upright Williams arcade games into "Multi-Williams" cabinets that play nearly every Williams video game created. The kit consists of a control panel, a circuit board, a marquee, and cabinet artwork. Williams multi-game machines are regularly found in online auctions, and usually sell for between $1,000 and $1,500 in good condition. The multigame upgrade kits are also available separately, but some electronics skill is required to install them.

Robotron: 2084 (Williams, 1982)

Unique gameplay is probably one of the reasons that the Williams video games stand out from the pack in the classic era. ***Robotron: 2084*** certainly exhibits this quality. Its control method—two eight-way joysticks, one that controls direction of movement and the other that controls direction of fire—is one that is shared by few other games, classic or otherwise. In addition to the unique control scheme, the game features hectic action and breakneck gameplay—a trademark of Williams designer Eugene Jarvis, whose first game, *Defender*, had set the high-water mark for game difficulty in the arcades two years earlier.

a **Tron** *recreates several key scenes from the Disney movie by the same name. A hit in its day, this game continues to be popular among classic arcade game collectors. (Photo courtesy of James Bright, http://www.quarterarcade.com.)*

b **Joust** *was one of the most popular games of 1982, and remains a fun and engaging game to this day. (From the author's collection.)*

If one were to survey a random group of video game professionals and hard-core gamers from any era, it is likely that a large percentage of these people would peg *Robotron* as their favorite video game of all time. This is definitely reflected in the collectors' market today, where *Robotron* machines are among the most consistently pricey classics that are regularly available. The upright version of the game, which is commonly available from online merchants and auctions (though not often at live auctions for some reason), seldom sells for less than $700 in working condition. The cocktail and cabaret versions of *Robotron* are extremely rare, and always sell for considerably more. If you are lucky enough to locate either of these cabinets, you're likely to pay well over $1,000 for a working specimen.

Robotron upright cabinets are among the easiest Williams games to restore due to their simple side art, which can be touched up by hand with decent results.

Defender (Williams, 1980)

Part of successful arcade video game design is achieving a balance of making a game fun from the get-go so that people are willing to drop a quarter in the slot, but difficult enough so that they don't play for more than a minute or two. The shorter the play time, the better the revenues—but making the game *too* difficult tends to keep people from trying it more than once.

Flying in the face of this basic arcade game principle, **Defender** broke this rule and was still a huge success. *Defender* is unabashedly difficult to play. It was one of the first games to feature a scrolling playfield—one that extends beyond the confines of a single screen—and that abnormally large game universe is chockfull of fast-moving enemies to kill and slow-moving innocent bystanders to rescue. In addition to all of the onscreen action, the game requires you to master a mind-boggling array of controls: a joystick and five buttons!

In spite of all of this, *Defender* was a very successful game. It had graphics and sound that were unrivaled at the time, and the challenge of the game drew players in droves. In fact, *Defender* was Williams's best-selling video game, with nearly 60,000 cabinets sold worldwide. The game was produced in both upright and cocktail versions. The more-common upright is more popular (and more pricey) than the less-common cocktail version. Despite the game's popularity among collectors, *Defender* is relatively easy to find. Upright models in good condition often sell for around $700 to $800.

Defender has the same side art caveat that applies to all Williams games—the stenciled side art is more difficult to replace than the stickers used by other game manufacturers. Electronically speaking, *Defender* boards suffer the same battery-related problems associated with most Williams board sets. (See the description of *Joust* earlier in this chapter for details.)

After *Defender* and *Robotron: 2084*, Eugene Jarvis continued his tradition of designing sadistically difficult games with *Stargate*, a sequel to *Defender* that features not five, but *six* control buttons in addition to a joystick. Although *Stargate* isn't in the top 20 list, it is still very popular among collectors.

Galaxian (Midway, 1979)

Despite the fact that color television sets had been all the rage since the mid-1960s, every video game from 1972 through 1979 featured not-so-state-of-the-art black-and-white graphics. *Galaxian* was the game that boldly broke that monochrome tradition.

Building on the alien shooter theme introduced and popularized by *Space Invaders*, *Galaxian* featured the added challenge of aliens that actually attacked aggressively rather than simply

a

b

a   **Robotron: 2084** *is consistently
counted as one of the most popular video games of all time—
despite its steep learning curve.
(Photo courtesy of James Bright,
http://www.quarterarcade.com.)*

b   **Defender.** *Designer Eugene Jarvis
established himself as one of the
first hard-core video game designers with this game. Whereas players had been put off by the
complicated gameplay of Computer Space in 1971, audiences a
mere nine years later flocked to
Defender despite its daunting
control scheme. (Photo courtesy
of James Bright, http://www.
quarterarcade.com.)*

marching back and forth waiting to be shot. Though the action seems slow when compared to later classics such as *Galaga* and *Gyruss*, both of which followed very similar themes, *Galaxian* was one of the biggest adrenaline rushes to hit the pre-1980 arcade scene.

Galaxian is a rather unique game in the top 20 list in that it is not very expensive today. The upright version of the game is rarer than other Midway games like *Galaga* and *Ms. Pac-Man*. The cocktail and cabaret versions are rarer still. Even so, the game is not particularly expensive. Auction prices typically run in the $400 range—not bad for such a nice piece of arcade history.

Like many Midway games, the upright *Galaxian* has elaborate cabinet art that covers the entire sides plus the area below the coin box. This art is stenciled on rather than applied with stickers, and so is difficult to restore when badly damaged. (Some restored machines feature smaller side art stickers that accurately reproduce the images but are considerably smaller than the original artwork.) Parts and reproduction marquees, bezels, and control panel overlays are fairly easy to come by, but the lime green t-molding used on the machine is often more expensive than common colors like black and white.

Donkey Kong Junior (Nintendo, 1982)

Nintendo knew they were on to something after the success of *Donkey Kong*, and it wasn't long until both the red- and blue-clad carpenter and the stubborn gorilla made their way back into arcades. Only this time, their roles were reversed. Mario, apparently rather miffed at Kong's antics in the first game, has captured the gorilla, and Kong's young offspring is out to save his papa.

Donkey Kong Junior, unlike many video game sequels, is completely fresh and innovative, and just as much fun (if not more fun) than the original game. *Donkey Kong Junior* is thematically unique in that it features the only appearance of Mario as a villain in a Nintendo video game. It is also the last time Mario and Kong appeared together in an arcade video game. (*Donkey Kong 3* starred the ape as the villain and a gardener named Stanley as the hero, and the *Mario Bros.* series featured Mario but not Kong.)

Donkey Kong Junior was produced in upright and cocktail versions. The upright, the more common and more popular of the two, is housed in a typical classic Nintendo cabinet. Dedicated machines were orange, although some *Donkey Kong Juniors* are found in converted *Donkey Kong* cabinets. Dedicated *Donkey Kong Junior* machines typically sell for a couple hundred dollars less than *Donkey Kong* machines in similar condition.

Like *Donkey Kong*, the replacement artwork and parts for upright *Donkey Kong Junior* machines are easy to find, making rebuilding this game among the easier restoration projects. Interestingly, the supply of *Donkey Kong Junior* PCBs is slowly dwindling due to the popularity of the *Double Donkey Kong* kit described earlier in this chapter, which can only be built on *Donkey Kong Junior* PCBs. This tends to make the price of *Donkey Kong Junior* PCBs on the market today a bit higher than those of the original game.

Frogger (Sega/Gremlin, 1981)

While some classic games will be remembered for their complexity, one of the most memorable things about **Frogger** is its simplicity. Following in the wake of the nonviolent games like *Pac-Man*, *Frogger* exhibits the same sort of cartoon-like graphics and whimsy and the same simple control scheme: a single, four-direction joystick. The object is simple: guide five frogs across the

a

b

a **Galaxian** *was the first arcade video game to feature full-color graphics. (Photo courtesy of James Bright, http://www.quarterarcade.com.)*

b **Donkey Kong Junior,** *the second in Nintendo's string of video game hits, is the one and only Nintendo game that portrays Mario as a villain. (Photo courtesy of James Bright, http://www. quarterarcade.com.)*

highway and the river and repeat until the pressure gets to be too much for you. *Frogger* is an easy game to learn but, like most of the best games, difficult to master.

Despite its enduring quality—there have been a number of PC and console games based on *Frogger* over the years, not counting the versions released for classic game consoles—and its popularity among collectors, *Frogger* remains a relatively inexpensive classic. The fairly common upright version averages $400 to $500, and the rarer cocktail version generally isn't much more expensive.

Like many popular classics, there are a number of online sources for *Frogger* side art, control panel overlays, and so on. Parts and boards are also reasonably easy to obtain. The combination of availability, affordability, and easy access to restoration materials makes *Frogger* an easy classic to add to your collection.

Recently, a number of combination games that feature *Frogger* along with other such disparate games as *Mr. Do!*, *Ms. Pac-Man*, and *Galaga* have been showing up in auctions (both live and online). These games are recent reproductions and *not* original classics.

Battlezone (Atari, 1980)

There are probably no classic video game fans that don't remember spending at least some time driving a tank through *Battlezone*'s alien landscape and doing battle with the faceless enemies that lurked there. The enemies were primitive black-and-white vector polygons (tinted green by a screen overlay), and the landscape was not much more than similarly rendered boxes and pyramids, but *Battlezone* had an uncanny ability to suspend disbelief and pull players into its world.

First-person games were few and far between in the '80s, and *Battlezone* was one of the first. (Atari's *Red Baron*, a first-person flying game, was developed at the same time, but *Battlezone* was the first of the two to make it into the arcades.) This then-unique point of view, the periscope viewer (on the upright model) and the dual joystick tank controls created a new experience in video gaming.

Today, *Battlezone* is considered a very collectible game. The upright version is far easier to find than the cabaret version, and is generally the more popular of the two. The cabaret version lacks the immersive feel of its larger counterpart—it is not equipped with the periscope viewer.

Aside from the usual problems that often plague games with vector monitors, the primary stumbling blocks for *Battlezone* owners are the joysticks. The rubber rings that center the joysticks are prone to breakage. Replacement parts are not easy to find and can be quite expensive.

Although the cabaret version of *Battlezone* is extremely rare, there is one version of the game that is rarer still. Shortly after *Battlezone* was released in the arcades, the U.S. Army contacted Atari and commissioned them to design a special version of the game to simulate the Bradley fighting vehicle. The military version, called *Bradley Trainer*, featured a complex control panel that emulated all of the real tank's knobs and switches, and a new hand controller (the same as the one that was eventually used on Atari's *Star Wars*).

There were only two *Bradley Trainers* built, and only one is known to exist today. It is unlikely that the owner of this game would *ever* sell it but, if it *were* to hit the market, it would sell for an astronomical price.

a **Frogger.** With a whole slew of PC and console games based on it and a memorable Seinfeld cameo in the 1990s, Frogger has maintained its visibility both inside and outside the collecting community. (Photo courtesy of James Bright, http://www.quarterarcade.com.)

b **Battlezone** might well be the first first-person 3-D game. (Photo courtesy of James Bright, http://www.quarterarcade.com.)

Dig Dug (Atari, 1982)

Many U.S. arcade game manufacturers imported some of their biggest hits from Japanese companies. Midway, for example, imported many of its biggest hits from other manufacturers like Taito (*Space Invaders*) and Namco (*Pac-Man*, *Galaxian*, and *Galaga*).

Atari refrained from this practice until 1982, at which point they made a deal with Namco to bring ***Dig Dug*** to U.S. arcades. At the time it was released, this game—where digging and inflating replaced the all-too-familiar arcade tasks of flying and shooting—was a truly unique experience. This game mechanic remained unique only until later that same year, when Universal released *Mr. Do!* Even so, *Dig Dug*, with Atari's powerful name behind it, remained the dominant digging game of the classic arcade era. However, despite its greater visibility in the arcades, *Dig Dug* only had one follow-up (the obscure and now hard-to-find *Dig Dug II*), while its digging rival *Mr. Do!* went on to have a number of fun and engaging sequels.

Atari produced three *Dig Dug* cabinet variations. The upright version is housed in a cabinet similar to that of the *Centipede* upright, and the cocktail version is a typical Atari cocktail table design. The cabaret version is extremely rare—rumor has it that only 500 were produced. The cabaret price is higher than that of the other two versions, but not significantly so.

Dig Dug uses standard, easy to find Atari hardware, and replacement artwork is readily available (for the upright version). This, combined with the relatively low street price of the game itself, makes *Dig Dug* a good buy for prospective collectors.

Space Invaders (Midway, 1978)

Few people realize that the video game crash of the mid-1980s was actually the *second* major slump for the fledgling industry. An onslaught of six years' worth of *Pong*-style games in the arcades combined with the release of a slew of home *Pong* systems resulted in a loss of interest in arcade video games in the late '70s.

This all changed in 1977 when, in Japan, Taito released a new game called ***Space Invaders***. *Space Invaders* was unique and gave birth to the "shooter" game genre. The game was so popular in Japan that it caused a coin shortage. Taito knew they had a hit on their hands, and they offered the U.S. distribution rights for the game to Midway. Midway introduced *Space Invaders* to U.S. audiences in 1978, sparking an era of unprecedented success in the coin-op video game industry that has never been repeated since.

Over 100,000 *Space Invaders* machines were produced in Japan, and another 60,000 were sold in the United States. Midway made both upright and cocktail versions of the game. There was also a cabaret version that seems to have made its way into U.S. arcades. This version carries the Taito label and uses a joystick controller for movement rather than the directional buttons used on the Midway versions. The Midway upright is fairly common today, while both the cocktail and the Taito cabaret are difficult to find.

Not counting vector games, *Space Invaders* is the only black-and-white game in the top 20 list. Authentic replacement monitors for black-and-white games are harder to find than their color counterparts, so repair is often a better option than replacement in a *Space Invaders* machine with monitor problems. Cosmetic restoration is a challenge as well since the side art is painted on, and the combination monitor bezel/marquee and the control panel overlay are not widely reproduced and can be difficult to find.

a

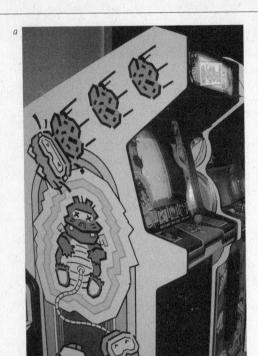

b

a **Dig–Dug.** *Although many U.S. arcade manufacturers had been importing Japanese games for years, Atari didn't start distributing games designed by other companies until they released this one in 1982. (Photo courtesy of James Bright, http://www.quarterarcade.com.)*

b **Space Invaders.** *Video game historians generally agree that the 1978 release of Space Invaders marked the beginning of the golden age of arcade video games. (Pictured: the 1980 sequel, Space Invaders Deluxe.) (Photo courtesy of James Bright, http://www.quarterarcade.com)*

a

a **Asteroids Deluxe,** *the first of three sequels to Atari's 1979 hit, was not a stellar success at the arcades; nevertheless, it has made its way into the top 20 most collected games today. (Photo courtesy of James Bright, http://www. quarterarcade.com.)*

Few arcade games are as historically significant in terms of industry impact as *Space Invaders*. Many hobbyists consider this machine among the crown jewels of their collections.

Asteroids Deluxe (Atari, 1981)

One of the reasons for Atari's success in the early days of arcade video games was their knack for innovation. Their string of *Pong* variants in the '70s aside, Atari was known for introducing new games that were nothing like any of their own previous games or the games produced by their competitors.

Asteroids Deluxe was certainly a standout exception to this rule. Aside from a deflector shield (activated by a sixth button that overcomplicated an already button-heavy control panel), there was very little difference between this game and *Asteroids*. This actually might be one of the reasons that the game has become popular among collectors today—collectors who aren't lucky enough to come across an original *Asteroids* machine might well be settling for its very similar sequel.

Whatever the reason, this game *is* popular among collectors. As is generally the case, the upright version is the most common and least expensive. *Asteroids Deluxe* cocktail and cabaret versions are extremely rare, although their prices generally aren't significantly higher than upright models.

Repair-wise, *Asteroids Deluxe* carries the usual vector monitor caveats. From a cosmetic restoration standpoint, this machine is difficult to deal with because, as of this writing, there are no ready sources for cabinet art.

Due to player complaints about glare, Atari changed the design of the upright cabinet slightly after *Asteroids Deluxe* was initially released. One cabinet variation features a vertical monitor bezel and another has a slightly slanted bezel with metal grillwork. This is important to note because the two bezels are not interchangeable. If you are purchasing a bezel for your *Asteroids Deluxe* upright, make sure your cabinet style matches the bezel. The variation between the two cabinets is described in detail online at the Killer List of Video Games web site (http://www.klov.com).

Coveted Classics—The Holy Grails of Arcade Video Game Collecting

Many of the games described in this chapter have attained their popularity among collectors today for a variety of reasons, including initial popularity, lasting gameplay value, and (perhaps most importantly) ready availability in today's collectors' market.

There are, however, some classic arcade games that are coveted among collectors but are difficult to find due to their age, their fragility, or their limited availability at the time they were released.

The following sections describe some of these classic arcade Holy Grails.

Computer Space (Nutting Associates, 1971)

To anyone who knows anything about the history of the video game industry—even if that knowledge is confined to the brief history at the beginning of this book—it is no surprise that *Computer Space* is one of the most coveted classic coin-op video games. Besides the fact that few games have ever aesthetically matched *Computer Space* in terms of cabinet style, this game has the distinction of being the *first*. Before *Computer Space*, there was no such thing as a coin-op video game.

This game's unique exterior is easily matched by its unique *interior*. Constructed before the availability of inexpensive microchips, *Computer Space*'s boards are primitive even by classic arcade game standards, and the monitor is nothing more than a black-and-white television set that is hardwired to the game.

Two versions of *Computer Space* were produced: a one-player version with pushbutton controls, and a much rarer two-player model that uses joysticks for movement. All versions were housed in futuristic-looking fiberglass cabinets that were molded in red, green, yellow, or blue.

Although complex gameplay appealed to arcade players after nearly a decade of video game conditioning, the combination of new technology and tremendously difficult game mechanics led to a lackluster commercial performance for *Computer Space*. Only about 1,500 machines were built. This small production run combined with 30 years of attrition accounts for the small number of *Computer Space* machines in existence today.

It is no surprise that most of these games, which have passed the three-decade mark in age, are no longer functional. Replacement parts are nonexistent, and circuit board sets—working or otherwise—sell for extraordinarily high prices.

Nonworking, complete single-player *Computer Space* machines typically sell for $3,000 or more, with working models garnering even higher prices. During the research for this book, no two-player *Computer Space* machines were offered for sale on the open market—at least none that I found.

It is safe to say that just about any classic arcade video game collector would be thrilled to add a *Computer Space* machine to his or her collection. It is equally safe to say that most collectors will never have the opportunity or the means to do so.

Pong (Atari, 1972)

In terms of historical significance, **Pong** holds two distinctions. It is the game that gave rise to the popularity of arcade video games, and it is the game that laid the foundation for Atari, the biggest name in video games during the classic era.

Pong, which started as a simple programming experiment for Atari engineer Al Alcorn, was exactly the type of game needed to introduce the idea of video games to the general public. Whereas *Computer Space* is very complicated, *Pong* is very simple. As Atari founder Nolan Bushnell puts it, it is a game that a guy in a bar can play with a beer in his hand. Two knobs, two paddles, one ball. *Pong* is simplicity in itself.

Like *Computer Space*, *Pong* is a very rudimentary game, with no microchips, very little in the way of electronic frills, and a black-and-white television for a monitor. *Pong*'s cabinet is a lot simpler than that of *Computer Space* as well, with plain wood grain sides, a yellow bezel/marquee, and a silver control panel imprinted with the game's simple instructions.

There is no shortage of games like *Pong*. When the game became popular, dozens of other companies got in on the act and produced their own versions of the game, different only in name and cabinet style. The *Pong* clones and, indeed, the many *Pong* sequels that Atari produced throughout the 1970s, do not hold a candle to the original in terms of collectible value. Working or not, an Atari *Pong* machine seldom sells for under $1,000.

Pong is not easy to find, and replacement parts and restoration materials for the game are pretty much nonexistent. Even so, any serious collector who has the means and the opportunity to purchase this piece of arcade history would likely jump at the chance to do so.

Warrior (Vectorbeam, 1979)

Games like *Computer Space* and *Pong* are considered Holy Grails because of their significance in arcade video game history. Others fall into the category of coveted collectibles because of their rarity and their considerable replay value.

Vectorbeam's **Warrior** is a game title that hard-core arcade video game collectors tend to whisper in awe. In many ways, this vector graphics game was way ahead of its time. Decades before games like *Mortal Kombat* brought player-versus-player fighting games to the public's attention, *Warrior* introduced the fighting game genre in a unique way. The game portrays two sword-wielding knights from an overhead perspective. The object of the game is a fight to the death. The playfield is deceptively elaborate, with multiple levels accessed via staircases, and two bottomless pits that the players must avoid. The monitor actually only displays the images of the players' characters and the score. All of the remaining graphics are rendered using detailed interior cabinet art and mirrors. The result is a visually amazing and extremely fun game.

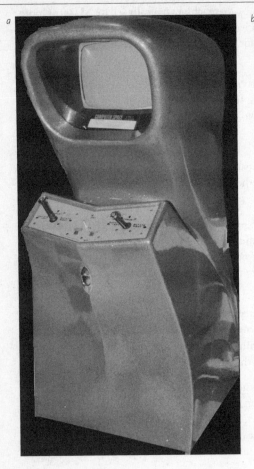

a **Computer Space,** *Nolan Bushnell's version of Steve Russell's mainframe computer game Spacewar, is a coveted collectible for good reason: it was the first arcade video game ever made. (From the collection of Cassidy Nolen. Photo by Bill Burton.)*

b **Pong.** *Computer Space was the first coin-op video game, but it was Pong that launched the arcade video game industry and a company called Atari. (Photo courtesy of James Bright, http://www.quarterarcade.com.)*

Warrior is one of the rarest vector graphics games—indeed, it is one of the rarest arcade games *period*. The demand for this game among serious collectors is quite high. It is seldom if ever available for sale, and when it *is*, a working model in good condition can go for as much as $3,000. As rare as the game itself is, the parts to restore and repair the game are rarer still. Any serious collector with the means to do so would gladly purchase a *Warrior* machine or any parts thereof in *any* condition just for a chance to eventually have a working model in his or her collection.

Quantum (Atari, 1982)

The rarest arcade games generally tend to be those manufactured by smaller companies. Most games by the big players like Atari, Midway, and Nintendo were generally widely distributed, making them relatively easy to find even two decades after their release.

One notable exception to this rule is an Atari color vector game called **Quantum**. The object of the game is to capture subatomic particles without colliding with them. The gameplay is quite abstract and the machine didn't do well in the arcade test markets. This is probably why the game never made it into wide distribution.

The cabinet, an upright, is heavily adorned with artwork. The sides are silk screened with a grid and abstract images, and the entire front panel around the coin door is also covered with artwork. The control panel, which features only a trackball and player start buttons, follows the same imagery scheme.

Rumor has it that there were only around 500 machines produced, and many of these were sold off to individuals when the game failed in the arcades. *Quantum*, like other color vector games, can be subject to monitor problems, though most *Quantum* machines, which have spent most of their existence in private collections, are generally in better condition than games that have seen a lot of use, like *Tempest*.

Despite the fact that it was a failure in its time, *Quantum* is certainly in high demand today. Serious collectors are willing to pay well over $2,000 for a working *Quantum* machine, no questions asked. If you are lucky, you might see one *Quantum* machine for sale each year.

If your goal is to collect truly rare arcade machines, you should put *Quantum* near the top of your "must have" list.

The Adventures of Major Havoc (Atari, 1983)

Another Atari color vector game that is difficult to find today and is thus very collectible is **The Adventures of Major Havoc** (usually known simply as *Major Havoc*). Besides the typical vector monitor difficulties, one of the reasons that *Major Havoc* is so difficult to find today is that it was released in the era when game conversions were becoming popular among arcade owners and game manufacturers. Many *Major Havoc* machines were conversion kits installed in other games. One version of the conversion kit was produced for *Tempest* upright cabinets and another was built to fit in *Gravitar*, *Black Widow*, and *Space Duel* cabinets. Although a dedicated version of the game was also released, many dedicated *Major Havoc* machines were themselves converted to other games.

The controller on the dedicated *Major Havoc* is truly unique. It is a roller that spins left and right—sort of a two-directional trackball. Replacements for this controller are difficult to find, but it is reparable if you have some electronics expertise. Conversion kit versions of the game use a spinner control like the one used on *Tempest*.

a

b

a **Vector Beam's Warrior** is one of the rarest and most collectible classic arcade games in existence. No one knows how many are in circulation today, but some collectors are willing to pay thousands of dollars to obtain one.

b **Quantum.** While most of Atari's games in the 1980s were widely distributed, Quantum is a notable exception to this rule. Only about 500 were made. (Photo courtesy of James Bright, http://www. quarterarcade.com.)

a

b

a **The Adventures of Major Havoc**
*is more common than Quantum,
yet it is another Atari color vector
game that is difficult to find
today, especially in the dedicated
cabinet pictured here. (Photo
courtesy of James Bright,
http://www.quarterarcade.com.)*

b *The* **Discs of Tron** *environmental
version is one of the most unique
classic video games ever made.*

Conversion *Major Havoc* machines, especially those housed in *Tempest* cabinets, are the most common today. The dedicated version, which is housed in a rather interesting upright cabinet that was also used for *Firefox, Return of the Jedi,* and *I, Robot,* is the most collectible version. The *Major Havoc* prices in this book reflect both conversions and dedicated games. Dedicated prices run closer to the upper end of the range, while conversions sell for prices at the lower end of the spectrum.

Discs of Tron (Environmental Version, Bally Midway 1983)

One of the more memorable scenes in the movie *Tron* was the disc battle where characters face off on floating platforms and try to knock each other off into the void below by pelting each other with glowing discs. An arcade version of this game was supposed to appear in the original *Tron* arcade game, but it didn't make the cut. Instead, Bally Midway released it separately as a sequel called **Discs of Tron**.

The upright version of *Discs of Tron,* while collectible in its own right (it's far rarer than the original *Tron*) is not generally counted among the Holy Grails of arcade collecting. The environmental version, on the other hand, is another story.

The environmental version of *Discs of Tron,* which weighs in at over 700 pounds, is one of the most massive classic video games ever built. It stands over six feet tall and is over six feet deep. Its interior—which is outfitted with black lights, fluorescent paint, and quadraphonic sound (including speech, which is omitted in most upright *Discs of Tron* cabinets)—is about the size of an average phone booth and is enclosed on all but the sides, completely immersing the player in the *Tron* game grid.

Because this game is so unwieldy, it is often cut into two sections and pieced back together to make it easier to handle. (Look for evidence of this on the floor and ceiling of the game if you're thinking of purchasing one.) A number of cut-off upright versions were also produced—environmental cabinets without the back, ceiling, and floor with a small marquee. These makeshift uprights have speech, whereas the dedicated upright cabinets do not.

An environmental *Discs of Tron* is obviously not a game for just anyone. You not only have to have a means to transport and move the game, you also have to have the space to display it. If you *do* happen to have the room, however, this game is sure to make you the envy of your fellow collectors.

Other Notable Holy Grail Machines

The classic arcade games described in the previous sections are all collectibles that experienced hobbyists agree are highly sought-after games that would be a valuable addition to any collection, but they are by no means the only coveted classic arcade collectibles. There are many games that are considered extremely valuable due to their rarity, popularity, or a combination of both. Some other arcade Holy Grails include:

- *Blaster* (Duramold version, Williams, 1983)

- *Cliff Hanger* (Stern, 1983)

- *Death Race* (Exidy, 1976)

- *I, Robot* (Atari, 1983)

- *Joust* (cocktail version, Williams, 1982)

- *Missile Command* (cockpit version, Atari, 1980)—reportedly, fewer than 100 were made

- *Reactor* (Gottlieb, 1982)

- *Tapper* (Budweiser version, Bally, Midway 1983)—not particularly rare, but highly sought-after

- *Zookeeper* (Taito, 1982)

Prototypes: The Holiest of Holy Grails

Arcade game manufacturers often test their games in select locations to gauge player reaction before the games are put into mass-production. For this purpose, the company builds prototype versions of the game.

As is true with any product, if a prototype isn't successful, the product is either redesigned or cancelled, and the prototypes are abandoned to the whims of fate.

Many classic arcade prototypes still exist today. They are usually discovered in the warehouses of manufacturers and former arcade owners, gathering dust in some forgotten corner. For a die-hard collector, the discovery of a prototype game—especially one that is legendary among collectors—is a truly momentous occasion.

There is no way to pin down the exact number of arcade game prototypes that exist (or that once existed). Classic arcade prototype machines are items that simply turn up from time to time. When a prototype is discovered, it is seldom offered for sale at any price. When a prototype *is* offered for sale, the price is likely to be very high indeed. The better known the game, the higher the price.

A number of classic game prototypes have been discovered over the years. A few of them include:

- *The Adventures of Major Havoc*. Some prototypes are actually alternate versions of games that were eventually released. A recent discovery is a dedicated *Major Havoc* prototype in a *Crystal Castles*–style cabinet (http://www.safestuff.com/protomh.htm).

- *Akka Arrh*. Only three cabinets housing this Atari game prototype are known to exist. You can see the third one that was discovered at http://www.safestuff.com/aa.htm.

- *Arcade Classics*. An Atari Games prototype with two new games: *Super Centipede and Missile Command II*. See it at http://www.safestuff.com/ac.htm.

- *Marble Madness 2: Marble Man*. A number of prototypes of this never-released *Marble Madness* sequel have been found. You can see them online at http://www.safestuff.com/marble-man.htm.

- *Pong*. The prototype version of *Pong*, which was tested by Al Alcorn and Nolan Bushnell in Andy Capp's Tavern, still exists, and can be seen at the Atari Museum Web site (http://www.klov.com).

You might note that many of the links in the previous list point to a single Web site. This is because one of the most amazing stashes of one-of-a-kind items was recently obtained by a collector who managed to purchase a large quantity of the arcade-related contents of Atari's Milpitas,

California, facility when it was shut down by Midway in the summer of 2003. To get an idea of the magnitude of this find, check out the "My Trip to Atari" link on http://www.safestuff.com. This is the kind of find that any arcade collector would kill to be a part of.

Arcade Games Price Guide

005
Manufacturer: Sega
Date: 1982
Cabinet Type: Upright
Rarity: 9
Price Range: $100–250*

10-YARD FIGHT
Manufacturer: Taito
Date: 1984
Cabinet Type: Upright
Rarity: 4
Price Range: $150–250

18 WHEELER
Manufacturer: Midway
Date: 1979
Cabinet Type: Upright
Rarity: 9
Price Range: $100–150*

1942
Manufacturer: Capcom
Date: 1984
Cabinet Type: Upright
Rarity: 3
Price Range: $250–400
Cabinet Type: Cocktail
Rarity: 7
Price Range: $300–450*

1943 THE BATTLE OF MIDWAY
Manufacturer: Capcom
Date: 1989
Cabinet Type: Upright
Rarity: 3
Price Range: $300–400
Cabinet Type: Cocktail
Rarity: 7
Price Range: $350–450*

280 ZZZAP
Manufacturer: Midway
Date: 1976
Cabinet Type: Upright
Rarity: 9
Price Range: $100–200*

3D-BOWLING
Manufacturer: Meadows
Date: 1978
Cabinet Type: Upright
Rarity: 9
Price Range: $100–150*
Cabinet Type: Cocktail
Rarity: 9
Price Range: $100–150*

4-D WARRIORS
Manufacturer: Sega
Date: 1985
Cabinet Type: Upright
Rarity: 9
Price Range: $75–150*

4-PLAYER BOWLING ALLEY
Manufacturer: Midway
Date: 1978
Cabinet Type: Upright
Rarity: 9
Price Range: $100–150*
Cabinet Type: Cocktail
Rarity: 9
Price Range: $125–175*
Notes: Cocktail called simply "Bowling Alley"

600
Manufacturer: Konami
Date: 1981
Cabinet Type: Upright
Rarity: 9
Price Range: $75–100*
Notes: Bootleg version of *Turtles*

720 DEGREES (720°)
Manufacturer: Atari Games
Date: 1986
Cabinet Type: Upright
Rarity: 6
Price Range: $250–350
Notes: Atari System II game

8 BALL ACTION (EIGHT BALL ACTION)
Manufacturer: Nintendo
Date: 1984
Cabinet Type: Upright
Rarity: 8
Price Range: $75–150*

800 FATHOMS
Manufacturer: U.S. Billiards
Date: 1981
Cabinet Type: Upright
Rarity: 9
Price Range: $100–200*
Notes: Also known as *Mariner*

A.P.B.
Manufacturer: Atari Games
Date: 1987
Cabinet Type: Upright
Rarity: 6
Price Range: $150–250
Notes: Atari System II game

AB$CAM
Manufacturer: U.S. Billiards
Date: 1981
Cabinet Type: Upright
Rarity: 9
Price Range: $100–200*

ACROBAT
Manufacturer: Taito
Date: 1978
Cabinet Type: Upright
Rarity: 9
Price Range: $50–100*

ADVENTURE MR. DO!
Manufacturer: Universal
Date: 1984
Cabinet Type: Upright
Rarity: Prototype
Price Range: $?
Notes: Laser disc game featuring *Mr. Do;* no pricing information available

THE ADVENTURES OF ROBBY ROTO
Manufacturer: Bally Midway
Date: 1982
Cabinet Type: Upright
Rarity: 8
Price Range: $150–200*
Notes: Usually known as simply *Robby Roto*
Cabinet Type: Cocktail
Rarity: 9
Price Range: $250–350*
Cabinet Type: Cabaret
Rarity: 9
Price Range: $250–350*

AFTER BURNER
Manufacturer: Sega
Date: 1987
Cabinet Type: Upright
Rarity: 3
Price Range: $100–200
Cabinet Type: Cockpit
Rarity: 7
Price Range: $500–700*
Notes: Moving cockpit

AFTER BURNER II
Manufacturer: Sega
Date: 1987
Cabinet Type: Upright
Rarity: 5
Price Range: $300–600
Notes: Usually found as conversions of *Afterburner* (price is for dedicated version)
Cabinet Type: Cockpit
Rarity: 8
Price Range: $650–800*
Notes: Usually found as conversions of *Afterburner* (price is for dedicated version)

AIR COMBAT
Manufacturer: Digital Games Incorporated
Date: 1976
Cabinet Type: Upright
Rarity: 9
Price Range: $100–300

AKKA ARRH
Manufacturer: Atari Games
Date: 1982
Cabinet Type: Upright
Rarity: Prototype
Price Range: $?
Notes: Only three are known to exist; no pricing information available; see http://www.safestuff.com for pictures and info

ALBEGAS
Manufacturer: Sega
Date: 1985
Cabinet Type: Upright
Rarity: 9
Price Range: $150–200*
Notes: Also known as *Cybernaut*

ALI BABA AND 40 THIEVES
Manufacturer: Sega
Date: 1982
Cabinet Type: Upright
Rarity: 9
Price Range: $75–150*

ALIEN INVADER
Manufacturer: Universal
Date: 1979
Cabinet Type: Upright
Rarity: 9
Price Range: $75–150*

ALIEN SECTOR
Manufacturer: Namco
Date: 1985
Cabinet Type: Upright
Rarity: 9
Price Range: $150–250*
Notes: Also known as *Baraduke*

ALLEY RALLY
Manufacturer: Exidy
Date: 1975
Cabinet Type: Upright
Rarity: 9
Price Range: $100–150*

ALPHA-1
Manufacturer: Atari
Date: 1983
Cabinet Type: Upright
Rarity: Prototype
Price Range: $?
Notes: Prototype of *Major Havoc;* no pricing information available

ALPHA MISSION
Manufacturer: SNK
Date: 1985
Cabinet Type: Upright
Rarity: 9
Price Range: $100–175*
Notes: Game for SNK's NEO-GEO system; there is a bootleg version called *ASO: Armored Scrum Object*

ALPHA MISSION II

Manufacturer: SNK
Date: 1991
Cabinet Type: Upright
Rarity: 9
Price Range: $100–175*
Notes: Game for SNK's NEO-GEO system (sequel to *Alpha Mission*)

ALPINE SKI

Manufacturer: Taito
Date: 1981
Cabinet Type: Upright
Rarity: 7
Price Range: $300–400

ALTERED BEAST

Manufacturer: Sega
Date: 1988
Cabinet Type: Upright
Rarity: 5
Price Range: $250–400

THE AMAZING MAZE GAME

Manufacturer: Midway
Date: 1976
Cabinet Type: Upright
Rarity: 9
Price Range: $50–100*

AMBUSH

Manufacturer: Nippon
Date: 1983
Cabinet Type: Upright
Rarity: 9
Price Range: $100–200*

AMIDAR

Manufacturer: Stern
Date: 1982
Cabinet Type: Upright
Rarity: 8
Price Range: $250–350*
Notes: There is a bootleg version of this game called *Amigo*

ANGLER DANGLER

Manufacturer: Data East
Date: 1982
Cabinet Type: Upright
Rarity: 9
Price Range: $150–250*

ANTEATER

Manufacturer: Tago Electronics
Date: 1982
Cabinet Type: Upright
Rarity: 9
Price Range: $100–200*

ANTI-AIRCRAFT

Manufacturer: Atari
Date: 1975
Cabinet Type: Upright
Rarity: 9
Price Range: $50–150*
Notes: Sometimes referred to as *Anti-Aircraft II*

ARABIAN

Manufacturer: Atari
Date: 1983
Cabinet Type: Upright
Rarity: 8
Price Range: $150–300
Notes: Licensed from Sun Electronics Corp.

ARCADE CLASSICS

Manufacturer: Atari Games
Date: 1992
Cabinet Type: Upright
Rarity: Prototype
Price Range: $?
Notes: Designed to play two never-released games: *Super Centipede* and *Missile Command II;* see http://www.safestuff.com for pictures and info

ARCH RIVALS

Manufacturer: Bally Midway
Date: 1989
Cabinet Type: Upright
Rarity: 7
Price Range: $200–300

ARIAN MISSION

Manufacturer: SNK
Date: 1985
Cabinet Type: Upright
Rarity: 9
Price Range: $100–175*
Notes: Also known as *Alpha Mission;* Game for SNK's NEO-GEO system

ARKANOID

Manufacturer: Taito
Date: 1986
Cabinet Type: Upright
Rarity: 3
Price Range: $100–250
Notes: This game is most commonly found as a conversion kit—few dedicated versions exist
Cabinet Type: Cocktail
Rarity: 7
Price Range: $250–300

ARKANOID—REVENGE OF DOH

Manufacturer: Taito
Date: 1987
Cabinet Type: Upright
Rarity: 7
Price Range: $150–250
Notes: JAMMA kit; dedicated cabinets probably do not exist
Cabinet Type: Cocktail
Rarity: 7
Price Range: $250–300

ARM WRESTLING

Manufacturer: Nintendo
Date: 1985
Cabinet Type: Upright
Rarity: 8
Price Range: $150–200*
Notes: Released as a conversion kit for *Punch-Out*

ARMOR ATTACK

Manufacturer: Cinematronics
Date: 1980
Cabinet Type: Upright
Rarity: 7
Price Range: $300–500

ARMORED CAR

Manufacturer: Stern
Date: 1981
Cabinet Type: Upright
Rarity: 9
Price Range: $75–150*

ASTEROID

Manufacturer: Midway
Date: 1973
Cabinet Type: Upright
Rarity: 10
Price Range: $50–100*
Notes: Repackaged version of *Space Race*, licensed
from Atari

ASTEROIDS

Manufacturer: Atari
Date: 1979
Cabinet Type: Upright
Rarity: 2
Price Range: $350–900
Cabinet Type: Cocktail
Rarity: 7
Price Range: $600–1,000
Cabinet Type: Cabaret
Rarity: 8
Price Range: $450–1,000
Notes: Early production models of the upright ver-
sion were released in *Lunar Lander* cabinets

ASTEROIDS DELUXE

Manufacturer: Atari
Date: 1981
Cabinet Type: Upright
Rarity: 4
Price Range: $325–600
Cabinet Type: Cocktail
Rarity: 8
Price Range: $350–700
Cabinet Type: Cabaret
Rarity: 9
Price Range: $350–700

ASTRO BATTLE

Manufacturer: Sidam
Date: 1978
Cabinet Type: Upright
Rarity: 9
Price Range: $50–100*

ASTRO BLASTER

Manufacturer: Sega/Gremlin
Date: 1981
Cabinet Type: Upright
Rarity: 8
Price Range: $150–250*

ASTRO CHASE

Manufacturer: Exidy
Date: 1984
Cabinet Type: Upright
Rarity: 9
Price Range: $75–150*

ASTRO COMBAT

Manufacturer: Thomas Automatics, Inc.
Date: 1981
Cabinet Type: Upright
Rarity: 9
Price Range: $50–150*
Notes: Bootleg version of *Tank Battalion*

ASTRO FANTASIA

Manufacturer: Data East
Date: 1981
Cabinet Type: Upright
Rarity: 9
Price Range: $75–150*

ASTRO FIGHTER

Manufacturer: Gremlin
Date: 1980
Cabinet Type: Upright
Rarity: 8
Price Range: $75–150
Date: 1980
Cabinet Type: Cocktail
Rarity: 8
Price Range: $100–200

ASTRO INVADER

Manufacturer: Stern
Date: 1980
Cabinet Type: Upright
Rarity: 8
Price Range: $150–250

ASTRO RACE

Manufacturer: Taito
Notes: Copy of *Space Race*
Date: 1973
Cabinet Type: Upright
Rarity: 10
Price Range: $50–100*

ASTRO HOCKEY

Manufacturer: Brunswick
Date: 1974
Cabinet Type: Upright
Rarity: 9
Price Range: $50–100*

ASTRON BELT

Manufacturer: Sega
Date: 1983
Cabinet Type: Upright
Rarity: 9
Price Range: $650–750*
Notes: Laser disc space combat game; licensed to
Bally Midway

ATARI BASEBALL

Manufacturer: Atari
Date: 1979
Cabinet Type: Cocktail
Rarity: 8
Price Range: $250–400

ATARI BASKETBALL

Manufacturer: Atari
Date: 1979
Cabinet Type: Upright
Rarity: 7
Price Range: $400–600

ATARI FOOTBALL (2-PLAYER)

Manufacturer: Atari
Date: 1979
Cabinet Type: Cocktail
Rarity: 6
Price Range: $500–750
Notes: First game to use a trackball controller

ATARI FOOTBALL (4-PLAYER)

Manufacturer: Atari
Date: 1979
Cabinet Type: Cocktail
Rarity: 9
Price Range: $600–900*

ATARI SOCCER

Manufacturer: Atari
Date: 1979
Cabinet Type: Cocktail
Rarity: 9
Price Range: $300–500

ATOMIC BOY

Manufacturer: Irem
Date: 1985
Cabinet Type: Upright
Rarity: 9
Price Range: $100–175*

ATOMIC CASTLE

Manufacturer: Laserdisc Computer Systems
Date: 1984
Cabinet Type: Upright
Rarity: 10
Price Range: $500–700*

ATTACK

Manufacturer: Taito
Date: 1976
Cabinet Type: Upright
Rarity: 9
Price Range: $75–150*

ATTACK

Manufacturer: Exidy
Date: 1977
Cabinet Type: Upright
Rarity: 9
Price Range: $75–150*

AUTO TEST

Manufacturer: Capitol Projector Corp.
Date: 1975
Cabinet Type: Upright
Rarity: 10
Price Range: $50–100*

AVALANCHE

Manufacturer: Atari
Date: 1978
Cabinet Type: Upright
Rarity: 9
Price Range: $200–300

AVENGER

Manufacturer: Electra
Date: 1975
Cabinet Type: Upright
Rarity: 9
Price Range: $75–150*

AZTARAC

Manufacturer: Centuri
Date: 1983
Cabinet Type: Upright
Rarity: 10
Price Range: $400–700*
Notes: Color vector game with a unique bezel that features a round, convex section in the center; it is rumored that only 500 were produced

AZURIAN ATTACK

Manufacturer: Rait Electronics
Date: 1982
Cabinet Type: Upright
Rarity: 10
Price Range: $75–150*

B-WINGS

Manufacturer: Data East
Date: 1985
Cabinet Type: Upright
Rarity: 10
Price Range: $150–250*

BABY PAC-MAN

Manufacturer: Bally Midway
Date: 1982
Cabinet Type: Upright
Rarity: 7
Price Range: $500–900
Notes: Hybrid video/pinball game

BADLANDS

Manufacturer: Konami
Date: 1984
Cabinet Type: Upright
Rarity: 10
Price Range: $600–700*
Notes: Western-themed laser disc game

BADLANDS

Manufacturer: Atari
Date: 1989
Cabinet Type: Upright
Rarity: 9
Price Range: $200–400
Notes: The seventh and final game in Atari's *Sprint* series (which began in 1976 with *Sprint 2*)

BAGMAN
Manufacturer: Stern
Date: 1982
Cabinet Type: Upright
Rarity: 7
Price Range: $180–260
Notes: Licensed to Stern for distribution in the U.S., but a direct release version from Valadon Automation also exists

BALL PARK
Manufacturer: Taito
Date: 1979
Cabinet Type: Upright
Rarity: 9
Price Range: $50–150*

BALL PARK II
Manufacturer: Taito
Date: 1979
Cabinet Type: Upright
Rarity: 9
Price Range: $50–150*

BALLOON BOMBER
Manufacturer: Taito
Date: 1980
Cabinet Type: Upright
Rarity: 9
Price Range: $75–150*

BANDIDO
Manufacturer: Exidy
Date: 1980
Cabinet Type: Upright
Rarity: 8
Price Range: $150–350

BANK PANIC
Manufacturer: Sega
Date: 1983
Cabinet Type: Upright
Rarity: 9
Price Range: $200–300*
Notes: Distributed by Bally Midway

BARADUKE
Manufacturer: Namco
Date: 1985
Cabinet Type: Upright
Rarity: 9
Price Range: $150–250*
Notes: Also known as *Alien Sector*

BARRACUDA
Manufacturer: Coinex
Date: 1981
Cabinet Type: Upright
Rarity: 9
Price Range: $75–150*
Notes: Bootleg version of *Piranha*

BARRICADE
Manufacturer: Ramtek
Date: 1976
Cabinet Type: Upright
Rarity: 9
Price Range: $50–150*

BARRICADE II
Manufacturer: Taito
Date: 1977
Cabinet Type: Upright
Rarity: 9
Price Range: $50–150*

BARRIER
Manufacturer: Vectorbeam
Date: 1978
Cabinet Type: Upright
Rarity: 9
Price Range: $450–650*

BASKETBALL
Manufacturer: Taito
Date: 1974
Cabinet Type: Upright
Rarity: 9
Price Range: $75–150*

BATTLE CROSS
Manufacturer: Omori Electronics Corporation
Date: 1982
Cabinet Type: Upright
Rarity: 10+
Price Range: $?
Notes: Only one boardset is known to exist; no pricing information available due to rarity

BATTLE CRUISER M-12
Manufacturer: Sigma
Date: 1982
Cabinet Type: Upright
Rarity: 9
Price Range: $75–150*

BATTLE OF ATLANTIS
Manufacturer: Comsoft/Game World
Date: 1981
Cabinet Type: Upright
Rarity: 9
Price Range: $100–200*

THE BATTLE ROAD
Manufacturer: Irem
Date: 1984
Cabinet Type: Upright
Rarity: 9
Price Range: $150–250*

BATTLE STATION
Manufacturer: Centuri
Date: 1977
Cabinet Type: Upright
Rarity: 9
Price Range: $50–150*

BATTLE WINGS
Manufacturer: Data East
Date: 1984
Cabinet Type: Upright
Rarity: 9
Price Range: $150–250*

BATTLEZONE

Manufacturer: Atari
Date: 1980
Cabinet Type: Upright
Rarity: 5
Price Range: $400–800
Cabinet Type: Cabaret
Rarity: 8
Price Range: $600–800*
Notes: A more complex version was produced for the military. Only two "Military *Battlezone*" machines are known to exist.

BAZOOKA

Manufacturer: Project Support Engineering
Date: 1977
Cabinet Type: Upright
Rarity: 9
Price Range: $100–200*

BEASTIE FEASTIE

Manufacturer: Cardinal Amusement Products
Date: 1984
Cabinet Type: N/A
Rarity: 9
Price Range: $100–200*
Notes: An add-on board to convert *Pac-Man* into a new game. No dedicated cabinets exist.

BEEZER

Manufacturer: Tong
Date: 1982
Cabinet Type: N/A
Rarity: 9
Price Range: $100–200*
Notes: A conversion kit for *Pac-Man* and *Galaxian* machines. No dedicated cabinets exist.

BEGA'S BATTLE

Manufacturer: Data East
Date: 1983
Cabinet Type: Upright
Rarity: 10
Price Range: $600–700*
Notes: An anime laser disc game

BERZERK

Manufacturer: Stern
Date: 1980
Cabinet Type: Upright
Rarity: 7
Price Range: $300–500
Cocktail
Rarity: 8
Price Range: $400–600

BIGFOOT BONKERS

Manufacturer: Meadows
Date: 1976
Cabinet Type: Upright
Rarity: 9
Price Range: $50–100*

BIO ATTACK

Manufacturer: Taito
Date: 1983
Cabinet Type: Upright
Rarity: 9
Price Range: $75–150*

BIPLANE

Manufacturer: Fun Games, Inc.
Date: 1976
Cabinet Type: Upright
Rarity: 9
Price Range: $50–100*

BIPLANE 4

Manufacturer: Fun Games, Inc.
Date: 1976
Cabinet Type: Upright
Rarity: 9
Price Range: $50–150*
Notes: Four-player version of *BiPlane*

BIRDIE KING

Manufacturer: Taito
Date: 1982
Cabinet Type: Upright
Rarity: 5
Price Range: $100–300

BIRDIE KING II

Manufacturer: Taito
Date: 1983
Cabinet Type: Upright
Rarity: 3
Price Range: $100–300
Notes: Often found as conversions in non-Taito cabinets

BIRDIE KING III

Manufacturer: Taito
Date: 1984
Cabinet Type: Upright
Rarity: 5
Price Range: $100–300

BLACK WIDOW

Manufacturer: Atari
Date: 1982
Cabinet Type: Upright
Rarity: 8
Price Range: $500–800
Notes: The dedicated version uses the same cabinet as *Gravitar*

BLAST OFF

Manufacturer: Namco
Date: 1989
Cabinet Type: Upright
Rarity: 9
Price Range: $150–250*
Notes: Sequel to *Bosconian*

BLASTER

Manufacturer: Williams
Date: 1983
Cabinet Type: Upright
Rarity: 8
Price Range: $600–900*
Cabinet Type: Cockpit
Rarity: 10
Price Range: $850–1,300*
Cabinet Type: Duramold
Rarity: 10
Price Range: $700–1,200
Notes: Williams games in Duramold cabinets are highly collectible.

BLASTEROIDS
Manufacturer: Atari Games
Date: 1987
Cabinet Type: Upright
Rarity: 5
Price Range: $250–400
Notes: Third sequel to *Asteroids*

BLASTO
Manufacturer: Gremlin
Date: 1978
Cabinet Type: Upright
Rarity: 9
Price Range: $50–150*
Cabinet Type: Cocktail
Rarity: 99
Price Range: $75–175*

BLOCK GAME
Manufacturer: Konami
Date: 1978
Cabinet Type: Upright
Rarity: 9
Price Range: $50–100*
Notes: Konami's first American release (a *Breakout* clone)

BLOCKADE
Manufacturer: Gremlin
Date: 1976
Cabinet Type: Upright
Rarity: 9
Price Range: $50–100*

BLUE PRINT
Manufacturer: Bally Midway
Date: 1982
Cabinet Type: Upright
Rarity: 8
Price Range: $100–200
Cabinet Type: Cocktail
Rarity: 9
Price Range: $100–300
Cabinet Type: Cabaret
Rarity: 9
Price Range: $150–350*

BLUE SHARK
Manufacturer: Bally Midway
Date: 1978
Cabinet Type: Upright
Rarity: 9
Price Range: $75–150*

BOGEY MANOR
Manufacturer: Technos
Date: 1985
Cabinet Type: Upright
Rarity: 9
Price Range: $100–200*

BOMB BEE
Manufacturer: Namco
Date: 1979
Cabinet Type: Upright
Rarity: 9
Price Range: $200–300*
Notes: Sequel to *Gee Bee;* designed by Toru Iwatani, designer of *Pac-Man*

BOMB JACK
Manufacturer: Tehkan
Date: 1984
Cabinet Type: Upright
Rarity: 9
Price Range: $250–350*

BOMBS AWAY
Manufacturer: Meadows
Date: 1976
Cabinet Type: Upright
Rarity: 9
Price Range: $50–100*

BOOMER RANG'R
Manufacturer: Data East
Date: 1983
Cabinet Type: Upright
Rarity: 9
Price Range: $200–300*
Notes: Also known as *Genesis*

BOOMERANG
Manufacturer: Sunsoft
Date: 1985
Cabinet Type: Upright
Rarity: 9
Price Range: $150–250*

BOOT HILL
Manufacturer: Midway
Date: 1977
Cabinet Type: Upright
Rarity: 8
Price Range: $150–300*
Notes: Sequel to *Gun Fight*

BORDERLINE
Manufacturer: Sega
Date: 1981
Cabinet Type: Upright
Rarity: 9
Price Range: $75–150*

BOSCONIAN
Manufacturer: Midway
Date: 1981
Cabinet Type: Upright
Rarity: 8
Price Range: $150–350
Notes: Licensed from Namco
Cabinet Type: Cocktail
Rarity: 9
Price Range: $300–400
Cabinet Type: Cabaret
Rarity: 9
Price Range: $400–500*

BOULDER DASH
Manufacturer: Exidy
Date: 1984
Cabinet Type: Upright
Rarity: 9
Price Range: $100–200*

BOULDER DASH
Manufacturer: Data East
Date: 1985
Cabinet Type: Upright
Rarity: 9
Price Range: $150–250*
Notes: A Data East Cassette (DECO) version of the Exidy game

BOUNCER
Manufacturer: Entertainment Sciences
Date: 1984
Cabinet Type: Upright
Rarity: 9
Price Range: $150–250*

THE BOUNTY
Manufacturer: Orca
Date: 1982
Cabinet Type: Upright
Rarity: 9
Price Range: $100–200*

BOWLING ALLEY
Manufacturer: Capcom
Date: 1979
Cabinet Type: Cocktail
Rarity: 9
Price Range: $75–150*
Notes: Not to be confused with *Capcom Bowling*, which is much more common.

BOXING BUGS
Manufacturer: Cinematronics
Date: 1981
Cabinet Type: Upright
Rarity: 9
Price Range: $500–700*
Notes: Rare Cinematronics color vector game

BREAKOUT
Manufacturer: Atari
Date: 1976
Cabinet Type: Upright
Rarity: 8
Price Range: $75–150
Cabinet Type: Cocktail
Rarity: 9
Price Range: $100–200

BRISTLES
Manufacturer: Exidy
Date: 1984
Cabinet Type: Upright
Rarity: 9
Price Range: $75–150*

BUBBLE BOBBLE
Manufacturer: Taito
Date: 1986
Cabinet Type: Upright
Rarity: 6
Price Range: $100–250

BUBBLES
Manufacturer: Williams
Date: 1982
Cabinet Type: Upright
Rarity: 7
Price Range: $400–600
Cabinet Type: Cocktail
Rarity: 9
Price Range: $500–700
Cabinet Type: Cabaret
Rarity: 9
Price Range: $500–700
Cabinet Type: Duramold
Rarity: 8
Price Range: $700–1,000
Notes: Williams games in Duramold cabinets are highly collectible.

BUCK ROGERS PLANET OF ZOOM
Manufacturer: Sega
Date: 1982
Cabinet Type: Upright
Rarity: 7
Price Range: $250–400*
Cabinet Type: Cockpit
Rarity: 8
Price Range: $350–550*

BUGGY CHALLENGE
Manufacturer: Taito
Date: 1984
Cabinet Type: Upright
Rarity: 9
Price Range: $200–350
Cabinet Type: Cabaret
Rarity: 9
Price Range: $250–400*

BULL FIGHT
Manufacturer: Sega
Date: 1984
Cabinet Type: Upright
Rarity: 9
Price Range: $150–250*
Notes: Distributed by Bally Midway

BULLFROG
Manufacturer: Unknown
Date: 1981
Cabinet Type: Upright
Rarity: 9
Price Range: $100–200
Notes: Bootleg of *Frogger* in its own dedicated cabinet

BUMP 'N JUMP
Manufacturer: Bally Midway
Date: 1982
Cabinet Type: Upright
Rarity: 6
Price Range: $100–375
Cabinet Type: Cocktail
Rarity: 9
Price Range: $150–400
Notes: Licensed from Data East (DECO)

BUMP 'N JUMP
Manufacturer: Data East
Date: 1982
Cabinet Type: Upright
Rarity: 8
Price Range: $200–400
Notes: The original Data East Cassette (DECO) version of the game.

BURGERTIME
Manufacturer: Bally Midway
Date: 1982
Cabinet Type: Upright
Rarity: 4
Price Range: $350–800
Notes: Licensed from Data East
Cabinet Type: Cocktail
Rarity: 9
Price Range: $500–1,100

BURGERTIME
Manufacturer: Data East
Date: 1982
Cabinet Type: Upright
Rarity: 9
Price Range: $200–400
Notes: The Data East Cassette (DECO) version of the game.

BURNIN' RUBBER
Manufacturer: Data East
Date: 1982
Cabinet Type: Upright
Rarity: 9
Price Range: $100–200
Notes: Copy of *Bump 'n Jump*

CALIPSO
Manufacturer: Tago Electronics
Date: 1982
Cabinet Type: Upright
Rarity: 9
Price Range: $75–150
Notes: Licensed by Stern

CANYON BOMBER
Manufacturer: Atari
Date: 1977
Cabinet Type: Upright
Rarity: 9
Price Range: $50–150*

CAPCOM BOWLING
Manufacturer: Capcom
Date: 1988
Cabinet Type: Upright
Rarity: 2
Price Range: $100–250
Notes: Dedicated versions of this game are very uncommon; most are conversions. All dedicated versions are uprights.

CARNIVAL
Manufacturer: Sega/Gremlin
Date: 1980
Cabinet Type: Upright
Rarity: 7
Price Range: $200–450
Cabinet Type: Cocktail
Rarity: 9
Price Range: $250–500

CASINO STRIP
Manufacturer: Status
Date: 1985
Cabinet Type: Upright
Rarity: 10
Price Range: $200–300*
Notes: A laser disc strip poker game.

CAVELON
Manufacturer: Jetsoft
Date: 1983
Cabinet Type: Upright
Rarity: 9
Price Range: $75–150*

CAVEMAN
Manufacturer: Gottleib
Date: 1981
Cabinet Type: Upright
Rarity: 8
Price Range: $350–500*
Notes: The first pinball/video game hybrid

CENTIPEDE
Manufacturer: Atari
Date: 1980
Cabinet Type: Upright
Rarity: 2
Price Range: $400–1,000
Cabinet Type: Cocktail
Rarity: 6
Price Range: $600–900
Cabinet Type: Cabaret
Rarity: 7
Price Range: $550–900

CENTIPEDE/MILLIPEDE/MISSILE COMMAND
Manufacturer: Team Play
Date: 2001
Cabinet Type: Upright
Rarity: 1
Price Range: $1,500–3,500
Notes: A recent release that combines three classic Atari games (and a bonus bowling game) in one cabinet.

CERBERUS
Manufacturer: Cinematronics
Date: 1985
Cabinet Type: Upright
Rarity: 9
Price Range: $200–300*

CHACK'N POP
Manufacturer: Taito
Date: 1983
Cabinet Type: Upright
Rarity: 9
Price Range: $100–200

CHALLENGE

Manufacturer: Micro
Date: 1974
Cabinet Type: Upright
Rarity: 9
Price Range: $50–100*

CHALLENGER

Manufacturer: Centuri
Date: 1981
Cabinet Type: Upright
Rarity: 9
Price Range: $75–150*

CHAMPION BASEBALL

Manufacturer: Sega
Date: 1982
Cabinet Type: Upright
Rarity: 8
Price Range: $100–200
Cabinet Type: Cocktail
Rarity: 9
Price Range: $150–250*
Notes: Often found as conversions in non-Sega cabinets

CHAMPION BASEBALL II

Manufacturer: Sega
Date: 1983
Cabinet Type: Upright
Rarity: 9
Price Range: $100–200*

CHAMPION BOXING

Manufacturer: Sega
Date: 1983
Cabinet Type: Upright
Rarity: 9
Price Range: $100–200*

CHAMPIONSHIP SPRINT

Manufacturer: Atari Games
Date: 1986
Cabinet Type: Upright
Rarity: 2
Price Range: $250–300
Notes: Atari System II game; sixth game in Atari's *Sprint* series

CHANGE LANES

Manufacturer: Taito
Date: 1983
Cabinet Type: Upright
Rarity: 8
Price Range: $100–250*

CHANGES

Manufacturer: Orca
Date: 1982
Cabinet Type: Upright
Rarity: 9
Price Range: $75–150*
Notes: Maze game similar to *Pac-Man*

CHECK MAN

Manufacturer: Zilec-Zenitone
Date: 1982
Cabinet Type: Upright
Rarity: 9
Price Range: $75–150*

CHECKMATE

Manufacturer: Midway
Date: 1977
Cabinet Type: Upright
Rarity: 9
Price Range: $50–100*

CHEEKY MOUSE

Manufacturer: Universal
Date: 1980
Cabinet Type: Upright
Rarity: 9
Price Range: $75–150*
Cabinet Type: Cocktail
Rarity: 9
Price Range: $100–200*

CHEYENNE

Manufacturer: Exidy
Date: 1984
Cabinet Type: Upright
Rarity: 8
Price Range: $100–300
Notes: One of several games in the Exidy shooting series that included *Crossbow, Chiller,* and *Crackshot*

CHICKEN SHIFT

Manufacturer: Bally Sente
Date: 1984
Cabinet Type: Upright
Rarity: 9
Price Range: $100–200*
Notes: Sente games often appear as conversions in non-Sente cabinets

CHILLER

Manufacturer: Exidy
Date: 1986
Cabinet Type: Upright
Rarity: 9
Price Range: $150–350*
Notes: One of several games in the Exidy shooting series that included *Crossbow, Cheyenne,* and *Crackshot*

CHINESE HERO

Manufacturer: Taiyo System
Date: 1984
Cabinet Type: Upright
Rarity: 9
Price Range: $100–200*

CHOPLIFTER

Manufacturer: Sega
Date: 1986
Cabinet Type: Upright
Rarity: 7
Price Range: $350–400
Notes: Often found as conversions in non-Sega cabinets

CIRCUS

Manufacturer: Exidy
Date: 1977
Cabinet Type: Upright
Rarity: 9
Price Range: $50–100*

CIRCUS CHARLIE

Manufacturer: Konami
Date: 1984
Cabinet Type: Upright
Rarity: 8
Price Range: $250–400
Notes: Distributed by Centuri

CISCO 400

Manufacturer: Taito
Date: 1977
Cabinet Type: Upright
Rarity: 9
Price Range: $50–100*
Notes: Clone of *Sprint 2*

CITY CONNECTION

Manufacturer: Jaleco
Date: 1985
Cabinet Type: Upright
Rarity: 9
Price Range: $100–200*

CKIDZO

Manufacturer: Meadows
Date: 1976
Cabinet Type: Upright
Rarity: 9
Price Range: $50–100*

CLEAN SWEEP

Manufacturer: Ramtek
Date: 1974
Cabinet Type: Upright
Rarity: 9
Price Range: $50–100*

CLIFF HANGER

Manufacturer: Stern
Date: 1983
Cabinet Type: Upright
Rarity: 9
Price Range: $1,000–2,500*
Notes: Laser disc game based on the Japanese cartoon film series *Lupin III;* very collectible

CLOAK AND DAGGER

Manufacturer: Atari
Date: 1983
Cabinet Type: Upright
Rarity: 9
Price Range: $350–500*
Notes: Often found as a conversion kit in Williams cabinets; price is for a dedicated machine (conversions should sell for $200–300)

CLOUD 9

Manufacturer: Atari
Date: 1983
Cabinet Type: Upright
Rarity: Prototype
Price Range: $?
Notes: No pricing information available

CLOWNS

Manufacturer: Bally Midway
Date: 1978
Cabinet Type: Upright
Rarity: 8
Price Range: $100–200*
Notes: Copy of Exidy's *Circus*
Cabinet Type: Cocktail
Rarity: 9
Price Range: $150–250*

CLUSTER BUSTER

Manufacturer: Data East
Date: 1983
Cabinet Type: Upright
Rarity: 9
Price Range: $75–150*

COBRA COMMAND

Manufacturer: Data East
Date: 1984
Cabinet Type: Upright
Rarity: 9
Price Range: $350–500*
Notes: Laser disc game made as a conversion kit for *Dragon's Lair, Space Ace,* and *M.A.C.H. III* cabinets

COBRA COMMAND

Manufacturer: Data East
Date: 1988
Cabinet Type: Upright
Rarity: 8
Price Range: $75–150
Notes: A horizontal shooter loosely based on the 1984 laser disc game

COBRA GUNSHIP

Manufacturer: Meadows
Date: 1976
Cabinet Type: Upright
Rarity: 9
Price Range: $50–100*

COLONY 7

Manufacturer: Taito
Date: 1981
Cabinet Type: Upright
Rarity: 9
Price Range: $200–300*

COMBAT

Manufacturer: Exidy
Date: 1985
Cabinet Type: Upright
Rarity: 9
Price Range: $150–350*
Notes: One of several games in the Exidy shooting series that included *Crossbow, Cheyenne,* and *Crackshot*

COMMANDO
Manufacturer: Data East
Date: 1985
Cabinet Type: Upright
Rarity: 4
Price Range: $150–300

COMMANDO
Manufacturer: Sega
Date: 1983
Cabinet Type: Upright
Rarity: 9
Price Range: $100–200*

COMOTION
Manufacturer: Gremlin
Date: 1977
Cabinet Type: Cocktail
Rarity: 9
Price Range: $50–100*

COMPETITION GOLF
Manufacturer: Data East
Date: 1985
Cabinet Type: Upright
Rarity: 9
Price Range: $100–200*

COMPUTER OTHELLO
Manufacturer: Nintendo
Date: 1978
Cabinet Type: Cocktail
Rarity: 9
Price Range: $50–100*

COMPUTER SPACE (1 PLAYER)
Manufacturer: Nutting Associates
Date: 1971
Cabinet Type: Upright
Rarity: 9
Price Range: $1,500–3,500
Notes: The first arcade video game ever made; single-player version; nonworking units often sell for over $3,000

COMPUTER SPACE (2 PLAYER)
Manufacturer: Nutting Associates
Date: 1971
Cabinet Type: Upright
Rarity: 10
Price Range: $2,500–4,500
Notes: Rarer 2-player version

COMPUTER SPACE BALL
Manufacturer: Nutting Associates
Date: 1972
Cabinet Type: Upright
Rarity: 10
Price Range: $75–150*

CONGO BONGO
Manufacturer: Sega
Date: 1983
Cabinet Type: Upright
Rarity: 7
Price Range: $350–550
Cabinet Type: Cocktail
Rarity: 9
Price Range: $400–600*
Notes: Known in Europe as *Tip Top*

CONGORILLA
Manufacturer: Orca
Date: 1981
Cabinet Type: Upright
Rarity: 9
Price Range: $150–250*
Notes: Bootleg of *Donkey Kong*

CONSTELLA
Manufacturer: Nichibutsu
Date: 1982
Cabinet Type: Upright
Rarity: 9
Price Range: $100–200*

CONTRA
Manufacturer: Konami
Date: 1987
Cabinet Type: Upright
Rarity: 7
Price Range: $125–300
Notes: Known in Europe as *Gryzor*

COP 01
Manufacturer: Nichibutsu
Date: 1985
Cabinet Type: Upright
Rarity: 9
Price Range: $75–150*

COPS 'N ROBBERS
Manufacturer: Atari
Date: 1976
Cabinet Type: Upright
Rarity: 9
Price Range: $50–100*

COSMIC ALIEN
Manufacturer: Universal
Date: 1980
Cabinet Type: Upright
Rarity: 8
Price Range: $100–200*
Cabinet Type: Cocktail
Rarity: 9
Price Range: $150–250*

COSMIC AVENGER
Manufacturer: Universal
Date: 1981
Cabinet Type: Upright
Rarity: 8
Price Range: $150–250*

COSMIC CHASM
Manufacturer: Cinematronics
Date: 1983
Cabinet Type: Upright
Rarity: 10
Price Range: $500–600*
Notes: Color vector game; originally produced for the Vectrex, this is the first home console game to be converted to an arcade game (instead of vice versa)

COSMIC GUERILLA
Manufacturer: Universal
Date: 1979
Cabinet Type: Upright
Rarity: 8
Price Range: $150–250

COSMIC MONSTERS
Manufacturer: Universal
Date: 1981
Cabinet Type: Upright
Rarity: 9
Price Range: $50–150*
Cabinet Type: Cocktail
Rarity: 9
Price Range: $100–200
Notes: Clone of *Space Invaders*

COSMIKAZE
Manufacturer: Game-A-Tron
Date: 1981
Cabinet Type: Upright
Rarity: 9
Price Range: $75–150*

COSMOS
Manufacturer: Century Electronics
Date: 1981
Cabinet Type: Upright
Rarity: 9
Price Range: $75–150*

COUNTDOWN
Manufacturer: Volley
Date: 1974
Cabinet Type: Upright
Rarity: 9
Price Range: $50–100*

CRACKSHOT
Manufacturer: Exidy
Date: 1987
Cabinet Type: Upright
Rarity: 9
Price Range: $150–350*
Notes: One of several games in the Exidy shooting series that included *Crossbow, Cheyenne,* and *Chiller*

CRASH
Manufacturer: Exidy
Date: 1979
Cabinet Type: Upright
Rarity: 9
Price Range: $75–150*

CRASH 'N SCORE
Manufacturer: Atari
Date: 1975
Cabinet Type: Upright
Rarity: 9
Price Range: $50–100*

CRASHING RACE
Manufacturer: Taito
Date: 1976
Cabinet Type: Upright
Rarity: 9
Price Range: $50–100*

CRATER RAIDER
Manufacturer: Bally Midway
Date: 1984
Cabinet Type: Upright
Rarity: 9
Price Range: $150–300*

CRAZY BALLOON
Manufacturer: Taito
Date: 1980
Cabinet Type: Upright
Rarity: 9
Price Range: $50–100*
Cabinet Type: Cocktail
Rarity: 9
Price Range: $75–150*

CRAZY CLIMBER
Manufacturer: Nichibutsu
Date: 1980
Cabinet Type: Upright
Rarity: 7
Price Range: $425–900
Cabinet Type: Cocktail
Rarity: 9
Price Range: $450–900
Notes: Licensed by Taito; several dedicated cabinets exist: Taito, Nichibutsu standard, and Nichibutsu Deluxe (which was taller)

CRAZY KONG
Manufacturer: Falcon
Date: 1981
Cabinet Type: Upright
Rarity: 8
Price Range: $250–400
Notes: *Donkey Kong* clone licensed by Nintendo for release in foreign markets

CRAZY KONG JR.
Manufacturer: Falcon
Date: 1982
Cabinet Type: Upright
Rarity: 9
Price Range: $200–350*
Notes: Copy of *Donkey Kong Junior*

CRAZYFOOT
Manufacturer: Bally Midway
Date: 1974
Cabinet Type: Upright
Rarity: 9
Price Range: $50–100*

CROSSFIRE
Manufacturer: Taito
Date: 1977
Cabinet Type: Upright
Rarity: 9
Price Range: $75–150*
Notes: Copy of *Bazooka*

CROSSBOW
Manufacturer: Exidy
Date: 1983
Cabinet Type: Upright
Rarity: 7
Price Range: $150–350*
Notes: One of several games in the Exidy shooting series that included *Crackshot, Cheyenne,* and *Chiller*

CROWN'S GOLF
Manufacturer: Sega
Date: 1984
Cabinet Type: Upright
Rarity: 7
Price Range: $150–250*
Notes: Distributed by Kitcorp

CROWN'S GOLF IN HAWAII
Manufacturer: Sega
Date: 1985
Cabinet Type: Upright
Rarity: 9
Price Range: $150–250*
Notes: Distributed by Kitcorp; upgrade kit for *Crown's Golf*

CRUISIN'
Manufacturer: Kitcorp
Date: 1984
Cabinet Type: Upright
Rarity: 9
Price Range: $100–200*
Notes: Licensed from Jaleco

CRUSH ROLLER
Manufacturer: Kural Samno
Date: 1981
Cabinet Type: Upright
Rarity: 9
Price Range: $100–200*
Notes: Released by Williams in the U.S. as *Make Trax*

CRYSTAL CASTLES
Manufacturer: Atari
Date: 1983
Cabinet Type: Upright
Rarity: 4
Price Range: $175–400
Cabinet Type: Cocktail
Rarity: 9
Price Range: $250–500*
Notes: Often seen as a conversion in *Missile Command* and other Atari trackball game cabinets

CUBE QUEST
Manufacturer: Simurtek
Date: 1984
Cabinet Type: Upright
Rarity: 9
Price Range: $600–800*
Notes: Laser disc game; for more info see http://www.dragons-lair-project.com

CURVE BALL
Manufacturer: Mylstar
Date: 1984
Cabinet Type: Upright
Rarity: 9
Price Range: $150–200*

CUTIE Q
Manufacturer: Namco
Date: 1979
Cabinet Type: Upright
Rarity: 9
Price Range: $75–150*
Notes: Designed by Toru Iwatani, the designer of *Pac-Man*

D-DAY
Manufacturer: Olympia
Date: 1981
Cabinet Type: Upright
Rarity: 9
Price Range: $75–150*

D-DAY
Manufacturer: Jaleco
Date: 1984
Cabinet Type: Upright
Rarity: 9
Price Range: $75–150*

DAMBUSTERS
Manufacturer: GAT
Date: 1981
Cabinet Type: Upright
Rarity: 9
Price Range: $75–150*

DANGER ZONE
Manufacturer: Leijac
Date: 1986
Cabinet Type: Upright
Rarity: 9
Price Range: $250–400*
Notes: Cabinet has a unique swiveling monitor with dual gun-grip joysticks

DARK INVADER
Manufacturer: Ramtek
Date: 1978
Cabinet Type: Upright
Rarity: 10
Price Range: $200–300*
Notes: The game actually has a real neon laser housed inside that shoots the targets

DARK PLANET

Manufacturer: Stern
Date: 1982
Cabinet Type: Upright
Rarity: 10
Price Range: $300–500*
Notes: Unique cabinet with a 3-D visual effect produced by detailed backdrops and mirrors

DARK WARRIOR

Manufacturer: Century Electronics
Date: 1981
Cabinet Type: Upright
Rarity: 9
Price Range: $75–150*

DAVIS CUP

Manufacturer: Taito
Date: 1973
Cabinet Type: Upright
Rarity: 9
Price Range: $50–100*

DAWN PATROL

Manufacturer: Micro
Date: 1978
Cabinet Type: Upright
Rarity: 9
Price Range: $75–150*

DAZZLER

Manufacturer: Century Electronics
Date: 1982
Cabinet Type: Upright
Rarity: 9
Price Range: $75–150*

DEAD EYE

Manufacturer: Meadows
Date: 1978
Cabinet Type: Upright
Rarity: 9
Price Range: $50–100*

DEATH RACE

Manufacturer: Exidy
Date: 1976
Cabinet Type: Upright
Rarity: 9
Price Range: $600–1,000
Notes: Has the distinction of being the first game to create an uproar over video game violence

DECO CASSETTE SYSTEM

Manufacturer: Data East
Date: 1981
Cabinet Type: Upright
Rarity: 8
Price Range: $200–300*
Notes: Cabinet that plays Data East Cassette (DECO) games including *Bump 'n Jump* and *BurgerTime*

DEEP SCAN

Manufacturer: Sega/Gremlin
Date: 1979
Cabinet Type: Upright
Rarity: 9
Price Range: $75–150*

DEFENDER

Manufacturer: Williams
Date: 1980
Cabinet Type: Upright
Rarity: 3
Price Range: $500–1,000
Cabinet Type: Cocktail
Rarity: 8
Price Range: $550–900
Notes: A very popular collectible

DEMOLITION DERBY

Manufacturer: Bally Midway
Date: 1984
Cabinet Type: Upright
Rarity: 8
Price Range: $200–300*
Cabinet Type: Cocktail
Rarity: 9
Price Range: $250–350*

DEMOLITION DERBY

Manufacturer: Chicago Coin
Date: 1977
Cabinet Type: Upright
Rarity: 9
Price Range: $50–100*

DEMON

Manufacturer: Rock-Ola
Date: 1982
Cabinet Type: Upright
Rarity: 9
Price Range: $75–150*

DEPTHCHARGE

Manufacturer: Gremlin
Date: 1977
Cabinet Type: Upright
Rarity: 9
Price Range: $50–100*

DESERT FOX

Manufacturer: Milwaukee Coin Industries, Ltd.
Date: 1976
Cabinet Type: Upright
Rarity: 9
Price Range: $50–100*

DESERT GUN

Manufacturer: Midway
Date: 1977
Cabinet Type: Upright
Rarity: 9
Price Range: $50–100*

DESERT PATROL

Manufacturer: Project Support Engineering
Date: 1977
Cabinet Type: Upright
Rarity: 9
Price Range: $50–100*

DESERT RACE

Manufacturer: Moppet Video
Date: 1982
Cabinet Type: Upright
Rarity: 9
Price Range: $200–300*
Notes: This is a miniature sized game (about 3 feet high) made for children

DESTROYER

Manufacturer: Atari
Date: 1977
Cabinet Type: Upright
Rarity: 9
Price Range: $75–150*

DESTRUCTION DERBY

Manufacturer: Exidy
Date: 1975
Cabinet Type: Upright
Rarity: 9
Price Range: $75–150*

DEVASTATOR

Manufacturer: Williams
Date: 1984
Cabinet Type: Upright
Rarity: Prototype
Price Range: $?
Notes: No pricing information available

DEVIL FISH

Manufacturer: Arctic
Date: 1982
Cabinet Type: Upright
Rarity: 9
Price Range: $75–150*

DEVIL ZONE

Manufacturer: Universal
Date: 1980
Cabinet Type: Upright
Rarity: 9
Price Range: $50–100*

DIG DUG

Manufacturer: Atari
Date: 1982
Cabinet Type: Upright
Rarity: 3
Price Range: $250–500
Cabinet Type: Cocktail
Rarity: 8
Price Range: $400–600
Cabinet Type: Cabaret
Rarity: 8
Price Range: $400–600
Notes: Licensed from Namco. Only about 500 cabaret *Dig Dugs* were produced

DIG DUG II

Manufacturer: Namco
Date: 1985
Cabinet Type: Upright
Rarity: 9
Price Range: $300–500*

DIGGER

Manufacturer: Sega/Gremlin
Date: 1980
Cabinet Type: Upright
Rarity: 9
Price Range: $50–150*

DISCS OF TRON

Manufacturer: Bally Midway
Date: 1983
Cabinet Type: Upright
Rarity: 8
Price Range: $650–800
Cabinet Type: Environmental
Rarity: 9
Price Range: $800–1,200
Notes: Very collectible

DO! RUN RUN

Manufacturer: Universal
Date: 1984
Cabinet Type: Upright
Rarity: 9
Price Range: $150–250
Notes: Fourth game in the *Mr. Do* series; only released as an upgrade kit for existing games (no dedicated version)

DOG FIGHT

Manufacturer: Thunderbolt
Date: 1983
Cabinet Type: Upright
Rarity: 9
Price Range: $75–150*

DOG PATCH

Manufacturer: Midway
Date: 1978
Cabinet Type: Upright
Rarity: 9
Price Range: $50–100*

DOMINO MAN

Manufacturer: Bally Midway
Date: 1983
Cabinet Type: Upright
Rarity: 9
Price Range: $200–300*
Cabinet Type: Cocktail
Rarity: 9
Price Range: $350–450*
Cabinet Type: Cabaret
Rarity: 9
Price Range: $350–450*

DOMINOS

Manufacturer: Atari
Date: 1977
Cabinet Type: Upright
Rarity: 9
Price Range: $50–100*

DONKEY KONG
Manufacturer: Nintendo
Date: 1981
Cabinet Type: Upright
Rarity: 2
Price Range: $400–1,000
Cabinet Type: Cocktail
Rarity: 6
Price Range: $400–800
Cabinet Type: Cabaret
Rarity: 8
Price Range: $500–800*

DONKEY KONG 3
Manufacturer: Nintendo
Date: 1983
Cabinet Type: Upright
Rarity: 4
Price Range: $300–500
Notes: Most are conversions in *Donkey Kong* or *Donkey Kong Junior* cabinets

DONKEY KONG JUNIOR
Manufacturer: Nintendo
Date: 1982
Cabinet Type: Upright
Rarity: 3
Price Range: $375–710
Cabinet Type: Cocktail
Rarity: 7
Price Range: $310–550

DOUBLE DRAGON
Manufacturer: Taito
Date: 1987
Cabinet Type: Upright
Rarity: 4
Price Range: $150–300
Notes: Often seen as a conversion in nondedicated cabinets

DOUBLE DRAGON II—THE REVENGE
Manufacturer: Technos
Date: 1988
Cabinet Type: Upright
Rarity: 5
Price Range: $250–300
Notes: Often seen as a conversion in nondedicated cabinets

DOUBLE DRIBBLE
Manufacturer: Konami
Date: 1986
Cabinet Type: Upright
Rarity: 4
Price Range: $50–150
Notes: Often seen as a conversion in nondedicated cabinets

DOUBLE PLAY
Manufacturer: Midway
Date: 1977
Cabinet Type: Upright
Rarity: 9
Price Range: $50–100*
Cabinet Type: Cocktail
Rarity: 9
Price Range: $75–150*

DRAG RACE
Manufacturer: Kee Games
Date: 1979
Cabinet Type: Upright
Rarity: 9
Price Range: $50–100*

DRAGON BUSTER
Manufacturer: Namco
Date: 1984
Cabinet Type: Upright
Rarity: 9
Price Range: $150–250*

DRAGON'S LAIR
Manufacturer: Cinematronics
Date: 1983
Cabinet Type: Upright
Rarity: 7
Price Range: $1,000–1,500
Notes: Very collectible; European versions were distributed by Atari

DRAGON'S LAIR II: TIME WARP
Manufacturer: Leland
Date: 1991
Cabinet Type: Upright
Rarity: 8
Price Range: $1,000–1,200
Notes: Belated sequel to *Dragon's Lair*

DRIBBLING
Manufacturer: Model Racing
Date: 1983
Cabinet Type: Cocktail
Rarity: 9
Price Range: $75–150*

DRIVING FORCE
Manufacturer: Shinkai, Inc.
Date: 1984
Cabinet Type: Upright
Rarity: 9
Price Range: $75–150*

DYNAMIC SKI
Manufacturer: Taiyo System
Date: 1984
Cabinet Type: Upright
Rarity: 9
Price Range: $100–200*

EAGLE
Manufacturer: Centuri
Date: 1980
Cabinet Type: Upright
Rarity: 9
Price Range: $100–200*
Cabinet Type: Cabaret
Rarity: 9
Price Range: $150–250*

EARTH FRIEND
Manufacturer: Bally Midway
Date: 1982
Cabinet Type: Environmental
Rarity: Prototype
Price Range: $?
Notes: No pricing information available

EGGS

Manufacturer: Universal
Date: 1983
Cabinet Type: Upright
Rarity: 9
Price Range: $75–150*
Notes: Copy of *Scrambled Eggs*

ELECTRA

Manufacturer: Electra Games, Inc.
Date: 1975
Cabinet Type: Cocktail
Rarity: 9
Price Range: $50–100*

THE ELECTRIC YO-YO

Manufacturer: Taito
Date: 1982
Cabinet Type: Upright
Rarity: 9
Price Range: $150–250*

ELEPONG

Manufacturer: Taito
Date: 1973
Cabinet Type: Upright
Rarity: 9
Price Range: $50–100*

ELEVATOR ACTION

Manufacturer: Taito
Date: 1983
Cabinet Type: Upright
Rarity: 4
Price Range: $300–500

ELEVATOR ACTION II

Manufacturer: Taito
Date: 1994
Cabinet Type: Upright
Rarity: 8
Price Range: $300–500*
Notes: Also known as *Elevator Action Returns*

ELIMINATION

Manufacturer: Kee Games
Date: 1974
Cabinet Type: Cocktail
Rarity: 9
Price Range: $50–100*
Notes: Copy of *Quadrapong*

ELIMINATOR

Manufacturer: Sega/Gremlin
Date: 1981
Cabinet Type: Upright
Rarity: 8
Price Range: $300–500*
Cabinet Type: Cocktail
Rarity: 9
Price Range: $500–600*
Cabinet Type: Cocktail (w/canopy)
Rarity: 10
Price Range: $600–800*
Notes: The cocktail version is the only 4-player vector game ever made

THE EMPIRE STRIKES BACK

Manufacturer: Atari Games
Date: 1985
Cabinet Type: Upright
Rarity: 8
Price Range: $600–900*
Cabinet Type: Cockpit
Rarity: 8
Price Range: $800–1,200*
Notes: This is a conversion kit for Atari's *Star Wars* game; it is not uncommon to find cabinets with both board sets in them

THE END

Manufacturer: Stern
Date: 1980
Cabinet Type: Upright
Rarity: 9
Price Range: $75–150*
Cabinet Type: Cocktail
Rarity: 9
Price Range: $100–200*
Notes: Licensed from Konami

ENIGMA II

Manufacturer: Game Plan
Date: 1981
Cabinet Type: Upright
Rarity: 9
Price Range: $100–200*

EQUITES

Manufacturer: Alpha Denshi/Sega
Date: 1984
Cabinet Type: Upright
Rarity: 9
Price Range: $75–150*

ESCAPE FROM THE PLANET OF THE ROBOT MONSTER

Manufacturer: Atari Games
Date: 1989
Cabinet Type: Upright
Rarity: 8
Price Range: $300–500

ESPIAL

Manufacturer: Venture Line
Date: 1983
Cabinet Type: Upright
Rarity: 9
Price Range: $75–150*
Notes: Licensed from Orca

EXCITING HOUR

Manufacturer: Technos
Date: 1985
Cabinet Type: Upright
Rarity: 9
Price Range: $100–200

EXCITING SOCCER

Manufacturer: Alpha Denshi
Date: 1983
Cabinet Type: Upright
Rarity: 9
Price Range: $75–150*

EXCITING SOCCER II

Manufacturer: Alpha Denshi
Date: 1984
Cabinet Type: Upright
Rarity: 9
Price Range: $75–150*

EXERION

Manufacturer: Taito
Date: 1983
Cabinet Type: Upright
Rarity: 8
Price Range: $200–300
Cabinet Type: Cabaret
Rarity: 8
Price Range: $150–250
Notes: Licensed from Jaleco

EXODUS

Manufacturer: Subelectro
Date: 1979
Cabinet Type: Upright
Rarity: 9
Price Range: $75–150*

EXPLORER

Manufacturer: Data East
Date: 1982
Cabinet Type: Upright
Rarity: 9
Price Range: $150–250*
Notes: Game for the Data East Cassette (DECO) system

EXPRESS RAIDER

Manufacturer: Data East
Date: 1985
Cabinet Type: Upright
Rarity: 9
Price Range: $100–200*
Notes: Also known as *Western Express*

EXTRA BASES

Manufacturer: Midway
Date: 1980
Cabinet Type: Upright
Rarity: 9
Price Range: $75–150*

EXTRA INNINGS

Manufacturer: Midway
Date: 1978
Cabinet Type: Upright
Rarity: 9
Price Range: $50–100*

EYES

Manufacturer: Rock-Ola
Date: 1982
Cabinet Type: Upright
Rarity: 9
Price Range: $150–250*

THE FAIRYLAND STORY

Manufacturer: Taito
Date: 1985
Cabinet Type: Upright
Rarity: 9
Price Range: $150–300*

FANTASY

Manufacturer: Rock-Ola
Date: 1981
Cabinet Type: Upright
Rarity: 9
Price Range: $75–150*
Cabinet Type: Cocktail
Rarity: 9
Price Range: $100–200*

FAST FREDDIE

Manufacturer: Atari
Date: 1982
Cabinet Type: Upright
Rarity: 9
Price Range: $200–350*

FAX

Manufacturer: Exidy
Date: 1983
Cabinet Type: Unique
Rarity: 10
Price Range: $75–150*
Notes: Trivia game; cabinet was the size and shape of a jukebox

FIELD COMBAT

Manufacturer: Jaleco
Date: 1985
Cabinet Type: Upright
Rarity: 9
Price Range: $100–200*

FIELD GOAL

Manufacturer: Taito
Date: 1979
Cabinet Type: Upright
Rarity: 9
Price Range: $75–150*
Cabinet Type: Cocktail
Rarity: 9
Price Range: $100–200*

FIGHTING ICE HOCKEY

Manufacturer: Data East
Date: 1984
Cabinet Type: Upright
Rarity: 9
Price Range: $100–200*

FINAL LAP

Manufacturer: Atari Games
Date: 1987
Cabinet Type: Upright
Rarity: 8
Price Range: $350–450
Cabinet Type: Cockpit
Rarity: 6
Price Range: $500–600
Notes: Licensed from Namco; the first multiplayer linked arcade racing game

FIRE ONE!

Manufacturer: Exidy
Date: 1979
Cabinet Type: Upright
Rarity: 9
Price Range: $75–150*

FIRE POWER
Manufacturer: Allied Leisure
Date: 1975
Cabinet Type: Upright
Rarity: 9
Price Range: $75–150*

FIRE TRUCK
Manufacturer: Atari
Date: 1978
Cabinet Type: Cockpit
Rarity: 9
Price Range: $100–200*

FIREFOX
Manufacturer: Atari
Date: 1984
Cabinet Type: Upright
Rarity: 9
Price Range: $500–600*
Cabinet Type: Cockpit
Rarity: 9
Price Range: $700–800*
Notes: Laser disc game based on the Clint Eastwood film

FISCO 400
Manufacturer: Taito
Date: 1977
Cabinet Type: Upright
Rarity: 9
Price Range: $100–200*

FISHING
Manufacturer: Data East
Date: 1982
Cabinet Type: Upright
Rarity: 9
Price Range: $75–150*

FITTER
Manufacturer: Taito
Date: 1981
Cabinet Type: Upright
Rarity: 9
Price Range: $100–200*
Cabinet Type: Cocktail
Rarity: 9
Price Range: $250–300*
Notes: Copy of *Round-Up*

FLASHGAL
Manufacturer: Sega
Date: 1985
Cabinet Type: Upright
Rarity: 9
Price Range: $75–150*

FLICKY
Manufacturer: Sega
Date: 1984
Cabinet Type: Upright
Rarity: 9
Price Range: $100–200
Notes: Distributed by Bally Midway

FLIM-FLAM
Manufacturer: Meadows
Date: 1974
Cabinet Type: Upright
Rarity: 9
Price Range: $50–100*
Cabinet Type: Cocktail
Rarity: 9
Price Range: $50–100*

FLIP AND FLOP
Manufacturer: Exidy
Date: 1984
Cabinet Type: Upright
Rarity: 9
Price Range: $75–150*

FLIP-OUT
Manufacturer: Volley
Date: 1975
Cabinet Type: Upright
Rarity: 9
Price Range: $50–100*
Cabinet Type: Cocktail
Rarity: 9
Price Range: $50–100*

FLY-BOY
Manufacturer: Kaneko
Date: 1982
Cabinet Type: Upright
Rarity: 9
Price Range: $75–150*

FLYING FORTRESS
Manufacturer: Electra Games, Inc.
Date: 1977
Cabinet Type: Upright
Rarity: 9
Price Range: $50–100*

FLYING FORTRESS II
Manufacturer: Taito
Date: 1977
Cabinet Type: Upright
Rarity: 9
Price Range: $50–100*

FLYING SHARK
Manufacturer: Model Racing
Date: 1977
Cabinet Type: Upright
Rarity: 9
Price Range: $50–100*

FONZ
Manufacturer: Sega/Gremlin
Date: 1976
Cabinet Type: Upright
Rarity: 10
Price Range: $150–300*
Notes: Based on the *Happy Days* character

FOOD FIGHT
Manufacturer: Atari
Date: 1983
Cabinet Type: Upright
Rarity: 7
Price Range: $500–800
Cabinet Type: Cocktail
Rarity: 8
Price Range: $600–800

FORMATION Z
Manufacturer: Jaleco
Date: 1984
Cabinet Type: Upright
Rarity: 9
Price Range: $200–300*
Notes: Also known as *Aeroboto* (released by Williams)

FORMULA K
Manufacturer: Kee Games
Date: 1974
Cabinet Type: Upright
Rarity: 9
Price Range: $50–100*

FORTRESS
Manufacturer: Sega/Gremlin
Date: 1978
Cabinet Type: Upright
Rarity: 9
Price Range: $50–100*

FREEZE
Manufacturer: Cinematronics
Date: 1982
Cabinet Type: Upright
Rarity: 9
Price Range: $100–200*
Notes: Licensed from Leijac

FRENZY
Manufacturer: Stern
Date: 1982
Cabinet Type: Upright
Rarity: 8
Price Range: $100–300
Cabinet Type: Cocktail
Rarity: 9
Price Range: $250–500*
Notes: Sequel to *Berzerk*

FRISKY TOM
Manufacturer: Nichibutsu
Date: 1981
Cabinet Type: Upright
Rarity: 9
Price Range: $100–200*
Cabinet Type: Cocktail
Rarity: 9
Price Range: $150–300*

FROGGER
Manufacturer: Sega/Gremlin
Date: 1981
Cabinet Type: Upright
Rarity: 3
Price Range: $400–650
Cabinet Type: Cocktail
Rarity: 7
Price Range: $450–750

FROGGER/MR. DO
Manufacturer: Unknown
Date: 2003
Cabinet Type: Cabaret
Rarity: 1
Price Range: $1,000–1,600
Cabinet Type: Cocktail
Rarity: 1
Price Range: $1,500–2000
Notes: New combo game in a cocktail cabinet with a 19″ monitor

FROGS
Manufacturer: Gremlin
Date: 1978
Cabinet Type: Upright
Rarity: 9
Price Range: $75–150*

FROGS AND SPIDERS
Manufacturer: Taito
Date: 1981
Cabinet Type: Upright
Rarity: 9
Price Range: $50–150*
Cabinet Type: Cocktail
Rarity: 9
Price Range: $75–200*

FRONT LINE
Manufacturer: Taito
Date: 1982
Cabinet Type: Upright
Rarity: 8
Price Range: $450–550

FUN FOUR
Manufacturer: Baily International, Inc.
Date: 1974
Cabinet Type: Cocktail
Rarity: 9
Price Range: $50–100*

FUNKY BEE
Manufacturer: Orca
Date: 1982
Cabinet Type: Upright
Rarity: 9
Price Range: $75–150*

FUNKY FISH
Manufacturer: Sun Electronics
Date: 1981
Cabinet Type: Upright
Rarity: 9
Price Range: $75–150*

FUNNY MOUSE

Manufacturer: Chuo Co. Ltd.
Date: 1982
Cabinet Type: Upright
Rarity: 9
Price Range: $75–150*
Notes: Bootleg of *Super Mouse*

FUTURE SPY

Manufacturer: Sega
Date: 1984
Cabinet Type: Upright
Rarity: 9
Price Range: $200–300*
Notes: A conversion manufactured for *Zaxxon* cabinets

GALACTIC WARRIORS

Manufacturer: Konami
Date: 1985
Cabinet Type: Upright
Rarity: 9
Price Range: $100–200*

GALAGA

Manufacturer: Midway
Date: 1981
Cabinet Type: Upright
Rarity: 1
Price Range: $400–1,200
Cabinet Type: Cocktail
Rarity: 3
Price Range: $600–1,200
Cabinet Type: Cabaret
Rarity: 5
Price Range: $600–1,000
Notes: Very popular collectible—expensive in spite of
the large number available; "new" reproductions of
the game also exist (very expensive). Cabaret price is
for the original version—a new cabaret version with a
19″ monitor exists, and is much more expensive

GALAGA 3

Manufacturer: Bally Midway
Date: 1984
Cabinet Type: Upright
Rarity: 7
Price Range: $400–520
Cabinet Type: Cocktail
Rarity: 9
Price Range: $500–600
Notes: Also known as *Gaplus*

GALAGA '88

Manufacturer: Namco
Date: 1987
Cabinet Type: Upright
Rarity: 7
Price Range: $200–450
Notes: Distributed by Atari Games

GALAXIAN

Manufacturer: Midway
Date: 1979
Cabinet Type: Upright
Rarity: 4
Price Range: $400–500
Cabinet Type: Cocktail
Rarity: 7
Price Range: $300–500

GALAXIAN3

Manufacturer: Namco
Date: 1990
Cabinet Type: Environmental
Rarity: 10
Price Range: $11,000–15,000
Notes: A massive 6-player Laser disc game with a
110-inch projection screen and a Bose sound system;
very big and very expensive (original price was over
$150,000)

GALAXY RANGER

Manufacturer: Sega
Date: 1984
Cabinet Type: Upright
Rarity: 10
Price Range: $500–800*
Notes: Laser disc game distributed by Bally Midway
in the U.S.; known as *Star Blazers* in Japan

GALAXY RESCUE

Manufacturer: Taito
Date: 1979
Cabinet Type: Upright
Rarity: 9
Price Range: $50–150*
Notes: Bootleg of *Lunar Rescue*

GALAXY WARS

Manufacturer: Taito
Date: 1979
Cabinet Type: Upright
Rarity: 9
Price Range: $50–150*

GALLAG

Manufacturer: Unknown
Date: 1982
Cabinet Type: Upright
Rarity: 8
Price Range: $250–1,100
Notes: Bootleg of *Galaga;* often found in restored
Galaga cabinets; shouldn't command as high a price as
the original (but often does)

THE GAME TREE

Manufacturer: Project Support Engineering
Date: 1977
Cabinet Type: Upright
Rarity: 10
Price Range: $50–100*

GAPLUS
Manufacturer: Namco
Date: 1984
Cabinet Type: Upright
Rarity: 6
Price Range: $350–550
Notes: Distributed by Bally Midway in the U.S.; also known as *Galaga 3*

GAUNTLET
Manufacturer: Atari Games
Date: 1985
Cabinet Type: Upright
Rarity: 4
Price Range: $500–700
Notes: The 4-player version is the most common; a rarer 2-player version also exists

GAUNTLET II
Manufacturer: Atari Games
Date: 1986
Cabinet Type: Upright
Rarity: 5
Price Range: $500–700*
Notes: Usually found as conversions of *Gauntlet*

GEE BEE
Manufacturer: Namco
Date: 1978
Cabinet Type: Upright
Rarity: 9
Price Range: $75–150*
Cabinet Type: Cocktail
Rarity: 9
Price Range: $100–200*
Notes: Designed by Toru Iwatani, the designer of *Pac-Man*

GHOSTS 'N GOBLINS
Manufacturer: Capcom
Date: 1985
Cabinet Type: Upright
Rarity: 4
Price Range: $250–370

GHOULS 'N GHOSTS
Manufacturer: Capcom
Date: 1988
Cabinet Type: Upright
Rarity: 9
Price Range: $300–400*
Notes: Sequel to *Ghosts 'n Goblins*

GIMME A BREAK
Manufacturer: Bally Sente
Date: 1985
Cabinet Type: Upright
Rarity: 9
Price Range: $100–200*
Cabinet Type: Cocktail
Rarity: 9
Price Range: $250–350*

GLADIATOR 1984
Manufacturer: SNK
Date: 1984
Cabinet Type: Upright
Rarity: 9
Price Range: $75–150
Date: 1983

THE GLOB
Manufacturer: Epos
Cabinet Type: N/A
Rarity: 9
Price Range: $100–200*
Notes: No dedicated version exists; almost always found as a conversion in a *Pac-Man* cabinet

GOAL IV
Manufacturer: Atari
Date: 1975
Cabinet Type: Cocktail
Rarity: 9
Price Range: $50–100*

GOAL TO GO
Manufacturer: Stern
Date: 1983
Cabinet Type: Upright
Rarity: 10
Price Range: $500–700*
Notes: Laser disc football game

GOALIE GHOST
Manufacturer: Bally Sente
Date: 1984
Cabinet Type: Upright
Rarity: 9
Price Range: $100–175*

GOLD BUG
Manufacturer: Century Electronics
Date: 1982
Cabinet Type: Upright
Rarity: 9
Price Range: $50–150*

GOLD MEDAL WITH BRUCE JENNER
Manufacturer: Stern
Date: 1984
Cabinet Type: Upright
Rarity: Prototype
Price Range: $?
Notes: Laser disc game featuring athlete Bruce Jenner; only 2 were manufactured; no pricing information available due to extreme rarity

GOLDEN AXE
Manufacturer: Sega
Date: 1989
Cabinet Type: Upright
Rarity: 5
Price Range: $200–425

GOLDEN INVADERS
Manufacturer: Sigma Entertainment, Inc.
Date: 1980
Cabinet Type: Upright
Rarity: 9
Price Range: $50–100*

GORF
Manufacturer: Midway
Date: 1981
Cabinet Type: Upright
Rarity: 3
Price Range: $200–800
Cabinet Type: Cocktail
Rarity: 8
Price Range: $400–800
Cabinet Type: Cabaret
Rarity: 7
Price Range: $300–600

GOT-YA
Manufacturer: Game-A-Tron
Date: 1981
Cabinet Type: Upright
Rarity: 9
Price Range: $50–150*

GOTCHA
Manufacturer: Atari
Date: 1973
Cabinet Type: Upright
Rarity: 9
Price Range: $50–100*

GP WORLD
Manufacturer: Sega
Date: 1984
Cabinet Type: Upright
Rarity: 10
Price Range: $500–600*
Notes: Laser disc game that simulates Gran Prix racing

GRADIUS
Manufacturer: Konami
Date: 1985
Cabinet Type: Upright
Rarity: 9
Price Range: $150–300*
Notes: Known in Europe as *Nemesis*

GRAN TRAK 10
Manufacturer: Atari
Date: 1974
Cabinet Type: Upright
Rarity: 8
Price Range: $100–175*
Notes: The first video driving game

GRAN TRAK 20
Manufacturer: Atari
Date: 1974
Cabinet Type: Upright
Rarity: 9
Price Range: $100–175*
Notes: 2-player version of *Gran Trak 10*

GRAND CHAMPION
Manufacturer: Taito
Date: 1974
Cabinet Type: Upright
Rarity: 9
Price Range: $100–175*

GRAND PRIX
Manufacturer: Taito
Date: 1983
Cabinet Type: Upright
Rarity: 9
Price Range: $100–200*

GRANNY AND THE GATORS
Manufacturer: Bally Midway
Date: 1983
Cabinet Type: Upright
Rarity: 8
Price Range: $450–600*
Notes: Hybrid video/pinball game

GRAVITAR
Manufacturer: Atari
Date: 1982
Cabinet Type: Upright
Rarity: 8
Price Range: $400–800

GREAT GUNS
Manufacturer: Stern
Date: 1983
Cabinet Type: Upright
Rarity: 9
Price Range: $75–150*

GREAT SWORDSMAN
Manufacturer: Taito
Date: 1984
Cabinet Type: Upright
Rarity: 9
Price Range: $150–250*
Notes: Distributed by Romstar in the U.S.

GREEN BERET
Manufacturer: Konami
Date: 1985
Cabinet Type: Upright
Rarity: 9
Price Range: $100–250*

GRIDIRON
Manufacturer: Meadows
Date: 1977
Cabinet Type: Upright
Rarity: 9
Price Range: $50–100*

GRIDIRON FIGHT
Manufacturer: Tehkan
Date: 1985
Cabinet Type: Cocktail
Rarity: 9
Price Range: $200–300*

GRIDLEE
Manufacturer: Videa
Date: 1983
Cabinet Type: Upright
Rarity: Prototype
Price Range: $?
Notes: Only one exists; no pricing information available due to extreme rarity

GROBDA

Manufacturer: Namco
Date: 1984
Cabinet Type: Upright
Rarity: 9
Price Range: $100–200

GT ROADSTER

Manufacturer: Ramtek
Date: 1979
Cabinet Type: Upright
Rarity: 9
Price Range: $50–100*

GUIDED MISSILE

Manufacturer: Midway
Date: 1977
Cabinet Type: Upright
Rarity: 9
Price Range: $50–100*

GUN BLADE

Manufacturer: Vic Tokai
Date: 1985
Cabinet Type: Upright
Rarity: 9
Price Range: $100–200*

GUN FIGHT

Manufacturer: Midway
Date: 1975
Cabinet Type: Upright
Rarity: 8
Price Range: $150–250
Cabinet Type: Cocktail
Rarity: 9
Price Range: $200–300*
Notes: Also known as *Western Gun*

GUNMAN

Manufacturer: Taito
Date: 1977
Cabinet Type: Upright
Rarity: 9
Price Range: $50–100*

GUNSMOKE

Manufacturer: Romstar
Date: 1985
Cabinet Type: Upright
Rarity: 9
Price Range: $150–300*
Notes: Licensed from Capcom

GUZZLER

Manufacturer: Tehkan
Date: 1983
Cabinet Type: Upright
Rarity: 9
Price Range: $100–200*
Notes: Distributed in the U.S. by Centuri

GYPSY JUGGLER

Manufacturer: Meadows
Date: 1978
Cabinet Type: Upright
Rarity: 9
Price Range: $50–100*

GYRODINE

Manufacturer: Taito
Date: 1985
Cabinet Type: Upright
Rarity: 9
Price Range: $75–150*

GYRUSS

Manufacturer: Konami
Date: 1983
Cabinet Type: Upright
Rarity: 4
Price Range: $250–500
Cabinet Type: Cocktail
Rarity: 8
Price Range: $300–500*
Notes: Distributed in the U.S. by Centuri

GYRUSS/1942

Manufacturer: Konami
Date: 2002
Cabinet Type: Cabaret
Rarity: 2
Price Range: $1,800–2,200
Notes: New combo game in a cabaret cabinet with a 19″ monitor

HAL 21

Manufacturer: SNK
Date: 1985
Cabinet Type: Upright
Rarity: 9
Price Range: $100–200*

HANG-ON

Manufacturer: Sega
Date: 1985
Cabinet Type: Upright
Rarity: 3
Price Range: $100–400
Cabinet Type: Cockpit
Rarity: 7
Price Range: $300–600*
Cabinet Type: Cockpit (Deluxe)
Rarity: 9
Price Range: $500–700*

HANG-ON JR.

Manufacturer: Sega
Date: 1985
Cabinet Type: Upright
Rarity: 8
Price Range: $70–350
Cabinet Type: Cockpit
Rarity: 9
Price Range: $200–500*

HANGMAN

Manufacturer: Status
Date: 1984
Cabinet Type: Upright
Rarity: 9
Price Range: $75–150*

HARD DRIVIN'
Manufacturer: Atari Games
Date: 1989
Cabinet Type: Upright
Rarity: 7
Price Range: $100–200
Cabinet Type: Cockpit
Rarity: 6
Price Range: $100–200
Notes: The upright version actually has a seat

HARD HAT
Manufacturer: Exidy
Date: 1982
Cabinet Type: Upright
Rarity: 9
Price Range: $100–200

HAT TRICK
Manufacturer: Bally Sente
Date: 1984
Cabinet Type: Upright
Rarity: 9
Price Range: $200–300*
Cabinet Type: Cocktail
Rarity: 9
Price Range: $350–400

HEAD ON
Manufacturer: Gremlin
Date: 1979
Cabinet Type: Upright
Rarity: 8
Price Range: $200–300*

HEAD ON 2
Manufacturer: Gremlin
Date: 1979
Cabinet Type: Upright
Rarity: 9
Price Range: $75–150*
Cabinet Type: Cocktail
Rarity: 9
Price Range: $75–150*
Notes: Also included in 2 Gremlin dual cabinets (with either *Invinco* or *Deep Scan*)

HEART ATTACK
Manufacturer: Century Electronics
Date: 1983
Cabinet Type: Upright
Rarity: 9
Price Range: $75–150*

HEAVY METAL
Manufacturer: Sega
Date: 1985
Cabinet Type: Upright
Rarity: 9
Price Range: $100–200*

HEAVYWEIGHT CHAMP
Manufacturer: Sega
Date: 1976
Cabinet Type: Upright
Rarity: 9
Price Range: $50–100*

HEAVYWEIGHT CHAMP
Manufacturer: Sega
Date: 1987
Cabinet Type: Upright
Rarity: 9
Price Range: $100–200*

HELIFIRE
Manufacturer: Nintendo
Date: 1980
Cabinet Type: Upright
Rarity: 9
Price Range: $75-150*
Cabinet Type: Cocktail
Rarity: 9
Price Range: $200–300*

HERO IN THE CASTLE OF DOOM
Manufacturer: Crown Vending
Date: 1984
Cabinet Type: Upright
Rarity: 9
Price Range: $75–150*

HI-WAY
Manufacturer: Atari
Date: 1975
Cabinet Type: Upright
Rarity: 9
Price Range: $50–100*

HIGH VOLTAGE
Manufacturer: Alpha Denshi
Date: 1985
Cabinet Type: Upright
Rarity: 9
Price Range: $100–200*

HIGH WAY RACE
Manufacturer: Taito
Date: 1983
Cabinet Type: Upright
Rarity: 9
Price Range: $100–200*

HIT 'N MISS
Manufacturer: Exidy
Date: 1987
Cabinet Type: Upright
Rarity: 9
Price Range: $150–350*
Notes: Built on the same hardware and cabinet as other Exidy shooters such as *Crossbow* and *Chiller*

HIT ME
Manufacturer: Ramtek
Date: 1976
Cabinet Type: Upright
Rarity: 9
Price Range: $50–100*

HOCCER
Manufacturer: Eastern Micro Electronics, Inc.
Date: 1983
Cabinet Type: Upright
Rarity: 9
Price Range: $75–150*

HOCKEY

Manufacturer: Ramtek
Date: 1973
Cabinet Type: Upright
Rarity: 9
Price Range: $50–100*

HOCKEY TV

Manufacturer: Sega
Date: 1973
Cabinet Type: Upright
Rarity: 9
Price Range: $50–100*

HOLE LAND

Manufacturer: Tecfri
Date: 1984
Cabinet Type: Upright
Rarity: 9
Price Range: $75–150*

HOLEY MOLEY

Manufacturer: Tai
Date: 1982
Cabinet Type: Upright
Rarity: 9
Price Range: $100–250*
Notes: Also known as *Mole Attack*

HOPPER

Manufacturer: Karateco
Date: 1982
Cabinet Type: Upright
Rarity: 9
Price Range: $50–150*

HOPPER ROBO

Manufacturer: Sega
Date: 1983
Cabinet Type: Upright
Rarity: 9
Price Range: $75–150*

HOPPING MAPPY

Manufacturer: Namco
Date: 1986
Cabinet Type: Upright
Rarity: 9
Price Range: $250–350*
Notes: Sequel to *Mappy*

HOT SHOCKER

Manufacturer: E. G. Felaco
Date: 1982
Cabinet Type: Upright
Rarity: 9
Price Range: $100–200*

HOVERCRAFT

Manufacturer: Leijac
Date: 1983
Cabinet Type: Upright
Rarity: Prototype
Price Range: $?
Notes: A 3-D hover tank game; no pricing information available due to rarity

HUNCHBACK

Manufacturer: Century Electronics
Date: 1983
Cabinet Type: Upright
Rarity: 9
Price Range: $75–150*

HUNCHBACK OLYMPICS

Manufacturer: CVS
Date: 1984
Cabinet Type: Upright
Rarity: 9
Price Range: $75–150*
Notes: Marquee reads "H.B.'s Olympics"

HUSTLE

Manufacturer: Gremlin
Date: 1977
Cabinet Type: Upright
Rarity: 9
Price Range: $75–150*

HYPER OLYMPIC

Manufacturer: Konami
Date: 1983
Cabinet Type: Upright
Rarity: 9
Price Range: $350–500*
Notes: More commonly known as *Track and Field*

HYPER OLYMPIC '84

Manufacturer: Konami
Date: 1984
Cabinet Type: Upright
Rarity: 9
Price Range: $300–500*
Notes: More commonly known as *Hyper Sports*

HYPER SPORTS

Manufacturer: Konami
Date: 1984
Cabinet Type: Upright
Rarity: 7
Price Range: $300–500*
Cabinet Type: Cocktail
Rarity: 8
Price Range: $500–600*

I, ROBOT

Manufacturer: Atari
Date: 1983
Cabinet Type: Upright
Rarity: 8
Price Range: $1,200–1,600
Notes: Designed by Dave Theurer (designer of *Missile Command* and *Tempest*); very collectible

I'M SORRY

Manufacturer: Coreland/Sega
Date: 1985
Cabinet Type: Upright
Rarity: 9
Price Range: $75–150*

IKARI WARRIORS
Manufacturer: Tradewest
Date: 1986
Cabinet Type: Upright
Rarity: 6
Price Range: $400–600

INDIAN BATTLE
Manufacturer: Taito
Date: 1980
Cabinet Type: Upright
Rarity: 9
Price Range: $50–150*
Cabinet Type: Cocktail
Rarity: 9
Price Range: $100–200*

INDIANA JONES AND THE TEMPLE OF DOOM
Manufacturer: Atari Games
Date: 1985
Cabinet Type: Upright
Rarity: 7
Price Range: $200–500
Notes: Atari System I game

INDOOR SOCCER
Manufacturer: Universal
Date: 1985
Cabinet Type: Upright
Rarity: 9
Price Range: $75–150*

INDY 4
Manufacturer: Atari
Date: 1976
Cabinet Type: Upright
Rarity: 9
Price Range: $150–250*
Notes: Actually housed in a large, square cabinet with four sets of driving controls and a flat table-height monitor in the center

INDY 800
Manufacturer: Kee Games
Date: 1975
Cabinet Type: Upright
Rarity: 10
Price Range: $200–300*
Notes: Similar to Atari's *Indy 4,* but playable by 8 players simultaneously

INFERNO
Manufacturer: Williams
Date: 1984
Cabinet Type: Upright
Rarity: 10
Price Range: $?
Notes: Possibly fewer than 50 exist; no pricing information available due to extreme rarity

INSECTOR
Manufacturer: Gottleib
Date: 1982
Cabinet Type: Upright
Rarity: Prototype
Price Range: $?
Notes: Designed by Tim Skelly, who also designed *Rip-Off, Star Castle,* and *Reactor* (among many others); no pricing information available due to rarity

INTERCEPTOR
Manufacturer: Taito
Date: 1976
Cabinet Type: Upright
Rarity: 9
Price Range: $50–100*

INTERSTELLAR
Manufacturer: Funai
Date: 1983
Cabinet Type: Upright
Rarity: 10
Price Range: $500–700*
Notes: Laser disc space fighter game

INTREPID
Manufacturer: Nova Games, Ltd.
Date: 1983
Cabinet Type: Upright
Rarity: 9
Price Range: $75–150*

INTRUDER
Manufacturer: Game Plan
Date: 1980
Cabinet Type: Upright
Rarity: 9
Price Range: $50–150*

INVADER WARS
Manufacturer: World Vending
Date: 1979
Cabinet Type: Cocktail
Rarity: 10
Price Range: $150–250*
Notes: Bootleg of *Space Invaders*

INVADER'S REVENGE
Manufacturer: Zenitone Microtech
Date: 1979
Cabinet Type: Upright
Rarity: 10
Price Range: $75–150*
Notes: Add-on/conversion for *Space Invaders;* found in *Space Invaders* cabinets

THE INVADERS
Manufacturer: Zaccaria
Date: 1978
Cabinet Type: Upright
Rarity: 10
Price Range: $75–150*
Notes: Copy of *Space Invaders*

INVINCO!

Manufacturer: Sega/Gremlin
Date: 1979
Cabinet Type: Upright
Rarity: 9
Price Range: $50–150*

IXION

Manufacturer: Sega
Date: 1983
Cabinet Type: Upright
Rarity: Prototype
Price Range: $?
Notes: No pricing information available due to extreme rarity

JACK RABBIT

Manufacturer: Zaccaria
Date: 1984
Cabinet Type: Upright
Rarity: 9
Price Range: $100–250*

JACK THE GIANT KILLER

Manufacturer: Cinematronics
Date: 1982
Cabinet Type: Upright
Rarity: 8
Price Range: $150–300*

JAIL BREAK

Manufacturer: Konami
Date: 1985
Cabinet Type: Upright
Rarity: 9
Price Range: $100–250*

JET FIGHTER

Manufacturer: Atari
Date: 1975
Cabinet Type: Upright
Rarity: 9
Price Range: $50–100*

JOSHI VOLLEYBALL

Manufacturer: Taito
Date: 1983
Cabinet Type: Upright
Rarity: 9
Price Range: $75–150*

JOURNEY

Manufacturer: Bally Midway
Date: 1983
Cabinet Type: Upright
Rarity: 8
Price Range: $200–400
Cabinet Type: Cocktail
Rarity: 9
Price Range: $350–550*

JOUST

Manufacturer: Williams
Date: 1982
Cabinet Type: Upright
Rarity: 3
Price Range: $475–900
Cabinet Type: Cocktail
Rarity: 8
Price Range: $800–1,100
Notes: Some sources say that only 250 were produced

JOUST II: SURVIVAL OF THE FITTEST

Manufacturer: Williams
Date: 1986
Cabinet Type: Upright
Rarity: 8
Price Range: $600–800
Notes: Only between 500 and 1,100 were produced

JR. PAC-MAN

Manufacturer: Bally Midway
Date: 1983
Cabinet Type: Upright
Rarity: 7
Price Range: $500–600
Notes: Dedicated versions of this game are worth more—most are found as conversions in *Pac-Man, Ms. Pac-Man,* or *Super Pac-Man* cabinets

JUMP BUG

Manufacturer: Rock-Ola
Date: 1981
Cabinet Type: Upright
Rarity: 9
Price Range: $75–150*

JUMP COASTER

Manufacturer: Kaneko
Date: 1983
Cabinet Type: Upright
Rarity: 9
Price Range: $100–250*

JUMP SHOT

Manufacturer: Bally Midway
Date: 1983
Cabinet Type: Upright
Rarity: 9
Price Range: $100–250*

JUMPING JACK

Manufacturer: Universal
Date: 1984
Cabinet Type: Upright
Rarity: 9
Price Range: $100–250*

JUNGLE BOY

Manufacturer: Taito
Date: 1982
Cabinet Type: Upright
Rarity: Prototype
Price Range: $?
Notes: Prototype of *Jungle King;* no pricing information available due to extreme rarity

JUNGLE HUNT
Manufacturer: Taito
Date: 1982
Cabinet Type: Upright
Rarity: 4
Price Range: $150–350
Cabinet Type: Cocktail
Rarity: 9
Price Range: $200–300*
Notes: The non-Tarzan version of *Jungle King*

JUNGLE KING
Manufacturer: Taito
Date: 1982
Cabinet Type: Upright
Rarity: 6
Price Range: $250–400
Cabinet Type: Cocktail
Rarity: 9
Price Range: $300–500*
Notes: The original version of the game; Taito
changed the main character to an explorer in a pith
helmet (and the name of the game to *Jungle Hunt*)
due to a copyright battle over the game's similarity to
the character of Tarzan

JUNGLER
Manufacturer: Stern
Date: 1981
Cabinet Type: Upright
Rarity: 9
Price Range: $100–200*
Notes: Licensed from Konami

JUNO FIRST
Manufacturer: Gottlieb
Date: 1983
Cabinet Type: Upright
Rarity: 9
Price Range: $100–200*
Notes: Licensed from Konami

KAMIKAZE
Manufacturer: Leijac
Date: 1979
Cabinet Type: Upright
Rarity: 9
Price Range: $50–150*
Notes: Copy of *Astro Invader*

KANGAROO
Manufacturer: Atari
Date: 1982
Cabinet Type: Upright
Rarity: 6
Price Range: $250–350
Notes: Licensed from Sun Electronics Corp.

KAOS
Manufacturer: Game Plan
Date: 1981
Cabinet Type: Upright
Rarity: 9
Price Range: $50–100*

KARATE CHAMP
Manufacturer: Data East
Date: 1984
Cabinet Type: Upright
Rarity: 9
Price Range: $200–400*
Notes: 1-player version

KARATE CHAMP
Manufacturer: Data East
Date: 1984
Cabinet Type: Upright
Rarity: 4
Price Range: $200–500*
Notes: 2-player version; the first of (seemingly) hundreds of player-vs.-player martial arts games

KARNOV
Manufacturer: Data East
Date: 1987
Cabinet Type: Upright
Rarity: 8
Price Range: $150–250

KICK
Manufacturer: Midway
Date: 1981
Cabinet Type: Upright
Rarity: 9
Price Range: $200–450
Notes: 1,600 games were released as *Kick* before the
name was changed to *Kick Man*

KICK MAN
Manufacturer: Midway
Date: 1981
Cabinet Type: Upright
Rarity: 8
Price Range: $250–350
Notes: The same game as *Kick*, but with some *Pac-Man* characters added to increase popularity

KICK RIDER
Manufacturer: Universal
Date: 1984
Cabinet Type: Upright
Rarity: 9
Price Range: $100–200*

KICK START
Manufacturer: Taito
Date: 1984
Cabinet Type: Upright
Rarity: 9
Price Range: $100–200*

KICKER
Manufacturer: Konami
Date: 1985
Cabinet Type: Upright
Rarity: 9
Price Range: $100–200*
Notes: Also known as *Shao-lin's Road*

KILLER COMET
Manufacturer: Game Plan
Date: 1980
Cabinet Type: Upright
Rarity: 9
Price Range: $75–150*
Notes: Licensed from Centuri

KING AND BALLOON
Manufacturer: Game Plan
Date: 1981
Cabinet Type: Upright
Rarity: 9
Price Range: $75–150*
Notes: Licensed from Namco

KNIGHTMARE
Manufacturer: Konami
Date: 1985
Cabinet Type: Upright
Rarity: 9
Price Range: $100–200*

KNIGHTS IN ARMOR
Manufacturer: Project Support Engineering
Date: 1976
Cabinet Type: Upright
Rarity: 9
Price Range: $50–100*

KNOCK OUT!
Manufacturer: Digital Games Incorporated
Date: 1975
Cabinet Type: Cocktail
Rarity: 9
Price Range: $50–100*
Notes: 4-player *Pong* clone

KNOCK OUT!
Manufacturer: KKK
Date: 1982
Cabinet Type: Upright
Rarity: 9
Price Range: $75–150*
Notes: Copy of *Triple Punch*

KNUCKLE JOE
Manufacturer: Taito
Date: 1985
Cabinet Type: Upright
Rarity: 9
Price Range: $100–200*
Notes: Licensed from Seibu Kaihatsu

KO PUNCH
Manufacturer: Sega
Date: 1981
Cabinet Type: Upright
Rarity: 9
Price Range: $50–150*

KONAMI GT
Manufacturer: Konami
Date: 1985
Cabinet Type: Upright
Rarity: 9
Price Range: $150–250*

KONAMI'S PING-PONG
Manufacturer: Konami
Date: 1985
Cabinet Type: Upright
Rarity: 9
Price Range: $100–200*

KONG
Manufacturer: Fun Games, Inc.
Date: 1976
Cabinet Type: Upright
Rarity: 9
Price Range: $50–100*
Notes: Also known as *King*

KOZMIK KROOZ'R
Manufacturer: Bally Midway
Date: 1982
Cabinet Type: Upright
Rarity: 9
Price Range: $250–400*

KRAM
Manufacturer: Taito
Date: 1982
Cabinet Type: Upright
Rarity: 9
Price Range: $250–350*

KREEPY KRAWLERS
Manufacturer: Exidy
Date: 1979
Cabinet Type: Upright
Rarity: 9
Price Range: $75–150*

KRULL
Manufacturer: Gottleib
Date: 1983
Cabinet Type: Upright
Rarity: 8
Price Range: $150–250*

KUNG FU MASTER
Manufacturer: Data East
Date: 1984
Cabinet Type: Upright
Rarity: 4
Price Range: $150–475
Cabinet Type: Cocktail
Rarity: 9
Price Range: $250–500*
Notes: Licensed from Irem; known as *Spartan X* in Japan

LA TRIVIA
Manufacturer: REM
Date: 1985
Cabinet Type: Upright
Rarity: 9
Price Range: $75–150*

LADY BUG
Manufacturer: Universal
Date: 1981
Cabinet Type: Upright
Rarity: 7
Price Range: $100–300
Cabinet Type: Cocktail
Rarity: 7
Price Range: $200–350

LAGUNA RACER
Manufacturer: Midway
Date: 1977
Cabinet Type: Upright
Rarity: 9
Price Range: $50–100

LASER
Manufacturer: Unknown
Date: 1980
Cabinet Type: Cocktail
Rarity: 10
Price Range: $50–150*
Notes: Copy of Space Laser with some gameplay differences

LASER BASE
Manufacturer: Amstar
Date: 1981
Cabinet Type: Upright
Rarity: 9
Price Range: $100–200*
Notes: Also known as *Future Flash*

LASER GRAND PRIX
Manufacturer: Taito
Date: 1984
Cabinet Type: Cockpit
Rarity: 10
Price Range: $500–600*
Notes: Laser disc racing game

LASSO
Manufacturer: SNK
Date: 1982
Cabinet Type: Upright
Rarity: 9
Price Range: $75–150*

LAZARIAN
Manufacturer: Bally Midway
Date: 1981
Cabinet Type: Upright
Rarity: 9
Price Range: $100–200*
Cabinet Type: Cocktail
Rarity: 9
Price Range: $200–350*
Cabaret
Rarity: 9
Price Range: $250–400*

LAZER COMMAND
Manufacturer: Meadows
Date: 1976
Cabinet Type: Upright
Rarity: 9
Price Range: $50–100*
Notes: 2-player only

LEADER
Manufacturer: Midway
Date: 1973
Cabinet Type: Upright
Rarity: 9
Price Range: $50–150*
Notes: 4-player *Pong* clone

THE LEGEND OF KAGE
Manufacturer: Taito
Date: 1985
Cabinet Type: Upright
Rarity: 8
Price Range: $100–250

LEMANS
Manufacturer: Atari
Date: 1976
Cabinet Type: Upright
Rarity: 9
Price Range: $50–150*

LEPRECHAUN
Manufacturer: Moppet Video
Date: 1982
Cabinet Type: Upright
Rarity: 9
Price Range: $200–300*
Notes: This is a miniature sized game (about 3 feet high) made for children; easier version of *Pot of Gold*

LEVERS
Manufacturer: Rock-Ola
Date: 1983
Cabinet Type: Upright
Rarity: 9
Price Range: $75–150*

LIBBLE RABBLE
Manufacturer: Namco
Date: 1983
Cabinet Type: Upright
Rarity: 9
Price Range: $100–200*
Notes: Designed by Toro Iwatani, designer of *Pac-Man*

LIBERATION
Manufacturer: Data East
Date: 1984
Cabinet Type: Upright
Rarity: 9
Price Range: $75–150*

LIBERATOR
Manufacturer: Atari
Date: 1982
Cabinet Type: Upright
Rarity: 8
Price Range: $300–450*

LIL' HUSTLER
Manufacturer: Dynamo
Date: 1981
Cabinet Type: Upright
Rarity: 9
Price Range: $75–150*
Notes: Also known as *Video Hustler*

LIMBO
Manufacturer: Universal
Date: 1979
Cabinet Type: Upright
Rarity: Prototype
Price Range: $?
Notes: No pricing information available due to rarity

LIZARD WIZARD
Manufacturer: Sunn
Date: 1985
Cabinet Type: Upright
Rarity: 9
Price Range: $100–200*

LOCK 'N' CHASE
Manufacturer: Data East
Date: 1981
Cabinet Type: Upright
Rarity: 9
Price Range: $200–300*
Notes: The Data East Cassette (DECO) version of the game

LOCK 'N' CHASE
Manufacturer: Taito
Date: 1981
Cabinet Type: Upright
Rarity: 8
Price Range: $200–350*
Notes: Dedicated version; licensed from Data East

LOCO-MOTION
Manufacturer: Centuri
Date: 1981
Cabinet Type: Upright
Rarity: 8
Price Range: $200–400

LODE RUNNER
Manufacturer: Irem
Date: 1984
Cabinet Type: Upright
Rarity: 9
Price Range: $250–450*

LODE RUNNER—THE BUNGELING STRIKES BACK
Manufacturer: Irem
Date: 1984
Cabinet Type: Upright
Rarity: 9
Price Range: $250–450*

LODE RUNNER—GOLDEN LABYRINTH
Manufacturer: Irem
Date: 1985
Cabinet Type: Upright
Rarity: 9
Price Range: $250–450*

LOGGER
Manufacturer: Century Electronics
Date: 1982
Cabinet Type: Upright
Rarity: 9
Price Range: $75–150
Notes: Obvious copy of *Donkey Kong* where you are a logger trying to retrieve your axe from the bird who stole it

LOOPER
Manufacturer: Orca
Date: 1982
Cabinet Type: Upright
Rarity: 9
Price Range: $50–150*

LOOPING
Manufacturer: Venture Line
Date: 1981
Cabinet Type: Upright
Rarity: 8
Price Range: $100–200

LOST TOMB
Manufacturer: Stern
Date: 1983
Cabinet Type: Upright
Rarity: 9
Price Range: $200–300

LUNAR BATTLE
Manufacturer: Atari
Date: 1982
Cabinet Type: Upright
Rarity: Prototype
Price Range: $?
Notes: Prototype of *Gravitar;* no pricing information available due to extreme rarity

LUNAR LANDER
Manufacturer: Atari
Date: 1979
Cabinet Type: Upright
Rarity: 7
Price Range: $500–800

LUNAR RESCUE
Manufacturer: Taito
Date: 1979
Cabinet Type: Upright
Rarity: 9
Price Range: $75–150*

LUPIN III
Manufacturer: Taito
Date: 1980
Cabinet Type: Upright
Rarity: 9
Price Range: $100–200*
Cabinet Type: Cocktail
Rarity: 9
Price Range: $150–250*

M-4
Manufacturer: Midway
Date: 1977
Cabinet Type: Upright
Rarity: 9
Price Range: $50–100*

M-79 AMBUSH
Manufacturer: Ramtek
Date: 1977
Cabinet Type: Upright
Rarity: 9
Price Range: $50–100

M.A.C.H. 3

Manufacturer: Mylstar
Date: 1983
Cabinet Type: Upright
Rarity: 9
Price Range: $450–550*
Cabinet Type: Cockpit
Rarity: 9
Price Range: $600–800
Notes: Laser disc air combat game

MACHO MOUSE

Manufacturer: Techstar
Date: 1982
Cabinet Type: Upright
Rarity: 9
Price Range: $75–150*

MAD ALIEN

Manufacturer: Data East
Date: 1980
Cabinet Type: Upright
Rarity: 9
Price Range: $75–150*
Cabinet Type: Cocktail
Rarity: 9
Price Range: $100–200*

MAD CRASHER

Manufacturer: SNK
Date: 1984
Cabinet Type: Upright
Rarity: 9
Price Range: $100–200*

MAD PLANETS

Manufacturer: Gottleib
Date: 1983
Cabinet Type: Upright
Rarity: 9
Price Range: $250–450*

MAGIC BRUSH

Manufacturer: Olympia
Date: 1981
Cabinet Type: Upright
Rarity: 9
Price Range: $75–150*
Notes: Bootleg of *Crush Roller*

MAGIC MAGGOT

Manufacturer: Digimatic Italia
Date: 1980
Cabinet Type: Upright
Rarity: 9
Price Range: $75–150*
Notes: Bootleg of *Centipede*

MAGICAL SPOT

Manufacturer: Universal
Date: 1980
Cabinet Type: Upright
Rarity: 9
Price Range: $75–150*
Cabinet Type: Cocktail
Rarity: 9
Price Range: $100–200*

MAGICAL SPOT II

Manufacturer: Universal
Date: 1980
Cabinet Type: Upright
Rarity: 9
Price Range: $75–150*
Cabinet Type: Cocktail
Rarity: 9
Price Range: $100–200

MAGMAX

Manufacturer: Nichibutsu
Date: 1985
Cabinet Type: Upright
Rarity: 9
Price Range: $100–200*

MAJOR HAVOC, THE ADVENTURES OF

Manufacturer: Atari
Date: 1983
Cabinet Type: Upright
Rarity: 8
Price Range: $560–1,000
Notes: Very collectible; often seen as conversions in other Atari vector cabinets such as *Gravitar* and *Tempest;* dedicated versions (of which it is rumored there were only around 300) sell for a higher price than conversions (closer to the top end of the quoted price range)

MAJOR LEAGUE

Manufacturer: Sega
Date: 1985
Cabinet Type: Upright
Rarity: 9
Price Range: $150–250*

MAKE TRAX

Manufacturer: Williams
Date: 1981
Cabinet Type: Upright
Rarity: 7
Price Range: $200–400
Notes: Also known as *Crush Roller*

MANEATER

Manufacturer: Project Support Engineering
Date: 1975
Cabinet Type: Upright
Rarity: 10
Price Range: $200–300*
Notes: Housed in a fiberglass cabinet shaped like a shark with an open mouth

MANHATTAN

Manufacturer: Data East
Date: 1981
Cabinet Type: Upright
Rarity: 9
Price Range: $50–150*

MANIA CHALLENGE

Manufacturer: Taito
Date: 1986
Cabinet Type: Upright
Rarity: 8
Price Range: $75–150
Notes: Sequel to *Mat Mania*

MAPPY

Manufacturer: Bally Midway
Date: 1983
Cabinet Type: Upright
Rarity: 5
Price Range: $250–450
Cabinet Type: Cocktail
Rarity: 9
Price Range: $350–550*

MARBLE MADNESS

Manufacturer: Atari Games
Date: 1985
Cabinet Type: Upright
Rarity: 6
Price Range: $500–800
Notes: Atari System I game

MARBLE MADNESS II: MARBLE MAN

Manufacturer: Atari Games
Date: 1991
Cabinet Type: Upright
Rarity: Prototype
Price Range: $?
Notes: No pricing information available due to rarity;
see http://www.safestuff.com for pictures and info

MARINE BOY

Manufacturer: Orca
Date: 1982
Cabinet Type: Upright
Rarity: 9
Price Range: $75–150*
Notes: Has nothing to do with the cartoon series of
the same name

MARINE DATE

Manufacturer: Taito
Date: 1981
Cabinet Type: Upright
Rarity: 9
Price Range: $75–150*
Cabinet Type: Cocktail
Rarity: 9
Price Range: $100–200*

MARINER

Manufacturer: Amenip
Date: 1981
Cabinet Type: Upright
Rarity: 9
Price Range: $50–150*
Notes: Also known as *800 Fathoms*

MARIO BROS.

Manufacturer: Nintendo
Date: 1983
Cabinet Type: Upright
Rarity: 4
Price Range: $225–500
Notes: Dedicated cabinet is wider than other Nin-
tendo cabinets of the time; more commonly found as
conversions in *Donkey Kong* and other cabinets

MARS

Manufacturer: Artic
Date: 1981
Cabinet Type: Upright
Rarity: 9
Price Range: $75–100*
Cabinet Type: Cocktail
Rarity: 9
Price Range: $100–200*
Cabinet Type: Cabaret
Rarity: 9
Price Range: $100–200*

MARVIN'S MAZE

Manufacturer: SNK
Date: 1983
Cabinet Type: Upright
Rarity: 9
Price Range: $100–200*

MAT MANIA

Manufacturer: Taito
Date: 1985
Cabinet Type: Upright
Rarity: 8
Price Range: $100–200
Notes: Licensed from Technos; sequel to *Tag Team Wrestling*

MAYDAY!!

Manufacturer: Hoei
Date: 1981
Cabinet Type: Upright
Rarity: 10
Price Range: $200–400*
Notes: Similar to *Defender;* Williams forced Hoei to
halt production due to copyright infringement

MAYHEM 2002

Manufacturer: Cinematronics
Date: 1985
Cabinet Type: Upright
Rarity: 9
Price Range: $75–150*

MAZER BLAZER

Manufacturer: Stern
Date: 1983
Cabinet Type: Upright
Rarity: 10
Price Range: $250–450*

MEADOWS 4 IN 1

Manufacturer: Meadows
Date: 1976
Cabinet Type: Cocktail
Rarity: 8
Price Range: $50–100*

MEADOWS LANES

Manufacturer: Meadows
Date: 1977
Cabinet Type: Upright
Rarity: 9
Price Range: $50–100*

MEGA FORCE
Manufacturer: Tehkan
Date: 1985
Cabinet Type: Upright
Rarity: 9
Price Range: $75–150*

MEGA ZONE
Manufacturer: Konami
Date: 1983
Cabinet Type: Upright
Rarity: 9
Price Range: $75–150*

MEGADON
Manufacturer: Photar
Date: 1982
Cabinet Type: Upright
Rarity: 9
Price Range: $100–200*

MEGATACK
Manufacturer: Game Plan
Date: 1980
Cabinet Type: Upright
Rarity: 9
Price Range: $75–150*
Notes: Licensed from Centuri

MERMAID
Manufacturer: Rock-Ola
Date: 1982
Cabinet Type: Upright
Rarity: 9
Price Range: $75–150*

METAL CLASH
Manufacturer: Data East
Date: 1985
Cabinet Type: Upright
Rarity: 9
Price Range: $75–150*

METAL SOLDIER ISAAC
Manufacturer: Taito
Date: 1984
Cabinet Type: Upright
Rarity: 9
Price Range: $100–200*

METEOR
Manufacturer: Hoei
Date: 1980
Cabinet Type: Upright
Rarity: 9
Price Range: $150–250*
Notes: Bootleg of *Asteroids* with its own dedicated cabinet

METEOROIDS
Manufacturer: Venture Line
Date: 1981
Cabinet Type: Upright
Rarity: 9
Price Range: $100–200*

METRO-CROSS
Manufacturer: Namco
Date: 1985
Cabinet Type: Upright
Rarity: 8
Price Range: $75–150

MIGHTY MONKEY
Manufacturer: Yih Lung
Date: 1982
Cabinet Type: Upright
Rarity: 9
Price Range: $75–150*

MIKIE
Manufacturer: Konami
Date: 1984
Cabinet Type: Upright
Rarity: 8
Price Range: $75–150

MILLIPEDE
Manufacturer: Atari
Date: 1982
Cabinet Type: Upright
Rarity: 3
Price Range: $300–650
Cabinet Type: Cocktail
Rarity: 8
Price Range: $400–700*

MINEFIELD
Manufacturer: Stern
Date: 1983
Cabinet Type: Upright
Rarity: 9
Price Range: $75–150*

MINI-GOLF
Manufacturer: Bally Sente
Date: 1985
Cabinet Type: Upright
Rarity: 7
Price Range: $75–150
Cabinet Type: Cocktail
Rarity: 7
Price Range: $75–150
Notes: Often found as a conversion in other trackball game cabinets (Centipede, etc.)

MINI-GOLF
Manufacturer: Digital Games Incorporated
Date: 1980
Cabinet Type: Upright
Rarity: 9
Price Range: $50–100

MINI GOLF DELUXE
Manufacturer: Bally Sente
Date: 1985
Cabinet Type: Upright
Rarity: 9
Price Range: $75–150*

MINKY MONKEY
Manufacturer: Technos
Date: 1982
Cabinet Type: Upright
Rarity: 9
Price Range: $75–150*

MIRAGE
Manufacturer: Jeutel
Date: 1981
Cabinet Type: Upright
Rarity: 10
Price Range: $200–400*
Notes: Copy of *Defender* with improved control, graphics, and gameplay

MIRAX
Manufacturer: Current Technology, Inc.
Date: 1985
Cabinet Type: Upright
Rarity: 9
Price Range: $100–200*

MISSILE COMMAND
Manufacturer: Atari
Date: 1980
Cabinet Type: Upright
Rarity: 4
Price Range: $500–800
Cabinet Type: Cocktail
Rarity: 8
Price Range: $400–800
Cabinet Type: Cabaret
Rarity: 8
Price Range: $500–800
Cabinet Type: Cockpit
Rarity: 10
Price Range: $1,000–1,400*
Notes: Licensed by Sega for release in some European countries. According to most sources, fewer than 200 were made

MISSILE COMMAND 2
Manufacturer: Atari
Date: 1982
Cabinet Type: Upright
Rarity: Prototype
Price Range: $?
Notes: No pricing information available due to extreme rarity

MISSILE DEFEND
Manufacturer: Digimatic Italia
Date: 1980
Cabinet Type: Upright
Rarity: 9
Price Range: $200–300*
Notes: Bootleg of *Missile Command*

MISSILE RADAR
Manufacturer: Nutting and Associates
Date: 1973
Cabinet Type: Upright
Rarity: 10
Price Range: $100–200*

MISSILE-X
Manufacturer: Taito
Date: 1977
Cabinet Type: Upright
Rarity: 9
Price Range: $50–100

MISSION X
Manufacturer: Data East
Date: 1982
Cabinet Type: Upright
Rarity: 9
Price Range: $100–200*
Notes: Game for the Data East Cassette (DECO) system

MISTER VIKING
Manufacturer: Sega
Date: 1984
Cabinet Type: Upright
Rarity: 9
Price Range: $100–200*

MOGUCHAN
Manufacturer: Orca
Date: 1982
Cabinet Type: Upright
Rarity: 9
Price Range: $75–150*

MOLE ATTACK
Manufacturer: Yachiyo Electronics
Date: 1982
Cabinet Type: Upright
Rarity: 9
Price Range: $100–250*
Notes: Also known as *Holey Moley*

MONACO GP
Manufacturer: Sega
Date: 1980
Cabinet Type: Upright
Rarity: 6
Price Range: $150–250
Cabinet Type: Cabaret
Rarity: 7
Price Range: $200–300
Cabinet Type: Cockpit
Rarity: 8
Price Range: $300–400

MONEY MONEY
Manufacturer: Zaccaria
Date: 1983
Cabinet Type: Upright
Rarity: 9
Price Range: $100–200*

MONSTER BASH
Manufacturer: Sega
Date: 1982
Cabinet Type: Upright
Rarity: 9
Price Range: $100–200*
Cabinet Type: Cocktail
Rarity: 9
Price Range: $150–250*

MONTE CARLO

Manufacturer: Atari
Date: 1980
Cabinet Type: Upright
Rarity: 8
Price Range: $75–150*

MOON ALIEN

Manufacturer: Nichibutsu
Date: 1980
Cabinet Type: Upright
Rarity: 9
Price Range: $75–150*

MOON ALIEN PART II

Manufacturer: Nichibutsu
Date: 1980
Cabinet Type: Upright
Rarity: 9
Price Range: $75–150*

MOON ALPHA

Manufacturer: Nichibutsu
Date: 1980
Cabinet Type: Upright
Rarity: 9
Price Range: $75–150*

MOON CRESTA

Manufacturer: Sega/Gremlin
Date: 1980
Cabinet Type: Upright
Rarity: 8
Price Range: $150–250
Notes: Licensed from Nichibutsu; dedicated
Nichibutsu versions also exist (price is about the same
for both versions)

MOON LANDER

Manufacturer: Taito
Date: 1980
Cabinet Type: Cocktail
Rarity: 9
Price Range: $100–200*
Notes: Housed in a tall cocktail cabinet that allows
players to stand and play

MOON PATROL

Manufacturer: Williams
Date: 1982
Cabinet Type: Upright
Rarity: 4
Price Range: $250–650
Notes: Licensed from Irem
Cabinet Type: Cocktail
Rarity: 8
Price Range: $300–500
Notes: Licensed from Irem

MOON QUASAR

Manufacturer: Nichibutsu
Date: 1980
Cabinet Type: Upright
Rarity: 9
Price Range: $50–150*

MOON RAKER

Manufacturer: Nichibutsu
Date: 1980
Cabinet Type: Upright
Rarity: 9
Price Range: $50–150*

MOON SHUTTLE

Manufacturer: Taito
Date: 1981
Cabinet Type: Upright
Rarity: 9
Price Range: $75–150*
Notes: Licensed from Nichibutsu
Cabinet Type: Cocktail
Rarity: 9
Price Range: $100–200*

MOON WAR

Manufacturer: Stern
Date: 1981
Cabinet Type: Upright
Rarity: 9
Price Range: $100–200*

MOTORACE U.S.A

Manufacturer: Williams
Date: 1983
Cabinet Type: Upright
Rarity: 9
Price Range: $150–300*
Notes: Licensed from Irem

MOTOS

Manufacturer: Namco
Date: 1985
Cabinet Type: Upright
Rarity: 9
Price Range: $100–200*

MOUSE TRAP

Manufacturer: Exidy
Date: 1981
Cabinet Type: Upright
Rarity: 8
Price Range: $200–300

MOUSER

Manufacturer: UPL
Date: 1983
Cabinet Type: Upright
Rarity: 9
Price Range: $75–100*

MR. DO!

Manufacturer: Universal
Date: 1982
Cabinet Type: Upright
Rarity: 6
Price Range: $150–375
Cabinet Type: Cocktail
Rarity: 9
Price Range: $200–400*

MR. DO!'S CASTLE

Manufacturer: Universal
Date: 1983
Cabinet Type: Upright
Rarity: 8
Price Range: $100–200
Cabinet Type: Cocktail
Rarity: 9
Price Range: $150–250*
Notes: The Japanese version is called *Mr. Do! Vs. Unicorns*

MR. DO!'S WILD RIDE

Manufacturer: Universal
Date: 1984
Cabinet Type: Upright
Rarity: 9
Price Range: $100–200*
Cabinet Type: Cocktail
Rarity: 9
Price Range: $150–250*

MR. F. LEA

Manufacturer: Pacific Novelty
Date: 1983
Cabinet Type: Upright
Rarity: 10
Price Range: $75–150*

MR. TNT

Manufacturer: Telko
Date: 1983
Cabinet Type: Upright
Rarity: 9
Price Range: $75–150*

MRS. DYNAMITE

Manufacturer: Universal
Date: 1982
Cabinet Type: Upright
Rarity: 9
Price Range: $75–150*

MS. PAC-MAN

Manufacturer: Midway
Date: 1981
Cabinet Type: Upright
Rarity: 1
Price Range: $500–1,200
Cabinet Type: Cocktail
Rarity: 3
Price Range: $850–1,600
Cabinet Type: Cabaret
Rarity: 5
Price Range: $500–1,200
Notes: Very popular collectible; because of popularity, many conversions exist (and are usually a little cheaper than dedicated models). Original version; new cabaret models with 19″ monitors are currently available (expect to pay $1,600+)

MS. PAC-MAN/GALAGA—CLASS OF 1981

Manufacturer: Namco
Date: 2000
Cabinet Type: Upright
Rarity: 1
Price Range: $1,900–3,300
Cabinet Type: Cocktail
Rarity: 2
Price Range: $1,900–3,300
Cabinet Type: Cabaret
Rarity: 2
Price Range: $2,200–3,300
Notes: New combo game with 25″ monitor. Cocktail and Cabaret models have 19″ monitors.

MUNCH MOBILE

Manufacturer: Centuri
Date: 1983
Cabinet Type: Upright
Rarity: 9
Price Range: $150–250*
Notes: Known in Japan as *Joyful Ride*

MY HERO

Manufacturer: Sega
Date: 1985
Cabinet Type: Upright
Rarity: 9
Price Range: $75–150*
Notes: Known in Japan as *Seishun Scandal*

MYSTIC MARATHON

Manufacturer: Williams
Date: 1984
Cabinet Type: Upright
Rarity: 9
Price Range: $150–250*

N-SUB

Manufacturer: Sega
Date: 1980
Cabinet Type: Upright
Rarity: 8
Price Range: $50–150*

N.Y. CAPTOR

Manufacturer: Taito
Date: 1985
Cabinet Type: Upright
Rarity: 9
Price Range: $75–150*

NAMCO CLASSIC COLLECTION VOLUME 1

Manufacturer: Namco
Date: 1995
Cabinet Type: Upright
Rarity: 7
Price Range: $250–400*
Notes: 4 Namco games (*Galaga, Mappy, Xevious,* and *Super Xevious*) in a single cabinet; most often seen as a conversion

NAMCO CLASSIC COLLECTION VOLUME 2
Manufacturer: Namco
Date: 1996
Cabinet Type: Upright
Rarity: 6
Price Range: $250–400
Notes: 4 Namco games (*Dig Dug, Pac-Man, Rally-X, and New Rally-X*) in a single cabinet; most often seen as a conversion

NAME THAT TUNE
Manufacturer: Bally Sente
Date: 1986
Cabinet Type: Upright
Rarity: 8
Price Range: $75–150*

NATO DEFENSE
Manufacturer: Pacific Novelty
Date: 1982
Cabinet Type: Upright
Rarity: 9
Price Range: $100–200*

NAUGHTY BOY
Manufacturer: Cinematronics
Date: 1982
Cabinet Type: Upright
Rarity: 9
Price Range: $100–200*
Notes: Licensed from Jaleco

NAVARONE
Manufacturer: Namco
Date: 1980
Cabinet Type: Upright
Rarity: 9
Price Range: $75–150*

NEBULA
Manufacturer: Data East
Date: 1980
Cabinet Type: Upright
Rarity: 9
Price Range: $100–200*

NEMESIS
Manufacturer: Konami
Date: 1985
Cabinet Type: Upright
Rarity: 9
Price Range: $150–250*
Notes: European version of *Gradius*

NEW RALLY-X
Manufacturer: Namco
Date: 1981
Cabinet Type: Upright
Rarity: 9
Price Range: $150–300*

NEW SINBAD 7
Manufacturer: ATW U.S.A.
Date: 1983
Cabinet Type: Upright
Rarity: 9
Price Range: $75–150*

NEW YORK! NEW YORK!
Manufacturer: Gottleib
Date: 1980
Cabinet Type: Upright
Rarity: 8
Price Range: $150–300

NFL FOOTBALL
Manufacturer: Bally Midway
Date: 1983
Cabinet Type: Upright
Rarity: 10
Price Range: $400–700*
Notes: CED video disc game (used the RCA video disc technology with a diamond needle like a record player, not a laser disc); extremely rare

NIBBLER
Manufacturer: Rock-Ola
Date: 1983
Cabinet Type: Upright
Rarity: 9
Price Range: $100–200*
Rarity: 9
Price Range: $150–250*

NIGHT DRIVER
Manufacturer: Atari
Date: 1976
Cabinet Type: Upright
Rarity: 8
Price Range: $150–300
Cabinet Type: Cockpit
Rarity: 9
Price Range: $300–500*
Notes: Sit-down version with a fiberglass cockpit

NIGHT RACER
Manufacturer: Micronetics
Date: 1977
Cabinet Type: Upright
Rarity: 9
Price Range: $50–100*
Rarity: 9
Price Range: $75–150*

NIGHT STAR
Manufacturer: Data East
Date: 1983
Cabinet Type: Upright
Rarity: 9
Price Range: $100–200*

NIGHT STOCKER
Manufacturer: Bally Sente
Date: 1986
Cabinet Type: Upright
Rarity: 9
Price Range: $75–150*

NINJA
Manufacturer: Data East
Date: 1981
Cabinet Type: Upright
Rarity: 9
Price Range: $75–150*

NO MAN'S LAND
Manufacturer: Gottleib
Date: 1980
Cabinet Type: Upright
Rarity: 9
Price Range: $75–150*
Notes: Licensed from Universal

NOVA 2001
Manufacturer: Universal
Date: 1984
Cabinet Type: Upright
Rarity: 9
Price Range: $100–200*

OLYMPIC TENNIS
Manufacturer: See-Fun
Date: 1973
Cabinet Type: Cocktail
Rarity: 9
Price Range: $50–100*

OMEGA RACE
Manufacturer: Midway
Date: 1981
Cabinet Type: Upright
Rarity: 6
Price Range: $200–300
Cabinet Type: Cocktail
Rarity: 8
Price Range: $400–700
Cabinet Type: Cabaret
Rarity: 8
Price Range: $300–600
Cabinet Type: Cockpit
Rarity: 9
Price Range: $500–600
Notes: The only vector graphics game produced by Midway

ONE ON ONE
Manufacturer: PMC
Date: 1974
Cabinet Type: Upright
Rarity: 9
Price Range: $50–100*

OPERATION BEAR
Manufacturer: Bear
Date: 1987
Cabinet Type: Upright
Rarity: 9
Price Range: $200–300*
Notes: Bootleg of *Operation Wolf* with a detachable machine gun

OPERATION THUNDERBOLT
Manufacturer: Taito
Date: 1988
Cabinet Type: Upright
Rarity: 4
Price Range: $100–350

OPERATION WOLF
Manufacturer: Taito
Date: 1987
Cabinet Type: Upright
Rarity: 4
Price Range: $75–320

ORBIT
Manufacturer: Atari
Date: 1978
Cabinet Type: Upright
Rarity: 8
Price Range: $375–400

ORBITRON
Manufacturer: Signatron U.S.A
Date: 1982
Cabinet Type: Upright
Rarity: 9
Price Range: $75–150*

OUT LINE
Manufacturer: Century Electronics
Date: 1982
Cabinet Type: Upright
Rarity: 9
Price Range: $75–150*
Notes: Also known as *Radar Zone*

OUT RUN
Manufacturer: Sega
Date: 1986
Cabinet Type: Upright
Rarity: 4
Price Range: $100–300
Cabinet Type: Cabaret
Rarity: 8
Price Range: $150–300*
Cabinet Type: Cockpit (standard)
Rarity: 7
Price Range: $200–350*
Notes: Standard version with limited movement
Cabinet Type: Cockpit (deluxe)
Rarity: 9
Price Range: $400–500*
Notes: Fully articulated deluxe version

OUTLAW
Manufacturer: Atari
Date: 1976
Cabinet Type: Upright
Rarity: 9
Price Range: $50–150*

OZMA WARS
Manufacturer: SNK
Date: 1979
Cabinet Type: Upright
Rarity: 9
Price Range: $50–150*

PAC & PAL
Manufacturer: Namco
Date: 1983
Cabinet Type: Upright
Rarity: 9
Price Range: $150–300*
Notes: Also known as *Pac-Man* and *Chomp Chomp*

PAC AND PAINT

Manufacturer: Kural Electronics
Date: 1986
Cabinet Type: Upright
Rarity: 9
Price Range: $100–200*
Notes: European copy of *Crush Roller* and *Make Trax*

PAC-LAND

Manufacturer: Bally Midway
Date: 1984
Cabinet Type: Upright
Rarity: 7
Price Range: $150–300

PAC-MAN

Manufacturer: Midway
Date: 1980
Cabinet Type: Upright
Rarity: 3
Price Range: $400–1,000
Cabinet Type: Cocktail
Rarity: 6
Price Range: $600–1,000
Cabinet Type: Cabaret
Rarity: 7
Price Range: $600–1,000

PAC-MAN PLUS

Manufacturer: Bally Midway
Date: 1982
Cabinet Type: Upright
Rarity: 7
Price Range: $400–600
Cabinet Type: Cocktail
Rarity: 8
Price Range: $450–650*
Cabinet Type: Cabaret
Rarity: 8
Price Range: $450–650*

PAC-MANIA

Manufacturer: Atari Games
Date: 1987
Cabinet Type: Upright
Rarity: 8
Price Range: $450–550*
Notes: Licensed from Namco

PACE CAR PRO

Manufacturer: Electra
Date: 1975
Cabinet Type: Upright
Rarity: 9
Price Range: $50–100*

PADDLE-BALL

Manufacturer: Williams
Date: 1973
Cabinet Type: Upright
Rarity: 9
Price Range: $75–250
Notes: Almost identical in style, size, and shape to Atari's *Pong*

PADDLE BATTLE

Manufacturer: Allied Leisure
Date: 1973
Cabinet Type: Upright
Rarity: 9
Price Range: $50–100*

PANDORA'S PALACE

Manufacturer: Konami
Date: 1984
Cabinet Type: Upright
Rarity: 9
Price Range: $100–200*

PAPERBOY

Manufacturer: Atari Games
Date: 1984
Cabinet Type: Upright
Rarity: 7
Price Range: $200–500

PARALLEL TURN

Manufacturer: Jaleco
Date: 1984
Cabinet Type: Upright
Rarity: 9
Price Range: $75–150*

PENGO

Manufacturer: Sega
Date: 1982
Cabinet Type: Upright
Rarity: 7
Price Range: $300–500
Cabinet Type: Cocktail
Rarity: 9
Price Range: $350–550*

PEPPER II

Manufacturer: Exidy
Date: 1982
Cabinet Type: Upright
Rarity: 9
Price Range: $200–350*

THE PERCUSSOR

Manufacturer: Orca
Date: 1981
Cabinet Type: Upright
Rarity: 9
Price Range: $75–150*

PETER PACK RAT

Manufacturer: Atari Games
Date: 1985
Cabinet Type: Upright
Rarity: 8
Price Range: $450–550*
Notes: Atari System I game

PETER PEPPER'S ICE CREAM FACTORY

Manufacturer: Data East
Date: 1984
Cabinet Type: Upright
Rarity: 9
Price Range: $250–350*
Notes: Sequel to *BurgerTime*

PHANTOM II
Manufacturer: Midway
Date: 1979
Cabinet Type: Upright
Rarity: 9
Price Range: $50–150*

PHOENIX
Manufacturer: Centuri
Date: 1980
Cabinet Type: Upright
Rarity: 7
Price Range: $300–650
Notes: Licensed from Amstar Electronics Corp.

PHOZON
Manufacturer: Namco
Date: 1983
Cabinet Type: Upright
Rarity: 9
Price Range: $75–150*

PICKIN'
Manufacturer: Valadon Automation
Date: 1983
Cabinet Type: Upright
Rarity: 9
Price Range: $75–150*

PIG NEWTON
Manufacturer: Sega
Date: 1983
Cabinet Type: Upright
Rarity: 9
Price Range: $100–200*

PIN-PONG
Manufacturer: Atari
Date: 1974
Cabinet Type: Upright
Rarity: 9
Price Range: $50–100*

PINBALL ACTION
Manufacturer: Tehkan
Date: 1985
Cabinet Type: Upright
Rarity: 9
Price Range: $100–200*

PINBO
Manufacturer: Jaleco
Date: 1984
Cabinet Type: Upright
Rarity: 9
Price Range: $75–150*

PING PONG KING
Manufacturer: Taito
Date: 1985
Cabinet Type: Upright
Rarity: 9
Price Range: $75–150*

PINK FLOYD THE WALL
Manufacturer: Bally Midway
Date: 1983
Cabinet Type: Upright
Rarity: Prototype
Price Range: $?
Notes: No pricing information available due to extreme rarity

PIONEER BALLOON
Manufacturer: Rock-Ola
Date: 1982
Cabinet Type: Upright
Rarity: 9
Price Range: $75–150*

PIRANHA
Manufacturer: GL
Date: 1981
Cabinet Type: Upright
Rarity: 8
Price Range: $100–200

PIRATE PETE
Manufacturer: Taito
Date: 1982
Cabinet Type: Upright
Rarity: 9
Price Range: $200–400*
Notes: *Jungle King* with pirates

PIRATE TREASURE
Manufacturer: Moppet Video
Date: 1982
Cabinet Type: Upright
Rarity: 9
Price Range: $200–300*
Notes: This is a miniature-sized game (about 3 feet high) made for children

PIT & RUN
Manufacturer: Taito
Date: 1984
Cabinet Type: Upright
Rarity: 9
Price Range: $75–150*

THE PIT
Manufacturer: Centuri
Date: 1981
Cabinet Type: Upright
Rarity: 9
Price Range: $50–150*

PITCHMAN
Manufacturer: Laserdisc Computer Systems
Date: 1983
Cabinet Type: Upright
Rarity: Prototype
Price Range: $?
Notes: Laser disc game; only one is known to exist; no pricing available due to extreme rarity

PITFALL II—LOST CAVERNS
Manufacturer: Sega
Date: 1985
Cabinet Type: Upright
Rarity: 8
Price Range: $150–250
Notes: Licensed from Activision

PLANET
Manufacturer: Alca
Date: 1979
Cabinet Type: Upright
Rarity: 9
Price Range: $200–300*
Notes: Bootleg of *Asteroids* with its own dedicated cabinet

PLAYCHOICE
Manufacturer: Nintendo
Date: 1986
Cabinet Type: Upright
Rarity: 6
Price Range: $200–400*
Notes: Plays a variety of Nintendo and licensed games (basically the ones available for the NES console, but in board form)

PLAYCHOICE 5
Manufacturer: Nintendo
Date: 1986
Cabinet Type: Upright
Rarity: 5
Price Range: $250–500*
Notes: PlayChoice prices can vary widely depending on the games included (and the number of games included)

PLAYCHOICE 10
Manufacturer: Nintendo
Date: 1986
Cabinet Type: Upright
Rarity: 4
Price Range: $300–600
Notes: Dedicated double-monitor version; single-monitor (conversion kit) versions are cheaper; a bartop version also exists

PLEIADES
Manufacturer: Centuri
Date: 1981
Cabinet Type: Upright
Rarity: 7
Price Range: $250–400*
Notes: The title screen calls the game "Pleiads"
Cabinet Type: Cocktail
Rarity: 8
Price Range: $300–450*

POLARIS
Manufacturer: Taito
Date: 1980
Cabinet Type: Upright
Rarity: 9
Price Range: $75–150*

POLE POSITION
Manufacturer: Atari
Date: 1982
Cabinet Type: Upright
Rarity: 4
Price Range: $250–550
Notes: Licensed from Namco
Cabinet Type: Cockpit
Rarity: 6
Price Range: $500–800

POLE POSITION II
Manufacturer: Atari
Date: 1983
Cabinet Type: Upright
Rarity: 5
Price Range: $300–550*
Cabinet Type: Cockpit
Rarity: 8
Price Range: $500–800*
Notes: Dedicated version is uncommon; most often found as conversions in *Pole Position* cabinets

PONG
Manufacturer: Atari
Date: 1972
Cabinet Type: Upright
Rarity: 9
Price Range: $900–1,200
Cabinet Type: Cocktail
Rarity: 10
Price Range: $1,100–1,500*
Notes: Certainly one of the most historically significant arcade games; rare to find one that's working. Barrel-shaped cocktail version; very rare

PONG DOUBLES
Manufacturer: Atari
Date: 1972
Cabinet Type: Upright
Rarity: 9
Price Range: $50–150*
Cabinet Type: Cocktail
Rarity: 9
Price Range: $100–200*

PONG TRON
Manufacturer: Sega
Date: 1973
Cabinet Type: Upright
Rarity: 9
Price Range: $50–100*

PONG TRON II
Manufacturer: Sega
Date: 1973
Cabinet Type: Upright
Rarity: 9
Price Range: $50–100*

PONPOKO
Manufacturer: Venture Line
Date: 1982
Cabinet Type: Upright
Rarity: 9
Price Range: $50–150*

POOL SHARK

Manufacturer: Atari
Date: 1977
Cabinet Type: Upright
Rarity: 9
Price Range: $50–150*

POOYAN

Manufacturer: Stern
Date: 1982
Cabinet Type: Upright
Rarity: 8
Price Range: $100–250*

POP FLAMER

Manufacturer: Stern
Date: 1982
Cabinet Type: Upright
Rarity: 9
Price Range: $75–150*
Notes: Licensed from Jaleco

POPEYE

Manufacturer: Nintendo
Date: 1982
Cabinet Type: Upright
Rarity: 4
Price Range: $150–500
Cabinet Type: Cocktail
Rarity: 7
Price Range: $300–600

POPPER

Manufacturer: Omori
Date: 1983
Cabinet Type: Upright
Rarity: 9
Price Range: $75–150*

PORT MAN

Manufacturer: Nova
Date: 1982
Cabinet Type: Upright
Rarity: 9
Price Range: $50–150*

POT OF GOLD

Manufacturer: Game Plan
Date: 1982
Cabinet Type: Upright
Rarity: 9
Price Range: $50–150*
Notes: Also known as *Leprechaun*

POWER PLAY

Manufacturer: Cinematronics
Date: 1985
Cabinet Type: Upright
Rarity: 9
Price Range: $100–200*

PRO BOWLING

Manufacturer: Data East
Date: 1983
Cabinet Type: Upright
Rarity: 9
Price Range: $50–150*

PRO HOCKEY

Manufacturer: Taito
Date: 1973
Cabinet Type: Upright
Rarity: 9
Price Range: $50–150*

PRO MONACO GP

Manufacturer: Sega
Date: 1980
Cabinet Type: Upright
Rarity: 9
Price Range: $75–150*

PRO SOCCER

Manufacturer: Data East
Date: 1983
Cabinet Type: Upright
Rarity: 9
Price Range: $50–150*

PRO SPORTS

Manufacturer: Data East
Date: 1983
Cabinet Type: Upright
Rarity: 10
Price Range: $50–150*

PRO TENNIS

Manufacturer: Data East
Date: 1983
Cabinet Type: Upright
Rarity: 10
Price Range: $50–150*

PRO TENNIS

Manufacturer: Williams
Date: 1973
Cabinet Type: Upright
Rarity: 8
Price Range: $50–100

PROFESSOR PAC-MAN

Manufacturer: Bally Midway
Date: 1983
Cabinet Type: Upright
Rarity: 10
Price Range: $250–450*
Notes: Trivia game with a *Pac-Man* theme; only 400 were made

PUCKMAN

Manufacturer: Namco
Date: 1979
Cabinet Type: Upright
Rarity: 9
Price Range: $500–700*
Cabinet Type: Cocktail
Rarity: 9
Price Range: $600–800*
Notes: The original Japanese version of *Pac-Man*

PULSAR

Manufacturer: Sega/Gremlin
Date: 1981
Cabinet Type: Upright
Rarity: 9
Price Range: $75–150*

PUNCH-OUT!!

Manufacturer: Nintendo
Date: 1984
Cabinet Type: Upright
Rarity: 6
Price Range: $300–600

PUPPY PONG

Manufacturer: Atari
Date: 1973
Cabinet Type: Unique
Rarity: 10
Price Range: $200–400*
Notes: Cabinet is actually a yellow dog house; game
was designed for use in Chuck E. Cheese restaurants

PURSUIT

Manufacturer: Atari
Date: 1974
Cabinet Type: Upright
Rarity: 9
Price Range: $50–100

Q*BERT

Manufacturer: Gottleib
Date: 1982
Cabinet Type: Upright
Rarity: 7
Price Range: $400–800
Cabinet Type: Cocktail
Rarity: 9
Price Range: $500–900*

Q*BERT'S QUBES

Manufacturer: Mylstar
Date: 1983
Cabinet Type: Upright
Rarity: 9
Price Range: $350–600*
Cabinet Type: Cocktail
Rarity: 9
Price Range: $650–800*

QB-3

Manufacturer: Rock-Ola
Date: 1982
Cabinet Type: Upright
Rarity: 9
Price Range: $50–150*

QIX

Manufacturer: Taito
Date: 1981
Cabinet Type: Upright
Rarity: 7
Price Range: $300–500
Notes: It's pronounced "kicks," not "quicks"
Cabinet Type: Cocktail
Rarity: 9
Price Range: $350–550*

QIX II: TOURNAMENT

Manufacturer: Taito
Date: 1981
Cabinet Type: Upright
Rarity: 9
Price Range: $350–600*
Cabinet Type: Cocktail
Rarity: 9
Price Range: $450–650*

QUADRA PONG

Manufacturer: Atari
Date: 1974
Cabinet Type: Cocktail
Rarity: 9
Price Range: $50–100*

QUANTUM

Manufacturer: Atari
Date: 1982
Cabinet Type: Upright
Rarity: 10
Price Range: $2,500–3,500
Notes: Only 500 were produced; very collectible

QUARTET

Manufacturer: Sega
Date: 1986
Cabinet Type: Upright
Rarity: 9
Price Range: $250–450*
Notes: Dedicated version was 4-player; also sold as a
2-player conversion kit; dedicated version is difficult
to find (price is for 4-player version)

QUARTET 2

Manufacturer: Sun Corporation of America
Date: 1986
Cabinet Type: Upright
Rarity: 9
Price Range: $200–400*
Notes: Licensed from Sega

QUASAR

Manufacturer: Zaccaria
Date: 1980
Cabinet Type: Upright
Rarity: 9
Price Range: $50–150*

QUIZ SHOW

Manufacturer: Kee Games
Date: 1976
Cabinet Type: Upright
Rarity: 9
Price Range: $50–100*

QWAK

Manufacturer: Atari
Date: 1982
Cabinet Type: Upright
Rarity: Prototype
Price Range: $?
Notes: Puzzle game; no pricing information available
due to rarity

QWAK!

Manufacturer: Atari
Date: 1974
Cabinet Type: Upright
Rarity: 9
Price Range: $50–100*
Notes: Duck hunting game

R-TYPE

Manufacturer: Nintendo
Date: 1987
Cabinet Type: Upright
Rarity: 8
Price Range: $150–250
Notes: Licensed from Irem

RACE

Manufacturer: Fun Games, Inc.
Date: 1976
Cabinet Type: Upright
Rarity: 9
Price Range: $50–100*

RACER

Manufacturer: Midway
Date: 1975
Cabinet Type: Upright
Rarity: 9
Price Range: $50–100*

RADAR SCOPE

Manufacturer: Nintendo
Date: 1980
Cabinet Type: Upright
Rarity: 9
Price Range: $75–150*
Cabinet Type: Cocktail
Rarity: 9
Price Range: $200–300
Notes: About 2,000 of the 3,000 in the U.S. were con-
verted to *Donkey Kong*—if you see a red *Donkey Kong*
cabinet, chances are it originally housed this game

RADICAL RADIAL

Manufacturer: Nichibutsu
Date: 1982
Cabinet Type: Upright
Rarity: 9
Price Range: $75–150*

RAIDERS 5

Manufacturer: UPL
Date: 1985
Cabinet Type: Upright
Rarity: 9
Price Range: $75–150*

RAINBOW ISLANDS

Manufacturer: Taito
Date: 1987
Cabinet Type: Upright
Rarity: 9
Price Range: $150–250*
Notes: Also known as *Jumping Islands;* sequel to *Bub-
ble Bobble*

RALLY

Manufacturer: For-Play
Date: 1973
Cabinet Type: Upright
Rarity: 9
Price Range: $50–100*

RALLY-X

Manufacturer: Midway
Date: 1980
Cabinet Type: Upright
Rarity: 7
Price Range: $200–350
Cabinet Type: Cocktail
Rarity: 8
Price Range: $150–300
Cabinet Type: Cabaret
Rarity: 9
Price Range: $200–350

RAMPAGE

Manufacturer: Bally Midway
Date: 1986
Cabinet Type: Upright
Rarity: 7
Price Range: $400–500

RASTAN

Manufacturer: Taito
Date: 1987
Cabinet Type: Upright
Rarity: 7
Price Range: $200–500
Notes: Known as *Rastan Saga* outside the U.S.

RAZZMATAZZ

Manufacturer: Sega
Date: 1983
Cabinet Type: Upright
Rarity: 9
Price Range: $75–150*

REACTOR

Manufacturer: Gottleib
Date: 1982
Cabinet Type: Upright
Rarity: 10
Price Range: $500–800*
Notes: Very collectible

REBOUND

Manufacturer: Atari
Date: 1974
Cabinet Type: Upright
Rarity: 9
Price Range: $50–100*
Notes: Released by Kee Games as *Spike*

RED ALERT

Manufacturer: Irem
Date: 1981
Cabinet Type: Upright
Rarity: 9
Price Range: $75–150*

RED BARON

Manufacturer: Atari
Date: 1980
Cabinet Type: Upright
Rarity: 8
Price Range: $450–600
Cabinet Type: Cockpit
Rarity: 9
Price Range: $650–1,000

RED CLASH

Manufacturer: Kaneko
Date: 1982
Cabinet Type: Upright
Rarity: 9
Price Range: $50–150*

REDLINE RACER

Manufacturer: Cinematronics
Date: 1986
Cabinet Type: Upright
Rarity: 9
Price Range: $100–200*
Notes: Manufactured by Tradewest

REGULUS

Manufacturer: Sega
Date: 1983
Cabinet Type: Upright
Rarity: 9
Price Range: $75–150*

REPULSE

Manufacturer: Sega
Date: 1985
Cabinet Type: Upright
Rarity: 9
Price Range: $75–150*
Notes: Also known as *Son of Phoenix*

RESCUE

Manufacturer: Stern
Date: 1982
Cabinet Type: Upright
Rarity: 9
Price Range: $100–200*

RETURN OF THE INVADERS

Manufacturer: Taito
Date: 1985
Cabinet Type: Upright
Rarity: 9
Price Range: $100–250*

RETURN OF THE JEDI

Manufacturer: Atari
Date: 1984
Cabinet Type: Upright
Rarity: 8
Price Range: $800–1,000

REVENGER '84

Manufacturer: Magic Electronics
Date: 1984
Cabinet Type: Upright
Rarity: 9
Price Range: $75–150*

REVOLUTION X

Manufacturer: Midway
Date: 1984
Cabinet Type: Upright
Rarity: 9
Price Range: $450–600*
Notes: Dedicated version is 3-player; also sold as a 2-player conversion kit for *Terminator 2: Judgment Day;* price is for the 3-player version (2-player is generally less expensive)

RING FIGHTER

Manufacturer: Taito
Date: 1984
Cabinet Type: Upright
Rarity: 9
Price Range: $100–200*

RING KING

Manufacturer: Data East
Date: 1985
Cabinet Type: Upright
Rarity: 7
Price Range: $150–275
Notes: Also known as *King of Fighters*

RING KING II

Manufacturer: Data East
Date: 1986
Cabinet Type: Upright
Rarity: 9
Price Range: $150–275*
Notes: Sequel to *Ring King*

RIP CORD

Manufacturer: Exidy
Date: 1979
Cabinet Type: Upright
Rarity: 9
Price Range: $50–150*

RIP OFF

Manufacturer: Cinematronics
Date: 1980
Cabinet Type: Upright
Rarity: 9
Price Range: $450–600*

RIVER PATROL

Manufacturer: Kersten
Date: 1981
Cabinet Type: Upright
Rarity: 9
Price Range: $50–150*

ROAD BLASTER

Manufacturer: Data East
Date: 1985
Cabinet Type: Upright
Rarity: 10
Price Range: $600–700*
Notes: Laser disc game; also known as *Road Avenger*

ROAD BLASTERS

Manufacturer: Atari
Date: 1987
Cabinet Type: Upright
Rarity: 4
Price Range: $75–250
Notes: Atari System I game
Cabinet Type: Cockpit
Rarity: 7
Price Range: $200–450*

ROAD CHAMPION

Manufacturer: Taito
Date: 1978
Cabinet Type: Upright
Rarity: 9
Price Range: $50–100*

ROAD FIGHTER

Manufacturer: Konami
Date: 1984
Cabinet Type: Upright
Rarity: 9
Price Range: $100–200*

ROAD RUNNER

Manufacturer: Atari Games
Date: 1985
Cabinet Type: Upright
Rarity: 8
Price Range: $400–500*
Notes: Atari System I game

ROAD RUNNER

Manufacturer: Midway
Date: 1977
Cabinet Type: Upright
Rarity: 9
Price Range: $50–100*

ROBOT

Manufacturer: Allied Leisure
Date: 1975
Cabinet Type: Upright
Rarity: 9
Price Range: $50–100*

ROBOT BOWL

Manufacturer: Exidy
Date: 1977
Cabinet Type: Cocktail
Rarity: 9
Price Range: $50–150*

ROBOTRON: 2084

Manufacturer: Williams
Date: 1982
Cabinet Type: Upright
Rarity: 3
Price Range: $700–1,200
Cabinet Type: Cocktail
Rarity: 7
Price Range: $1,200–3,000
Cabinet Type: Cabaret
Rarity: 8
Price Range: $1,300–2,000
Notes: One of the most collectible games around

ROC'N ROPE

Manufacturer: Konami
Date: 1983
Cabinet Type: Upright
Rarity: 9
Price Range: $200–300*

ROCK CLIMBER

Manufacturer: Taito
Date: 1981
Cabinet Type: Upright
Rarity: 9
Price Range: $100–200*

ROCKET RACER

Manufacturer: Rock-Ola
Date: 1983
Cabinet Type: Upright
Rarity: 9
Price Range: $75–150*

ROLLER ACES

Manufacturer: Williams
Date: 1983
Cabinet Type: Upright
Rarity: 9
Price Range: $75–150*

ROLLER JAMMER

Manufacturer: Nichibutsu
Date: 1984
Cabinet Type: Upright
Rarity: 9
Price Range: $75–150*

ROLLING CRASH

Manufacturer: Nichibutsu
Date: 1979
Cabinet Type: Upright
Rarity: 9
Price Range: $50–150*

ROLLING THUNDER

Manufacturer: Atari Games
Date: 1986
Cabinet Type: Upright
Rarity: 6
Price Range: $100–250

ROOT BEER TAPPER

Manufacturer: Bally Midway
Date: 1984
Cabinet Type: Upright
Rarity: 7
Price Range: $500–650
Cabinet Type: Cocktail
Rarity: 9
Price Range: $550–700*
Notes: Bally Midway replaced the original *Tapper* with this game when it was decided that the Budweiser version was advertising beer to minors

ROOTIN' TOOTIN'

Manufacturer: Data East
Date: 1983
Cabinet Type: Upright
Rarity: 9
Price Range: $75–150*

ROUND-UP

Manufacturer: Centuri
Date: 1981
Cabinet Type: Upright
Rarity: 9
Price Range: $75–150*
Cabinet Type: Cocktail
Rarity: 9
Price Range: $100–200*
Notes: Also known as *Fitter*

ROUTE 16

Manufacturer: Centuri
Date: 1981
Cabinet Type: Upright
Rarity: 9
Price Range: $75–150*

RUG RATS

Manufacturer: Nichibutsu
Date: 1983
Cabinet Type: Upright
Rarity: 9
Price Range: $75–150*
Notes: Also known as *Wiping*

RUMBA LUMBER

Manufacturer: Taito
Date: 1984
Cabinet Type: Upright
Rarity: 9
Price Range: $75–150*

RUNAWAY

Manufacturer: Atari
Date: 1982
Cabinet Type: Upright
Rarity: Prototype
Price Range: $?
Notes: No pricing information available due to extreme rarity

RUSH 'N ATTACK

Manufacturer: Konami
Date: 1985
Cabinet Type: Upright
Rarity: 7
Price Range: $75–250

RYGAR

Manufacturer: Tecmo
Date: 1986
Cabinet Type: Upright
Rarity: 8
Price Range: $150–300*

SAFARI

Manufacturer: Sega/Gremlin
Date: 1977
Cabinet Type: Upright
Rarity: 9
Price Range: $50–100*

SAFARI RALLY

Manufacturer: SNK
Date: 1979
Cabinet Type: Upright
Rarity: 9
Price Range: $50–150*

SAMURAI

Manufacturer: Sega
Date: 1980
Cabinet Type: Upright
Rarity: 9
Price Range: $100–250*

SARGE

Manufacturer: Bally Midway
Date: 1985
Cabinet Type: Upright
Price Range: $150–250*
Rarity: 9
Price Range: $200–300*

SATAN OF SATURN

Manufacturer: SNK
Date: 1981
Cabinet Type: Upright
Rarity: 9
Price Range: $75–150*
Cabinet Type: Cabaret
Rarity: 9
Price Range: $100–200*
Notes: Licensed from Taito; also known as *Zarzon*

SATAN'S HOLLOW

Manufacturer: Bally Midway
Date: 1982
Cabinet Type: Upright
Rarity: 7
Price Range: $175–650
Cabinet Type: Cocktail
Rarity: 9
Price Range: $300–600*

SATURN

Manufacturer: Jaleco
Date: 1983
Cabinet Type: Upright
Rarity: 9
Price Range: $75–150*

SAVAGE BEES

Manufacturer: Memetron
Date: 1985
Cabinet Type: Upright
Rarity: 9
Price Range: $100–200*
Notes: Also known as *Exed Exes* and *Attack of the Savage Bees;* licensed from Capcom

SCION

Manufacturer: Cinematronics
Date: 1984
Cabinet Type: Upright
Rarity: 9
Price Range: $100–200*
Notes: Licensed from Seibu Denshi

SCORE

Manufacturer: Exidy
Date: 1977
Cabinet Type: Upright
Rarity: 9
Price Range: $50–100*

SCORPION

Manufacturer: Zaccaria
Date: 1982
Cabinet Type: Upright
Rarity: 9
Price Range: $50–150*

SCRAMBLE

Manufacturer: Stern
Date: 1981
Cabinet Type: Upright
Rarity: 8
Price Range: $400–700
Cabinet Type: Cocktail
Rarity: 9
Price Range: $500–800*
Notes: Licensed from Konami

SCRAMBLED EGG

Manufacturer: Technos
Date: 1983
Cabinet Type: Upright
Rarity: 9
Price Range: $75–150*

SCREW LOOSE

Manufacturer: Gottleib
Date: 1983
Cabinet Type: Upright
Rarity: Prototype
Price Range: $?
Notes: Designed by Tim Skelly, who also designed
Rip-Off, Star Castle, and *Reactor* (among many others);
only 3 exist; no pricing information available due to
extreme rarity

SCRUM TRY

Manufacturer: Data East
Date: 1984
Cabinet Type: Upright
Rarity: 9
Price Range: $50–150*

SEA BATTLE

Manufacturer: Ramtek
Date: 1976
Cabinet Type: Upright
Rarity: 9
Price Range: $50–100*

SEA FIGHTER POSEIDON

Manufacturer: Taito
Date: 1984
Cabinet Type: Upright
Rarity: 9
Price Range: $75–150*

SEA WOLF

Manufacturer: Midway
Date: 1976
Cabinet Type: Upright
Rarity: 7
Price Range: $100–250
Notes: Fairly easy to find, but not in working condition

SEA WOLF II

Manufacturer: Midway
Date: 1978
Cabinet Type: Upright
Rarity: 9
Price Range: $150–300*

SECRET BASE

Manufacturer: Sega
Date: 1978
Cabinet Type: Upright
Rarity: 9
Price Range: $50–100*

SECTION Z

Manufacturer: Capcom
Date: 1985
Cabinet Type: Upright
Rarity: 9
Price Range: $100–200*

SECTOR ZONE

Manufacturer: Nichibutsu
Date: 1984
Cabinet Type: Upright
Rarity: 9
Price Range: $100–200*

SEGA NINJA

Manufacturer: Sega
Date: 1985
Cabinet Type: Upright
Rarity: 9
Price Range: $75–150*

SEICROSS

Manufacturer: Nichibutsu
Date: 1984
Cabinet Type: Upright
Rarity: 9
Price Range: $100–200*

SENJYO

Manufacturer: Tehkan
Date: 1983
Cabinet Type: Upright
Rarity: 9
Price Range: $100–200*

THE SHANGHAI KID

Manufacturer: Taiyo
Date: 1985
Cabinet Type: Upright
Rarity: 9
Price Range: $100–200*

SHARK

Manufacturer: U.S. Billiards
Date: 1975
Cabinet Type: Upright
Rarity: 9
Price Range: $50–100*

SHARK ATTACK
Manufacturer: Game Plan
Date: 1981
Cabinet Type: Upright
Rarity: 9
Price Range: $50–150*
Cabinet Type: Cocktail
Rarity: 9
Price Range: $100–200*

SHARK JAWS
Manufacturer: Atari
Date: 1975
Cabinet Type: Upright
Rarity: 9
Price Range: $50–150*

SHERIFF
Manufacturer: Nintendo
Date: 1980
Cabinet Type: Upright
Rarity: 9
Price Range: $75–150*
Notes: Copy of *Bandido*

SHINOBI
Manufacturer: Sega
Date: 1987
Cabinet Type: Upright
Rarity: 7
Price Range: $150–350

SHOOT THE BULL
Manufacturer: Bally Midway
Date: 1985
Cabinet Type: Upright
Rarity: 10
Price Range: $75–150*
Notes: Released as a conversion kit for *Pac-Man*

SHOOTING MASTER
Manufacturer: Sega
Date: 1984
Cabinet Type: Upright
Rarity: 9
Price Range: $150–250*

SHOOTOUT
Manufacturer: Data East
Date: 1985
Cabinet Type: Upright
Rarity: 9
Price Range: $75–150*

SHRIKE AVENGER
Manufacturer: Bally Sente
Date: 1984
Cabinet Type: Cockpit
Rarity: Prototype
Price Range: $?
Notes: As many as 12 of these machines were constructed; no pricing information available due to rarity

SHUFFLEBOARD
Manufacturer: Midway
Date: 1978
Cabinet Type: Upright
Rarity: 9
Price Range: $50–100

SIDE TRACK
Manufacturer: Exidy
Date: 1979
Cabinet Type: Upright
Rarity: 9
Price Range: $50–150*

SILVER LAND
Manufacturer: Falcon
Date: 1981
Cabinet Type: Upright
Rarity: 9
Price Range: $50–150*

SINBAD MYSTERY
Manufacturer: Sega
Date: 1983
Cabinet Type: Upright
Rarity: 9
Price Range: $75–150*

SINISTAR
Manufacturer: Williams
Date: 1982
Cabinet Type: Upright
Rarity: 7
Price Range: $500–700
Cabinet Type: Cockpit
Rarity: 8
Price Range: $800–1,000
Cabinet Type: Duramold
Rarity: 10
Price Range: $800–1,000*

SKELAGON
Manufacturer: Nichibutsu
Date: 1983
Cabinet Type: Upright
Rarity: 9
Price Range: $100–200*
Notes: Also known as *SF-X*

SKI
Manufacturer: Allied Leisure
Date: 1975
Cabinet Type: Upright
Rarity: 9
Price Range: $50–100*

SKY ARMY
Manufacturer: Shoei
Date: 1982
Cabinet Type: Upright
Rarity: 9
Price Range: $50–150*

SKY BUMPER
Manufacturer: Venture Line
Date: 1982
Cabinet Type: Upright
Rarity: 9
Price Range: $50–150*

SKY CHUTER
Manufacturer: Irem
Date: 1980
Cabinet Type: Upright
Rarity: 9
Price Range: $50–150*

SKY JAGUAR

Manufacturer: Konami
Date: 1984
Cabinet Type: Upright
Rarity: 9
Price Range: $100–200*

SKY KID

Manufacturer: Namco
Date: 1985
Cabinet Type: Upright
Rarity: 9
Price Range: $100–250*

SKY KID DELUXE

Manufacturer: Namco
Date: 1986
Cabinet Type: Upright
Rarity: 9
Price Range: $100–250*

SKY LANCER

Manufacturer: Orca
Date: 1983
Cabinet Type: Upright
Rarity: 9
Price Range: $75–150*

SKY RAIDER

Manufacturer: Atari
Date: 1978
Cabinet Type: Upright
Rarity: 9
Price Range: $50–100*

SKY SKIPPER

Manufacturer: Nintendo
Date: 1982
Cabinet Type: Upright
Rarity: 9
Price Range: $75–150*

SKYDIVER

Manufacturer: Atari
Date: 1978
Cabinet Type: Upright
Rarity: 9
Price Range: $75–150*

SKYWARS

Manufacturer: Micro Amusements, Inc.
Date: 1976
Cabinet Type: Upright
Rarity: 9
Price Range: $50–100*
Cabinet Type: Cocktail
Rarity: 9
Price Range: $75–150*

SLALOM

Manufacturer: Orca
Date: 1982
Cabinet Type: Upright
Rarity: 10
Price Range: $75–100*

SLITHER

Manufacturer: GDI
Date: 1982
Cabinet Type: Upright
Rarity: 8
Price Range: $450–600*

SMASH TV

Manufacturer: Williams
Date: 1990
Cabinet Type: Upright
Rarity: 6
Price Range: $400–600

SMOKEY JOE

Manufacturer: Atari
Date: 1978
Cabinet Type: Upright
Rarity: 9
Price Range: $75–150*
Notes: 1-player version of *Fire Truck*

SNACKS 'N JAXSON

Manufacturer: Bally Sente
Date: 1984
Cabinet Type: Upright
Rarity: 9
Price Range: $100–200*

SNAKE PIT

Manufacturer: Bally Sente
Date: 1984
Cabinet Type: Upright
Rarity: 9
Price Range: $100–200*

SNAP JACK

Manufacturer: Universal
Date: 1981
Cabinet Type: Upright
Rarity: 9
Price Range: $75–150*

SNOOPY PONG

Manufacturer: Atari
Date: 1973
Cabinet Type: Upright
Rarity: Prototype
Price Range: $?
Notes: Only one was made due to copyright issues; eventually became *Puppy Pong;* pricing information unavailable due to extreme rarity

SOCCER

Manufacturer: Ramtek
Date: 1973
Cabinet Type: Upright
Rarity: 9
Price Range: $50–100*

SOLAR FOX

Manufacturer: Bally Midway
Date: 1981
Cabinet Type: Upright
Rarity: 9
Price Range: $150–250*
Cabinet Type: Cocktail
Rarity: 9
Price Range: $300–400*
Cabinet Type: Cabaret
Rarity: 9
Price Range: $350–450*

SOLAR QUEST

Manufacturer: Cinematronics
Date: 1981
Cabinet Type: Upright
Rarity: 9
Price Range: $400–600*
Notes: Color vector game

SON OF PHOENIX

Manufacturer: Associated Overseas MFR, Inc.
Date: 1985
Cabinet Type: Upright
Rarity: 9
Price Range: $75–150*

SON SON

Manufacturer: Capcom
Date: 1984
Cabinet Type: Upright
Rarity: 9
Price Range: $100–200*

SOS

Manufacturer: Namco
Date: 1979
Cabinet Type: Upright
Rarity: 9
Price Range: $50–150*

SPACE ACE

Manufacturer: Cinematronics
Date: 1984
Cabinet Type: Upright
Rarity: 7
Price Range: $1,000–1,500
Notes: Very collectible; European version distributed by Atari; re-released in 1991 as a conversion kit for *Dragon's Lair II: Time Warp*

SPACE ATTACK

Manufacturer: Sega
Date: 1979
Cabinet Type: Upright
Rarity: 9
Price Range: $50–150*

SPACE ATTACK II

Manufacturer: Video Games (UK) Ltd.
Date: 1980
Cabinet Type: Upright
Rarity: 9
Price Range: $50–150*

SPACE BEAM

Manufacturer: Nanao
Date: 1980
Cabinet Type: Upright
Rarity: 9
Price Range: $50–150*

SPACE BIRD

Manufacturer: Hoei
Date: 1980
Cabinet Type: Upright
Rarity: 9
Price Range: $50–150*

SPACE CHASER

Manufacturer: Taito
Date: 1980
Cabinet Type: Upright
Rarity: 9
Price Range: $75–150*

SPACE CYCLONE

Manufacturer: Taito
Date: 1980
Cabinet Type: Upright
Rarity: 9
Price Range: $75–150*

SPACE DEMON

Manufacturer: Fortrek
Date: 1980
Cabinet Type: Upright
Rarity: 9
Price Range: $75–150*

SPACE DUEL

Manufacturer: Atari
Date: 1982
Cabinet Type: Upright
Rarity: 7
Price Range: $200–450
Cabinet Type: Cocktail
Rarity: 8
Price Range: $400–600

SPACE DUNGEON

Manufacturer: Taito
Date: 1981
Cabinet Type: Upright
Rarity: 9
Price Range: $150–300*

SPACE ENCOUNTERS

Manufacturer: Midway
Date: 1980
Cabinet Type: Upright
Rarity: 9
Price Range: $50–150
Cabinet Type: Cabaret
Rarity: 9
Price Range: $100–200*

SPACE FEVER

Manufacturer: Nintendo
Date: 1980
Cabinet Type: Cocktail
Rarity: 9
Price Range: $75–150*
Notes: Some versions include a color monitor overlay

SPACE FIGHTER

Manufacturer: Sega
Date: 1979
Cabinet Type: Upright
Rarity: 9
Price Range: $50–150*

SPACE FIGHTER MARK II

Manufacturer: Data East
Date: 1980
Cabinet Type: Upright
Rarity: 9
Price Range: $50–150*

SPACE FIGHTER X

Manufacturer: Nichibutsu
Date: 1982
Cabinet Type: Upright
Rarity: 9
Price Range: $50–150*

SPACE FIREBIRD

Manufacturer: Gremlin
Date: 1980
Cabinet Type: Upright
Rarity: 8
Price Range: $100–200
Cabinet Type: Cocktail
Rarity: 9
Price Range: $150–250*
Notes: Licensed from Nintendo

SPACE FORCE

Manufacturer: Venture Line
Date: 1980
Cabinet Type: Upright
Rarity: 9
Price Range: $50–150*

SPACE FORTRESS

Manufacturer: Century Electronics
Date: 1981
Cabinet Type: Upright
Rarity: 9
Price Range: $50–150*

SPACE FURY

Manufacturer: Sega/Gremlin
Date: 1981
Cabinet Type: Upright
Rarity: 9
Price Range: $500–900
Cabinet Type: Cocktail
Rarity: 9
Price Range: $700–900*

SPACE HARRIER

Manufacturer: Sega
Date: 1985
Cabinet Type: Upright
Rarity: 7
Price Range: $275–400
Cabinet Type: Cockpit
Rarity: 9
Price Range: $300–500
Notes: Nonmoving version
Cabinet Type: Cockpit
Rarity: 10
Price Range: $400–600*
Notes: Full-motion cockpit

SPACE INTRUDER

Manufacturer: Shoei
Date: 1980
Cabinet Type: Upright
Rarity: 9
Price Range: $100–200*
Notes: Bootleg of *Space Invaders*

SPACE INVADERS

Manufacturer: Midway
Date: 1978
Cabinet Type: Upright
Rarity: 3
Price Range: $350–700
Cabinet Type: Cocktail
Rarity: 8
Price Range: $300–500*
Manufacturer: Taito
Cabinet Type: Cabaret
Rarity: 8
Price Range: $350–550*
Notes: Licensed from Taito; there is no Taito upright version of the game. Only Taito released the game in cabinet form

SPACE INVADERS II

Manufacturer: Midway
Date: 1980
Cabinet Type: Cocktail
Rarity: 9
Price Range: $400–500*
Notes: 2-player simultaneous play

SPACE INVADERS DELUXE

Manufacturer: Midway
Date: 1980
Cabinet Type: Upright
Rarity: 4
Price Range: $350–600
Cabinet Type: Cocktail
Rarity: 9
Price Range: $400–600
Notes: Title screen says "Space Invaders Part II" (which is the overseas name of the game)

SPACE INVADERS PART II
Manufacturer: Taito
Date: 1980
Cabinet Type: Upright
Rarity: 9
Price Range: $400–600*
Cabinet Type: Cocktail
Rarity: 9
Price Range: $400–600*
Notes: Released in the U.S. as *Space Invaders Deluxe*

SPACE INVASION
Manufacturer: Capcom
Date: 1985
Cabinet Type: Upright
Rarity: 9
Price Range: $100–200*
Notes: The European version of *Commando*

SPACE LASER
Manufacturer: Taito
Date: 1980
Cabinet Type: Upright
Rarity: 9
Price Range: $50–150*

SPACE LAUNCHER
Manufacturer: Nintendo
Date: 1979
Cabinet Type: Upright
Rarity: 9
Price Range: $75–150*

SPACE ODYSSEY
Manufacturer: Sega/Gremlin
Date: 1981
Cabinet Type: Upright
Rarity: 9
Price Range: $100–200*

SPACE PANIC
Manufacturer: Universal
Date: 1980
Cabinet Type: Upright
Rarity: 8
Price Range: $100–200
Cabinet Type: Cocktail
Rarity: 9
Price Range: $150–250*

SPACE PHANTOMS
Manufacturer: Zilec
Date: 1979
Cabinet Type: Upright
Rarity: 9
Price Range: $50–150*
Notes: *Ozma Wars* with different graphics

SPACE RACE
Manufacturer: Atari
Date: 1973
Cabinet Type: Upright
Rarity: 10
Price Range: $75–150*
Notes: Also licensed to Midway and sold as *Asteroid*

SPACE SEEKER
Manufacturer: Taito
Date: 1981
Cabinet Type: Upright
Rarity: 9
Price Range: $75–150*

SPACE TACTICS
Manufacturer: Sega
Date: 1980
Cabinet Type: Cockpit
Rarity: 9
Price Range: $200–300*

SPACE TANK
Manufacturer: Tehkan
Date: 1983
Cabinet Type: Upright
Rarity: 9
Price Range: $75–150*

SPACE TREK
Manufacturer: Sega
Date: 1980
Cabinet Type: Upright
Rarity: 9
Price Range: $50–150*

SPACE WALK
Manufacturer: Midway
Date: 1978
Cabinet Type: Upright
Rarity: 9
Price Range: $50–100*

SPACE WAR
Manufacturer: Konami
Date: 1979
Cabinet Type: Upright
Rarity: 9
Price Range: $50–150*
Notes: Copy of *Space Laser*

SPACE WAR
Manufacturer: Vectorbeam
Date: 1977
Cabinet Type: Upright
Rarity: 9
Price Range: $400–600*
Notes: Same game as Cinematronics' *Space Wars*, but in a smaller cabinet and released under the Vectorbeam label

SPACE WARP
Manufacturer: Century Electronics
Date: 1983
Cabinet Type: Upright
Rarity: 9
Price Range: $75–150*
Notes: Conversion kit

SPACE WARS
Manufacturer: Cinematronics
Date: 1977
Cabinet Type: Upright
Rarity: 8
Price Range: $450–750
Notes: The first game to use vector (X-Y) graphics

SPACE ZAP
Manufacturer: Midway
Date: 1980
Cabinet Type: Upright
Rarity: 8
Price Range: $150–250
Cabinet Type: Cocktail
Rarity: 9
Price Range: $200–300*
Cabinet Type: Cabaret
Rarity: 9
Price Range: $200–300

SPATTER
Manufacturer: Sega
Date: 1984
Cabinet Type: Upright
Rarity: 9
Price Range: $75–150*

SPECIAL BREAK
Manufacturer: Rene Pierre
Date: 1977
Cabinet Type: Upright
Rarity: 9
Price Range: $50–100*

SPECIAL FORCES
Manufacturer: Magic Conversions, Inc.
Date: 1985
Cabinet Type: Upright
Rarity: 9
Price Range: $75–200*
Notes: Conversion kit for *Donkey Kong*

SPECTAR
Manufacturer: Exidy
Date: 1980
Cabinet Type: Upright
Rarity: 9
Price Range: $75–150*
Cabinet Type: Cocktail
Rarity: 9
Price Range: $100–200*
Cabinet Type: Cabaret
Rarity: 9
Price Range: $150–250*

SPEED BUGGY
Manufacturer: Data East
Date: 1984
Cabinet Type: Upright
Rarity: 9
Price Range: $150–250*
Cabinet Type: Cockpit
Rarity: 9
Price Range: $250–350*

SPEED COIN
Manufacturer: Stern
Date: 1984
Cabinet Type: Upright
Rarity: Prototype
Price Range: $?
Notes: No pricing information available due to extreme rarity

SPEED FREAK
Manufacturer: Vectorbeam
Date: 1978
Cabinet Type: Upright
Rarity: 9
Price Range: $450–650*
Notes: Vector (X-Y) driving game

SPEED RACE
Manufacturer: Taito
Date: 1974
Cabinet Type: Upright
Rarity: 9
Price Range: $50–100*

SPEED RACE GP-5
Manufacturer: Taito
Date: 1980
Cabinet Type: Upright
Rarity: 9
Price Range: $50–150*

SPEED RACE TWIN
Manufacturer: Taito
Date: 1976
Cabinet Type: Upright
Rarity: 9
Price Range: $75–150*

SPELUNKER
Manufacturer: Irem
Date: 1985
Cabinet Type: Upright
Rarity: 9
Price Range: $75–150*

SPELUNKER II
Manufacturer: Irem
Date: 1985
Cabinet Type: Upright
Rarity: 9
Price Range: $75–150*

SPIDERS
Manufacturer: Venture Line
Date: 1981
Cabinet Type: Upright
Rarity: 8
Price Range: $50–150
Notes: Licensed from Sigma Ent., Inc.

SPIKE
Manufacturer: Kee Games
Date: 1974
Cabinet Type: Upright
Rarity: 9
Price Range: $50–100*
Notes: Released by Atari as *Rebound*

SPIKER
Manufacturer: Bally Sente
Date: 1986
Cabinet Type: Upright
Rarity: 9
Price Range: $100–200*

SPITFIRE

Manufacturer: Innovative Coin
Date: 1976
Cabinet Type: Upright
Rarity: 9
Price Range: $50–100*

SPLAT!

Manufacturer: Williams
Date: 1982
Cabinet Type: Upright
Rarity: 10
Price Range: $200–400*
Notes: Designed by John Newcomer, designer of *Joust*

SPRINGER

Manufacturer: Orca
Date: 1982
Cabinet Type: Upright
Rarity: 9
Price Range: $50–150*

SPRINT 1

Manufacturer: Kee Games
Date: 1978
Cabinet Type: Upright
Rarity: 8
Price Range: $50–150
Notes: 1-player version of *Sprint 2*

SPRINT 2

Manufacturer: Kee Games
Date: 1976
Cabinet Type: Upright
Rarity: 7
Price Range: $100–150

SPRINT 4

Manufacturer: Atari
Date: 1977
Cabinet Type: Upright
Rarity: 9
Price Range: $100–200*
Notes: Essentially a 4-player version of *Sprint 2*

SPRING 8

Manufacturer: Atari
Date: 1977
Cabinet Type: Upright
Rarity: 9
Price Range: $100–250*
Notes: Essentially an 8-player version of *Sprint 4*

SPY HUNTER

Manufacturer: Bally Midway
Date: 1983
Cabinet Type: Upright
Rarity: 4
Price Range: $350–700
Cabinet Type: Cockpit
Rarity: 6
Price Range: $600–1,000

SPY HUNTER II

Manufacturer: Bally Midway
Date: 1987
Cabinet Type: Upright
Rarity: 8
Price Range: $250–350
Notes: Sequel to *Spy Hunter*

STAR ATTACK

Manufacturer: Nichibutsu
Date: 1982
Cabinet Type: Upright
Rarity: 9
Price Range: $75–150*

STAR BLAZER

Manufacturer: Sega
Date: 1983
Cabinet Type: Upright
Rarity: 9
Price Range: $75–150*

STAR CASTLE

Manufacturer: Cinematronics
Date: 1980
Cabinet Type: Upright
Rarity: 7
Price Range: $450–650*

STAR CRUISER

Manufacturer: Ramtek
Date: 1977
Cabinet Type: Upright
Rarity: 9
Price Range: $50–100*

STAR FIGHTER

Manufacturer: Ace Vending Corp.
Date: 1980
Cabinet Type: Upright
Rarity: 9
Price Range: $50–150*
Notes: Copy of *Eagle*

STAR FIRE

Manufacturer: Exidy
Date: 1980
Cabinet Type: Upright
Rarity: 9
Price Range: $100–200*
Cabinet Type: Cockpit
Rarity: 9
Price Range: $200–400*

STAR FORCE

Manufacturer: Tehkan
Date: 1984
Cabinet Type: Upright
Rarity: 9
Price Range: $100–200*

STAR INVADERS

Manufacturer: Potomac Mortgage Company
Date: 1980
Cabinet Type: Cocktail
Rarity: 9
Price Range: $50–150*

STAR JACKER

Manufacturer: Sega
Date: 1983
Cabinet Type: Upright
Rarity: 9
Price Range: $75–150*

STAR JAGUAR

Manufacturer: Sega
Date: 1983
Cabinet Type: Upright
Rarity: 9
Price Range: $75–150*

STAR LAKER

Manufacturer: Sega
Date: 1981
Cabinet Type: Upright
Rarity: 9
Price Range: $50–150*

STAR LUSTER

Manufacturer: Namco
Date: 1985
Cabinet Type: Upright
Rarity: 9
Price Range: $75–150*

STAR RIDER

Manufacturer: Williams
Date: 1983
Cabinet Type: Upright
Rarity: 10
Price Range: $500–600*
Cabinet Type: Cockpit
Rarity: 10
Price Range: $600–800*
Notes: Laser disc jet cycle racing game

STAR TREK

Manufacturer: For-Play
Date: 1972
Cabinet Type: Upright
Rarity: 9
Price Range: $75–150*

STAR TREK (STRATEGIC OPERATIONS SIMU-LATOR)

Manufacturer: Sega
Date: 1982
Cabinet Type: Upright
Rarity: 7
Price Range: $500–800
Cabinet Type: Cockpit
Rarity: 8
Price Range: $600–1,000
Notes: Often seen as conversions in *Asteroids, Tempest,* and other game cabinets. Cockpit is known as the "captain's chair" version

STAR WARRIOR

Manufacturer: Potomac Mortgage Company
Date: 1981
Cabinet Type: Cocktail
Rarity: 9
Price Range: $50–150*

STAR WARS

Manufacturer: Atari
Date: 1983
Cabinet Type: Upright
Rarity: 5
Price Range: $800–1,200
Cabinet Type: Cockpit
Rarity: 8
Price Range: $1,000–1,500
Notes: One of the most collectible games around

STARGATE

Manufacturer: Williams
Date: 1981
Cabinet Type: Upright
Rarity: 4
Price Range: $550–900
Notes: Sequel to *Defender*
Cabinet Type: Cocktail
Rarity: 7
Price Range: $500–650
Cabinet Type: Cabaret
Rarity: 8
Price Range: $550–900

STARHAWK

Manufacturer: Cinematronics
Date: 1977
Cabinet Type: Upright
Rarity: 9
Price Range: $500–600*

STARSHIP 1

Manufacturer: Atari
Date: 1976
Cabinet Type: Upright
Rarity: 9
Price Range: $50–150*

STEEPLECHASE

Manufacturer: Atari
Date: 1975
Cabinet Type: Upright
Rarity: 9
Price Range: $50–100*

STINGER

Manufacturer: Seibu Denshi
Date: 1983
Cabinet Type: Upright
Rarity: 9
Price Range: $75–100*

STOCKER

Manufacturer: Bally Sente
Date: 1984
Cabinet Type: Upright
Rarity: 9
Price Range: $100–200*

STOMPIN'

Manufacturer: Bally Sente
Date: 1986
Cabinet Type: Upright
Rarity: 9
Price Range: $100–200*

STRATEGY X
Manufacturer: Stern
Date: 1981
Cabinet Type: Upright
Rarity: 9
Price Range: $75–150*

STRATOVOX
Manufacturer: Taito
Date: 1980
Cabinet Type: Upright
Rarity: 9
Price Range: $150–250*

STREAKING
Manufacturer: Shoei
Date: 1982
Cabinet Type: Upright
Rarity: 9
Price Range: $50–150*

STREET BURNERS
Manufacturer: Allied Leisure
Date: 1975
Cabinet Type: Upright
Rarity: 9
Price Range: $50–100*

STREET FOOTBALL
Manufacturer: Bally Sente
Date: 1985
Cabinet Type: Upright
Rarity: 9
Price Range: $100–200*

STREET HEAT
Manufacturer: Cardinal Amusement Products
Date: 1985
Cabinet Type: Upright
Rarity: 9
Price Range: $75–150*
Notes: Usually found as a conversion kit in *Donkey Kong* cabinets

STRENGTH & SKILL
Manufacturer: Sun/Kitco
Date: 1984
Cabinet Type: Upright
Rarity: 9
Price Range: $50–150*

STRIKE BOWLING
Manufacturer: Taito
Date: 1982
Cabinet Type: Upright
Rarity: 9
Price Range: $50–150*

STROKE & MATCH GOLF
Manufacturer: Nintendo
Date: 1984
Cabinet Type: Upright
Rarity: 9
Price Range: $75–150*
Cabinet Type: Cocktail
Rarity: 9
Price Range: $100–200*

STUNT CYCLE
Manufacturer: Atari
Date: 1976
Cabinet Type: Upright
Rarity: 9
Price Range: $50–150

SUBMARINE
Manufacturer: Midway
Date: 1979
Cabinet Type: Upright
Rarity: 9
Price Range: $50–150

SUBROC—3D
Manufacturer: Sega
Date: 1982
Cabinet Type: Upright
Rarity: 8
Price Range: $150–250*
Cabinet Type: Cockpit
Rarity: 9
Price Range: $300–400*

SUBS
Manufacturer: Atari
Date: 1977
Cabinet Type: Upright
Rarity: 9
Price Range: $75–150*
Notes: 2-player game with 2 monitors and sets of controls

SUNDANCE
Manufacturer: Cinematronics
Date: 1979
Cabinet Type: Upright
Rarity: 10
Price Range: $500–700*
Notes: Rare black-and-white vector game

SUPER ASTRO FIGHTER
Manufacturer: Data East
Date: 1982
Cabinet Type: Upright
Rarity: 9
Price Range: $50–150*

SUPER BAGMAN
Manufacturer: Stern
Date: 1984
Cabinet Type: Upright
Rarity: 9
Price Range: $150–250*
Notes: Licensed from Valadon Automation

SUPER BASKETBALL
Manufacturer: Konami
Date: 1984
Cabinet Type: Upright
Rarity: 8
Price Range: $100–200

SUPER BLOCK
Manufacturer: Taito
Date: 1978
Cabinet Type: Upright
Rarity: 9
Price Range: $50–100*

SUPER BOND

Manufacturer: Alpha
Date: 1982
Cabinet Type: Upright
Rarity: 9
Price Range: $50–150*

SUPER BOWL

Manufacturer: Sega/Gremlin
Date: 1977
Cabinet Type: Upright
Rarity: 9
Price Range: $50–100*

SUPER BREAK

Manufacturer: Data East
Date: 1978
Cabinet Type: Upright
Rarity: 9
Price Range: $50–100*

SUPER BREAK 2

Manufacturer: Data East
Date: 1978
Cabinet Type: Upright
Rarity: 9
Price Range: $50–100*

SUPER BREAKOUT

Manufacturer: Atari
Date: 1978
Cabinet Type: Upright
Rarity: 9
Price Range: $50–150

SUPER BUG

Manufacturer: Kee Games
Date: 1977
Cabinet Type: Upright
Rarity: 9
Price Range: $50–100*
Notes: First video game to use a scrolling playfield

SUPER COBRA

Manufacturer: Stern
Date: 1981
Cabinet Type: Upright
Rarity: 8
Price Range: $200–300
Cabinet Type: Cocktail
Rarity: 9
Price Range: $250–350*

SUPER DEATH CHASE

Manufacturer: Exidy
Date: 1977
Cabinet Type: Upright
Rarity: 10
Price Range: $400–500*

SUPER DON QUIXOTE

Manufacturer: Universal
Date: 1984
Cabinet Type: Upright
Rarity: 10
Price Range: $500–700*
Notes: Laser disc game similar to *Dragon's Lair*

SUPER DOUBLES TENNIS

Manufacturer: Data East
Date: 1983
Cabinet Type: Upright
Rarity: 9
Price Range: $75–150*

SUPER EARTH INVASION

Manufacturer: Competitive Video
Date: 1980
Cabinet Type: Upright
Rarity: 10
Price Range: $75–150*
Notes: Copy of *Space Invaders*

SUPER FLIPPER

Manufacturer: Chicago Coin
Date: 1975
Cabinet Type: Special
Rarity: 9
Price Range: $75–150*
Notes: A video pinball game housed in a pinball machine cabinet

SUPER GALAXIANS

Manufacturer: Midway
Date: 1979
Cabinet Type: Upright
Rarity: 9
Price Range: $200–300*
Notes: A faster version of *Galaxian;* released as an upgrade for *Galaxian* machines

SUPER GLOB

Manufacturer: Epos
Date: 1983
Cabinet Type: Upright
Rarity: 10
Price Range: $150–350*
Notes: Only released as an upgrade kit; usually found in *Pac-Man* cabinets

SUPER HANG-ON

Manufacturer: Sega
Date: 1987
Cabinet Type: Upright
Rarity: 5
Price Range: $300–400

SUPER HIGH-WAY

Manufacturer: Taito
Date: 1977
Cabinet Type: Upright
Rarity: 9
Price Range: $50–100

SUPER INVADER ATTACK

Manufacturer: Zaccaria/Zelco
Date: 1978
Cabinet Type: Upright
Rarity: 10
Price Range: $75–150*
Notes: Copy of *Space Invaders*

SUPER INVADERS

Manufacturer: EMAG Corporation
Date: 1978
Cabinet Type: Upright
Rarity: 10
Price Range: $75–150
Notes: Bootleg of *Space Invaders;* Zenitone-Microsec
and another unknown company also released *Space
Invaders* clones under this name

SUPER LOCOMOTIVE

Manufacturer: Sega
Date: 1982
Cabinet Type: Upright
Rarity: 9
Price Range: $50–150*

SUPER MARIO BROS.

Manufacturer: Nintendo
Date: 1985
Cabinet Type: Upright
Rarity: 5
Price Range: $200–300

SUPER MISSILE ATTACK

Manufacturer: General Computer Corp.
Date: 1981
Cabinet Type: Upright
Rarity: 10
Price Range: $200–300*
Notes: Sold as an upgrade board for *Missile Command;*
found in *Missile Command* cabinets

SUPER MOON CRESTA

Manufacturer: Sega/Gremlin
Date: 1981
Cabinet Type: Upright
Rarity: 9
Price Range: $100–200*

SUPER MOUSE

Manufacturer: Taito
Date: 1982
Cabinet Type: Upright
Rarity: 9
Price Range: $50–150*

SUPER OFF ROAD, IRON MAN IVAN STEW-ART'S

Manufacturer: Leland
Date: 1989
Cabinet Type: Upright (3-player)
Rarity: 2
Price Range: $280–850
Cabinet Type: Upright
Rarity: 5
Price Range: $200–250
Notes: Worth slightly more with the updated "Track
Pak" boards installed

SUPER PAC-MAN

Manufacturer: Bally Midway
Date: 1982
Cabinet Type: Upright
Rarity: 7
Price Range: $300–400
Cabinet Type: Cocktail
Rarity: 8
Price Range: $550–650
Cabinet Type: Cabaret
Rarity: 8
Price Range: $400–600

SUPER PUNCH-OUT!!

Manufacturer: Nintendo
Date: 1985
Cabinet Type: Upright
Rarity: 8
Price Range: $400–600*

SUPER QIX

Manufacturer: Taito
Date: 1987
Cabinet Type: Upright
Rarity: 8
Price Range: $200–350
Notes: Sequel to *Qix*

SUPER RIDER

Manufacturer: Venture Line
Date: 1983
Cabinet Type: Upright
Rarity: 9
Price Range: $50–150*

SUPER SOCCER

Manufacturer: Allied Leisure
Date: 1973
Cabinet Type: Upright
Rarity: 9
Price Range: $50–100*

SUPER SPEED RACE

Manufacturer: Midway
Date: 1979
Cabinet Type: Upright
Rarity: 9
Price Range: $50–150*

SUPER SPEED RACE GP V

Manufacturer: Taito
Date: 1980
Cabinet Type: Upright
Rarity: 9
Price Range: $50–150*

SUPER SPEED RACE JR.

Manufacturer: Bally Midway
Date: 1985
Cabinet Type: Upright
Rarity: 9
Price Range: $100–250*
Notes: Licensed from Taito

SUPER SPEED RACE V
Manufacturer: Taito
Date: 1978
Cabinet Type: Upright
Rarity: 9
Price Range: $50–150*

SUPER SPRINT
Manufacturer: Atari Games
Date: 1986
Cabinet Type: Upright
Rarity: 4
Price Range: $350–700

SUPER TANK
Manufacturer: Computran
Date: 1981
Cabinet Type: Upright
Rarity: 9
Price Range: $50–150*
Cabinet Type: Cocktail
Rarity: 9
Price Range: $100–200*

SUPER XEVIOUS
Manufacturer: Namco
Date: 1984
Cabinet Type: Upright
Rarity: 9
Price Range: $300–400*
Notes: Updated version of *Xevious*

SUPER ZAXXON
Manufacturer: Sega
Date: 1982
Cabinet Type: Upright
Rarity: 9
Price Range: $300–400*

SUPERBIKE
Manufacturer: Crown Vending
Date: 1984
Cabinet Type: Upright
Rarity: 9
Price Range: $75–150*
Notes: Sold as a conversion kit for *Donkey Kong* machines

SURVIVAL
Manufacturer: Rock-Ola
Date: 1982
Cabinet Type: Upright
Rarity: 9
Price Range: $50–150*

SWAT
Manufacturer: Bally Midway
Date: 1984
Cabinet Type: Upright
Rarity: 9
Price Range: $100–200*
Notes: Licensed from Coreland/Sega

SWIMMER
Manufacturer: Centuri
Date: 1982
Cabinet Type: Upright
Rarity: 9
Price Range: $150–250*
Notes: Licensed from Tehkan

T.T. BLOCK
Manufacturer: Taito
Date: 1977
Cabinet Type: Upright
Rarity: 9
Price Range: $50–100*

TABLE TENNIS
Manufacturer: Nutting Associates
Date: 1973
Cabinet Type: Upright
Rarity: 9
Price Range: $50–100*

TAC/SCAN
Manufacturer: Sega
Date: 1982
Cabinet Type: Upright
Rarity: 8
Price Range: $250–450

TACTICIAN
Manufacturer: Konami
Date: 1981
Cabinet Type: Upright
Rarity: 9
Price Range: $75–150*
Notes: Licensed from Sega

TAG TEAM WRESTLING
Manufacturer: Data East
Date: 1984
Cabinet Type: Upright
Rarity: 7
Price Range: $150–250
Notes: Also known as *The Big Pro Wrestling;* licensed from Technos

TAILGUNNER
Manufacturer: Cinematronics
Date: 1979
Cabinet Type: Upright
Rarity: 9
Price Range: $500–700*

TAILGUNNER II
Manufacturer: Exidy
Date: 1980
Cabinet Type: Cockpit
Rarity: 10
Price Range: $600–800*
Notes: Cockpit version of *Tailgunner*

TAKE 7
Manufacturer: Fun Games, Inc.
Date: 1975
Cabinet Type: Upright
Rarity: 9
Price Range: $50–100*

TANK

Manufacturer: Kee Games
Date: 1974
Cabinet Type: Upright
Rarity: 9
Price Range: $75–150*
Cabinet Type: Cocktail
Rarity: 10
Price Range: $100–200*

TANK 8

Manufacturer: Kee Games
Date: 1976
Cabinet Type: Upright
Rarity: 9
Price Range: $150–250*

TANK BATTALION

Manufacturer: Game Plan
Date: 1981
Cabinet Type: Upright
Rarity: 9
Price Range: $50–150*
Cabinet Type: Cocktail
Rarity: 9
Price Range: $100–200*
Notes: Licensed from Namco

TANK BUSTERS

Manufacturer: Valadon Automation
Date: 1985
Cabinet Type: Upright
Rarity: 9
Price Range: $50–150*

TANK II

Manufacturer: Kee Games
Date: 1974
Cabinet Type: Upright
Rarity: 9
Price Range: $75–150

TANK III

Manufacturer: Kee Games
Date: 1975
Cabinet Type: Upright
Rarity: 9
Price Range: $75–150*

TANKERS

Manufacturer: Fun Games, Inc.
Date: 1975
Cabinet Type: Upright
Rarity: 9
Price Range: $50–100*
Notes: Copy of Tank

TAPPER

Manufacturer: Bally Midway
Date: 1984
Cabinet Type: Upright
Rarity: 5
Price Range: $600–1,200
Notes: Very collectible
Cabinet Type: Cocktail
Rarity: 8
Price Range: $500–800

TARG

Manufacturer: Exidy
Date: 1980
Cabinet Type: Upright
Rarity: 8
Price Range: $100–200

TARG

Manufacturer: Centuri
Date: 1980
Cabinet Type: Cocktail
Rarity: 9
Price Range: $100–200
Notes: Cocktail version of the Exidy game

TAZZ-MANIA

Manufacturer: Stern
Date: 1982
Cabinet Type: Upright
Rarity: 9
Price Range: $50–150

TEHKAN WORLD CUP

Manufacturer: Tehkan
Date: 1985
Cabinet Type: Upright
Rarity: 9
Price Range: $150–250*
Cabinet Type: Cocktail
Rarity: 8
Price Range: $100–200*

TEMPEST

Manufacturer: Atari
Date: 1980
Cabinet Type: Upright
Rarity: 4
Price Range: $550–1,200
Cabinet Type: Cocktail
Rarity: 8
Price Range: $550–1,200
Cabinet Type: Cabaret
Rarity: 7
Price Range: $650–900
Notes: One of the most collectible games around

TEMPEST TUBES

Manufacturer: Atari
Date: 1980
Cabinet Type: N/A
Rarity: 8
Price Range: $100–200*
Notes: Upgrade that adds new playfields to *Tempest*;
the price listed indicates price for the *upgrade only*—
add this to the cost of the *Tempest* machine itself

TEN YARD FIGHT '85

Manufacturer: Memetron
Date: 1985
Cabinet Type: Upright
Rarity: 9
Price Range: $100–200*

TENNIS

Manufacturer: Nintendo
Date: 1983
Cabinet Type: Upright
Rarity: 9
Price Range: $75–150*
Notes: Not the same game as *VS. Tennis*

TENNIS TOURNEY

Manufacturer: Allied Leisure
Date: 1973
Cabinet Type: Upright
Rarity: 9
Price Range: $50–100*

TERRA CRESTA

Manufacturer: Nichibutsu
Date: 1985
Cabinet Type: Upright
Rarity: 9
Price Range: $100–200*

TERRANEAN

Manufacturer: Data East
Date: 1980
Cabinet Type: Upright
Rarity: 9
Price Range: $75–150*

TETRIS

Manufacturer: Atari Games
Date: 1988
Cabinet Type: Upright
Rarity: 4
Price Range: $200–400
Cabinet Type: Cocktail
Rarity: 9
Price Range: $300–400
Notes: Found as conversions in a wide variety of cabinet types

TETRIS

Manufacturer: Sega
Date: 1988
Cabinet Type: Upright
Rarity: 9
Price Range: $200–400*
Notes: Same basic game as the Atari version, but with different graphics

THAYER'S QUEST

Manufacturer: RDI Video Systems
Date: 1984
Cabinet Type: Upright
Rarity: 10
Price Range: $800–1000
Notes: Rare Laser disc adventure game; produced only as a conversion kit for *Dragon's Lair*—no dedicated versions exist

THIEF

Manufacturer: Pacific Novelty
Date: 1981
Cabinet Type: Upright
Rarity: 9
Price Range: $75–150*

THE THREE STOOGES

Manufacturer: Mylstar
Date: 1984
Cabinet Type: Upright
Rarity: 9
Price Range: $150–300*

TIC TAC QUIZ

Manufacturer: Sega
Date: 1977
Cabinet Type: Upright
Rarity: 9
Price Range: $50–100*

TIC TAC TRIVIA

Manufacturer: Merit
Date: 1985
Cabinet Type: Upright
Rarity: 9
Price Range: $50–150*
Notes: Also available in a bar-top version

TIGER-HELI

Manufacturer: Romstar
Date: 1985
Cabinet Type: Upright
Rarity: 9
Price Range: $150–250*
Notes: Licensed from Taito

TIMBER

Manufacturer: Bally Midway
Date: 1984
Cabinet Type: Upright
Rarity: 9
Price Range: $400–600*
Notes: Dedicated cabinets are *Tapper* cabinets with new art pasted over the *Tapper* art

TIME GAL

Manufacturer: Taito
Date: 1985
Cabinet Type: Upright
Rarity: 9
Price Range: $75–150*
Notes: Laser disc adventure released only in Japan (and for the Sega CD home system)

TIME LIMIT

Manufacturer: Chou Co., Ltd.
Date: 1983
Cabinet Type: Upright
Rarity: 9
Price Range: $75–150*

TIME PILOT

Manufacturer: Centuri
Date: 1982
Cabinet Type: Upright
Rarity: 5
Price Range: $150–300
Cabinet Type: Cocktail
Rarity: 9
Price Range: $200–350
Notes: Designed by Yoshiki Okamoto, who also designed *Gyruss, 1942,* and the *Street Fighter* games; dedicated version from Konami also exists

TIME PILOT '84

Manufacturer: Konami
Date: 1984
Cabinet Type: Upright
Rarity: 7
Price Range: $150–250
Cabinet Type: Cocktail
Rarity: 10
Price Range: $200–300*

TIME TUNNEL

Manufacturer: Taito
Date: 1982
Cabinet Type: Upright
Rarity: 9
Price Range: $75–150*

THE TIN STAR

Manufacturer: Taito
Date: 1983
Cabinet Type: Upright
Rarity: 9
Price Range: $100–200*

TNK-III

Manufacturer: SNK
Date: 1985
Cabinet Type: Upright
Rarity: 9
Price Range: $100–200*

TOGGLE

Manufacturer: Bally Sente
Date: 1985
Cabinet Type: Upright
Rarity: 9
Price Range: $100–200*

TOMAHAWK 777

Manufacturer: Data East
Date: 1980
Cabinet Type: Upright
Rarity: 9
Price Range: $75–150*
Cabinet Type: Cocktail
Rarity: 9
Price Range: $100–200*

TOMAHAWK MISSILE

Manufacturer: Electro Sport
Date: 1980
Cabinet Type: Upright
Rarity: 9
Price Range: $50–150*

TOMCAT

Manufacturer: Atari Games
Date: 1983
Cabinet Type: Upright
Rarity: Prototype
Price Range: $?
Notes: Pricing information unavailable due to rarity

TOP BOWLER

Manufacturer: Taito
Date: 1978
Cabinet Type: Upright
Rarity: 9
Price Range: $50–100*

TOP GEAR

Manufacturer: Universal
Date: 1984
Cabinet Type: Cockpit
Rarity: 10
Price Range: $600–800*
Notes: Laser disc racing game

TOP GEAR II

Manufacturer: Universal
Date: 1985
Cabinet Type: Cockpit
Rarity: 10
Price Range: $600–800*
Notes: Sequel to *Top Gear*

TOP ROLLER

Manufacturer: Jaleco
Date: 1983
Cabinet Type: Upright
Rarity: 9
Price Range: $75–150*

TOP RUNNER

Manufacturer: Sega
Date: 1978
Cabinet Type: Upright
Rarity: 9
Price Range: $50–100*

TOP SECRET

Manufacturer: Exidy
Date: 1986
Cabinet Type: Upright
Rarity: 9
Price Range: $200–400*
Notes: Released only as a conversion kit for Exidy
Crossbow (and similar) cabinets

TORA TORA

Manufacturer: Game Plan
Date: 1980
Cabinet Type: Upright
Rarity: 9
Price Range: $50–150*

TORNADO

Manufacturer: Data East
Date: 1981
Cabinet Type: Upright
Rarity: 9
Price Range: $100–200*
Notes: Released only as a conversion kit

TORNADO BASEBALL

Manufacturer: Midway
Date: 1976
Cabinet Type: Upright
Rarity: 9
Price Range: $50–150
Cabinet Type: Cocktail
Rarity: 9
Price Range: $75–150*

TOURNAMENT ARKANOID

Manufacturer: Romstar
Date: 1987
Cabinet Type: Upright
Rarity: 9
Price Range: $200–500
Cabinet Type: Cocktail
Rarity: 9
Price Range: $350–600*
Notes: Sequel to *Arkanoid*

TOURNAMENT PRO GOLF

Manufacturer: Data East
Date: 1982
Cabinet Type: Upright
Rarity: 9
Price Range: $75–150*

TOURNAMENT TABLE

Manufacturer: Atari
Date: 1978
Cabinet Type: Cocktail
Rarity: 9
Price Range: $50–150*

THE TOWER OF DRUAGA

Manufacturer: Namco
Date: 1984
Cabinet Type: Upright
Rarity: 9
Price Range: $75–150*

TRACK & FIELD

Manufacturer: Konami
Date: 1983
Cabinet Type: Upright
Rarity: 7
Price Range: $300–500
Cabinet Type: Cocktail
Rarity: 8
Price Range: $600–800
Notes: Known as *Hyper Olympic* outside the U.S.

TRAMPOLINE

Manufacturer: Taito
Date: 1978
Cabinet Type: Upright
Rarity: 9
Price Range: $50–100*
Cabinet Type: Cocktail
Rarity: 9
Price Range: $75–150*

TRANQUILIZER GUN

Manufacturer: Sega
Date: 1980
Cabinet Type: Upright
Rarity: 8
Price Range: $50–150*

TRAVERSE U.S.A

Manufacturer: Irem
Date: 1983
Cabinet Type: Upright
Rarity: 9
Price Range: $75–150*
Notes: Also known as *Zippy Race*

TREASURE HUNT

Manufacturer: Hara Industries
Date: 1982
Cabinet Type: Upright
Rarity: 9
Price Range: $75–150*
Notes: Same game as *Jack the Giant Killer*

TREASURE ISLAND

Manufacturer: Data East
Date: 1981
Cabinet Type: Upright
Rarity: 9
Price Range: $75–150*

TRIPLE HUNT

Manufacturer: Atari
Date: 1977
Cabinet Type: Upright
Rarity: 9
Price Range: $50–100*

TRIPLE PUNCH

Manufacturer: KKI
Date: 1982
Cabinet Type: Upright
Rarity: 9
Price Range: $75–150*

TRIV-QUIZ

Manufacturer: Status
Date: 1982
Cabinet Type: Upright
Rarity: 9
Price Range: $50–150*

TRIVIA CHALLENGE

Manufacturer: Kramer
Date: 1985
Cabinet Type: Upright
Rarity: 9
Price Range: $50–150*

TRIVIA MASTER

Manufacturer: PGD
Date: 1985
Cabinet Type: Upright
Rarity: 9
Price Range: $50–150*

TRIVIA WHIZ

Manufacturer: Merit
Date: 1984
Cabinet Type: Upright
Rarity: 9
Price Range: $100–200*
Cabinet Type: Cocktail
Rarity: 8
Price Range: $150–250

TRIVIAL PURSUIT—ALL-STAR SPORTS

Manufacturer: Bally Sente
Date: 1984
Cabinet Type: Upright
Rarity: 10
Price Range: $100–200*

TRIVIAL PURSUIT—BABY BOOMER
Manufacturer: Bally Sente
Date: 1984
Cabinet Type: Upright
Rarity: 9
Price Range: $100–200*

TRIVIAL PURSUIT—GENUS I
Manufacturer: Bally Sente
Date: 1984
Cabinet Type: Upright
Rarity: 9
Price Range: $100–200*

TRIVIAL PURSUIT—GENUS II
Manufacturer: Bally Sente
Date: 1984
Cabinet Type: Upright
Rarity: 9
Price Range: $100–200*

TRIVIAL PURSUIT—SPANISH VERSION
Manufacturer: Bally Sente
Date: 1984
Cabinet Type: Upright
Rarity: 10
Price Range: $100–200*

TRIVIAL PURSUIT—YOUNG PLAYERS
Manufacturer: Bally Sente
Date: 1984
Cabinet Type: Upright
Rarity: 10
Price Range: $100–200*

TRON
Manufacturer: Bally Midway
Date: 1982
Cabinet Type: Upright
Rarity: 6
Price Range: $600–1,200
Cabinet Type: Cocktail
Rarity: 8
Price Range: $700–900
Cabinet Type: Cabaret
Rarity: 9
Price Range: $700–1,000
Notes: Very collectible

TROPICAL ANGEL
Manufacturer: Irem
Date: 1983
Cabinet Type: Upright
Rarity: 9
Price Range: $50–150*

TUBE PANIC
Manufacturer: Nichibutsu
Date: 1984
Cabinet Type: Upright
Rarity: 8
Price Range: $75–150*
Cabinet Type: Cocktail
Rarity: 8
Price Range: $100–200*
Cabinet Type: Cockpit
Rarity: 9
Price Range: $150–250*

TUGBOAT
Manufacturer: Moppet Video
Date: 1982
Cabinet Type: Upright
Rarity: 10
Price Range: $200–300*
Notes: This is a miniature-sized game (about 3–4 feet high) made for children

TUNNEL HUNT
Manufacturer: Centuri
Date: 1982
Cabinet Type: Upright
Rarity: 9
Price Range: $75–150*
Notes: Licensed by Atari

TURBO
Manufacturer: Sega
Date: 1981
Cabinet Type: Upright
Rarity: 3
Price Range: $100–200
Cabinet Type: Cabaret
Rarity: 8
Price Range: $150–250*
Cabinet Type: Cockpit
Rarity: 7
Price Range: $200–300*

TURBO OUT RUN
Manufacturer: Sega
Date: 1989
Cabinet Type: Upright
Rarity: 3
Price Range: $150–450
Notes: Sequel to *Out-Run*
Cabinet Type: Cabaret
Rarity: 8
Price Range: $250–400*
Cabinet Type: Cockpit
Rarity: 8
Price Range: $300–500*

TURBO SUB
Manufacturer: Entertainment Sciences
Date: 1985
Cabinet Type: Upright
Rarity: 9
Price Range: $150–250*

TURBO TAG
Manufacturer: Bally Midway
Date: 1985
Cabinet Type: Upright
Rarity: Prototype
Price Range: $?
Notes: Licensed from Simon and Schuster; no pricing information available due to rarity

TURKEY SHOOT
Manufacturer: Williams
Date: 1984
Cabinet Type: Upright
Rarity: 9
Price Range: $400–500*

TURPIN

Manufacturer: Sega
Date: 1981
Cabinet Type: Upright
Rarity: 9
Price Range: $50–150*
Notes: Copy of *Turtles*

TURTLES

Manufacturer: Stern
Date: 1981
Cabinet Type: Upright
Rarity: 9
Price Range: $75–150*

TUTANKHAM

Manufacturer: Stern
Date: 1982
Cabinet Type: Upright
Rarity: 8
Price Range: $200–450
Notes: Licensed from Konami

TV BASKETBALL

Manufacturer: Midway
Date: 1974
Cabinet Type: Upright
Rarity: 9
Price Range: $50–100*

TV FLIPPER

Manufacturer: Midway
Date: 1975
Cabinet Type: Upright
Rarity: 9
Price Range: $50–100*

TV PINBALL

Manufacturer: Exidy
Date: 1975
Cabinet Type: Upright
Rarity: 9
Price Range: $50–100*

TV PING PONG

Manufacturer: Chicago Coin
Date: 1973
Cabinet Type: Upright
Rarity: 9
Price Range: $50–100*

TV PINGAME

Manufacturer: Chicago Coin
Date: 1973
Cabinet Type: Upright
Rarity: 9
Price Range: $50–100*

TV TENNIS

Manufacturer: U.S. Billiards
Date: 1973
Cabinet Type: Upright
Rarity: 9
Price Range: $50–100*

TWO TIGERS

Manufacturer: Bally Midway
Date: 1984
Cabinet Type: Upright
Rarity: 9
Price Range: $150–250

TX-1

Manufacturer: Atari
Date: 1984
Cabinet Type: Cockpit
Rarity: 9
Price Range: $400–600*
Notes: Licensed from Namco; has 3 monitors which
provide a wrap-around view

UFO CHASE

Manufacturer: Electra
Date: 1975
Cabinet Type: Upright
Rarity: 9
Price Range: $50–100*

ULTRA TANK

Manufacturer: Kee Games
Date: 1978
Cabinet Type: Upright
Rarity: 9
Price Range: $50–150*

U.N. COMMAND

Manufacturer: Project Support Engineering
Date: 1977
Cabinet Type: Upright
Rarity: 9
Price Range: $75–150*
Notes: 2-player version of *Bazooka*

UNIWARS

Manufacturer: Irem
Date: 1980
Cabinet Type: Upright
Rarity: 9
Price Range: $50–150*

UP'N DOWN

Manufacturer: Bally Midway
Date: 1983
Cabinet Type: Upright
Rarity: 9
Price Range: $150–250*
Notes: Licensed from Sega

US VS. THEM

Manufacturer: Mylstar
Date: 1984
Cabinet Type: Upright
Rarity: 10
Price Range: $500–700*
Notes: Laser disc space-themed shooter

VAMPIRE

Manufacturer: Entertainment Enterprise, Ltd.
Date: 1983
Cabinet Type: Upright
Rarity: 9
Price Range: $75–150*

VAN-VAN CAR
Manufacturer: Karateco
Date: 1983
Cabinet Type: Upright
Rarity: 9
Price Range: $50–150*

VANGUARD
Manufacturer: Centuri
Date: 1981
Cabinet Type: Upright
Rarity: 7
Price Range: $300–375
Notes: Licensed from SNK
Cabinet Type: Cocktail
Rarity: 8
Price Range: $350–450
Notes: Cinematronics produced the cocktail version, which was actually a stand-up cocktail version (taller than the usual cocktail cabinet)

VANGUARD II
Manufacturer: SNK
Date: 1984
Cabinet Type: Upright
Rarity: 8
Price Range: $150–250

VENTURE
Manufacturer: Exidy
Date: 1981
Cabinet Type: Upright
Rarity: 8
Price Range: $350–500*

VERTIGO
Manufacturer: Exidy
Date: 1985
Cabinet Type: Cockpit
Rarity: Prototype
Price Range: $?
Notes: Supposedly the last vector (X-Y) game made; pricing information unavailable due to extreme rarity

VICTORY
Manufacturer: Exidy
Date: 1982
Cabinet Type: Upright
Rarity: 9
Price Range: $250–500*

VIDEO 8 BALL
Manufacturer: Century Electronics
Date: 1982
Cabinet Type: Upright
Rarity: 9
Price Range: $50–150*

VIDEO ACTION
Manufacturer: UPL
Date: 1975
Cabinet Type: Cocktail
Rarity: 9
Price Range: $50–100

VIDEO ACTION 2
Manufacturer: UPL
Date: 1976
Cabinet Type: Cocktail
Rarity: 10
Price Range: $50–100

VIDEO PINBALL
Manufacturer: Atari
Date: 1978
Cabinet Type: Upright
Rarity: 8
Price Range: $100–250

VIDEO POOL
Manufacturer: U.S. Billiards
Date: 1975
Cabinet Type: Upright
Rarity: 9
Price Range: $50–100*

VIDEO TRIVIA
Manufacturer: Greyhound
Date: 1985
Cabinet Type: Upright
Rarity: 9
Price Range: $50–150*

VOLLEY BALL
Manufacturer: Nintendo
Date: 1986
Cabinet Type: Upright
Rarity: 9
Price Range: $150–250*

VS. GAME SYSTEM
Manufacturer: Nintendo
Date: 1984
Cabinet Type: Upright (Unisystem)
Rarity: 3
Price Range: $100–300
Notes: UniSystem (one monitor); plays Nintendo Vs. games (listed individually below); add the cabinet cost to the individual game cost to determine approximate value
Cabinet Type: Upright (Duosystem)
Rarity: 7
Price Range: $200–300
Cabinet Type: Cocktail
Rarity: 3
Price Range: $100–300
Notes: Duo System (2 monitors, 2 control panels); plays Nintendo Vs. games (listed individually below); add the cabinet cost to the individual game cost to determine approximate value

VS. 10-YARD FIGHT
Manufacturer: Irem
Date: 1985
Cabinet Type: N/A
Rarity: 9
Price Range: $50–100*
Notes: Price does not include cabinet (see above for VS. Game System cabinet prices)

VS. BALLOON FIGHT

Manufacturer: Nintendo
Date: 1984
Cabinet Type: N/A
Rarity: 9
Price Range: $30–90*
Notes: Price does not include cabinet (see above for
VS. Game System cabinet prices)

VS. BASEBALL

Manufacturer: Nintendo
Date: 1984
Cabinet Type: N/A
Rarity: 8
Price Range: $45–95*
Notes: Price does not include cabinet (see above for
VS. Game System cabinet prices)

VS. BATTLE CITY

Manufacturer: Nintendo
Date: 1984
Cabinet Type: N/A
Rarity: 9
Price Range: $75–125*
Notes: Price does not include cabinet (see above for
VS. Game System cabinet prices)

VS. CASTLEVANIA

Manufacturer: Nintendo
Date: 1987
Cabinet Type: N/A
Rarity: 8
Price Range: $50–75
Notes: Price does not include cabinet (see above for
VS. Game System cabinet prices)

VS. CLU CLU LAND

Manufacturer: Nintendo
Date: 1985
Cabinet Type: N/A
Rarity: 9
Price Range: $50–75*
Notes: Price does not include cabinet (see above for
VS. Game System cabinet prices)

VS. DR. MARIO

Manufacturer: Nintendo
Date: 1990
Cabinet Type: N/A
Rarity: 9
Price Range: $70–100*
Notes: Price does not include cabinet (see above for
VS. Game System cabinet prices)

VS. DUCK HUNT

Manufacturer: Nintendo
Date: 1984
Cabinet Type: N/A
Rarity: 7
Price Range: $100–150*
Notes: Includes 2 guns; price does not include cabinet
(see above for VS. Game System cabinet prices)

VS. EXCITEBIKE

Manufacturer: Nintendo
Date: 1984
Cabinet Type: N/A
Rarity: 7
Price Range: $50–100
Notes: Price does not include cabinet (see above for
VS. Game System cabinet prices)

VS. FREEDOM FORCE

Manufacturer: Nintendo
Date: 1988
Cabinet Type: N/A
Rarity: 9
Price Range: $45–95*
Notes: Price does not include cabinet (see above for
VS. Game System cabinet prices)

VS. GOLF

Manufacturer: Nintendo
Date: 1984
Cabinet Type: N/A
Rarity: 6
Price Range: $50–100*
Notes: Price does not include cabinet (see above for
VS. Game System cabinet prices)

VS. GRADIUS

Manufacturer: Nintendo
Date: 1986
Cabinet Type: N/A
Rarity: 9
Price Range: $75–125*
Notes: Price does not include cabinet (see above for
VS. Game System cabinet prices)

VS. GUMSHOE

Manufacturer: Nintendo
Date: 1987
Cabinet Type: N/A
Rarity: 9
Price Range: $75–125*
Notes: Price does not include cabinet (see above for
VS. Game System cabinet prices)

VS. HOGAN'S ALLEY

Manufacturer: Nintendo
Date: 1984
Cabinet Type: N/A
Rarity: 7
Price Range: $100–150*
Notes: Includes 2 guns; price does not include cabinet
(see above for VS. Game System cabinet prices)

VS. ICE CLIMBER

Manufacturer: Nintendo
Date: 1984
Cabinet Type: N/A
Rarity: 8
Price Range: $50–100
Notes: Price does not include cabinet (see above for
VS. Game System cabinet prices)

VS. LADIES GOLF

Manufacturer: Nintendo
Date: 1985
Cabinet Type: N/A
Rarity: 9
Price Range: $50–75*
Notes: Price does not include cabinet (see above for VS. Game System cabinet prices)

VS. MACH RIDER

Manufacturer: Nintendo
Date: 1985
Cabinet Type: N/A
Rarity: 9
Price Range: $50–125*
Notes: Price does not include cabinet (see above for VS. Game System cabinet prices)

VS. PINBALL

Manufacturer: Nintendo
Date: 1984
Cabinet Type: N/A
Rarity: 9
Price Range: $50–100*
Notes: Price does not include cabinet (see above for VS. Game System cabinet prices)

VS. PLATOON

Manufacturer: Nintendo
Date: 1988
Cabinet Type: N/A
Rarity: 8
Price Range: $25–50
Notes: Price does not include cabinet (see above for VS. Game System cabinet prices)

VS. RAID ON BUNGELING BAY

Manufacturer: Nintendo
Date: 1985
Cabinet Type: N/A
Rarity: 9
Price Range: $30–60*
Notes: Licensed from Broderbund; price does not include cabinet (see above for VS. Game System cabinet prices)

VS. SKY KID

Manufacturer: Namco
Date: 1985
Cabinet Type: N/A
Rarity: 9
Price Range: $75–100*
Notes: Price does not include cabinet (see above for VS. Game System cabinet prices)

VS. SLALOM

Manufacturer: Nintendo
Date: 1986
Cabinet Type: N/A
Rarity: 9
Price Range: $100–150*
Notes: Controls include skis for steering; price does not include cabinet (see above for VS. Game System cabinet prices)

VS. SOCCER

Manufacturer: Nintendo
Date: 1986
Cabinet Type: N/A
Rarity: 9
Price Range: $75–100*
Notes: Price does not include cabinet (see above for VS. Game System cabinet prices)

VS. SUPER CHINESE

Manufacturer: Nintendo
Date: 1988
Cabinet Type: N/A
Rarity: 9
Price Range: $50–75*
Notes: Price does not include cabinet (see above for VS. Game System cabinet prices)

VS. SUPER MARIO BROS.

Manufacturer: Nintendo
Date: 1986
Cabinet Type: N/A
Rarity: 5
Price Range: $100–200
Notes: Price does not include cabinet (see above for VS. Game System cabinet prices)

VS. TENNIS

Manufacturer: Nintendo
Date: 1984
Cabinet Type: N/A
Rarity: 3
Price Range: $75–100
Notes: Price does not include cabinet (see above for VS. Game System cabinet prices)

VS. TETRIS

Manufacturer: Tengen
Date: 1987
Cabinet Type: N/A
Rarity: 9
Price Range: $50–100*
Notes: Price does not include cabinet (see above for VS. Game System cabinet prices)

VS. THE GOONIES

Manufacturer: Nintendo
Date: 1985
Cabinet Type: N/A
Rarity: 8
Price Range: $50–100
Notes: Price does not include cabinet (see above for VS. Game System cabinet prices)

VS. TOP GUN

Manufacturer: Konami
Date: 1987
Cabinet Type: N/A
Rarity: 9
Price Range: $45–95*
Notes: Price does not include cabinet (see above for VS. Game System cabinet prices)

VS. TROJAN
Manufacturer: Nintendo
Date: 1987
Cabinet Type: N/A
Rarity: 9
Price Range: $50–100*
Notes: Price does not include cabinet (see above for VS. Game System cabinet prices)

VS. URBAN CHAMPION
Manufacturer: Nintendo
Date: 1985
Cabinet Type: N/A
Rarity: 9
Price Range: $30–60*
Notes: Price does not include cabinet (see above for VS. Game System cabinet prices)

VS. VOLLEYBALL
Manufacturer: Nintendo
Date: 1986
Cabinet Type: N/A
Rarity: 9
Price Range: $45–95*
Notes: Price does not include cabinet (see above for VS. Game System cabinet prices)

VS. WILD GUNMAN
Manufacturer: Nintendo
Date: 1984
Cabinet Type: N/A
Rarity: 9
Price Range: $100–150*
Notes: Includes two guns; price does not include cabinet (see above for VS. Game System cabinet prices)

VS. WRECKING CREW
Manufacturer: Nintendo
Date: 1985
Cabinet Type: N/A
Rarity: 9
Price Range: $30–60*
Notes: Price does not include cabinet (see above for VS. Game System cabinet prices)

VULGUS
Manufacturer: SNK
Date: 1984
Cabinet Type: Upright
Rarity: 9
Price Range: $150–250*
Notes: Licensed from Capcom

WACKO
Manufacturer: Bally Midway
Date: 1983
Cabinet Type: Upright
Rarity: 9
Price Range: $250–450
Notes: Has a unique angled cabinet (slants down from left to right)

WANTED
Manufacturer: Sigma Ent., Inc
Date: 1984
Cabinet Type: Upright
Rarity: 9
Price Range: $75–150*

WAR OF THE BUGS
Manufacturer: Food and Fun Corp./Armenia
Date: 1981
Cabinet Type: Upright
Rarity: 9
Price Range: $50–150*
Notes: Also known as *Monstrous Maneuvers in a Mushroom Maze*

WAR OF THE WORLDS
Manufacturer: Cinematronics
Date: 1982
Cabinet Type: Upright
Rarity: 10
Price Range: $400–500*
Notes: Rare color vector game

WARLORDS
Manufacturer: Atari
Date: 1980
Cabinet Type: Upright
Rarity: 8
Price Range: $200–400
Cabinet Type: Cocktail
Rarity: 8
Price Range: $400–600
Notes: Upright version is black and white and accommodates only 1 or 2 players. Cocktail version is color and accommodates 1–4 players

WARP WARP
Manufacturer: Rock-Ola
Date: 1981
Cabinet Type: Upright
Rarity: 9
Price Range: $75–150*
Notes: Licensed from Namco; Namco dedicated version is known as *Warp & Warp*

WARRIOR
Manufacturer: Vectorbeam
Date: 1979
Cabinet Type: Upright
Rarity: 10
Price Range: $1,000–3,000
Notes: One of the most collectible games around; the first player-vs.-player simultaneous fighting game

WATER MATCH
Manufacturer: Bally Midway
Date: 1984
Cabinet Type: Upright
Rarity: 9
Price Range: $100–200*
Notes: Licensed from Sega

WATER SKI
Manufacturer: Taito
Date: 1983
Cabinet Type: Upright
Rarity: 9
Price Range: $75–150*

WHEELS

Manufacturer: Midway
Date: 1975
Cabinet Type: Upright
Rarity: 9
Price Range: $50–100

WHEELS II

Manufacturer: Midway
Date: 1975
Cabinet Type: Upright
Rarity: 10
Price Range: $50–100
Notes: 2-player version of *Wheels*

WHEELS RUNNER

Manufacturer: I G Spa
Date: 1982
Cabinet Type: Upright
Rarity: 9
Price Range: $75–150*
Notes: Copy of *Super Sprint*

WILD WESTERN

Manufacturer: Taito
Date: 1982
Cabinet Type: Upright
Rarity: 9
Price Range: $150–250*
Cabinet Type: Cocktail
Rarity: 9
Price Range: $200–300*

WILLIAMS MULTIGAME

Manufacturer: Williams
Date: 2003
Cabinet Type: Upright
Rarity: 3
Price Range: $1,250–1,700
Notes: Williams upright cabinet (*Joust, Defender,* and others) user-modified to play a number of Williams's arcade games; some have Williams Multigame marquees and side art

WIMBLEDON

Manufacturer: Nutting Associates
Date: 1974
Cabinet Type: Upright
Rarity: 9
Price Range: $50–100*

WINGS

Manufacturer: Electra
Date: 1976
Cabinet Type: Upright
Rarity: 9
Price Range: $50–100*

WINNER

Manufacturer: Midway
Date: 1973
Cabinet Type: Upright
Rarity: 9
Price Range: $50–100*

WINNER IV

Manufacturer: Midway
Date: 1973
Cabinet Type: Upright
Rarity: 8
Price Range: $75–150
Notes: 4-player version of *Winner*

WIPE OUT

Manufacturer: Ramtek
Date: 1974
Cabinet Type: Upright
Rarity: 9
Price Range: $50–100*

WIPING

Manufacturer: Nichibutsu
Date: 1982
Cabinet Type: Upright
Rarity: 9
Price Range: $100–200*

WIZARD OF WOR

Manufacturer: Midway
Date: 1981
Cabinet Type: Upright
Rarity: 7
Price Range: $200–450*
Cabinet Type: Cocktail
Rarity: 9
Price Range: $300–500*
Cabinet Type: Cabaret
Rarity: 8
Price Range: $250–450

WORLD SERIES BASEBALL

Manufacturer: Cinematronics
Date: 1984
Cabinet Type: Upright
Rarity: 9
Price Range: $100–200*

WORLD SERIES—THE SEASON

Manufacturer: Cinematronics
Date: 1985
Cabinet Type: Upright
Rarity: 9
Price Range: $100–200

WYVERN F-0

Manufacturer: Taito
Date: 1985
Cabinet Type: Upright
Rarity: 9
Price Range: $100–200*

XENOPHOBE

Manufacturer: Bally Midway
Date: 1987
Cabinet Type: Upright
Rarity: 9
Price Range: $150–400

XEVIOUS

Manufacturer: Atari
Date: 1982
Cabinet Type: Upright
Rarity: 7
Price Range: $350–500
Notes: Licensed from Namco

XYBOTS

Manufacturer: Atari Games
Date: 1987
Cabinet Type: Upright
Rarity: 7
Price Range: $200–350

YAMATO

Manufacturer: Sega
Date: 1983
Cabinet Type: Upright
Rarity: 9
Price Range: $50–150*

YIE-AR KUNG-FU

Manufacturer: Konami
Date: 1985
Cabinet Type: Upright
Rarity: 8
Price Range: $200–400

ZAXXON

Manufacturer: Sega
Date: 1982
Cabinet Type: Upright
Rarity: 4
Price Range: $300–550
Cabinet Type: Cocktail
Rarity: 8
Price Range: $400–600

ZEKTOR

Manufacturer: Sega/Gremlin
Date: 1982
Cabinet Type: Upright
Rarity: 9
Price Range: $300–400*

ZERO HOUR

Manufacturer: Universal
Date: 1981
Cabinet Type: Upright
Rarity: 9
Price Range: $50–150*

ZERO TIME

Manufacturer: Petaco S.A.
Date: 1979
Cabinet Type: Upright
Rarity: 9
Price Range: $75–150*
Notes: Spanish version of *Galaxian*

ZOAR

Manufacturer: Tago Electronics
Date: 1982
Cabinet Type: Upright
Rarity: 9
Price Range: $75–150*
Notes: Licensed from Data East

ZODIACK

Manufacturer: Orca
Date: 1983
Cabinet Type: Upright
Rarity: 9
Price Range: $75–150*

ZOO KEEPER

Manufacturer: Taito
Date: 1982
Cabinet Type: Upright
Rarity: 8
Price Range: $600–1,000
Notes: 2 cabinet versions exist—a common version with blue animals on orange, and one with full-color side art (which is very rare)

ZUN ZUN BLOCK

Manufacturer: Taito
Date: 1979
Cabinet Type: Upright
Rarity: 9
Price Range: $50–100

ZZYZZYXX

Manufacturer: Cinematronics
Date: 1982
Cabinet Type: Upright
Rarity: 9
Price Range: $75–150*
Notes: Also known as *Brix*

15 Classic Arcade Game Setup, Restoration, and Repair

For most collectors of classic arcade video games, owning and playing the games is only part of the appeal of the hobby. Like collectors of vintage automobiles, classic arcade game hobbyists enjoy tinkering with, restoring, and repairing their collectibles nearly as much as showing them off.

If you're new to the hobby, you probably think that you'll never have to deal with the intricacies of setup, restoration, and repair. In some instances—especially if you purchase your games fully restored from a dealer—you might be right. But, in most cases, even the most reluctant and mechanically challenged arcade collectors eventually take a more hands-on approach to the hobby.

Many arcade repairs require specialized knowledge of electronics and a great deal of practice and skill to perform. Such repairs are outside the scope of this book, and should be handled (or taught) by electronics professionals. There are, however, quite a few things that just about anyone can do to improve the value, appearance, and operation of arcade collectibles. That's what this chapter is all about.

The information provided in this chapter is a result of my personal experience in arcade restoration and repair. The techniques described herein have worked successfully for me, but your results might vary. Use this information at your own risk when working on your own games.

CAUTION: Before you go poking around inside an arcade game, always be sure that it is turned off and unplugged. Be aware that arcade video games have a number of high-voltage connections that can cause serious injury or death if touched, even when the game is powered down and unplugged. If you are not comfortable with working inside your game, have a knowledgeable fellow collector or electronics expert show you the danger zones inside the game before you attempt any repairs or internal restoration.

Basic Arcade Game Operation

If you've decided to collect classic arcade games, chances are that you are quite familiar with the exterior of a video game. However, if you're like most people, you've probably never seen what an arcade game looks like on the inside.

Most arcade games are basically identical to one another internally, although board and component layout varies from game to game. Obviously, the **internal layout of a game** varies by cabinet style as well—the inside of a cocktail-style game is laid out much differently than that of an upright model.

If you are unfamiliar with the components and layout of your game, the best thing you can do is to obtain a service manual for the game. Service manuals generally describe the game's operation, option settings, and components. Many even include schematics of the printed circuit boards (PCBs), wiring diagrams, and service information on the monitor as well.

Original manuals for most popular classic arcade games appear on eBay from time to time, and generally range in price from $5 to $30 depending on the game. If you don't mind working from a scanned copy, just about every game manual ever printed is available for download somewhere on the Internet. Unfortunately, due to increasing pressure from groups like the Interactive Digital Software Association (IDSA), some of the best archives of arcade manuals have been removed from the Internet. This is unfortunate, since these manuals are no longer readily available in their original form, especially for rarer games. There are still a number of collectors' sites that store digital versions of arcade manuals, however. Rather than getting these collectors in trouble by listing the sites here, I'll just recommend that you use your trusty Internet search engine. You should eventually find what you need.

In some cases, the original service manual is included with a game when you buy it (either intentionally or accidentally). Before you go out and buy or download a manual, check inside the game. Most of the time, if the manual is included, it can be found in one of three places: in a plastic pouch attached to the inside of the game's back door, in the bottom of the game, or shoved into the coin box.

Powering Up

Powering up many classic arcade games is as easy as simply plugging them into the wall—a surprising number of games are not equipped with power switches. Other games *do* have power switches, though, so if you plug your game in and it doesn't immediately power up, don't despair! It might just be switched off.

Of course, as you might expect, the locations of power switches on classic arcade video games are as varied as the design of the game cabinets. In general, the switch is located in one of the following places:

- On the back of the game, near the bottom, next to the power cord (Atari, Nintendo).

- On the back of the game, near the top (Williams).

- On the top of the game, in a recessed hole near the front (Centuri) or the back (Bally Midway).

- Inside the game, behind the coin door (Data East).

Note that not necessarily *all* of the games manufactured by the companies noted in the previous list have power switches in the specified locations.

If, after you plug in the game and flip the switch, the game still doesn't power up, you've got a problem of some sort. (See Changing Fuses later in this chapter for details on symptoms and a possible simple and quick, cheap fix for this problem.)

Coin Mechanisms

Most classic arcade games have two coin mechanisms—the hardware that sits behind the coin slots and registers credits on the game. These mechanisms may or may not work on your games, but chances are that you don't want to be forced to drop quarters into the game every time you want to play anyway. That's one of the reasons you bought the game in the first place! The important thing you need to know is how to put credits on the machine so that you *can* play.

One easy way to put credits on the machine is to operate the coin mechanisms manually. Coin mechanisms used by different manufacturers vary, but all of them have one thing in common: a small lever, located somewhere on the side or the back of the mechanism that moves up and down. Sliding this lever down generally registers a credit on the machine.

In **the interior of some arcade video games**, a credit switch is factory-installed just inside the coin door. Some Bally Midway games, for instance, have a small panel with a red credit button mounted on the right just inside the coin door. Each press of this button adds a credit to the machine.

Often, dealers and electronically savvy collectors install their own makeshift credit switches on the game. Many classic games you find today have such switches, and they range in execution from subtle and professional to jury-rigged and ugly. Purist collectors prefer that such a switch not be installed in their games or, if it is, that it be installed in a discreet location.

Of course, the easiest way to put credits on a game is to set it to free-play mode. Not all games have this option but, on those that do, setting the option is quite easy. See the next section, Setting Game Options, for details.

Setting Game Options

Most classic arcade video games have adjustable option settings. These options range from number of lives, time limit settings, and general game difficulty to the activation of the ever-popular free-play option.

Classic arcade video games employ one of two methods for setting game options: dual inline package (DIP) switches and on-screen menus.

Setting DIP Switches

Most classic games use the **DIP switch** method for setting options. This setup method requires that you open the game and locate the proper bank of DIP switches on the appropriate game PCB.

Locating and setting the DIP switches is much easier if you have the game manual or a circuit diagram of the PCB. Some games have multiple banks of DIP switches that perform different functions, so it is important that you find the right bank before you start flipping switches.

The manual also describes the functions of the various switch combinations—a vital element to properly setting the game options. DIP switch settings are also sometimes listed on a sticker or information sheet attached to the inside of the cabinet, usually on the back door. DIP switch settings for hundreds of games are listed on sites all over the Internet. Try a search for "arcade switch settings" and you should find the information you need for most games.

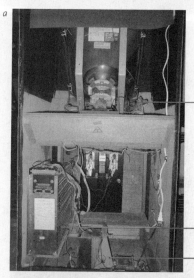

a

Monitor

PCB (Inside Cage)

Power Supply

NOTE ✲✲

Throughout the text,
BOLD indicates that an
item appears in a picture.

b

a **The interior of a classic arcade video game.**

b **A typical coin mechanism.** *Moving the small lever (indicated here by the arrow) down on a coin mechanism registers a credit on the game.*

a **DIP switches.** *The options on most classic arcade games are set via banks of DIP switches like the ones pictured here.*

Before you reset any DIP switches, it is a good idea to note the original setting for each switch. That way, if you set something incorrectly, you have a reference for returning the game to its original option settings.

To change the DIP switch settings:

1. Turn off and unplug the machine and open the game to access the PCBs.

2. Toggle the appropriate switches for the options you want to change. DIP switches are very small, so it is easiest to toggle them using a pen or other pointy object.

3. When the switches are set, close the machine and power it up.

On-Screen Setup

A number of classic arcade games, particularly those that were manufactured from the early '80s on, have on-screen setup menus through which the game options are set. This is usually a much easier way to set game options but, on many games, the settings are lost as soon as the game is switched off, forcing you to reset the options each time you power up the machine.

The methods of setting game options in this manner vary widely from game to game. Most machines have a switch located on a PCB or on a panel inside the coin door that puts the game into test or setup mode. In some machines, this switch is clearly labeled. In others, you need a manual or circuit board diagram in order to find it.

In any case, to set the game options, power the machine up and set the test/options switch to the appropriate position. In most cases, the game's controls are used to step through the various options and settings. Follow the on-screen instructions to set the options you want. When the setup is complete, you must exit the test/setup mode. Some games have an "exit and save" option on the menu that, once selected, returns the machine to play mode. Other machines require that you manually exit the setup mode by flipping the test/options switch again.

If you are new to arcade games, it is best to consult the game manual or talk to an experienced hobbyist before attempting the setup procedure.

Saving High Scores

Starting with *Space Invaders*, displaying players' high scores has been a function common to just about every arcade video game. Early games displayed only the highest score achieved. As the high score feature evolved, games provided an option for players to enter their initials to identify their scores. Many games also displayed an entire list of the highest scores at the end of each game and during the game's attract mode.

Unfortunately, most classic arcade games save high scores only until they are powered down. Once they are switched off, the high score list is reset.

There are some exceptions to this rule. *Centipede*, for example, permanently saves the top three scores in the list. Williams games, like *Joust*, actually save as many 50 high scores (provided that the machine's batteries are working properly). Games that store high scores generally have an option for erasing the high score list. (Check your machine's manual for details.)

In most cases, there is no way short of leaving your games running 24/7—a practice that is *not* recommended—to save your high score lists in games that are not factory-equipped to do so. For some games, however, clever hobbyists have come up with high score save kits that you can install (provided you have the electronics expertise to do so). Some games for which high score save kits are available include *Asteroids*, *Super Pac-Man*, *Donkey Kong*, and *Donkey Kong Jr.* These kits are available from many vendors on the Internet, including Arcade Shop Amusements (http://www.arcadeshop.com).

Basic Restoration Techniques

Many people get into the arcade game collecting hobby with the intention of doing little more than playing their games. There's nothing wrong with that approach—just owning and playing a classic arcade video game is a very satisfying experience. If you purchase your games from a dealer or from a fellow hobbyist who has taken good care of them, chances are that you won't have to worry about the game's physical appearance.

Some hobbyists, however, take their collecting to the next level by seeking out less-than-perfect games and turning them into museum-quality collectibles that look as if they were just pulled off the assembly line in the 1980s. The level of satisfaction one achieves by turning a worn-out game into a collectible classic is nothing short of amazing.

You might feel like you're not qualified to cosmetically restore a video game, but you'd be surprised what a little bit of elbow grease (along with some rudimentary painting skill and patience) can do for the appearance of your games.

On my Web site (http://www.davesclassicarcade.com), you can view two complete classic arcade game restorations—the conversion of a *Donkey Kong 3* machine to an original *Donkey Kong* and the conversion of *Super Mario Bros.* to *Mario Bros.*—from start to finish. Click the Restoration Projects button on the main page to see step-by-step pictorial logs of the restoration process.

Cleaning

The easiest bit of restoration you can perform on a classic arcade game is some basic cleaning. Most classic games, especially those purchased at auctions or from musty old warehouses, have about 20 years' worth of dust and grime caked on them, inside and out. By simply removing the dirt, you can greatly improve the appearance of your game.

Start on the inside. Remove all large, loose objects from the bottom of the game. You'll be surprised what you find in some games—screws, nails, tokens, and coins are just some of the things you'll find rattling around the bottom of a cabinet. Next, use a vacuum cleaner with a soft brush attachment to thoroughly vacuum out the dust and grime on the bottom of the cabinet and on the circuit boards. Be gentle when vacuuming the PCBs so as not to dislodge any vital components. If the dust on the boards resists your vacuuming efforts, you can remove the boards and carefully clean them with a small, soft bristle paintbrush.

After the inside is cleaned out, it's time to hit the outside of the machine. Arcade cabinets and their artwork are pretty tough. You can use a soft, damp cloth to wipe down the cabinet. Clean the marquee and bezel using any common glass cleaner.

Control panel overlays (CPOs) are particularly susceptible to grime buildup since they are the part of the game that players are constantly touching. You can purchase replacement CPOs for most popular classic games, but before you spend the money to do so, try cleaning the one you already have.

Using a soft cloth and some standard household kitchen cleaner with grease-cutting capabilities, spray a small section of the CPO and start scrubbing. Generally, you should see some improvement almost immediately. For ground-in dirt and grease, it can take some significant scrubbing to get the CPO clean.

A commercial cleaner called C-Pop is specifically designed to clean and bring out the color in dirty, faded CPOs. A number of online sites sell this product. Most collectors agree that the best results are achieved by **cleaning the CPO** first and then applying C-Pop to bring out the colors.

Replacing CPOs

Sometimes, all of the cleaning in the world won't save a CPO. Often, repeated contact with the overlay rubs out the graphics or, worse, tears and rips the CPO. This is common around the controls themselves, particularly on machines that use trackball controllers, and along the edges of the control panel. Sometimes, damage isn't always gameplay induced. Back in the bad old days when people could smoke pretty much anywhere they wanted to, arcade patrons often rested their lit cigarettes on game control panels while they played, resulting in burn marks and melting.

There are a couple of ways to deal with a CPO that is damaged beyond repair. One is to replace the entire control panel with one that has a better overlay. This is overkill in many cases, but it

a

a **Joust CPO, before and after cleaning**. *It's amazing what a soft cloth, some common household kitchen cleaner, and a little elbow grease can do to restore a dirty control panel overlay.*

does solve the problem. If you can find an inexpensive replacement control panel that is in working condition (they are often sold in online auctions), this is certainly the easiest way to restore the appearance of your machine.

The more common restoration method, which is more labor-intensive but usually less expensive, is to simply replace the overlay itself with a new one. From time to time, you can find original new old stock (NOS) overlays for sale in online auctions. These overlays were produced by the game's manufacturer when the game was still in production. You can also buy reproduction overlays for most popular classic arcade games from companies that specialize in this business, like Arcade Shop Amusements (http://www.arcadeshop.com) and Arcade Renovations (http://www.arcaderenovations.com).

The basic process of replacing a CPO is as follows:

1. **Remove the control panel.** Most control panels are held in place by a pair of latches, one on either side of the control panel. To get to these latches, you must reach through the coin door and unhook them. In some cases, these latches are the only thing that holds the panel in place, but some control panels are also attached with a long hinge or several bolts. Every game is dif-

ferent, so you'll have to examine your control panel to see how it is connected. This is yet another instance where having a copy of the game's service manual is very useful.

2. **Remove the controls.** Before you can strip off the old CPO, you need to remove the buttons, joysticks, and other controls from the panel. This is usually a fairly straightforward process. Be sure to mark all of the connectors on both the controls themselves and the wiring harnesses in the game cabinet to indicate what wire connects to what. (This makes things a lot easier when you reattach the controls later on.) Price tags with string ties, which you can find at just about any office supply store, make great temporary wire labels.

3. **Remove the old overlay.** There's no reason to save the old overlay, so there's no reason to be subtle here. Use a razor blade to peel the old CPO loose. It sometimes takes a lot of scraping to do this. Another method that works well is to apply paint thinner to dissolve the glue holding the CPO in place, and use a paint scraper to peel off the overlay.

4. **Clean the control panel surface.** When the old overlay is removed, scrape away as much excess glue as possible using a razor blade. If the glue is particularly stubborn, use a solvent (available at paint stores) to remove the glue. When you're done, sand the surface of the control panel to remove any rust or rough spots. If the overlay doesn't cover the entire control panel—that is, there are parts of the control panel that are exposed around the edges of the overlay—repaint the control panel before you continue.

5. **Attach the new overlay.** Most overlays have an adhesive backing and will stick pretty well. Even so, you might want to use a thin layer of spray adhesive on the control panel itself to ensure a tight bond. Line up the new overlay using the controller holes as a reference point. Peel a small section of the backing loose and, after rechecking the alignment, attach the overlay to the control panel along one edge. Remove the backing slowly—an inch or so at a time—and press down as you go, smoothing out any bubbles that form, until the entire overlay is attached.

6. **Reinstall the controls and attach the control panel.** After letting the glue set for a while, re-install the controls. Use a sharp knife to trim any overlapping edges and to cut the controller holes (if necessary). After the controls are installed, reattach the wire harnesses and replace the control panel.

Because CPOs can be expensive, you want to make sure you get the job done right the first time. Seek out the help of a fellow collector who has restoration experience if you're not comfortable doing the job yourself.

Replacing Side Art Decals

Next to CPOs, the most common cosmetic damage to a game is usually the cabinet art, particularly the side art. In an arcade setting, games are typically crammed together side-by-side and, when they are moved, they rub against one another. This rips side art stickers and puts scratches and chips in painted side art.

Like CPOs, both NOS and reproduction classic arcade side art is available online for games that use decals for side art. In some ways, replacing cabinet art stickers is easier than replacing CPOs, although the large size and high price of the decals makes the process nerve-wracking to the uninitiated.

To replace side art decals:

1. **Remove the old decals.** If there is anything remaining of the original side art decals, use a razor blade to remove them, taking care not to scratch the paint on the cabinet. For particularly tough decals, you might need to use a heat gun to loosen the adhesive. (Heat guns are available at most large hardware stores.) If the decal you're removing is the same as the one that you're replacing it with, you might want to make some small reference marks (in pencil or grease marker) on the cabinet around the existing decal's edges to provide a reference for the positioning of the new art.

2. **Clean and fill the side of the cabinet.** Wipe the side of the cabinet down with a damp towel and dry it off, making sure you remove all of the excess glue from the old side art. If there are any deep gashes in the wood, use wood filler to fill them and sand the filled sections smooth. If you're planning to do some touch-up painting, do it before you apply the new side art.

3. **Find your starting point.** If you haven't already done so, find the topmost point on the machine where the side art will start and make an erasable mark. Use a level to draw a light, level line on the cabinet to mark the adhesion point for the top edge of the decal (if the decal is straight along the top edge).

4. **Begin applying the decal.** Peel the top inch or so of the backing and align the sticker with your mark. Press down just hard enough along the top edge to hold the sticker in place. Double-check the positioning before you move on. Continue this process, peeling back an inch or so of backing at a time as you proceed down the side of the machine. If any bubbles form under the art, carefully squeeze them out. Most replacement decals have a protective sheet on the front of the art to protect them from scratching and tearing during installation. If your sticker is not protected in this manner, use a soft cloth to do the smoothing rather than your bare hands. Take your time during this process so that you don't rip the decal or leave any bubbles under the artwork.

5. **Final touches.** When the decal is completely secured, carefully rub it down to remove any remaining bubbles, and rub firmly along the edges to make sure it is secure. Finally, carefully remove the protective coating (if there is one) from the face of the decal.

One trick recommended by a number of collectors that supposedly makes side art stickers easier to position and install is to spray down the side of the machine with a light coat of water or ammonia-based window cleaner before applying the decal. This prevents the glue from immediately adhering to the machine and allows you to slide it around a bit to get it in place. After the decal is properly positioned, allow several hours for the water or window cleaner to evaporate. Afterward, the decal is firmly attached.

As you know, some classic video games have painted cabinet art as opposed to decals. Replacing the art on these machines is a little more involved. Stencil kits are available for some games with painted side art. These kits usually come with painting instructions and color-matching information. You can also do some freehand touch-up work, or create your own set of stencils using clear stencil material (available at most craft stores).

Basic Repairs

When you are dealing with 20- to 30-year-old electronic devices, it is almost inevitable that you'll run into mechanical and electronic problems eventually. Because most classic arcade video games spent the better part of their existence running 18 hours a day and being used and abused by the general public, it's no wonder that they tend to fail today.

Many video game repairs are beyond the ability of the average hobbyist, and are therefore not discussed in this guide. However, there are a number of minor repairs that you can make on your own even if you've never even picked up a soldering iron. Learning how to take care of the simple repairs on your own makes you more independent and gives you a sense of accomplishment.

Light Fixtures

One of the most common problems in an arcade video game is a dead marquee light. Obviously, an unlit marquee doesn't prevent the game from functioning, but it does detract from the game's appearance.

If your marquee is dark, follow these simple steps to troubleshoot the problem:

1. **Remove the marquee.** Most video arcade marquees are very easy to remove. Generally, along the top edge of the marquee glass, there is a plastic or metal strip attached to the top of the game by several screws. Remove the screws and the strip, and the marquee should lift right out, revealing the light fixture. (Some machines are designed differently. A quick examination of the marquee usually reveals how it is attached.)

2. **Check all the connections.** Trace the wire from the marquee light fixture as far as you can through the machine, and make sure that all of the wiring connections are tight. If so, the problem is probably in the fixture itself.

3. **Replace the starter.** About 99% of classic arcade video games have fluorescent light fixtures, and the most common failure in these fixtures is the starter—a small cylinder that twists into the fixture. Start by replacing this. To remove the starter, twist it about a quarter-turn to the left until it is loose and then lift it out. Fluorescent starters are available in most hardware stores. Take the original starter with you to make certain you get the proper replacement, since many different varieties are available. Because starters are cheap and often need replacing, it's not a bad idea to have a few on hand at all times.

4. **Replace the bulb.** If replacing the starter doesn't do the trick, replace the bulb itself. Most arcade video games use standard 15 watt fluorescents that are either 18 or 24 inches in length. (Take the old bulb with you to the store if you're not sure what you need.) You can save yourself a trip to the store by testing the existing bulb in another machine (if you have one that takes the same size bulb) to see if it is, in fact, defective.

If the connections are solid and replacing the starter and the bulb doesn't fix the problem, the **ballast** is probably the culprit. This is the small rectangular box that is the heart of the light fixture. A new ballast can be purchased at just about any hardware store for less than $10. Take the old ballast with you to the store to ensure that you get a proper replacement.

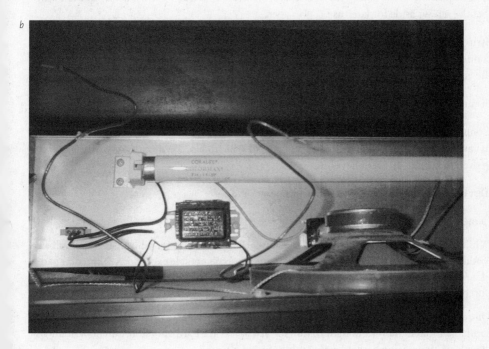

a **The starter** *is one of the first things you should check and replace when troubleshooting a fluorescent light fixture.*

b **The ballast** *(the square black box shown here) is the heart of a fluorescent light fixture.*

Replacing a ballast requires some rudimentary electronics skill, but it's nothing that an amateur can't master. You'll need the following tools and supplies to proceed:

- A wire cutter/stripper

- A screwdriver

- Two wire nuts

Follow these steps to remove and replace a fluorescent ballast:

1. **Remove the old ballast.** Start by snipping the two wires connected to the ballast. Cut them as close as possible to the ballast itself. Use a screwdriver to remove the ballast from the fixture. (Set the screws aside for later use.)

2. **Strip the wires.** Strip about half an inch of insulation off of the wires in the light fixture that connected to the old ballast. If the two wires on the new ballast are not already stripped, strip the ends of these as well.

3. **Secure the new ballast.** Using the screws you set aside, secure the new ballast into the fixture.

4. **Connect the wires.** Secure each of the stripped wires in the cabinet to one of the wires on the ballast. (It doesn't matter which wire attaches to which.) Use a wire nut to twist the ends together and create solid connections.

5. **Test the fixture.** Plug in the machine and power it up.

In most cases, marquee light problems can be solved by following the procedures described above.

While most classic arcade video games use standard **light fixtures** for which parts and bulbs are readily available in most hardware stores, there are some notable exceptions. Nintendo games like *Donkey Kong* use a nonstandard fixture. Bulbs and starters for this light fixture must be purchased from dealers who specialize in lighting or arcade parts.

One other solution to an ailing light fixture is to replace the entire thing. You can usually get a complete 18-inch fluorescent light fixture for $20 or less at a hardware store and hook it into the game's existing wiring harness with a minimum of effort.

An experienced fellow hobbyist should be able to guide you through simple light fixture repairs if you're uncomfortable with performing them yourself.

Replacing Fuses

Good troubleshooting techniques dictate that you eliminate the simplest possible causes for a problem before you jump to the conclusion that there is something major involved. If an arcade video game fails to power up when you plug it in and flip the power switch, this can indicate that there is a major problem with the power supply, the PCBs, or the monitor. On the other hand, the problem might be as simple as a bad fuse. Often, if the marquee lights when the game is powered up but there is no other response from the machine, this is an indicator of a blown fuse.

Most arcade video games have one or more fuses located on or near the game's power supply and/or on the PCBs. On some power supplies, the fuses are exposed and easy to see. In other

a

a **Light fixture repair.** *Use wire nuts to ensure a solid connection when connecting the ballast to the light fixture.*

power supplies, the fuses are installed with screw-on fuse caps. Most video games use the same type of small glass fuses used in older automobiles, and these are available at most auto supply, electronics, and hardware stores.

Before you remove any fuses, make sure that you document the location of each fuse. When multiple fuses are present, chances are that each has a different amperage rating. Installing a fuse with an incorrect amperage rating can cause damage to your game.

If the fuses are installed under screw-on caps, removal is as easy as unscrewing the cap: the fuse should come out with the cap when it is removed. Fuses that are installed in an exposed fuse block are usually much more difficult to remove. You might have to gently pry the metal ends up with a screwdriver to release them. Take care not to put too much pressure on the fuse—it is easy to break the glass tube. Ideally, you should use a fuse puller to remove the fuses. These tools are available at most electronics stores.

It is usually easy to see when a fuse has been blown. Remove the fuse from the game and hold it up to a light. If there are burn marks on the inside of the glass tube or the thin metal filament inside the fuse is separated, the fuse is bad. Make sure you check all of the fuses while you're re-placing one in case the problem isn't limited to a single fuse.

When you purchase replacement fuses, make sure that the new fuses have the same amperage as the ones you remove. The number of amps for which the fuse is rated is generally inscribed on the metal connector at the end of the fuse. The service manual for the game should also in-dicate the location and amperage of all of the fuses.

Once the fuses have been checked and the bad ones replaced, close up the cabinet and power up the game. If the game works, the problem is solved. If the game still doesn't power up or the new fuses blow immediately, this points to a more serious problem, and it's time to call in some-one with more experience.

Replacing Boards

Repairing a circuit board—troubleshooting a problem and replacing chips, capacitors, and other components—is a job for a person with electronics experience and the proper tools. It takes time to get the hang of board-level repair, and it's not something that casual hobbyists generally attempt, at least not when they first start collecting.

Something that a casual hobbyist *can* do, on the other hand, is replace entire boards. Usually, replacing a PCB is as easy as disconnecting a few cables and removing some screws.

Some common indications of a bad PCB include:

- The graphics are scrambled during gameplay.

- The game is stuck in startup mode when powered on.

- The self-test at startup displays an error message.

- The game repeatedly restarts or freezes after playing for a short time.

Most people can master board-swapping with little effort, but there are a few things to keep in mind:

- Try to work in a static-free environment when handling boards. Avoid rooms with low humidity and carpet.

- As you disconnect cables, carefully label each one so that you know where it connects to the PCB when you're putting the game back together. Also note the orientation of each connector to avoid reconnecting them backwards or upside down.

- Hold onto the old boards after you remove them. As your skills and knowledge increase over the years, you might learn how to repair the board. Extra PCBs can be kept as backups or sold to other collectors who need them.

PCBs for many popular classic video games are regularly available in online and live auctions. Also, companies like El Dorado Games (http://www.eldoradogames.com) swap working boards for defective ones for a fee. Prices for PCBs vary greatly—working main boards for common popular games like *Centipede* run as high as $125 or so, and working boards for rare games are considerably more expensive. It's a good idea to have a knowledgeable individual confirm that the problem is in a particular board before you purchase a new board. Most games have several PCBs, and the problem is generally localized to only one board.

When you are ready to purchase a board, buy only boards that the seller confirms are in working condition. Most sellers won't guarantee boards once they are in your possession—it is easy to damage a board when handling or installing it, and the seller has no control over the installation process—but you should confirm as best you can that the board is working before it is shipped to you.

Installing a Joystick

It is not uncommon after 20 or more years of use for arcade video game controllers to fail. Joysticks are among the only moving parts in most video games, and they take the most abuse. If the joystick on your game sticks when you try to move it or is too loose, it makes playing the game all but impossible. Luckily, most common joysticks are very easy to replace, even if you're not electronically inclined.

The first step is to obtain a replacement joystick. In order to do so, you must determine the type of joystick you need. If your game has a specialized controller, like the tank controllers on *Battlezone* or the yoke controller on *Star Wars*, you probably have quite a search ahead of you. You can't replace these controllers with generic parts.

Luckily, most classic arcade games use standard joysticks, and these are easy to find on Internet auction sites and from vendors who sell video game parts. It's best to purchase a new stick when possible, since most new joysticks are sold with diagrams that show you how to disassemble and assemble them.

Even if your game uses a common joystick type, you have to determine what type of stick your game requires. Specifically, you need to know how many directions the stick needs to move in order to play the game.

Some examples of different joystick directional requirements are as follows:

- Games like *Galaxian* and *Galaga*, where the ship only moves left and right, use two-way joysticks.

- Most maze games like *Pac-Man* and *Pengo* have characters that move in four directions (left, right, up, and down). These games use four-way joysticks.

- Other games that allow greater freedom of movement like *Time Pilot* require eight-way joysticks.

It is important to install the proper joystick type. Although eight-way joysticks will technically work in all of the aforementioned games, the extra directional input causes the stick to be imprecise in games that don't require eight directions of movement. If you are unsure what type of joystick your game requires, look up your game on the Killer List of Video Games (http://www.klov.com). The joystick types for most games are described in the listings.

In addition to purchasing the correct joystick type, you must also purchase a joystick that is of an appropriate length. Most joystick models are available in both long- and short-shaft versions. If the control panel on your game is wooden, you need a long-shaft joystick. If the control panel is metal, purchase a short-shaft stick. You should also measure the "foot print" of your existing stick (the distance between the bolts that attach it to the control panel) to ensure that you get a new stick that fits your cabinet.

When you have purchased your new joystick, you're ready to begin the installation process.

1. **Remove the control panel.** See Replacing Control Panel Overlays earlier in this chapter for details on this process.

2. **Document the connections.** Before you disconnect any wires, you should document each and every wiring connection on the joystick (there are usually eight wires, two on each switch). If you have a digital camera, take a picture of the bottom of the original joystick to document the wiring positions. Otherwise, draw a diagram, taking care to label wire colors and all connection locations.

3. **Disconnect the old stick**. Usually, the wires are connected to the joystick switches using slip-on connectors that pull off easily. If the connections are soldered, you'll need a soldering iron to install a new stick. If you're uncomfortable with using a soldering iron, it's best to have someone install the new joystick for you.

4. **Remove the old joystick.** Joysticks are generally connected to the control panel using four bolts. Simply remove the nuts (setting them aside for later use), and slide the joystick free. In most cases, the ball on top of the stick is too big to fit through the hole in the control panel. If this is the case, you must remove the stick from the joystick base. At the base of the stick, there is a thin C-shaped connector notched into the shaft that holds the stick in place. Pry this loose using a screwdriver and the stick should slide free.

5. **Attach the new stick**. If you purchased a new joystick, chances are that it came with a diagram showing how the stick is assembled. Start by attaching the base to the control panel using the four bolts and nuts that held the original stick in place. Note that the orientation of the joystick base doesn't matter as long as the holes line up. Next, slide the new joystick through the hole in the top of the control panel and attach it to the base as per the joystick instructions. (If you don't have instructions, you can download instructions for most typical joysticks at the Happ Controls web site—http://www.happcontrols.com.)

6. **Connect the wires.** It is important that you connect the wires in the same locations from which they were removed. If you don't, left could be right, up could be down, and so on. This is where your diagram or photo comes in handy. When you compare the switches on your new joystick to those on the original, you might notice that, while the old switches have two-connector terminals, the new switches have *three*—two on the end of the switch and one on the side (bent at a 90-degree angle). The connector on the side is known as the "common" connector. You'll always use this one. The other two switches are usually labeled "NO" (normally open) and "NC" (normally closed). "Normally open" means that, when the stick is not moved in that direction, the switch is inactive. "Normally closed" means that the switch is active even when the joystick is *not* being pushed in that direction. When connecting the wires, you must connect them to the normally open and common connectors. If you connect the normally closed connector, your onscreen character or ship moves when you're *not* moving the joystick rather than when you *are* moving it.

After the installation is complete, it's time to test your work. Reconnect the control panel, power up the game, and start playing. Common problems you might encounter include:

- **Incorrect directional movement.** If moving the stick right moves the ship/character left and so on, you've rewired the stick incorrectly. It's helpful to remember that, when you're looking at the bottom of the joystick, the switches are reversed. When you push a joystick up, it's actually the *bottom* switch that is activated, when you push the stick left, the *right* switch is activated, and so on.

- **No movement in one or more directions.** This usually means that one of your connections is loose. Make sure all of the connections are tight. Also check the wiring harness that connects the control panel to the machine to make sure that connection is secure.

a

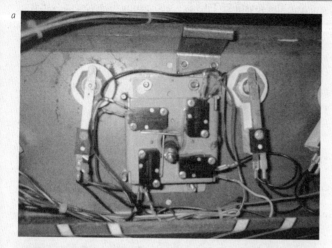

b

c

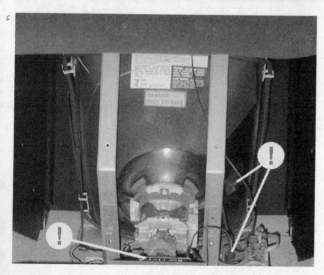

a **Disconnecting a joystick.** *Using a digital camera or a hand-drawn diagram, document all of the wiring connections on the old joystick before you disconnect it.*

b **A new joystick, installed and connected.** *Note the terminals to which the wires are attached on the newer-style switches.*

c **The inside of a video game monitor.** *There are several notable danger zones (marked with exclamation points in the illustration) inside the monitor, but if you are not well-versed in monitor repair, the best way to avoid serious injury is to not touch anything you see here.*

- **Character/ship moves without moving the joystick.** This is a good sign that you've wired a connection to an "NC" connector. Switch the wires to the "NO" connectors to alleviate the problem.

About Monitors

Another part of a classic video game that is prone to failure after 20 years of hard labor is the monitor. Indications of a dead or dying monitor include:

- Wavy lines in the picture.

- Bright or dim spots on the screen.

- Red, green, or blue missing from the picture.

- The picture is squashed or bent on the side, top, or bottom.

- The picture flickers.

- There is no picture whatsoever, but you can hear the game playing.

If you're expecting to find a guide to fixing common monitor problems in this book, you're going to be disappointed. Of all of the parts of an arcade video game that inexperienced hobbyists should *never* touch, the monitor is highest on the list. Monitors are extremely dangerous if you don't know what you're doing. The high voltage coursing through them can cause serious injury or even death if you touch the wrong component. Even when the machine has been powered down and unplugged for several days, a residual high-voltage charge can remain in the monitor.

Monitor repair requires advanced electronics knowledge. Unless you have the proper training, you should never touch any components **inside a video game monitor** (apart from the picture adjustment controls, which are generally located in a safe area), nor should you attempt to disconnect or remove the monitor from the machine. If your game is suffering from monitor problems, defer to a professional or an experienced hobbyist rather than risking electrocution.

APPENDIX A

Glossary of Classic Video Game Terms

If you're new to classic video game collecting, there are probably many terms that you're unfamiliar with. Since you're going to be hearing them a lot in this hobby, it's a good idea to know what they mean.

The following are some of the most common terms used by classic video game collectors. Each term is identified as to the branch of video game collecting—arcade, console, or handheld—to which it is related.

Attract Mode (arcade)
The series of images, game play, titles, and instructions that run continuously onscreen when no one is playing an arcade video game.

Bezel (arcade)
The glass or Plexiglas cover that sits in front of the monitor on an arcade video game. (Also known as monitor glass.)

Bootleg (arcade, console)
An unauthorized copy of a game that is released by a rival company. For example, several bootleg versions of Nintendo's *Donkey Kong* arcade game exist, including *Crazy Kong* and *Congorilla*, both of which have game play and graphics that are nearly identical to those of the original game.

Burn In (arcade, console)
Burn in generally refers to a "ghost" image of certain elements of a video game's graphics that are permanently imprinted in the phosphor coating of the monitor screen. Burn in results

from a static image that displayed for a long period of time. Burn in is unsightly on an arcade game, but doesn't affect the game itself. Burn in is also possible on a television set when a console game image is displayed for a long period of time.

Cabaret (arcade).
A style of arcade video game cabinet that is usually about one-hird the size of a full-sized upright cabinet. Also known as a mini-cabinet or mini-game.

Cabinet (arcade)
The wood or Fiberglas shell that houses an arcade video game.

Cap Kit (arcade)
A set of capacitors and other electronic parts used to repair a video game monitor.

Cart (console)
Short for cartridge.

Case (console, handheld)
The plastic shell that houses a video game cartridge. Case also refers to the plastic shell that houses a video game console or a handheld/tabletop game.

Clone (arcade, console, handheld)
A game that is an obvious copy of another game.

Cockpit (arcade)
A style of arcade video game cabinet that allows the player to sit inside. Also known as a sit-down or deluxe cabinet.

Cocktail (arcade)
A style of arcade cabinet that is the size and shape of a small table, with the monitor set into the surface of the table under a sheet of glass. Players generally sit to play this style of game.

Coin-op (arcade)
Short for coin-operated. Arcade video games are also referred to as coin-op video games.

Control Panel (arcade)
A metal, wood, or plastic panel on the front of a video game cabinet upon which the game's controls are mounted.

Control Panel Overlay (arcade).
The artwork that covers an arcade game control panel; usually a decal.

Console (console)
Generic term for a home video game system that connects to a television.

Conversion (arcade)

An arcade game cabinet that houses a different game than the one for which the cabinet was originally designed.

CPO (arcade)

Short for "control panel overlay."

Dedicated (arcade)

An arcade game cabinet that houses the game for which it was originally designed; opposite of conversion.

Detachable Controllers (console)

Controllers (paddles, joysticks, and so on) that can be completely disconnected from the console base unit. (See also: *Wired Controllers*.)

DIP switches (arcade)

Short for dual inline package switches. A bank of small switches that is generally used to set game options in arcade video games.

Emulator (arcade, console, handheld)

A software program that allows you to play arcade, console, or handheld video game ROM images on a personal computer or other electronic device. Popular emulators include Stella, an Atari 2600 emulator, and MAME (Multiple Arcade Machine Emulator), which plays arcade video game ROMs.

Environmental (arcade)

A type of arcade cabinet that encloses the player and attempts to create an extension of the game environment. Bally Midway's *Discs of Tron* is a prime example of a classic environmental cabinet.

Free Play (arcade)

Many arcade games have a switch setting that allows people to play without inserting coins or manipulating the coin mechanisms. This is known as free play mode. Not all arcade games have free play settings.

Gatefold Box (console, handheld)

A type of box that opens like a book.

Hack (arcade, console)

A game that has been altered from its original form in some way, usually by changing the graphics or game play slightly.

Handheld (handheld)

A portable electronic or video game that is small enough to hold in one's hand when it is played.

Homebrew (console)

A new, contemporary game designed for play on a classic console, usually programmed by a collector or hobbyist.

In the wild (arcade, console, handheld)

A collector's term that refers to randomly finding a video game collectible in any non-video game location, like a flea market or a thrift store.

JAMMA (arcade)

Short for Japanese Arcade Machine Manufacturers Association. JAMMA is a standard for arcade PCBs that allows game circuit boards to be interchangeable from one cabinet to another. A JAMMA PCB works in any cabinet that is wired for JAMMA boards.

JAMMA-tized (arcade)

Collector slang for an arcade board or game cabinet that has been converted to the JAMMA standard.

Label Variation (console)

A single video game cartridge that is available with two or more label styles. Some label variations greatly enhance the value of a cartridge, especially for Atari 2600 games.

LCD (handheld)

Short for liquid crystal display; a type of image display technology (usually black and white) used in more advanced handheld games from the classic era; capable of displaying more complex images and animations than LED or VFD displays.

LED (handheld)

Short for light-emitting diode; a type of image display used in the earliest handheld classic games. Usually produces no more than a very simple red-on-black image. Eventually replaced in handheld game applications by VFD and LCD displays.

Licensed Game (arcade, console, handheld)

A game that is produced by one manufacturer and sold by another. Licensed games are often sold under different titles and in packaging different from that of the original manufacturer. For example, Sears department stores sold licensed versions of Atari and Intellivision cartridges under the Sears Tele-Games brand label.

MAME (arcade)

Acronym for Multiple Arcade Machine Emulator. A program that allows arcade ROM images to run on a home computer.

Marquee (arcade)

Translucent plastic or glass artwork mounted on the front of an arcade machine to display the game's title. This backlit panel is usually located on front, top section of the game, above the monitor.

MIB (console, handheld)

Acronym for mint in box; refers to an item that is in like-new condition and includes all original packing materials.

Multi-Cart (console)

A game cartridge that includes many different games on a single cartridge.

NOS (arcade)

Acronym for new old stock; a replacement part or piece of artwork that was produced by a game's original manufacturer when the game was new, but has never been used.

NTSC (console)

Short for National Television Standards Committee; the television display standard for North America and Japan. Cartridges for many classic video game systems were produced in both NTSC and PAL format (see PAL). Generally speaking, PAL games do not display properly on NTSC televisions.

Operator (arcade)

A person who earns a living by placing arcade video games in locations such as arcades, hotel lobbies, and so on.

PAL (console)

Short for Phase Alternating Lines; the television display standard for most of Western Europe and Central/South America. Many classic video game cartridges were produced in both PAL and NTSC format (see NTSC). Generally speaking, NTSC games do not display properly on PAL televisions.

Part out (arcade)

Selling the parts of an arcade game—the monitor, control panel, boards, and so on—individually rather than selling the game as a whole.

PCB (arcade, console, handheld)

Short for printed circuit board.

Pocket-sized (handheld)

Any handheld game that is small enough to easily fit in a pocket.

Prototype (arcade, console, handheld)

A pre-production or test version of an arcade game, cartridge, or piece of video game hardware that is not meant for public release. Prototypes exist for items that were eventually released commercially and for items that were never released. Prototype classic video game items are highly sought by collectors.

Raster monitor (arcade)

A black-and-white or color video monitor that displays images in the same manner as a television set, by constantly redrawing the entire screen row by row. Raster monitors are the most common monitors found in classic arcade games.

Reproduction (arcade, console)

A product, piece of artwork, etc., that is an almost exact copy of the original item. In arcade collecting, reproductions of marquees, side art, bezels, and control panel overlays are commonly available. In console collecting, reproductions of rare and prototype game cartridges are often produced.

RGVAC (arcade)

Short for rec.games.video.arcade.collecting; the most popular online newsgroup for arcade video game collectors.

ROM (arcade, console, handheld).

Acronym for Read-Only Memory. Generally, the chip that contains the program code for a game.

ROM Image (arcade, console, handheld).

A software copy of a video game's program code. Video game ROM images for many arcade and console games (and some handheld games) are available for download from the Internet and played on home computers via an emulator.

SECAM (console)

Short for Sequential Color and Memory; the television display standard for France, Poland, and most of Eastern Europe. Generally speaking, PAL video games work on SECAM televisions, but NTSC games do not.

Shopped (arcade)

Refers to an arcade video game (or pinball machine) that has been at least thoroughly cleaned and tested and (often) partially or fully restored.

Side Art (arcade)

The graphics on the side of an arcade cabinet. Side art is painted on or applied as decals.

Sprite (arcade, console)

An on-screen graphic that moves.

Standalone (console).

A video game console with a built-in monitor that requires no television in order to play. Milton Bradley's Vectrex is an example of a standalone console.

T-Molding (arcade)

Plastic molding that is applied to the leading edges of a game's sides to give the game a finished appearance. T-molding on classic arcade video games comes in a wide variety of colors.

Tabletop (handheld)

A portable game larger than a handheld game that rests on a table (or other surface) when played.

Third-Party (console)

A software company that produces video game software for another company's console. Activision and Imagic were two of the first third-party software manufacturers.

Upright (arcade)

The most common type of arcade video game cabinet; usually stands five- to six-feet tall.

VCS (console)

Short for video computer system; the original name for the Atari 2600.

Vector monitor (arcade, console)

A black and white or color monitor that traces lines directly on the screen rather than refreshing entire rows of the screen. This is the type of monitor used in games like *Asteroids* and *Tempest*. A vector monitor was also used in the Vectrex home video game console. Also known as an X-Y monitor.

VFD (handheld)

Short for vacuum fluorescent display; an image display technology used in many handheld and tabletop classic games. This type of display is capable of generating very colorful images, but is not as versatile as an LCD display.

Wired Controllers (console)

Controllers (paddles, joysticks, and so on) that are attached to the console base unit with wires, usually two- to six-feet in length. Wired controllers allow you to play at a distance, but the wires themselves cannot be easily disconnected from the console. Also known as hard-wired controllers. (See also: *Detachable Controllers*.)

Wristwatch Game (handheld)

A tiny portable video game that is built into a wristwatch.

X-Y monitor (arcade, console)

See Vector monitor.

APPENDIX B

Additional Resources

The classic video game collecting hobby is constantly growing, and there are a huge number of resources available, from books on the history of video games to websites with information and resources for buying, selling, trading, repairing, and collecting classic video games of all types.

The following sections list only a small sampling of the books, magazines, and Web sites that every classic video game collector should be aware of.

Books and Publications

Arcade Fever (John Sellers, Running Press, 2001). A whimsical, nostalgic profile of a number of popular arcade games from 1971 through 1985.

Game Over, Press Start to Continue (David Sheff, GamePress, 1999). A fascinating, comprehensive history of Nintendo.

GameRoom Magazine (http://www.gameroommagazine.com). A magazine for collectors of arcade video games, pinball machines, and other coin-operated collectibles.

High Score! (Rusel DeMaria and Johnny Lee Wilson, Osborne/McGraw-Hill, 2002). A history of video and computer games and game companies from the birth of the industry through 2001.

Phoenix: The Fall and Rise of Video Games (Leonard Herman, Rolenta Press, 2003). An excellent history of the home video game industry from the start to the present.

Supercade (Van Burnham, MIT Press, 2001). A pictorial and textual history of arcade and home video games from 1971 to 1984, with many chapters written by video game designers and programmers from the classic era.

The Ultimate History of Video Games (Steven L. Kent, Prima Publishing, 2001). A comprehensive history of home video games (with some arcade game information as well), from the start of the industry through 2001. Originally published as *The First Quarter*.

Zap! The Rise and Fall of Atari (Scott Cohen, Xlibris Corporation, 1984). A brief history of Atari, written in the midst of the video game crash of the 1980s.

Classic Gaming Conventions and Events

Austin Gaming Expo (http://www.austingamingexpo.com). One of the newer conventions catering primarily to console game enthusiasts. The first Austin Gaming Expo was held on July 26, 2003 in Austin, Texas.

California Extreme (http://www.caextreme.org). A national classic arcade video game and pinball show held every summer in San Jose, California.

CinciClassic (http://www.cinciclassic.com). A classic gaming convention in the Midwest, held in the fall of each year in Cincinnati, Ohio.

Classic Gaming Expo (http://www.cgexpo.com). CGE, one of the largest national classic gaming conventions, is held every August.

Northwest Classic Gaming Enthusiasts (http://www.nwcge.com). A classic game group that holds a spring event in Kirkland, Washington, every year.

PhillyClassic (http://www.phillyclassic.com). One of the east coast's premier classic gaming events, PhillyClassic is held every spring in Philadelphia, Pennsylvania.

Console Games—General Information

AtariAge (http://www.atariage.com). The nexus for the Atari collecting community and the definitive source for collecting information for all Atari video game consoles; also has an online store that sells original, homebrew, and reproduction titles.

Atari History Museum (http://www.atarimuseum.com). The history of Atari console and arcade video games, with lots of pictures and information.

Intellivision Lives (http://www.intellivisionlives.com). The official Intellivision Web site, with historical information, loads of pictures, and an online store.

INTV Funhouse (http://www.intvfunhouse.com). An excellent collector site dedicated to Intellivision hardware and games.

The Odyssey² Home Page (http://www.classicgaming.com/museum/o2/index/shtml). The definitive online source for information on the Magnavox Odyssey².

Pong-**Story** (http://www.pong-story.com). A video game history site dedicated primarily to *Pong* and its many home console derivatives.

Console and Arcade Games—Online Dealers

Atari2600.com (http://www.atari2600.com). Sells games and hardware for nearly every classic video game console.

Atarionline.com (http://www.atarionline.com). Offers local arcade video game sales and service (in the northern Virginia area) and classic console and cartridge sales worldwide.

Classic Game Creations (http://www.classicgamecreations.com). Has a variety of homebrew games for Vectrex, ColecoVision, and Magnavox Odyssey² for sale and download, as well as a great deal of collecting information.

Good Deal Games (http://www.gooddealgames.com/ForSale.html). Offers software and hardware for classic and contemporary video game consoles.

Mark's Video Game Manufacturing (http://www.vectrexcarts.com). Offers a variety of homebrew, reproduction, and updated (hacked) Vectrex games at very reasonable prices. Also sells parts for manufacturing Vectrex cartridges.

Opcode Games (http://www.opcodegames.com). Relatively new company that has recently embarked on a mission to bring faithful reproductions of classic arcade games to the ColecoVision. Their first release, *Space Invaders Collection*, is available now.

Packrat Video Games (http://www.packratvg.com). Packrat sells games and hardware for just about every classic video game and computer system. Their selection includes many homebrew and reproduction titles for the 2600.

ResQsoft Productions (http://home.earthlink.net/~resqsoft/products.htm). Hobbyist Lee Krueger's Website, which offers a number of homebrew titles for the Atari 2600 and 7800 systems.

Telegames (http://www.telegames.com). Sells games and hardware for most classic console systems. Also sells the ColecoVision-compatible DINA game console.

QuarterArcade (http://www.quarterarcade.com). One of the East Coast's premier online arcade video game dealers, with a huge selection of fully-restored classic arcade video games, parts, restoration artwork, and PCBs. Delivery is available throughout the continental U.S.

Arcade Games—General Information

Arcade Restoration Workshop (http://www.arcaderestoration.com). A hobbyist Website with lots of information on restoring classic arcade video games.

The Dragon's Lair Project (http://www.dragons-lair-project.com). A Website with detailed information on *Dragon's Lair* and just about every other laser disc video game ever made.

Duramold.com (http://www.duramold.com). A recently-established hobbyist Website dedicated to Williams arcade video games.

The Killer List of Video Games (http://www.klov.com). A comprehensive online encyclopedia of arcade video games, with pictures, technical information, and descriptions.

Video Arcade Preservation Society (http://www.vaps.org). An organization of arcade game collectors dedicated to the preservation of the hobby. Includes contact information and site links for hundreds of arcade collectors worldwide.

Arcade Games—Parts and Restoration

Arcade Grafix/PC Amusements (http://www.arcadegrafix.com). Carries a huge selection of reproduction cabinet art, CPOs, marquees, and bezels.

Arcade Renovations (http://www.arcaderenovations.com). A dealer in reproduction arcade art and accessories, with some of the highest-quality classic arcade art reproductions available.

Arcadeshop Amusements (http://www.arcadeshop.com). Carries a wide selection of new and used parts, reproduction artwork, and complete arcade machines.

Bob Roberts (http://www.therealbobroberts.com). Bob carries a huge assortment of replacement parts for classic and contemporary arcade video games. Fast, personal service.

Happ Controls (http://www.happcontrols.com). Sells brand new replacement parts, from joysticks to monitors, for classic and contemporary coin-operated games and equipment.

Arcade Games—Live Auctions

Auction Game Sales (http://www.auctiongamesales.com). Regularly holds auctions in Tennessee, Georgia, North Carolina, and Maryland.

Super Auctions (http://www.superauctions.com) holds auctions in California, Missouri, New Jersey, Texas, Florida, Georgia, Ohio, and Wisconsin.

U.S. Amusement Auction (http://www.usamusement.com). Holds auctions in New Jersey, Indiana, and Ohio.

Handheld Games—General Information

Handheld Games Museum (http://www.handheldmuseum.com). Provides a comprehensive listing of classic and recent handheld and tabletop games, with hundreds of pictures and detailed descriptions.

Handhelden (http://www.handhelden.com). An ever-growing collection of pictures and detailed information on hundreds of handhelds and tabletops from the classic era.

Mini-Arcade.com (http://www.miniarcade.com). A site with pictures and descriptions of over 250 classic handheld and tabletop games.

INDEX

Entries in italics are game titles.
Page numbers in italics indicate illustrations.